Communications in Computer and Information Science 1009

Commenced Publication in 2007
Founding and Former Series Editors:
Phoebe Chen, Alfredo Cuzzocrea, Xiaoyong Du, Orhun Kara, Ting Liu,
Krishna M. Sivalingam, Dominik Ślęzak, Takashi Washio, and Xiaokang Yang

More information about this series at http://www.springer.com/series/7899

Guangtao Zhai · Jun Zhou ·
Ping An · Xiaokang Yang (Eds.)

Digital TV and Multimedia Communication

15th International Forum, IFTC 2018
Shanghai, China, September 20–21, 2018
Revised Selected Papers

 Springer

Editors
Guangtao Zhai (iD)
Shanghai Jiao Tong University
Shanghai, China

Jun Zhou
Shanghai Jiao Tong University
Shanghai, China

Ping An
Shanghai University
Shanghai, China

Xiaokang Yang
Shanghai Jiao Tong University
Shanghai, China

ISSN 1865-0929 ISSN 1865-0937 (electronic)
Communications in Computer and Information Science
ISBN 978-981-13-8137-9 ISBN 978-981-13-8138-6 (eBook)
https://doi.org/10.1007/978-981-13-8138-6

This Springer imprint is published by the registered company Springer Nature Singapore Pte Ltd.
The registered company address is: 152 Beach Road, #21-01/04 Gateway East, Singapore 189721, Singapore

Preface

The present book includes extended and revised versions of papers selected from the 15th International Forum of Digital TV and Multimedia Communication (IFTC 2018), held in Shanghai, China, during September 20–21, 2018.

IFTC is a summit forum in the field of digital TV and multimedia communication. The 2018 forum was co-hosted by SIGA, the China International Industry Fair 2018 (CIIF 2018) and Shanghai Association for Science and Technology, and co-sponsored by Shanghai Jiao Tong University (SJTU), IEEE BTS Chapter of Shanghai Section. The 15th IFTC served as an international bridge for extensively exchanging the latest research advances in digital TV and multimedia communication around the world as well as the relevant policies of industry authorities. The forum also aims to promote the technology, equipment, and applications in the field of digital TV and multimedia by comparing the characteristics, framework, significant techniques and their maturity, analyzing the performance of various applications in terms of scalability, manageability and portability, and discussing the interfaces among varieties of networks and platforms.

The conference program included invited talks delivered by six distinguished speakers from China, Canada, Korea, as well as an oral session of six papers and a poster session of 33 papers. The topics of these papers range from audio/image processing to image and video compression as well as telecommunications. This book contains 39 papers selected from IFTC 2018. We would like to thank the authors for contributing their novel ideas and visions that are recorded in this book.

December 2018

Guangtao Zhai
Jun Zhou
Ping An
Xiaokang Yang

Organization

General Chairs

Xiaokang Yang   Shanghai Jiao Tong University, China
Ping An   Shanghai University, China
Guangtao Zhai   Shanghai Jiao Tong University, China

Program Committee

Jun Zhou   Shanghai Jiao Tong University, China
Hua Yang   Shanghai Jiao Tong University, China
Xianming Liu   Harbin Institute of Technology, China
Jiantao Zhou   University of Macau, China

International Liaisons

Weisi Lin   Nanyang Technological University, Singapore
Patrick Le Callet   Nantes University, France
Lu Zhang   INSA de Rennes, France

Finance Chairs

Yi Xu   Shanghai Jiao Tong University, China
Lianghui Ding   Shanghai Jiao Tong University, China

Publications Chairs

Yue Lu   East China Normal University, China
Qiudong Sun   Shanghai Second Polytechnic University, China
Liquan Shen   Shanghai University, China

Award Chairs

Changwen Chen   SUY Buffalo, USA
Wenjun Zhang   Shanghai Jiao Tong University, China

Publicity Chairs

Xiangyang Xue   Fudan University, China
Yuming Fang   Jiangxi University of Finance and Economics, China

Industrial Program Chairs

Yiyi Lu	China Telecom Shanghai Branch, China
Yongjun Fei	Giant Interactive Group Inc., China
Guozhong Wang	Shanghai University, China

Organizing Committee

Cheng Zhi	Secretary-General, SIGA, China
Tiantian He	Shanghai Jiao Tong University, China

Contents

Quality Assessment

Virtual Reality

Image Processing

An Image Enhancement Based CDVS
Matching Algorithm

Linlin Zhu$^{(\boxtimes)}$, Guozhong Wang, Guowei Teng, Zhenglong Yang, Ming He,
and Tao Wang

School of Communication and Information Engineering,
Shanghai University, Shanghai, China
2528636507@qq.com

Abstract. Compact Descriptor for Visual Search (CDVS) provides a standardized bitstream syntax for mobile image retrieval and matching applications. Although the standard CDVS algorithm has significant advances in the images with the good lighting condition, this approach often fails on dealing with the low-light images. A CDVS matching algorithm based on image enhancement is proposed. Firstly, a histogram equalization method is used for improving the quality of the pictures on low-light conditions to increase the matching number of the key points. Then, a same image enhancement method, which is mainly according to the homomorphic filtering, is adopt as the preprocessing for enhancing the contrast of the image with suppressing the low frequency signal and highlighting the high frequency signal to better extract the descriptors. Experimental results show that the proposed algorithm performs favorably against the standard CDVS algorithm on low-light images. Furthermore, the histogram equalization based CDVS matching algorithm has the best performance comparing with the homomorphic filtering method and the standard CDVS matching algorithm.

Keywords: CDVS · Image matching · Histogram equalization ·
Homomorphic filtering

1 Introduction

Compact Descriptor for Visual Search(CDVS), it is a recently completed standard from the ISO/IEC Moving Picture Experts Group (MPEG). The primary goal of this standard is to provide a standardized bitstream syntax to get the interoperability of image retrieval applications [1]. The process of standardization has made significant progress in reducing image feature data, calculations of the feature extraction process and memory usage. The key building blocks of CDVS [1] are shown in Fig. 1.

From Fig. 1, we can see that CDVS mainly includes the following steps: interest point detection, local feature selection, local feature description, local feature descriptor compression, local feature position compression, and local feature

© Springer Nature Singapore Pte Ltd. 2019
G. Zhai et al. (Eds.): IFTC 2018, CCIS 1009, pp. 3–15, 2019.
https://doi.org/10.1007/978-981-13-8138-6_1

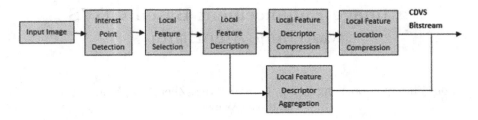

Fig. 1. Normative blocks of the CDVS standard. Compressed global and local features are extracted from the query image and combined to form the final bitstream.

descriptor aggregation. The CDVS evaluation data set is an order of magnitude larger than other popular data sets, such as $INRIA\ Holidays$ and $Oxford\ Buildings$. The data set has more variations in the type of objects, scale, rotation, occlusion and lighting conditions than the $INRIA\ Holidays$ and $Oxford$ data sets. Ground-truth data of 10155 matching image pairs and 112175 non-matching image pairs for the pairwise matching experiment. For the retrieval experiment, it uses 8314 query images, 18840 reference images, and a distractor set of one million images from Flickr [2].

In the experiment, we selected "buildings" and "objects" in the CDVS datasets for testing. It is found that matching images with good lighting conditions has a good matching effect, and the average accuracy of matching can reach to about 90%. However, the average accuracy of matching images under low-light conditions is only about 70%. It is obvious that the lighting condition has a great influence on the accuracy of matching. Therefore, this paper proposes that we first perform image enhancement processing to those images with low light conditions, and then apply the standard CDVS algorithm to the processed images for feature extraction and matching, which can greatly improve the matching accuracy. The remainer of the paper is as follows. Section 2 gives the related works. Section 3 presents the proposed method. The experimental results are shown in Sect. 4. In Sect. 5, we give the conclusion.

2   Related Works

In order to solve the above problem of low-light images, many solutions have been proposed. The histogram equalization algorithm, the Retinex enhancement method, the gradient domain image enhancement algorithm and the homomorphic filter algorithm are described in [3]. The global histogram equalization [4,5] method can enhance the overall image contrast and is suitable for enhancing the overall low grayscale image with low dynamic range; The local histogram equalization method can enhance the image detail information and stretch the local gray scale range of the image. However, there are problems such as the blockiness and the computational efficiency [6]. The Retinex method [7] mainly consists in estimating the luminance image, which can enhance the information in the dark part of the image while maintaining the brightness of the image. The gradient domain [8] method can expand the local gradient range while compressing the dynamic range of the image. Compared with other methods, it performs well in the shadow and highlight parts of the image. However, reconstruction of the image in the gradient domain requires a certain numerical algorithm and the computational complexity is high. The homomorphic filtering method [9] converts the image to the logarithmic domain, which makes the calculation more efficient. It can compress the overall dynamic range of the image, and at the same time enhance the contrast of the low-value region of the grayscale, and is suitable for enhancing the image with a low gray value.

Local histogram equalization method, Retinex method, and gradient method are effective, but the lack of fast algorithms makes these methods only applicable to image analysis and cannot be used in real time, limiting their application range, they do not apply to the real-time requirements of CDVS. Therefore, the paper uses global histogram equalization and homomorphic filtering to enhance the image, and then the enhanced image is applied to the CDVS algorithm.

3   Image Enhancement Based CDVS Matching Algorithm

Image enhancement is an important part in image processing. In the process of image generation, transmission or transformation, the image quality is degraded due to the influence of many factors, which makes it difficult to analyze and identify the images. Therefore, the main ideas of image enhancement highlight the features of interest in the image according to specific needs, attenuating unwanted features, and improving image analysis. For the images with low light conditions, the histogram equalization and the homomorphic filtering [10] are commonly used for the image enhancement.

3.1   CDVS Matching Algorithm Based on Histogram Equalization

Histogram equalization, also known as histogram flattening, is a non-linear process and a method for contrast adjustment using image histograms in order to obtain a more open and more balanced distribution. By using a method that is more suitable for the human visual analysis, it increases the contrast to enhance the brightness of the image. This method is suitable for the case where the image exhibits a very compact pixel contrast. The implementation of the histogram equalization depends on a scheme that can effectively expand the most commonly used pixel grayscale values step by step, using multiple histograms to complete local contrast adjustment instead of completing the overall contrast adjustment, which is an adaptive histogram equalization. To adjust the local contrast of the image. The histogram equalization is a histogram correction method based on the cumulative distribution function transformation method. The relationship between the transformation function $T(r)$ and the original image probability density function $P_r(r)$ is

$$s = T(r) = \int_0^r P_r(w)dw \tag{1}$$

Discretization of formula (1) yields the following formula

$$s_k = T(r_k) = \sum_{j=0}^{k} P_r(r_j) = \sum_{j=0}^{k} \frac{n_j}{n} \quad k = 0, 1, 2, ..., L - 1 \qquad (2)$$

s_k is called histogram equalization, and the pixels in the input image with the gray level of r_k are mapped to the corresponding pixels in the output image with the gray level of s_k.

The effect of the image after histogram equalization is shown in Fig. 2. As can be seen from the figure, the details of the original image are not very clear, and the contrast between the objects is not strong enough. The gray level range of the histogram is very narrow. After the process of histogram equalization, the contrast of the image is obviously enhanced and the degree range of the histogram gray becomes wider, the grayscale distribution of the image is more balanced, so we can obtain a satisfactory image effect. To separate the high-frequency part and the low-frequency part of the image by using the frequency information of the image, to make the image retain more original grayscale image distribution while achieving a more attractive balance.

The standard image is respectively matched with the low-light image and the histogram image based on the CDVS standard algorithm. From Fig. 3(a), it can be seen that when matching a standard image with a low-light image, there are a lot of false matching points, and a little successful matching pairs. Figure 3(b) shows that the matching between the standard image and the histogram equalizes image. It can be seen that the number of matching successes is obviously increased, and the points of successful matching are mostly distributed around the face, it proves that the image features are enhanced, the details of the image are more prominent, and it is more conducive to the extraction and matching of descriptors.

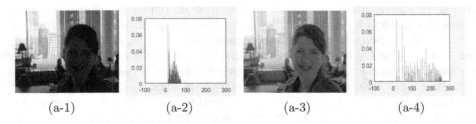

(a-1)   (a-2)   (a-3)   (a-4)

Fig. 2. Image histogram equalization preprocessing results. (a-1) Original images; (a-2) Histogram of original image; (a-3) Histogram-equalized of original images; (a-4) Histograms after histogram equalization.

3.2   CDVS Matching Algorithm Based on Homomorphic Filtering

Homomorphic filtering is a method often used in image enhancement. Classical homomorphic filter processing is operated in the frequency domain. It uses the

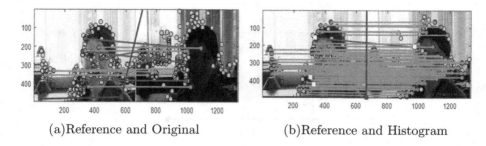

(a)Reference and Original   (b)Reference and Histogram

Fig. 3. Image matching results (Yellow points: not matched descriptors Red lines: matches discarded by DISTRAT Green lines: matches maintained by DISTRAT) (Color figure online)

image model as the basis of frequency domain processing and it is a processing technique to improve the image quality by both performing the compression of the grayscale range and the enhancement of the contrast. The basic idea of homomorphic filtering is shown in the Fig. 4 below.

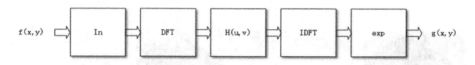

Fig. 4. Processing of homomorphic filter

Among it: ln is the logarithm of $F(x, y)$, the purpose is to transform the multiplication into a simple addition in the image model

$$z(x, y) = \ln f(x, y) = \ln i(x, y) + \ln r(x, y) \tag{3}$$

DFT is a Fourier transform to the data, the purpose is to convert the image to the frequency domain

$$F(z(x, y)) = F(\ln i(x, y)) + F(\ln r(x, y)) \tag{4}$$

That is $Z = I + R$; then is data filtering, selecting appropriate transfer function, compressing the variation range of the irradiation component $i(x, y)$, reducing $I(x, y)$, and enhancing reflection component $r(x, y)$ contrast, promoting $R(x, y)$ and enhancing high-frequency components, that is to determine a suitable $H(u, v)$. As the above analysis shows, the approximate shape of $H(u, v)$ [9] is shown Fig. 5. $IDFT$ is inverse Fourier transform to the data; exp is the exponential transformation to the data; $g(x, y)$ is the image data obtained after processing.

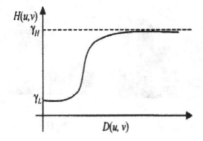

Fig. 5. Homomorphic filtering transfer function H(u,v)

After the image passes the homomorphic filter, the resulting image is shown in Fig. 6. According to the processing effect, if the appropriate filter parameters are selected, the parts of the low-frequency and the high-frequency information of the image can be retained and enhanced respectively, which will complete the compression of the dynamic range and the enhancement of the contrast. Obviously, the image after the homomorphic filter processing, the visual effect is significantly better than the original image.

(a-1)   (a-2)   (a-3)   (a-4)

Fig. 6. Preprocessing results of image homomorphism filtering. (a-1) Original images; (a-2) spectrum before filtering; (a-3) Applying homomorphic filter to original image; (a-4) spectrum after filtering.

The standard image is respectively matched with the low-light image and the homomorphic filter image based on the CDVS standard algorithm. From Fig. 7(a), it can be seen that when matching a standard image with a low-light image, the number of successful matching pairs is small. Figure 7(b) shows the matching between the standard image and the homomorphic filter image, there is a significant increase in matching, it is proved that the matching accuracy of the image is also improved.

3.3   CDVS Matching Algorithm Based on Image Enhancement

The specific processing of the algorithm in this paper is shown in Fig. 8. The image under low light conditions is processed with histogram equalization or

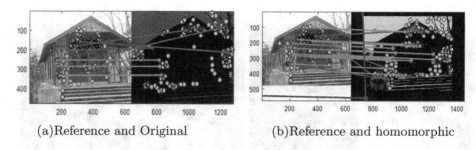

(a)Reference and Original (b)Reference and homomorphic

Fig. 7. Image matching results (Yellow points: not matched descriptors Red lines: matches discarded by DISTRAT Green lines: matches maintained by DISTRAT) (Color figure online)

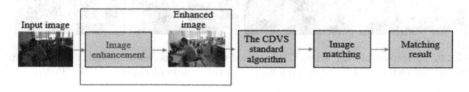

Fig. 8. Flow chart of CDVS algorithm based on image enhancement

homomorphic filtering before matching by the CDVS standard algorithm. Then the image after enhancement processing is matched by the standard algorithm.

4 Experimental Results and Analysis

4.1 Objective Performance

In this experiment, 12 low-light images in the CDVS datasets of "building" were randomly selected as the images to be processed, and the good conditions corresponding to the 12 low-light images were tested as reference images, and simulated in Matlab2016. The image under low-light conditions, the histogram equalized image, and the homomorphic filtered image are respectively matched with the reference image. Examples of test images show in Fig. 9.

From Table 1, it can be seen that when the low-light image is matched with the standard image, the number of matching key points is obviously smaller than the number of key points that are matched after the image is enhanced. For example, in test image 3, the matching key points of the histogram equalization and the homomorphic filtering are increased from 47 to 216 and 141 respectively, and the geometric proofs show that the number of matching key points increases from 16 to 153 and 83 respectively, and the matching final score increases from 0.6670 to 0.9724 and 0.9333 respectively. It shows that on low light conditions, the image details are lost, the image features are weakened, and the useful information of the image is not extracted well. These will result

reference   low-light   histogram   homomorphic

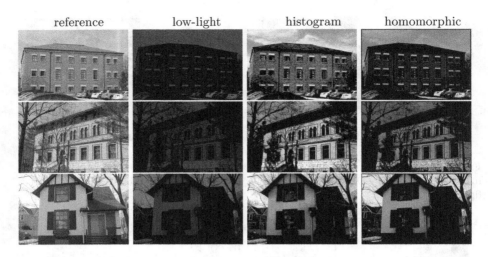

Fig. 9. Examples of test images. The rows show the reference image, the low-light image, the results of histogram equalized and the results of homomorphic filtered.

Table 1. The experimental results

Reference image	Low light conditions matching			Histogram equalization matching			Homomorphic filtering matching		
	Match	Verify	Score	Match	Verify	Score	Match	Verify	Score
1	52	20	0.6997	118	63	0.9241	77	39	0.8723
2	31	0	0	57	26	0.7904	20	0	0
3	47	16	0.667	216	153	0.9724	141	83	0.9333
4	82	41	0.9163	131	82	0.9415	123	70	0.9311
5	35	15	0.718	138	75	0.9266	52	27	0.8141
6	94	49	0.8858	220	189	0.9781	127	91	0.9442
7	65	26	0.8636	104	72	0.9312	74	38	0.8797
8	84	37	0.826	233	188	0.9785	133	98	0.9487
9	45	17	0.6316	80	48	0.9091	63	29	0.8186
10	52	21	0.793	130	95	0.956	90	47	0.9051
11	82	42	0.8744	206	164	0.9806	124	79	0.9455
12	77	27	0.6683	204	180	0.977	145	111	0.9579

in the reduction of image descriptors and the decrease of matching accuracy. After image enhancement, the gray value distribution of the image is wider, the physical characteristics of the image are highlighted, and the detailed information of the image is enriched, which is favorable for the extraction and matching of the image descriptor.

Table 2. The experimental results

Reference image	Original	Histogram		Homomorphic		△score
	Score	Score	Gain	Score	Gain	Gain
1	69.97%	92.41%	22.44%	87.23%	17.26%	5.18%
2	0.00%	79.04%	79.04%	0.00%	0.00%	79.04%
3	66.70%	97.24%	30.54%	93.33%	26.63%	3.91%
4	91.63%	94.15%	2.52%	93.11%	1.48%	1.04%
5	71.80%	92.66%	20.86%	81.41%	9.61%	11.25%
6	88.58%	97.81%	9.23%	94.42%	5.84%	3.39%
7	86.36%	93.12%	6.76%	87.97%	1.61%	5.15%
8	82.60%	97.85%	15.25%	94.87%	12.27%	2.98%
9	63.16%	90.91%	27.75%	81.86%	18.70%	9.05%
10	79.30%	95.60%	16.30%	90.51%	11.21%	5.09%
11	87.44%	98.06%	10.62%	94.55%	7.11%	3.51%
12	66.83%	97.70%	30.87%	95.79%	28.96%	1.91%
Average	77.67%	95.23%	17.56%	90.46%	12.79%	4.77%

From Table 2, we most concern about the matching accuracy, which are 95.23% for histogram equalization algorithm and 90.46% for homomorphic filter algorithm. Histogram equalization algorithm matching accuracy increases 17.56% and homomorphic filter algorithm increases 12.79% compared to low light images. The histogram equalization algorithm improves 4.77% compared to the homomorphic filter algorithm. From the table, we can see that the test image 2 matching fails and the matching total score is 0 before processed. After the histogram equalization processing, the image matching is successful and the matching total score reaches 79.04%. The image is illustrated after the histogram equalization processing. The features are more prominent, which facilitates the extraction of image descriptors and improves the matching accuracy of images. From the table we can also see that the matching effect of homomorphic filtering on the image has also been improved, but the total score of the matching decreases 5% comparing with the histogram equalization.

In Fig. 10, the image key points, matching points after geometric verification and total match scores are compared respectively. We can see that the histogram equalization based CDVS matching algorithm has the best performance comparing with the homomorphic filtering method and the standard CDVS matching algorithm.

4.2 Subjective Performance

Due to the decrease of image matching rate caused by low light conditions, the experiment is performed using the following method in this paper. Image A

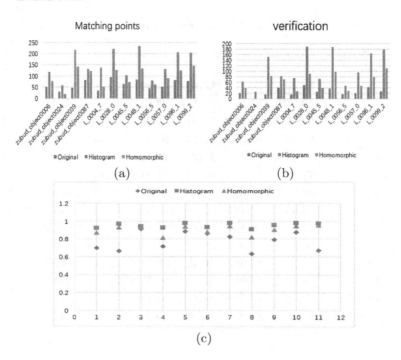

(a)   (b)

(c)

Fig. 10. Quantitative comparison on the dataset. The numbers below the horizontal axis denote the image index.

(a)Image A   (b)Image B   (c)Image C   (d)Image D

Fig. 11. (a) the reference image (b) low-light image (c) image dealt with histogram equalization (d) image dealt with homomorphic-filtered

is the reference image. The remaining three images are as follows. Image B is the low-light image, image C is histogram equalization image and image D is homomorphic filtering image. They are shown in Fig. 11.

In Fig. 11, the image A is matched with the B, C, and D images respectively, the corresponding experimental results are shown in Fig. 12. It can be seen that when the image A matches the image B, the number of matching points is not many, even matching error occurs. These indicate that the characteristics of the image are reduced under low light conditions. The details are also covered, which makes it difficult to read the image information and brings great difficulty to the matching between the images. The results of the matching between image A and

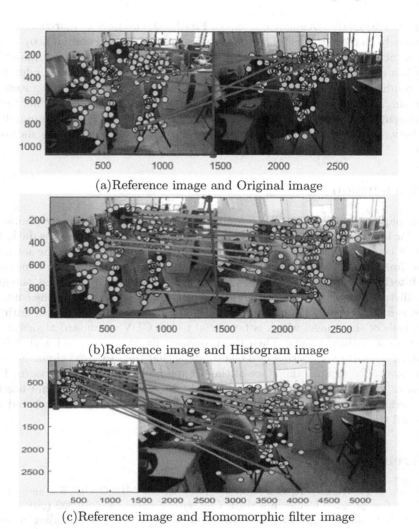

(a)Reference image and Original image

(b)Reference image and Histogram image

(c)Reference image and Homomorphic filter image

Fig. 12. Image matching results (Yellow points: not matched descriptors Red lines: matches discarded by DISTRAT Green lines: matches maintained by DISTRAT) (Color figure online)

Table 3. The experimental results

	Original	Histogram	Homomorphic
Matching points	76	99	82
Verification	33	53	37
Total score	0.8492	0.9111	0.8707

images C and D are obviously enhanced. Firstly, the number of matching points is obviously increased. Most of the descriptors are distributed around people, and the characteristics of the image can be extracted very well, and the matching error has also been corrected well. These indicate that the image under low-light conditions has more outstanding image features after image enhancement processing, and the details of the image are also strengthened. According to the experiments above, it is illustrated that the matching enhancing, the matching rate between the images can be improved. The matching results are shown in Table 3.

5   Conclusion

In this paper, we propose a CDVS matching algorithm based on image enhancement for low-light image. Since the brightness of the low light image is dark, the contrast is poor and the details of the image are lost, which result in the accuracy of the image matching is reduced, so the histogram equalization or homomorphic filtering is applied to the image before matching. After processing, the gray value distribution of the image is wide, the brightness is smooth and the contrast is obvious. It highlights the physical characteristics of the image and enriches the details of the image, which is beneficial to the CDVS standard algorithm to detect more feature points. Then the processed image is matched with CDVS standard algorithm. Experimental results show that the proposed algorithm performs favorably against the state-of-the-art methods on low-light images. Furthermore, the histogram equalization based CDVS matching algorithm has the best performance comparing with the homomorphic filtering method and the standard CDVS matching algorithm.

References

1. Duan, L.Y., Huang, T., Gao, W.: Overview of the MPEG CDVS standard. In: Data Compression Conference IEEE Computer Society, pp. 323–332 (2015)
2. Lin, J.: Compact aggregated descriptors for mobile visual search. Beijing Jiaotong University (2014)
3. Wang, H., et al.: Review of image enhancement algorithms. Chin. Opt. **10**(4), 438–448 (2017)
4. Wang, Y., Chen, Q., Zhang, B.: Image enhancement based on equal area dualistic sub-image histogram equalization method. IEEE Trans. Consum. Electron. **45**(1), 68–75 (1999)
5. Kim, Y.T.: Contrast enhancement using brightness preserving bi-histogram equalization. IEEE Trans. Consum. Electron. **43**(1), 1–8 (2002)
6. Kim, J.Y., Kim, L.S., Hwang, S.H.: An advanced contrast enhancement using partially overlapped sub-block histogram equalization. In: IEEE International Symposium on Circuits and Systems, Proceedings, ISCAS IEEE, vol. 4, pp. 537–540 (2002)
7. Lin, L., Weiping, H., Lei, L., Wei, Z., Hongxiao, W.: Survey on enhancementhods for non-uniform illumination image. Appl. Res. Comput. **27**(5), 1625–1628 (2010)

8. Fattal, R., Lischinski, D., Werman, M.: Gradient domain high dynamic range compression. In: Conference on Computer Graphics and Interactive Techniques ACM, pp. 249–256 (2002)
9. Chunning, C., Yanjie, W.: Image contrast enhancement by homomorphic filtering in frequency field **23**(2), 2606–2613 (2007)
10. Liu, Y.J., Liu, Q.: Ultrasound image enhancement based on homomorphic filter and histogram equalization. J. Clin. Rehabil. Tissue Eng. Res. **15**(48), 9031–9034 (2011)

An Improved Seam-Line Searching Algorithm Based on Object Detection

Rui Sun, Chuanzhen Li, Wei Zhong, and Long Ye[(✉)]

Key Laboratory of Media Audio and Video of Ministry of Education,
Communication University of China, Beijing, China
542838455@qq.com, {lichuanzhen,wzhong,
yelong}@cuc.edu.cn

Abstract. Seam-line searching algorithm is one of the widely used image fusion method to stitch images. The major methods of generating seam-line mainly take considering the correlation between the pixels, resulting in a so-called "seam-line crossing the object" phenomenon, which greatly deteriorates the visual experience of the final stitching result. To overcome the above problem, this paper proposes an improved seam-line searching algorithm based on object detection. After image registration of reference and target images with the as-projective-as-possible warp or the adaptive as-natural-as-possible warp, the Single-Shot Detector model is applied to detect objects in the overlapping regions of the registered images. Considering the smallest difference in color and structure, the seam-line is allowed to extend along the edge of these objects which are not supposed to be crossed as much as possible if this line crosses these objects. The experimental results show that our method can effectively avoid "seam-line crossing the object" phenomenon and make the mosaic images look more natural. At the same time, our method can also be combined with global warp and other more advanced local-warp-based alignment methods to obtain better stitching results.

Keywords: Seam-line · Image fusion · Object detection

1 Introduction

With the rapid development of virtual reality and ultra-high definition technologies, image stitching became a hot research topic as it can merge two or more images with overlapping regions into a wider and larger image [1]. The final purpose of image stitching is to merge images as seamlessly as possible even in the presence of parallax, lens distortion and illumination difference, and eliminate artificial traces such as ghosting and blurring, and make the mosaic images look as natural and real as possible [2].

There are two basic steps to stitch images: image registration and image fusion. The representative method of image registration is using global projective warp to transform the stitched images from different perspectives into the same one, and then solve the problem on image alignment [3]. Global warp is robust, but it is often not flexible enough to satisfy all types of scene [4]. In order to solve the shortcomings of global warp and improve the alignment quality, some local warps have been proposed.

© Springer Nature Singapore Pte Ltd. 2019
G. Zhai et al. (Eds.): IFTC 2018, CCIS 1009, pp. 16–30, 2019.
https://doi.org/10.1007/978-981-13-8138-6_2

The as-projective-as-possible (APAP) warp aims to be globally projective, yet allow local non-projective deviations to account for violations to the assumed imaging conditions [5]. The shape-preserving half-projective (SPHP) warp is a combination of projection transformation and similarity transformation in space, thus improving the quality of alignment in the overlapping regions and preserving the perspective of each image [6]. The adaptive as-natural-as-possible (AANAP) warp combines local homography with global similarity transformation. AANAP warp reduces the perspective distortion and it improves the view of non-overlapping regions comparing with APAP [2]. The mesh-based image stitching with linear structure protection (MISwLP) applies constraints to the lines extracted from images to protect them from being distorted by the mesh deformation process, thus obtaining natural panoramas with reduced distortion [7].

In image fusion, the weighted fusion algorithms are generally used to merge multi-images because they are often easy to realized. The main idea of weighted mean methods is that pixels at different part of the overlapping regions contribute differently to the final composite [8]. According to the different settings of weighting function, the weighted fusion algorithms can be divided into two classes–linear and nonlinear. Among linear methods, the linear cross-fade function works relatively well, but it sudden changes at the edge of overlapping regions, resulting in blurring and not robust enough. The weighting function based on Gaussian model proposed by Fang et al. [9] is more representative among nonlinear weighting functions. Because the Gaussian function ranges smoothly between 0 and 1, it overcomes the shortcoming of linear function and reduces blurring to a certain extent. But when the objects in the overlapping regions are moving or more complex, the effect of weighted fusion algorithm will be very poor. On the contrary, the seam-line searching algorithm can deal with this situation well. The basic idea of seam-line searching algorithm is to find a line in the overlapping regions, and the corresponding part of the right and left sides of the line can just be merged into a complete, vivid image. The advantages of seam-line searching algorithm are simple principle and easy implementation. Meanwhile, the performance of the seam-line searching algorithm is also better than the weighted fusion algorithm when the overlapping regions are more complex. Fang et al. [10] proposed a solution criterion and the optimal seam-line is searched by making the color and neighborhood structure difference as small as possible in the overlapping regions, so when a small object with single color and symmetrical structure appears, the color and the neighborhood structure difference will not be enough to restrain the direction of the seam-line. At this time, the seam-line will cross the object and lead to the final mosaic images deformity and unnaturalness [11]. To this end, Liu et al. [11] tried to change the direction of the seam-line by adding the item of image contour energy on the basis of the solution criterion, and then find a more reasonable seam-line. Li et al. [12] proposed a new cost energy function combining the color difference, the gradient magnitude and the texture complexity in the graph cuts energy minimization framework to detect an optimal seam-line. But their methods can not solve the "seam-line crossing the object" phenomenon fundamentally.

At present, image mosaic is mainly applied to the stitching of aerial images, orthoimages and panoramic images. The overlapping regions of the first two kinds are relatively flat and having no obvious objects, but our work focuses on panoramic images and there are often obvious and various objects in the overlapping regions.

Therefore, aiming at the weakness of traditional seam-line searching algorithm, this paper proposes an improved seam-line searching algorithm based on object detection to solve the "seam-line crossing the object" phenomenon. The rest of the paper is organised as follows: Sect. 2 surveys related work. Section 3 introduces the proposed method in detail. Results are presented in Sect. 4, and we conclude in Sect. 5.

2   Related Work

2.1   Image Registration

In terms of image registration, the existed state-of-the-art methods like APAP or AANAP have shown satisfactory performance, with the basic idea that transforming the stitched images of different perspectives into the same one through coordinate transformation. Specifically, APAP warp partitions the source image into a grid of C1 × C2 cells and obtains the local homography corresponding to each cell by giving each cell a different weight [5]. AANAP warp linearizes the homography and slowly changes it to the estimated global similarity transformation by considering all the local warp variables [2]. After registration, the overlapping regions are often complex, blurring, ghosting so that the final mosaic images' fusion results are often not visual pleasure. Therefore, our work focuses on better mosaic images by improving seam-line searching algorithm.

2.2   Solution Criterion

The seam-line theory holds that for two images after registration, there is an ideal seam-line in the overlapping regions, which can well synthesize images, or even eliminate ghost completely [11]. This line requires that the difference in color intensity between the pixel on it and the two stitched images is least, and the pixels around the seam-line have the most similar values.

Based on this theory, Fang et al. [10] proposed the optimal seam-line solution criterion:

$$E(x, y) = E_{color}(x, y)^2 + E_{geometry}(x, y) \qquad (1)$$

where E_{color} represents the difference in color intensity of the corresponding pixels on and around seam-line in the overlapping regions, and $E_{geometry}$ represents neighborhood structure difference. The search strategy of the seam-line searching algorithm in [10] can be summarized as the following three steps:

(1) Initialize the criterion value for each pixel in the first row of the overlapping regions.
(2) Search downwards in three directions: lower left, vertically below and lower right.
(3) Find the line with the smallest criterion value as the optimal seam-line.

However, when the overlapping regions have objects with uniform color and simple regional structure, the seam-line found by the traditional seam-line searching algorithm often crosses these objects, that is the so-called "seam-line crossing the object" phenomenon, resulting in the mosaic image's deformity and unnaturalness [11]. In order to solve this problem, we perform object detection in the overlapping regions.

2.3   The Object Detection Model

With the application of artificial intelligence becoming more and more extensive, the importance of object detection has become more prominent. At present, Faster R-CNN, R-FCN and SSD are the most widely used object detection models. We choose the SSD model because SSD is the fastest of these three models, and its execution performance has a certain amount of observability. Unlike Faster R-CNN and R-FCN, SSD performs region proposal and region category simultaneously in the "single shot" and predicts box and category at the same time when processing images. Specifically, for an input image and a set of ground truth labels, SSD will perform the following operations:

(1)   The image is transmitted through a series of convolution layers, and several different feature maps are generated on different scales.
(2)   For each position in each of these feature maps, use a 3×3 convolution filter to evaluate a group of default bounding boxes.
(3)   For each box, predict both the a-boundary box offset and the b-category probability at the same time.
(4)   In the training process, the ground truth box is matched with the prediction box which is based on IoU. The best prediction box and all other IoU boxes with actual values >0.5 will be marked as "positive" [13].

By using SSD model, we detect some objects which are not supposed to be crossed in the overlapping regions of the stitched images. The results of object detection are as Fig. 1.

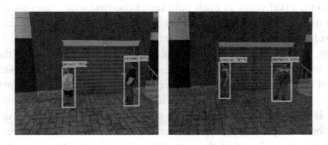

Fig. 1. The results of object detection.

3   Seam-Line Searching Based on Object Detection

The steps of the proposed method are shown as Fig. 2.

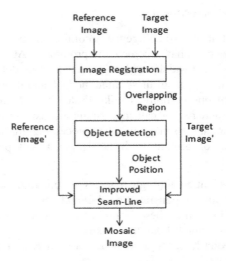

Fig. 2. System design.

Firstly, APAP or AANAP is applied to transform the reference image and the target image into a same perspective. After image registration, we perform object detection in the overlapping regions to detect if there are some objects which are not supposed to be crossed. Finally, based on the traditional seam-line solution criterion and SSD-based object detection, we improved the searching strategy of the optimal seam-line as follows:

(1) Initialization. Pixel point in each column of the first row corresponds to a seam-line, and its intensity value are initialized as the criterion value of each pixel point. Each pixel point is the starting point of each seam-line;

(2) Extension. A line which has calculated the intensity value of the seam-line extends downward until the last line. For current point of each seam-line, the method of extension is to calculate the criterion values of the three pixel points in the next row which are close to the current point, and find out the minimum value of them. If these three pixel points are not in the object regions we detected, then we take the pixel point with the smallest criterion value as the extension direction of the seam-line and update the intensity value of this seam-line (plus this minimum criterion value). If one or two of these three pixel points are located in the detected object regions that can not be crossed, a penalty factor will be added to guarantee the pixels on seam-line are not in object regions. If these three pixel points are both in the detected object regions, we will take the closest boundary point which is in the same row as these three pixel points in the object regions as the extension direction of the seam-line, and then update the intensity value of this

seam-line with the criterion value corresponding to the boundary point. The minimum criterion value selection theory is as Eq. 2.

$$E_{total} = E_{pre} + \min\{E_i(x,y) + P_i(x,y), E_b(x,y) + P_b(x,y)\}, i = 1, 2, 3 \quad (2)$$

$$P_i(x,y) = \begin{cases} 0, I_i(x,y) \notin S \\ \\ \infty, I_i(x,y) \in S \end{cases} \quad i = 1, 2, 3 \quad (3)$$

$$P_b(x,y) = \begin{cases} 0, \{I_1(x,y), I_2(x,y), I_3(x,y)\} \subset S \\ \infty, else \end{cases} \quad (4)$$

where I_i(x, y) and I_b(x, y) represent one pixel point among the three pixel points for each searching downward and the closest boundary point respectively, E_i(x, y) and E_b(x, y) represent the criterion values of corresponding points. S represents the detected object regions (rectangle frame), E_{pre} represents the sum of the criterion values for all points that have been calculated. P_i(x, y) and P_b(x, y) are the penalty items that we add, so that the seam-line can avoid these objects which are not supposed to be crossed as far as possible.

(3) Select the optimal seam-line. Select the line with the smallest intensity value from all lines as the optimal seam-line.

4 Experimental Results

Our experimental pictures are mainly divided into two parts: virtual scene and real scene. The pictures of the virtual scene are from SYNTHIA-Rand dataset (Fig. 3), and the pictures of the real scene are from the photos taken by ourselves (Fig. 4) and the dataset provided by the author of APAP (Fig. 5). We choose these pictures because they can fully demonstrate that our method is applicable for both virtual and real scenes and show the superiority of our method against other methods. In detail, We combine our method with APAP (AANAP) and compare the stitching results with APAP, AANAP, linear or nonlinear blending and the traditional seam-line searching algorithm.

The results for the people image pair are provided in Fig. 3. Each row is a result of different methods. Two areas of each results have been highlighted. The results of APAP and AANAP all show obvious ghosting because of the different people in the overlapping regions of the two stitched images. The results of linear blending on the third and fourth rows are still blurry to some extent in red boxes. The Gaussian function's results look good visually in red boxes, but its performance in blue boxes is very poor. As for the results on the seventh and eighth rows, the seam-line found by traditional seam-line searching algorithm failed to avoid people in red boxes, leading to deformity in the final mosaic images. Conversely, our algorithm avoids these people successfully and shows satisfactory results both in blue boxes and red boxes on the last two rows.

Algorithm: Object Detection-based Seam-Line

Input: Reference image R and target image T

  I: Obtain registered images R' and T' by APAP or AANAP

  II: Get object regions S by performing object detection in the overlapping
      regions

  III: Improved seam-line searching algorithm:

      (i) Calculate initialized intensity value E_{pre} for each column and criterion
         values E_1, E_2, E_3 in the next row

      (ii) If $\{I_1, I_2, I_3\} \subset S$ then

$$E_{total} = E_{pre} + E_b$$

      else

$$E_{total} = E_{pre} + \min\{E_1, E_2, E_3\}$$

      (iii) Select the line with the smallest E_{total} as the optimal seam-line

Output: Mosaic image

Fig. 3. The proposed algorithm.

Figure 4 compares the results for the car image pair. The results of APAP and AANAP are relatively fuzzy on the whole. The linear blending shows better results than APAP and AANAP on the third and fourth rows but it is still not clear enough in the overlapping regions. The results of Gaussian function perform well in blue boxes, but the cars in red boxes are obviously unnatural. The results of the traditional seam-line searching algorithm are clear. However, the cars in the red boxes are obviously deformed because the selected seam-line crosses the cars. Oppositely, our stitching results are relatively clear in the overlapping regions, and the cars in red boxes look more real and natural.

In Fig. 5, APAP and AANAP all show blurry results. The linear blending works well for simple scene in blue boxes, but it still shows bad results in red boxes. The results of Gaussian function are very unnatural in the edge of overlapping regions. As for the traditional seam-line searching algorithm, you can see clearly that the seam-line crosses people and car, resulting in the incompleteness of people and the unnaturalness of the car. On the contrary, the optimal seam-line selected by our method avoids these objects which are not supposed to be crossed successfully.

The panorama examples demonstrate the performance of our proposed method with multiple images. The image dataset in Fig. 6 consists of some cars, a roundabout, and people. Our method works well in the dataset, maintaining the integrity of image contents, and providing a natural look to the panorama. There are no visible parallax errors and perspective distortions. What's more, the experimental results show that our method can find a more reasonable seam-line in the overlapping regions and ensure the authenticity and naturalness of the final mosaic images, so our method has a certain value of application (Fig. 7).

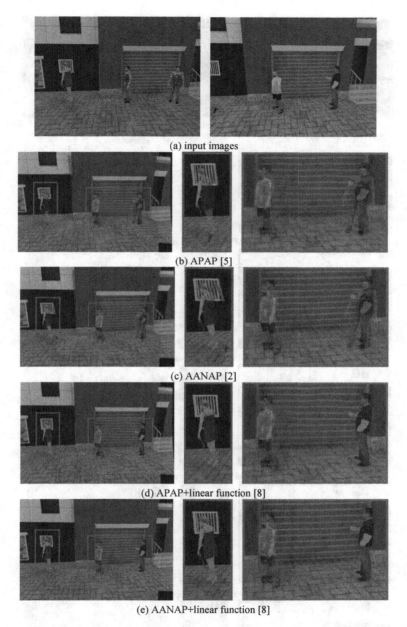

(a) input images

(b) APAP [5]

(c) AANAP [2]

(d) APAP+linear function [8]

(e) AANAP+linear function [8]

Fig. 4. Qualitative comparisons (best viewed on screen) on the people image pair. (Color figure online)

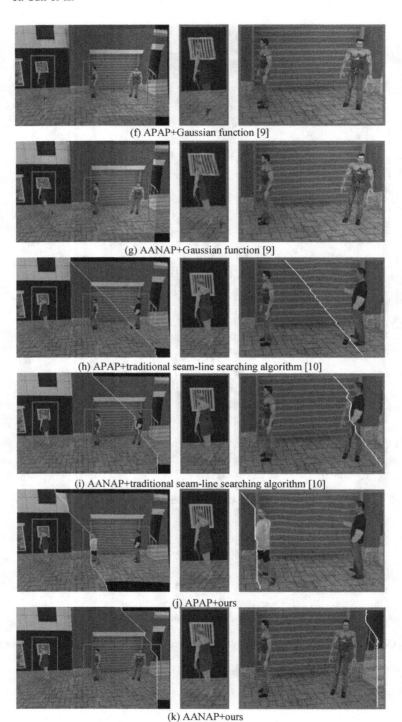

(f) APAP+Gaussian function [9]

(g) AANAP+Gaussian function [9]

(h) APAP+traditional seam-line searching algorithm [10]

(i) AANAP+traditional seam-line searching algorithm [10]

(j) APAP+ours

(k) AANAP+ours

Fig. 4. (*continued*)

(a) input images

(b) APAP [5]

(c) AANAP [2]

(d) APAP+linear function [8]

(e) AANAP+linear function [8]

Fig. 5. Qualitative comparisons (best viewed on screen) on the car image pair. (Color figure online)

(f) APAP+Gaussian function [9]

(g) AANAP+Gaussian function [9]

(h) APAP+traditional seam-line searching algorithm [10]

(i) AANAP+traditional seam-line searching algorithm [10]

(j)APAP+ours

(k) AANAP+ours

Fig. 5. (*continued*)

(a) input images

(b) APAP [5]

(c) AANAP [2]

(d) APAP+linear function [8]

(e) AANAP+linear function [8]

Fig. 6. Qualitative comparisons (best viewed on screen) on the people and car image pair.

(f) APAP+Gaussian function [9]

(g) AANAP+Gaussian function [9]

(h) APAP+traditional seam-line searching algorithm [10]

(i) AANAP+traditional seam-line searching algorithm [10]

(j)APAP+ours

(k) AANAP+ours

Fig. 6. (*continued*)

(a) input images

(b) mosaic image by our method

Fig. 7. Panorama of roundabout images.

5 Conclusion

This paper proposes an improved seam-line searching algorithm based on object detection. Our method overcomes the shortcoming of the traditional seam-line searching algorithm with the seam-line crossing objects with small differences in color and structure. By adding object detection, our seam-line can avoid these objects effectively and make the mosaic images look more real. Specially, our method is mainly applicable for the situation that there are some obvious objects in the overlapping regions. That means other methods are still perfect when the overlapping regions are simple or there are no important objects.

Another major contribution of this paper is that the proposed method can be combined with APAP, AANAP and other warps. While obtaining better alignment accuracy, the fusion effect of mosaic images is also greatly improved. The experimental results also fully demonstrate the effectiveness of our method.

Acknowledgment. This work is supported by the National Natural Science Foundation of China under Grant Nos. 61631016 and 61371191, and the Project of State Administration of Press, Publication, Radio, Film and Television under Grant No. 2015-53.

References

1. Zhang, F., Liu, F.: Parallax-tolerant image stitching. In: CVPR 2014, pp. 3262–3269 (2014)
2. Lin, C.-C., Pankanti, S., Ramamurthy, K.N., Aravkin, A.Y.: Adaptive as-natural-as-possible image stitching. In: CVPR 2015, pp. 1155–1163 (2015)
3. Szeliski, R.: Image alignment and stitching. In: Paragios, N., Chen, Y., Faugeras, O. (eds.) Handbook of Mathematical Models in Computer Vision, pp. 273–292. Springer, Boston (2005). https://doi.org/10.1007/0-387-28831-7_17
4. Chen, Y.-S., Chuang, Y-Yu.: Natural image stitching with the global similarity prior. In: Leibe, B., Matas, J., Sebe, N., Welling, M. (eds.) ECCV 2016. LNCS, vol. 9909, pp. 186–201. Springer, Cham (2016). https://doi.org/10.1007/978-3-319-46454-1_12
5. Zaragoza, J., Chin, T.-J., Brown, M.S., Suter, D.: As-projective-as-possible image stitching with moving DLT. In: CVPR 2013, pp. 2339–2346 (2013)
6. Chang, C.-H., Sato, Y., Chuang, Y.-Y.: Shape-preserving half-projective warps for image stitching. In: CVPR 2014, pp. 3254–3261 (2014)
7. He, C., Zhou, J.: Mesh-based image stitching algorithm with linear structure protection. J. Image Graph. 23(7), 973–983 (2018)
8. Zhang, J., Chen, G., Jia, Z.: An image stitching algorithm based on histogram matching and sift algorithm. IJPRAI 31(4), 1–14 (2017)
9. Tian, F., Shi, P.: Image mosaic using orb descriptor and improved blending algorithm. JMPT 5(3), 98–108 (2014)
10. Fang, X., Pan, Z., Xu, D.: An improved algorithm for image mosaic. J. Comput. Aided Des. Comput. Gra 15(11), 1362–1365 (2003)
11. Liu, Q., Cai, H., Chen, G., Dou, S., Yang, Y.: An image mosaic method based on improving seam line. In: ICNC-FSKD, pp. 414–418 (2016)
12. Li, L., Yao, J., Li, H., Xia, M., Zhang, W.: Optimal seamline detection in dynamic scenes via graph cuts for image mosaicking. Mach. Vis. Appl. 28(8), 819–837 (2017)
13. Liu, W., et al.: SSD: single shot MultiBox detector. In: Leibe, B., Matas, J., Sebe, N., Welling, M. (eds.) ECCV 2016. LNCS, vol. 9905, pp. 21–37. Springer, Cham (2016). https://doi.org/10.1007/978-3-319-46448-0_2

Enhanced Saliency Prediction
via Free Energy Principle

Peng Ye[2], Yongfang Wang[1,2(✉)], Yumeng Xia[2], Ping An[1,2],
and Jian Zhang[3]

[1] Shanghai Institute for Advanced Communication and Data Science,
Shanghai, China
yfw@shu.edu.cn
[2] School of Communication and Information Engineering,
Shanghai University, Shanghai 200444, China
[3] Global Big Data Technologies Center, University of Technology Sydney,
Sydney, NSW 2007, Australia

Abstract. Saliency prediction can be treated as the activity of human brain. Most saliency prediction methods employ features to determine the contrast of an image area relative to its surroundings. However, only few studies have investigated how human brain activities affect saliency prediction. In this paper, we propose an enhanced saliency prediction model via free energy principle. A new AR-RTV model, which combines the relative total variation (RTV) structure extractor with autoregressive (AR) operator, is firstly utilized to decompose an original image into the predictable component and the surprise component. Then, we adopt the local entropy of 'surprise' map and the gradient magnitude (GM) map to estimate the component saliency maps-sub-saliency respectively. Finally, inspired by visual error sensitivity, a saliency augment operator is designed to enhance the final saliency combined two sub-saliency maps. Experimental results on two benchmark databases demonstrate the superior performance of the proposed method compared to eleven state-of-the-art algorithms.

Keywords: Saliency prediction · Free energy principle ·
RTV structure extractor · Image decomposition · Visual error sensitivity

1 Introduction

Saliency prediction is an important mechanism developed in Human Visual System (HVS) to cope with a vast amount of visual information. With this mechanism, HVS would selectively process the most important (salient) part that attracts much more human attention and ignore other parts. Saliency prediction is an important technique to promote the performances of different multimedia processing applications such as video coding [1], object recognition [2, 3], and quality assessment [4–6]. Therefore, a more effective and efficient saliency prediction model is always required.

Generally, there are two main categories approaches in saliency prediction: bottom-up and top-down. Bottom-up approach, which only uses input signal information itself,

© Springer Nature Singapore Pte Ltd. 2019
G. Zhai et al. (Eds.): IFTC 2018, CCIS 1009, pp. 31–44, 2019.
https://doi.org/10.1007/978-981-13-8138-6_3

is fast and data-driven [7–19]. While top-down approach, which requires prior knowledge, is slow and task-driven [20].

Up to now, numerous saliency prediction models have been proposed and the number is supposed to increase at a high rate [21]. A majority of saliency prediction models are proposed by calculating center-surround differences from features such as intensity, edge, color and orientation [7–10]. Itti et al. designed the earliest center-surround architecture based on the neuronal architecture of the primate early visual system [7]. This model firstly subsamples the input image into a Gaussian pyramid and decomposes the pyramid into intensity, color and orientation channels. Then, It implements a set of center-surround operations [22] to yield the feature map of each channel, and the final saliency map is computed by summing and normalizing feature maps. Also, some saliency prediction models are to find visual "pop-outs" in frequency domain [11–14]. Hou et al. proposed the classical saliency prediction model based on residual Fourier amplitude spectrum [11]. Some researchers proposed to make use of natural image statistics for saliency prediction [15, 16]. Bruce et al. introduced a saliency prediction algorithm by taking into account information maximization [15]. Recently, some saliency prediction models based on deep learning are proposed to achieve promising performance [17–19]. Tavakoli et al. [18] presented an unsupervised multi-scale hierarchical saliency prediction model, which adopted independent subspace analysis (ISA) to train an unsupervised framework by combining local and global concept.

Since visual saliency is decided by human beings themselves, the most effective model should consider the activity of human brain to input information. Recently, a free-energy principle has been proposed, which unifies several brain theories within a framework and tries to formulate the internal generative mechanism (IGM) [23, 24]. The principle points out that the HVS cannot fully process all of the input scenes and tries to avoid some surprises (i.e., the difference between an input image and its inferred one) [23]. Such surprises reveal the important characteristics of human perception and highly correlate with visual saliency [25].

In this paper, we propose an enhanced saliency prediction model for images based on free energy principle. By simulating the IGM of brain, we firstly propose a new AR-RTV model to decompose the image into the predictable component and the surprise component (similar to the AR-bi-lateral model of Gu et al. [25]), which combines the auto-regressive (AR) operator and the relative total variation (RTV) structure extractor. Then, we compute the saliency of surprise component by using its local entropy and the saliency of predictable part by using the local entropy of its gradient magnitude (GM) map, respectively. Finally, inspired by visual error sensitivity, a saliency augment operator is designed to further enhance the final saliency map which is the combination of the above two parts. Experimental results on two databases (Toronto [15] and MIT [26]) confirm the superior performance of the proposed model.

The remainder of this paper is organized as follows. In Sect. 2, we introduce the enhanced free energy principle based saliency prediction model in detail. Experiment results are presented in Sect. 3. Section 4 draws the conclusion of this paper.

2 Enhanced Saliency Prediction via Free Energy Principle

The overview of the saliency prediction flow chart is showed in Fig. 1. The input RGB image is firstly decomposed into three LAB channels. A sub-saliency map is generated by the proposed saliency prediction model for each channel respectively, and the final saliency map is generated with above three sub-saliency maps. Figure 2 depicts the framework of the proposed model. Firstly, the AR-RTV model (integrate AR operator and RTV structure extractor) is introduced to decompose an image into two components. Then we utilize local entropy to compute the sub-saliency maps of the two component parts, respectively. Next, the saliency map is gained by the weighted sum of sub-saliency. Finally, the final saliency map is enhanced with a saliency augment operator after across aforementioned two maps.

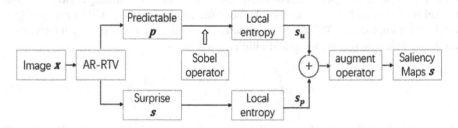

Input Image   LAB Color Channels   Free Energy Inspired Enhanced Saliency Prediction   Channel Maps   Final Saliency Map

Fig. 1. An overview of the saliency prediction flow chart

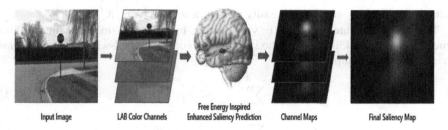

Fig. 2. The framework of the enhanced free energy inspired saliency prediction model

2.1 Image Decomposition via Free Energy Principle

According the inference in [27], the IGM tries to represent the sensor information probabilistically with minimum prediction error. Generally speaking, the motivation for the free energy principle rests upon the fact that self-organizing biological agents resist a tendency to unpredictable and therefore try to minimize the entropy of their sensory states (correspond to suppress surprise) [23].

Though an AR model is useful to imitate the IGM of brain by minimizing the probability of prediction error [27–29], it sometimes works unsteadily at image structure. Therefore, a new AR-RTV model, which integrates AR operator and the RTV structure extractor with an excellent structure-preserving capacity, is proposed to model the free energy principle. To specify, the expression of the AR operator is defined as:

$$x_i = \Delta^h(x_i)\boldsymbol{a} + e_i \tag{1}$$

where x_i represents a pixel value at location i in image $\boldsymbol{x}$, $\Delta^h(x_i)$ is the h member neighborhood of x_i and is set to 8 through experiments, $\boldsymbol{a} = (a_1, a_2, \ldots, a_h)^T$ denotes an AR parameter vector, and e_i is the error value between the original value and the prediction. With regard to $\boldsymbol{a}$, the matrix form of linear system can be defined as:

$$\hat{\boldsymbol{a}} = arg \min_{\boldsymbol{a}} \|\boldsymbol{x} - \boldsymbol{X}\boldsymbol{a}\|_2 \tag{2}$$

in which $\boldsymbol{x} = (x_1, x_2, \ldots, x_h)^T$ and $\boldsymbol{X}(i,:) = \Delta^h(x_i)$. By utilizing the least square method, the linear system can be easily solved as $\boldsymbol{a} = \left(\boldsymbol{X}^T\boldsymbol{X}\right)^{-1}\boldsymbol{X}^T\boldsymbol{x}$.

The RTV structure extractor is very simple but effective to make meaningful structures stand out [30]. The method contains a common pixel-wise *windowed total variation (WTV)*, computed as:

$$\mathcal{D}_x(p) = \sum\nolimits_{q \in R(p)} g_{p,q} \cdot \left|(\partial_x S)_q\right| \tag{3}$$

$$\mathcal{D}_y(p) = \sum\nolimits_{q \in R(p)} g_{p,q} \cdot \left|(\partial_y S)_q\right| \tag{4}$$

where q represents any pixel unit of $R(p)$, the rectangular surrounding region centered at pixel p. $\mathcal{D}_x(p)$ and $\mathcal{D}_y(p)$ measure the absolute spatial imparity within region $R(p)$, which are computed as WTV of the directions x and y of pixel p. $g_{p,q}$ represents a weighting function related to spatial affinity, written as:

$$g_{p,q} \propto exp\left(-\frac{(x_p - x_q)^2 + (y_p - y_q)^2}{2\sigma^2}\right) \tag{5}$$

where σ regulates the spatial size of the region. By exploiting $\mathcal{D}_x(p)$ and $\mathcal{D}_x(p)$, both salient textures and structure pixels will be detected.

Besides $\mathcal{D}$, a novel *windowed inherent variation* method is contained in the method, which is used to help separate structures from texture pixels, expressed as:

$$\mathcal{L}_x(p) = \left|\sum\nolimits_{q \in R(p)} g_{p,q} \cdot (\partial_x S)_q\right| \tag{6}$$

$$\mathcal{L}_y(p) = \left|\sum\nolimits_{q \in R(p)} g_{p,q} \cdot (\partial_y S)_q\right| \tag{7}$$

where $\mathcal{L}$ measures the overall spatial variation, which is responsive to the consistency of the gradients (i.e., their directions) in a region. Then $\mathcal{L}$ and $\mathcal{D}$ are combined to establish a more effective regularization term for structure extraction, written as:

$$\hat{s} = arg \min_{S}(S_p - I_p)^2 + \lambda \cdot \left(\frac{\mathcal{D}_x(p)}{\mathcal{L}_x(p) + \varepsilon} + \frac{\mathcal{D}_y(p)}{\mathcal{L}_y(p) + \varepsilon} \right) \tag{8}$$

in which the part $(S_p - I_p)^2$ limits the result not significantly deviated from the input. The regularization term $\mathcal{D}_x(p)/(\mathcal{L}_x(p) + \varepsilon) + \mathcal{D}_y(p)/(\mathcal{L}_y(p) + \varepsilon)$, which is called *relative total variation* (RTV), is designed to extract structures from an image. λ is a weighting factor. ε is a small positive number used to avoid denominator 0.

By decomposing the RTV term into a quadratic term and a non-linear term, Eq. (8) can be quickly solved by an efficient solver in [30] and therefore the vector representation of structure image can be easily obtained. In order to facilitate the expression, we define the structure extractor to be:

$$x_i = \Delta^{h'}(x_i)\boldsymbol{b} + e_i' \tag{9}$$

where $\Delta^{h'}(x_i)$ is the h' member neighborhood of x_i, $\boldsymbol{b} = (b_1, b_2, \ldots, b_h)^T$ is a vector of RTV coefficients, and e_i' is an error term.

Finally, by combining AR operator and RTV structure extractor, a AR-RTV model can be used to estimate the predictable component $\boldsymbol{p}$, defined as:

$$\tilde{x}_i = \frac{\Delta^h(x_i)\boldsymbol{a} + \alpha\Delta^{h'}(x_i)\boldsymbol{b}}{1 + \alpha} \tag{10}$$

in which $\tilde{x}_i$ is the inferred pixel value at position i in $\boldsymbol{p}$, and α is a positive constant to control the relative significance of above two parts and is set to 0.3 [25]. Then the surprise component $\boldsymbol{s}$ can be computed as:

$$\boldsymbol{s} = \boldsymbol{x} - \boldsymbol{p} \tag{11}$$

Figure 3 shows the comparison results between AR-based model and AR-RTV model. With respect to the predicted map with AR-based model in Fig. 3(b), the predicted map with AR-RTV model in Fig. 3(c) has a clearer and more visible structure, which plays a big role in saliency prediction. Compared to the saliency map with AR-based model in Fig. 3(e), the saliency map in Fig. 3(f) is more similar to the ground truth, which intuitively present the superiority of AR-RTV model.

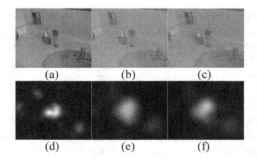

Fig. 3. Comparison between AR-based model and AR-RTV model. (a) Input image. (b) Predicted map with AR-based model. (c) Predicted map with AR-RTV model. (d) Ground truth map. (e) Saliency map (computed by the proposed algorithm) with AR-based model. (f) Saliency map with AR-RTV model.

2.2   Saliency Prediction Based on AR-RTV

In general, the saliency is regarded as rarity, visual attention, unpredictability, or surprise. It's meaningful for us to take into account the impact of the human brain on saliency prediction. In the paper, we utilize the AR-RTV model inspired by free energy principle to decompose an image into the predictable and the surprise components for saliency prediction, respectively.

According to [31], the procedure of free energy minimization highly resembles the predictive coding, which can be naturally regarded as the entropy of the difference between the input signal and the predicted one. Therefore, the sub-saliency of the surprise component is computed as its local entropy, written as:

$$S_u = \mathbb{N}(\mathbb{G}(\mathcal{H}(s))) \tag{12}$$

where $\mathbb{G}$ is a Gaussian filter and $\mathbb{N}$ represents the normalization procedure.

As for the predictable component, in which we human-beings can accurately infer the content, we simply adopt a GM map to capture the saliency. Some studies have pointed out that a gradient operator combined with Gaussian postprocessing at a small scale is competent for saliency prediction [4, 14]. Thus, given an input predictable component p, the classic Sobel operator [32] which is more effective than other similar operators in our experiment, is used to compute its sub-saliency as:

$$S_p = \mathbb{N}(\mathbb{G}(\mathcal{H}(g))) \tag{13}$$

where g is the GM map produced by processing the predictable component p with the Sobel operator.

Combining the sub-saliency above two parts, we can obtain the saliency map as:

$$S_c = \frac{S_u + \beta S_p}{1 + \beta} \tag{14}$$

where β is a positive constant to control the relative weights of above two parts and is set to 1 for the best performance.

To illustrate the validity of the proposed method used to predict the saliency of image decomposition components, we chose five sample images including various scenes from the classical Toronto dataset [15] to make a comparison for different saliency prediction methods, as presented in Fig. 4. It's obvious that the combined saliency map computed by Eq. (14) is greatly closer to the ground truth compared to the two component sub-saliency maps computed by Eqs. (12) and (13).

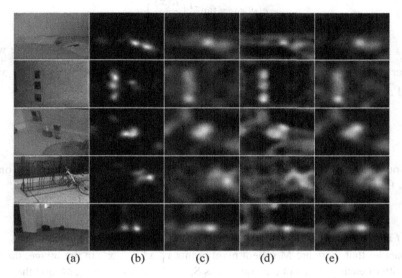

(a)   (b)   (c)   (d)   (e)

Fig. 4. Visual comparison samples of saliency prediction methods. (a) five sample images from the Toronto dataset [15]. (b) Ground truth maps. (c) Saliency maps computed by Eq. (12). (d) Saliency maps computed by Eq. (13). (e) Saliency maps computed by Eq. (14).

2.3   Visual Error Sensitivity Augmented Saliency

Some studies have shown that the HVS is highly space-variant on account of the density distributions of cone and ganglion cells [33–35]. On the retina, the distribution of cone receptors is highly non-uniform, and thus the density of the cone cells is highest at the fovea and decreases very fast with the increase of eccentricity [33]. The distribution of ganglion cells is also highly uneven and the density of the ganglion cells decreases even faster than the density of the cone receptors [35]. So salient region projected on the fovea is perceived at the highest resolution and thus is most sensitive to error. Meanwhile, the resolution and the error sensitivity drop very fast with the increased eccentricity from the focused region.

Itti et al. designed a map normalization operator to globally augment saliency maps which have a small number of strong peaks of activity (conspicuous locations) and globally suppress maps which contain plentiful comparable peak responses in [7]. More recently, a Hadamard product operator is used to achieve the same purpose [13, 25]. Inspired by the visual error sensitivity [35], we intend to address this problem from a local and global perspective. The foveation-based error sensitivity $S_f(v,f,x)$ can defined as [35]:

$$S_f(v,f,x) = \begin{cases} \exp(-0.0461f \cdot e(v,x)) & \text{for } f \leq f_m(x) \\ 0 & \text{for } f > f_m(x) \end{cases} \tag{15}$$

where f is the spatial frequency measured in cycles/degree and $f_m(x)$ is the cutoff frequency for a given location x; $e(v,x)$ is the retinal eccentricity, written as:

$$e(v,x) = \tan^{-1}\left(\frac{d(x)}{Nv}\right) \tag{16}$$

where $x = (x_1, x_2)^T$ is any pixel in an image, v is the viewing distance, N is the width of observed image, $d(x)$ is the distance from x to the salient point $x^f = \left(x_1^f, x_2^f\right)^T$, defined as:

$$d(x) = \left\|x - x^f\right\|_2 = \sqrt{\left(\left(x_1 - x_1^f\right)^2 + \left(x_2 - x_2^f\right)^2\right)} \tag{17}$$

In our experiments, we find that the spatial frequency f has little effect on the results, thus we simplify Eq. (15) as:

$$S(v,x) = \exp(-0.0461f \cdot e(v,x)) \tag{18}$$

where f is a constant number and is setted to 256 in our experiment.

Consider that there are M salient pixel points $x_1^f, x_2^f, \ldots, x_M^f$ in the image, the error sensitivity of each pixel can be computed as $S_i(v,x)$ for $i = 1, 2, \ldots, M$, and the overall error sensitivity computed as the maximum of them can be given by:

$$S_o(v,x) = \max_{i=1,2,\ldots,M} (S_i(v,x)) \tag{19}$$

In practice, it is not necessary and time-consuming to compute each of the $S_i(v,x)$. Since visual error sensitivity decreases with increasing distance from any pixel to salient pixel, in order to promote the meaningful pixel and suppress other noise pixel to a large extent, we choose the largest distance between x and M salient pixel to compute the overall error sensitivity, written as:

$$S_o(v,x) = S_j(v,x),$$
$$\text{where } j \in \underset{j \in \{1,2,\ldots,M\}}{\arg\max} \left\{\left\|x - x_i^f\right\|_2\right\} \tag{20}$$

The final saliency map S' is locally enhanced by visual error sensitivity and globally enhanced by Hadamard product operator, written as:

$$S' = \langle S_c, S_o(v,x)\rangle \circ \langle S_c, S_o(v,x)\rangle \tag{21}$$

where $\langle S_c, S_o(v,x)\rangle$ is the inner product of the combined saliency map S_c and the overall error sensitivity model $S_o(v,x)$, $\circ$ is a Hadamard product operator.

Figure 5 shows comparison of different saliency augmented methods. As shown in Fig. 5, the augmented saliency map with proposed operator (Fig. 5(c)) is more similar with the ground truth map (Fig. 5(b)). Meanwhile, from this figure, it is clear that the Hadamard product operator can globally augment the saliency better than map normalization operator. But both of them cannot address the local noise, which can be well handled with the visual error sensitivity model.

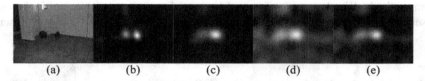

(a)   (b)   (c)   (d)   (e)

Fig. 5. Comparison sample of saliency augmented methods: (a) Input image. (b) Ground truth map. (c) Augmented saliency map with proposed operator. (d) Augmented saliency map with map normalization operator. (e) Augmented saliency map with Hadamard product operator.

The detailed steps of the proposed saliency prediction method are summarized as follows: First, an input RGB image is converted to LAB image and is resized to a 28×38 image representation similar to the program in [13, 14, 25]; Second, the enhanced saliency map in each color channel is computed by the proposed saliency prediction model. Third, the final saliency map is composed of the weighted sum across three enhanced saliency maps, defined as:

$$S = \sum_{i=\{L,A,B\}} W_i S_i'$$ (22)

where S_L', S_A' and S_B' are the enhanced saliency maps in L, A and B channels, W_L, W_A and W_B are positive constants to adjust the relative importance across color channels, and are set to 0.47, 0.34 and 0.19 respectively.

3 Experimental Results

Bylinskii et al. [36] distinguish kinds of performance metrics which is used to evaluate the calculated saliency maps into two types. Distribution-based metrics require a ground truth map with continuous distribution, while location-based metrics utilize a binary ground truth map with fixation values at discrete locations. Six metrics are employed to evaluate our method: the Area under ROC curve-Judd (AUC-J), the Area under ROC curve-Borji (AUC-B), the pearson's Correlation Coefficient (CC), the Kullback-Leibler divergence (KL), the Normalized Scanpath Saliency (NSS) and the similarity (SIM). Among these measures, the CC, KL and SIM metrics are distribution-based metrics, whereas the AUC-J, AUC-B and NSS are location-based. With larger AUC-J, AUC-B, CC, NSS and SIM values, the saliency prediction model can detect fixation regions more precisely. On the contrary, smaller KL value between the generated saliency map and the fixation map demonstrates better performance of the saliency prediction model.

All of these metrics which can be found in the MIT saliency benchmark are used to evaluate scores of saliency prediction models on two databases: most widely-used Toronto dataset [15] and largest MIT dataset [26]. Eleven models in total, including five classical Itti [7], WMAP [8], GBVS [9], AIM [15], SUN [16], and five state-of-the-art CovMean [10], SigSal [13], HFT [14], FES [25], IM [37], and one latest deep learning model UHM [18], are chosen for performance comparison.

First, we give a qualitative comparison between the proposed model and other eleven methods. We show several typical images of various natural scenes in Toronto dataset and the corresponding saliency maps in Fig. 6. In which, the first row presents

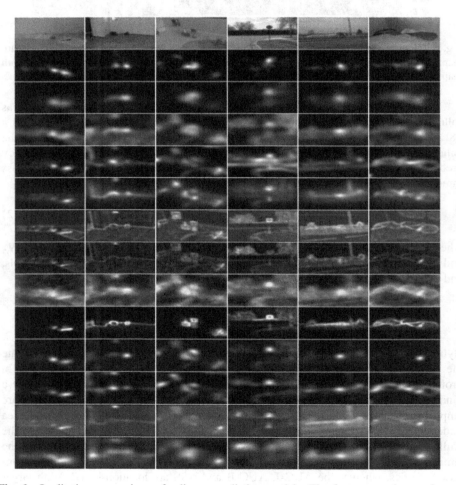

Fig. 6. Qualitative comparison of saliency prediction models: The first row and second row show the typical images in the Toronto dataset [15] and the associated ground truth (fixation maps). The images from the third row to the fourteenth row show the saliency map computed by the proposed model, FES [25], Itti [7], GBVS [9], AIM [15], SUN [16], WMAP [8], IM [36], SigSal [13], HFT [14], CovMean [10], UHM [18].

several representative sample images, the second and third rows show the associated ground truth maps and the saliency map computed by the proposed approach, the fourth to fourteenth rows show the saliency maps generated by other models. From this figure, it is easily found that the proposed method can predict human fixation points accurately, and the corresponding saliency map is more consistent with the ground truth than other state-of-the-art competitors. This is primarily achieved by simulating the brain mechanism and the visual property.

Second, we give a quantitative comparison between the proposed model and other eleven methods on Toronto dataset and MIT dataset in Table 1 and Table 2. The best two performing models for each metrics are shown in bold type. From the comparison results of Table 1, relative to the model ranked second place on the score, the AUC-J, AUC-B, CC, NSS and SIM values have an increase of 0.0218, 0.0207, 0.1014, 0.2088, 0.0726 respectively. Meanwhile, the KL value has a decrease of 0.1836. From the comparison results of Table 2, relative to the model ranked second place on the score, the AUC-J, AUC-B, CC, NSS and SIM values have an increase of 0.0297, 0.0274, 0.0701, 0.1973, 0.0387 respectively. Meanwhile, the KL value has a decrease of 0.2181. In summary, although other algorithms such as the classical model GBVS and the latest deep learning model UHM also have good performance, the proposed method is superior to other algorithms for all metrics, which is the result of the consideration of human brain activity and human visual property.

Table 1. Performance comparisons of the saliency models on the Toronto dataset.

Models	AUC-J	AUC-B	CC	KL	NSS	SIM
Itti [7]	0.7431	0.7278	0.3514	1.0231	0.9397	0.4369
GBVS [9]	**0.8127**	**0.8008**	**0.5372**	**0.8672**	**1.3835**	**0.4737**
AIM [15]	0.7453	0.7331	0.3519	1.1461	0.9773	0.3963
SUN [16]	0.6927	0.6805	0.2611	1.2377	0.7585	0.3846
WMAP [8]	0.7594	0.6749	0.3914	2.3347	1.2510	0.4267
IM [36]	0.7701	0.7488	0.4431	2.6238	1.1935	0.4528
SigSal [13]	0.7849	0.7612	0.4890	0.9295	1.3832	0.4588
HFT [14]	0.7302	0.7122	0.3670	1.0769	1.0248	0.4316
CovMean [10]	0.7687	0.7445	0.3874	1.1637	1.0789	0.3907
FES [25]	0.7886	0.7803	0.4508	0.9839	1.1659	0.4386
UHM [18]	0.7882	0.7777	0.4685	0.9642	1.1749	0.4485
Ours	**0.8345**	**0.8215**	**0.6386**	**0.6836**	**1.5923**	**0.5473**

Table 2. Performance comparisons of the saliency models on the MIT dataset.

Models	AUC-J	AUC-B	CC	KL	NSS	SIM
Itti [7]	0.7048	0.6950	0.2307	1.6512	0.7768	0.2938
GBVS [9]	0.7569	0.6910	0.2516	1.8354	0.8285	0.2832
AIM [15]	0.7217	0.7133	0.2530	1.7049	0.8828	0.2655
SUN [16]	0.6833	0.6751	0.2134	1.7885	0.7509	0.2713
WMAP [8]	0.7392	0.6737	0.2900	2.4135	1.0563	0.3276
IM [36]	0.7732	0.7518	0.3435	2.2658	1.1732	**0.3430**
SigSal [13]	0.7552	0.7398	0.3172	1.5177	1.0730	0.3115
HFT [14]	0.7223	0.7076	0.2759	1.6026	0.9380	0.3090
CovMean [10]	0.7755	0.7591	0.3111	1.7023	1.0175	0.2646
FES [25]	0.7686	0.7636	0.3163	1.5489	1.0309	0.2999
UHM [18]	**0.7915**	**0.7851**	**0.3708**	**1.4732**	**1.2009**	0.3164
Ours	**0.8212**	**0.8125**	**0.4409**	**1.2551**	**1.3982**	**0.3817**

4 Conclusion

In this paper, we propose an enhanced saliency prediction model via free energy principle. By mathematically modeling free energy principle, the AR-RTV model is firstly established to decompose an input image into predictable component and surprise component. Then, the saliency maps of above two components are computed by employing the local entropy of the 'surprise' map and the GM map separately. Finally, through analyzing human visual property, the saliency augmented operator which consists of a visual error sensitivity inspired operator and a Hadamard product operator, is designed to augment the saliency map. Experiment results on two benchmark datasets show that the proposed method is more competent to other eleven state-of-the-art models in saliency prediction.

For future research, we will further explore the effect of the brain activity on stereoscopic image saliency, omni-directional image saliency.

Acknowledgment. This work was supported by Natural Science Foundation of China under Grant No. 61671283, 61301113.

References

1. Shang, X., Wang, Y., Luo, L., et al.: Perceptual multiview video coding based on foveated just noticeable distortion profile in DCT domain. In: IEEE International Conference on Image Processing, pp. 1914–1917. IEEE (2014)
2. Han, J., Zhang, D., Cheng, G., et al.: Object detection in optical remote sensing images based on weakly supervised learning and high-level feature learning. IEEE Trans. Geosci. Remote Sens. **53**(6), 3325–3337 (2015)
3. Han, J., Chen, C., Shao, L., et al.: Learning computational models of video memorability from fMRI brain imaging. IEEE Trans. Cybern. **45**(8), 1692 (2015)

4. Gu, K., Li, L., Lu, H., et al.: A fast reliable image quality predictor by fusing micro- and macro-structures. IEEE Trans. Ind. Electron. **64**(5), 3903–3912 (2017)
5. Gu, K., Lin, W., Zhai, G., et al.: No-reference quality metric of contrast-distorted images based on information maximization. IEEE Trans. Cybern. **47**(12), 4559–4565 (2017)
6. Gu, K., Wang, S., Yang, H., et al.: Saliency-guided quality assessment of screen content images. IEEE Trans. Multimedia **18**(6), 1098–1110 (2016)
7. Itti, L., Koch, C., Niebur, E.: A model of saliency-based visual attention for rapid scene analysis. IEEE Computer Society (1998)
8. López-García, F., Fdez-Vidal, X.R., Pardo, X.M., et al.: Scene recognition through visual attention and image features: a comparison between SIFT and SURF approaches. Intech (2011)
9. Harel, J.: Graph-based visual saliency. Nips **19**, 545–552 (2007)
10. Erdem, E., Erdem, A.: Visual saliency estimation by nonlinearly integrating features using region covariances. J. Vis. **13**(4), 11 (2013)
11. Hou, X., Zhang, L.: Saliency detection: a spectral residual approach. In: IEEE Conference on Computer Vision and Pattern Recognition 2007, CVPR 2007, pp. 1–8. IEEE (2007)
12. Achanta, R., Hemami, S., Estrada, F., et al.: Frequency-tuned salient region detection. In: IEEE Conference on Computer Vision and Pattern Recognition 2009, CVPR 2009, pp. 1597–1604. IEEE (2009)
13. Hou, X., Harel, J., Koch, C.: Image signature: highlighting sparse salient regions. IEEE Trans. Pattern Anal. Mach. Intell. **34**(1), 194 (2012)
14. Li, J., Levine, M.D., An, X., et al.: Visual saliency based on scale-space analysis in the frequency domain. IEEE Trans. Pattern Anal. Mach. Intell. **35**(4), 996–1010 (2013)
15. Bruce, N., Tsotsos, J.: Attention based on information maximization. J. Vis. **7**(9), 950 (2007)
16. Zhang, L., Tong, M.H., Marks, T.K., et al.: SUN: a Bayesian framework for saliency using natural statistics. J. Vis. **8**(7), 32.1 (2008)
17. Zhao, Q., Koch, C.: Learning visual saliency by combining feature maps in a nonlinear manner using AdaBoost. J. Vis. **12**(6), 22 (2012)
18. Tavakoli, H.R., Laaksonen, J.: Bottom-up fixation prediction using unsupervised hierarchical models. In: Chen, C.-S., Lu, J., Ma, K.-K. (eds.) ACCV 2016. LNCS, vol. 10116, pp. 287–302. Springer, Cham (2017). https://doi.org/10.1007/978-3-319-54407-6_19
19. Pan, J., Ferrer, C.C., Mcguinness, K., et al.: SalGAN: visual saliency prediction with generative adversarial networks (2017)
20. Fang, Y., Lin, W., Lau, C.T., et al.: A visual attention model combining top-down and bottom-up mechanisms for salient object detection. In: IEEE International Conference on Acoustics, Speech and Signal Processing, pp. 1293–1296. IEEE (2011)
21. Borji, A., Itti, L.: State-of-the-art in visual attention modeling. IEEE Trans. Pattern Anal. Mach. Intell. **35**(1), 185–207 (2012)
22. Leventhal, A.G.: The Neural Basis of Visual Function: Vision and Visual Dysfunction, vol. 4. CRC Press, Boca Raton (1991)
23. Friston, K.: The free-energy principle: a unified brain theory? Nat. Rev. Neurosci. **11**(2), 127 (2010)
24. Zhai, G., Wu, X., Yang, X., et al.: A psychovisual quality metric in free-energy principle. IEEE Trans. Image Process. **21**(1), 41–52 (2012)
25. Gu, K., Zhai, G., Lin, W., et al.: Visual Saliency detection with free energy theory. IEEE Signal Process. Lett. **22**(10), 1552–1555 (2015)
26. Judd, T., Ehinger, K., Durand, F., et al.: Learning to predict where humans look. In: IEEE, International Conference on Computer Vision, pp. 2106–2113. IEEE (2010)
27. Wu, J., Shi, G., Lin, W., et al.: Just noticeable difference estimation for images with free-energy principle. IEEE Trans. Multimedia **15**(7), 1705–1710 (2013)

28. Gu, K., Zhai, G., Yang, X., et al.: Hybrid no-reference quality metric for singly and multiply distorted images. IEEE Trans. Broadcast. **60**(3), 555–567 (2014)
29. Gu, K., Zhai, G., Yang, X., et al.: Using free energy principle for blind image quality assessment. IEEE Trans. Multimedia **17**(1), 50–63 (2014)
30. Xu, L., Yan, Q., Xia, Y., et al.: Structure extraction from texture via relative total variation. ACM Trans. Graph. **31**(6), 1–10 (2012)
31. Attias, H.: A variational Bayesian framework for graphical models. In: International Conference on Neural Information Processing Systems, pp. 209–215. MIT Press (1999)
32. Qu, Y.D., Cui, C.S., Chen, S.B., et al.: A fast subpixel edge detection method using Sobel – Zernike moments, operator. Image Vis. Comput. **23**(1), 11–17 (2005)
33. Wandell, B.A.: Foundations of Vision. Sinauer Associates, Sunderland (1995)
34. Geisler, W.S.: Real-time foveated multiresolution system for low-bandwidth video communication. Proc. SPIE – Int. Soc. Opt. Eng. **3299**, 294–305 (1998)
35. Wang, Z., Bovik, A.C.: Embedded foveation image coding. IEEE Trans. Image Process. **10**(10), 1397–1410 (2001)
36. Bylinskii, Z., Judd, T., Oliva, A., et al.: What do different evaluation metrics tell us about saliency models? IEEE Trans. Pattern Anal. Mach. Intell. **41**(3), 740–757 (2019)
37. Margolin, R., Tal, A.: Saliency for image manipulation. Vis. Comput. **29**(5), 381–392 (2013)

Design of 2D Checkboard Nonuniform Directional Filter Banks and Its Application to Image Nonlinear Approximation

Wei Zhong[✉], Kaiyang Xia, Li Fang, Long Ye, and Qin Zhang

Key Laboratory of Media Audio and Video (Communication University of China), Ministry of Education, Communication University of China, No. 1 Dingfuzhuang East Street, Chaoyang District, Beijing 100024, People's Republic of China
{wzhong, xiakaiyang, yelong, zhangqin}@cuc.edu.cn,
fangly2000@gmail.com

Abstract. In this paper, we propose a class of 2D nonuniform directional filter banks (DFBs) with checkboard frequency partitioning. It is constructed by cascading 1D nonuniform filter banks and 2D quadrant filter bank, which can efficiently separate two different directional subbands mixed in one frequency subband. Since the involved 1D nonuniform filter banks and 2D quadrant filter bank are both non-redundant, the resulted 2D nonuniform DFBs also have the non-redundancy property, which is extremely crucial to the application of image nonlinear approximation. In the experiments, we apply the designed 2D checkboard nonuniform DFB to decompose the input image to validate its capability of extracting directions. Further by choosing certain percent of large coefficients to perform the reconstruction, the experiment results show that the proposed nonuniform checkboard DFBs have better nonlinear approximation performance than the conventional wavelet transform and uniform checkboard DFBs.

Keywords: Nonuniform directional filter bank ·
Checkboard frequency partitioning · Image nonlinear approximation

1 Introduction

The direction information of image edge contour and texture plays an important role in image denoising, compression and feature extraction. It is well known that the traditional wavelet transform can represent the singularity of one dimensional (1D) signal [1, 2]. But for the two-dimensional (2D) image, the 2D separable wavelet, which is the tensor product of 1D wavelet, can only extract the information of three directions, horizontal, vertical and diagonal. It cannot efficiently describe the rich direction information contained in the texture image. Therefore, the researchers have been putting efforts to find a new transformation which can extract and analyze the texture direction of images effectively.

As a class of tools to extract texture direction information, directional filter banks (DFBs) have developed rapidly in recent years. The original critical sampling DFBs were proposed by Bamberger and Smith in 1992 [3]. It is constructed by a cascade of

© Springer Nature Singapore Pte Ltd. 2019
G. Zhai et al. (Eds.): IFTC 2018, CCIS 1009, pp. 45–54, 2019.
https://doi.org/10.1007/978-981-13-8138-6_4

two-channel 2D wedge-shaped filter banks and parallel quadrilateral filter banks through the tree structure, which can realize the direction decomposition of the number of subbands being 2^n. But the resulted DFBs lack multi-resolution characteristics, and this characteristic is very important in image representation. To solve this problem, the DFBs with critical sampling and multi-resolution characteristics have been proposed [4–6]. However, since the 2D filters and sampling structure used in such DFBs are both non-separable, the design and implementation complexities of the whole system are very high. In 2005, Lu et al. proposed a directional wavelet transform [7]. Later, it is extended to the multi-channel uniform DFBs with checkboard frequency partitioning [8, 9]. This transformation not only preserves the non-redundancy property of the 2D separable critical sampling uniform filter banks, but also separates the information of two different directions mixed in each subband. But it is still restricted by the traditional scheme of uniform frequency partitioning in terms of the direction subband division. In the actual application of image processing, the texture distribution of natural images is always rich and irregular, and thus it also needs more flexible direction division to realize the effective representation of the image. The multi-scale geometric transformation, which is guided by wavelet transform, is another important tool to extract the texture information of images. This kind of transformations, such as curvelet [10], contourlet [11] and shearlet [12], etc., can extract the texture direction information of image by using the special geometric features of the image data itself. However, their performance in image processing depends to a large extent on that of the involved 2D DFBs. But most of the existing DFBs are not flexible in the direction division, which makes these multi-scale geometric transformations not meet the needs of the actual application when dealing with irregular texture images. In addition, most of these multi-scale geometric transformations are over-complete and cannot be used well in image processing requiring economic expense, such as image compression and nonlinear approximation.

In this paper, we extend the construction of uniform checkboard DFBs to the nonuniform cases, breaking the limits of the traditional uniform frequency partitioning. The proposed 2D nonuniform checkboard DFB is constructed by cascading 1D M-channel linear-phase (LP) nonuniform filter banks (NUFBs) and 2D quadrant filter bank. Firstly, we design a 2D separable NUFB with channel number of $M_x \times M_y$ by the tensor product of two 1D LP NUFBs with the channel numbers being M_x and M_y, respectively. And then the 2D quadrant filter bank is used to deal with the subbands other than the lowpass one in the 2D separable NUFB and thus the two different directional information mixed in one frequency subband can be efficiently separated. As a result, we can obtain a 2D checkboard nonuniform DFB with only one lowpass subband and $2\big((M_x \times M_y) - 1\big)$ directional subbands. Since the involved 1D NUFBs and 2D quadrant filter bank are both non-redundant, the resulted 2D nonuniform DFBs also have the non-redundancy property. By choosing certain percent of large coefficients to perform the reconstruction, the experiment results show that the proposed nonuniform checkboard DFBs have better nonlinear approximation performance than the traditional wavelet transform and uniform checkboard DFBs.

The outline of this paper is organized as follows. Section 2 proposes the design method of 2D nonuniform DFBs with checkboard frequency partitioning. The constructed 2D checkboard nonuniform DFB is applied in Sect. 3 to perform the nonlinear approximation of images. Finally, some conclusions are drawn in Sect. 4.

2 Design of 2D Checkboard Nonuniform DFBs

The traditional 2D separable wavelet can only extract three directional information of horizontal, vertical and diagonal, as shown in Fig. 1(a), and thus it cannot efficiently describe the rich direction information contained in the texture image. Further by using the wavelet transform to decompose the image, the obtained subbands are mixed with different directional information. Figure 1(b) gives the result of LH subband by employing 9/7 wavelet to perform the one-level decomposition of image Barbara. It can be seen from Fig. 1(b) that, the traditional separable wavelet cannot separate the directional information of 45° and 135° from image Barbara effectively.

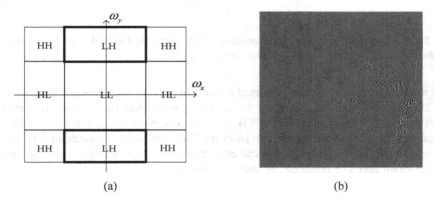

(a)   (b)

Fig. 1. The 2D separable wavelet. (a) The scheme of frequency spectrum division and (b) the result of LH subband by using 9/7 wavelet to perform the one-level decomposition of image Barbara.

In this section, in order to represent the texture image more effectively, we further generalize the construction of uniform checkboard DFBs [8, 9] to the nonuniform cases, breaking the limits of the traditional uniform frequency partitioning. According to the texture direction distribution and the needs of actual applications, we first design two 1D LP NUFBs with the channel numbers being respectively M_x and M_y to form a 2D separable NUFB with channel number of $M_x \times M_y$. For simple demonstration, Fig. 2 shows the frequency spectrum decomposition of 2D separable LP NUFB with the channel number $M_x = M_y = 5$ and sampling factors being [4 8 8 4 4].

It can be seen from Fig. 2 that, the constructed 2D separable LP NUFB can divide the entire frequency spectrum into $M_x \times M_y$ checkboard subbands. However, it should be noticed that each subband involves two different directional information. Take the 2D separable LP NUFB with the channel number $M_x = M_y = 5$ and sampling factors being [4 8 8 4 4] as an example, the directional information of 22° and 158° are both clustered in the subband indexed with 5 as shown in Fig. 2, which will greatly weaken the direction sensitivity of the constructed 2D separable DFB and reduce its effect in image processing. Especially in the application of low bit rate image coding, this may

$\uparrow \omega_y$

24	19	14	9	4	4	9	14	19	24
23	18	13	8	3	3	8	13	18	23
22	17	12	7	2	2	7	12	17	22
21	16	11	6	1	1	6	11	16	21
20	15	10	5	0	0	5	10	15	20
20	15	10	5	0	0	5	10	15	20
21	16	11	6	1	1	6	11	16	21
22	17	12	7	2	2	7	12	17	22
23	18	13	8	3	3	8	13	18	23
24	19	14	9	4	4	9	14	19	24

$\omega_x \rightarrow$

Fig. 2. The frequency spectrum decomposition of 2D separable LP NUFB with the channel number $M_x = M_y = 5$ and sampling factors being $[4\,8\,8\,4\,4]$.

lead to fuzzy regions in the reconstructed images. In order to solve this problem, we use the 2D quadrant filter bank to filter the subbands other than the lowpass one in the constructed $M_x \times M_y$ channel LP NUFB, so as to effectively separate the two different directional information mixed in each subband. The employed 2D quadrant filter bank is made up of a pair of filters, which can extract information in the spectrum regions of 2–4 quadrant and 1–3 quadrant, as shown in Fig. 3.

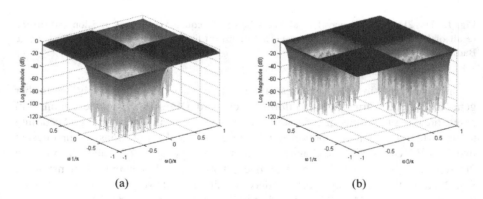

      (a)   (b)

Fig. 3. The frequency supports of 2D quadrant filter bank. (a) 2–4 quadrant and (b) 1–3 quadrant

In the proposed design method, by cascading the constructed 2D separable LP NUFB and 2D quadrant filter bank, we can obtain the block diagram of the proposed 2D non-redundant nonuniform DFB with checkboard frequency partitioning, as shown in Fig. 4. It can be seen from Fig. 4 that, the obtained 2D nonuniform checkboard DFB can produce one lowpass subband and $2\big((M_x \times M_y) - 1\big)$ directional subbands. In contrast to Fig. 2, Fig. 5(a) illustrates the spectral direction division of the obtained 49-channel nonuniform checkboard DFB with the channel number $M_x = M_y = 5$ and sampling factors being $[4\,8\,8\,4\,4]$. We can see from Fig. 5(a) that, the constructed 49-channel nonuniform checkboard DFB can generate 48 directional subbands denoted respectively by $1, 2, \cdots, 48$ and one lowpass subband represented by 0. Each directional subband corresponds to one direction, which well solves the problem of direction confusion in the original $M_x \times M_y$ channel 2D separable NUFB. At the same time, the reservation of lowpass subband can achieve the multi-resolution characteristic of the obtained nonuniform checkboard DFB. Compared with the 31-channel uniform checkboard DFB given in [8], as shown in Fig. 5(b), the 49-channel nonuniform checkboard DFB constructed in this section is capable of providing more precise and flexible spectrum partitioning scheme. In addition, since the involved 1D M-channel LP NUFBs and 2D quadrant filter bank are both critically sampled, the resulted 2D nonuniform checkboard DFB also has the non-redundancy property, which is extremely crucial to the application of image nonlinear approximation.

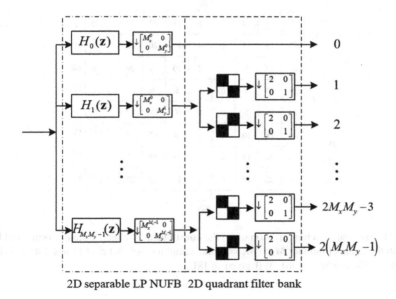

2D separable LP NUFB 2D quadrant filter bank

Fig. 4. The block diagram of the proposed 2D non-redundant nonuniform DFB with checkboard frequency partitioning.

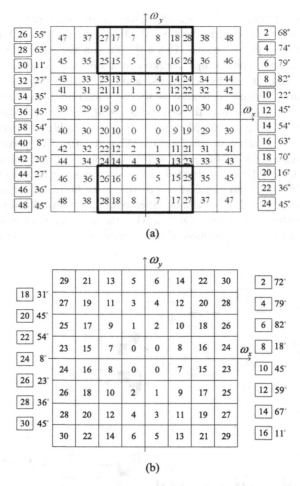

(a)

(b)

Fig. 5. The spectral direction division of (a) the constructed 49-channel nonuniform checkboard DFB with the channel number $M_x = M_y = 5$ and sampling factors being [4 8 8 4 4] and (b) the 31-channel uniform checkboard DFB given in [8].

3   Experiments of Image Nonlinear Approximation

Nonlinear approximation is an effective method to evaluate the performance of filter banks in image processing. In this section, we apply the constructed nonuniform checkboard DFBs to the nonlinear approximation of images.

Firstly, we will test the direction extraction performance of the constructed nonuniform DFBs with checkboard frequency partitioning. Here, the image "Barbara" with the size of 512×512 is selected as the test image. Taking the 5-channel LP NUFB with sample factors [4 8 8 4 4] as an example, we employ the method of partial cosine modulation [13] to perform the design and the length of filters is selected to be 49. Figure 6 shows respectively the magnitude responses of the prototype filters and analysis filters, as well as aliasing and amplitude distortions. The maximum value of aliasing error and peak-to-peak value of amplitude distortion are $E_a = 5.74 \times 10^{-3}$, $E_{pp} = 1.83 \times 10^{-2}$. By cascading the designed 25-channel 2D separable LP NUFB and quadrant filter bank, the 49-channel nonuniform checkboard DFB can be obtained with the channel number $M_x = M_y = 5$ and sampling factors being [4 8 8 4 4]. Then we apply the constructed 49-channel nonuniform checkboard DFB to extract the directional information of image Barbara. For convenient comparison, here we give the decomposition results of subbands 5–8, 15–18 and 25–28 as shown in Fig. 7. This region corresponds to the LH subband obtained by using 9/7 wavelet as shown in Fig. 1(b). With the comparison of Figs. 1(b) and 7, it can be seen that the constructed 49-channel nonuniform checkboard DFB can distribute the directional information from 45° to 135° contained in the image into 12 different directional subbands, so as to extract the texture direction information more accurately than the traditional wavelet.

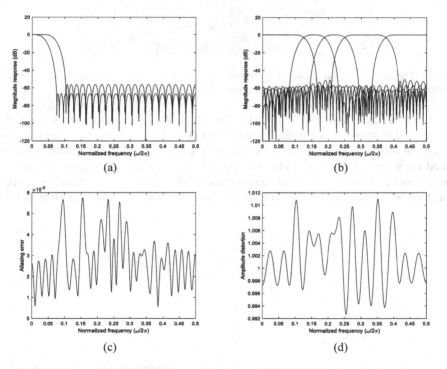

Fig. 6. The 5-channel LP NUFB with sampling factors [4 8 8 4 4]. (a) Magnitude responses of prototype filters, (b) magnitude responses of analysis filters, (c) aliasing error and (d) amplitude distortion.

Next we take the image "Zoneplate" with rich texture as an example and perform the nonlinear approximation by using the constructed 49-channel nonuniform checkboard DFB, 9/7 separable wavelet and the 31-channel uniform checkboard DFB in [8], respectively. In the experiment, the $K\%$ of large coefficients are selected after decomposition to perform the reconstruction and the performance of nonlinear approximation is measured by peak signal to noise ratio (PSNR). Figure 8 shows the comparison results of PSNR values of reconstructed images obtained by the three methods mentioned above, respectively.

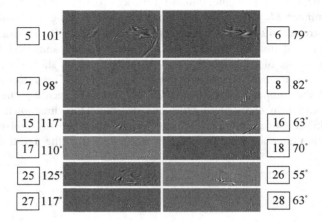

Fig. 7. The decomposition results of subbands 5–8, 15–18 and 25–28 obtained by applying the constructed 49-channel nonuniform checkboard DFB to image Barbara.

It can be seen from Fig. 8 that, for the image Zoneplate with rich texture, the constructed 49-channel nonuniform checkboard DFB can achieve more fine extraction of texture direction information, so as to make the image information more concentrated on a few large coefficients. And thus the constructed 49-channel nonuniform checkboard DFB is capable of obtaining better performance on nonlinear approximation than 9/7 separable wavelet and the 31-channel uniform checkboard DFB in [8].

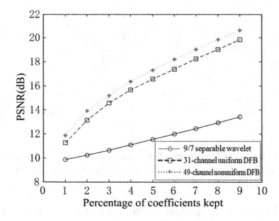

Fig. 8. The comparison results of PSNR values of reconstructed images obtained by the constructed 49-channel nonuniform checkboard DFB, 9/7 separable wavelet and the 31-channel uniform checkboard DFB in [8], respectively.

Further in order to compare the perceptual visual quality, Fig. 9 shows the results of reconstructed images by using the proposed 49-channel nonuniform checkboard DFB and the 31-channel uniform checkboard DFB in [8], when retaining 7% of large coefficients to perform the nonlinear approximation. We can see from Fig. 9 that, compared to the 31-channel uniform checkboard DFB in [8], the proposed 49-channel nonuniform checkboard DFB are more advantageous in preserving the information of the edge direction of image.

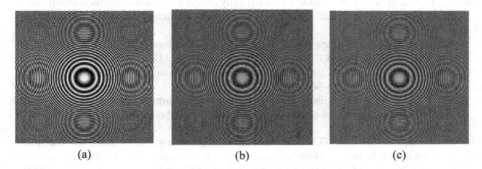

(a)   (b)   (c)

Fig. 9. The results of reconstructed images when retaining 7% of large coefficients to perform the nonlinear approximation. (a) The original image Zoneplate, (b) the 31-channel uniform checkboard DFB in [8] with PSNR = 18.27 dB, and (c) the proposed 49-channel nonuniform checkboard DFB with PSNR = 19.04 dB.

4   Conclusion

In this paper, we propose a simple but efficient design method for 2D nonuniform DFBs with checkboard frequency partitioning. It is constructed by cascading 1D LP NUFBs and 2D quadrant filter bank, which can efficiently separate two different directional subbands mixed in one frequency subband. Since the involved 1D NUFBs and 2D quadrant filter bank are both non-redundant, the resulted 2D nonuniform DFBs also have the non-redundancy property. The experiment on direction extraction demonstrates that the designed 2D checkboard nonuniform DFB can extract the texture direction information more accurately than the traditional wavelet. Further by choosing certain percent of large coefficients to perform the reconstruction, the experiment results show that the proposed 49-channel nonuniform checkboard DFBs have better nonlinear approximation performance than the 9/7 separable wavelet and 31-channel uniform checkboard DFB in [8].

Acknowledgment. This work is supported by the National Natural Science Foundation of China under Grant No. 61631016, and the Fundamental Research Funds for the Central Universities under Grant Nos. 2018XNG1824 and YLSZ180226.

References

1. Mallat, S.G., Peyré, G.: A Wavelet Tour of Signal Processing: The Sparse Way. Elsevier, Academic Press, Cambridge (2009)
2. Yan, R.Q., Gao, R.X., Chen, X.F.: Wavelets for fault diagnosis of rotary machines: a review with applications. Signal Process. **96**, 1–15 (2014)
3. Bamberger, R.H., Smith, M.J.T.: A filter bank for directional decomposition of images: theory and design. IEEE Trans. Signal Process. **40**(4), 882–893 (1992)
4. Lu, Y., Do, M.N.: CRISP-contourlets: a critically sampled directional multiresolution image representation. In: Wavelets: Applications in Signal and Image Processing X, vol. 5207, pp. 655–665 (2003)
5. Eslami, R., Radha, H.: A new family of nonredundant transforms using hybrid wavelets and directional filter banks. IEEE Trans. Image Processing **16**, 1152–1167 (2007)
6. Nguyen, T.T., Oraintara, S.: A class of multiresolution directional filter banks. IEEE Trans. Signal Process. **55**(3), 949–961 (2007)
7. Lu, Y., Do, M.N.: The finer directional wavelet transform. In: Proceedings of IEEE International Conference on Acoustics, Speech, and Signal Processing, vol. IV, pp. 573–576 (2005)
8. Liang, L.L., Ye, S.H., Shi, G.M., Xie, X.M., Zhong, W., Wang, C.: A class of non-redundant directional filter banks. In: Muneesawang, P., Wu, F., Kumazawa, I., Roeksabutr, A., Liao, M., Tang, X. (eds.) PCM 2009. LNCS, vol. 5879, pp. 982–987. Springer, Heidelberg (2009). https://doi.org/10.1007/978-3-642-10467-1_92
9. Rahulkar, A.D., Holambe, R.S.: Partial iris feature extraction and recognition based on a new combined directional and rotated directional wavelet filter banks. Neurocomputing **81**, 12–23 (2012)
10. Ma, J., Plonka, G.: The curvelet transform. IEEE Signal Process. Mag. **27**(2), 118–133 (2010)
11. Da Cunha, A.L., Zhou, J., Do, M.N.: The nonsubsampled contourlet transform: theory, design, and applications. IEEE Trans. Image Process. **15**(10), 3089–3101 (2006)
12. Kutyniok, G., Lim, W.Q., Reisenhofer, R.: ShearLab 3D: faithful digital shearlet transforms based on compactly supported shearlets. ACM Trans. Math. Softw. **42**(1), 5–44 (2016)
13. Fang, L., Zhong, W., Zhang, Q.: Design of M-channel linear-phase nonuniform filter banks with arbitrary rational sampling factors. IET Signal Proc. **10**(2), 106–114 (2016)

Super-Resolution Restoration for Sonar Images: Comprehensive Comparison

Weiling Chen[1](✉), Zhuang Yang[2], Huiqing Zhang[2], Yi Zhu[1], and Yutao Liu[3]

[1] Key Laboratory of Underwater Acoustic Communication and Marine Information Technology Ministry of Education, Xiamen University, Xiamen 361005, China
weiling.chen@stu.xmu.edu.cn
[2] Faculty of Information Technology, Beijing University of Technology, Beijing 100124, China
[3] Graduate School at Shenzhen, Tsinghua University, Shenzhen 518055, China

Abstract. This paper investigates the performance of advanced super-resolution restoration algorithms on sonar images. Because of the ability of being able to shoot images in relatively dim light underwater, sonar has been more and more widely used during recent years. However, images taken by sonar usually have low resolution due to the positive correlation between sonar image resolution and frequency of sonar sensors, as well as the negative relationship between working range and frequency of sonar sensors. For more accurate observation, resolution of sonar image should be increased. Since few super-resolution restoration algorithm has been designed for sonar images, we selected eight existing state-of-the-art or classical super-resolution restoration algorithms designed for optical images. Then we tested their performances on sonar images using classical and state-of-the-art image quality assessment (IQA) methods. Finally we analyze the relationship between their performances and the content of sonar images by comparing the visual qualities of reconstructed magnified super-resolution sonar images.

Keywords: Sonar image · Super-resolution restoration · Image quality

1 Introduction

There has been a big demand for imaging in many underwater applications, such as marine charting, underwater target detection. Underwater imaging technology is mainly composed of optical imaging and sonar imaging. The resolution of underwater optical image is relatively high. However, the effective work range of underwater optical imaging device is generally low, and it will be useless in muddy water field. Instead, because of the ability to take images in relatively

This work was supported in part by the National Science Foundation of China (Grant 61703009), the Young Elite Scientist Sponsorship Program by China Association for Science and Technology (Grant 2017QNRC001), and Young Top-Notch Talents Team Program of Beijing Excellent Talents Funding (Grant 2017000026833ZK40).

© Springer Nature Singapore Pte Ltd. 2019
G. Zhai et al. (Eds.): IFTC 2018, CCIS 1009, pp. 55–64, 2019.
https://doi.org/10.1007/978-981-13-8138-6_5

Fig. 1. An example of optical natural scene image and sonar image. (a) a sonar image captured by a acoustic lens sonar; (b) an optical natural scene image captured by a camera.

dim light underwater, sonar has been more and more widely used during recent years. According to underwater acoustic behavior, the lower the frequency of underwater acoustic signal is, the slower its attenuation is, that is, the working range of sonar is inversely proportional to frequency [1]. On the other hand, sonar devices work in higher frequency will produce images with higher resolution. Therefore, there is a trade-off between working range and image resolution in most sonar image applications, it is important to develop a method to increase the resolution of sonar image without increasing frequency of acoustic signal.

There have been many super-resolution models for optical natural scenes images [2–6], in contrast, limited efforts have been denoted to sonar image super-resolution restoration. There are also many differences between sonar images and natural scene images. For imaging principle, most optical natural scenes images are created using a camera, which uses a lens to transform the optical wavelength of a scene to a picture of what the human eye can see. For sonar image, it is captured by a sonar sensor which emits pulses of sounds and listens for echoes, the sonar image is formed according to the arrival time and intensity of echoes. From visual perspective as Fig. 1 shows, (1) optical natural scene images are usually colourful and have rich color variations, thick lines, more details and complex texture content; (2) sonar images are mostly characterized by small variation of pixel values, low contrast, less details and gray levels. Due to the differences between optical natural scene images and sonar images, main contribution of this paper is to test the validity of existing super-resolution restoration methods on sonar images.

In this paper, we first briefly review some classical or advanced super-resolution restoration algorithms. Then the performance of the selected super-resolution methods are tested and compared on sonar images with different content, which is followed by the conclusion.

2   Methodology and Analysis

2.1   Related Work

We will first introduce some approaches proposed for increasing the resolution of sonar images. Since speckle noise is a kind of typical noise in sonar images because of oceanic reverberation, it is a major factor resulting in resolution degradation on sonar captured images. Some researchers try to increase the resolution and sharpness of sonar images by reducing speckle noise [7,8], however, there is a limit to the resolution that can be increased with these methods. Besides, mosaicing has also been employed for sonar image super-resolution restoration [9,10]. It takes effect by dividing the target region, and then taking sonar images with higher resolution for subregions, finally constructing higher resolution images through registration and mosaicing process according to a fusion algorithm. But mosaicing-based super-resolution restoration algorithms may lead to non-uniform resolution in resolution-enhanced images. Common sonar imaging technologies includes beam-forming technique, acoustic lens imaging and acoustic holographic imaging. The abovementioned methods are mostly designed for sonar images based on beam-forming technique. Since acoustic lens imaging has been more and more widely used in recent years, we will test the performances of the existing classical and state-of-the-art super-resolution restoration algorithms on acoustic lens sonar images in this paper.

There are many impressive researches addressing the optical image super resolution restoration task, and most of them have shown superior performance in corresponding testing images. The Bicubic interpolation [11] is one of the most classical methods among them, which has been commonly used for resizing videos and images. Fine details can be better maintained by Bicubic interpolation than by common bilinear algorithm, because the Bicubic interpolation takes 16 pixels (4×4) into account instead of 4 pixels (2×2). Since the Bicubic interpolation is based on the assumption that images are limited in band, which has been proved to be not applicable to most cases, it might exhibit some unexpected visual artifacts. But for smooth areas, the Bicubic might provide relatively good performance. During the last decades, large amounts of effort have been devoted to dictionary-based super-resolution methods. Among them, Neighbor Embedding approaches [3,12–16], which were proposed based on the assumption that the local geometry of local low resolution patches and their corresponding high resolution versions are similar, and Sparse Coding approaches [17,18], which reduce the pool of training samples by introducing compact dictionaries on basis of sparse signal representation, are the main branches of the dictionary-based methods. A distinct category in dictionary-based super resolution restoration methods is learning-based approach. These methods learn to regress from low resolution patches to high resolution patches directly with the help of learning machine, such as Support Vector Regression (SVR) [19], and Convolutional Neural Network (CNN) [1].

2.2 Experimental Protocol

Algorithms. We have selected eight common-used super-resolution restoration methods for performance comparison on sonar images. The Bicubic interpolation has been selected as the representation of classical invariant linear filters. Since dictionary-based methods hold important position in super-resolution restoration, five Neighbor Embedding methods and one Sparse Coding-based methods, which were considered or proposed in [3,15–17], are also selected for comparison. For a more comprehensive comparison, Super-Resolution Convolutional Neural Network (SRCNN) [1] is selected to represent the super-resolution based on deep learning in this paper. Following are the brief introduction of selected super-resolution restoration methods.

The Bicubic interpolation is built on the assumption that images are limited in band. The Bicubic interpolation can achieve good performance for smooth regions because it assumes smoothness of image data. Since smooth region is not the only component of most images, images are also composed of thick lines and complex texture content. The Bicubic interpolation may introduce visual artifacts like blocking and blurring into high resolution reconstructed images. The Bicubic interpolation of a low resolution image I can be written as

$$I(i + u, j + v) = ABC \tag{1}$$

where A, B, and C can be represented as

$$A = [S(1 + u)S(u)S(1 - u)S(2 - u)] \tag{2}$$

$$B = \begin{bmatrix} I(i-1, j-2) & I(i, j-2) & I(i+1, j-2) & I(i+2, j-2) \\ I(i-1, j-1) & I(i, j-1) & I(i+1, j-1) & I(i+2, j-1) \\ I(i-1, j) & I(i, j) & I(i+1, j) & I(i+2, j) \\ I(i-1, j+1) & I(i, j+1) & I(i+1, j+1) & I(i+2, j+1) \end{bmatrix} \tag{3}$$

$$C = [S(1 + v)S(v)S(1 - v)S(2 - v)]^T. \tag{4}$$

$S(\omega)$ is fundamental interpolation function as shown below

$$S(\omega) = \begin{cases} 1 - 2|\omega|^2 + |\omega|^3 & |\omega| < 1 \\ 4 - 8|\omega| + 5|\omega|^2 - |\omega|^3 & 1 \leq |\omega| < 2 \\ 0 & |\omega| \geq 2 \end{cases} \tag{5}$$

Zeyde *et al.* use sparse-representation model for optical image super-resolution restoration in [17]. The foundation of this work is the local *Sparse-Land* model and the Sparse Coding-based super-resolution approach published by Yang [20]. In Yang's work, the Sparse Coding-based super-resolution was described as Eq. 6 shows:

$$\mathbf{X}^* = arg \min_{X, \{\alpha_{i,j}\}} \{ \|DH\mathbf{X} - \mathbf{Y}\|_2^2 + \gamma \sum_{i,j} \|\alpha_{ij}\|_0$$
$$+ \beta \sum_{i,j} \|\widehat{D}\alpha_{ij} - P_{ij}\mathbf{X}\|_2^2 + \kappa\rho(\mathbf{X}) \} \tag{6}$$

where $\mathbf{Y}$ represents low resolution image, $\mathbf{X}$ and $\mathbf{X}^*$ denote its high resolution version and super-resolution magnified version, respectively. H is a low-pass filter, $\widehat{D}$ denotes a down-sampling operator, α_{ij} is the coefficient vector representing the sparsity constraint. Besides, P_{ij} is a projection matrix and $\rho(\cdot)$ represents a penalty function. Zeyde *et al.* exploit this framework and introduce some important changes to get less execution time, better objective quality, which is usually measured by Peak Signal-to-Noise Ratio (PSNR), and less artifacts. The most important modifications include removing redundant steps, applying Orthogonal Matching Pursuit (OMP) and Principal Component Analysis (PCA) to reduce the dimensionality, training dictionary pair using different training approach.

When considering Neighbor Embedding approaches, an application that applies unconstrained least squares to solve the regression, which is denoted by 'LS' [15] is selected in this paper for comparison. Another works based on Neighbor Embedding are Anchored Neighborhood Regression (ANR) and Global Regression (GR) [15]. By reformulating the aforementioned least square regression in Neighbor Embedding or Sparse Coding approaches with the help of l_2 norm of the coefficients and Ridge Regression [21], the patch representation problem becomes:

$$\min_{\beta} \|y_F - N_l\beta\|_2^2 + \lambda\|\beta\|_2 \tag{7}$$

where y_F is the input feature, β denotes the coefficient vector, while λ is a parameter to stabilize the solution and lighten the singularity problems. The K nearest neighbors of dictionary are denoted as N_l. Then the y_F can be projected to high resolution space as

$$x = N_h(N_l^T N_l + \lambda I)^{-1} N_l^T y_F. \tag{8}$$

The whole low resolution dictionary is used for GR, that is $(N_h, N_l) = (D_h, D_l)$. Therefore projection matrix can be denoted as Eq. 9 shows, which means the high resolution image x can be calculated using the procomputed P_G and y_F as Eq. 10 shows.

$$P_G = D_h(D_l^T D_l + \lambda I)^{-1} D_l^T. \tag{9}$$

$$x = P_G y_F. \tag{10}$$

As mentioned before, Eq. 7 to Eq. 10 are the main points of GR. When the local neighbors are considered instead of the whole dictionary, the Eq. 10 becomes

$$x_i = P_j y_{iF}. \tag{11}$$

where y_{iF} is the input patch feature, while P_j is a separated projection matrix of each dictionary atom d_j, and x_i denotes the reconstructed high resolution image patch. Then Timofte proposed A+ by utilizing the features and anchored regressors from ANR and learning the regressors on the full training material as Simple Function (SF) [22] in [3]. Another direction of Neighbor Embedding approaches is represented by Jointly Optimized Regressor (JOR) [16], which learns multiple regressors and adaptively select the most applicable one for current low resolution image patch.

In recent years, deep learning has been widely developed because of its superior performance in many applications. Super-Resolution Convolutional Neural Network (SRCNN) is one of the earliest works employing deep learning in super-resolution. It obtains high resolution image by sending Bicubic interpolated version of the low resolution image into three layer convolutional networks. It has been proved that SRCNN can achieve pretty good performance in natural scene optical images.

Criteria and Experimental Settings. To compare the performance of selected super-resolution methods on sonar images, high resolution sonar images reconstructed using different super-resolution methods are compared quantitatively and qualitatively in the following part. In our experimental part, 30 sonar images are selected as the reference high resolution samples, and their downscaled versions (by fixed upscaling factor, $\times 3$) will be obtained as corresponding low resolution images. Then the low resolution sonar images will be reconstructed using abovementioned eight super-resolution methods using the same fixed upscaling factor, that is $\times 3$. For comprehensive comparison, the objective qualities of reconstructed sonar images will be reported. Ten kinds of classical or state-of-the-art image quality assessment (IQA) methods are used in this part, which fall into three categories, that is: (1) classical natural scene IQA metric, such as PSNR; (2) state-of-the-art natural scene image quality metrics, like ARISM [23], CPCQI [24], NFERM [25], ADD-SSIM [26], PSIM [27], RIQMC [28], SISBLIM [29]; (3) quality assessment methods designed for sonar images, PSIQP [30], LESQP [31], and NSIQM [32]. Among these quality metrics, NSIQM, ARISM, RIQMC, and SISBLISM are no-reference approaches, which are more applicable to the applications of super-resolution restoration.

2.3   Experimental Analysis

Objective Quality. To assess the performance of eight super-resolution methods comprehensively, IQA methods including reference-based methods and reference-free methods are selected in this paper for performance evaluation. Different objective qualities of reconstructed images made by eight super-resolution methods are tabulated in Table 1, where the best performance is highlighted in bold font, and the second performance is highlight in underline. All the objective qualities in Table 1 have been normalized to [0, 1], where higher score represents the better quality. For upscaling factor $\times 3$ as shown in Table 1, according to the common used PSNR, SRCNN shows its superiority over selected super-resolution restoration methods on sonar images, and A+ performs second only to SRCNN. When systematically considering about other IQA metrics designed for optical images, SRCNN and Zeyde *et al.* are the best-performance super-resolution methods among selected methods on sonar images. For IQA metrics designed for sonar images, A+ performs better than other seven super-resolution methods, while JOR also shows comparable performance.

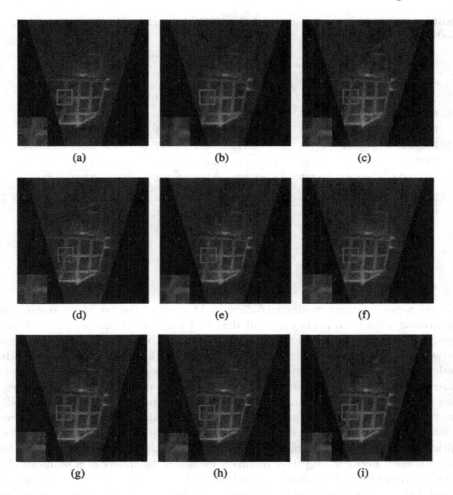

Fig. 2. Results of super-resolution magnified image with an upscaling factor ×3. (a) Original image; (b) Bicubic; (c) Zeyde *et al.*; (d) GR; (e) ANR; (f) NE+LS; (g) A+; (h) SRCNN; (i) JOR.

Visual Quality. The visual quality of magnified sonar images with upscaling factor ×3 is displayed in Fig. 2. For clear observation, details in red box are further magnified in the lower left corner of each sonar image. In Fig. 2, most details and important textures are retained in the reconstructed images, though the edge of the objects may be not sharp enough. Among eight super-resolution methods, Zeyde *et al.* seems to provide with good visual quality, while the Bicubic interpolation still underperforms other selected methods. In can be concluded from Fig. 2: (1) JOR, A+ and SRCNN can recover sharper edges of sonar images, especially for sonar images with more details; (2) for smooth regions, all selected super-resolution methods yield good performance.

Table 1. Performance comparison of the NSIQM metric and reference-based IQA methods on the SIQD database.

IQA	Bicubic	Zeyde *et al.*	ANR	GR	NE+LS	A+	SRCNN	JOR
ADD_ SSIM	0.590	0.623	0.626	0.582	0.625	0.609	**0.722**	0.623
CPCQI	0.222	**0.452**	0.226	0.214	0.229	0.232	0.270	0.227
PSIM	0.542	0.554	0.609	**0.611**	0.601	0.606	0.597	0.607
PSNR	0.472	0.438	0.459	0.451	0.474	0.503	**0.519**	0.467
RIQMC	**0.472**	0.446	0.417	0.412	0.425	0.407	0.423	0.405
ARISM	0.352	0.488	0.375	**0.499**	0.461	0.407	0.472	0.395
SISBLIM	**0.644**	0.549	0.599	0.590	0.562	0.562	0.608	0.547
LESQP	0.729	0.610	0.726	0.717	0.729	**0.745**	0.728	0.741
PSIQP	0.642	0.483	**0.704**	0.586	0.617	0.612	0.530	0.570
NSIQM	0.552	0.599	0.624	0.625	0.625	**0.666**	0.614	0.644

3   Conclusion

In this paper, we first briefly introduce eight state-of-the-art super-resolution restoration algorithms. They are all designed for optical images and achieve good performances in consideration of PSNR. Since there exist many differences between camera captured optical images and sonar captured images, methods designed for optical images may not be successful in sonar images. We have evaluated the performances of selected super-resolution methods on sonar images. To make a general evaluation, ten IQA methods including common used PSNR are used in this paper to measure the objective qualities of reconstructed super-resolution sonar images. In can be concluded that IQA methods designed for optical images and sonar images focus on different standard, which leads to inconsistency between objective qualities measured by different IQA methods. IQA metric technically designed according to the characteristics and utilities of magnified super-resolution sonar images is in demand. As for visual quality of reconstructed sonar images, it can be seen that most selected super-resolution methods fail at generating sharp and clear edges. But nearly all methods can recover rough shape of the objects and smooth regions.

References

1. Gordon, H.: Can the Lambert-Beer law be applied to the diffuse attenuation coefficient of ocean water. Limnol. Oceanogr. **34**(8), 1389–1490 (1989)
2. Dai, D., Timofte, R., Van, G.: Jointly optimized regressors for image super-resolution. Comput. Graph. Forum **34**(2), 95–104 (2015)
3. Timofte, R., De Smet, V., Van Gool, L.: A+: adjusted anchored neighborhood regression for fast super-resolution. In: Cremers, D., Reid, I., Saito, H., Yang, M.-H. (eds.) ACCV 2014. LNCS, vol. 9006, pp. 111–126. Springer, Cham (2015). https://doi.org/10.1007/978-3-319-16817-3_8

4. Timofte, R., De, V., Gool, L.: Anchored neighborhood regression for fast example-based super-resolution. In: IEEE International Conference on Computer Vision, pp. 1920–1927 (2013)
5. Dong, C., Loy, C.C., He, K., Tang, X.: Learning a deep convolutional network for image super-resolution. In: Fleet, D., Pajdla, T., Schiele, B., Tuytelaars, T. (eds.) ECCV 2014. LNCS, vol. 8692, pp. 184–199. Springer, Cham (2014). https://doi.org/10.1007/978-3-319-10593-2_13
6. Zeyde, R., Elad, M., Protter, M.: On single image scale-up using sparse-representations. In: Boissonnat, J.-D., Chenin, P., Cohen, A., Gout, C., Lyche, T., Mazure, M.-L., Schumaker, L. (eds.) Curves and Surfaces 2010. LNCS, vol. 6920, pp. 711–730. Springer, Heidelberg (2012). https://doi.org/10.1007/978-3-642-27413-8_47
7. James, R., Supriya, M.: Spatial resolution enhancement of sonar images using one step pixel prediction. In: International Conference on Control Communication & Computing India, pp. 553–557 (2016)
8. Huo, G., Li, Q., Fan, X.: A fast super-resolution algorithm with despeckling for multi-frame sonar images. In: International Conference on Information Science and Engineering, pp. 3412–3415 (2010)
9. Kim, K., Intrator, N., Neretti, N.: Image registration and mosaicing of noisy acoustic camera images. In: IEEE International Conference on Electronics, Circuits and Systems, pp. 527–530 (2005)
10. Hurtos, N., Cuf, X., Petillot, Y., Salvi, J.: Fourier-based registrations for two-dimensional forward-looking sonar image mosaicing. In: IEEE/RSJ International Conference on Intelligent Robots and Systems, vol. 57(1), pp. 5298–5305 (2012)
11. Keys, R.: Cubic convolution interpolation for digital image processing. IEEE Trans. Acoust. Speech Signal Process. 29(6), 1153–1160 (1981)
12. Chang, H., Yeung, D., Xiong, Y.: Super-resolution through neighbor embedding. In: Computer Vision and Pattern Recognition 2004 (2004)
13. Roweis, S., Saul, L.: Nonlinear dimensionality reduction by locally linear embedding, vol. 2001 (2001)
14. Bevilacqua, M., Roumy, A., Guillemot, C., Morel, A.: Low-complexity single-image super-resolution based on nonnegative neighbor embedding. In: British Machine Vision Conference (2012)
15. Timofte, R., De, V., Gool, L.: Anchored neighborhood regression for fast example-based super-resolution. In: IEEE International Conference on Computer Vision, pp. 1920–1927 (2014)
16. Dai, D., Timofte, R., Van, G.: Jointly optimized regressors for image super-resolution. Comput. Graph. Forum 34, 95–104 (2015)
17. Roman, Z., Michael, E., Matan, P.: On single image scale-up using sparse-representations. In: International Conference on Curves and Surfaces, pp. 711–730 (2010)
18. Yang, J., Wright, J., Huang, T., Ma, Y.: Image super-resolution via sparse representation. IEEE Trans. Image Process. 19(11), 2861–2873 (2010)
19. Ni, K., Nguyen, T.: Image superresolution using support vector regression. IEEE Trans. Image Process. 16(6), 1596–1610 (2007)
20. Yang, J., Wright, J., Huang, T., Ma, Y.: Image super-resolution as sparse representation of raw image patches. In: Computer Vision and Pattern Recognition, pp. 1–8 (2008)
21. Tikhonov, A., Arsenin, V.: Solution of Ill-Posed Problems. Winston & Sons, New York (1977)

22. Yang, C., Yang, M.: Fast direct super-resolution by simple functions. In: IEEE International Conference on Computer Vision, pp. 561–568 (2013)
23. Gu, K., Zhai, G., Lin, W., Yang, X., Zhang, W.: No-reference image sharpness assessment in autoregressive parameter space. IEEE Trans. Image Process. Publ. IEEE Signal Process. Soc. **24**(10), 3218–3231 (2015)
24. Gu, K., Zhai, G., Lin, W., Yang, X., Zhang, W.: Learning a blind quality evaluation engine of screen content images. Neurocomputing **196**(C), 140–149 (2016)
25. Gu, K., Zhai, G., Yang, X., Zhang, W.: Using free energy principle for blind image quality assessment. IEEE Trans. Multimed. **17**(1), 50–63 (2014)
26. Gu, K., Wang, S., Zhai, G., Lin, W., Yang, X., Zhang, W.: Analysis of distortion distribution for pooling in image quality prediction. IEEE Trans. Broadcast. **62**(2), 446–456 (2016)
27. Gu, K., Li, L., Lu, H., Min, X., Lin, W.: A fast reliable image quality predictor by fusing micro- and macro-structures. IEEE Trans. Industr. Electron. **64**(5), 3903–3912 (2017)
28. Gu, K., Zhai, G., Lin, W., Liu, M.: The analysis of image contrast: from quality assessment to automatic enhancement. IEEE Trans. Cybern. **46**(1), 284–297 (2017)
29. Gu, K., Zhai, G., Yang, X., Zhang, W.: Hybrid no-reference quality metric for singly and multiply distorted images. IEEE Trans. Broadcast. **60**(3), 555–567 (2014)
30. Chen, W., Gu, K., Min, X., Yuan, F., Cheng, E.: Partial-reference sonar image quality assessment for underwater transmission. IEEE Trans. Aerosp. Electron. Syst. (2018)
31. Chen, W., Yuan, F., Cheng, E., Lin, W.: Subjective and objective quality evaluation of sonar images for underwater acoustic transmission. In: IEEE International Conference on Image Processing, pp. 176–180 (2017)
32. Chen, W., Yuan, F., Cheng, E., Gao, C.: Sonar image quality assessment based on degradation measurement. Oceans (2018)

How to Reliably Upsample Screen Content Images?

Jun Wu[1(✉)], Zhuang Yang[2], Du Peng[2], Cong Guo[2], and Huiqing Zhang[2]

[1] School of Electronics and Information, Northwestern Polytechnical University,
Xi'an, Shaanxi, China
wujun318@mail.nwpu.edu.cn
[2] Beijing University of Technology, Beijing, China

Abstract. In this paper, we investigate the performance of super-resolution restoration (SR) algorithms for the screen content images (SCIs), which emerged with the rapid development of multi-device communication. SR is a crucial technique to improve the perceptual-quality of low-resolution SCIs captured from low-cost imaging sensors. However, most of existing SR algorithms are designed for natural scene images (NSIs), and their performance for SCIs is rarely studied. In order to verify the effectiveness of the existing NSIs-oriented SR algorithms on SCIs, we select eight classical or advanced SR algorithms as representative. Then, their performance for SCIs is measured by nine state-of-the-art image quality assessment (IQA) metrics which have been proven to be consistent with human perception. Finally, we can verify the effectiveness of those SR algorithms on SCIs by comparing the objective quality scores derived from those IQA metrics.

Keywords: Screen content image · Super-resolution restoration · Image quality

1 Introduction

With the rapid development of multi-device communication, the screen content images (SCIs) have been more closely and frequently related to our daily lives [1]. Different from natural scene images (NSIs) which are captured by an optical camera under the condition of visible light, the SCIs are collected from the screens of various digital display devices, for example, the computer monitors, mobile phone screens. Figure 1 demonstrates a typical comparison between the screen content image and natural scene image. From the perspective of image content, the SCIs are mixed with natural scene images, character pictures and

This work was supported in part by the National Science Foundation of China (Grant 61703009), the Young Elite Scientist Sponsorship Program by China Association for Science and Technology (Grant 2017QNRC001), Young Top-Notch Talents Team Program of Beijing Excellent Talents Funding (Grant 2017000026833ZK40), and Beijing Natural Science Foundation (Grant 8184064).

© Springer Nature Singapore Pte Ltd. 2019
G. Zhai et al. (Eds.): IFTC 2018, CCIS 1009, pp. 65–73, 2019.
https://doi.org/10.1007/978-981-13-8138-6_6

computer created graphics. From the point of image structure, the SCIs always composed of fewer colors, simpler shapes, and a larger frequency of thin lines than NSIs [2]. Due to those differences between SCIs and NSIs, many traditional image processing algorithms designed for NSIs are proven to be invalid on SCIs, e.g., image compression [3], image quality assessment [1].

(a) Screen content image

(b) Natural scene image

Fig. 1. An example of natural scene image and screen content image.

In practical applications, some low-resolution SCIs are often generated from low-cost imaging sensors, e.g., monitoring image and screen-shots of smartphones with poor communication networks. Those low-resolution SCIs always fail to meet the requirements of subsequent image processing system, so we need to improve the resolution of the SCIs. Under this demand, we can consider that the super-resolution restoration (SR) is a crucial technique to improve the quality of low-resolution images. However, most of existing SR algorithms are proposed for enhancing the resolution of NSIs, because of the different characteristics between the SCIs and NSIs mentioned before. Therefore, the research of the effectiveness of those NSIs-oriented SR algorithms on SCIs becomes a meaningful question. In this research, we reveals the validity of several representative SR algorithms on SCIs, and the research result is high related to the development of SR algorithms dedicated to SCIs.

In this paper, eight representative SR algorithms are selected to enhance the resolution of a set of low-resolution SCIs. Then, nine state-of-the-art perception-aware image quality assessment (IQA) metrics are employed to evaluate the objective quality of those enhanced images. Finally, the validity of those SR algorithms on SCIs is analyzed by combining the objective IQA result and subjective observation.

The rest of this paper is organized as follows. The selected SR algorithms are briefly introduced in Sect. 2. The employed IQA metrics and experimental settings are introduced in Sect. 3. The performance of those SR algorithms on SCIs is demonstrated and analyzed in Sect. 4. Finally, we draw a conclusion in Sect. 5.

2   Related Work

In this section, we briefly introduce the selected super-resolution restoration algorithms and image quality assessment methods.

2.1   Super-Resolution Restoration Algorithms

We roughly classified the selected SR algorithms into three categories.

Interpolation Based Methods. We select three classical interpolation algorithms, including nearest-neighbor interpolation, bilinear interpolation, and bicubic interpolation. Nearest-neighbor is the simplest interpolation method. It chooses the value of the nearest point and does not consider the values of neighboring points. Bilinear interpolation is to perform linear interpolation in two directions alternately. The smoothing effect of bilinear interpolation may degrade the details of the image. Bicubic interpolation is an extension of cubic interpolation for interpolating data points on a two-dimensional regular grid [4]. The interpolated surface is smoother than corresponding surfaces obtained by bilinear interpolation or nearest-neighbor interpolation.

Sparse-Representation Based Methods. Sparse-coding-based SR methods are proposed based on the assumption that the low resolution patch and their corresponding high resolution version have similar sparse representation coefficients under different sparse dictionaries. Yang *et al.* proposed a SR method by calculating a sparse representation for low-resolution input, and then using the coefficients to generate the high-resolution output with a high resolution dictionary [5]. Mallat *et al.* developed a SR method with sparse mixing estimators, which derived from a mixture model of the signal measurement [6]. Dong *et al.* designed a SR algorithm by adaptive sparse domain selection and adaptive regularization [6]. Moreover, Dong proposed an image interpolation method by incorporating the image non-local self-similarity into sparse representation model [6].

Deep-Learning Based Methods. Deep learning (DL) has been widely used in various image processing algorithms, we select one advanced DL-based SR algorithms which derived with the convolution neural network (CNN). The proposed CNN-based SR approach learns an end-to-end mapping between low- and high-resolution images. With a lightweight structure, this method has achieved state-of-the-art performance for NSIs.

2.2   Image Quality Assessment Methods

The goal of image quality assessment is to automatically evaluate the quality of images in accordance with human visual perception. Therefore, the IQA methods are always employed to evaluate the performance of other image processing algorithms. Compared with subjective evaluation, the IQA methods can give an objective and robust performance evaluation to the results of the image processing algorithm. In this paper, we employ several advanced IQA methods dedicated to the SCIs to assess the results of super-resolution algorithms. According to the availability of a reference image, the IQA methods can be classified into three categories: full-reference (FR) method, reduced-reference (RR) method, and no-reference (NR) method.

Full-Reference Method. In full-reference methods, the reference image with perfect quality is fully available for quality assessment process. The FR-IQA method always calculates the difference between the test image and the reference image and evaluates the fidelity of the test image. Due to sufficient reference information, the FR-IQA methods are often achieved higher evaluation accuracy. However, the whole reference information is hardly to be obtained in the practical applications, which limited the scope of application of the FR-IQA method.

Reduced-Reference Method. In reduced-reference methods, only partial reference information is accessible, and the amount of reference information is always very small. This situation generally occurs in communication systems with limited bandwidth resources. In those situations, the quality characteristics of images are represented by features with a small amount of data. With the development of image quality assessment techniques, there is no clear distinction between RR-IQA methods and FR-IQA methods, and they are all limited by the reference information.

No-Reference Method. In no-reference methods, the reference information is not available, and the quality assessment task is solely conducted based on the information of test images. Therefore, the NR-IQA methods are more difficult than the FR- and RR-IQA methods. At the same time, the NR-IQA methods have a wider range of applications, because they get rid of the requirement for the reference information. The most critical part of the NR-IQA method is to describe the quality variation of the image with an appropriate image features. With the development of the deep learning algorithms, this process has become more promising.

Table 1. The basic information of IQA metrics

Images	Types	Metrics
NSIs	FR	PSIM [10]
	NR	NFERM [11], ARISM [12], NIQMC [13], BIQME [14]
SCIs	FR	SQMS [1], SVQI [15]
	NR	ASIQE [2], UCA [16]

3   Criteria and Experimental Settings

To compare the performance of SR algorithms for screen content images, we choose ten high-resolution SCIs as reference images. Then, those reference SCIs are downsampled with factor 2 to generate the low-resolution versions. An example is shown in Fig. 2, we can find that the downsampling image has lost many structural information, which make a great impact on the text area of the SCI. In order to enhance the image fidelity and intelligibility, eight classical or advanced SR algorithms are implied for the ten low-resolution SCIs to reconstruct the corresponding high-resolution versions. The effectiveness of the SR algorithms can be evaluated by measure the fidelity between the resolution-enhanced image and corresponding reference image, as well as the intelligibility of the reconstructed image.

In the traditional SR algorithms, the performance of those algorithms is always evaluated by the simplest IQA metric: mean square error (MSE) or peak signal-to-noise (PSNR). However, it has been proven that the MSE and PSNR cannot accurately reflect human perception in many situations [10]. To overcome the drawback of MSE and PSNR, the researchers have developed many perception-aware IQA metrics according to the human visual perception.

In this paper, we employ nine state-of-the-art IQA metrics to comprehensively compare the performance of the selected SR algorithms, so that the evaluation results are more consistent with human visual perception. The selected IQA metrics can be classified into two categories, including: (1) the IQA metrics designed for the NSIs, e.g., PSIM [10], NFERM [11], ARISM [12], NIQMC [13], BIQME [14]; (2) the IQA metrics proposed for the SCIs, e.g., SQMS [1], ASIQE [2], SVQI [15], UCA [16]. Among those IQA metrics, the PSIM, SQMS and SVQI are full-reference (FR) methods, and the remaining metrics are no-reference (NR) methods. The basic information of those IQA metrics is concluded in Table 1.

4   Experimental Analysis

We analysis the performance of selected super-resolution restoration algorithms from two aspects: visual quality and objective assessment quality.

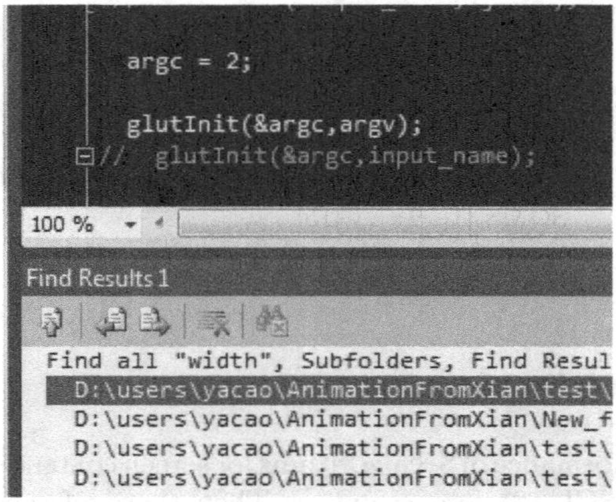

(a) Original image

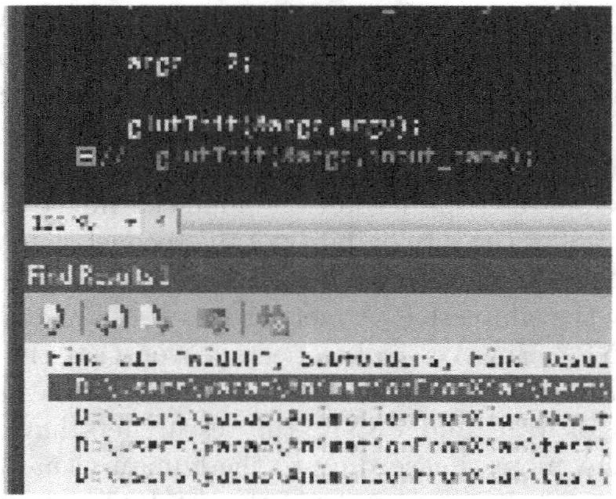

(b) Downsamlping image

Fig. 2. An example of image downsampling.

4.1 Visual Quality

In order to intuitively evaluate the performance of the selected SR algorithms, we demonstrate an example in Fig. 3. In Fig. 3, (a)–(h) are the eight reconstructed images derived from Fig. 2(b). We can judge the performance of the SR algorithms by compare the corresponding results to the reference image (Fig. 2(a)). The example screen content image is composed of text region and software icons. Therefore, the reconstruction effect of the text region determines the performance of the SR algorithm. Form Fig. 3, we can find the following observations: (1) The SRCNN algorithm has demonstrated the best visual perception, the text region and software icons are well reconstructed in (h); (2) The reconstructed images of three interpolation-based algorithms have induced serious blurring effect, which reduce the visual quality of reconstructed images; (3) The reconstructed images of four sparse-coding based algorithms have shown

(a) Nearest interpolation

(b) Bilinear interpolation

(c) Bicubic interpolation

(d) ScSR [5]

(e) SME-SR [6]

(f) ADSDIR [7]

(g) NARM-SR [8]

(h) SRCNN [9]

Fig. 3. Results of eight selected SR algorithms for SCIs.

different visual perception. The ScSR algorithm has caused serious details lost effect, and the ADSD-IR algorithm has induced slight blurring effect to the reconstructed image. The SME-SR has well reconstructed the edge of image but involved slight color distortion. The NARM-SR has obtained a comparable result with the SRCNN algorithm.

Table 2. Performance comparison of the SR algorithms for the SCIs.

IQA metrics	Nearest	Bilinear	Bicubic	ScSR	SME-SR	ASDS-IR	NARM-SR	SRCNN
NFERM [11]	8	5	6	7	3	1	4	2
ARISM [12]	8	7	6	3	4	5	2	1
NIQMC [13]	8	7	6	4	1	3	5	2
BIQME [14]	7	5	6	8	2	3	4	1
PSIM [10]	8	5	7	3	2	6	3	1
SQMS [1]	7	5	6	8	2	4	1	3
ASIQE [2]	7	5	6	8	3	1	2	4
SVQI [15]	7	5	6	8	2	4	3	1
UCA [16]	8	4	5	6	3	7	2	1
Average	7.5	5.3	6	6.1	2.4	3.8	2.9	1.8

4.2   Objective Quality

In this section, we demonstrate the average performance of the SR algorithms for all SCIs in Table 2. In order to show the performance comparison more clearly, we report the ranking of all SR algorithms under each IQA metric. Meanwhile, in order to verify the comprehensive performance of the SR algorithms under all criteria, we also calculate the average ranking value of each SR algorithm. A small average value indicates that the corresponding SR algorithm has better performance for the SCIs. From Table 2, we can draw the following conclusions: (1) The SRCNN algorithms has obtained the best performance under all criteria, this is consistent with the visual perception performed in Sect. 4.1; (2) Most of the sparse-coding based SR algorithms have moderate resolution-enhanced effect for SCIs; (3) The interpolation-based method and the ScSR algorithms show weak ability for the resolution-improvement of SCIs.

5   Conclusion

In this paper, we first briefly introduced eight state-of-the-art super-resolution restoration algorithms. They are all designed for natural scene images and achieve good performances in consideration of MSE and PSNR. Since there existing many differences between NSIs and SCIs, the SR algorithms designed for NSIs may not be successful in SCIs. Therefore, we evaluated the performances of the selected SR algorithms for a set of SCIs. To make a perception-aware evaluation, nine advanced IQA methods were used to measure the objective qualities of reconstructed super-resolution SCIs, and the average results of all IQA metrics were also calculated. Combining subjective observation and objective quality assessment results, we could conclude that most SR algorithms designed for NSIs obtained similar performance for SCIs. However, there are some advanced NSIs-oriented SR algorithms generate poor reconstruction effects for SCIs, e.g., the ScSR algorithms. This conclusion proved that we cannot recklessly employ the NSIs-oriented SR algorithms for the SCIs.

References

1. Gu, K., Wang, S., Yang, H., et al.: Saliency-guided quality assessment of screen content images. IEEE Trans. Multimed. **18**(6), 1098–1110 (2016)
2. Gu, K., Zhou, J., Qiao, J.F., et al.: No-reference quality assessment of screen content pictures. IEEE Trans. Image Process. **26**(8), 4005–4018 (2017)
3. Wang, S., Gu, K., Zeng, K., et al.: Perceptual screen content image quality assessment and compression. In: IEEE International Conference on Image Processing, pp. 1434–1438. IEEE (2015)
4. Keys, R.: Cubic convolution interpolation for digital image processing. IEEE Trans. Acoust. Speech Signal Process. **29**(6), 1153–1160 (2003)
5. Yang, J., Wright, J., Huang, T.S., et al.: Image super-resolution via sparse representation. IEEE Trans. Image Process. **19**(11), 2861–2873 (2010)
6. Mallat, S., Yu, G.: Super-resolution with sparse mixing estimators. IEEE Trans. Image Process. **19**(11), 2889–2900 (2010)
7. Dong, W., Zhang, L., Shi, G., et al.: Image deblurring and super-resolution by adaptive sparse domain selection and adaptive regularization. IEEE Trans. Image Process. **20**(7), 1838–1857 (2011)
8. Dong, W., Lukac, R., et al.: Sparse representation based image interpolation with nonlocal autoregressive modeling. IEEE Trans. Image Process. **22**(4), 1382–1394 (2013)
9. Dong, C., Chen, C.L., He, K., et al.: Image super-resolution using deep convolutional networks. IEEE Trans. Pattern Anal. Mach. Intell. **38**(2), 295–307 (2016)
10. Gu, K., Li, L., Lu, H., et al.: A fast reliable image quality predictor by fusing micro- and macro-structures. IEEE Trans. Industr. Electron. **64**(5), 3903–3912 (2017)
11. Gu, K., Zhai, G., Yang, X., et al.: Using free energy principle for blind image quality assessment. IEEE Trans. Multimed. **17**(1), 50–63 (2014)
12. Gu, K., Zhai, G., Lin, W., et al.: No-reference image sharpness assessment in autoregressive parameter space. IEEE Trans. Image Process. **24**(10), 3218–3231 (2015)
13. Gu, K., Lin, W., Zhai, G., et al.: No-reference quality metric of contrast-distorted images based on information maximization. IEEE Trans. Cybern. **47**(12), 4559–4565 (2017)
14. Gu, K., Tao, D., Qiao, J.F., et al.: Learning a no-reference quality assessment model of enhanced images with big data. IEEE Trans. Neural Netw. Learn. Syst. **29**(4), 1301–1313 (2017)
15. Gu, K., Qiao, J., Min, X., et al.: Evaluating quality of screen content images via structural variation analysis. IEEE Trans. Visual. Comput. Graph. **24**, 2689 (2018)
16. Min, X., Ma, K., Gu, K., et al.: Unified blind quality assessment of compressed natural, graphic and screen content images. IEEE Trans. Image Process. **26**, 5462 (2017)

Design of Online Annotation and Incision System for IVUS Images

Yaowen Zhu[1], Yankun Cao[1], Pengfei Zhang[2], Haixia Hou[3], and Zhi Liu[1(✉)]

[1] School of Information Science and Engineering,
Shandong University, Qingdao 266237, China
liuzhi@sdu.edu.cn
[2] Qilu Hospital, Shandong University, Jinan 250014, China
[3] Qingdao Agricultural University, Qingdao 266109, China

Abstract. The Online Annotation and Incision System (OAIS) system proposed in this paper is a digital hospital application software designed and developed by browser/server (B/S) structure after the comprehensive investigation of the work flow of the relevant departments of hospitals and the actual needs of small domestic hospitals, which can complete the processing, classification, storage, delivery and display of intravascular ultrasound (IVUS) image data. This system is a distributed system, which is divided into three layers: the presentation layer, the background service layer and the data storage layer. The presentation layer adopts Html5, Boostrap and jQuery technologies to provide users with simple and friendly interaction interfaces. The background service layer makes use of Nginx load balancing, and integrates JavaEE frameworks including SpringMVC, Mybatis and Hessian to provide stable and reliable services for the system. The data storage layer combines the MySQL database with the Redis cache server to help the system store and retrieve data quickly. This system can make up for the shortcomings of simple screenshot function of the relevant software in the current market, and can basically meet the medical needs of hospitals. By using this system, the leadership of relevant departments of the hospital can strengthen the unified work management of medical staff. Meanwhile, by using this system, medical staff can not only annotate, cut and store the IVUS image data efficiently, but also maintain personal information and bulletin information effectively, so as to enhance work communication and improve diagnostic efficiency.

Keywords: IVUS images · Annotation and incision · Distributed system · MySQL

1 Introduction

At present, cardiovascular diseases occur frequently and there are a wide range of patients. Therefore, how to effectively diagnose and treat vascular diseases is particularly important. The structure of human blood vessels is relatively complex [1], with multi-layer tissue structure, which can be roughly divided into intima and adventitia. When the vascular tissue of human body changes, its structure and tissue will change

G. Zhai et al. (Eds.): IFTC 2018, CCIS 1009, pp. 74–90, 2019.
https://doi.org/10.1007/978-981-13-8138-6_7

accordingly. In the diagnosis of vascular diseases, medical staff usually first take X-ray or IVUS images of the patient's blood vessels, and then diagnose the disease through the structural morphology of the intima and adventitia of the patient's blood vessels. If the medical staff annotates the IVUS image of the patient and intercepts the useful image information according to the need, the interference of irrelevant information can be reduced and the diagnostic efficiency of the medical staff can be improved. According to the survey, most of the software with image annotation and cutting function in the market requires local installation. The installation process is complex and the data interconnection cannot be realized, which makes it difficult for medical staffs to communicate with each other. However, some existing online screenshot tools on the network cannot save and manage the image data well, which cannot meet the professional medical needs.

In order to improve the diagnostic efficiency of doctors and meet the needs of professional vascular image cutting, we designed an OAIS system based on B/S structure. The OAIS system uses the Canvas control of Html5 to screen the pixels in the IVUS image one by one, retaining the part between the intima and adventitia of blood vessels, and indirectly realizes the function of annotating and cutting the IVUS image. The system makes up for the shortcomings of simple cutting function and image management function of the similar software in the current market, which can basically meet the professional medical needs of the hospital. By connecting with the database, the system can help the hospital leadership to conduct unified management and work arrangement for medical staff, and strengthen communication among medical staff. The system also has a simple and friendly interface, which can help medical staff annotate, cut and store IVUS image data efficiently, manage personal information and bulletin information effectively. The whole operation process of the system complies with the operating habits of the medical staff, thus effectively improving the diagnostic efficiency of the medical staff.

In the paper, the detailed design of OAIS system are described. The rest of the paper is organized as follow. Section 2 introduces the system functional and non-functional requirements analysis. The overall technical architecture of the system is introduced in detail in Sect. 3. Section 4 introduces the data model and database, the annotation and incision function and interactive interface of this system. At last, we give the conclusion and future work.

2 System Requirements Analysis

Requirement analysis is a crucial first step in the system design process. Requirement analysis makes perfect and detailed analysis of the system, determines the functional and reliability requirements of the system, and transforms "what is needed" into "what is done". Good requirement analysis can promote the system development process and save development costs.

2.1   Functional Requirements and Use-Case Analysis

By using the OAIS system, medical staff can annotate and cut IVUS images online, diagnose and manage the cropped IVUS images, meanwhile the administrator personnel can manage user information and bulletin information, and review user qualification. This system not only needs to meet users' functional requirements, but also needs to meet users' requirements of security, usability, reliability and rationality, providing users with friendly user interface and safe and reliable user experience, helping to reduce the working intensity of user and improve their work efficiency. Therefore, the system needs to provide the following services:

(1)   At the most basic level, medical staff can manage personal information, and manage data which mainly refer to IVUS images, by using the system. Administrators can review user qualification, manage userinfo and bulletin information through this system.

(2)   Traditional diagnosis of vascular diseases requires observation of IVUS images, but the images are not effectively classified and managed. As a result, the IVUS images of lesions are not easy to be collected, which is not conducive to repeated query and comparative analysis of diseases by medical staff. In order to solve this problem, the computer information technology is used to effectively collect, classify and manage medical images which are not easy to collect, so as to facilitate the follow-up examination by medical staff. Further, during diagnosis, medical staff need analyze the disease by observing the structural morphology of the patient's inner and outer vascular membranes. In order to reduce the interference of irrelevant information, it may be necessary to intercept part of the IVUS image for observation, so the image manipulation function should be designed. Medical staff can annotate the inner and outer membrane boundary of the IVUS image through the browser, and the system can automatically cut out the image information between the inner and outer membranes by the design of the image cutting algorithm, which can help medical staff improve the diagnostic efficiency.

Before dividing the functional modules of the system, we need to determine the system use-case diagram in order to divide the modules more clearly. The use-case diagram contains two parts: Actor and User Case. The first step is to identify the actor, who is the person or system that interacts with the system, that is, the user or the usage environment [2]. The actor of this system mainly include users and administrators, among which users mainly refer to the medical staff who use the system, and administrators refer to the hospital leadership that use the system. The actor relationship is shown in Fig. 1. Secondly, the use-case are determined. The use-case is the service provided by the system to the actor. The functional requirements of each user can be clearly divided by the use-case and its sub-modules. The use case of this system is divided into the following two parts:

(1)   Users can annotate, cut, add, delete, modify and query IVUS images, maintain personal information, and view notices. The user use-case diagram is demonstrated in Fig. 2.

(2)   The main tasks of the administrator are user qualification review, user information management and bulletin information management. The administrator use-case, as shown in Fig. 3.

Fig. 1. The actor relationship.

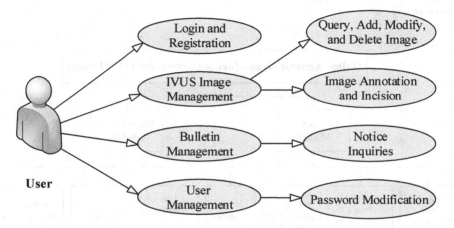

Fig. 2. The user use-case.

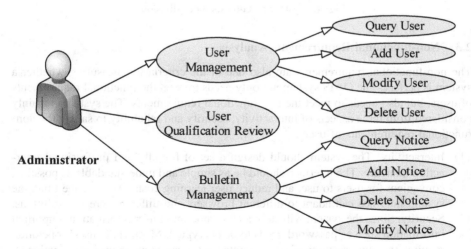

Fig. 3. The administrator use-case.

2.2   Division of System Function Modules

In Sect. 2.1, we have a detailed analysis of the functional requirements of the system, so that we can clearly understand the functions the system needs to implement. Combining with business scenario and requirement analysis, we divide the system functions into two modules, namely user module and administrator module. The user module is also divided into login and registration module, IVUS image management module, user information module and notice inquiries module. The administrator module is mainly divided into user qualification review module, user management module and bulletin management module. The system function modules is divided as shown in Fig. 4.

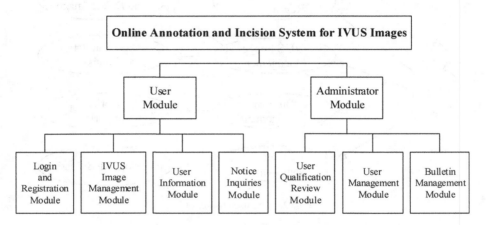

Fig. 4.   System function modules division.

2.3   Non-functional Requirements Analysis

The non-functional requirements are also one of the criteria for measuring whether a system is perfect. The OAIS system not only needs to meet the functional requirements of users, but also needs to meet the non-functional requirements. The system is mainly considered from three aspects of interactivity, security and reliability to satisfy the non-functional requirements of users.

(1) Interactivity. The system should design a set of friendly and professional inter-action interface. The interface should be as simple and understandable as possible, convenient for users to use, and reduce user learning costs. At the same time, the system interface can adapt to different browsers and different screen resolutions.
(2) Security. Since the system will store a large amount of user information, important information such as password needs to be encrypted. Meanwhile, user's operation requires the authorization of administrator, who can manage user information.
(3) Reliability. When the system runs, it needs to ensure stable and reliable operation. Even if there is a fault, the system can also have a good exception handling mechanism and information feedback.

3   Design of System Framework

3.1   System Overview

The summary design is responsible for transforming the functional modules obtained from requirements analysis into system structure and data structure [2]. The OAIS system is a distributed system based on B/S structure design, which is divided into three layers, including presentation layer, background service layer and data storage layer, as shown in Fig. 5. At the presentation layer, users and administrators access their respective system interfaces through the browser. Users manage IVUS images, maintain personal information and query notices through user interface, while administrators operate the background management system to review user qualifications, grant permissions to users, and manage the user information and bulletin information. The background service layer is mainly responsible for processing the business logic, receiving the user's HTTP request, operating the database, and finally feeding back the processing results and related static resources (such as HTML, pictures) to the user. The data storage layer is responsible for storing user related information, user cache information, and IVUS images.

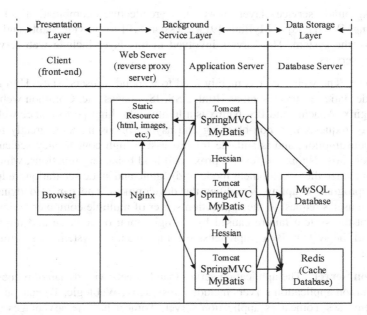

Fig. 5. The overall architecture and technical structure of the system. The system dynamically dispatches tasks to multiple logical processing nodes running on multiple Tomcat through Nginx load balancing, and each node performs the image storage function through Hessian remote service call.

3.2 Design of the Presentation Layer

The presentation layer mainly refers to the front end, and the front end adopts Html5 + Bootstrap + jQuery technology. Bootstrap is a Web framework based on Html, JavaScript and CSS, developed by Twitter's designers Jacob Thornton and Mark Otto, which can quickly build a responsive layout website [3]. Responsive layout means that web pages can automatically adjust page layout and display according to the resolution of the display screen, so that users can have a better user experience on the PC. Bootstrap provides a complete, concise and standard web interaction design style, which helps developers to quickly develop front-end interaction interfaces. JQuery is a simple and excellent JavaScript library that aims to "write less code and do more" [4]. This simple and efficient JavaScript library significantly simplifies DOM manipulation, animation effects, event handling and Ajax interactions [5]. By using jQuery technology, developers can effectively perform Dom manipulations, Ajax interactions and animation effects, process page logic, simplify JavaScript code, and save development costs and time. Through the combination of Bootstrap and jQuery technology, the system provides users with a friendly interactive experience.

3.3 Design of the Background Service Layer

The background service layer uses the architecture combination of Nginx [6] + SpringMVC [7, 8] + MyBatis [9] + Hessian [10] to provide stable and reliable services for the system. The servers involved in this layer include web servers and application servers.

Web Server. The web server is mainly used to respond to users' static Http requests and provide static resources such as Html, CSS, JS, images, etc. Common web servers include Nginx, Apache, and IIS. Nginx is a lightweight, high-performance web server that handles requests in a non-blocking and asynchronous manner, greatly reducing resource consumption, and is suitable for processing high concurrency scenarios [6]. More importantly, Nginx has reverse proxy and load balancing functions, which helps the system realize the development mode of dynamic and static separation, reduces the degree of program coupling, simplifies the development, and can also dynamically allocate the user's request to the application server of multiple computer nodes, which can prevent the system failure caused by a single point of collapse and improve the reliability of the system. By comprehensive comparison, the system uses Nginx as the web server.

Application Server. The application server mainly deals with dynamic requests from users. Common application servers include JBoss, Jetty, Weblogic, Tomcat, and so on. This system uses Tomcat as application server. Tomcat has the advantages of lightweight, stability and security, and is widely used in production and development by a large number of enterprises. With Tomcat and Nginx combined, you can deploy more programs.

Development Framework. SpringMVC + MyBatis, as the main development framework of the backstage, has the advantages of fast and stable development and clear module division. The SpringMVC design conforms to the MVC [11] model and the three-layer model [12]. The MVC model divides the system into three parts: Controller, Model, and View. The Model part is used to store data, the View part is used to represent the presentation content, and the Controller part is responsible for processing the business logic, querying and manipulating the data in the Model part, and packaging the data into a View and returning it to the user. The three-layer model refers to the presentation layer, the business layer, and the persistence layer. As the presentation layer, SpringMVC interacts with users by creating a Controller class, and responds to user requests as a presentation layer. The business layer generates Service classes to provide specific business logic processing. DAO class (Data Access Object) and POJO (Plain Ordinary Java Object) class maintain the persistence layer and take charge of data storage. Controller, Service, and DAO are all generated by dependency injection. Further, integrating MyBatis [9] with SpringMVC is responsible for maintaining the development of the persistence layer and improving the development efficiency. Finally, Hessian [10] remote service is used to be responsible for communication between services.

3.4 Design of the Data Storage Layer

The data storage layer adopts the architecture combination of MySQL and Redis [13], specifically involving two kinds of servers: database server and cache server.

Database Server. Data storage is an indispensable part of a system. The stability and reliability of data is one of the guarantees for the normal operation of the program. Common database servers include MySQL, SQLServer, Oracle, and more. Compared with other database systems, MySQL's storage engine architecture separates query processing and other server tasks from the storage/extraction of data, which can be applied and functioned in a variety of different scenarios [14]. This system uses MySQL as the database server to store and retrieve data.

Cache Server. In order to achieve distributed deployment, this system needs to use cache database. Redis [13] is a NoSQL (non-relational) database with high-speed memory cache. Because it uses memory to store data, it is very fast for reading and writing speed, which is very suitable as a cache server.

4   Detailed Design of System

4.1   Design of Data Model and Database

Design of Data Model. In Sects. 2 and 3, we elaborated on the system requirements analysis and the overall technical architecture of the system, and we need to design the data model before our formal development. As a method of data model design, the E-R (Entity Relationship Diagram) Diagram can help us to view the data model more intuitively. The E-R diagram of this system is shown in Fig. 6.

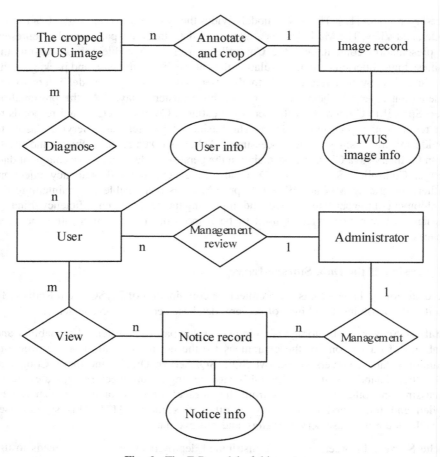

Fig. 6. The E-R model of this system.

Design of Database. According to the E-R diagram in Sect. 4.1, we designed the database table and its table structure fields. The following tables list the main tables involved in this system, and the system can run stably by operating these tables.

The User Information Table. The user information table (as shown in Table 1) is used to record user's personal information, including user's ID number, name, password, etc. To ensure user privacy, the login password is encrypted by using MD5. Meanwhile, in order to ensure the security of the system, users need the qualification review, and the auth field is used to record the authorization status of users.

The Cropped IVUS Images Record Table. The field name of The cropped IVUS images record table includes the cropped IVUS images name, image type, image record ID, and so on, as shown in Table 2. This table is used to record the information of IVUS images after cutting, so as to facilitate the user to repeatedly query the diagnostic data.

Table 1. The user information table.

Field name	Data type	Length	IS NULL	Comment
id	int	11	N	Primary key, user ID number
user_account	varchar	10	N	Use the user's real name as the user's login account
password	varchar	50	N	User login password,MD5 encryption
auth	int	1	N	If the authorization is indicated, 0 means unauthorized, and 1 means authorized
create_time	datetime	19	N	User creation date
update_time	datetime	19	N	User modified date

Table 2. The cropped IVUS images record table.

Field name	Data type	Length	IS NULL	Comment
id	int	11	N	Primary key, user ID number
Imagesrc_on	varchar	100	N	The original name of the IVUS image
Imagesrc_nn	varchar	100	N	The new name of the IVUS image
Imagedst_n	varchar	100	N	The name of the cropped IVUS image
image_type	varchar	30	Y	Image type
image_id	int	11	N	Foreign key, image record ID number
create_time	datetime	19	N	User creation date
update_time	datetime	19	N	User modified date
memo	varchar	50	Y	Comment

The Bulletin Information Table. The bulletin information (as shown in Table 3) table includes the notice title, the notice content, the publish date of notices and other field names. Users can view relevant notices through the system and adjust their work arrangements in a timely manner.

Table 3. The bulletin information table.

Field name	Data type	Length	IS NULL	Comment
id	int	11	N	Primary key, notice number
title	varchar	100	N	Notice title
content	varchar	300	N	Notice content
create_time	varchar	19	N	Publish date of the notice

4.2   Design of Online Annotation and Incision Function

The core function of the system is to annotate and cut IVUS images online. There are four steps to achieve this function:

> Step 1: Click to annotate the contour points of the inner and outer membranes in the IVUS image.
> Step 2: Determine the relationship between each pixel point on the image and the polygon connected by the annotation point.
> Step 3: Cut off the image, which inside the intima and outside the adventitia.
> Step 4: Save the cropped image to the database.

The Implementation Method of Annotation Function. The implementation uses the element <canvas> of Html5. The canvas element is used to draw graphics on a web page, and developers can use JavaScript scripts to draw 2D images on a web page. The front end first loads the image. After the system receives the request of the user to select the IVUS image, the image data is loaded into the Canvas control of Html5. At this point, Canvas can be seen as a canvas, and there is a mask layer on the Canvas. The user can select the label point on the mask layer. When choosing to annotate the adventitia, the system first clears the array of storing the adventitia data defined in the script, and then displays the labeled point on the page in the form of serial number through every click of the user, and obtains the relative coordinates of the corresponding canvas clicked by the mouse, and stores the coordinate data into the adventitia array. After the adventitia is selected, the user then choose the intima. Similarly, the intimal coordinate data will be stored in the intima array.

The Implementation Method of Incision Function. The system adopts an image segmentation method based on conditional judgment. we uses the winding number method to judge, that is, when the winding number is zero, the point is outside the closed curve. Firstly, each pixel on the IVUS image is regarded as a two-dimensional array, which is represented by row and column. Secondly, we wire each pixel to all the label points on the intima and adventitia, and the system will judge the pixels on the image one by one. By judging whether the sum of the angles at which the pixel is wired to all the label points is $360°$, we determine if the pixel is within the selected contour. Thirdly, we use a logic AND to filter out the pixels that inside the intima and outside the adventitia. Finally, the RGBA model of the IVUS image is introduced. We assign the alpha channel in the RGBA model of the pixel in the filtered part of the image to a value of zero. Thus, the filtered pixels will appear transparent on the browser page, resulting in a cropped IVUS image.

4.3   Design of Interactive Interface

The whole interface is designed with the classic structure of the left menu bar and the right workspace. Among them, the menu bar is divided into the top menu bar and the left menu bar, its function is roughly the same, the difference is that the top menu bar is a simplification of the left menu bar. There are three modules in the menu bar: diagnostic management, user management and bulletin management.

Module of Diagnostic Management. This interface contains the main functions of the system, annotating and cutting images, querying diagnostic data. Users firstly use the "Diagnose Image" interface to process the IVUS images, and then analyzes the cropped IVUS images through the "Diagnostic Records" interface.

The "Diagnose Image" interface is shown in Fig. 7(a). The user clicks the "Select File" button to upload the local IVUS image to the browser page. At this point, there will be two side-by-side images on the workspace. On the left is the IVUS image that needs to be annotated and cut, and on the right is the original IVUS image uploaded. The image on the right cannot be edited, only for reference comparison. By clicking on the "Annotate Intima" and "Annotate Adventitia" buttons, users can select the labeling points of the inner and outer membranes on the IVUS image in turn. The labeling points are expressed in the form of serial numbers, which will increase with order of user clicks. After the annotation action is completed, the user clicks the "Preview" button, and the cropped IVUS image will be displayed on the left side of workspace. Users can click the "Submit" button to upload the cropped image to the database, or click the "Reset" button to re-mark the image.

The "Diagnostic Records" interface is shown in Fig. 7(b). Users can query their own diagnostic records from the database and manage them to better analyze the patient's condition.

Module of User Management. Users and administrators have different user management modules. The administrator has high privilege, and the user management interface of the administrator is shown in Fig. 8(a) and (b). By using the "Add User" interface, the administrator can create a new user and submit the information of the new user to the database. At this time, the new user can log into the system within his own authority. By using the "Query User" interface, the administrator can view all user information from the database and modify or delete the user. The user management interface of users is shown in Fig. 8(c), and users can only manage their own passwords.

Module of Bulletin Management. The establishment of the bulletin management module is conducive for all users to understand the relevant dynamics and adjust their work schedules timely. The administrator's bulletin management interface is shown in Fig. 9(a) and (b). By using these interfaces, administrators can add, query, modify, and delete notices. The user can only query notices, and the bulletin information management interface of the user is shown in the Fig. 9(c).

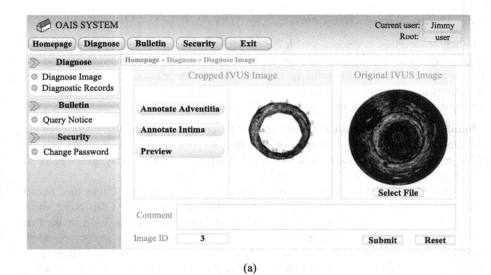

(a)

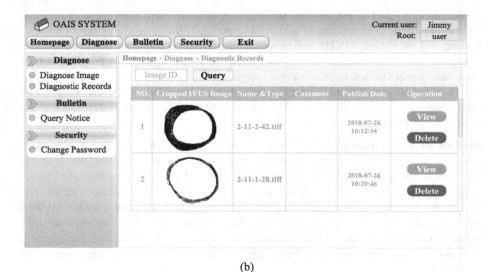

(b)

Fig. 7. Interfaces of diagnostic management module. (a) the "Diagnose Image" interface, (b) the "Diagnostic Records" interface.

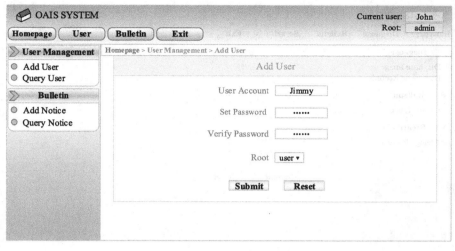

(a)

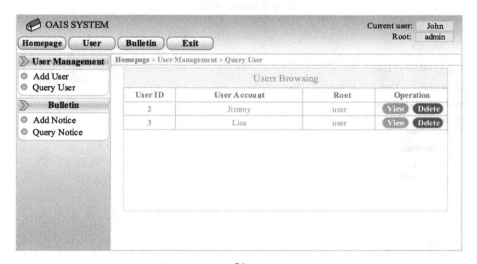

(b)

Fig. 8. Interfaces of user management module. (a) the "Add User" interface of the administrator, (b) the "Query User" interface of the administrator, (c) the user management interface of the user.

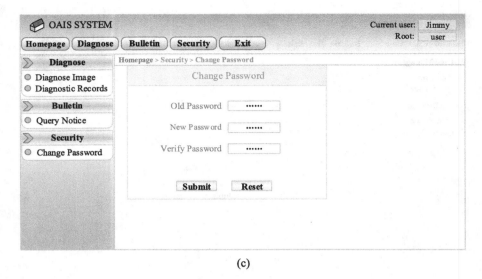

(c)

Fig. 8. (*continued*)

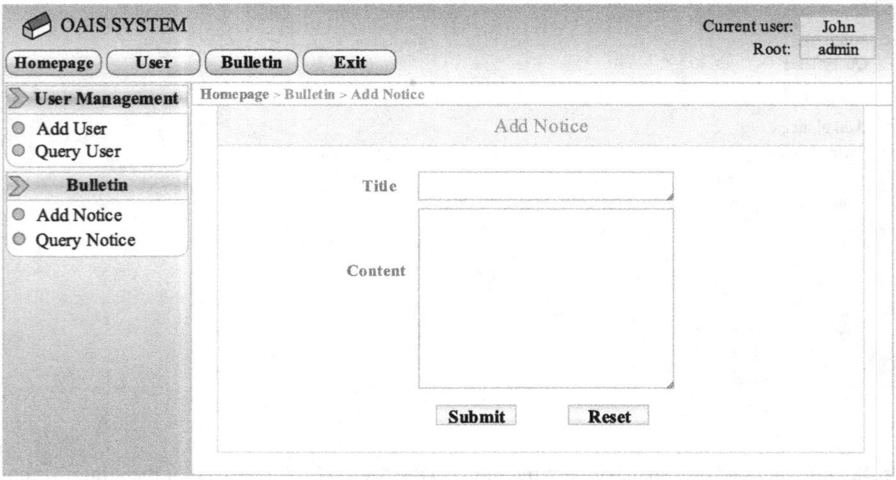

(a)

Fig. 9. Interfaces of bulletin management module. (a) the "Add Notice" interface of the administrator, (b) the "Query Notice" interface of the administrator, (c) the "Query Notice" interface of the user.

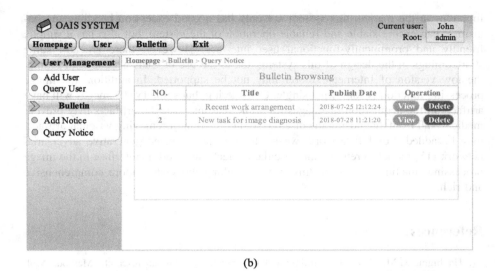

(b)

(c)

Fig. 9. (*continued*)

5   Conclusions and Future Work

In order to solve the practical problems encountered in the diagnosis of vascular diseases, the online annotation and incision for IVUS images system based on B/S distributed architecture was designed in this paper, which can help medical staff improve the diagnostic efficiency and facilitate the management of medical staff information and IVUS image data. Compared with other software with similar functions in the market, this system not only has a good exception handling mechanism, it can ensure stable and reliable operation of the system, but also has a simple, friendly and prominently-functional user interface. However, there are still some shortcomings in the design of this system: due to the use of Canvas control of Html5, the low version of Internet explorer may not be supported. In addition, the image processing function is somewhat single. Considering that some IVUS images will have artifacts in the acquisition of images for some reasons, vascular artifacts may prevent medical staff from diagnosing the disease, so the function of removing vascular artifacts may be added. For future work, we try to use the advanced generative adversarial network [15] model to remove the vascular artifacts, and add its interface to the image processing function module of this system, making the system more comprehensive and rich.

References

1. Haghighi, M.M., Ayer, J.: Cardiovascular assessment in human research. Methods Mol. Biol. **1735**, 297 (2018)
2. Pressman, R., Maxim, B.: Software Engineering: A Practitioner's Approach, 8th edn. McGraw Hill Science, Columbus (2014)
3. Jiang, W., Zhang, M., Zhou, B., Jiang, Y., Zhang, Y.: Responsive web design mode and application. In: 2014 IEEE Workshop on Advanced Research and Technology in Industry Applications (2014)
4. jQuery Foundation jquery.org: Jquery: the write less, do more, javascript library (2011)
5. Bibeault, B., Katz, Y.: jQuery in Action, 3rd Edition. Manning Publications Co. (2015)
6. Reese, W.: Nginx: the high-performance web server and reverse proxy. Linux J. **2008**(173), 2 (2008)
7. Roman, E., Ambler, S.W., Marinescu, F.: Mastering Enterprise Javabeans, pp. 217–224. Wiley, New York (2005)
8. Johnson, R., Hoeller, J.: Expert One-on-One J2EE Development without EJB. Wiley, Indianapolis (2004)
9. Prasad Reddy, K.S.: Working with MyBatis. In: Prasad Reddy, K.S. (ed.) Beginning Spring Boot 2. Apress, Berkeley (2017)
10. Surhone, L.M., Tennoe, M.T., Henssonow, S.F., Thrift, A.: Hessian (web service protocol). Betascript Publishing (2010)
11. Liu, Y., Quan, L.I.: Research and application of network public opinion management system based on MVC model. Modern Electronics Technique (2017)
12. Fouad, M.M., Aly, H.A.: A modified multiview video streaming system using 3-tier architecture. Adv. Electr. Electron. Eng. **14**(2), 196 (2016)
13. Baron, C.A.: NoSQL key-value DBs riak and redis. Database Syst. J. **4**, 3–10 (2016)
14. Schwartz, B., Zaitsev, P., Tkachenko, V.: High Performance MySQL: Optimization, Backups, and Replication. O'Reilly Media Inc., Sebastopol (2012)
15. Goodfellow, I.J., et al.: Generative adversarial nets. In: International Conference on Neural Information Processing Systems 2014, vol. 3, pp. 2672–2680 (2014)

Locally Adaptive Noise Covariance
Estimation for Color Images

Li Dong[(⊠)] and Jiantao Zhou

University of Macau, Macau 999078, People's Republic of China
{yb47452,jtzhou}@umac.mo

Abstract. Noise estimation is crucial in many image processing tasks such as denoising. Most of the existing noise estimation methods are specially developed for grayscale images. For color images, these methods simply handle each color channel independently, without considering the correlation across channels. Moreover, these methods often assume a globally fixed noise model throughout the entire image, neglecting the adaptiveness to the local structures. In this work, we propose a locally adaptive multivariate Gaussian approach to model the noise in color images, in which both the content-dependence and inter-dependence among color channels are explicitly considered. We design an effective method for estimating the noise covariance matrices. Specifically, by exploiting the image self-similarity property, we could estimate a distinct noise covariance matrix for each local region via a linear shrinkage estimator. Experimental results show that our method can effectively estimate the noise covariance matrices. The usefulness is demonstrated with real color image denoising.

Keywords: Noise modeling · Noise estimation · Color image denoising

1 Introduction

Noise is one of the most fundamental issues in image processing. It is unavoidably introduced during image acquisition, transmission and storage [2]. To develop noise-resistant algorithms, many works assume certain prior knowledge of the noise, e.g., the noise model and its parameters [3,7]. Unfortunately, in practice, this information is not always known beforehand, which has triggered the research on noise estimation. As a crucial preprocessing, noise estimation has been widely used in many vision tasks such as image denoising [27], motion deblurring [25], super-resolution [11], object recognition [16].

Currently, most of the existing noise estimation methods are specifically proposed for grayscale images [9,21,24,26], in which the identical independent distributed (i.i.d.) additive white Gaussian noise (AWGN) noise model is assumed

This work was supported in part by the Macau Science and Technology Development Fund under Grant FDCT/022/2017/A1, and in part by the Research Committee, University of Macau, under Grants MYRG2016-00137-FST and MYRG2018-00029-FST.

G. Zhai et al. (Eds.): IFTC 2018, CCIS 1009, pp. 91–105, 2019.
https://doi.org/10.1007/978-981-13-8138-6_8

because of its simplicity. For the color images, it is a convention to extend these methods by treating each color channel separately. For instance, Chen *et al.* [5] assumed an AWGN model for each color channel, and treated the noise levels in different color channels the same. Based on the statistical relationship between the noise level and the covariance matrix of the collected image patches, they derived a nonparametric noise level estimation algorithm. In another work [22], Liu *et al.* also employed the AWGN noise model but allowed each channel a different noise level. An iterative image patch selection scheme was proposed to select homogeneous regions from a noisy image. The noise estimation was made on those selected regions using principal component analysis (PCA).

The key underlying assumption behind this natural extension is that the noise is independent across the color channels. This is valid for some specific scenarios such as the RAW image, which consists of the unprocessed light measurements generated by the imaging sensor. In the RAW image case, the main noises (i.e., shot noise, fixed pattern noise, thermal noise, readout and quantization noise) all occur in a pixel-by-pixel fashion. Therefore, the present noise can be regarded as channel-independent [14]. But this assumption becomes improper for real color images [4,15]. This is because, for a modern consumer digital camera, the RAW image often undergoes a very complex in-camera processing pipeline, which typically includes demosaicking, white balance, color space transformation, gamma correction and image compression. This complicated processing procedure consists of highly non-linear filtering operations, which could heavily mix the noise in each color channel together. More concretely, three operations shall be responsible for such noise correlation among channels. First, the color space transformation, which transforms from one RGB space to another RGB space via 3D nonlinear mapping [17]. Second, sophisticated color filter array (CFA) demosaickings, e.g., [20,30], which interpolate the CFA image to a full-color image by jointly considering the color values in all channels. Third, the lossy image compression such as JPEG, which mix-ups the color channels during pixel-to-frequency domain transformations [6]. As already pointed out in [29], to perform high-quality filtering for real color images, it is necessary to take account of the correlation across color channels. In addition, most of the existing works also assume a globally fixed noise model throughout the entire image. However, a single globally-fixed noise model is clearly inadequate. This is because the in-camera image processing pipeline is actually content-dependent [15]. These operations manipulate or filter the image signals based on the local contents, making the incurred noise of the color image content-dependent. For instance, the conventional lossy image JPEG compression, which tends to remove more image details for a highly textured region, comparing with a smooth region. This makes the compression noise to be locally content-dependent.

Compared with extensive works on noise estimation for grayscale image, the topic of noise estimation for the real color image is less explored. One of the most related work is Nam *et al.* [23]. The authors proposed a holistic approach to the cross-channel image noise modeling, where the model parameters were determined with a multilayer perceptron (MLP) neural network. Essentially, [23] was a data-driven approach. To handle the images coming from a variety of cameras, Nam suggested using multiple networks, each of which was trained on the data from a specific camera brand with a particular capture setting. Nevertheless, when handling the color images from a never-seen camera, the performance of noise estimation was degraded. This weak generalization capability limits the practical usage of [23].

In this work, we propose a locally adaptive multivariate Gaussian noise model to characterize the noise in color images. By examining the noise in real-world color images, we observe that different local image regions exhibit different the noise strengths. To this end, we design a practical method for estimating the noise covariance matrices for each local region. Specifically, by utilizing the image self-similarity property, the noise estimation can be performed via a linear shrinkage estimator. Experimental results show that our method could accurately estimate the noise covariance matrices. The practical usefulness is illustrated with real color image denoising.

The rest of this paper is organized as follows. In Sect. 2, we motivate and validate the noise model for color images. Our proposed noise estimation is then described in Sect. 3. The experimental results on the real-world color images are given in Sect. 4, and Sect. 5 finally concludes this work.

2   Noise Model for Color Images

In this work, we use content-adaptive multivariate Gaussian noise model to describe the noise in color images. Unlike the conventional methods such as Chen *et al.* [5] and Liu *et al.* [22], we do *not* restrict the noise covariance matrix to be diagonal. By this relaxation, the correlation across the channels can be captured by the off-diagonal entries of the covariance matrix. Moreover, instead of estimating a globally fixed covariance matrix, we propose a content-adaptive noise estimation strategy, which could adapt the covariance estimate to the local image structures. In the next, we first experimentally verify that the proposed multivariate Gaussian model could effectively describe the incurred noise in the real color images.

We fix the camera position and capture settings, and shoot 300 images under the constant lighting for a static scene (see Fig. 1(a)). Upon recording these images, we randomly select one pixel position in the image and temporally collect all the intensity values for each channel. The histogram of the intensity for each color channel is shown in Figs. 1(b)–(d). As can be seen, the histogram can be well fitted with as univariate Gaussian model. Then, the scatter-plots for the intensity pair between different channels are given in Figs. 1(e)–(g). With these intensity pair data samples, one can easily compute the covariance matrices for cov(R,G) cov(R,B) and cov(G,B). By using the covariance matrix, we could plot multiple confidence ellipses for a bivariate Gaussian distribution. That is, these ellipse contours represents the bivariate Gaussian distribution with the computed covariance matrix. As clearly shown, those ellipse contours could effectively characterize the distribution of data samples. To conclude, the Gaussianity of distributions for intensity and intensity-pair indicates that the noise in color images can be empirically modeled as a 3D multivariate Gaussian.

(a) A sample test image from the image sequence

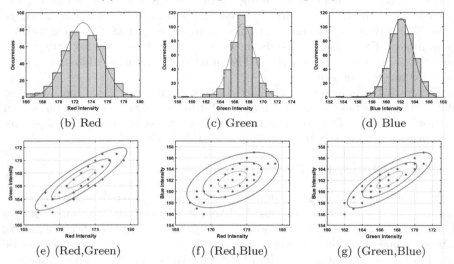

(b) Red   (c) Green   (d) Blue

(e) (Red,Green)   (f) (Red,Blue)   (g) (Green,Blue)

Fig. 1. Validation of the multivariate Gaussian noise model on real images. (a) Test image, where the selected pixel is pointed by the red arrow; (b) (c) (d) the intensity distribution of the selected pixel in each channel; (e) (f) (g) the scatter-plot for the intensity pair between different color channels. The ellipse contours represent 95%, 75% and 55% confidence of a bivariate Gaussian, respectively. (Color figure online)

Fig. 2. The heat-map for illustrating the pixel-wise generalized variance of the test image sequence. The region with highly active image structures exhibiting stronger noise strength (labeled with more yellowish color). (Color figure online)

However, assuming a globally fixed noise model is not adequate. This is because the in-camera image processing contains many operations that manipulate or filter the image signals based on the local contents, making the incurred noise content-dependent. To understand this situation, let us examine the noise strength associated with each pixel. As the above experiments indicated, the multivariate Gaussian noise model can effectively describe the noise at a pixel. To quantify the noise strength for a multivariate Gaussian model, we need a scalar statistic. Analogous to the variance for a univariate Gaussian model, we use the *generalized variance* to characterize the noise strength of the multivariate Gaussian model [1]. Formally, the generalized variance is defined as the determinant of the covariance matrix, squeezing a noise covariance matrix into a scaler. The generalized variances for the test image are shown in Fig. 2. As one can see, different regions exhibit different noise strengths. Specifically, the noise strength of the region exhibiting strong image structures is large, while the smooth regions are typically associated with low noise strengths.

Overall, the observations, drawn from Figs. 1 and 2, motivate us to develop a locally adaptive multivariate Gaussian noise model for the color images.

Mathematically, we describe the kth noisy pixel with an additive noise model

$$\mathbf{o}_k = \mathbf{u}_k + \mathbf{m}_k, \tag{1}$$

where $\mathbf{o}_k, \mathbf{u}_k \in \mathbb{R}^3$, denoting the observed noisy and the underlying clean pixels in the 3D color space, respectively; and $\mathbf{m}_k \in \mathbb{R}^3$ is the zero-mean, multivariate Gaussian noise

$$\mathbf{m}_k \sim \mathcal{N}(\mathbf{0}, \boldsymbol{\Sigma}_k), \tag{2}$$

where $\boldsymbol{\Sigma}_k$ is the unknown noise covariance matrix to be estimated. In this setting, our goal is to adaptively estimate the noise covariance matrices $\boldsymbol{\Sigma}_k$'s from the single given noisy color image.

3   Proposed Noise Covariance Estimation Method

The basic idea of the proposed estimation is as follows. By utilizing the image self-similarity property [3,7], a number of similar patches can be collected into a patch group from a searching region. Then, the estimation can be performed on the basis of this patch group. Note that the key assumption made here is that the noise strength of each patch in the patch group is same. This assumption is reasonable because those collected patches share similar image contents and the incurred noise is actually content-dependent.

For a $s \times s \times 3$ color image patch, we first vectorize the 2D patch in each channel, and stack them into a tall and thin vector $\mathbf{x} = [\mathbf{x}_r; \mathbf{x}_g; \mathbf{x}_b] \in \mathbb{R}^{3s^2 \times 1}$ (see Fig. 3), where the subscripts r, g and b are used to indicate the red, green and blue channels, respectively. Suppose $\mathcal{A}$ is a set that contains all possible vectorized patches of the given image. Then, for the kth image patch $\mathbf{x}_k \in \mathcal{A}$, we search M patches that most resemble it (including $\mathbf{x}_k$ itself) in terms of Euclidean distance, in a large searching window. Those matched patches form a dataset $\mathcal{Q}_k = \{\mathbf{x}_i\}_{i=1}^M$. Now, we can perform the noise estimation on this dataset.

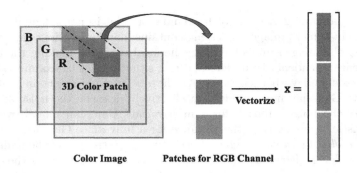

Fig. 3. Vectorize a 3D color patch into a column vector. (Color figure online)

However, in experiments, we find that a few textured patches are inevitably selected. This phenomenon is severe for highly textured images, where the number of smooth patches is quite limited. To mitigate this issue, we propose to first perform discrete cosine transform (DCT) high-pass filtering on $\mathcal{Q}_k$ before estimation. This could eliminate prominent image structures that reside in low-frequency bands, while still retaining the high-frequency components that are dominated by noise.

Suppose the complete orthonormal DCT base is $\mathbf{B} = [\mathbf{b}_1, \mathbf{b}_2, \ldots, \mathbf{b}_{s^2}] \in \mathbb{R}^{s^2 \times s^2}$. We construct the reduced DCT base $\widehat{\mathbf{B}}$ by equating the first K low-frequency bandpass filters to zeros, i.e.,

$$\widehat{\mathbf{B}} = [\underbrace{\mathbf{0}, \mathbf{0}, \ldots, \mathbf{0}}_{K}, \mathbf{b}_{K+1}, \ldots, \mathbf{b}_{s^2}]. \tag{3}$$

Then, for each vectorized color patch $\mathbf{x}_k \in \mathcal{Q}_k$, its corresponding reconstructed patch on $\widehat{\mathbf{B}}$ can be expressed as

$$\hat{\mathbf{x}}_k = (\mathbf{I}_3 \otimes \widehat{\mathbf{B}})(\mathbf{I}_3 \otimes \widehat{\mathbf{B}})^T \mathbf{x}_k. \tag{4}$$

Upon collecting all the $\hat{\mathbf{x}}_k$ into a new dataset $\widehat{\mathcal{Q}}_k$, our goal is converted into estimating the noise covariance from $\widehat{\mathcal{Q}}_k$. Note that, after excluding the prominent intrinsic image signals, $\hat{\mathbf{x}}_k$ is dominated by the noise. Further considering a vectorized color patch with *pure noise* under the noise model (1), $\hat{\mathbf{x}}_k$ can thus be treated as noise with distribution

$$\hat{\mathbf{x}}_k \sim \mathcal{N}(\mathbf{0}, \mathbf{C}_k), \tag{5}$$

where $\otimes$ denotes the Kronecker product, and $\mathbf{I}_d$ is the $d \times d$ identity matrix. Here, we define the covariance matrix

$$\mathbf{C}_k \triangleq \mathbf{\Sigma}_k \otimes \mathbf{I}_{s^2}. \tag{6}$$

In the following, we first estimate the covariance for $\mathbf{C}_k \in \mathbb{R}^{3s^2 \times 3s^2}$ from $\widehat{\mathcal{Q}}$, and then solve the covariance estimate for $\mathbf{\Sigma}_k \in \mathbb{R}^{3 \times 3}$ the equality (6).

One straightforward approach for estimation is to apply the conventional maximum likelihood (ML) method on the dataset $\widehat{\mathcal{Q}}_k$. However, the ML covariance estimate cannot be fully trusted. This is because the number of collected samples (e.g., $M = 10$) from a local region is small, especially comparing with the dimension of vectorized patch (e.g., when the patch size $s = 8$, the dimension of the vectorized patch is $3s^2 = 192$). To alleviate this problem, we propose to incorporate a prior on the covariance matrix during the estimation for the texture regions. The complete our proposed noise covariance estimation procedure is summarized in Algorithm 1. Specifically, the form of our estimator is imposed in the form of linear shrinkage [13,18,19], which can be expressed as

$$\widehat{\mathbf{C}}_k = \rho\boldsymbol{\Phi} + (1-\rho)\mathbf{S}_k, \tag{7}$$

where $\boldsymbol{\Phi}$ is the prior covariance matrix, which reflects the prior belief on the covariance to be estimated, and $\mathbf{S}_k$ is the sample covariance matrix of $\widehat{\mathcal{Q}}_k$, i.e.,

$$\mathbf{S}_k = \frac{1}{|\widehat{\mathcal{Q}}_k - 1|} \sum_{\hat{\mathbf{x}} \in \widehat{\mathcal{Q}}_k} \hat{\mathbf{x}}\hat{\mathbf{x}}^T. \tag{8}$$

The coefficient ρ is used to balance the importance between the prior matrix $\boldsymbol{\Phi}$ and the sample covariance $\mathbf{S}_k$. In [18], Ledoit et al. suggested a scaler multiples of identity matrix as a general setting for $\boldsymbol{\Phi}$. Instead, in this work, we set $\boldsymbol{\Phi} = \widehat{\mathbf{S}} \otimes \mathbf{I}_{s^2}$, in which $\widehat{\mathbf{S}}$ takes the average of all the $\widehat{\mathbf{S}}_k$'s, i.e.,

$$\widehat{\mathbf{S}} = \frac{1}{|\mathcal{A}|} \sum_{k=1}^{|\mathcal{A}|} \mathbf{S}_k, \tag{9}$$

In general, the imposed prior is related to sample covariance matrices. The reason for choosing this prior is based on the following observation: overall, the noise shall be locally adaptive for each patch; but part of the noise such as thermal and circuits noise is content-independent. These types of noise are shared among all the image patches.

As can be seen, (7) is actually a convex linear combination of the prior matrix $\boldsymbol{\Phi}$ and sample covariance $\mathbf{S}_k$, in which the setting of coefficient ρ and the prior $\boldsymbol{\Phi}$ play a crucial role. The coefficient ρ can be determined by solving the following optimization problem [18]

$$\min_{\rho} \mathbb{E}[\|\widehat{\mathbf{C}}_k - \boldsymbol{\Sigma}\|^2]$$
$$\text{s.t.:} \ \widehat{\mathbf{C}}_k = \rho\boldsymbol{\Phi} + (1-\rho)\mathbf{S}_k, \tag{10}$$

where $\rho = \frac{a}{b}$, where a and b are given by

$$a = \|\mathbf{S}_k - \boldsymbol{\Phi}\|^2; \tag{11}$$

$$b = \min(\bar{b}, a), \ \text{where} \ \bar{b} = \frac{1}{M} \sum_{k=1}^{M} \|\hat{\mathbf{x}}_k\hat{\mathbf{x}}_k^T - \mathbf{S}_k\|^2. \tag{12}$$

Algorithm 1. Locally adaptive noise covariance matrices estimation

---

Input: Noisy color image.

Output: Estimated noise covariance matrix $\widehat{\boldsymbol{\Sigma}}_k$ associated with the kth pixel

1: **for** the patch $\mathbf{x}_k$ centered at kth pixel **do**

2:    Find its M most similar patches in the local searching region.
     This forms dataset $\mathcal{Q} = \{\mathbf{x}_i\}_{i=1}^{M}$.

3:    Perform DCT filtering on $\mathcal{Q}$ using (4), which converts $\mathcal{Q}$ to $\widehat{\mathcal{Q}} = \{\hat{\mathbf{x}}_i\}_{i=1}^{M}$.

4:    Set the prior $\boldsymbol{\Phi} = \widehat{\mathbf{S}} \otimes \mathbf{I}_{s^2}$, where $\mathbf{S}_k$ is computed using (9); compute the
     coefficient $\rho = \frac{a}{b}$, where a and b are given by (11) and (12), respectively.

5:    Fuse the prior and the sample covariance matrix $\widehat{\mathbf{C}}_k = \rho\boldsymbol{\Phi} + (1-\rho)\mathbf{S}_k$.

6:    Solve each element of $\widehat{\boldsymbol{\Sigma}}_k$ using (13)
     $\widehat{\boldsymbol{\Sigma}}_k(i,j) = \mathsf{mean}\left(\mathsf{diag}\left(\widehat{\mathbf{C}}^{(i,j)}\right)\right)$, for $i,j = 1,2,3$.

7: **end for**

8: **return** Estimated noise covariance $\widehat{\boldsymbol{\Sigma}}_k$.

The above estimator (7) was rigorously proved being a consistent estimator for $\boldsymbol{\Sigma}$. For more details on the proof, please refer to the Sections 3.3 and 3.4 in [18].

The estimator (7) can be interpreted from the perspective of Bayesian. The estimate $\widehat{\boldsymbol{\Sigma}}_k$ can be regarded as a trade-off two components: prior information and data fitting fidelity. Prior information states that the underlying true covariance matrix is nearby the given prior $\boldsymbol{\Phi}$; while the data fitting fidelity states that the true covariance should also resides nearby the sample covariance $\mathbf{S}_k$. Putting those prior and the data fidelity together, a reasonable estimate for the true covariance is lying in somewhat the middle point between $\boldsymbol{\Phi}$ and $\mathbf{S}_k$. Such trade-off is controlled by the ρ, which balance the relative importance of the prior and data fitting fidelity. In fact, the setting of ρ depends on which one is more accurate. When the sample size is limited, the $\mathbf{S}_k$ merely inferred from the data is biased. One shall put more trust on the prior information, and shrink the estimate towards the prior $\boldsymbol{\Phi}$.

Once the estimate of $\widehat{\mathbf{C}} \in \mathbb{R}^{3s^2 \times 3s^2}$ is obtained, each element of $\widehat{\boldsymbol{\Sigma}}_k \in \mathbb{R}^{3\times 3}$ can be efficiently computed as follows

$$\widehat{\boldsymbol{\Sigma}}_k(i,j) = \mathsf{mean}\left(\mathsf{diag}\left(\widehat{\mathbf{C}}^{(i,j)}\right)\right), \text{ for } i,j = 1,2,3. \tag{13}$$

where $\mathsf{mean}(\cdot)$ computes the mean of the input vector; $\mathsf{diag}(\cdot)$ returns a vector with the entries of the input diagonal matrix, and $\widehat{\mathbf{C}}^{(i,j)} \in \mathbb{R}^{s^2 \times s^2}$ is the (i,j)th uniformly-partitioned square block matrix of $\widehat{\mathbf{C}} \in \mathbb{R}^{3s^2 \times 3s^2}$.

4 Experimental Results

4.1 Experiment Setup

To validate the effectiveness of our proposed estimation method, we need the ground-truth noise covariance matrices as reference. We prepare such ground-truths from the real-world images, which are captured by following the procedure given below. Under the constant lighting environment, the static scene is shot multiple times with the same camera brand and fixed capture settings. Because the camera position and the scene are all static, no fluctuation or motion is introduced during imaging. This makes the recorded images well-aligned spatially. Moreover, since the camera settings and lighting are fixed, the incurred variation across the image sequence can be attributed to the camera itself. With the obtained image sequence, we can compute the ground-truth noise covariance matrix and its associated the ground-truth 'clean' image. The covariance matrix calculated throughout each pixel location can be regarded as the ground-truth noise covariance matrix. The temporal mean of the image sequence, i.e., the mean image, can be regarded as the ground-truth 'clean' image. Using this mean image, the quantitative measures for evaluating the image quality such as PSNR and SSIM can be calculated. Note that this strategy for computing the ground-truth clean image and the noise statistics has already been practiced in many existing works, e.g., [10,23,28].

In this work, we capture image sequences with two mobile phone cameras: OnePlus 3T (one sequence) and iPhone 6 Plus (one sequence). Each image sequence contains 300 images. In addition, to make our test image set diverse, we also collect 3 image sequences from the existing datasets, which are all captured with digital single-lens reflex (DSLR) cameras. The first 4 sequences are from [23], which are captured by Nikon D800 (two sequences), and Canon 5D Mark III (one sequence), respectively; each image sequence contains 500 images. The above 5 image sequences compose our entire test image set. The detailed camera settings for each image sequences are listed in Table 1. For better visual illustration in the following experiments, we randomly crop a part of image in size of 512×512 from the original image. The representative sample images for each image sequence are shown in Fig. 4.

The algorithmic parameters of our proposed method are empirically set as follows: the patch size $s = 8$, the number of excluded bands $K = 4$, the searching window size is 20×20, and the number of searched patches $M = 10$. To compare the estimated noise covariance $\hat{\Sigma}$ with the ground-truth Σ, we use the metric introduced by [12], which can be expressed as

$$\xi(\hat{\Sigma}, \Sigma) = \left[\sum_{i=1}^{n} \ln^2 \lambda_i(\hat{\Sigma}, \Sigma) \right]^{\frac{1}{2}}, \tag{14}$$

where $\lambda_i(\hat{\Sigma}, \Sigma)$ is the ith generalized eigenvalue that can be obtained by solving $(\hat{\Sigma} - \lambda\Sigma)\mathbf{x} = 0$. Clearly, a smaller ξ indicates better estimation performance. In the next, we first evaluate the estimation accuracy of our method. Then the practical usage is demonstrated with real color image denoising.

#1   #2   #3   #4   #5

Fig. 4. The sample image from each image sequence of our dataset.

Table 1. The camera settings for the test image sequences.

Image #	Camera settings			
	Camera brand	ISO	Aperture	Exposure time
1	Nikon D800	3200	$f/11$	$1/30\,\text{s}$
2		6400	$f/11$	$1/50\,\text{s}$
3	Canon 5D Mark III	3200	$f/11$	$1/30\,\text{s}$
4	OnePlus 3T	400	$f/2$	$1/25\,\text{s}$
5	iPhone 6 Plus	160	$f/2.2$	$1/33\,\text{s}$

4.2 Estimation Accuracy

Our method is compared with three state-of-the-art noise estimation works, Chen *et al.* [5] and Liu *et al.* [22], and Nam *et al.* [23]. Note that in [23], Nam suggested training a series of multilayer perceptrons (MLP), each of which handles the images generated by a specific camera brand and setting (e.g., the ISO). We refer this version of [23] as *MLP(specific)*. However, the side information of camera brand and capture setting is not always available in practice. Therefore, we train a single unified network to handle all the images in a generic way. The training/validation data are provided by [23]. To avoid confusion, this unified-network approach is denoted by *MLP(generic)*.

Table 2. Comparison of the estimation error on our image set. The data in each cell is represented in the format MEAN ± STD.

Img. #	[5]	[22]	MLP(generic) [23]	MLP(specific) [23]	Ours
1	8.391 ± 0.975	6.717 ± 1.152	3.243 ± 1.489	1.082 ± 0.608	1.032 ± 1.185
2	7.247 ± 0.880	7.839 ± 1.921	2.758 ± 1.126	1.262 ± 1.129	1.178 ± 1.002
3	6.578 ± 1.317	8.605 ± 1.788	2.121 ± 1.202	2.471 ± 0.899	2.106 ± 0.961
4	6.627 ± 2.008	6.056 ± 1.786	3.328 ± 1.684	2.839 ± 1.591	1.797 ± 1.263
5	6.688 ± 1.208	7.451 ± 1.797	3.306 ± 1.240	2.020 ± 0.934	1.338 ± 0.846

First, the comparison results of the estimation error ξ are tabulated in Table 2. It can be seen that our method outperforms the other three competing works on all test images. Compared with the work [5, 22], both our method could estimate the covariance matrix in a more accurate way. This can be explained by that both [5, 22] totally neglect the correlation across color channels, and merely estimate the diagonal entries of the covariance matrix. In contrast, our approach explicitly account for the correlations among different color channels, and not confine the off-diagonal entries in the covariance matrix to be zeros during estimation.

Compared with *MLP(generic)*, one can observe that our method achieves superior performance at a large margin for all test images. *MLP(generic)* is a data-driven approach that is trained on the collected images generated by many camera brands with multiple capture settings. In essence, it attempts to achieve a *trade-off* among all the seen camera brands and capture settings. As clearly shown in Table 2, this trade-off leads to certain degradation on the estimation accuracy when comparing with *MLP(specific)*. Finally, compared with *MLP(specific)*, our method achieves moderately superior estimation performance. This implies that our approach could adapt to the images output by different cameras and capture settings.

4.3 Application to Color Image Denoising

One direct application of our noise estimation method is color image denoising. In this subsection, we show that the incorporation of our estimated covariances could improve the denoising performance. Although there exist many color image denoisers, we here adopt one of the state-of-the-art methods named *Multi-Channel Weighted Nuclear Norm* (MC-WNNM[1]) [29]. Essentially, MC-WNNM performs the denoising by solving the optimization problem

$$\hat{\mathbf{X}} = \arg \min_{\mathbf{X}} \|\mathbf{W}(\mathbf{Y} - \mathbf{X})\|_F^2 + \|\mathbf{X}\|_{w,*}, \tag{15}$$

where $\mathbf{Y}$ is the noisy patch matrix, in which each column is a vectorized color image patch; $\mathbf{X}$ is the corresponding clean patch matrix; $\mathbf{W}$ is the weighting matrix to balance the reconstruction error among the color channels. $\|\mathbf{X}\|_{w,*} = \sum_i w_i \sigma_i(\mathbf{X})$ is the weighted nuclear norm of $\mathbf{X}$, where $\sigma_i(\mathbf{X})$ is the ith singular value of $\mathbf{X}$. The weighting vector w is set as the same way in [29].

The optimization problem (15) is solvable only when the weighting matrix $\mathbf{W}$ is known as a prior. In [29], $\mathbf{W}$ is set as follows

$$\mathbf{W} = \begin{bmatrix} \hat{\sigma}_r^{-1}\mathbf{I}_{s^2} & 0 & 0 \\ 0 & \hat{\sigma}_g^{-1}\mathbf{I}_{s^2} & 0 \\ 0 & 0 & \hat{\sigma}_b^{-1}\mathbf{I}_{s^2} \end{bmatrix} = \hat{\mathbf{\Sigma}}^{-\frac{1}{2}} \otimes \mathbf{I}_{s^2}, \tag{16}$$

where $\hat{\sigma}_r, \hat{\sigma}_g$ and $\hat{\sigma}_b$ are the estimated noise levels for red, green and blue channels, respectively. In [29], those parameters are estimated with method [5] or [22]. That is, the covariance matrix $\hat{\mathbf{\Sigma}}$ takes a diagonal matrix structure

$$\hat{\mathbf{\Sigma}} = \mathsf{diagm}\left([\hat{\sigma}_r^2, \hat{\sigma}_g^2, \hat{\sigma}_b^2]\right). \tag{17}$$

---

[1] Matlab source code available: https://github.com/csjunxu/MCWNNM_ICCV2017.

Here, diagm($\cdot$) returns a diagonal matrix with the entries of the input vector at main diagonal. Obviously, this setting takes no account of the correlation across the color channels. To remedy this issue, we can adaptively replace the globally fixed diagonal covariance matrix $\widehat{\Sigma}$ with our estimated one $\widehat{\Sigma}_k$ for denoising the kth color image patch.

Table 3. Comparison of denoising performance (in terms of PSNR and SSIM) using MC-WNNM denoiser [29]. The C-BM3D denoiser is included as a baseline.

Img. #	C-BM3D [8]		[5]		[22]		MLP(generic) [23]		MLP(specific) [23]		Ours	
	PSNR	SSIM	PSNR	SSIM	PSNR	SSIM	PSNR	SSIM	PSNR	SSIM	PSNR	SSIM
1	35.17	0.947	35.85	0.954	35.95	0.962	36.90	0.972	37.05	0.964	37.29	0.974
2	29.66	0.749	29.74	0.749	30.19	0.753	31.24	0.810	32.08	0.836	32.62	0.870
3	36.14	0.962	36.95	0.955	36.32	0.954	36.17	0.972	36.71	0.974	36.63	0.970
4	31.29	0.930	31.77	0.931	31.68	0.930	33.19	0.976	33.46	0.964	33.58	0.966
5	31.14	0.909	31.89	0.930	31.35	0.920	32.02	0.935	34.04	0.943	34.30	0.947
Avg	35.56	0.927	36.08	0.932	35.97	0.932	37.01	0.951	37.27	0.955	37.41	0.960

For comparison, the well-known denoiser C-BM3D [8] is also included as a baseline. Its required single noise level is estimated by [5]. The detailed denoising results on the 5 test images are provided in Table 3. As can be seen, our method could boost the denoising performance of MC-WNNM. For instance, the method C-BM3D with [5], MC-WNNM with [5] and MC-WNNM with [22] give the averaged PSNR of the denoised image as 35.56 dB, 36.08 dB and 35.97 dB, respectively, while MC-WNNM with our estimated noise covariance matrices achieves 37.41 dB. Further compared with *MLP(generic)* and *MLP(specific)*, *Ours(adaptive)* also achieves a higher PSNR value, at the gains of 0.40dB and 0.14 dB, respectively. As a final remark, it is worth pointing out that, a more accurate noise estimate does not always lead to better denoising performance. For example, on the test image #3, *MLP(specific)* gives the estimation error 2.471 ± 0.899, which is worse than that of ours 2.106 ± 0.961. However, the resultant PSNR value of *MLP(specific)* is 36.71 dB, which is better than that of *Ours(adaptive)* 36.63 dB. This phenomenon implies that the covariances fed to a specific denoiser need further fine-tuned occasionally; but the in-depth investigation of this issue is beyond the scope of this work.

In Fig. 5, we present one visual example denoised results using different noise covariance matrix settings. It can be seen that the denoised image produced with ours is more visually closer to the mean image. Specifically, [5, 22] cannot effectively help MC-WNNM remove all the noise. In a more detailed inspection, one could observe that the results generated with [5, 22] slightly suffer chromatic aberration when compared with the mean image. We believe this can be attributed to the negligence of correlation across the color channels. Instead, our method could aid MC-WNNM to better preserve the fine color details. The results given by *MLP(generic)* is somewhat over-smoothed.

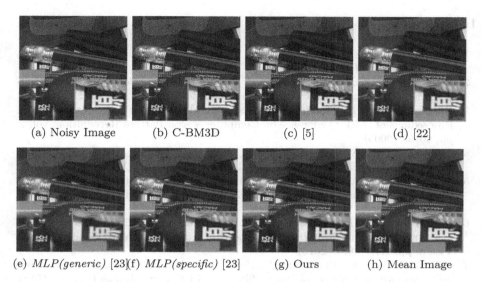

(a) Noisy Image   (b) C-BM3D   (c) [5]   (d) [22]

(e) *MLP(generic)* [23](f) *MLP(specific)* [23]   (g) Ours   (h) Mean Image

Fig. 5. Comparison of denoising results with different noise covariance settings. (a) Noisy image, PSNR = 29.97 dB; (b) [5] + C-BM3D [8], PSNR = 31.14 dB; (c) [5] + MC-WNNM, PSNR = 31.89 dB; (d) [22] + MC-WNNM, PSNR = 31.35 dB; (e) *MLP(generic)* [23] + MC-WNNM, PSNR = 32.02 dB; (f) *MLP(specific)* [23] + MC-WNNM, PSNR = 34.04 dB; (g) Ours + MC-WNNM, PSNR = **34.30** dB; (h) mean image. Zoom in for better visual comparison.

Both *MLP(specific)* and our method could help MC-WNNM produce visually pleasing denoised results. However, for the denoised image of *MLP(specific)*, one may still notice some subtle color artifacts near the edges.

5   Conclusion

In this work, we propose a practical noise covariance estimation method from a single noisy color image, based on the locally adaptive multivariate Gaussian noise model. The local-adaptiveness of noise indicates each local textured region possesses a unique noise model parameter. To this end, we design an effective method for estimating the noise covariance matrices. Specifically, by grouping the non-local similar patches, we could adaptively estimate a covariance matrix for each local patch via a linear shrinkage estimator. Extensive experiments show that our method can effectively estimate the noise covariance matrices, which could boost the performance of many color image processing algorithms such as color image denoising. Our method can be readily adopted into other vision tasks that require the noise covariance as a crucial parameter. As for the future works, we would like to investigate the mathematical relationship between the local noise levels and the patch texture strengths.

References

1. Anderson, T.W.: An Introduction to Multivariate Statistical Analysis, vol. 2. Wiley, New York (1958)
2. Bovik, A.C.: Handbook of Image and Video Processing. Communications, Networking and Multimedia. Academic Press, Orlando (2005)
3. Buades, A., Coll, B., Morel, J.M.: A non-local algorithm for image denoising. In: Proceedings of IEEE Conference on Computer Vision Pattern Recognition, vol. 2, pp. 60–65 (2005)
4. Chakrabarti, A.: Modeling radiometric uncertainty for vision with tone-mapped color images. IEEE Trans. Pattern Anal. Mach. Intell. **36**(11), 2185–2198 (2014)
5. Chen, G., Zhu, F., Pheng, A.H.: An efficient statistical method for image noise level estimation. In: Proceedings of IEEE International Conference on Computer Vision (2015)
6. Choi, I., Kim, S., Brown, M.S., Tai, Y.W.: A learning-based approach to reduce JPEG artifacts in image matting. In: Proceedings of IEEE Conference on Computer Vision, pp. 2880–2887 (2013)
7. Dabov, K., Foi, A., Katkovnik, V., Egiazarian, K.: Image denoising by sparse 3-D transform-domain collaborative filtering. IEEE Trans. Image Process. **16**(8), 2080–2095 (2007)
8. Dabov, K., Foi, A., Katkovnik, V., Egiazarian, K.: Color image denoising via sparse 3D collaborative filtering with grouping constraint in luminance-chrominance space. In: Proceedings of IEEE International Conference on Image Processing (2007)
9. Dong, L., Zhou, J., Tang, Y.Y.: Noise level estimation for natural images based on scale-invariant kurtosis and piecewise stationarity. IEEE Trans. Image Process. **26**(2), 1017–1030 (2017)
10. Dong, L., Zhou, J., Tang, Y.Y.: Effective and fast estimation for image sensor noise via constrained weighted least squares. IEEE Trans. Image Process. **27**(6), 2715–2730 (2018)
11. Dong, W., Zhang, L., Shi, G., Wu, X.: Image deblurring and super-resolution by adaptive sparse domain selection and adaptive regularization. IEEE Trans. Image Process. **20**(7), 1838–1857 (2011)
12. Förstner, W., Moonen, B.: A metric for covariance matrices. In: Grafarend, E.W., Krumm, F.W., Schwarze, V.S. (eds.) Geodesy-The Challenge of the 3rd Millennium. Springer, Heidelberg (2003). https://doi.org/10.1007/978-3-662-05296-9_31
13. Haff, L.: Empirical Bayes estimation of the multivariate normal covariance matrix. Ann. Stat. **8**, 586–597 (1980)
14. Healey, G.E., Kondepudy, R.: Radiometric CCD camera calibration and noise estimation. IEEE Trans. Pattern Anal. Mach. Intell. **16**(3), 267–276 (1994)
15. Jiang, H., Tian, Q., Farrell, J., Wandell, B.A.: Learning the image processing pipeline. IEEE Trans. Image Process. **26**(10), 5032–5042 (2017)
16. Kang, B.J., Park, K.R.: Real-time image restoration for iris recognition systems. IEEE Trans. Syst. Man Cybern. B (Cybern.) **37**(6), 1555–1566 (2007)
17. Kim, S.J., Lin, H.T., Lu, Z., Süsstrunk, S., Lin, S., Brown, M.S.: A new in-camera imaging model for color computer vision and its application. IEEE Trans. Pattern Anal. Mach. Intell. **34**(12), 2289–2302 (2012)
18. Ledoit, O., Wolf, M.: A well-conditioned estimator for large-dimensional covariance matrices. J. Multivar. Anal. **88**(2), 365–411 (2004)

19. Leonard, T., Hsu, J.S.: Bayesian inference for a covariance matrix. Ann. Stat. **20**(4), 1669–1696 (1992)
20. Lian, N.X., Chang, L., Tan, Y.P., Zagorodnov, V.: Adaptive filtering for color filter array demosaicking. IEEE Trans. Image Process. **16**(10), 2515–2525 (2007)
21. Liu, W., Lin, W.: Additive white Gaussian noise level estimation in SVD domain for images. IEEE Trans. Image Process. **22**(3), 872–883 (2013)
22. Liu, X., Tanaka, M., Okutomi, M.: Noise level estimation using weak textured patches of a single noisy image. In: Proceedings of IEEE International Conference on Image Processing (2012)
23. Nam, S., Hwang, Y., Matsushita, Y., Kim, S.: A holistic approach to cross-channel image noise modeling and its application to image denoising. In: Proceedings of IEEE Conference on Computer Vision Pattern Recognition (2016)
24. Pyatykh, S., Hesser, J., Zheng, L.: Image noise level estimation by principal component analysis. IEEE Trans. Image Process. **22**(2), 687–699 (2013)
25. Shan, Q., Jia, J., Agarwala, A.: High-quality motion deblurring from a single image. ACM Trans. Graph. (SIGGRAPH) **27**(3), 1–5 (2008)
26. Tang, C., Yang, X., Zhai, G.: Noise estimation of natural images via statistical analysis and noise injection. IEEE Trans. Circuits Sys. Video Technol. **25**(8), 1283–1294 (2015)
27. Wen, Y.W., Ng, M.K., Huang, Y.M.: Efficient total variation minimization methods for color image restoration. IEEE Trans. Image Process. **17**(11), 2081–2088 (2008)
28. Xu, J., Li, H., Liang, Z., Zhang, D., Zhang, L.: Real-world noisy image denoising: a new benchmark. arXiv preprint arXiv:1804.02603 (2018)
29. Xu, J., Zhang, L., Zhang, D., Feng, X.: Multi-channel weighted nuclear norm minimization for real color image denoising. In: Proceedings of IEEE International Conference on Computer Vision (2017)
30. Zhang, L., Wu, X.: Color demosaicking via directional linear minimum mean square-error estimation. IEEE Trans. Image Process. **14**(12), 2167–2178 (2005)

SAR Image Change Detection
Using Several Filters Combined with Log
Difference Image

Jiaqi Yu[✉]

Xidian University, Xi'an, China
yujiaqi@stu.xidian.edu.cn

Abstract. In this paper, in order to study the increasingly hot SAR image change detection, several simple and effective filtering methods based on existing SAR images are combined, and the difference image is generated by the method of log difference map. Here we try to use LEE filtering, Frost filtering, and wavelet threshold denoising SAR images using hard threshold and soft threshold functions to suppress the speckle noise of the symlet4 wavelet basis function, and then use the log difference image. Next, we perform median filtering on the resulting difference image. Then in order to enhance the difference image effect, the threshold method was used to binarize the obtained difference image. The existing SAR image data was applied to compare the above three methods, and exploit three evaluation indicators to verify the effectiveness of our algorithm. We use log difference image combined with K-Means algorithm as our compared algorithm. It is concluded that the wavelet method has the fastest speed and the Lee filter combined with the log difference map algorithm is more robust.

Keywords: SAR image · Filter · Log difference image · Threshold method

1 Introduction

It is a hot topic about SAR (Synthetic Aperture Radar) image change detection [20]. Image change detection is the process of analyzing images of the same scene taken at different times, which allows us to identify changes that may occur between the acquired dates considered. Change detection technology plays an extremely important role in the field of remote sensing image. Through the local texture change information and radiation value of remote sensing image, it can be used in agriculture [17], environment [18], land and resource utilization [19], crop growth, natural disaster situation, and even military field. They have played a pivotal role. However, the most serious problem in SAR image processing is its speckle noise [11], and this kind of noise is a kind of multiplicative noise, which will seriously affect the interpretation efficiency of SAR images.

© Springer Nature Singapore Pte Ltd. 2019
G. Zhai et al. (Eds.): IFTC 2018, CCIS 1009, pp. 106–117, 2019.
https://doi.org/10.1007/978-981-13-8138-6_9

In general, SAR image change detection is divided into three steps: (1) image preprocessing (2) generation of difference maps (3) difference map analysis ([12–15] mentioned). In the image preprocessing section, the first thing we consider is to remove the speckle noise. Since the noise here is multiplicative noise, it is difficult to use a simple mean filtering operation to achieve our goal. In view of this situation, we consider using wavelet denoising because it can both achieve noise reduction while keep the main information of the images. After completing this step, we need to generate the difference map. The easiest way to realize this is to do the difference calculation. However, the previous literature [1] proves that the effect is not very good. Document [2] tells us that the ratio operator performs better than the additive operator. For the convenience of operation, we convert the multiplication and division relationship into the addition and subtraction relationship. We naturally think of the logarithmic operation, and at the same time weaken the large difference that may be caused by the ratio relationship. After completing the generation of the difference map, we need to enhance the contrast between the changed area and the unchanged area. Therefore, the idea of binarization is used to enhance the difference, and we consider using the threshold method to enhance this contrast, which can be seen more clearly the change between the two SAR images.

2   Related Work

In recent years, there have been many algorithms for denoising (such as Lee filtering, Frost filtering, and wavelet threshold denoising) for SAR images, and some algorithms for generating difference graphs (such as log difference maps). Although these methods are well studied, they can be considered for combining the two. In view of the SAR image change detection to be studied in this paper, our start is to suppress the speckle noise and carry out in-depth SAR image change detection. This is in line with our start for image research, while at the same time combining some of the existing classic methods.

3   Algorithm

In this section we will describe the steps mentioned in the introduction. First, we use a block diagram to show the process (Fig. 1).

Next, we begin to introduce the algorithm in detail.

3.1   Some Filters

3.1.1   Frost Filter

The Frost filtering algorithm assumes that speckle noise is a multiplicative noise and assumes that the SAR image is a smooth process. We filter the image. The impulse response of the Frost filter is a bilateral exponential function, approximated as a low-pass filter whose filter parameters are determined by the image

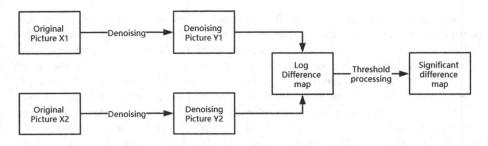

Fig. 1. SAR image change detection algorithm block diagram

local variance coefficient. The attenuation of the impulse response depends on the magnitude of the local variance coefficient and is proportional to it. The idea is similar to local weighted regression. Its mathematical expression is as follows:

$$g_j' = \frac{\sum\limits_{i=1}^{n}\sum\limits_{j=1}^{n} g_j' M_{ij}}{M_{ij}},$$
$$M_{ij} = exp(-A_{ij}T_{ij})$$
$$A_{ij} = \frac{\sigma_{ij}}{\overline{g}_{ij}^2}$$

$$(1)$$

where σ_{ij} and $\overline{g}_{ij}^2$ are the internal mean and variance of the window, respectively.

3.1.2   Lee Filter

Lee filter is one of the typical methods for image speckle filtering using image local statistical properties. It is based on a fully developed speckle noise model, selecting a window of a certain length as a local region. We assume that the prior mean and variance can be calculated by calculating the local mean and variance is obtained. The filtered new image can be obtained by using the weighted sum by the obtained mean and variance. Its mathematical expression is as follows:

$$\hat{x} = \overline{y} + b(y - \overline{y}) \tag{2}$$

where $var(x) = \frac{var(y)-\sigma_v^2}{1+\sigma_v^2}$, $b = \frac{var(x)}{var(y)}$, $\sigma_v^2 = \frac{1}{N}$, N is equivalent visual number.

3.1.3   Wavelet Threshold Denosing

The basic idea of wavelet threshold denoising is to set a threshold. For the signals of each scale, we consider the part larger than the threshold to be the signal, and the part smaller than the threshold is considered as noise, and the noise part is filtered and the signal part is retained. Then, the most important thing is the choice of threshold function. Here we introduce two threshold selection methods, hard threshold and soft threshold. The hard threshold method is to assign a value of 0 to the portion smaller than the threshold, and the rest remains unchanged. We use the following formula to express:

$$w_\lambda = \begin{cases} w, |w| \geq \lambda \\ 0, |w| < \lambda \end{cases} \tag{3}$$

The soft threshold function is similar to the hard threshold method except that when the absolute value of the signal is greater than the threshold, the threshold is subtracted from the threshold to become the difference between itself and the threshold. We use the following formula to express:

$$w_\lambda = \begin{cases} [sgn(w)] \, (|w| - \lambda), |w| \geq \lambda \\ 0, |w| < \lambda \end{cases} \tag{4}$$

3.2 Log Difference Image

The log difference graph algorithm is mentioned in [6] and [10]. We will get the ratio of the two filtered SAR images and take the logarithm and then obtain the absolute value. In order to avoid the phenomenon that the denominator is 0, we add 1 to two images. The specific formula is as follows:

$$D_l = |log(Y_1 + 1) - log(Y_2 + 1)| \tag{5}$$

D_l is generated by the logarithm difference image. Then we normalize the difference image to the grayscale interval of $[0, 255]$. After that, the resulting difference image is subjected to median filtering because the median filtering can better preserve the edge information.

3.3 Threshold Method

After completing the generation of the logarithmic difference image, in order to further enhance the contrast, we use the threshold method to binarize the difference image. To do this, we first get the gray histogram of the log difference image. Using the idea of the filter, more than half of the difference in the gray value is used as the selection point of the threshold. For example, let's assume we have 10,000 pixels and draw the grayscale histogram (using half of the difference in the gray value as example). The number is counted from the gray value of 0 until there are 5000 pixels, rounded up to get our gray threshold.

3.4 Compared Algorithm

An existing algorithm for SAR image change detection is introduced here (mentioned in [10]). The generated log difference image binarized by k-Means algorithm. K-Means algorithm will be introduced here.

At first, we choose two points as initial clustering center. And then, the distance from each pixel to the center of the initial cluster center is calculated. Each pixel is classified as that class if it is closer to one of initial cluster center.

Next, we calculate the mean of each category as the new cluster center. Repeat the process mentioned above until the cluster center doesn't change.

Finally, assign the smaller part of the mean to 0 and the other to 255 to get the final difference.

4   Experiment and Result

4.1   Dataset Description

In this section, we will experiment to verify the effectiveness of our algorithm. We will introduce three datasets here. The first are two SAR images taken at Red River in Vietnam on 1996.08.24 (Fig. 2(a)) and 1999.08.14 (Fig. 2(b)), with an image size of 512×512 pixels.

(a)   (b)

Fig. 2. SAR images of Red River in Vietnam.

The second set of data are captured at De Gaulle Airport on 1997.7.24 (Fig. 3(a)) and 1998.10.24 (Fig. 3(b)) respectively. The SAR image has an image size of 370×240 pixels.

The third set of data are two SAR images taken on Java Island in 1994.02.06 (Fig. 4(a)) and 1994.03.06 (Fig. 4(b)), respectively, with an image size of 512×512 pixels.

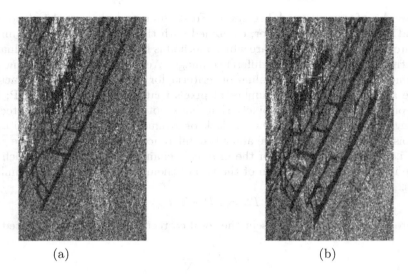

Fig. 3. SAR images of De Gaulle Airport.

Fig. 4. SAR images of Java Island.

4.2   Compared Algorithm Evaluation Mechanism

We use the aforementioned Lee filter, Frost filter and the wavelet denoising method mentioned in this paper, combined with the latter log difference image and threshold method to compare which method is better. The effect is evaluated subjectively by displaying the difference image. We will use the two parameters mentioned in [7,15] as the evaluation criteria for our test. One is the actual change and also detects the number of pixels that change, termed as TP; the other one is the number of pixels that have not changed and also detected unchanged, termed as TN. (Due to lack of ground graph and the multiplicative noise of the SAR image, we allow the difference to float by 10% of the gray value, i.e. the absolute value of the grayscale change is less than 26, which we believe is unchanged.) The sum of the two of them is the total correct number, that is,

$$TS = TP + TN. \tag{6}$$

Here, we use OPP to represent the total correct rate, which is calculated as:

$$OPP = \frac{TS}{N}. \tag{7}$$

where N represents the number of total pixels. In addition, we also decide to use the full code runtime as one of our evaluation criteria to evaluate the efficiency of the algorithm. (Matlab is used to experiment).

4.3   Experiment Results

For wavelet threshold denoising, we choose Symlet4 as our wavelet basis function [9] and the global threshold as our threshold (mentioned in [8]), the formula is as follows:

$$\lambda = \sigma \sqrt{2log(M \times N)}, \tag{8}$$

where σ s the standard deviation of noise and M, N are the image sizes, respectively.

The first dataset's result is as follows (Table 1 shows the number of each evaluation index and Fig. 5 shows the final difference map. We use half of the difference in the gray value):

Table 1. The first data results

	TP	TS	TN	OPP	Time(s)
K-Means	12318	154170	166488	63.51%	2.27
Frost	35866	150106	185972	70.94%	9.77
Lee	36181	149399	185580	70.79%	13.78
Wavelet(soft)	36060	149939	185999	70.95%	2.25
Wavelet(hard)	36710	149852	186562	71.17%	2.29

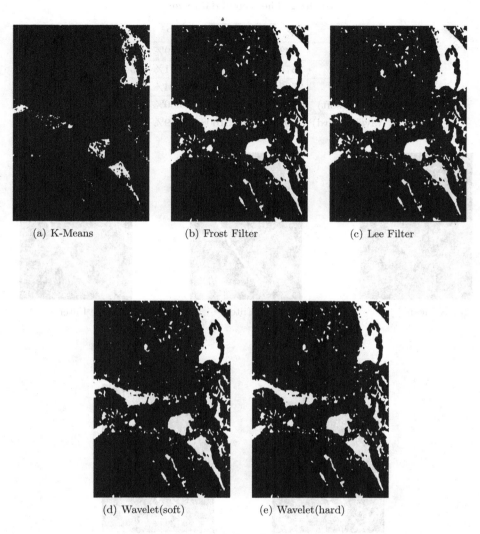

(a) K-Means   (b) Frost Filter   (c) Lee Filter

(d) Wavelet(soft)   (e) Wavelet(hard)

Fig. 5. The results of second data

The second dataset's result is as follows (Table 2 shows the number of each evaluation index and Fig. 6 shows the final difference map. We use 90% of the difference in the gray value):

Table 2. The second data results

	TP	TS	TN	OPP	Time(s)
K-Means	843	29780	30623	34.49%	1.89
Frost	2575	29399	31974	36.01%	4.54
Lee	2598	29402	32000	36.04%	5.34
Wavelet(soft)	2227	29387	31614	35.60%	2.26
Wavelet(hard)	2202	29406	31608	35.59%	3.00

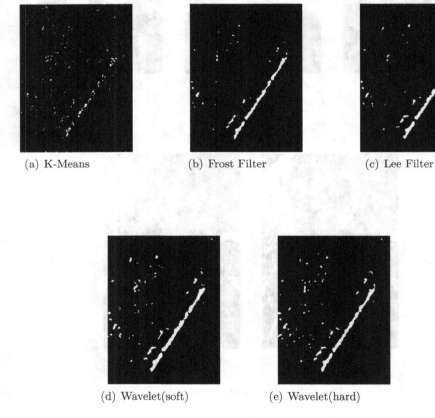

(a) K-Means   (b) Frost Filter   (c) Lee Filter

(d) Wavelet(soft)   (e) Wavelet(hard)

Fig. 6. The results of second data

The third dataset's result is as follows (Table 3 shows the number of each evaluation index and Fig. 7 shows the final difference map. We use half of the difference in the gray value):

Table 3. The third data results

	TP	TS	TN	OPP	Time(s)
K-Means	2821	110958	113799	43.4%	2.70
Frost	34962	103680	138642	52.89%	10.37
Lee	35989	103267	139256	53.12%	12.80
Wavelet(soft)	35455	102958	137502	52.45%	2.29
Frost	33643	103410	137053	52.28%	2.66

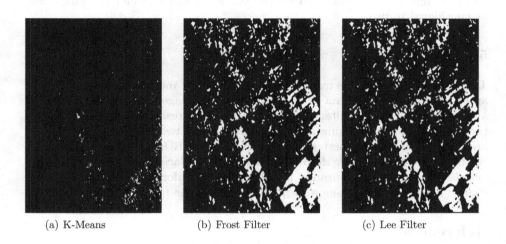

(a) K-Means   (b) Frost Filter   (c) Lee Filter

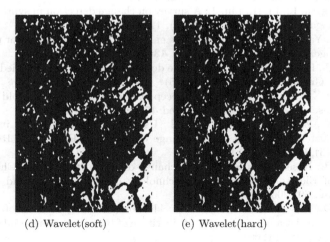

(d) Wavelet(soft)   (e) Wavelet(hard)

Fig. 7. The results of third data

4.4   Result Analysis

From the subjective results, except for the results in Fig. 6, the difference is not significant. Objectively speaking, each algorithm has its own merits. In comparison, the algorithm based on Lee filter is more robust in the log difference image, but its efficiency is lower (because of its local nature, the need for pixel-by-pixel traversal lead complexity to increase), especially the running time is too long. However, in terms of speed, wavelet threshold denoising is significantly faster than other algorithms. This is also a fast algorithm based on wavelet transform, which makes it more efficient. Therefore, if we need to pursue efficiency, SAR image change detection based on wavelet denoising and log difference image can be considered to use.

5   Conclusion

This article introduces the method of filter to denoise and uses logarithmic operator to extend the logarithm of the ratio difference image to the whole gray scale and then do the median filtering. Next, we use the threshold method to enhance the contrast of the changing region to get the final two SAR image difference images. Our model can better detect changes in SAR images and increase the correct amount of change. However, our model still lacks the grasp of the edge details. How to more accurately identify the edge information to make better change detection is the issue we will investigate in the future.

References

1. Rignot, E.J.M., Zyl, J.J.V.: Change detection techniques for ERS-1 SAR data. IEEE Trans. Geosci. Remote Sens. **31**(4), 896–906 (1993)
2. Gong, M., Su, L., Li, H., Liu, J.: A survey on change detection in synthetic apeture radar imagery. J. Comput. Dev. **53**(1), 123–127 (2016)
3. Lang, F., Yang, J., Li, D.: An adaptive enhanced Lee speckle filter for polarimetric SAR image. Acta Geod. Cartogr. Sin. **43**(7), 690–697 (2014)
4. Zhang, C., Pan, C., Ma, S.: SAR image de-speckling based on modified Frost filter. J. Image Graph. **10**(4), 431–435 (2005)
5. Chen, X.-X., Wang, Y.-J., Liu, L.: Deep study on wavelet threshold method for image noise removing. Laser & Infrared **42**(1), 105–110 (2012)
6. Zheng, Y., Zhang, X., Hou, B., et al.: Using combined difference image and k-means clustering for SAR image change detection. IEEE Geosci. Remote Sens. Lett. **11**(3), 691–695 (2014)
7. Zhang, H.: Research on SAR image change detection technology. Chengdu, University of Electronic Science and Technology of China, Signal and Information Processing, 60 (2008)
8. Xu, X.-D.: Research on coherent speckle noise filtering method of SAR image based on wavelet analysis, pp. 12–14. Institute of Remote Sensing, and GIS. Peking University, Beijing (2001)
9. An, Z.-H., Han, X., Dong, X.-L.: Comparative study on wavelets performance in transient power quality detection. Electrotechnice Electric No. 8 (2010)

10. Wu, S.: The research of SAR image change detection based on difference image fusion and difference image denoising, p. 20. Xidian University, School of Electronic Engineering (2017)
11. Zhu, J.: The research on some filtering algorithms in the SAR image speckle, pp. 6–12. Information and Communication of Engineering in the Graduate School of Hunan University (2014)
12. Gong, M., Cao, Y., Wu, Q.: A neighborhood-based ratio approach for change detection in SAR image. IEEE Geosci. Remote Sens. Lett. **9**(2), 307–311 (2012)
13. Su, L., Gong, M., Sun, B., et al.: Unsupervised change detection in SAR images based on locally fitting model and semi-EM algorithm. Int. J. Remote Sens. **35**(2), 621–650 (2014)
14. Ma, J., Gong, M., Zhou, Z.: Wavelet fusion on ration images for change detection in SAR images. IEEE Geosci. Remote Sens. Lett. **9**(6), 1122–1126 (2012)
15. Gong, M., Su, L., Jia, M., et al.: Fuzzy clustering with a modified MRF energy function for change detection in synthetic aperture radar images. IEEE Trans. Fuzzy Syst. **22**(1), 98–109 (2014)
16. Fu, L.: Change detection based on local information statistic in SAR image, pp. 6–7. Xidian University (2012)
17. Bruzzone, L., Serpico, S.B.: An iterative technique for the detection of land cover transitions in multi temporal remote sensing images. IEEE Trans. Geosci. Remote Sens. **35**(4), 858–867 (1997)
18. Chavez, P.S., Mackinnon, D.J.: Automatic detection of vegetation changes in the Southwestern United States using remotely sensed images. ISPRS J. Photogramm. Remote Sens. **60**(5), 1285–1294 (1994)
19. Hame, T., Heiler, I., Migual-Ayanz, J.S.: An unsupervised change detection and recognition system for forestry. Int. J. Remote Sens. **19**(6), 1079–1099 (1998)
20. Gong, M.G., Zhao, J., Liu, J., et al.: Change detection in synthetic aperture radar images based on deep neural networks. IEEE Trans. Neural Netw. Learn. Syst. **27**(1), 125–138 (2016)

Simulation and Experiment on Artificial Landmark-Based Monocular Visual Navigation System for Mobile Robot

Jing Hu[1,2], Xianbin Xu[1], Yuanhua Yang[1(✉)], and Mengjia Yin[1]

[1] School of Computer, Wuhan University, Hubei 430074, China
yangyuanhua123@163.com
[2] School of Computer, Wuhan Qingchuan University, Hubei 430204, China

Abstract. With regard to the automatic navigation of mobile robots working in a relatively fixed scene, this paper studies an artificial landmark-based monocular visual navigation system for mobile robot. The artificial landmark is designed to be conical in order to adapt to the rotation and distortion arising from the change of the angle of view during the movement of the robot. To better divide the artificial signpost, the inverse value of the H-channel mean of the background image has been calculated is selected as the main hue of the artificial landmark. The vision system adopts the template matching to detect and track the artificial landmarks that are previously installed in the working field within the field of view to determine the initial distance and heading. When the robot is approaching an artificial landmark, the node number of this landmark in the topological map is identified by detecting and decoding the Quick Response (QR) code pasted on the landmark, then the distance and position of the robot and the QR code plane are measured by using the monocular distance measurement technology based on an arbitrary plane constraint. The experimental results show that the detection of artificial landmark reaches 95% accuracy rate and averagely consumes 0.12 ms regardless of the changes in illumination intensity, angle of view, and dimension. The average root-mean-square error (RMSE) of the measurement by using the algorithm of monocular distance measuring is 10.9 mm, and the relative average error is 0.45%. In a word, the monocular visual navigation system proposed in this paper has a simple structure, fast detection speed, high precision and practical value.

Keywords: Visual navigation · Monocular vision · Artificial landmark · Distance measuring

1 Introduction

The robot's visual system simulates the visual function of the human eye, which can be used to detect and locate the target of the operation and to navigate the robot. Its performance is directly related to the efficiency and accuracy of the operation [1].

G. Zhai et al. (Eds.): IFTC 2018, CCIS 1009, pp. 118–130, 2019.
https://doi.org/10.1007/978-981-13-8138-6_10

Visual navigation can be divided into binocular (multi-ocular) visual navigation and monocular visual navigation according to the number of sensors used. Compared with monocular visual navigation, binocular visual navigation is more costly and slower in calculating, but more accurate in positioning. For example, Sinisterra developed a stereovision based methodology to estimate the position, speed and heading of a moving marine vehicle from a pursuing unmanned surface vehicle (USV), in support of enabling a USV to follow a target vehicle in motion [2]. Monocular visual navigation is a better choice in fields which pose stringent limitation on the cost and less-demanding requirement on positioning accuracy. Monocular visual navigation only requires a camera, with simple structure, and convenient and flexible operation, which makes it suitable for robot navigation in the field environment.

Monocular visual positioning is a mathematical model that uses the camera to establish the projection transformation relationship between spatial target and image feature point, and then calculates the position information of target feature point. For example, Lee presented a new implementation method for efficient simultaneous localization and mapping using a forward-viewing monocular vision sense, which was developed to be applicable in real time on a low-cost embedded system for indoor service robots [3]. Hu et al. proposed a low-cost yet accurate localization method for intelligent vehicles, which only needs a monocular camera and a GPS receiver [4]. Basiri used the method of presetting artificial landmark to assist mobile robot in target detection for monocular visual navigation technology, so as to increase the number of identifiable features in the environment and simplify the process of iden-tification and positioning. The robot can identify the landmark, then establish the relationships of all the landmark positions and finally construct the navigation map [5]. Song et al. presented a heterogeneous landmark-based visual navigation approach for a monocular mobile robot by using heterogeneous visual features and their inner geo-metric constraints managed by a novel multilayer feature graph (MFG) [6]. In order to solve the problem in indoor target searching, Wang et al. guided the robot to move to a designated area and located the robot by taking the QR code as artificial landmark, and eventually judged whether the robot reached the target nearby by finding out whether the area of the target region reached the threshold [7]. Wang used MR code as artificial landmark in the visual navigation of robot and proposed a real-time posi-tioning method for map by using monocular vision and odometer [8]. In addition to robot's self-positioning, measuring the distance between the target or obstacle and the robot is also one of the essential functions of visual navigation. Monocular visual measurement uses one camera to capture images for measurement. This method has such advantages as easy calibration of the camera, simple structure and fast operation, and in the meantime, it solves the problems that the stereoscopic visual measuring has a limited field of view and stereo matching is difficult. Scholars have studied the distance measurement by taking advantage of the perspective principle, and the established model only entailed a lens or a camera [9]. Recently, with the development of SLAM technology, in regard to the monocular SLAM (ORB-SLAM), a method for distance measuring is proposed, which uses the monocular camera to estimate the camera position based on motion and calculate the KF depth [10]. Zhang proposed a navigation method for weeding robot based on SUSAN (smallest univalve segment assimilating nucleus) corner and improved sequential clustering algorithm, which was effective in complicated environment [11].

Relying on the visual navigation system, mobile robot can autonomously move in a broad complex natural environment, automatically search and locate the operating site, detect and position the operating target at the site, and provide key parameters for follow-up operations. Mobile robot positioning and navigation vision system have been met the requirements. First, according to the system requirements to accurately identify the target and has a certain anti-jamming ability. Second, it can locate the target object, provide the position information for the robot's motion control, and satisfy the accuracy requirement. To meet those demand, this paper studies a monocular visual system, which combines artificial landmark and monocular ranging function to equip the mobile robot with automatic navigation and target detection. All algorithms are implemented by using VS2015 programming environment and OpenCV, which have wide range and excellent value of application.

2 Method

2.1 Processes of Artificial Landmark-Based Visual Navigation System

The robot uses a mounted camera to take pictures of the scenery in front of it, identifies and positions the artificial landmark and calculates the navigation route through image analysis. The workflow of the visual navigation system designed in this paper: (1) Prior to formal operation of the robot, a topology map is drawn by taking the artificial landmark as node. (2) The robot sets an initial course by detecting and tracking the artificial landmarks previously placed at the site. (3) The robot moves to the operating site nearby and detects and decodes the QR code pasted on the operating site to recognize the node number of this operating site in the entire topological map. (4) After identifying and locating the operating target, the robot's actuator performs the operation. (5) Monocular distance measuring method is applied to measure the spatial position of the QR code region to accurately position the robot in an automatic manner and provide the information including the distance and steering angle for the module that controls the robot movement. (6) Next operating site is scanned and a new course is set (Fig. 1).

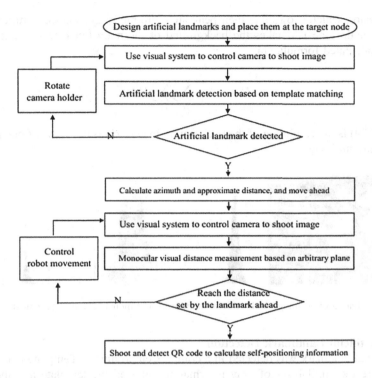

Fig. 1. Process of artificial landmark-based visual system

2.2 Artificial Landmark Design and Detection

2.2.1 Artificial Landmark Design

The design of artificial landmark has a direct influence on the performance of navigation system. The design of landmark color should consider the avoidance of overlapping with the main color of background in order to facilitate the image segmentation in the site where the landmarks are located. The color of the landmark was designed by taking the method of finding threshold for minimum overlapping in H channel histogram. This study took the environmental images to calculated H-channel histogram in the HSV color model of the image, analyzed the histogram distribution and peak characteristics, found the threshold point that distinguishes the artificial landmark and the environment, and eventually selected the color corresponding to the area with smallest overlap to the histogram as the main color of the artificial landmark. The shape of the artificial landmark should take into consideration the rotation and distortion arising from the change of the angle of view during the movement of the robot. The conical shape is chosen as the standardized shape for the landmark to adapt to the change in the visual angle of robot. An artificial landmark designed for grassland or woodland environment was proposed by this paper, as shown in Fig. 2. The artificial landmark color can be designed to be red which is a strong contrast to the background and its shape is conical. Figure 2 compares the H component histograms of background and landmark, which shows that their peak areas are rarely overlapped. Artificial road Signs the main tone HM takes the background of the main tonal mean value of the inverse, calculated formula (1).

$$H_M = 1 - \sum_{j=0}^{M-1} \sum_{j=0}^{N-1} H_B \qquad (1)$$

where (M, N) is the resolution of the background image, H_B is the value of one pixel in the background image.

Fig. 2. The background image and artificial landmarks and their H channel statistical histogram

2.2.2 Artificial Landmark Detection

The artificial landmark was detected in a complex environment. Template matching is to compare the similarities of gray information between the template and the input image to find the region with high similarity to the template image [12]. The establishment process of mathematical model of template matching is as follows: the template image is represented as T, and its size is $m \times n$, where gray value corresponding to each pixel is $T(x, y)$, $x \in (1, m), y \in (1, n)$. The input image is represented as I, its size is $M \times N$, and the gray value is $I(x, y)$, $x \in (1, M), y \in (1, N)$. The template is translated in the input image I to search the most similar area with the same size as the template, and the search range is $(x, y) \in (M - m + 1, N - n + 1)$, and the size of the obtained similarity matrix is $(M - m + 1, N - n + 1)$. Considering that the egg-collecting robot has low requirements for real-time performance and high precision, the normalized correlation coefficient matching method is selected to calculate the similarity $R(x, y)$.

$$R(x, y) = \frac{\sum_{x'y'} (T'(x', y') \cdot I'(x + x', y + y'))}{\sqrt{\sum_{x'y'} (T'(x', y'))^2 \sum_{x'y'} (I'(x + x', y + y'))^2}} \qquad (2)$$

where (x, y)——the coordinate of any pixel in the source image, (x', y')——the coordinate of any pixel in the template image, $R(x, y)$——the similarity of the two images. The smaller the $R(x, y)$, the smaller the difference and the higher the match.

The process of artificial landmark detection: (1) Manual production of the template image T of artificial landmark. A number of scene images with artificial landmarks are photographed, and the Grabcut algorithm [13] is used to segment the areas where the artificial landmarks are located in the environmental image and save it as a template image. (2) Visual model automatically performs template matching for artificial landmark. In the input environmental image I, the template image T is traversed from left to right and from top to bottom, and $R(x, y)$ is calculated in each area. After all the searches are completed, the minimum value $R_{\min}(x_m, y_m)$ is found, and the corresponding sub-image $I_{x_m y_m}$ is the matching target, and (x_m, y_m) is the pixel coordinate of the detection target. This coordinate is converted to physical unit that can be transmitted to the robot's motion control system.

2.2.3   QR Code Detection

QR code is generally designed as a square black and white pattern and is pasted on node as the unique number of this node. This study uses the Hamming code to encode the QR code. Figure 3 shows the algorithm flow chart of QR code detection. First, the colorful input image is converted into gray image, and then the adaptive threshold segmentation algorithm is used to binarize the image. The relative position of QR code to the camera is random, so the image should undergo perspective transformation to transform the distorted image into a square image. The outlines in square image are continually detected, and four-angle rectangle fitting is used to select the outline for subsequent decoding.

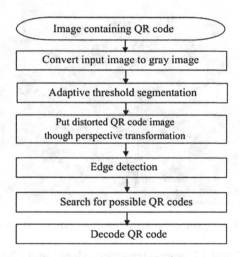

Fig. 3. Basic processes of QR code detection.

2.3   Camera Calibration and Monocular Distance Measuring

2.3.1   Camera Calibration

The camera calibration uses the calibration object with a known shape and size to provide the reference point, and then uses image processing and mathematical transformation to obtain the internal and external parameters of camera. The method proposed by Zhang Zhengyou is used for camera calibration [14]. The calibration board used in this experiment has angular points with an area of. First, the camera's focal length and aperture are adjusted for clear imaging. The camera's visual view is changed to capture 21 calibration images. Then the camera calibration program is implemented to process the calibrated image, extract the angular point and calculate the camera's internal parameter matrix. Figure 4 shows the calibration images collected and the angular points extracted. The camera internal parameters obtained in this paper through calibration: optical center coordinate (245.4, 334.7), scale factors in x and y directions (1007.32, 998.76), and camera distortion coefficient (0.4317, −10.2, 0.01, −0.016, 64.64). Based on this, the coordinate transformation relationship between the camera coordinate system and the world coordinate system, that is, the rotation matrix R and the translation matrix T is further calculated. The ground is set to be the constraint plane. The calibration board is placed on the ground, i.e. the world coordinate system is established on the ground plane. The solve PnP function in OpenCV is used to solve the external parameters, namely, the rotation vector r and the translation vector T of the world coordinate system relative to the camera coordinate system. The outcome of this function is a 1 × 3 rotation vector r. The singular value decomposition (SVD) of the rotation vector r is performed using the Rodrigues function, and rotation vector is converted to the rotation matrix R.

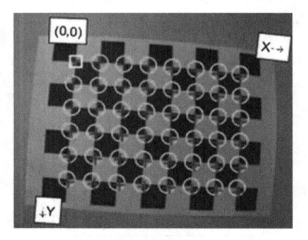

Fig. 4. Angular point extraction from calibration image

2.3.2 Monocular Visual Distance-Measuring Model and Method

Figure 5 shows the perspective imaging principle and its model. The monocular visual distance-measuring model based on arbitrary plane constraints that draws on the principle of perspective imaging has three assumptions. First, the world coordinate system is built on an arbitrary plane and coincides with the plane, and the Z axis is perpendicular to any plane. Secondly, the camera has a fixed position with an arbitrary plane (world coordinate system) in one distance measure, and the two have a certain coordinate transformation relationship. Finally, the world coordinate system can be set at will, and a specific relationship with the camera is not required. The position of the camera in this paper is basically fixed relative to the ground, so the ground can be used as the constraint plane to construct the monocular distance measuring model for the mobile robot. The ground is the constraint plane. The calibration board is placed on the ground, i.e. the world coordinate system is established on the ground plane.

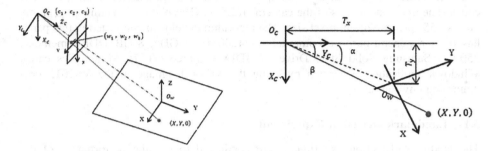

Fig. 5. The camera model of distance measure based on arbitrary plane constraint.

The main idea on this distance measuring model is to transform the coordinate of camera origin and image projection point into world coordinate system, establish the intersection coordinate of the line equation and the arbitrary plane $Z = 0$, and then calculate the distance by the method of solid geometry equation calculation. Any point in space can be transformed to another point through rotation and translation, as shown in Eq. (3).

$$\begin{bmatrix} x \\ y \\ z \end{bmatrix} = R \begin{bmatrix} X \\ Y \\ Z \end{bmatrix} + t \tag{3}$$

where R and T are rotation matrix and translational vector, respectively, which are obtained by camera calibration. The pixel coordinate of any point $P(X, Y, Z)$ in space is $p(u, v)$. According to Eq. (3), the world coordinate system can be expressed as (w_1, w_2, w_3), where $w_3 = F = f_x \cdot S_x$, F represents the real focal length, f_x is the scale factor in x direction, and S_x is the pixel size which can be found in the manufacturing parameters of camera's imaging chip. The connecting line of the camera's optical point to spatial point can be expressed as Eq. (4).

$$\frac{X - c_1}{w_1 - c_1} = \frac{Y - c_2}{w_2 - c_2} = \frac{Z - c_3}{w_3 - c_3} \tag{4}$$

With the existing constraint condition $Z = 0$ of the distance-measuring model, $Z = 0$ is substituted into Eq. (4) to obtain an equation set. X and Y is obtained by solving this equation set, and then substituted into Eq. (5) to calculate the distance from any point in space to the camera.

$$Dis = \sqrt{(X - c_1)^2 + (Y - c_2)^2} \tag{5}$$

3   Experiment and Discussion

The experimental platform includes a 300,000-pixel industrial camera, two-degree-of-freedom camera holder, notebook computer, homemade artificial landmarks, and QR codes. The main parameters of the camera: 1/2.5 in. CMOS color imaging chip, frame number 55 fps, resolution, pixel size. The algorithm developed and tested in this paper has been a general-purpose computer (i5 4200M 2.5 GHz, 8 GB DDR3 memory, 250 GB Samsung Solid State Drive, NVIDIA GeForce GT 755M graphics card). Windows application is written by using the VC++ language in the VS2015 programming environment.

3.1   Landmark Detection Experiment

The landmark detection experiments are conducted to test the performance of the landmark detection algorithm used in this paper. In the experiment, artificial landmarks are placed in the environment of various light intensities (main background color is green), and images are taken. The landmark detection performance is tested under the condition of uniform illumination and no obstruction. In order to verify the advanced performance of the proposed algorithm, artificial landmarks are detected by using a matching algorithm that is based on the feature of Scale Invariant Feature Transform (SIFT) [15], and the matched feature points are filtered by using the RANSAC algorithm. Figure 6(a) shows two test image, H-channel image and matching result, respectively. The artificial landmarks are detected, which consumes 0.11 ms. The landmark detection performance is also tested under the condition of uneven illumination and obvious obstruction. Figure 6(b) shows the test image using the SIFT method in RGB color. The artificial landmarks are not detected, which consumes 0.47 ms. The experimental results show that, in the outdoor environment, the SIFT method can not detect the target, the effect is very poor, not for the detection of artificial road signs. The present algorithm is able to detect the target regardless of the change in illumination intensity, angle of view, and dimension.

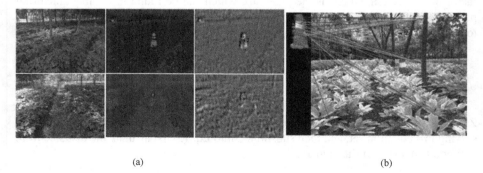

(a)   (b)

Fig. 6. Artificial landmarks in different environment are detected using the present method and SIFT method. (Color figure online)

In order to verify the influence of the color channel on the algorithm and the advantage of using normalized correlation coefficient matching method in the template matching method, this study tests 40 experimental pictures in different environments and applies 6 different similarity calculation methods provided by OpenCV to the image's H channel and S channel respectively. Accurate rates of matching are listed in Table 1. The similarity calculation methods mainly include squared error, normalized squared error, correlation, normalized correlation, correlation coefficient, and corresponding normalized correlation coefficient, which are sequentially labeled as TM1 to TM6 in Table 1. The matching results using the SIFT method are also listed in Table 1 for comparison. It is shown in Table 1 as **SIFT-RANSAC**. Comparing the results in Table 1, it can be seen that using H channel of the image yields the accurate rate in template matching which is higher than that of using S channel, and Method 6 (normalized correlation coefficient method) has the highest matching accurate rate. The SIFT feature point matching method has a poor detection effect in the outdoors and cannot be applied to artificial landmark detection.

Table 1. Accurate rate of artificial landmarks detection in both H channel and S channel of the test image using different matching methods

Matching method		TM1	TM2	TM3	TM4	TM5	TM6	SIFT-RANSAC
Matching accurate rate	H Channel	80%	80%	85%	50%	35%	95%	25%
	S Channel	60%	60%	20%	50%	35%	20%	20%

In the QR code detection experiment, as shown in Fig. 7, the printed QR code is posted on a flat plate and placed in an outdoor and indoor environment in a random posture. Experimental results show that QR code can be accurately detected and decoded. Finally, according to the method of decoding the code, the binary encoding is 11010101.

Fig. 7. The image of QR code placed on the grassland and the procedures and result of image processing.

3.2 Monocular Distance-Measuring Experiment

The distance-measuring experiment robot is built as shown in Fig. 8(a). The camera is fixed on a robot base with the lens pointing to the ground. As shown in Fig. 8(b), a wooden board painted with 18 black dots is placed on the ground as the constraint plane. The side length of the board is 600 mm, and the spacing of the dots is 200 mm. A tape measure with a minimum scale of 1 mm is used to measure the distance from the projection point of the camera on the constraint plane to the sample point. Then, the position of the board is changed, the measurement is repeated twice, and the data on a total of 26 sampling points are obtained. The result of distance calculation needs to be multiplied by 50, which depends on the mutual distance between the four feature points taken in the PnP algorithm as described above. The experimental results have been shown in Table 2. The greater the distance, the greater the absolute error. The average RMSE of 26 measurements is 10.9 mm, and the relative mean error is 0.45%. Using Excel software to fit the linear relationship between the distance and the actual distance based on the least square method, the correction equation is $y = 51.523x + 2.586$. Figure 8(c) shows the scatter diagram of the calculated distance and the actual distance. Their correlation is $R = 0.99892$ and the linear fitting equation is $y = 1.028x + 2.8407$.

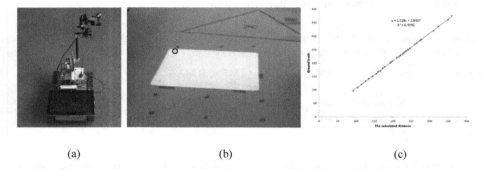

(a)   (b)   (c)

Fig. 8. The robot and monocular distance-measuring model and the experimental result.

Table 2. Calculated distance and actual distance for test set of sample points

Number	Calculated distance	Actual distance	Number	Calculated distance	Actual distance
1	173.5	182	14	237.6	240
2	175.5	185	15	239.6	244.5
3	177.6	187.2	16	245.2	249.5
4	195.4	202	17	241.6	250
5	196.3	204	18	249.6	254.2
6	198.8	207.4	19	260.3	269.5
7	212.1	219.7	20	265.3	274
8	213.2	220	21	278.8	287.5
9	218.6	224.5	22	285.3	294.2
10	220.6	229.5	23	299.6	304.5
11	221.4	230	24	311.2	319.5
12	225.1	234.5	25	325.5	337
13	230.6	239.5	26	378.5	394

4 Conclusion

This paper proposes a design method for artificial landmark-based visual navigation system. In this paper, the artificial landmark is designed to be conical, and select the HSI color model that has been least affected by the illumination and used the H-Channel feature of the background to design the main color of the artificial signpost. The correlation-based template matching method is used to detect artificial landmark, which has an optimal detection effect in indoor and outdoor and takes an average time of 0.11 ms, with high accuracy and efficiency. This study designs a distance-measuring method that is based on arbitrary plane, which can measure the distance in an efficient manner. Its average relative error is 0.45%, which can meet the requirements of the mobile robot on distance measurement. The distance-measuring model has the advantages of convenient adjustment, fast ranging, high accuracy of ranging, and simple model. The system is a simple and effective visual navigation system with good practicality.

References

1. Li, J., Chen, B., Yang, L., Tao, Z.: Detection for navigation route for cotton harvester based on machine vision. Trans. Chin. Soc. Agric. Eng. **29**(11), 11–19 (2013)
2. Sinisterra, A.J., Dhanak, M.R., von Ellenrieder, K.: Stereovision-based target tracking system for USV operations. Ocean Eng. **133**, 197–214 (2017)
3. Lee, T., Kim, C., Cho, D.: A monocular vision sensor-based efficient SLAM method for indoor service robots. IEEE Trans. Ind. Electron. **99**, 1 (2018)
4. Hu, Z., Li, Y., Hu, Y., Chu, D.: Integration of vision and topological self-localization for intelligent vehicles. Mechatronics **51**, 46–58 (2018)
5. Basiri, A., Amirian, P., Winstanley, A.: The use of quick response (QR) codes in landmark-based pedestrian navigation. Int. J. Navig. Obs. **7**, 1–7 (2014)
6. Song, D., Lu, Y.: Visual navigation using heterogeneous landmarks and unsupervised geometric constraints. IEEE Trans. Robot. **31**(3), 736–749 (2017)
7. Tian, Q., Wang, S.-P., Fu, S.-C., Shao, X.-P.: Study of indoor object search robot based on QR code navigation. Comput. Syst. Appl. **23**(1), 193–196 (2014)
8. Indelman, V., Choudhary, S., Christensen, H.I.: Information-based reduced landmark SLAM. In: 2015 IEEE International Conference on Robotics and Automation (ICRA), pp. 4620–4627 (2015)
9. Wu, G., Cheng, L.: Monocular distance measuring algorithm for visual navigation of robot inspecting high-tension line. J. Optoelectron. Laser **27**(9), 941–948 (2017)
10. Xu, F., Wang, Z.: An embedded visual SLAM algorithm based on Kinect and ORB features. In: 34th Chinese Control Conference (CCC), pp. 6026–6031 (2015)
11. Zhang, Q., Chen, M., Li, B.: A visual navigation algorithm for paddy field weeding robot based on image understanding. Comput. Electron. Agric. **143**, 66–78 (2017)
12. Korman, S., Reichman, D., Tsur, G., Avidan, S.: Fast-Match: fast affine template matching. Int. J. Comput. Vis. **121**(1), 111–125 (2017)

13. Deng, L.L.: Pre-detection technology of clothing image segmentation based on GrabCut algorithm. Wirel. Pers. Commun. **1**, 1–12 (2017)
14. Zhang, Y., Zhou, L., Liu, H., Shang, Y.: A flexible online camera calibration using line segments. J. Sens., 1–16 (2016)
15. Ghoualmi, L., Draa, A., Chikhi, S.: An ear biometric system based on artificial bees and the scale invariant feature transform. Expert Syst. Appl. **57**(c), 49–61 (2016)

Machine Learning

Deep Neural Network Acceleration Method Based on Sparsity

Ming He[✉], Haiwu Zhao, Guozhong Wang, Yu Chen, Linlin Zhu,
and Yuan Gao

School of Communication and Information Engineering, Shanghai University,
Shanghai, China
heming_199510@163.com

Abstract. With the development of deep learning, deep learning has
become more and more widely used in artificial intelligence. At this
stage, the deep neural network (DNN) based on high-performance GPU
and CPU devices has achieved remarkable results in the fields of object
detection and recognition. The DNNs have also been applied to social
media, image processing and video processing. With the improvement of
neural networks, the depth and complexity of various neural networks are
also increasing. On the basis of the sparsity of DNN weights, our method
analyzes the influence of the weights on the feature map and obtains the
relations between convolution layers. The sparsity of the network channel
is deduced from the L1 norm and the L2 norm. And the weights of the
DNN are pruned according to sparsity. In the vgg-16 experiment, we can
accelerate the neural network by 2.7 times without affecting the accuracy
of the neural network. Compared to the unstructured pruning, structured
pruning based on the sparsity can effectively improve the speed of the
forward and backward process, which has a certain significance for the
application of DNNs.

Keywords: DNNs · L1 norm · L2 norm · Sparsity ·
Structured pruning

1 Introduction

At present, the development of artificial intelligence takes deep neural networks
and big data as the research directions and has achieved results in image recognition and detection. It has been applied to social media and image video processing. At the same time, with the development of the information society, the
amount of image data generated every day keeps increasing. Therefore, for a
DNN, it is not only necessary to improve the accuracy of the network model for
the target recognition, but also to increase the speed of the network model [1].

Computer vision is the most widely used artificial intelligence technology.
Based on the deep neural network of computer vision research, various deep

© Springer Nature Singapore Pte Ltd. 2019
G. Zhai et al. (Eds.): IFTC 2018, CCIS 1009, pp. 133–145, 2019.
https://doi.org/10.1007/978-981-13-8138-6_11

models have achieved good results in the field of object recognition. But the complexity of deep model is increasing. In order to reduce the complexity of deep neural networks, the development trend of the neural networks is to reduce the full-connection layer and the storage of weights through sparse connections and weight sharing [2]. However, the computational complexity of the convolution layer for image data processing is still very large [3]. For example, the number of floating-point operations for a three-channel color image with a resolution of 224×224 by the vgg-16 reaches 15 GFLOPS, so the scale of operation of the deep model is still not reduced.

In the past work, the research direction of model compression tends to design smaller models to meet the requirements [4,5]. Compared with deep neural models, such models lose a lot of middle layer information. It is of great significance to compress the deep model and retain the middle layer information of the deep neural network. In 2016, Mao et al. [6] proposed the model compression method of pruning, weight quantization and Huffman coding for the deep model. Unstructured pruning has achieved good compression at the full connection layer. To achieve the acceleration effect on the deep model, the convolution layer still needs to be structured pruning [7,8]. In this paper, a structured pruning method based on sparsity is introduced to accelerate the deep model.

2   Related Work

At present, after learning from the data set, the parameters of the deep model are stored in binary files as floating-point numbers. These parameters are divided into weight parameters and bias parameters. When the deep model is used, the operation result is obtained by the convolution operation of the parameters and the input feature maps, and the object recognition or detection result is obtained by the value of the output feature maps.

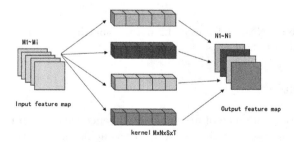

Fig. 1. Convolutional layer structure, input feature maps: M1-Mi, output feature maps: N1-Ni

The format of the storage and operation of these floating-point numbers in the model is based on the convolution operation channel order and the convolution kernel order, as shown in Fig. 1. The input feature maps are from M1 to Mi, and the number is M. The output feature maps are output after convolution, which are from N1 to Ni. Therefore, the convolution kernel of a convolutional layer is stored in the channel dimension corresponding to the number of input feature maps and the kernel dimension corresponding to the output feature maps. In addition, the size of each convolution kernel is SxT. Each convolution layer has N convolution kernels, each convolution kernel has M channels. Thus, in the deep model, the weights parameter of a convolutional layer is a four-dimensional vector of MxNxSxT.

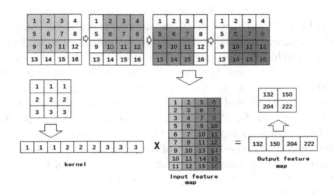

Fig. 2. Im2col operation of input feature map and kernel

When using the deep model, the convolution operation is expanded by im2col and the convolution operation is converted to matrix multiplication. As shown in Fig. 2, the input feature map is transformed into a column matrix by im2col. The 16×16 input feature map will expand the four parts involved in the convolution operation into a column vector of length 9, and then combine the four column vectors into an input feature map matrix. The convolution kernel is also expanded into a row vector with a length of 9. The convolution kernel is multiplied by the input feature map matrix to obtain the output result, and then restored to the 4×4 output feature map matrix. The result of adding the results of multiple channels is the output feature map. In the operation process, the floating-point multiplication of the convolution layer accounts for most of the computational scale of a forward process.

In the existing work, the compression and acceleration of the convolutional layer mainly focus on small-scale models such as AlexNet and LeNet models [7]. Although good acceleration and compression are achieved on these models, the models themselves are smaller in size and the fine-tuning after compression is less difficult. However, these small models have little scope of application. The LeNet model is used for handwriting recognition. The input feature map is a 28×28 grayscale image. The AlexNet network is less commonly used because of its poor accuracy on the ILSVRC-2012 data set. The vgg-16 network not only achieved good results in the ILSVRC-2012 data set contest, but also the vgg-16 network has a wide range of applications in object detection, target tracking and so on. In the latest research, feature maps obtained in the middle layer of the Vgg-16 network can be applied to multi-target tracking and image feature extraction. In the work of Song Han et al., the compression method focuses on compressing the number of weights, while the weights of the depth model are mainly concentrated in the full connection layer. The pruning method is used to change the fully connected layer into a sparse connection. However, in the computational scale, the operation of the fully connected layer accounts for only 0.8% of all operations, and the acceleration of the deep model is not obvious. Moreover, unstructured pruning produces a lot of holes in the convolution operation. These holes are completely random. There is work to recombine these holes into a complete matrix, but the pruning process for DNN is more complicated and in practice it is very Difficult to achieve. Therefore, in the deep model acceleration methods, the structured pruning scheme is more adopted. In the case of a reduced scale of operation, the accuracy of the deep network is not changed after fine-tuning.

In this paper, the pruning of the deep model is performed in the convolutional channel. The GPU we use for the server is 1080ti and the CPU is Intel i-7700k. The sparsity of each convolution kernel in the previous layer is obtained from the L1 norm of the weights and the L2 norm of the weights, and then the convolution kernel of the next layer is pruned according to the sparsity of the previous layer. In the vgg-16 model, the best pruning effect is obtained based on the depth of the layer and the scale of operations.

3   Proposal Methods

In this section, we proposed a pruning method based on the sparseness of the weights matrix based on the forward operations implemented by the DNN. In the DNN implementation process, it is obtained by the product of im2col transformed input feature maps and im2col transformed convolution kernel. The process of im2col is shown in Fig. 2. The calculation process of a layer of convolution kernel is as follows

$$\overrightarrow{z} = W^{(l)} \overrightarrow{x} + b^{(l)}, \forall l \in 1, 2...L - 1 \tag{1}$$

Where $W^{(l)}$ is the weight parameters of a convolutional layer. According to Fig. 1, we know that $W^{(l)}$ is a four-dimensional vector of MxNxSxT, where M is the number of input feature maps and N is the number of output feature maps. $b^{(l)}$ is the bias parameters of each layer, and there is an uniform bias parameter for each output feature map. Since there are fewer bias parameters, there is less redundancy in comparing the weight parameters. Therefore, the method of parameter compression in this paper is applied to the weight parameters.

For a DNN, after inputting a feature map, the operation process in the middle-hidden layer is the nesting of the convolution process. The process is as follows,

$$\phi(\overrightarrow{x}) = \phi_{L-1}(\phi_{L-2}(...\phi_2(\phi_1(\overrightarrow{x})))) \tag{2}$$

Where $\phi_l(\overrightarrow{x})$ is a convolutional layer or fully connected layer. In addition, in the DNN, there are also operations such as the activation layer and the pooling layer. Since the reference information used by these operations is not stored in the parameter matrix, these layers are not discussed in this paper.

3.1 L1 Norm and L2 Norm Sparse Neural Network

In a DNN, not only must show good performance on the training data set, but also have better generalization ability. Too many parameters will remember the training data set, so that the accuracy of the depth model on other samples will decrease. The sparse parameters can improve the generalization ability of the model and thus perform better on the newly input samples. During the deep learning, over-fitting of the model is reduced by various regularization algorithms. When the parameters are updated, add a penalty term $\Omega(\omega)$, which λ is a hyperparameter in the Lagrangian multiplier, as shown below,

$$\omega^* = argmin_\omega \Sigma_{i=1}^L L(y_i, f(x_i, \omega)) + \lambda\Omega(\omega) \tag{3}$$

Where $L(\bullet)$ is the loss function in the process of deep learning. In the process of parameters learning, the adjustment of the learning rate makes the weight parameters update to the value that minimizes the loss function and adds the penalty item to accelerate the fitting of the model. However, if the penalty item is too large, it will also cause the model to be under-fitted, causing the parameters of the model to become sparse. Here, when training the network generally, only the penalty parameter is added to the weight parameters, and the penalty item is not added to the biases.

Such penalties are used as regularization of weights in deep learning. In deep learning, common regularization terms are L0 norm, L1 norm, and L2 norm. From the sparse process, the weight matrix can be sparse by using the L0 norm. However, since the L0 norm regularization has NP-hard problems, the L0 norm is an exhaustive method in finding the optimal solution. For deep neural network training, using greedy algorithm to achieve regularization is too costly. In practice, the loss function using the L1 weight constraint is shown in (4).

$$\omega^* = argmin_\omega \Sigma_{i=1}^L L(y_i, f(x_i, \omega)) + \lambda\Omega(\omega)$$
$$s.t. \|\omega\|_1 \leq M \tag{4}$$

Where $\|\omega\|_1$ is $\Sigma_{i=1}^n \mid \omega_i \mid$. In the L1 norm constraint, it obtains the sum of the absolute values of the weights, that is, the absolute value function. The absolute value function is not divisible at 0, so the regularization process is converted to a summation process of weights. In order to meet the requirements of regularization constraints, many weights will become 0 during the implementation. The depth model obtained from the L1 norm is more generalized and sparser. However, in the deep model, some small weights need to be preserved. At this time, the L2 norm constraint of the model needs to be obtained. The depth model can get some non-zero weights.

In practice, L2 norm regularization is a commonly used constraint for deep learning regularization. The L2 norm is implemented as shown in (5),

$$\omega^* = argmin_\omega \Sigma_{i=1}^L L(y_i, f(x_i, \omega)) + \lambda \Omega(\omega)$$
$$s.t. \|\omega\|_2^2 \leq M \tag{5}$$

Where $\|\omega\|_2^2$ is $\sqrt{\Sigma_{i=1}^n \omega_i^2}$. In the L2 norm constraint, it is the square root of the sum of the squares of the weights. In practical applications, in order to facilitate the gradient, it is multiplied by 0.5 before the Lagrangian constraint, i.e., $\Omega(\omega) = \frac{1}{2n}\|\omega\|_2^2$. In the process of solving regularization, we can use the Hessian matrix to solve the problem. We can constrain learning too large weights from the data set. But in the regularization process, due to the differential of $\|\omega\|_2^2$, these weights do not become 0 in operation. Therefore, compared to the L1 norm, although the L2 norm can sparse the matrix, it does not change the weight value to zero.

Due to the difference between the L1 norm and the L2 norm, the L1 norm can obtain more zero solutions, so the result of summing the L1 norm of a matrix is smaller than that of the L2 norm. Then the L1 norm divided by the L2 norm, a sparsity can be obtained. It is shown in (6).

$$S = \frac{\|\omega\|_1}{\|\omega\|_2^2} = \frac{\Sigma_{i=1}^n |\omega_i|}{\sqrt{\Sigma_{i=1}^n \omega_i^2}} \tag{6}$$

Considering the weights scale and normalization, the number of weights added in (6) is rewritten as (7), so that the calculated result is between 0 and 1. In (7), the matrix sparsity calculation is based on the convolution kernel, so n = N, that is, the number of one-level convolution kernels. In this calculation, the normalized sparsity calculation formula can be obtained as follows.

$$S = \frac{\sqrt{n} - \frac{\Sigma_{i=1}^n |\omega_i|}{\sqrt{\Sigma_{i=1}^n \omega_i^2}}}{\sqrt{n} - 1} \tag{7}$$

In the actual application process, the sparsity S is larger, and the parameter matrix is numerically sparser. Taking filter 1 and filter 2 in Fig. 3 as an example, two parameters are taken in both filter 1 and filter 2 for calculation and comparison. The sparsity calculated in filter 1 is 0.034. The sparse degree in filter 2 is 0.82, and it is also sparser in value. Therefore, in the actual use of sparsity, if the sparsity is greater, the more weight parameters with smaller values in the matrix. After passing through the deep neural network, the smaller-sized convolution kernels will get sparse solutions and sparse feature maps. These sparse feature maps have little effect on the final result. The sparse weight matrix can be obtained by increasing pruning in the convolution kernel with larger sparsity.

3.2 Pruning Method

As described in Sect. 3.1, the sparsity of the matrix can be measured by the L1 norm and the L2 norm. The convolutional layer consists of a four-dimensional

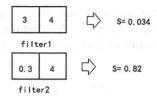

Fig. 3. Comparison of sparsity of different filters

vector. As shown in Fig. 4, if the feature map obtained in the previous layer is a sparse solution, the degree of prune may be increased in the weight parameters of the next layer, and the redundant convolution parameters may be removed. At the same time, pruning the convolution kernel of the corresponding channel from the pruning process can round off the convolution operation in the forward process.

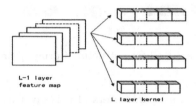

Fig. 4. The influence of the sparsity of the previous layer on the weight parameter of the next layer

In the use of deep neural networks, the convolution operation takes up most of the time in the forward process. For deep neural networks, such as vgg-16, the convolutional layer floating-point operations accounted for 99.2% of all floating-point operations. Therefore, in the pruning, according to the floating-point operations of this layer, more pruning efforts are set for the layers with more floating-point operands, which will have better acceleration effect. At the same time, according to the previous content, the convolution operation of the depth process is a nested process. As the layer is deepened, the errors caused by the sparseness will also be accumulated, so the shallow network has a lower degree of pruning. The calculation of the degree of pruning based on floating-point operands is (8).

$$G_{i,l} = min(kF_l S_{i',l-1}, 1)$$
$$\forall i \in 1, 2..M; \forall i' \in 1, 2..M; \forall l \in 2, 3..L \tag{8}$$

$S_{i',L-1}$ is the sparsity of the convolution kernel corresponding to the input channel of this layer., which is calculated from (7). l is the layer depth of this layer, the first layer is directly connected to the input image, the last layer is the L layer. F_l is the ratio of floating-point operations to total floating-point operations at this level. k is the coefficient. As the layer is deepened, the weights is more. We can set the pruning degree calculation formula according to the number of weights as (9),

$$G_{i,l} = min(kW_lS_{i',l-1}, 1)$$
$$\forall i \in 1, 2..M; \forall i' \in 1, 2..M; \forall l \in 2, 3..L \tag{9}$$

The difference from (8) is that the influence parameter F_l is changed to W_l, and W_l is the ratio of the number of weights in this layer to the total number of weights.

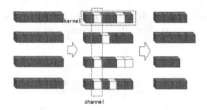

Fig. 5. Sparse-based structured pruning process

In the pruning process, all parameters of this layer are divided into channel granularity and convolution kernel granularity. As shown in Fig. 5, the parameters in the different convolution kernels acting on the same input feature map are the channel granularity as indicated by the vertical dashed box in the figure, and they act on the different input feature maps to approve the convolution kernel. The parameters are marked by a horizontal dashed box as the convolution kernel granularity. When the sparsity calculated by the upper layer, the degree of pruning of different channels can be determined according to the sparsity. Although the number of parameters pruned by each channel is different, it does not affect the number of output channels, and it can maintain more applications of the depth model.

4   Experimental Results

In this section, we prune the vgg-16 model and test the acceleration effect. As for the vgg-16 network, the top-1 accuracy of the ILSVRC-2012 test data set can reach 68.34%, and top-5 accuracy can reach 88.45%. So, in the experiment, based on the ILSVRC-2012 data set, the top-1 and top-5 accuracy of the pruned network will be tested.

In the experiment process, Python code was used to run on the caffe platform. The training data set of ILSVRC-2012 was used during fine-tuning and training. The verification data set of ILSVRC-2012 was used during testing.

The compressed depth model is a caffemodel of vgg-16 for object recognition that can achieve the recognition of 1000 categories of objects. We bring the trained model into the pruning algorithm. During the pruning process, fine-tuning trains the parameters of the unpruned. The algorithm is shown in Table 1. The $G0_i$ is the sparsity of each channel corresponding to the previous layer.

Table 1. Algorithm implementation

Algorithm: Pruning of Deep Neural Networks Based on Sparsity

Input: ILSVRC-2012 training data set, ILSVRC-2012 verification data set,pre-trained vgg-16 caffemodel, Preset Pruning Sparse Matrix G
 output: Sparse model after structured pruning
 initialization: Read model parameters, read sparsity, calculate the sparsity of each convolution layer
 for each l **in** [2 , L] do
 Determine the pruning sparsity matrix $G0$ for each convolution kernel based on the sparseness values of the output channels of the previous layer
 if $\Sigma_{i=0}^{N} G0_i == 1$do
 for $G0_i$ **in** $G0$ do
 $G0_i = G0_i \times G_j, G_j \in G$
 else
 for $G0_i$ **in** $G0$ do
 $G0_i = G0_i \times G_j \div \Sigma_{i=0}^{N} G0_i, G_j \in G$
 Prune the parameters of this layer according to $G0$ matrix
 fine-tuning

In this paper, the compression of the deep model concentrates on the convolution layers, and the compression of the full-connection layers has achieved good compression effects in the past work and articles. And in the latest application of the deep model, the number of fully connected layers is gradually reduced, and it is changed to sparsely connected. Therefore, based on the latest development trend of the depth model, the application of compression and acceleration techniques for the full-connection layers is limited. In this paper, for each convolution layer, a structured pruning is performed for each layer according to the number of parameters and the amount of computations. The obtained pruning results were compared with the unstructured pruning results to obtain the program results.

Before pruning, the sparseness of the convolutional layer of the vgg-16 network is firstly counted. The results are shown in Fig. 6. The sparseness of each convolutional layer in the figure is based on the convolution kernel. In the figure, the horizontal axis shows the order of the convolution kernels according to the sparsity degree, and the vertical axis shows the sparsity. According to the results, the larger sparse degree convolution kernels will also be sparser. In the input to

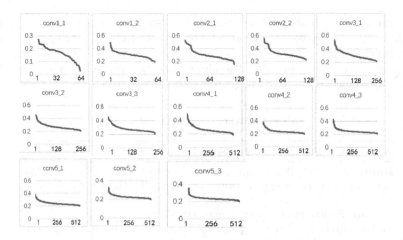

Fig. 6. Sparseness of convolutional layers

the next layer, when the feature map of the layer is convoluted with the next-level convolution kernel, relatively sparse feature maps will be sparser. We can set a larger degree of prune for the sparser channels.

4.1   Accelerating Method Based on Depth of Layer and Number of Weights

In this section, the model is pruned according to the number of weights. Referring to the result of (9), the progressive training process is used to fine-tune the network parameters after pruning Test the top-5 and top-1 accuracy of the deep network during training. The fine-tuning process is shown in Fig. 7.

In the figure, the horizontal axis represents the number of trainings and a total of 8,000 trainings are performed. The vertical axis indicates the accuracy of top-5 and top-1. After a certain number of trainings, the final accuracy can be restored to the original top-5 accuracy of 88.45%, and top-1 is slightly decreased compared to 68.34%. In a wide range of deep network applications, top-5 accuracy can be guaranteed for normal use in most application scenarios.

4.2   Acceleration Method Based on Floating Point Calculation

Compared with the pruning method based on the number of parameters, the pruning method based on floating-point calculations is more effective for accelerating the use of the network, and also uses a progressive training process. Test the top-1 and top-5 accuracy of the network during training. The training process is shown in Fig. 8.

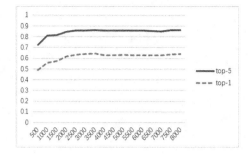

Fig. 7. Progressive training results after pruning based on the number of weights

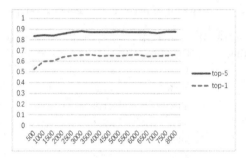

Fig. 8. Progressive training results after pruning based on floating-point computations

In the figure, the horizontal axis represents the number of trainings, a total of 8,000 trainings, and the vertical axis represents the accuracy of top-1 and top-5. Compared to the pruning method based on the amount of weights, the accuracy of top-1 has improved.

The comparison results in Fig. 9 can be obtained, in which top-1(F) denotes the process of fine-tuning the model after pruning based on the floating-point calculation amount, and top-1(W) represents the process of fine-tuning the model after pruning according to the amount of weights. As can be seen from the figure, in the process of fine-tuning the network, it is easier to obtain better top-1 performance based on the pruning method of floating-point numbers.

4.3   Comparison of Two Pruning Methods

Compared to unstructured pruning, structured convolutional pruning saves convolutional operations on partial feature maps. At the same time, if the accuracy is acceptable, more weights can be pruned, and the size of the convolutional layer can also be compressed.

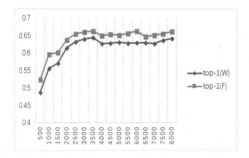

Fig. 9. Top-1 accuracy comparison of the two pruning methods

Table 2. Comparison of acceleration effect after pruning

Layer	Unstructured Pruning	Structure Pruning(W)	Speed-up	Structure Pruning(F)	Speed-up
Conv1_1	58%	1	x1.0	1	x0
Conv1_2	22%	66%	x1.8	50%	x2.0
Conv2_1	34%	65%	x1.8	56%	x1.8
Conv2_2	36%	54%	x2.3	52%	x1.9
Conv3_1	53%	56%	x2.2	54%	x1.9
Conv3_2	24%	47%	x2.7	36%	x2.8
Conv3_3	42%	45%	x2.9	35%	x2.9
Conv4_1	32%	42%	x3.1	28%	x3.6
Conv4_2	27%	38%	x3.6	19%	x5.3
Conv4_3	34%	28%	x4.0	18%	x5.6
Conv5_1	35%	22%	x4.5	41%	x2.8
Conv5_2	29%	18%	x5.6	38%	x2.9
Conv5_3	36%	18%	x5.6	35%	x3.1
Sum	32%	30%	X2.1	31%	x2.7

In Table 2, the pruning results based on the number of convolution kernels and floating-point calculations, and their acceleration effects are also calculated. Among them, Structure Pruning(W) is the result of Pruning according to the number of parameters, and Structure Pruning(F) is the result of Pruning based on floating-point calculation. From the data in the table, although the number of weights reduced by the two methods is almost the same, the effect of pruning based on floating point calculations is better than the effect of pruning based on the number of weights. In the unstructured pruning method, since the distribution of pruning is random, it is difficult to achieve an accelerated effect without the support of a specific device. In the results, pruning based on floating-point calculations can speed up the deep neural network by 2.7 times.

5   Conclusion

In this paper, we introduce a pruning method for convolutional layers based on sparsity. Based on the floating-point calculations, the pruning of the channels is structured, and the pruning results in the convolution layer can be accelerated 2.7 times. The feature maps obtained by sparse convolution kernels also affect the next level of operations, thus setting different pruning sparseness for the convolutional parameters of the corresponding channel in the next layer. The deep model after pruning according to different sparsity can achieve the original accuracy in object detection and object recognition. In the future, because the feature map output of each layer is maintained, the deep neural network can be applied to feature coding, target tracking, etc. However, there are still some shortcomings in this paper. Due to the lack of experimental data, only one deep network has been pruned, and in the future, more pruning work will be implemented for deep neural networks.

References

1. Sun, F., Wang, C., Gong, L., et al.: A high-performance accelerator for large-scale convolutional neural networks. In: 2017 IEEE International Symposium on Parallel and Distributed Processing with Applications and 2017 IEEE International Conference on Ubiquitous Computing and Communications (ISPA/IUCC), pp. 622–629. IEEE (2017)
2. Han, S., Mao, H., Dally, W.J.: Deep compression: compressing deep neural networks with pruning, trained quantization and Huffman coding. In: International Conference on Learning and Representation (ICLR), San Juan, pp. 233–242. IEEE (2016)
3. Anwar, S., Hwang, K., Sung, W.: Structured pruning of deep convolutional neural networks. ACM J. Emerg. Technol. Comput. Syst. (JETC) **13**(3), 32 (2017)
4. Yu, N., Qiu, S., Hu, X., et al.: Accelerating convolutional neural networks by group-wise 2D-filter pruning. In: 2017 International Joint Conference on Neural Networks (IJCNN), pp. 2502–2509. IEEE (2017)
5. He, Y., Zhang, X., Sun, J.: Channel pruning for accelerating very deep neural networks. In: International Conference on Computer Vision (ICCV), vol. 2(6) (2017)
6. Mao, H., et al.: Exploring the Regularity of Sparse Structure in Convolutional Neural Networks. CoRR (2017)
7. Han, S., Pool, J., Tran, J., et al.: Learning both weights and connections for efficient neural network. In: Advances in Neural Information Processing Systems, pp. 1135–1143 (2015)
8. Luo, J.H., Wu, J., Lin, W.: ThiNet: a filter level pruning method for deep neural network compression. In: 2017 IEEE International Conference on Computer Vision (ICCV), Venice, pp. 5068–5076 (2017)

Feature-Selecting Based Hashing via Deep Convolutional Neural Networks

Honghe Zheng, Ran Ma[⊠], Ping An, and Tong Li

Shanghai Institute for Advanced Communication and Data Science,
Key Laboratory of Advanced Displays and System Application,
Ministry of Education, Shanghai University, Shanghai 200444, China
maran@shu.edu.cn

Abstract. In the task of image retrieval, the nearest neighbor algorithm is widely used because of its high efficiency, where hashing algorithm is one of typical representatives. In recent years, with the development of deep convolutional neural networks, there have been many deep hashing algorithms for image retrieval. This paper proposes a new deep hashing algorithm that adds a hash layer to the image classification networks to obtain hash codes. A constraint item be added to the classification loss function, which is used to pick out some important nodes from the hash layer, and these selected nodes representing the picture are encoded. Compared with other existing algorithms, the performance of our algorithm has a certain improvement.

Keywords: Image retrieval · Deep learning · Convolutional neural networks · Hashing

1 Introduction

The aim of image retrieval is finding images that meet the user's needs from the dataset, according to the information provided by the user. Image retrieval technology can be mainly divided into two categories: text-based image retrieval (TBIR) and content-based image retrieval (CBIR), where CBIR is the current mainstream technology. Different from traditional TBIR, CBIR analyzes and retrieves the color, texture, and layout of an image. This technique need to extracts the features of the images in the image database and stores them into the feature library in advance. When retrieving for an input image, the similarity matching algorithm is used to calculate the similarity between the input image's features and the image features in the feature library. Thereafter, some images are shown to users in descending order of similarity.

However, when calculating the similarity of a large number of features, CBIR needs plenty of time and cannot satisfy people's need. In recent years, the amount of work relating to hashing algorithm used for image retrieval is immense, because the binary code (hash code) constructed by the hashing algorithm can retain similar information of the image and can be used for efficient image retrieval [1–3]. As a typical nearest neighbor algorithm, the key of the hashing algorithm is to design a hash transformation that can map similar pictures to hash codes that are close in Hamming space. This is a process of mapping high-dimensional feature vectors into low-dimensional Hamming

© Springer Nature Singapore Pte Ltd. 2019
G. Zhai et al. (Eds.): IFTC 2018, CCIS 1009, pp. 146–155, 2019.
https://doi.org/10.1007/978-981-13-8138-6_12

spaces. In this way, an approximate nearest neighbor (ANN) search can be performed by calculating the Hamming distance between the images' hash codes. Based on the hashing processing, the memory costs of image retrieval system can be greatly reduced and the efficiency of image retrieval is also greatly improved.

As the pioneering work, random projections were used as hash functions in Locality Sensitive Hashing (LSH) [4]. It is a data-independent algorithm, because the random projections do not need to be trained. LSH is one of the most well-known hashing algorithms, which is widely used for large scale image retrieval. Many similar algorithms have been derived from LSH, such as [5–7]. However, this kind of algorithm has a fatal shortcoming. Since no data is trained to get the hash function, the obtained hash codes can't preserve the semantic information of the image effectively.

On the contrary, some data-dependent algorithms were proposed, which use training data to learn the hash function and are also named learning to hashing algorithms. The hash functions after training on the dataset preserve similar information of images better. Based on whether the training data contains supervisory information or not, data-dependent algorithms are divided into two types: unsupervised hashing and supervised hashing. The common unsupervised hashing algorithms include [8–10]. These unsupervised hashing all use unlabeled datasets to learning hashing functions that map input data points into binary codes. Supervised hashing can achieve better accuracy than unsupervised hashing, because it can make full use of the information of the input data. Typical supervised hashing algorithms include [11–14]. But, the performance of these algorithm largely depends on the features extracted in the first stage, and they also do not perform well on image retrieval of large-scale data.

In recent years, a lot of studies have tested that deep learning has achieved excellent performance in image classification [15], target detection [16], face detection [17] and other computer vision tasks [18], which show the powerful feature extraction capabilities of deep convolutional neural networks. Therefore, hashing algorithms via deep learning have been proposed to simultaneously learn the image representation and hash codes, such as [19–25], which have shown superior performance over the traditional hashing algorithms. But most of algorithms based on deep learning have a common problem that they need to take input in the form of images pairs or image triples, which makes them unsuitable for situations with large amounts of data. Furthermore, these algorithms do not handle well on which nodes are selected to represent the image.

In this paper, we propose a new deep hashing algorithm for large-scale image retrieval. Like common deep hash algorithms [22, 24, 26], we add a hash Layer between the image representation layer and classification outputs in an image classification network. The hash layer with k units is the hash function. But, our hash layer do not use hyperbolic tangent (tanh) activation or other activation functions. We insert the hash layer served as linear transition into the original two layers. And the outputs of the hash layer are hash codes after being mapping by hash function. Moreover, a node with a positive value in hash layer is a valid node and the importance of each node in representing the image is not the same. So, we added additional one constraint to the loss function. This constrain can help to pick out the most important nodes of the picture in the hash layer. And these nodes are encoded to 1. When we minimize an objective function defined over classification error and a constraints item on the outputs of the hash layer, we can get the hash code we want. In order to adapt to the hash learning task, the structure of the classification network has also been modified.

2   The Proposed Algorithm

This section mainly introduces the proposed deep hashing algorithm. The system framework is shown in Fig. 1. The network takes inputs from images and learns image representations, hash codes through the optimization of the loss function. The output of the hash layer is converted to hash code by hash function.

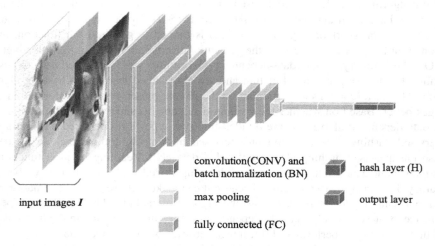

Fig. 1. System framework.

Give N images $I = \{I_1, I_2, \ldots, I_N\}$ and their associated label vectors $Y = \{y_n \in \{0, 1\}^M\}^N$, where M is the total number of class labels. The entry of the vector y_n is 1 if an image I_n belongs to the corresponding class, otherwise 0. N images get their hash codes ($B = \{b_n\} \in \{0, 1\}^{K \times N}$, where K is the number of bits in hash codes) after passing through the network that we have been trained before. The goal of our supervised hashing algorithm is to learning a mapping: $I \to B$ that B can retain information similarity in I.

2.1   Feature Extraction

In order to obtain the semantic information of the image, we make use of deep convolutional neural networks (CNNs) that have been proven to have good feature extraction capabilities. And we suppose that the classification network can extract features that contain image semantic information. So we can add the hash layer to the existing CNN classification models, such as AlexNet and VGG etc. But, to better adapt to hashing learning task, we modify the structure of VGG. The parameters of the new network are shown in Table 1. It has seven convolution layers (CONV) with seven batch normalization layers (BN) and three max-pooling operations followed by two fully connected layers (FC), one hash layer (H) and one output layer. In each CONV layer, units are organized into feature maps and are connected locally to patches in the outputs (i.e., feature maps) of the previous layer. The BN layers can speed up the convergence of the model. The FC layers can be viewed as a classifier. The seven CONV layers and two FC layers are composed of the rectified linear units (ReLUs) because the ReLUs lead to faster training. The output layer is a classification layer having the units of the same number of class labels.

Table 1. The architecture for feature extraction.

Layer	Size of filter	Number of filters	Others
CONV 1_1	3 × 3	64	Stride = 1, padding = SAME
BN	None	None	ReLU
CONV 1_2	3 × 3	64	Stride = 1, padding = SAME
BN	None	None	ReLU
Max pooling	3 × 3	None	Stride = 2
CONV 2_1	3 × 3	128	Stride = 1, padding = SAME
BN	None	None	ReLU
CONV 2_2	3 × 3	128	Stride = 1, padding = SAME
BN	None	None	ReLU
Max pooling	3 × 3	None	Stride = 2
CONV 3_1	3 × 3	256	Stride = 1, padding = SAME
BN	None	None	ReLU
CONV 3_2	3 × 3	256	Stride = 1, padding = SAME
BN	None	None	ReLU
CONV 3_2	3 × 3	256	Stride = 1, padding = SAME
BN	None	None	ReLU
Max pooling	3 × 3	None	Stride = 2
FC6	None	384	ReLU
FC7	None	384	ReLU
H	None	K	None

Many existing deep hashing algorithm [22, 24, 26] usually use sigmoid or tanh as activation functions in the hash layer. But these activation functions cause the training speed to decrease. It should be noted that our hash layer does not use any activation functions. This is because the deep hashing algorithm considers the pictures in the same class as the similar picture, which is same to the image classification task. In other words, the output of the FC layers of the classification network has the similar target to the output of the deep hash. Therefore, we add one hash layer without activation functions to perform a linear transformation after the FC layers. The output of the hash layer is converted to hash code which can be used for image retrieval by hash function.

2.2   Hash Function

Let W^H denote the weights (i.e. the projection matrix) between the second FC layer (FC7) and the hash layer. And $a_n^{F_2}$ denotes the output of Layer FC7, the output of the units in Layer H can be computed as $a_n^H = W^H a_n^{F_2} + b^H$, where a_n^H is a K-dimensional vector and b^H is the bias term. This is a linear transformation. And combined with the role of the activation function ReLU, we consider that a node with a positive value in Layer H is a valid node. So a node with a value greater than 0 is encoded to 1, otherwise 0. The binary encoding function given by

$$b_n = \frac{\left(sign\left(a_n^H - \varepsilon \right) + 1 \right)}{2} \qquad (1)$$

where $sign(x) = 1$ if $x > 0$ and -1 otherwise, and $sign(\cdot)$ performs element-wise operations for a matrix or a vector; ε is a positive number close to 0. In this paper, ε is set to 0.0001.

2.3   Loss Function

Our main goal is to learn a map from image I_n to a K-bit binary code b_n, such that similar images are encoded to similar binary codes. So we should make codes of similar images to be as similar as possible, while the binary codes of dissimilar image being far away. And we also considered that the image classification label contains semantic information of the image, so the label of image is useful for learning a hash function. Based on the above considerations, the loss function defined on the classification error is optimized in this paper, which can ensure that semantically similar images are mapped to similar binary codes. In terms of the classification formulation, we can choose to optimize the following loss function

$$\mathcal{L}_1 = \sum_{n=1}^{N} L(y_n, \hat{y}_n) + \lambda \|W\|^2 \qquad (2)$$

where W is the weights of the entire network, λ governs the relative importance of the regularization term, $L(\cdot)$ is a loss function that minimizes classification loss and $\hat{y}_n$ denote the prediction of our network for an image I_n. The choice of the loss function depends on the dataset. For multi-class classification, we use softmax outputs and minimizes the cross-entropy error function

$$L(y_n, \hat{y}_n) = -\sum_{n=1}^{N} y_{nm} ln \hat{y}_{nm} \qquad (3)$$

where y_{nm} and $\hat{y}_{nm}$ are the desired output and the prediction of the mth unit, respectively. For multi-label classification, we use the loss function in [26].

Besides, for different images, the importance of different node in Layer H is different. So different images should choose different nodes to be represented. And for an image, each node's degree of importance in representing the image is also different. Therefore, the most effective nodes should be pick out to represent the image. However, some important nodes maybe be missing when picking out. For this reason, we uniformly pick the first half of the nodes, that is, half of bits in hash codes are 1 and the other half are 0. So we added the constraint to guarantee the probability of a positive value for nodes of hash layer are fifty percent, which is to select the top 50% of the nodes to represent the image. We design such a constraint function

$$\mathcal{L}_2 = \left| mean\left(\frac{\left(sign\left(a_n^H - \varepsilon e\right) + 1\right)}{2}\right) \right| \tag{4}$$

where e is the K-dimensional vector with all elements having the value of 1, $mean(\cdot)$ computes the average of the elements in a vector.

But the $sign(x)$ function is non-convex and non-smooth. Especially, the function value definition is also not clear at $x = 0$, which leads to standard backward propagation not possible during training deep networks. So it need to find an alternative function. In [27], it design such a smooth function $f(x)$

$$f(x) = tanh(\beta x) \tag{5}$$

And the relationship between the $sign(x)$ function and $f(x)$ are shown in Eq. (6).

$$sign(x) = \lim_{\beta \to \infty} f(x) = \lim_{\beta \to \infty} tanh(\beta x) \tag{6}$$

where β is a hyperparameter. In [27], β is set to 3. So Eq. (4) is rewritten as

$$\mathcal{L}_2 = \left| mean\left(\frac{tanh\left(3\left(a_n^H - \varepsilon e\right)\right) + 1}{2}\right) \right| \tag{7}$$

Ultimately, we aim to optimize the following objective to obtain the binary codes

$$\mathcal{L}_{full} = \mathcal{L}_1 + \mathcal{L}_2 \tag{8}$$

3 Experimental Results

In this part, we test with our proposed algorithm on two public benchmark datasets and compare with other traditional hashing algorithms and deep hashing algorithms. We mainly use mean average precision (MAP), Top-K precision curve as our evaluation metrics which widely adopted in the literature for performance comparison. The MAP results for NUS-WIDE dataset are calculated on the top 5,000 returned samples.

3.1 Datasets

CIFAR-10 is a dataset containing 60,000 color images in size 32 × 32. The images are divided into 10 categories, each of which is 6,000 images. The entire dataset is divided into two non-overlapping parts, of which the larger part has 50,000 images for training and the other part has 10,000 images for testing. Following the setting in [20, 21, 25], we pick 1000 images, 100 images in each category from test part, as query images for performance evaluation. We consider two images with the same label to be similar images.

NUS-WIDE is a dataset containing about 270,000 color images collected from Flickr. The images are divided into 81 categories, and each image belongs to one or more than one category. We only pick 195,834 images that belong to the 21 most frequent concepts, and each concept containing at least 5,000 images. We select 2,100 images, 100 images in each concept from test part, as query images for performance evaluation. If two images share at least one common semantic label, we consider they as similar images.

3.2 Analysis of Results

We roughly divide the comparison algorithm into two groups: the traditional hashing ones and the deep hashing ones. The compared traditional hashing algorithms we selected consist of unsupervised and supervised algorithms, which. Unsupervised ones include LSH [4] and SH [8] and supervised ones include LFH [12], KSH [11] and SDH [13]. For those algorithms, following [25], both the hand-crafted features and the features extracted by CNN-F network architecture are used as the input. The hand-crafted features contain a 512-dimensional GIST descriptor to represent images of CIFAR-10 dataset, and a 1134-dimensional feature vector to represent images of NUS-WIDE dataset. The deep hashing algorithms we selected include CNNH [19], NINH [20], DHN [22], DSH [23], DPSH [21] and DSDH [25]. Please note that DHN and DSH are based on AlexNet network architecture, while DPSH and DSDH are based on the CNN-F network architecture. Both the CNN-F network architecture and AlexNet architecture network contain five CONV layers and two FC layers. In order to make fair comparison, most of the results are directly reported from previous works. The MAP results of all algorithms on CIFAR-10 and NUS-WIDE are shown in Table 2, where the best results for MAP are shown in bold. From Table 2, we can see that most deep hashing algorithms perform better than traditional hashing ones and the performance of our proposed algorithm is also better than other comparison ones. DSDH achieves the best performance among all the other algorithms except ours on both CIFAR-10 dataset and NUS-WIDE dataset. Compared with DSDH, our algorithm improves the performance by 3%–11% on CIFAR-10 dataset and 1%–5% on NUS-WIDE dataset, respectively.

Table 2. MAP for different algorithms.

Algorithm	CIFAR-10				NUS-WIDE			
	12 bits	24 bits	32 bits	48 bits	12 bits	24 bits	32 bits	48 bits
Ours	**0.824**	**0.837**	**0.839**	**0.848**	**0.812**	**0.827**	**0.831**	**0.835**
DSDH	0.740	0.786	0.801	0.820	0.776	0.808	0.820	0.829
DPSH	0.713	0.727	0.744	0.757	0.752	0.790	0.794	0.812
DSH	0.644	0.742	0.770	0.799	0.712	0.731	0.740	0.748
DHN	0.555	0.594	0.603	0.621	0.708	0.735	0.748	0.758
NINH	0.552	0.566	0.558	0.581	0.674	0.697	0.713	0.715
CNNH	0.439	0.511	0.509	0.522	0.611	0.618	0.625	0.608
SDH	0.285	0.329	0.341	0.356	0.568	0.600	0.608	0.637
KSH	0.303	0.337	0.346	0.356	0.556	0.572	0.581	0.588
LFH	0.176	0.231	0.211	0.253	0.571	0.568	0.568	0.585
SH	0.127	0.128	0.126	0.129	0.454	0.406	0.405	0.400
LSH	0.121	0.126	0.120	0.120	0.403	0.421	0.426	0.441

We also report Top-5 K precision in Fig. 2 on two datasets. Once again, we can find that the proposed algorithm can significantly outperform other ones in most cases especially for all code length.

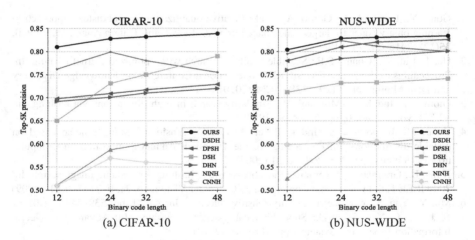

(a) CIFAR-10   (b) NUS-WIDE

Fig. 2. Top-5K precision on two datasets.

The previous experimental results are based on all selected 50% of the nodes code that are encoded to 1. Here, the impact of different number of nodes that are encoded to 1 is tested. We select 40%, 50% and 60% bits from the 48-bit hash codes to encode to 1. The test results are shown as Table 3, from which selecting 50% of the bits is the best.

Table 3. MAP with 48 bits for different number of bits encoded to 1 on the CIFAR-10 dataset.

Number of bits	19 bits (40%)	24 bits (50%)	29 bits (60%)
MAP	0.843	0.848	0.844

4 Conclusion

In this paper, we propose a novel deep hashing algorithm for large-scale image search. We get hash code by adding one hash layer to an image classification network and minimizing an objective function defined over classification error and the constraint we added. Extensive experiments have shown that our algorithm have better performance than other existing ones on benchmark image retrieval datasets. But we have not explicitly considered the quantization error, so a certain amount of quantization error still exists when converting the output of the hash layer into hash code. It need further works to deal with.

Acknowledgment. This work is supported in part by the National Natural Science Foundation of China under Grants 61301112 and 61422111.

References

1. Gong, Y., Lazebnik, S., Gordo, A., et al.: Iterative quantization: a procrustean approach to learning binary codes for large-scale image retrieval. IEEE Trans. Pattern Anal. Mach. Intell. **35**(12), 2916–2929 (2013)
2. He, J., Liu, W., Chang, S.F.: Scalable similarity search with optimized Kernel hashing. In: Proceedings of the 16th ACM SIGKDD International Conference on Knowledge Discovery and Data Mining, pp. 1129–1138. ACM (2010)
3. Gionis, A., Indyk, P., Motwani, R.: Similarity search in high dimensions via hashing. In: VLDB, vol. 99, no. 6, pp. 518–529 (1999)
4. Datar, M., Immorlica, N., Indyk, P., et al.: Locality-sensitive hashing scheme based on p-stable distributions. In: Proceedings of the Twentieth Annual Symposium on Computational Geometry, pp. 253–262. ACM (2004)
5. Kulis, B., Grauman, K.: Kernelized locality-sensitive hashing for scalable image search. In: 2009 IEEE 12th International Conference on Computer Vision, pp. 2130–2137. IEEE (2009)
6. Mu, Y., Yan, S.: Non-metric locality-sensitive hashing. In: AAAI, pp. 539–544 (2010)
7. Ji, J., Li, J., Yan, S., et al.: Super-bit locality-sensitive hashing. In: Advances in Neural Information Processing Systems, pp. 108–116 (2012)
8. Weiss, Y., Torralba, A., Fergus, R.: Spectral hashing. In: Advances in Neural Information Processing Systems, pp. 1753–1760 (2009)
9. Jiang, Q.Y., Li, W.J.: Scalable graph hashing with feature transformation. In: IJCAI, pp. 2248–2254 (2015)
10. Liu, H., Ji, R., Wu, Y., et al.: Towards optimal binary code learning via ordinal embedding. In: AAAI, pp. 1258–1265 (2016)
11. Liu, W., Wang, J., Ji, R., et al.: Supervised hashing with Kernels. In: 2012 IEEE Conference on Computer Vision and Pattern Recognition (CVPR), pp. 2074–2081. IEEE (2012)

12. Zhang, P., Zhang, W., Li, W.J., et al.: Supervised hashing with latent factor models. In: Proceedings of the 37th International ACM SIGIR Conference on Research & Development in Information Retrieval, pp. 173–182. ACM (2014)
13. Shen, F., Shen, C., Liu, W., et al.: Supervised discrete hashing. In: CVPR, vol. 2, no. 3, p. 5 (2015)
14. Shi, X., Xing, F., Xu, K., Sapkota, M., Yang, L.: Asymmetric discrete graph hashing. In: AAAI, pp. 2541–2547 (2017)
15. Krizhevsky, A., Sutskever, I., Hinton, G.E.: Imagenet classification with deep convolutional neural networks. In: Advances in Neural Information Processing Systems, pp. 1097–1105 (2012)
16. Szegedy, C., Toshev, A., Erhan, D.: Deep neural networks for object detection. In: Advances in Neural Information Processing Systems, pp. 2553–2561 (2013)
17. Sun, Y., et al.: Deep learning face representation by joint identification-verification. In: Advances in Neural Information Processing Systems, pp. 1988–1996 (2014)
18. Long, J., Shelhamer, E., Darrell, T.: Fully convolutional networks for semantic segmentation. In: Proceedings of the IEEE Conference on Computer Vision and Pattern Recognition, pp. 3431–3440 (2015)
19. Xia, R., Pan, Y., Lai, H., et al.: Supervised hashing for image retrieval via image representation learning. In: AAAI, vol. 1, p. 2 (2014)
20. Lai, H., Pan, Y., Liu, Y., et al.: Simultaneous feature learning and hash coding with deep neural networks. arXiv preprint arXiv:1504.03410 (2015)
21. Li, W.J., Wang, S., Kang, W.C.: Feature learning based deep supervised hashing with pairwise labels. arXiv preprint arXiv:1511.03855 (2015)
22. Zhu, H., Long, M., Wang, J., et al.: Deep hashing network for efficient similarity retrieval. In: AAAI, pp. 2415–2421 (2016)
23. Liu, H., Wang, R., Shan, S., et al.: Deep supervised hashing for fast image retrieval. In: Proceedings of the IEEE Conference on Computer Vision and Pattern Recognition, pp. 2064–2072 (2016)
24. Shen, F., Gao, X., Liu, L., et al.: Deep asymmetric pairwise hashing. In: Proceedings of the 2017 ACM on Multimedia Conference, pp. 1522–1530. ACM (2017)
25. Li, Q., Sun, Z., He, R., et al.: Deep supervised discrete hashing. In: Advances in Neural Information Processing Systems, pp. 2479–2488 (2017)
26. Yang, H.F., Lin, K., Chen, C.S.: Supervised learning of semantics-preserving hash via deep convolutional neural networks. IEEE Trans. Pattern Anal. Mach. Intell. **40**(2), 437–451 (2018)
27. Song, J.: Binary generative adversarial networks for image retrieval. arXiv preprint arXiv:1708.04150 (2017)

Efficient and Robust Homography Estimation Using Compressed Convolutional Neural Network

Guoping Wang, Zhixiang You, Ping An$^{(\boxtimes)}$, Jiadong Yu,
and Yilei Chen

Shanghai Institute for Advanced Communication and Data Science,
School of Communication and Information Engineering,
Shanghai University, Shanghai 200444, China
anping@shu.edu.cn

Abstract. Homography estimation is one of the important ways to calculate the transformation between images. For most embedded terminal devices, an efficient and robust homography estimation algorithm is extremely necessary. In this paper, we design an innovative compressed convolutional neural network to estimate homographies which work very well. The model size of the network is less than 10 MB, which is small enough to be used on mobile devices. In addition, to improve the estimated accuracy in challenging environment, we present a novel loss function to train our network. Finally, we compare our algorithm with traditional methods and other learning-based methods. Experiments on our compressed network demonstrate that the innovative network achieves better accuracy compared to other learning-based algorithms, and is more robust to illumination changes compared to traditional algorithms.

Keywords: Homography estimation · Convolutional neural network ·
Model compression · Loss function

1 Introduction

Homographies are usually used to describe the transformation of some points in the same plane between two images. If the camera shoots the same plane of the scene or moves with a pure rotation, we can use homographies to estimate the ego-motion of the camera. Homography estimation plays an important role in many computer vision tasks such as simultaneous localization and mapping (SLAM) [1], image stitching [2], video stabilization [3]. In ORB-SLAM [1], when the camera rotates purely, the homography and the fundamental matrix need to be calculated simultaneously to reduce the estimation error. Homographies are also used to handle the processing of Unmanned Aerial Vehicle (UAV) aerial video which is viewed from a far distance to the earth. [3] proposed a homography consistency based algorithm to directly stabilize the video recorded on moving cameras.

The classic homography estimation methods are mainly divided into two major categories: traditional methods and learning-based methods. Similar to the SLAM

© Springer Nature Singapore Pte Ltd. 2019
G. Zhai et al. (Eds.): IFTC 2018, CCIS 1009, pp. 156–168, 2019.
https://doi.org/10.1007/978-981-13-8138-6_13

system implementation scheme, the traditional approaches include feature-based methods and direct methods. Early work of the feature-based methods is mainly to carefully extract efficient hand-crafted features and match them across images robustly. Enormous work has been done to design satisfied local features and the typical pipeline of it is to find key-points, and compute their descriptors and match them. Edward Rosten and Tom Drummond proposed an algorithm named FAST [4] which used machine learning to derive a fast corner detector. SIFT [5] presented a method for extracting distinctive invariant features from images and it is robust to change in light, noise, and microscopic viewing angles. The main drawback of SIFT is time-consuming calculation because it does not use binary descriptors. ORB [6] features solve the definition of the key-points' directions and scales that FAST corner points do not have. Another important process of feature-based homography estimation is matching feature points between images. RANSAC [7] is a commonly used algorithm to eliminate a certain number of false matches. The accuracy of homography estimation relies to a large extent on the ingenious design of the feature points and the robustness of the elimination of false matching algorithm.

The second traditional approaches are direct methods, which do not need to know the point-to-point correspondence across frames, but instead estimate homographies by minimizing photometric errors. Direct methods can make full use of the information of the whole image and are capable of exploiting all the pixels for SLAM under the assumption of photometric consistency, e.g., SVO in [8] and LSD-SLAM in [9]. Direct methods do not need to calculate descriptors even key points while feature-based methods take a lot of time to compute, so its efficiency can be improved. In addition, direct methods are robust to texture-less environments. However, direct methods easily fail under the circumstances that illumination changes destroy the assumption of photometric consistency and result in large photometric error values. Many robust algorithms have been proposed to solve this problem, such as the enhanced correlation coefficient (ECC) [10].

Deep learning has made remarkable achievements in many computer vision tasks, especially in image classification [11, 12] and image retrieval tasks [13, 14]. In recent years, some work on learning-based SLAM begins to appear, like [15–17]. Considering that homography estimation is similar in spirit to CNN-SLAM, it is reasonable to expect that the capability of CNN-based features can be leveraged in devising a solution to the task of estimating homographies across images. [18] presents a deep convolutional neural network for homography estimation between a pair of images. It replaces 3 by 3 homography with the 4-point parameterization as training labels because the matrix only has 8° of freedom. Inspired by direct methods, [19] develops an unsupervised neural network and takes the photometric error as a loss function. It can be seen from the results that the accuracy of the unsupervised network is slightly higher than that of the supervised network. However, all the above networks are modified based on VGG-16 which has a large number of parameters and calculations. Therefore, their training models are nearly 500 MB in size. In addition, they have relatively lower accuracy of homography estimation than traditional methods in the case of more texture and stable light conditions.

Recent research in neural network model compression achieves promising results, such as MobileNets [20], ResNeXt [21] and ShuffleNet [22]. All of them utilize group convolution and depthwise separable convolution to reduce network parameters and compress model size on the premise of ensuring the accuracy. Concurrently, ShuffleNet proposes a new operation, channel shuffle, to maintain accuracy. Most of them test their compressed neural network performance on image classification rather than complex regression tasks.

In this paper, we present a novel learning-based approach by building a new neural network and introducing a better loss function than [18, 19]. Our main contributions are summarized as follows.

- We design a ShuffleNet-style network (see Fig. 1) for homography estimation based on pointwise group convolution and channel shuffle which are suitable for embedded device calculation. Our CNN model size is only 9.9 MB and is much more efficient than VGG-Net when exporting new models to clients.
- Considering the shortcomings of the existing networks, we build a new loss function to improve the accuracy of homography estimation under favorable environmental conditions.
- Our network is robust to large displacements and large illumination variation. We test it on the MS-COCO dataset that [18] mentioned.

The rest of this paper is organized as follows. Section 2 presents the details of our compressed network architecture and loss function. After that, we evaluate our methods in Sect. 3. Finally, conclusion and future work are discussed in Sect. 4.

2   Proposed Method

In this section, we will give an overview of our ShuffleNet-style compressed network architecture, which is shown in Fig. 1.

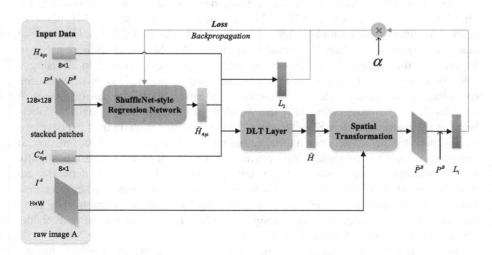

Fig. 1. Overview of ShuffleNet-style compressed network architecture.

In order to compare our algorithm with [18, 19], the pipeline of our network is similar to the unsupervised deep learning method [19]. Considering that most of the network parameters are in the regression module, we replace the VGG-style regression model with a new feature extraction network for homography estimation. In addition, we introduce a combined loss function for backward propagation to train our network. Firstly, the raw images and the warped images are stacked together as the input of the whole network. Through the ShuffleNet-style Regression Network module, the stacked images can be regressed to predict the 4-point homography parameterization $\tilde{H}_{4pt}$ which is an equivalent form of homography H. We can easily convert H_{4pt} to H using the direct linear transformation (DLT) method. Supervised approach builds a loss function based on the estimated 4-point homography $\tilde{H}_{4pt}$ and the ground truth H_{4pt}. Unsupervised method requires the $\tilde{H}_{4pt}$ to transform the raw image patch P_A into the warped patch $\tilde{P}_B$ through the Spatial Transformation module and minimizes pixel-wise photometric error between patch $\tilde{P}_B$ and patch P_B. In our network, we combine supervised and unsupervised algorithms as a new supervised method to train our model together for the purpose of improving accuracy.

2.1 ShuffleNet-Style Regression Network

Our ShuffleNet-style network benefits from efficient depthwise separable convolution and novel channel shuffle operation. Depthwise separable convolution is the key to our lightweighted model, it is able to effectively reduce the amount of convolution parameters. The parameters and computational costs of standard convolution can be calculated by:

$$params_{std} = C_{in} \times C_{out} \times K_h \times K_w \tag{1}$$

$$costs_{std} = C_{in} \times C_{out} \times K_h \times K_w \times H \times W \tag{2}$$

where $K_h \times K_w$ is the kernal size, C_{in} is the number of input channels, C_{out} is the number of output channels, and $H \times W$ is the size of output feature map. Depthwise separable convolution consists of two layers: depthwise convolutions and pointwise convolutions. Depthwise convolution only filters input channels and it does not combine them to create new features. Hence, pointwise convolution computes a linear combination of the result of depthwise convolution via 1×1 convolution [20]. We can calculate the parameters and computational costs of depthwise separable convolution by:

$$params_{dsc} = C_{in} \times K_h \times K_w + C_{in} \times C_{out} \tag{3}$$

$$costs_{dsc} = C_{in} \times K_h \times K_w \times H \times W + C_{in} \times C_{out} \times H \times W \tag{4}$$

It is easy to find the reduction of parameters and calculation costs by comparing equations of standard convolution and depthwise separable convolution.

Taking advantage of depthwise separable convolution, we modify the ShuffleNet unit by removing all batch normalization (BN) layers after each convolution layer (see Fig. 2) because BN layers introduce extra parameters and computational costs. Besides, our estimation task does not benefit from the BN layer when testing the networks we designed. Firstly, we apply group convolution to obtain input data from different groups followed by ReLU activation function. Secondly, to enhance information flow between channel groups, we exploit channel shuffle operations which can divide the channels in each group into serval subgroups and feed each group in the next layer with different subgroups [22]. Then, we apply depthwise separable convolution followed by another 1×1 group convolution. Finally, the input information is combined with the result of the group convolution. ShuffleNet unit has two ways of combination: channel concatenation through adding a 3×3 average pooling on the shortcut path (Fig. 2(a)) and direct element-wise addition (Fig. 2(b)).

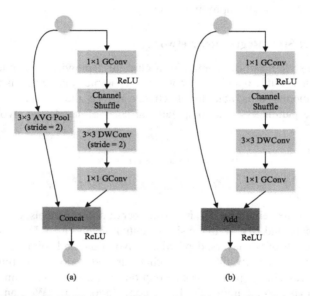

Fig. 2. Modified ShuffleNet units. (a) unit with stride = 2; (b) unit with stride = 1.

According to the formulas derived above, we can easily infer the parameters and computational costs of one ShuffleNet unit. Because channel concatenation and element-wise addition do not have any parameters, unit with stride = 2 is equal in parameters to unit with stride = 1. Similar to [22], we set the number of bottleneck channels M to 1/4 of the input channels C for each unit. So the number of the parameters in one unit is

$$params = 9C + \frac{C^2 + 2MC}{g} \tag{5}$$

where g is the number of subgroups. Only considering the costs of convolutional operations, we can infer the calculation of the unit with stride = 2 by:

$$costs_2 = H \times W \times \left(9C + \frac{4C^2 + 2MC}{g}\right) \tag{6}$$

where $H \times W$ is the size of output feature map. Similarly, the calculation of the unit with stride = 1 is

$$costs_1 = H \times W \times \left(9C + \frac{C^2 + 2MC}{g}\right) \tag{7}$$

Built on modified ShuffleNet units, the overall of our ShuffleNet-style regression network is shown in Table 1. The presented network is mainly made up of a stack of ShuffleNet units grouped into three stages. Each stage's first building block applies the unit with stride = 2 (Fig. 2(a)), like Stage2-1, Stage3-1 and Stage4-1. Then we deepen the network with some repeated units with stride = 1 (Fig. 2(b)) to improve the representation capability, such as Stage2-2, Stage3-2 and Stage4-2. Each layer's parameters and complexity which are infered by Eqs. (1–7) are listed in Table 1.

Table 1. ShuffleNet-style regression network's architecture and complexity.

Layer	Input size	Kernal size	Stride	Repeat	Parameters	Complexity (MFLOPs)
Conv1	$128 \times 128 \times 2$	3×3	2	1	288	1.180
MaxPool	$64 \times 64 \times 16$	3×3	2	1	0	0
Stage2-1	$32 \times 32 \times 16$		2	1	240	0.111
Stage2-2	$16 \times 16 \times 272$		1	3	90576	23.187
Stage3-1	$16 \times 16 \times 272$		2	1	30192	5.484
Stage3-2	$8 \times 8 \times 544$		1	7	811104	51.911
Stage4-1	$8 \times 8 \times 544$		2	1	115872	5.405
Stage4-2	$4 \times 4 \times 1088$		1	3	1361088	21.777
GlobalPool	$4 \times 4 \times 1088$	4×4	1	1	0	0
Conv5	$1 \times 1 \times 1088$	1×1	1	1	8704	0.009

2.2 DLT Layer and Spatial Transformation

The DLT Layer is used to solve for the homography matrix H given a set of four points correspondences. The Spatial Transformation Layer aims to apply the output of the DLT Layer to the first image I^A in order to generate the estimated patch $\tilde{P}^B$. We extend the two layers introduced in [19] by combining them with our ShuffleNet-style Regression Network module.

In order to simplify the training task, we introduce the 4-point parameterization H_{4pt} as the ground turth instead of the 3×3 homography matrix H. DLT algorithm is a commonly used method for the transformation between H_{4pt} and H. Under the assumption that the last element of H is set to 1, we can use the four-point coordinates C_{4pt}^{A} of the first patch P^{A} to obtain the homography by using differentiable operations. The back-propagation process can be performed automatically by implementing the DLT algorithm with the operators defined in TensorFlow.

It is very important to ensure that this transformation layer must be differentiable so that the photometric loss gradients can flow back. The Spatial Transformation Layer computes a normalized inverse $\tilde{H}_{inv}$ of estimated $\tilde{H}$, then uses the inverse for warping the raw image. The estimated patch $\tilde{P}^{B}$ and the real patch P^{B} are necessary to build the loss in Eq. (9).

2.3 Combined Loss Function

Supervised deep learning method like [18] use the Euclidean $L2$ norm of the predicted homography $\tilde{H}_{4pt}$ and the ground truth H_{4pt} as the loss function, defined as L_2. The function specifically used for training is

$$L_2 = \sqrt{\frac{1}{8}\left|\tilde{H}_{4pt} - H_{4pt}\right|^2} \tag{8}$$

Drawing inspiration from the traditional direct methods, unsupervised approach in [19] design an average $L1$ pixel-wise photometric loss

$$L_1 = \frac{1}{|p_i|}\sum_{p_i}\left|\tilde{P}_B(p_i) - P_B(p_i)\right| \tag{9}$$

where p_i is the homogeneous coordinate of the i-th pixel and $\tilde{H}_{4pt}$ defines the homography transformation $\tilde{P}_B(p_i)$.

However, both the supervised and unsupervised methods have their own unique flaws. For the L_2 loss function, different estimated homographies can have the same root mean square error (RMSE). As shown in Fig. 3, red bounding box represents the ground truth correspondences and yellow is the prediction. Though the regression network tries to fit the ground truth by minimizing RMSE, it must have inevitable deviations. In the case of the same L_2 error, using L_1 error can easily distinguish between the two situations of Fig. 3(a) and (b).

When we reproduced the work of [19], we found the unsupervised network is hard to train because the learning rate should be small to ensure any three points are not on the same line. Another reason for it is the L_1 loss is too large when the illumination condition across the images changes obviously. In the extreme, the L_2 error keeps increasing while the L_1 error decreases.

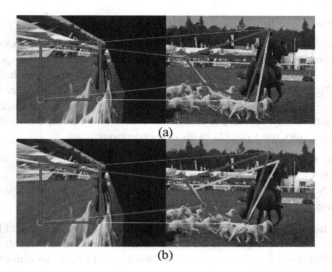

Fig. 3. Different estimated homographies with the same RMSE = 10. (Color figure online)

Hence, taking into account the simplicity of L_2 and the distinguishability of L_1, we combine them with a weigh hyperparameter α to build a novel loss function:

$$L = \sqrt{\frac{1}{8}\left|\tilde{H}_{4pt} - H_{4pt}\right|^2} + \alpha \times \frac{1}{|p_i|}\sum\nolimits_{p_i}\left|\tilde{P}_B(p_i) - P_B(p_i)\right| \qquad (10)$$

The network can be boldly trained with a big learning rate until it converges. By setting an appropriate value of α, the combined loss function is able to utilize L_2 to fit the label as quickly as possible at the early stage, and the L_1 loss fine-tuning is used to achieve the best accuracy in the later period.

3 Experiments

3.1 Datasets

To evaluate our compressed model, we select the same dataset MS-COCO as [18]. We generate 250000 pairs training images and 5000 pairs testing images respectively using the method introduced in [18]. All images are preprocessed to the same size 320×240 in order to ensure successful data generation. We choose $\rho = 45$ as the maximum perturbation value to wrap the images which means that the training data contains approximately all cases less than or equal to 45. We randomly crop a 128×128 patch out of the middle of the image as the input of the neural network while the traditional methods use the whole image. In addition, we standardize all data and do data augmentation by injecting random color, brightness and gamma shifts [19] to make our network more robust to these conditions.

3.2 Training

We train our ShuffleNet-style convolutional neural network for 150000 iterations over ~18 h on a single NVIDIA GeForce GTX 1080 Ti GPU. All experiments are implemented with TensorFlow open-source framework. We use a stochastic gradient descent (SGD) strategy with a batch size of 128, and an Adam Optimizer with default parameters. We set an initial learning rate of 0.0005 and adopt an exponential descent strategy to continuously decrease it to 0.0001. We follow most of the training settings and hyper-parameters used in [22], with two exceptions:

- We set the number of groups g equal to 4, which helps to encode more channel information;
- The penalty weight is decayed to 2e−05 instead of 4e−05 because the compressed network has too few parameters to overfit.

We can't use the models for transfer learning that [18] or [19] trained because our regression network is completely different. Instead, we take the result of the first random initialization training as a pre-trained model, and follow-up training processes can greatly reduce the time.

3.3 Experimental Results

In order to consider the influence of different weight parameter α values on the results, we specifically design a set of experiments to find the more appropriate α. We use models trained from different α loss functions to evaluate the test data which is augmented at a ratio of 0.5. The results of our experiments are presented in Table 2. For better comparison, we sort the results by dividing RMSEs from small to large into six levels, and calculate the average error for each level. Obviously, the performance of homography estimation is the best when α is 6. The reason we think may be that the proportion of L_1 loss function is too small to fine-tune the bounding box when α is less than 5, and the constraint of the L_2 loss function on the box is weakened when α is too big. Both cases can lead to poor homography estimation.

Table 2. 4pt-Homography RMSE with different α values.

α	Average RMSE	Performance percentile					
		Top 0–5%	Top 5–10%	Top 10–20%	Top 20–50%	Top 50–70%	Top 70–100%
2	7.34	2.49	3.27	3.97	5.40	7.31	11.92
4	6.69	2.11	2.83	3.46	4.74	6.60	11.18
5	6.70	2.12	2.80	3.47	4.76	6.55	11.23
6	**6.67**	**2.07**	**2.76**	**3.39**	**4.75**	**6.53**	**11.18**
8	6.69	2.07	2.77	3.41	4.74	6.53	11.27
10	7.45	2.48	3.28	3.97	5.40	7.40	12.21

To fairly compare the performances of all learning-based methods in a favorable environmental conditions, we test their models with no data augmentation and the same displacement ($\rho = 45$). Figure 4 displays the results of learning-based method divided by performance percentile. The 4pt-Homography RMSE of our ShuffleNet-style network is significantly better than the other two networks because we combine their respective advantages to make up for the shortcomings. Besides, to get the results of the other two methods we directly test the models that [19] published.

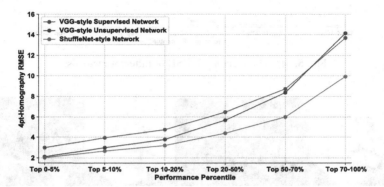

Fig. 4. 4pt-Homography RMSE of different learning-based methods.

For complete comparison, we compare our proposed ShuffleNet-style network method with some typical traditional methods, such as ORB [6], SIFT [5] and ECC [10]. We adjust the data augmentation ratio to 0.7 to verify the robustness of all the approaches. As shown in the Fig. 5, the performance of ECC is the worst of all, and even the best is over 9. ORB and SIFT algorithms perform very well 50% of the time, but in the remaining 50% of the time they do very poorly. Different from the results described in [19], the VGG-style networks do not have much more consistent performance when we test their trained models. On the other hand, our novel network is superior to other two networks. Even in the top 50% of the time, the accuracy of our ShuffleNet-style network is the closest to that of traditional methods. Figure 6 displays the qualitative visualization of all methods for homography estimation under the same illumination conditions. The metric we use to evaluate the performance of these algorithms is the 4pt-Homography RMSE. When dealing with hard cases, learning-based methods basically outperforms traditional methods because it can benefit from sufficient training data. ECC usually fails in the case of large displacements or intense light changes. SIFT is better than ORB but still has big error. In general, our approach is the most robust to illumination variation and large displacements ($\rho = 45$).

Table 3 depicts the complexity of VGG-style [18, 19] and ShuffleNet-style neural networks respectively. The size of our model is only 9.9 MB, which is 1/40 of the model that trained by VGG-style networks. Less computational costs and smaller models make it easier to update the model online and run on mobile devices, such as FPGAs, smartphones and other embedded platforms.

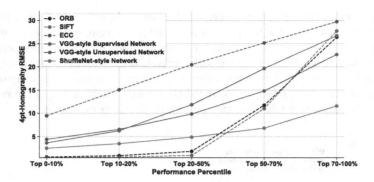

Fig. 5. 4pt-Homography RMSE of different methods.

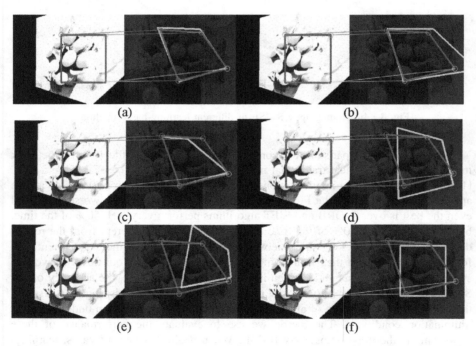

Fig. 6. Homography estimation results of all methods. (a) ShuffleNet-style network (RMSE = 4.88); (b) SIFT (RMSE = 22.38); (c) VGG-style unsupervised network (RMSE = 15.05); (d) ORB (RMSE = 27.26); (e) VGG-style supervised network (RMSE = 26.16); (f) ECC (Fail).

Table 3. VGG-style and ShuffleNet-style networks' complexity.

Network	Parameters	Complexity (MFLOPs)	Model size (MB)
VGG-style	34192264	9819.99	**410.3**
ShuffleNet-style	2418064	109.06	**9.9**

4 Conclusion

In this paper, we propose a novel end-to-end homography estimation model based on ShuffleNet-style compressed convolutional neural network. Leveraging the power of deep learning, this new network is able to estimate homographies more efficient and robust. Based on the MS-COCO datasets, it is verified that our combined loss function can produce more accurate 4-point homography parameterization H_{4pt} in the top 50% performance percentile and is robust to illumination variation. The size of our model is only 9.9 MB while maintaining accuracy, so it is suitable for computing on embedded devices because of the uniqueness of depthwise separable convolution.

For future work, it is reasonable to try to introduce Recurrent Neural Network (RNN) into the regression module to handle the temporal relationship between the two images because we usually use homography estimation to process video sequences. Inspired by the work of [17], we believe that sequential modelling of videos with RNN will be a feasible solution.

Acknowledgment. This work was supported in part by the National Natural Science Foundation of China under Grants 61571285, and Shanghai Science and Technology Commission under Grant 17DZ2292400 and 18XD1423900.

References

1. Mur-Artal, R., Tardos, J.D.: ORB-SLAM: tracking and mapping recognizable features. IEEE Trans. Rob. **31**(5), 1147–1163 (2015)
2. Wang, G., Zhai, Z., Xu, B., et al.: A parallel method for aerial image stitching using ORB feature points. IEEE/ACIS. In: International Conference on Computer and Information Science, pp. 769–773. IEEE (2017)
3. Hsu, Y.F., Chou, C.C., Shih, M.Y.: Moving camera video stabilization using homography consistency, pp. 2761–2764 (2012)
4. Rosten, E., Drummond, T.: Machine learning for high-speed corner detection. In: Leonardis, A., Bischof, H., Pinz, A. (eds.) ECCV 2006. LNCS, vol. 3951, pp. 430–443. Springer, Heidelberg (2006). https://doi.org/10.1007/11744023_34
5. Lowe, D.G.: Distinctive image features from scale-invariant keypoints. Int. J. Comput. Vision **60**(2), 91–110 (2004)
6. Rublee, E., Rabaud, V., Konolige, K., et al.: ORB: an efficient alternative to SIFT or SURF. In: International Conference on Computer Vision, Barcelona, pp. 2564–2571 (2011)
7. Fischler, M.A., Bolles, R.C.: Random sample consensus: a paradigm for model fitting with applications to image analysis and automated cartography. Commun. ACM **24**, 381–395 (1981)
8. Forster, C., Pizzoli, M., Scaramuzza, D.: SVO: fast semi-direct monocular visual odometry. In: IEEE International Conference on Robotics and Automation, pp. 15–22. IEEE (2014)
9. Engel, J., Schöps, T., Cremers, D.: LSD-SLAM: large-scale direct monocular SLAM. In: Fleet, D., Pajdla, T., Schiele, B., Tuytelaars, T. (eds.) ECCV 2014. LNCS, vol. 8690, pp. 834–849. Springer, Cham (2014). https://doi.org/10.1007/978-3-319-10605-2_54
10. Evangelidis, G.D., Psarakis, E.Z.: Parametric image alignment using enhanced correlation coefficient maximization. IEEE Trans. Pattern Anal. Mach. Intell. **30**(10), 1858–1865 (2008)

11. Krizhevsky, A., Sutskever, I., Hinton, G.E.: ImageNet classification with deep convolutional neural networks. In: International Conference on Neural Information Processing Systems, pp. 1097–1105. Curran Associates Inc. (2012)

12. Chatfield, K., Simonyan, K., Vedaldi, A., et al.: Return of the devil in the details: delving deep into convolutional nets. Comput. Sci. **50**(1), 815–830 (2014)

13. Wan, J., Wang, D., Hoi, S.C.H., et al.: Deep learning for content-based image retrieval: a comprehensive study. In: The ACM International Conference, pp. 157–166. ACM (2014)

14. Babenko, A., Slesarev, A., Chigorin, A., Lempitsky, V.: Neural codes for image retrieval. In: Fleet, D., Pajdla, T., Schiele, B., Tuytelaars, T. (eds.) ECCV 2014. LNCS, vol. 8689, pp. 584–599. Springer, Cham (2014). https://doi.org/10.1007/978-3-319-10590-1_38

15. Kendall, A., Grimes, M., Cipolla, R.: PoseNet: a convolutional network for real-time 6-DOF camera relocalization. Educ. Inform. **31**, 2938–2946 (2015)

16. Tateno, K., Tombari, F., Laina, I., et al.: CNN-SLAM: real-time dense monocular SLAM with learned depth prediction, pp. 6565–6574 (2017)

17. Wang, S., Clark, R., Wen, H., et al.: DeepVO: towards end-to-end visual odometry with deep recurrent convolutional neural networks, pp. 2043–2050 (2017)

18. Detone, D.: Deep image homography estimation. In: RSS Workshop on Limits and Potentials of Deep Learning in Robotics (2016)

19. Nguyen, T., Chen, S.W., Skandan, S., et al.: Unsupervised deep homography: a fast and robust homography estimation model. IEEE Robot. Autom. Lett. **PP**(99), 1 (2018)

20. Howard, A.G., Zhu, M., Chen, B., et al.: MobileNets: efficient convolutional neural networks for mobile vision applications (2017)

21. Xie, S., Girshick, R., Dollar, P., et al.: Aggregated residual transformations for deep neural networks. In: IEEE Conference on Computer Vision and Pattern Recognition, pp. 5987–5995. IEEE Computer Society (2017)

22. Zhang, X., Zhou, X., Lin, M., et al.: ShuffleNet: an extremely efficient convolutional neural network for mobile devices (2017)

Improving Semantic Style Transfer
Using Guided Gram Matrices

Chung Nicolas[1,2(✉)], Rong Xie[1,2], Li Song[1,2], and Wenjun Zhang[1,2]

[1] Institute of Image Communication and Network Engineering,
Shanghai Jiao Tong University, Shanghai, China
nicolas.chung@insa-lyon.fr,
{xierong,song_li,zhangwenjun}@sjtu.edu.cn
[2] Cooperative Medianet Innovation Center,
Shanghai Jiao Tong University, Shanghai, China

Abstract. Style transfer is a computer vision task that attempts to transfer the style of an artistic image to a content image. Thanks to the advance in Deep Convolutional Neural Networks, exciting style transfer results has been achieved, but traditional algorithms do not fully understand semantic information. Those algorithms are not aware of which regions in the style image have to be transferred to which regions in the content image. A common failure case is style transfer involving landscape images. After stylization, the textures and colors of the land are often found in incoherent places such as in the river or in the sky. In this work, we investigate semantic style transfer for content images with more than 2 semantic regions. We combine guided Gram matrices with gradient capping and multi-scale representations. Our approach simplifies the parameter tuning problem, improves the style transfer results and is faster than current semantic methods.

Keywords: Semantic style transfer · Guided gram matrices · Gradient capping · Multi-scale representation · Deep learning

1 Introduction

Much study in the past three years has focus on style transfer using Deep Convolutional Neural Networks. Style transfer on images aims to transfer the style of an artistic image to a content image. It has been widely investigated - in the field of computer vision and graphics - to solve problems such as: headshot portrait, weather transfer, texture synthesis and object transfiguration. In order to produce good results, style transfer algorithms must preserve the content features of the content image while changing important style features such as texture, colors and line stokes.

One way to address that problem is to solve an image optimization problem. Gatys *et al.* achieve astonishing results by considering a 19-layers VGG network pre-trained on image classification [7]. The objective to minimize is composed of

© Springer Nature Singapore Pte Ltd. 2019
G. Zhai et al. (Eds.): IFTC 2018, CCIS 1009, pp. 169–183, 2019.
https://doi.org/10.1007/978-981-13-8138-6_14

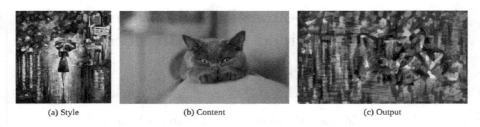

Fig. 1. Style: Rain princess, Leonid Afremov, 2014. An example of poor style transfer. Traditional methods consider the content image as a whole. These algorithms cannot distinguish the background and the object of interest (the cat here). In this case, too much content information is lost. A better style/content weight ratio need to be used. The process can be long and tedious.

a content loss and a style loss. The stylized images are obtained by performing gradient descent on white noisy images. Image optimization methods are flexible but computationally expensive. To overcome that problem, Justin *et al.* introduce a style transfer network based on model optimization [6]. Stylized images are generated 3 times faster, but the model has lost flexibility: a model has to be trained for each style images.

However, although traditional models (whether based on image optimization or model optimization) can achieve exciting results, more work is needed to exploit semantic information. Traditional models apply the style on the whole image. If the content and style weight are not well chosen, the results are poor (see Fig. 1). Semantic style transfer aims to spatially control neural style transfer. With semantic style transfer, the user selects which style to apply to each region in the content image. In [13], the authors attempt to mask the gradient using a simple threshold, but they were not completely successful. In [4], the authors try to combine capped gradient with Gram matrices manipulation, but the results are far from perfect. Recently, the authors in [9] introduce guided Gram matrices and have shown good results for simple content images.

In this study, we show how simple modifications of the original guided Gram matrices [9] improve the results of semantic style transfer. Our work concentrates on content images with more than 2 semantics regions. We simplify the parameter tunning problem by considering pixel ratio of the segmentation masks. By doing so, our approach can represent the different styles uniformly. As a second contribution, we demonstrate that spatial control can be reinforced by combining Gram matrices with gradient capping. During backpropagation, the idea is to update each region in the stylized image by stopping the gradient of the other regions. We also introduce a multi-scale semantic style transfer algorithm. Our model produces qualitatively better results and is faster than current semantic style transfer methods.

The rest of this paper is organized as follow. We summarize the current existing work in Sect. 2. We briefly introduce the neural style transfer algorithm in Sect. 2. We present our proposed model in Sect. 4. We detail the experiment in Sect. 5. We show and analyze the results in Sect. 6. We draw conclusion in Sect. 7.

2   Related Work

Style Transfer. Traditional style transfer methods solve an image optimisation problem. Gatys *et al.* demonstrate that content and style features can be extracted directly from the hidden activation layers of the VGG [7]. Extracted style features are then used to compute features correlation known as Gram matrices. Alternative methods replace Gram matrices with a Markov random fields (MRFs) regularizer [3,10]. MRFs are patch-based approaches that improve the precision of photo-realistic style transfer. In some cases, the colors of the content image should be preserved. Authors in [9] accomplish color preservation by implementing two simple linear methods. In [13] a better per-layer content and style weighting scheme is investigated. The same authors demonstrate that more style layers leads to better results. In [14], an histogram loss is used to improve stability of style transfer. These methods solve an image optimization problem: the quality of the resulting images is high but generating them is time-consuming. Moreover, these methods do not exploit semantic information.

Fast Style Transfer. Image optimization models are slow. To speed up style transfer, Justin *et al.* propose a model optimization problem [6]. They formulate the style transfer problem as an image transformation task. A feed-forward transformation network is trained. The per-pixel loss functions are replaced by perceptual losses. Compared to image optimization problems, stylized images are generated three times faster. It was found that generated images can be qualitatively improved using instance normalization [15]. Other methods like [5,12] developed a single network that can represent several styles. Even though these methods are faster than image optimization models, model optimization models cannot perform semantic style transfer. Those models lack flexibility: a model would need to be trained for each content images and combination of style images.

Semantic Style Transfer. The aim of semantic style transfer is to spatially control style transfer. In [9], the authors introduce Guided Gram Matrices. Unlike full style transfer, a Gram Matrix is computed for each region in the content image. The authors obtain good results for content images with 2 semantic regions. In [11] the authors address the computation bottleneck of backpropagation of semantic style transfer with a decoder network. Other works attempt to perform semantic style transfer using patch based methods [3,17]. All these methods have in common that they consider 1 content image and 1 style image with similar semantic regions. Those methods perform well for portrait style transfer. In this work, we consider 1 content image and n style images. It is harder since each style images does not necessarily have the same semantics as the content image. We demonstrate the efficiency of our method for content images with more than 2 semantic regions.

3   Neural Style Transfer

In this section, we briefly review the style transfer method proposed by Gatys *et al.* [7]. Our work solves the same image optimization problem but combines several reconstruction losses. We review them below.

Content and Style Losses. Gatys *et al.* generate stylized images by minimizing a content and style loss [7]. We denote C the content image, S the style image, I the generated image and F^l the activation map of convolutional layer l. The content of an image is represented by the activation of one convolutional layer lc. The content loss compares the content representation of C and I:

$$L_{content} = \|F^l(C) - F^l(I)\|^2 \tag{1}$$

Statistical features known as Gram Matrices represent the style of I [7]. When those statistics are computed for each region r in I, they are known as guided Gram Matrices [9]. Guided Gram matrices require semantic segmentation masks. Contrary to content features, multiple layers represent the style of an image. Let G_r^l be the guided Gram Matrices of the r-th region at layer l and β_r its associated weighting factor. The style loss is:

$$L_{style} = \sum_r \beta_r \sum_l \|G_r^l(S) - G_r^l(I)\|^2 \tag{2}$$

Regularizer Loss. Justin *et al.* [6] show that a regularizer loss improve results for fast style transfer methods. It is a per pixel loss function that encourages spatial smoothness by reducing distortions and visual artifacts. It is defined as [16]:

$$L_{regularizer} = \sum_{i,j} ((x_{i,j+1} - x_{i,j})^2 + (x_{i+1,j} - x_{i,j})^2)^{1/2} \tag{3}$$

4   Proposed Model

Our algorithm takes as input a content image (an ordinary photograph), n segmentation masks (each mask is associated to a region in the content image) and n style images. Figure 2 illustrates our method.

4.1   Loss Function

We generate stylized images by jointly minimizing a content, style and regularizer loss. Refer to the previous section for the detail of each loss. We control the tradeoff between content, style and regularizer by the weighting factors α, β and γ. As in [9], we used 19-layers VGG network pre-trained on image classification to extract the high levels features.

$$L_{total} = \alpha L_{content} + \beta L_{style} + \gamma L_{regularizer} \tag{4}$$

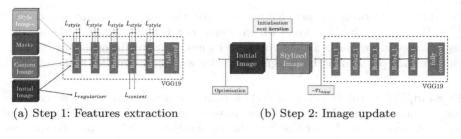

(a) Step 1: Features extraction   (b) Step 2: Image update

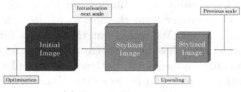

(c) Step 3: Next scale

Fig. 2. System overview. (a) *Features extraction.* We input the styles, masks, content and initialize the optimisation with the content. We extract content and style features and compute their associated loss. (b) *Image update.* We cap the gradient and update the stylized image. We repeat step (a) and (b) N times. (c) *Next scale.* We upscale the current stylized image and set it as initialisation for the next scale. We repeat the whole process until the final resolution is reached.

4.2 Improved Guided Gram Matrices

Auto-tuning of Weights. To understand our auto-tuning approach, we have to understand how guided Gram Matrices are computed. Consider an image X with R number of regions. Let G_r^l and T_r^l, respectively, be the guided Gram Matrix and the guidance channel at layer l for r-th region, $r \in [0, R]$. Let F_r^l be the activations maps masked by T_r^l. We denote $\odot$ the element-wise multiplication operator. G_r^l is the inner product between the F_r^l.

$$F_r^l(X) = T_r^l \odot F^l(X) \tag{5a}$$

$$G_r^l(X) = F_r^l(X)^T F_r^l(X) \tag{5b}$$

The main difficulty to obtain good results comes from parameters tuning. A content image composed of R semantic regions introduces R more parameters. We simplify that problem by tuning β_r (defined in Eq. 2) automatically. For a region r in C, we compute β_r as the ratio between the number of pixels in that region and the total number of pixels:

$$\beta_r = \frac{p_r}{\sum_i p_i} \tag{6}$$

where p_i is the number of pixel of region i. Because of masking (Eq. 5a), bigger regions contribute more to the style loss than smaller regions (more pixels).

To address that problem, we tried to normalize the guidance channels such that $\sum_i (T_r^l)_i^2 = 1$ [9], but by doing so, we found out that the style of the smaller regions was more marked than the bigger ones. Our weighting factor counterbalance that phenomena by assigning smaller weights to smaller regions.

Erosion/Dilation. Recall that style features are represented with several layers. Because neurons in deeper layers have bigger receptive field, the styles of adjacent regions overlap at the boundaries. Authors in [8] attempt to increase spatial control by using erosion and dilation on the guidance channels. The results are good but the numbers and the shapes of the considered regions are simple: only two large regions. We found out that results for small regions are poor. For small regions, only few neurons capture style features (see Eq. 5a). After erosion the remaining neurons are not enough to well represent the style.

We propose a method that could improve the blending problem but that we did not implement yet. Our idea is to define a zone of pixels at the boundaries using morphological filtering. The weight of two-adjacent style are set to 0.5 and 0.5. For n overlapping stylized regions, the weights are set to $1/n$. The aim is to smooth transition between the different stylized regions.

4.3   Gradient Capping

In the previous subsection, we saw that the styles overlap at the boundaries. To address that problem, we combine guided Gram Matrices with gradient capping. We ensure that only the desired regions are updated by stopping the propagation of the gradient through the unwanted regions. Consider X_r^t the r-th region of the stylized image X at iteration t, T_r the associated segmentation mask, λ the learning rate, ∇ the gradient and L_{tot} the loss function defined in Eq. 4. At each iteration we have:

$$X_r^{t+1} = X_r^t - \lambda \cdot T_r \cdot \nabla_{X^t} L_{tot} \tag{7}$$

Note that guided Gram Matrices mask style features. To match the dimension of those features (see Eq. 5a), the masks T_r have to be downsampled with pooling. Gradient capping masks regions in the stylized image itself (the input masks T_r are enough). With gradient capping, the transition between objects is sharp at the boundaries. We solve this problem by increasing the regularization weight γ (see Eq. 4).

As suggested in [4], we tried to independently minimize the content, style and regularizer loss, but the results were bad. The reason is that the minimum of a sum of functions is not equal to the sum of the minimun of the functions. This property can be easily verified by considering functions with positive and negative numbers such as the gradient. Thus, we have to jointly minimize the three losses.

4.4   Multi-scale Representation

In order to generate high resolution stylized images, multi-scale representation has been used in traditional style transfer methods [7,14]. The first step is to

---

Algorithm 1. Multi scale semantic style transfer. X^0 indicates image X at resolution α_0, N number of scales, $\uparrow$ upscaling, $\downarrow$ downscaling.

---

input : Content image C
         Style images S
         Masks content T_c
         Masks styles T_s
output: Stylized image I^k at scale α_k

begin
   /* Initialization with the smallest scale   */
   $C^0, S^0, T_c^0, T_s^0 \leftarrow C, S, T_c, T_s \downarrow \alpha_0$
   $I^0 \leftarrow C^0$
   /* Multi-scale representation   */
   for $k = 0, ..., N-1$ **do**
      /* Image optimization   */
      $I^k \leftarrow$ semantic-style-transfer$(C^k, S^k, T_c^k, T_s^k, I^k)$
      /* Initialization next scale   */
      $I^{k+1} \leftarrow I^k \uparrow \alpha_{k+1}$
      /* Upscale content image, style images and masks   */
      $C^{k+1}, S^{k+1}, T_c^{k+1}, T_s^{k+1} \leftarrow C^k, S^k, T_c^k, T_s^k \uparrow \alpha_{k+1}$

---

generate a low resolution image. This stylized image is then upscaled and set as the initialization image for the next scale. The process is then repeated until the final resolution is reached. By doing so, details are added between each successive scale and fewer iterations are required at high resolution.

We extend this multi-scale representation to semantic style transfer. In addition to content and style images, our algorithms requires the segmentation masks. We upscale images with bilinear interpolation. Refer to Algorithm 1 for the details.

Even though multi-scale representation requires less iterations at high resolution, it is not always faster than one-scale representation. There exists a preprocessing phase that is not negligeable. We empirically found that using 2 scales is a good trade-off between speed and quality of the generated images.

5 Experiment Details

The number of iteration was fixed to $N = 700$. Content features are extracted from layer ReLU4_2. Style features are extracted from layer ReLU1_1, ReLU2_1, ReLU3_1, ReLU4_1, ReLU5_1. The optimization process is initialized from the content image (cleaner results than white noise initialization). We use the content masks as style masks. Adam optimizer is used with learning rate $1e+1$. The content weight is $5e+0$. The style weight is $5e+2$. When not mentioned, we used the geometric weighting scheme defined in [13]. The strength of the total variation loss is $1e+3$. Our implementation is based on the work of [1]. We plan

Table 1. Running time comparison in second (s) of different semantic methods. Time is averaged over 20 samples. $N = 700$ iterations, r: number of semantic regions. A 400×400 content image was used.

Number regions	Castillo et al. [2]	Gatys et al. [9]	Our	Speed up	
				vs. [2]	vs. [9]
$r = 2$	92.1	62.1	**52.4**	1.8×	1.2×
$r = 3$	139.4	72.2	**58.7**	2.4×	1.2×
$r = 4$	185.3	82.7	**67.6**	2.7×	1.2×

to render our code publicly available upon acceptance for future research. On two NVIDIA k20c, it takes around 1 min to process one frame of size 400×400.

6   Results and Discussion

6.1   Proposed vs Others Semantic Methods

In this section, we qualitatively compare targeted style transfer [2], guided Gram Matrices [9] and our method. Two semantic regions are considered and the style is applied only on the background. The results are presented in Fig. 3.

With [2], the foreground is the same as in the content image. This method applies style transfer on the whole content and then segments the stylized regions. This method is simple but it cannot control which regions in the style images has to be transferred to which regions in the content image.

Our method and [9] produce close imitation of the foreground but ours better blends regions. In Fig. 3(a), the background between the arms and the lower body of the person riding the bike should be orange but is somewhat greyish with [9]. With ours, the background stays orange. In Fig. 3(b) with [9] the semantic style transfer failed around the head and the tail of the horse (because of erosion). With ours it does not. For [2], stylized regions blend naturally but another optimization problem is solved to avoid crude results.

6.2   Mutiple Semantic Regions

One of the main drawbacks of targeted transfer [2] is that the running time increases linearly with the number of semantic regions. When R styles are applied, [2] solve the style transfer problem R times. Our method and [9] solve the problem only once whatever value of R.

A running time comparison is shown in Table 1. It takes 92 s to [2] to produce a stylized image with 2 semantic regions and 185 s with 4 semantic regions: the time complexity is linear. With ours and [9], the running time increases approximately by 10 s for each additional regions. Ours is the fastest and beats [9] by 10–15 s. We show some generated images with our method in Fig. 4.

(a) Motorbike

(b) Horse

Fig. 3. Targeted transfer [2] vs Guided Gram matrices [9] vs Ours. Results obtained with [2] are pleasing, but ours offers more spatial control. Compared to [9] our method gives better blending results. With [9], the background is not consistent in (a) around the motorbike and in (b) around the head and the tail of the horse. Content images were extracted from the DAVIS dataset and were resized to 427×240 pixels.

(a) Mask   (b) Style 1   (c) Style 2   (d) Style 3

(e) Content   (f) 3 styles combination

(g) Mask   (h) Style 1   (i) Style 2   (j) Style 3   (k) Style 4

(l) Content   (m) 4 styles combination

Fig. 4. Our results for (f) 3, (m) 4 semantic regions. Numbers in the masks correspond to the style number which is applied. Mixing styles with the same predominant colors looks good ((m) yellow/orange). Content and maks are from the COCO dataset. (Color figure online)

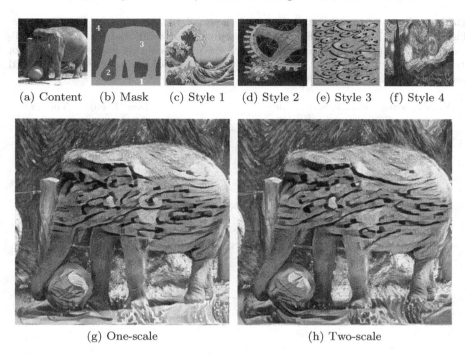

(a) Content   (b) Mask   (c) Style 1   (d) Style 2   (e) Style 3   (f) Style 4

(g) One-scale   (h) Two-scale

Fig. 5. (g) One-scale transfer, (h) Two-scale transfer. We used 700 iterations for both methods. We detailed the 2-scale process in Fig. 6. Multi-scaling generates a more pleasing image: with (g) ghosting instabilities can be seen in the soil. The perceptual loss curves are shown in Fig. 7.

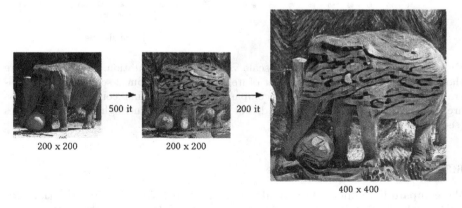

200 x 200   200 x 200

400 x 400

Fig. 6. Multi-scale transfer: 500 iterations (it) are performed at low resolution (200 × 200). The resulting image is then upscaled and set as initialisation for the next scale (400 × 400). We performed 200 more iterations. We report quantitative results for different scale in Table 2.

Table 2. Comparison of content loss, style loss and running time for different scale. The image used is the one in Fig. 5. The total number of iterations is fixed to $N = 700$. Values are averaged over 20 samples. For each successive scale, we halves the number of iterations by approximately 2. Using 2 scales offers a good compromise between speed and quality of the generated images.

Number scales	Iterations per scale				Loss (1e+6)		Time (s)
	50×50	100×100	200×200	400×400	Content	Style	
1	-	-	-	700	1.71	0.86	82.9
2	-	-	**500**	**200**	**1.82**	**0.87**	**67.8**
3	-	400	200	100	1.95	0.98	64.6
4	350	200	100	50	2.27	1.28	65.8

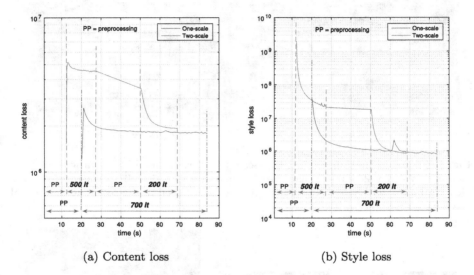

(a) Content loss   (b) Style loss

Fig. 7. Perceptual loss curves for 1-scale vs 2-scale representation. Visual results are shown in Fig. 5. With a same number of iterations (700 it), our 2-scale algorithm generates the stylized image faster (68 s compared to 83 s). The final content and style loss are roughly the same for both methods but multi-scaling reduces ghosting instabilities (see Fig. 5).

6.3 One-Scale vs Multi-scale

We compare here one-scale vs multi-scale methods. We used 700 iterations for both methods. We used the weighting scheme in [1] (better results in this case). Results with two-scale are presented in Figs. 5 and 6. We also report quantitative results with more scale in Table 2.

Our two-scale algorithm Fig. 5h produces visually more pleasing results than one-scale method Fig. 5g. Even after 700 iterations, the one-scale method does

(a) Gram matrices ($\gamma = 0$)
2.79 / 2.42

(b) Gram matrices ($\gamma = 1e+2$)
2.79 / 2.43

(c) Auto-tuning + Fig. 8b
2.24 / **1.32**

(d) Gradient capping + Fig. 8b
2.19 / 2.81

(e) Final ($\gamma = 1e+2$)
2.07 / 1.42

(f) Final ($\gamma = 1e+3$)
1.92 / **1.39**

Fig. 8. Ablation study. The image used is the same one as in Fig. 4e. γ is the regularization weight defined in Eq. 4. We report content/style loss ($1e+6$) below each image. Zoom in for details, especially around the right side of the shoes.

not well capture the style for the soil: this problem is known as ghosting. Our two-scale method does not show those instabilities.

Loss curves are shown in Fig. 7. Each optimisation begins with a preprocessing phase. During this phase, we extract the content features from the content image and the style features from the style images. This phase is longer for higher resolution images (10 s for 200×200 image, 20 s for 400×400 image).

Increasing iterations is not efficient to reduce the style loss. With one-scale, the style loss remains almost constant after 330 iterations (50 s). After optimisation, both methods present roughly the same content ($2e+6$) and style loss ($1e+6$). However, care has to be taken at the analysis of those values. As it can be seen in Fig. 5, the style loss fails to take ghosting instabilities into account.

The two-scale method generate images faster than the one-scale one (68 s compared to 83 s). Using more scales is slightly faster but the quantity of the generated images is worse (see Table 2).

6.4   Ablation Study

To study which part of our model is effective we perform an ablation study. Results are shown in Fig. 8. Figure 8a demonstrates that not using regularization results in a noisy image. It can be seen in Fig. 8b that with guided Gram matrices alone, the semantics are not well respected (especially around the shoes). Auto-tuning halves the style loss by 2 (Fig. 8c). It also reduces the content loss. With Gradient capping the semantics are respected (smaller content loss) but the contours are visible. It explains why the style loss is higher (see around the body and ear of the cat in Fig. 8d). Combining Gram matrices, auto-tuning and gradient capping offers a good trade off between content and style loss (Fig. 8e). We can observe in Fig. 8f that blending at the boundaries can be improved by increasing the regularization weight.

7   Conclusion

In this work we proposed a semantic style transfer that can process content images with more than 2 semantic regions. We have shown how simple modifications of the original guided Gram matrices can simplify the parameter tunning problem and improve the style transfer results. This study indicates that gradient capping is an efficient solution to spatial control of neural style transfer. We further proposed a multi-scale algorithm that generates high quality images faster than single scale methods. In current implementation, our method requires the segmentation masks of both the style and content images. We are working on developing a better solution that could perform both segmentation and style transfer at the same time.

Acknowledgment. This work was supported by NSFC (61671296 and 61521062) and the Shanghai Key Laboratory of Digital Media Processing and Transmissions.

References

1. Athalye, A.: Neural style (2015). github.com/anishathalye/neural-style
2. Castillo, C., De, S., Han, X., Singh, B., Yadav, A., Goldstein, T.: Son of Zorns lemma: targeted style transfer using instance-aware semantic segmentation (2017). arXiv:1701.02357
3. Champandard, A.J.: Semantic style transfer and turning two-bit doodles into fine artwork (2016). arXiv:1603.01768
4. Chan, E., Bhargava, R.: Show, divide and neural: weighted style transfer. CS231n: Convolutional Neural Networks for Visual Recognition, Project Reports (2016)
5. Dumoulin, V., Shlens, J., Kudlur, M.: A learned representation for artistic style (2017). arXiv:1610.07629
6. Johnson, J., Alahi, A., Fei-Fei, L.: Perceptual losses for real-time style transfer and super-resolution (2016). arXiv:1603.081155
7. Leon, A., Alexander, S., Matthias, B.: Image style transfer using convolutional neural networks (2015). arXiv:1508.06576
8. Leon, A., Alexander, S., Matthias, B., Hertzmann, A., Shechtman, E.: Supplementary material: controlling perceptual factors in neural style transfer. bethgelab.org (2016)
9. Leon, A., Alexander, S., Matthias, B., Hertzmann, A., Shechtman, E.: Controlling perceptual factors in neural style transfer (2017). arXiv:1611.07865
10. Li, C., Wand, M.: Combining markov random fields and convolutional neural networks for image synthesis (2016). arXiv:1601.04589
11. Lu, M., Zhao, H.L., Yao, A., Xu, F., Chen, Y., Zhang, L.: Decoder network over lightweight reconstructed feature for fast semantic style transfer. In: The IEEE International Conference on Computer Vision (ICCV) (2017)
12. Mahendran, A., Vedaldi, A.: Multi-style generative network for real-time transfer (2017). arXiv:1412.0035
13. Novak, R., Nikulin, Y.: Improving the neural algorithm of artistic style (2016). arXiv:1605.04603
14. Risser, E., Wilmot, P., Barnes, C.: Stable and controllable neural texture synthesis and style transfer using histogram losses (2017). arXiv:1701.08893
15. Ulyanov, D., Vedaldi, A., Lepitsky, V.: Instance normalization: the missing ingredient for fast stylization (2017). arXiv:1611.07865
16. Zhang, H., Dana, K.: Understanding deep image representation by inverting them (2017). arXiv:1703.06953
17. Zhao, H., Rosin, P.L., Lai, Y.: Automatic semantic style transfer using deep convolutional neural networks and soft masks (2017). arXiv:1708.09641

Multi-CNNs Bootstrap Against Label Noise with Applications in Age Estimation

Yuying Su, Guangling Sun[(⊠)], and Weiqi Fan

School of Communication and Information Engineering,
Shanghai University, Shanghai 200444, China
sunguangling@shu.edu.cn

Abstract. The age estimation has achieved great success in recent years. For learning an age estimation model, the age label of each facial image is required. If the age labels depend on subjective perception and are supplied by a diversity of amateur users, there inevitably exists improper labels. We name the improper labels as label noise. It is undoubted that the performance of learned model will decrease due to the label noise. Current typical works first identify the mislabeled examples and then remove them before training. Obviously, the discarding strategy does not fully use the valuable training data. In this paper, we explore how to use all training data in spite of the existing label noise. First, a part of the training set is separated into several subsets. Then, multiple Convolutional Neural Networks (multi-CNNs) share low and middle layers and are fine-tuned to the last two full-connected layers respectively using different subsets. In particular, we choose the VGG-Face as the base network. Next, the multi-CNNs determine the label of the remaining training data respectively. If one of the CNNs outputs the same result as the given label and also obtains the highest probability, the corresponding data is absorbed and the corresponding sub-CNN is retrained from the enlarged training data. Such a bootstrap procedure is repeated till no consistent labels are found. Once the bootstrap ends, the inconsistent labels are modified in terms of the consequence given by multi-CNNs decisions with statistical average and combined with previous learned data to compose a label noise reduced training set. Finally, a CNN model is learned from the label noise reduced training set. The empirical results have demonstrated the effectiveness of our proposed method on two age estimation datasets including our new Yitong dataset and WIKI dataset.

Keywords: Label noise · Age estimation · Multi-CNNs bootstrap

1 Introduction

The task of age estimation [1] based on convolutional neural networks (CNNs) [2] has achieved great success due to its superior performance compared with conventional methods in recent years. For a supervised learning of an age estimation task, the genuine age of each facial image needs to be labeled. If the age label is obtained relying on facial appearance, it belongs to a subjective perception. In addition, such labels are usually provided by a diversity of amateur users [3]. There inevitably exists disagreements among individuals for such an age label in that the age perception is associated with each

© Springer Nature Singapore Pte Ltd. 2019
G. Zhai et al. (Eds.): IFTC 2018, CCIS 1009, pp. 184–193, 2019.
https://doi.org/10.1007/978-981-13-8138-6_15

one's responsibility, experience and psychology. Consequently, the age label quality cannot be ensured and the improper labels are considered as label noise. Some examples with label noise in our new Yitong dataset have been shown in Fig. 1.

| 0-15 | 16-25 | 56-70 | 41-55 | 56-70 |

Fig. 1. Some examples of improper age labels in Yitong dataset. The label is an age interval.

The performance of classification/regression in age estimation problem might decrease because of mislabeled examples and many more training data are required for learning an accurate enough CNNs. Thus, to alleviate the negative effect of noisy labels in learning deep models, some approaches have been developed. Yang et al. [4] estimated the probability of mislabeled class with an adaptive sampling by iteratively reducing the possibility of selecting mislabeled examples for training model. Wei et al. [5] proposed multiple filtering with the aid of unlabeled data using confidence measurement to increase the effect of noise filter. This method has a high accuracy in identifying mislabeled data. Krawczyk et al. [6] intended to reduce the influence of label noise by using fuzzy one-classifier support vector machines that allows membership values to be associated with each training object. Sukhbaatar et al. [7] proposed to learn the noise distribution through an extra noise layer inserted into the deep model. Xiao et al. [8] solved this problem from a probabilistic graphical model perspective and trained a classifier with an end-to-end learning manner. Feng et al. [9] handled arbitrary outliers hidden in the data through a robust logistic regression via estimating the parameters in a linear programming method. Hamid et al. [10] studied a robust logistic regression method for classification with user-supplied tags in the case of label noise. Azadi et al. [11] automatically exploited the mutual context information from auxiliary images and propelled the model to select reliable images to boost the robustness of the learning process. Gamberger [12] divided the training dataset into n subsets and one of them was considered as the remaining dataset. The other n-1 sets were used to train a set of models. If the classification results of the remaining dataset disagree with their given labels, they were removed from the training dataset.

The discarding strategy mentioned above have wasted lots of valuable training data. We explore how to use all training data without discarding any data. Our proposed method is to identify the label noise in a novel strategy and then modify them as illustrated in Fig. 2. We present a multi-CNNs bootstrap scheme. First, a part of the training set is separated into several subsets. Then, multi-CNNs share low and middle layers and are fine-tuned to the last two fully connected layers respectively using different subsets. Next, the multi-CNNs determine the labels of the remaining training data respectively. If one of the CNNs outputs the same result as the given label and also obtains the highest probability, the corresponding data is absorbed and the corresponding sub-CNN is retrained from the enlarged learning data. Such a procedure is repeated till no consistent labels are found. And then, the inconsistent labels are modified in terms of the final obtained multi-CNNs decisions via statistical average and the label modified data and the consistent label data are combined to compose a label noise reduced data set. Finally, a CNN model is learned from the label noise reduced training set.

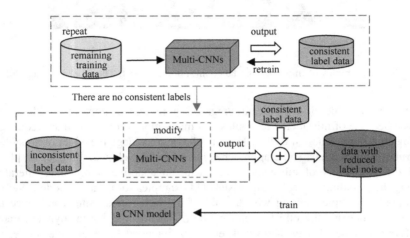

Fig. 2. An overview of the proposed method.

The contributions in this paper are summarized as follows:

(1) The bootstrap scheme is designed. During the repeated bootstrap procedure, the correctly classified samples are continuously relearned so as to improve the performance of the CNNs.
(2) The multi-CNNs scheme is employed. The labels of the samples that cannot be absorbed into any subset are altered to be the results output by CNNs and the samples are relearned. To increases the reliability of the estimated results, statistical average is utilized to combine the decisions of the multiple CNNs.
(3) The fine-tuning strategy is utilized. To effectively reduce the training data, fine-tuning the last two fully connected layers is adopted.

The remaining of the paper is organized as follows. Section 2 gives a brief introduction for VGG-Face network. Section 3 analyzes the proposed approach in detail. Section 4 shows the experimental results on two age estimation datasets including our new Yitong dataset and WIKI dataset. Section 5 draws a conclusion.

2 VGG-Face Network

We adopt VGG-Face [13] as a base network in the proposed framework. Thus, we give a brief introduction of VGG-Face in this section.

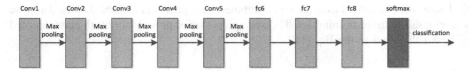

Fig. 3. An illustration of VGG-Face architecture.

The VGG-Face is trained from 2.6M facial images of 2622 unique individuals and used to perform identification recognition. As Fig. 3 illustrates, the network comprises 5 convolutional blocks and 3 fully connected layers. Each convolutional block consists of linear operators followed by one or more non-linear layers, such as ReLU or max pooling. These fully connected layers follow a stack of convolutional layers. The first two fully connected layers obtain 4096 dimensional feature sets. The last fully connected layer of 2622 dimensions is learned relying on the loss function. And the resulting vector is fed into a softmax layer to compute the class posterior probabilities.

3   Proposed Method

In this paper, we treat age estimation as classification task in that the age is labeled as one of the 5 age intervals. The 5 age intervals are 0–15, 16–25, 26–40, 41–55 and 56–70 respectively. Accordingly, the last fully connected layer is altered to be 5 dimensions. Our work attempts to reduce the label noise in an age estimation dataset and improve label quality with the purpose of increasing the age classification accuracy. The two key components of the proposed method involve the multi-CNNs bootstrap scheme and modifying inappropriate labels.

3.1   Multi-CNNs Bootstrap

We randomly divide the whole dataset S into training set and testing set. Then, a part of the training set is initially separated into n subsets. These initial training subsets are named as $A_1, A_2, \ldots \ldots, A_n$. Accordingly, we name the remaining training set as A_{extra}.

Each sub-CNN in multi-CNNs is only fine-tuned to the last two fully connected layers of VGG-Face using different subset. Once fine-tuning is finished, each sample in current A_{extra} is classified by the learned multi-CNNs. If one of the CNNs outputs the same result as the given label and also obtains the highest probability, the corresponding data is absorbed. Afterwards, corresponding sub-CNN will be relearned from the enlarged training subsets. As the process goes, the training subsets will gradually expand and the results obtained by multi-CNNs tend to be more reliable. Such a procedure is repeated till no data with consistent labels are found.

3.2   Modifying Inappropriate Labels

Once the bootstrap procedure ends, some inconsistent label training data leave. The inconsistent labels are modified in terms of the consequence given by multi-CNNs decisions with statistical average and combined with previous learned data to compose a label noise reduced training set. The average posterior probability of ith class denoted as $\overline{\alpha}_i$ is calculated as the Eq. (1).

$$\overline{\alpha}_i = \frac{\sum_{j=1}^{K} p_i(j)}{K} \tag{1}$$

Where K is the number of sub-CNN; i is a class index $(i = 1, 2, \ldots, 5)$; $p_i(j)$ is the posterior probability of ith class output by jth sub-CNN $(j = 1, 2, \ldots, K)$.

If the average posterior probability of someone class is the highest, the label of this class is considered to be a correct label. With such label alterations, all training samples with label noise can be modified and then will be combined with previous learned data to compose a label noise reduced training set. The age training set with reduced label noise will be used to learn the final CNN model.

The whole process is summarized in Algorithm 1.

Algorithm 1: Proposed method

Input: an age dataset S with label noise

Output: an age dataset with the reduced label noise and a CNN model

---

1   Divide S into training set and testing set

---

2   Separate a part of the training set into n subsets and the remaining training data set is denoted as A_{extra}

---

3   repeat

While the result agrees with the given label

- fine-tune each sub-CNN using each training subset

- classify A_{extra} (As the iteration goes, the size of A_{extra} gradually reduces)

- rearrange the data with consistent labels into respective training subset according to each sub-CNN output

---

4   For each mislabeled example s

- classify s using finally obtained multi-CNNs

- compute the posterior probability of each class using equation(1)

- modify the label of s to be a class label obtaining the highest posterior probability

---

5   Combine the data with modified labels and the data with consistent labels to produce a label noise reduced training set

---

6   Train a CNN model using the label noise reduced training set

---

4 Implementation and Experimental Results

4.1 Network Implementation and Parameter Setting

The Caffe library [14] and NVIDIA TITAN X GPUs are used to implement the proposed framework. VGG-Face is adopted as a base network. The input of the network is a three channel and spatial resolution of 224×224 image subtracted by an average face image. The number of subnets is 5. The training algorithm is stochastic gradient descent with 5 mini-batch and 0.01 learning rate. The momentum and weight decay is 0.9 and 0.0005 respectively. The iteration number is 50k.

4.2 Dataset

We test two datasets: one is our new Yitong dataset and the other is WIKI dataset. Yitong dataset is collected through a crowdsourcing platform and the age of each facial image is labeled by human subjective perception for the facial appearance. The dataset contains a total of 7912 images in which 5000 images for training and 2912 images for testing. The label of each facial image in WIKI dataset is biological age and the images are crawled by Rothe et al. [15] from celebrities of Wikipedia. Although the label of WIKI is biological age, it is still effective for learning and evaluating our proposed approach since the labeled biological ages agree with human perception in most cases. Some samples in WIKI are shown in Fig. 4. We divide samples in WIKI dataset into 5 age intervals. Table 1 has listed the sample numbers in different age intervals of both Yitong and WIKI. Notice that in our experiments, all images are preprocessed using methods in [16].

Table 1. Sample numbers in different age intervals of Yitong and WIKI.

	0–15	16–25	26–40	41–55	56–70	Total
Yitong						
Training set	1000	1000	1000	1000	1000	5000
Testing set	568	648	536	616	544	2912
WIKI						
All	245	7019	10497	5172	2866	25799

14/0-15   25/16-25   35/26-40   44/41-55   68/56-70

Fig. 4. Biological age/age group of some samples for WIKI dataset.

4.3   Experimental Results for Yitong Dataset

In this experiment, Yitong dataset is utilized to verify the effectiveness of the proposed method.

After each iteration during multi-CNNs bootstrap, the absorbed data with consistent label will enlarge the training subsets. To confirm this trend, the cumulative ratios of consistent label data number to size of A_{extra} corresponding to 6 iterations are shown in Fig. 5. The gradually increased ratios can been observed from this figure.

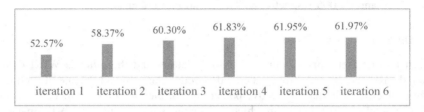

Fig. 5. The cumulative ratio of consistent label data number to size of A_{extra} after each iteration.

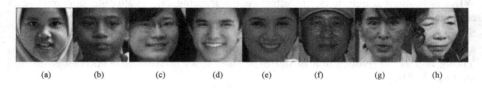

Fig. 6. Samples in Yitong dataset.

We randomly choose several testing images shown in Fig. 6 to demonstrate the effectiveness of our proposed method. The corresponding results are listed in Table 2. The $model_{noise}$ denotes the model trained using original Yitong dataset and $model_{reduced}$ denotes the model trained using Yitong dataset with reduced label noise. Table 2 shows that for most cases, the classification confidences obtained by $model_{reduced}$ are higher than those obtained by $model_{noise}$. In particular, the pairs of data emphasized in bold validate the significant advantage of $model_{reduced}$ over $model_{noise}$ for age estimation.

We also test the performance of $model_{noise}$ and $model_{reduced}$ on testing set. The results are listed in Table 3.

The results indicate that the proposed method actually has an effect for improving performance.

Table 2. Classification results obtained by $model_{noise}$ and $model_{reduced}$ for samples shown in Fig. 6.

Index	$model_{noise}$		$model_{reduced}$	
	Age interval	Probability	Age interval	Probability
(a)	0–15	**0.8335**	0–15	**0.9819**
(b)	0–15	0.9998	0–15	1.0000
(c)	16–25	**0.5357**	16–25	**0.9985**
(d)	16–25	0.9839	16–25	0.9971
(e)	16–25	**0.7088**	16–25	**0.9867**
(f)	41–55	**0.5828**	41–55	**0.9623**
(g)	56–70	0.9508	56–70	0.9630
(h)	56–70	0.9837	56–70	0.9930

Table 3. The accuracy of age classification for Yitong

$model_{noise}$	$model_{reduced}$
48.86%	**49.48%**

4.4 Experimental Results for Yitong-WIKI Dataset

While the above experimental results validate the effectiveness of our method, the improvement is not evident. We think that two factors have affected the testing results: One is the initial subsets option and the other is the testing set option. The label noise in former influences the performance of the proposed method and the label noise in latter influences the evaluation of the proposed method. We notice that the biological age labels of WIKI are objective so the label quality can be ensured. Thus, in this experiment, we evaluate the proposed method on testing samples chosen from WIKI dataset. In addition, the initial training subsets are also chosen from WIKI dataset. However, the training set except initial subsets still comes from Yitong dataset. So we name the combined dataset as Yitong-WIKI dataset. Specifically, 848 images and 23255 images are chosen from WIKI dataset as initial subsets and testing set respectively. Table 4 has listed the sample numbers in different age intervals of Yitong-WIKI dataset.

Table 4. Sample numbers in different age intervals of Yitong-WIKI.

	0–15	16–25	26–40	41–55	56–70	Total
Training set	1592	2368	2496	2216	1784	10456
Testing set	221	6299	9537	4572	2626	23255

The results in Table 5 indicate the essential roles of initial subsets as when the initial subsets are chosen from WIKI, the accuracy is improved approximately 10% for both $model_{noise}$ and $model_{reduced}$. On the other hand, the using of WIKI testing set highlights the advantage of $model_{reduced}$ over $model_{noise}$ for the improvement obtained

Table 5. The accuracy of age classification for Yitong-WIKI using $model_{noise}$ $model_{reduced}$.

Initial subset	$model_{noise}$	$model_{reduced}$
WIKI	38.25%	**47.82%**
Yitong	29.25%	33.57%

by $model_{reduced}$ has been more than 10% when the initial subsets are chosen from WIKI. The results confirm the effectiveness of our proposed multi-CNNs bootstrap against label noise.

5 Conclusion

Since the age labels produced by observing a facial image depend on subjective perception and are usually provided by a diversity of amateur users, there inevitably exists inappropriate labels. Most of works identify the mislabeled examples and then remove them before training. While the idea is straightforward, it introduces a serious wasting of training data. In this paper, we investigate a multi-CNNs bootstrap framework that the generalization of an ensemble of CNNs is increased gradually by a bootstrap way and the eventual multi-CNNs is employed to correct the improper labels in a satisfied accuracy. The experimental results have demonstrated the effectiveness of the proposed method on an age estimation task. In the future, we will apply the multi-CNNs bootstrap against label noise to other tasks, such as age regression, attribute analysis and general image classification.

Acknowledgment. This work is supported by Shanghai Municipal Natural Science Foundation under Grant No. 16ZR1411100.

References

1. Huerta, I., Fernández, C., et al.: A deep analysis on age estimation. Pattern Recogn. Lett. **68**(2), 239–249 (2015)
2. LeCun, Y., Boser, B., et al.: Backpropagation applied to handwritten zip code recognition. Neural Comput. **1**(4), 541–551 (1989)
3. Rajmadhan, E., Goldgof, D., Hall, L.: Finding label noise examples in large scale datasets. In: Proceedings of the IEEE International Conference on Systems Man and Cybernetics (SMC), Banff, AB, Canada, pp. 2420–2424 (2017)
4. Yang, P., Ormerod, J., et al.: AdaSampling for positive-unlabeled and label noise learning with bioinformatics applications. IEEE Trans. Cybern. **99**, 1–12 (2018)
5. Wei, H., Zhu, Q., et al.: Improved label noise identification by exploiting unlabeled data. In: Proceedings of the International Conference on Security, Pattern Analysis, and Cybernetics (SPAC), Shenzhen, pp. 284–289 (2017)
6. Krawczyk, B., Sáez, J., Woźniak, M.: Tackling label noise with multi-class decomposition using fuzzy one-class support vector machines. In: IEEE International Conference on Fuzzy Systems, pp. 915–922 (2016)

7. Sukhbaatar, S., Bruna, J., et al.: Training convolutional networks with noisy labels. In: ICLR, pp. 1–11 (2015)
8. Xiao, T., Xia, T., et al.: Learning from massive noisy labeled data for image classification. In: Proceedings of the IEEE Conference on Computer Vision and Pattern Recognition, pp. 2691–2699 (2015)
9. Feng, J., Xu, H., et al.: Robust logistic regression and classification. In: Advances in Neural Information Processing Systems, pp. 253–261 (2014)
10. Hamid, I., Ali, F., et al.: Image classification and retrieval from user-supplied tags. Comput. Res. Repository (2014)
11. Azadi, S., Feng, J., et al.: Auxiliary image regularization for deep CNNs with noisy labels. In: ICLR, pp. 1–12 (2016)
12. Gamberger, D., Lavrac, N., Groselj, C.: Experiments with noise filtering in a medical domain. In: Proceedings of the 16th International Conference on Machine Learning (ICML), Bled, Slovenia, pp. 143–151 (1999)
13. Parkhi, O.M., Vedaldi, A., Zisserman, A.: Deep face recognition. In: BMVC, vol. 1, no. 3, p. 6 (2015)
14. Jia, Y., Shelhamer, E., Donahue, J., et al.: Caffe: convolutional architecture for fast feature embedding. In: Proceedings of the 22nd ACM international conference on Multimedia, pp. 675–678. ACM, Orlando (2014)
15. Rothe, R., Timofte, R., et al.: Deep expectation of real and apparent age from a single image without facial landmarks. Int. J. Comput. Vis. **126**(2–4), 144–157 (2018)
16. Schroff, F., Kalenichenko, D., Philbin, J.: FaceNet: a unified embedding for face recognition and clustering. In: The IEEE Conference on Computer Vision and Pattern Recognition (CVPR), pp. 815–823 (2015)

Real-Time Semantic Mapping of Visual SLAM Based on DCNN

Xudong Chen, Yu Zhu[✉], Bingbing Zheng, and Junjian Huang

School of Information Science and Engineering,
East China University of Science and Technology, Shanghai, China
zhuyu@ecust.edu.cn

Abstract. Visual SLAM (Simultaneous Localization and Mapping) has been widely used in location and path planning of unmanned systems. However, the map created by visual SLAM system only contain low-level information. The unmanned system can work better if high-level semantic information is included. In this paper, we proposed a visual semantic SLAM method using DCNN (Deep Convolution Neural Network). The network is composed of feature extraction, multi-scale process and classification layers. We apply atrous convolution to GoogLeNet for feature extraction to increase the speed of network and to increase the resolution of the feature map. Spatial pyramid pooling is used in multi-scale process and Softmax is used in classification layers. The results reveals that the mIoU of our network on PASCAL 2012 is 0.658 and it takes 101 ms to infer an image with the size of 256×212 on NVIDIA Jetson TX2 embedded module, which can be used in real-time visual SLAM.

Keywords: Visual SLAM · Semantic mapping · Atrous convolution · Real-time · Embedded system

1 Introduction

Unmanned systems such as robot and unmanned aircraft have been widely used in daily life. The basic technology used in those systems is SLAM (Simultaneous Localization and Mapping), which uses the information obtained by sensors to locate the system and create the map of surrounding environment. SLAM using visual sensors such as camera is called visual SLAM. The first visual SLAM method is proposed by Davison in 2007, called MonoSLAM [1, 2]. It uses monocular camera and compute robot location through EKF (Extended Kalman Filter). Later, PTAM [3], ORB-SLAM [4] and other SLAM methods [5–8] are proposed.

The mainly used SLAM method only takes low-level information, such as distance and color, into consideration when creating the map. However, high-level information, such as semantic information, can help the unmanned system to move and serve better in the environment. [9] applies a pop-up 3D plane model to each image to obtain layout of the scene.

Semantic information of an image can be obtained by DCNN (Deep Convolution Neural Network), since DCNN has achieved great success in image classification [10–12], object detection [13–15] and semantic segmentation task [16, 17]. [18] applies

© Springer Nature Singapore Pte Ltd. 2019
G. Zhai et al. (Eds.): IFTC 2018, CCIS 1009, pp. 194–204, 2019.
https://doi.org/10.1007/978-981-13-8138-6_16

CNN to predict the depth map of an image and the semantic label. Despite the great performance of DCNN, the time consumed on inference is usually up to several seconds because of the depth of the network and the amount of calculation, which makes it hard to be applied in the real-time SLAM task on embedded system or mobile devices.

In this paper, we proposed a visual semantic SLAM method, as illustrated in Fig. 1. The input RGB image and depth image collected by RGB-D camera is first sent to the visual SLAM part. We can get the key frames and the robot pose of each key frame. Then RGB image of each key frame is sent to the DCNN network for semantic segmentation. Finally, the segmentation result and the robot pose of key frames are combined to create the semantic map. Our method can realize semantic SLAM real-time on NVIDIA Jetson TX2 embedded module. The map created through our method is shown in Fig. 2.

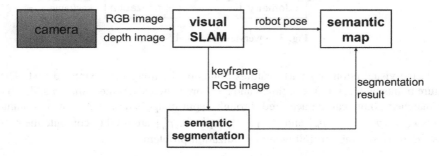

Fig. 1. Overview of visual semantic SLAM method

Fig. 2. Semantic map

2 Visual Semantic SLAM

Visual SLAM uses the images collected by camera to compute the pose of robot. Our SLAM method is based on ORB-SLAM, as illustrated in Fig. 3. The images are first sent to a visual odometry to get the preliminary pose, and then the pose is optimized through non-linear optimization. To further reduce the accumulative error, loop closing is also applied.

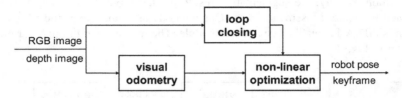

Fig. 3. Overview of visual SLAM

At the visual odometry part, features points of the image are extracted first. Then feature points between frame at time t and $t+1$ are matched. At the same time, depth of the matched points can be acquired through depth image. After that, matched feature points $\boldsymbol{P}_t = \{p_1, p_2, \ldots, p_n\}$ and $\boldsymbol{P}_{t+1} = \{p'_1, p'_2, \ldots, p'_n\}$ are used to compute the robot pose $[\boldsymbol{R}, \boldsymbol{t}]$ by solving the following optimization problem

$$\min_{\boldsymbol{R}, \boldsymbol{t}} \left\{ \frac{1}{2} \sum_{i=1}^{n} \left\| p'_i - (\boldsymbol{R} p_i + \boldsymbol{t}) \right\|^2 \right\} \tag{1}$$

If the pose of the current frame changes greatly, the frame will be added to the key frame list for mapping.

At the non-linear optimization part, the pose of each key frame is optimized by solving the following optimization problem

$$argmin \frac{1}{2} \sum_{i=1}^{m} \sum_{j=1}^{n} \left\| z_{ij} - h(\boldsymbol{\xi}_i, \boldsymbol{p}_j) \right\|_2^2 \tag{2}$$

Here, z_{ij} is coordinates of point $\boldsymbol{p}_j$ in the image and $h(\boldsymbol{\xi}_i, \boldsymbol{p}_j)$ is coordinates of point $\boldsymbol{p}_j$ computed through the pose $\boldsymbol{\xi}_i$.

We can get the key frame image and the pose of key frame through visual SLAM above. Map created by traditional visual SLAM use the color information and the pose of the key frame. However, the semantic information of the key frame is also needed to get semantic map in visual semantic SLAM. The semantic map not only covers spatial coordinate and color of the point but also contains semantic information of it, which means what object the point is. We propose the DCNN network in Sect. 3 for semantic segmentation.

3   Semantic Segmentation

We use DCNN for semantic segmentation task. The import image is first fed to the feature extraction network to get feature maps. Then the output feature maps pass through the multi-scale part. Finally, feature maps of different scales are fed into convolutional layers for classification. Figure 4 illustrates the structure of our network.

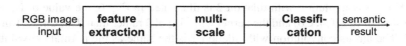

Fig. 4. Overview of the semantic segmentation network

3.1   Feature Extraction

There are two problems of applying DCNN for semantic segmentation for real-time mapping in SLAM. First, deep convolution neural networks are often very deep with many parameters so that it takes a long time to infer one image. Second, with the operation of convolution and pooling, the spatial resolution of the image decrease rapidly which is advantageous in classification task but disadvantageous in semantic segmentation task.

For the former problem, we use the architecture of GoogLeNet [11]. The core part in GoogLeNet is the inception module, as illustrated in Fig. 5. This module replaces the conv-pool layers. The convolution layers with the same spatial size (i.e. 3×3) are replaced by several convolution layers with different spatial size (i.e. 1×1, 3×3 and 5×5) so that the output feature map can represent the features from different resolutions. In addition, the 1×1 kernel helps to combine the information at the same spatial place in different channels. With the help of this module, features can be better extracted with fewer layer and fewer parameters. To further increase the speed of the net, the naïve net is improved as illustrated in Fig. 5(right). 1×1 convolutions are added before 3×3 and 5×5 convolutions. If the output size of the previous layer is $112 \times 112 \times 64$, the output size will become $112 \times 112 \times 256$ through 256 5×5 kernels with the parameters of $64 \times 5 \times 5 \times 256$. However, if 32 1×1 convolutions are added, the parameters will decrease to $64 \times 1 \times 1 \times 32 + 32 \times 5 \times 5 \times 256$, which is almost half of the naïve one.

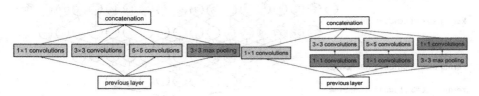

Fig. 5. Inception module (Left: naïve inception module, Right: improved inception module)

For the latter problem, we apply atrous convolution or dilated convolution proposed in [19] to GoogLeNet. Atrous convolution can be computed as following

$$y(i) = \sum_j x(i + d \times j) w(j) \tag{3}$$

where $y(i)$ is the output signal at position i, x is the input signal, w is the filter and d is the dilation.

1D atrous convolution with dilation 2 is illustrated in Fig. 6, the value of B2 is the dot product of (C2, C4, C6) and the kernel with size of 3 rather than (C3, C4, C5) and the kernel. The atrous convolution with dilation 1 is the same as the normal convolution.

We view the operation of pooling as the similar operation of convolution in which the kernel size is the same and the pooling operation treated as filter. We convert the normal convolution to atrous convolution as illustrated in Fig. 6, the original 1D signal is at the center in blue. The upper half is the process of the normal convolution or pooling operation with the kernel size and stride shown on the left. The lower half is the process of atrous convolution. We first change the stride of the first operation to 1, and then change the dilation of the second operation to 2 to insure the output has the same receptive field as the normal convolution. The receptive field of (B1, B2, ..., B5) is the same as that of (A1, A2, A3), which is (1, 2, ..., 11) of the original signal, but with higher resolution. We can conclude that by changing the stride of precious layer from $stride_{old}$ to $stride_{new}$, all the dilation of the operation afterwards should be multiplied by $\frac{stride_{old}}{stride_{new}}$. The dilation of the current operation can be computed as following

$$\text{dilation} = \frac{stride_{old}^1}{stride_{new}^1} \times \frac{stride_{old}^2}{stride_{new}^2} \times \cdots \times \frac{stride_{old}^N}{stride_{new}^N} \tag{4}$$

where N is the number of the stride changed.

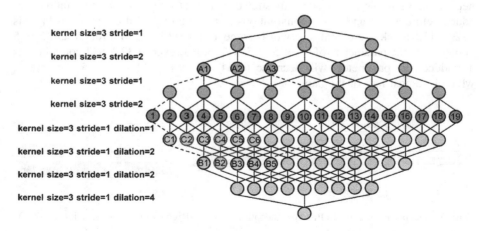

Fig. 6. Atrous convolution (Color figure online)

With the help of atrous convolution, we get the higher resolution output feature maps but do not change the receptive field so that we can use the pre-trained parameters.

We apply the method above to GoogLeNet. We change the stride of pooling operation after inception 3b and 4b and also change the input image size from $224 \times 224 \times 3$ to $321 \times 321 \times 3$ to get better semantic segmentation results when training. The architecture of GoogLeNet with and without dilated convolution are illustrated in Table 1, where changed part is shown in bold and italic.

Table 1. Architecture of GoogLeNet with and without atrous convolution.

Layer type	Without dilated convolution			With dilated convolution		
	Filter	Stride	Input size	Filter	Stride	Input size
Conv	$7 \times 7 \times 64$	2	$224 \times 224 \times 3$	$7 \times 7 \times 64$	2	*321 × 321 × 3*
Max Pool	Pool 3×3	2	$112 \times 112 \times 64$	Pool 3×3	2	$161 \times 161 \times 64$
Conv	$3 \times 3 \times 192$	1	$56 \times 56 \times 64$	$3 \times 3 \times 192$	1	$81 \times 81 \times 64$
Max Pool	Pool 3×3	2	$56 \times 56 \times 192$	Pool 3×3	2	$81 \times 81 \times 192$
Inception (3a)		1	$28 \times 28 \times 192$		1	$41 \times 41 \times 192$
Inception (3b)		1	$28 \times 28 \times 256$		1	$41 \times 41 \times 256$
Max Pool	Pool 3×3	2	$28 \times 28 \times 480$	Pool 3×3	*1*	$41 \times 41 \times 480$
Inception (4a)		1	$14 \times 14 \times 480$	*dilation = 2* *Pool = 5 × 5*	1	$41 \times 41 \times 480$
Inception (4b)		1	$14 \times 14 \times 512$	*dilation = 2* *Pool = 5 × 5*	1	$41 \times 41 \times 512$
Inception (4c)		1	$14 \times 14 \times 512$	*dilation = 2* *Pool = 5 × 5*	1	$41 \times 41 \times 512$
Inception (4d)		1	$14 \times 14 \times 512$	*dilation = 2* *Pool = 5 × 5*	1	$41 \times 41 \times 512$
Inception (4e)		1	$14 \times 14 \times 528$	*dilation = 2* *Pool = 5 × 5*	1	$41 \times 41 \times 528$
Max Pool	Pool 3×3	2	$14 \times 14 \times 832$	*Pool 5 × 5*	*1*	$41 \times 41 \times 832$
Inception (5a)		1	$7 \times 7 \times 832$	*dilation = 4* *Pool = 9 × 9*	1	$41 \times 41 \times 832$
Inception (5b)		1	$7 \times 7 \times 832$	*dilation = 4* *Pool = 9 × 9*	1	$41 \times 41 \times 832$
Output			$7 \times 7 \times 1024$			$41 \times 41 \times 1024$

3.2 Multi-scale

We use spatial pyramid pooling to capture multi-scale context, as illustrated in Fig. 7. The feature maps output from the feature extraction part are convoluted with kernels of different sizes, and then concatenated together.

We also use atrous convolution for spatial pyramid pooling, as illustrated in Fig. 8. We use the kernel of size 3×3 with dilation 6, 12, 18 and 24 to get kernels of different sizes. All these feature maps are concatenated together and convoluted with a 1×1 kernel to get the final feature maps.

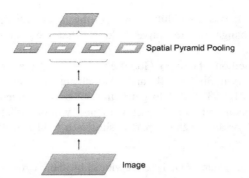

Fig. 7. Spatial pyramid pooling

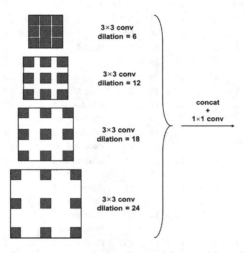

Fig. 8. Atrous convolution for spatial pyramid pooling

3.3   Classification

We fix the input image size to $321 \times 321 \times 3$ so that the output feature map size is 41×41 with n channels, where n is the number of classes. We use one-hot label with size $41 \times 41 \times n$, and convert it to the $n \times 1681$ matrix. The j-th row k-th column of the matrix is denoted as a_j^k. The output feature map is also convert to the $n \times 1681$ matrix and the j-th row k-th column of the matrix is denoted as y_j^k. We use Softmax loss as following

$$p_j^k = \frac{exp\left(a_j^k\right)}{\sum_{i=1}^{n} exp(a_i^k)} \tag{5}$$

$$loss = -\sum_{k=1}^{1681} \sum_{j=1}^{n} y_j^k log\left(p_j^k\right)$$ (6)

Because of the one-hot structure, the loss matrix is sparse. We only need to calculate 41×41 gradients, which is the spatial size of the output feature map.

4 Experimental Results

We test our network on PASCAL VOC 2012 dataset. The training set has 10582 images and the validation set has 1449 images. We compare our result with [19]. The feature extraction network of our net is GoogLeNet with atrous convolution applied while in [19] the feature extraction network is ResNet with atrous convolution applied. The result of segmentation is shown in Fig. 9. The visualization results obtained through our network can reveal the semantic information of the input image with a little decrease in mIoU but three times increase in speed, as shown in Table 2.

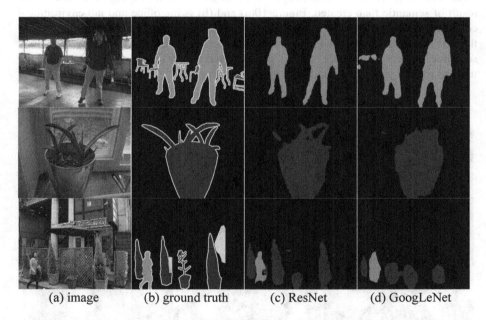

| (a) image | (b) ground truth | (c) ResNet | (d) GoogLeNet |

Fig. 9. Comparisons of results of different networks on semantic segmentation

We test our network on PASCAL VOC 2012 validation set. The input size is the original image size. The mean IoU of validation images is shown in Table 2. We also test the time consumed on inferring one image on NVIDIA Jetson TX2 embedded module with different input image sizes since the input image size can be changed when inferring. The result is also shown in Table 2.

Table 2. Comparisons of performance of different networks on semantic segmentation

Feature extraction network	mIoU	Time consume on Jetson TX2		
		256×212	321×321	640×480
ResNet101	0.749	0.311 s	0.527 s	1.126 s
GoogLeNet	0.658	0.101 s	0.168 s	0.425 s

The result shows that ResNet feature extraction layer has better result on semantic segmentation task, but the time consumed for inferring a 256×212 image is over 300 ms, which is not suitable for real-time task. The GoogLeNet feature extraction layer takes about 100 ms to infer a 256×212 image and has the mIoU of 0.658. By changing the extraction network from ResNet to GoogLeNet, the speed on inference is increased with not so much accuracy decrease so that our network can be used in the real-time visual SLAM task.

We applied our visual semantic SLAM method to the RGB-D images collected by a robot with RGB-D camera and images in TUM RGB-D dataset. Figure 10 shows the result of semantic map created. Figure 10(a) and (b) is the office and lab environment collected by camera, while Fig. 10(c) is from TUM dataset. We compare our result in the first row with the map without semantic information in the second row. The main semantic objects indoor are chairs, people, green plants and monitors, which are marked in red, pink, green and blue respectively.

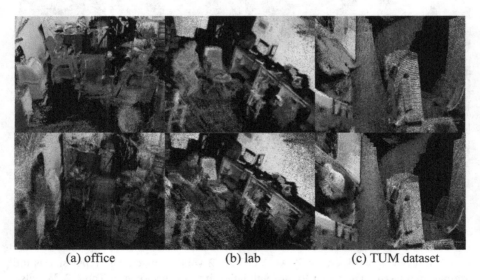

(a) office   (b) lab   (c) TUM dataset

Fig. 10. Semantic map created by visual SLAM. (First row: Semantic map, Second row: Map without semantic information) (Color figure online)

5   Conclusion

We have developed a visual semantic SLAM method which can understand the surrounding environment by adding semantic segmentation DCNN into visual SLAM process. The semantic segmentation network can do segmentation task real-time and has the acceptable mIoU. By understanding the environment around while SLAM, the unmanned system can have better implementations.

Acknowledgment. The authors greatly appreciate the financial supports of Shanghai Science and Technology Committee under Grant 17DZ1100808 and 17DZ1100803 and Shanghai Aerospace Science and Technology Innovation Fund under Grand SAST2016096.

References

1. Davison, A.J.: Real-time simultaneous localisation and mapping with a single camera. In: IEEE International Conference on Computer Vision, p. 1403. IEEE Computer Society (2003)
2. Davison, A.J., Reid, I.D., Molton, N.D., et al.: MonoSLAM: real-time single camera SLAM. IEEE Trans. Pattern Anal. Mach. Intell. **29**(6), 1052–1067 (2007)
3. Klein, G., Murray, D.: Parallel tracking and mapping for small AR workspaces. In: IEEE and ACM International Symposium on Mixed and Augmented Reality, pp. 1–10. IEEE Computer Society (2007)
4. Mur-Artal, R., Montiel, J.M.M., Tardós, J.D.: ORB-SLAM: a versatile and accurate monocular SLAM system. IEEE Trans. Robot. **31**(5), 1147–1163 (2017)
5. Engel, J., Cremers, D.: Semi-dense visual odometry for a monocular camera. In: IEEE International Conference on Computer Vision, pp. 1449–1456. IEEE Computer Society (2013)
6. Engel, J., Schöps, T., Cremers, D.: LSD-SLAM: large-scale direct monocular SLAM. In: Fleet, D., Pajdla, T., Schiele, B., Tuytelaars, T. (eds.) ECCV 2014, Part II. LNCS, vol. 8690, pp. 834–849. Springer, Cham (2014). https://doi.org/10.1007/978-3-319-10605-2_54
7. Forster, C., Pizzoli, M., Scaramuzza, D.: SVO: fast semi-direct monocular visual odometry. In: IEEE International Conference on Robotics and Automation, pp. 15–22. IEEE (2014)
8. Labbé, M., Michaud, F.: Online global loop closure detection for large-scale multi-session graph-based SLAM. In: IEEE/RSJ International Conference on Intelligent Robots and Systems, pp. 2661–2666. IEEE (2014)
9. Yang, S., Song, Y., Kaess, M., et al.: Pop-up SLAM: semantic monocular plane SLAM for low-texture environments. In: IEEE/RSJ International Conference on Intelligent Robots and Systems, pp. 1222–1229. IEEE (2016)
10. Simonyan, K., Zisserman, A.: Very deep convolutional networks for large-scale image recognition. In: NIPS (2015)
11. Szegedy, C., Liu, W., Jia, Y., et al.: Going deeper with convolutions. In: IEEE Conference on Computer Vision and Pattern Recognition, pp. 1–9. IEEE (2015)
12. He, K., Zhang, X., Ren, S, et al.: Deep residual learning for image recognition. In: IEEE Conference on Computer Vision and Pattern Recognition, pp. 770–778. IEEE Computer Society (2016)
13. Girshick, R.: Fast R-CNN. In: IEEE International Conference on Computer Vision, pp. 1440–1448. IEEE (2015)

14. Ren, S., He, K., Girshick, R., et al.: Faster R-CNN: towards real-time object detection with region proposal networks. In: International Conference on Neural Information Processing Systems, pp. 91–99. MIT Press (2015)

15. He, K., Gkioxari, G., Dollár, P., et al.: Mask R-CNN. In: IEEE International Conference on Computer Vision, pp. 2980–2988. IEEE (2017)

16. Long, J., Shelhamer, E., Darrell, T.: Fully convolutional networks for semantic segmentation. In: IEEE Conference on Computer Vision and Pattern Recognition, pp. 3431–3440. IEEE Computer Society (2015)

17. Zhao, H., Shi, J., Qi, X., et al.: Pyramid scene parsing network. In: IEEE Conference on Computer Vision and Pattern Recognition, pp. 6230–6239. IEEE Computer Society (2017)

18. Tateno, K., Tombari, F., Laina, I., et al.: CNN-SLAM: real-time dense monocular SLAM with learned depth prediction. In: IEEE Conference on Computer Vision and Pattern Recognition, pp. 6565–6574. IEEE Computer Society (2017)

19. Chen, L.C., Papandreou, G., Kokkinos, I., et al.: DeepLab: semantic image segmentation with deep convolutional nets, atrous convolution, and fully connected CRFs. IEEE Trans. Pattern Anal. Mach. Intell. 40(4), 834–848 (2018)

DDoS Attacks Detection Using Machine Learning Algorithms

Qian Li[1(✉)], Linhai Meng[2], Yuan Zhang[3], and Jinyao Yan[3]

[1] School of Information and Communication Engineering,
Communication University of China, Beijing, China
liqian0716@cuc.edu.cn
[2] Computer NIC Center, Communication University of China, Beijing, China
menglinhai@cuc.edu.cn
[3] Laboratory of Media Audio & Video, Communication University of China,
Beijing, China
{yuanzhang, jyan}@cuc.edu.cn

Abstract. A distributed denial-of-service (DDoS) attack is a malicious attempt to disrupt normal traffic of a targeted server, service or network by overwhelming the target or its surrounding infrastructure with a flood of Internet traffic. It has caused great harm to the security of the network environment. This paper develops a novel framework called PCA-RNN (Principal Component Analysis-Recurrent Neural Network) to identify DDoS attacks. In order to comprehensively understand the network traffic, we select most network characteristics to describe the traffic. We further use the PCA algorithm to reduce the dimensions of the features in order to reduce the time complexity of detection. By applying PCA, the prediction time can be significantly reduced while most of the original information can still be contained. Data after dimensions reduction is fed into RNN to train and get detection model. Evaluation result shows that for the real dataset, PCA-RNN can achieve significant performance improvement in terms of accuracy, sensitivity, precision, and F-score compared to the several existing DDoS attacks detection methods.

Keywords: DDoS attacks detection · RNN · PCA · Machine learning

1 Introduction

DDoS attack is a variants of DoS attack in which attacker uses authorized user IP address to attack on a particular victim. There are several types of DDoS attacks [1], namely, SYN-flood, ACK-flood, UDP-flood, Connection DDoS, DNS Reflect, ICMP-flood and so on. The main aim of the attackers is to jam the resources in order to deny services to the recipients. Attackers can use several strategies to achieve this goal, one of which is by flooding the network with bogus requests. DDoS attack is distributed in the way that the attacker is using multiple computers to launch the denial of service attack.

DDoS attacks pose an immense threat to the Internet, and many defense mechanisms have been proposed to combat the problem. A new study that tries to measure the direct cost of that one DDoS attack for IoT (Internet of Things) device users whose

© Springer Nature Singapore Pte Ltd. 2019
G. Zhai et al. (Eds.): IFTC 2018, CCIS 1009, pp. 205–216, 2019.
https://doi.org/10.1007/978-981-13-8138-6_17

machines were swept up in the assault found that it may have cost device owners a total of $323,973.75 in excess power and added bandwidth consumption [2]. It is urgent to do more in-depth research on DDoS attacks, and DDoS attacks detection as a very important part has become a hot topic of the research area.

Currently, there exist many statistical DDoS detection methods, such as network traffic statistics features based detection, source IP and destination IP addresses-based detection, port entropy values-based detection, and wavelet-based analysis [3–5], and destination entropy [6], etc. However, with the development of Internet technology, the DDoS attack model is changing faster and faster. Construction of a new statistical model requires a lot of time to build, so that it does not adapt well to the rapidly changing network environment. The statistical model has a single application scenario and a lot of complexity of building or upgrading the model.

In order to solve the above problems, the way of DDoS attacks detection through machine learning algorithms has gradually become the focus of research. The machine learning algorithm can find out the abnormal information behind the massive data, which is widely loved by researchers. Bilge et al. [7] use the flow size, client access patterns, and temporal behavior as features, and employ machine learning model to construct the difference between the normal network and the abnormal network to detect the Botnet Command and Control Servers. The advantage of the machine learning detection model is that new data can quickly update the detection model. There are still some deficiencies. Due to the high computational complexity of machine learning algorithms, it requires longer prediction time. The machine learning algorithms used to detect DDoS attacks do not consider the time correlation of traffic data.

Motivated by these challenges, this paper presents Principal Component Analysis-Recurrent Neural Network (PCA-RNN) to identify DDoS attacks. We first extract all relevant features to ensure our algorithm can cover all the attack types, which improves single application scenario problem. The features include four aspects, namely, flood feature, slow attack feature, flow time feature and web attack feature. Due to the large number of features selected in the first step, the computational complexity of the detection algorithm is largely increased. We handle this problem by reducing the dimension of input features. We use PCA as our dimension-reduction method, which is an efficient and flexible linear dimension-reduction method. Finally, since network traffic has short time correlation, it is beneficial if the detection algorithm could incorporate the short time features of the input data. In this way, we select RNN algorithm which has short-term memory and is timely efficient as our training module.

The rest of the paper is as follows: in the second part, we describe the related work of DDoS attacks detection; in the third Part, we propose our PCA-RNN detection model; in the fourth part, we conduct a series of comparative experiments and present the results in terms of accuracy and efficiency. We summarize our work in the last part.

2 Related Work

The basis for ensuring the normal operation of the network and having a high quality of service (QoS) lies in the effective detection of abnormal network traffic. The DDoS attacks detection methods at home and abroad are constantly researching and innovating, the common detection methods are statistical-based and machine learning, such as entropy detection, SVM (Support Vector Machine).

Statistical-Based Methods. Tao [3] uses entropy change to detect attacks in traffic. Once the detection system detects an attack, it will block or limit abnormal traffic and isolate the attacker's location. Information distance is employed to differentiate DDoS attacks from flash crowds. If the information distance in the suspicious flow is less than a given threshold, it will be described as a DDoS attack, otherwise it is a network transient congestion. Mousavi [4] proposes a method based on destination entropy to detect attacks. The paper uses the correspondence between source IP addresses and destination IP addresses to calculate entropy, sets the threshold by statistics to judge whether an attack has occurred. Relatively speaking, entropy is also not considered as a good measure [3] because it has relatively high false positive or false negative. Dong et al. [6] propose a new method which is designed to detect the DDoS attack and to further locate the compromised ports that have been connected by the malicious attackers. First, they classify the flow events associated with a port, then make a decision using SPRT (Sequential Probability Ratio Test), which has bounded false negative and false positive error rates. Zhang et al. [8] use ARIMA (Autoregressive Integrated Moving Average) method to detect DDoS. Kumar [9, 10] studies help understanding the relationship between the Smurf attack flow amplification factor and the original attack traffic.

Machine Learning-Based Methods. Kim et al. [11] determine whether an HTTP DDoS attack occurs by counting the difference between the average number of different destination domains, the average number of different requests, the average number of bytes of exchanged data, the average refer tree depth, and the similarity in the normal traffic and the abnormal traffic. Jacob et al. [12] present a system utilizes machine-learning to build graph-based model, and judge when an attack occurs through the difference between the normal network and the abnormal connection. BOTFINDER [13] detects infected hosts in the network only using high-level properties of the bot's network traffic. It uses machine learning to identify the key features of command-and-control communication, based observing traffic that bots produce in the controlled environment. Using these features, BOTFINDER creates models that can be deployed at network egress points to identify infected hosts.

The study found that the statistical detection method has high detection efficiency, but it takes a long time to build the model. Machine learning algorithm detection accuracy is high, but the detection efficiency is low.

3 Framework Design

The architecture of the proposed framework is illustrated in Fig. 1. It has three phases: extraction of features, feature preprocessing, detection model.

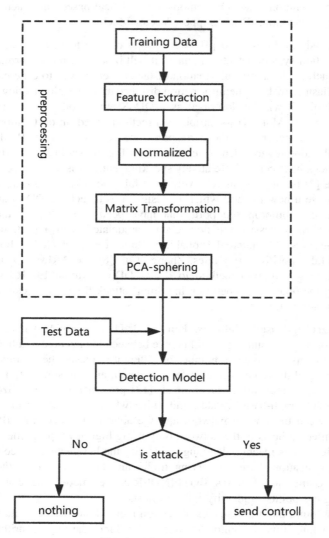

Fig. 1. PCA-RNN model

3.1   Extraction of Features

In order to more comprehensively understand the characteristics of network traffic, the most network traffic features are selected. As shown in Tables 1, 2, 3 and 4. We extract 34 features from four aspects: flood feature, slow attack feature, flow time feature, web attack feature. The 34 features generated by the four categories can basically represent most scenarios of a DDoS attack network. More eigenvalues lead to higher computational complexity and fewer eigenvalues cannot fully represent a DDoS attack, so we chose 34 eigenvalues. Because our features extract the core features of a DDoS attack, our model can work even if a new type of DDoS attack occurs.

Table 1. Flood features

Feature	Description
duration	length (number of seconds) of the connection
flag	normal or error status of the connection
src_bytes	number of data bytes from source to destination
dst_bytes	number of data bytes from destination to source
src_ip	source ip
dst_ip	destination ip
src_port	source port
dst_port	destination port
Wrong fragment	number of "wrong" fragments
urgent	number of urgent packets

Flood attack uses botnets to attack single node. Any flood attack is related to src_bytes. dst_bytes, src_ip, dst_ip, src_port, dst_port. Syn flood and ack flood are strongly associated with TCP flag, wrong fragment, urgent, etc. Hence, we choose the features in Table 1.

Table 2. Slow connection attack feature

Feature	Description
dst_host_count	count for destination host
dst_host_srv_count	srv_count for destination host
dst_host_same_srv_rate	same_srv_rate for destination host
dst_host_diff_srv_rate	diff_srv_rate for destination host
dst_host_same_src_port_rate	same_src_port_rate for destination host
dst_host_srv_diff_host_rate	diff_host_rate for destination host
dst_host_serror_rate	serror_rate for destination host
dst_host_srv_serror_rate	srv_serror_rate for destination host
dst_host_rerror_rate	rerror_rate for destination host
dst_host_srv_rerror_rate	srv_serror_rate for destination host

Slow connection attacks are very different from flood attacks. They mainly occupy ports or services for a long time to prevent legitimate users from accessing them by tcp connections. Based on this, we use the statistical information in 100 connection windows as the features of the slow connection attacks in Table 2.

Table 3. Flow time feature

Feature	Description
count	number of connections to the same host as the current connection in the past two seconds
srv_count	number of connections to the same service as the current connection in the past two seconds
serror_rate	% of connections that have "SYN" errors
srv_serror_rate	% of connections that have "SYN" errors
rerror_rate	% of connections that have "REJ" errors
srv_rerror_rate	% of connections that have "REJ" errors
same_srv_rate	% of connections to the same service
diff_srv_rate	% of connections to different services
srv_diff_host_rate	% of connections to different hosts

The RNN can find out the time correlation of network traffic, judging this connection through only one record is high randomness, so we construct a time window of the past two seconds to assist the RNN neural network to perform time correlation. The features are select as Table 3.

Table 4. Web attack feature.

Feature	Description
is_guest_login	1 if the login is a "guest" login; 0 otherwise
num_file_creations	number of file creation operations
hot	number of "hot" indicators
num_failed_logins	number of failed login attempts
logged_in	1 if successfully logged in; 0 otherwise

Application-layer DDoS attacks use script queries, upload and download files, and query databases to consume computing and bandwidth resources. This attack traffic is very similar to normal traffic. It cannot detect an attack through the header information, but it can judge the attack status through the data access system. Therefore, we extract the application layer features as shown in Table 4.

3.2 Features Preprocessing

We select 34 network features to describe the traffic, however, this would result in too many dimensions in the feature domain. Through the PCA matrix transformation, the number of principal components can be flexibly selected. Compared with Linear Discriminant Analysis (LDA) and other linear dimensionality reduction methods, PCA is more flexible to select the output dimension according to actual requirements, and PCA is more efficient than nonlinear dimensionless method, so we chose PCA as the dimension reduction method.

PCA is a statistical procedure that uses an orthogonal transformation to convert a set of correlated variables into a set of values of linearly uncorrelated variables. This transformation is defined in such a way that the first principal component has the largest possible variance (that is, accounts for as much of the variability in the data as possible), and each succeeding component in turn has the highest variance possible under the constraint that it is orthogonal to the preceding components. The resulting vectors are an uncorrelated orthogonal basis set. PCA is sensitive to the relative scaling of the original variables.

The following procedures illustrate the steps of data preprocessing:

(1) Samples normalization:

$$Y_j = \frac{X_j - \overline{X}}{\sigma_j} \tag{1}$$

Where X_j represents the sample of dimension j, $\overline{X}$ represents the average of the samples, σ_j represents the standard deviation of dimension j, Y_j represents the normalized sample.

(2) Correlation (covariance) matrix calculation: m represents the number of all samples, C represents correlation matrix.

$$C = \frac{1}{m-1} \sum_{i=1}^{m} (Y_j)(Y_j)^T \tag{2}$$

(3) Singular value decomposition of the correlation matrix: U is a $m * m$ matrix, S is a $m * n$ matrix, S is a $n * n$ matrix.

$$[U, S, V] = svd(C) \tag{3}$$

(4) Feature vector (corresponding to the largest K) selection:

$$U = \{u(1), u(2), u(3), \cdots, u(k)\} \tag{4}$$

(5) Feature dimensions reduction.

3.3   Detection Model

RNN is a class of artificial neural network where connections between units form a directed graph along a sequence. This allows it to exhibit dynamic temporal behavior for a time sequence. Unlike feedforward neural networks, RNNs can use their internal state (memory) to process sequences of inputs. This makes them applicable to tasks such as unsegmented, connected handwriting recognition or speech recognition.

As shown in the RNN cell in Fig. 2, t is set to indicate the state at time t, X_t indicates the input status at the time t, S_t indicates the output of the hidden layer at time t, and O_t indicates the output at time t, $\hat{y}_t$ indicates the estimated value at time t. The difference from the BP neural network is that there are two inputs to the RNN, one is the input at the current time t, and the other is the output of the state hidden layer at time $t - 1$. W, U, and V are parameters. Use the formula to indicate:

$$S_t = tanh(Ux_t + Ws_{t-1}) \tag{5}$$

$$\hat{y}_t = softmax(Vs_t) \tag{6}$$

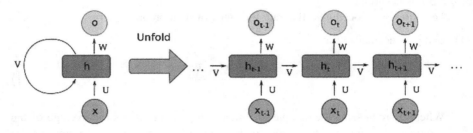

Fig. 2. Unfolded basic RNN

Due to network traffic has short time correlation, it is beneficial if the detection algorithm could incorporate the short time features of the input data. In this way, we select RNN algorithm which has short-term memory and is timely efficient as our training module.

Firstly, the detection model is optimized in terms of the number of layers, the number of nodes, the activation function, etc. and then the model is trained using dimensionality reduction data. Finally, the detection model is used for attack detection.

4   Experiments and Results

We evaluate our algorithm and compare with several existing detection algorithm using KDD data set [14]. The KDD data set is a 9 weeks network connection data collected from a simulated United States Air Force LAN, divided into identified training data and not identified test data. The test data and the training data have a different probability distribution, and the test data contains some types of attack that do not appear in the training data, which makes the intrusion detection more realistic.

We use accuracy, precision, sensitivity and F-score as the evaluation criteria. The accuracy in (7) provides the ratio between the attacks correctly classified to the overall attacks. Precision in (8) conveys the fraction of predictions that correct. Recall is the fraction of DDoS attacks that are correctly predicted in (9). F-score is the weighted average of sensitivity and precision in (10). Prediction time is the time it takes to predict the DDoS attacks on the test data.

$$\text{Accuracy(acc.)} = \frac{TP + TN}{TP + TN + FP + FN} \tag{7}$$

$$\text{Precision(pre.)} = \frac{TP}{TP + FP} \tag{8}$$

$$\text{Sensitivity(sen.)} = \frac{TP}{TP + FN} \tag{9}$$

$$\text{F} - \text{score} = \left(1 + \beta^2\right) \frac{pre \cdot sen}{\beta^2 pre + sen} \tag{10}$$

TP represents the number of true DDoS attack; TN represents the number of true normal traffic; FP represents the number of false DDoS attack; FN represents the number of false normal traffic.

This section experimented with the proposed method, and compared our approach to other machine learning algorithms, and common statistical-based methods.

Table 5. Performance of algorithms

Algorithms	acc	sen	pre	F1	Prediction time (s)
BP	0.9785	0.9785	0.9626	0.9702	0.7306
PCA-BP	0.9744	0.9744	0.9582	0.9661	0.6286
LSTM	0.9852	0.9852	0.9735	0.9791	7.0948
PCA-LSTM	0.9840	0.9840	0.9782	0.9785	1.7977
PCA-SVM	0.9865	0.9865	0.9833	0.9828	83.3326
RNN	0.9895	0.9895	0.9893	0.9872	3.9124
PCA-RNN	0.9872	0.9872	0.9810	0.9830	1.2162

Table 5 shows the results that our method achieves state of the art on all evaluation criteria. Since F-core is the weighted average of sensitivity and precision, we only compare F1, accuracy and prediction time here. We can easily notice that the prediction time can be significantly reduced through adding PCA in Fig. 3. In order to extract more attacks information, we select more features, a total of 34 features. However, more features also mean more input units, and the higher computational complexity, the more time it takes. After using the PCA algorithm to reduce the dimensions of the features, the original 34 features are converted into 6 features, and the prediction time is greatly reduced. Comparing the PCA-RNN and RNN algorithms, PCA-RNN prediction time significantly decreased, but the accuracy rate and F1 value only slightly decreased, in Fig. 4.

Because the SVM algorithm is more suitable for small datasets and takes too long time, it is not suitable for big datasets, so we only retain the experimental results of PCA-SVM. Although the prediction performance is not significantly different from that of PCA-RNN, the prediction time is 68.5 times as that of PCA-RNN. Overall, we have already demonstrated that PCA-RNN is a superior neural network algorithm in terms of accuracy and detection efficiency.

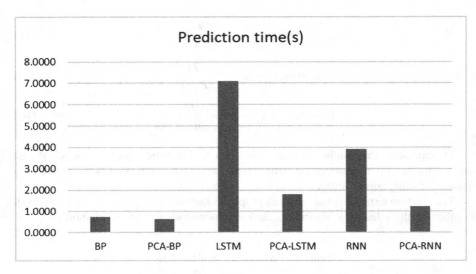

Fig. 3. Prediction time of PCA-RNN compared with existing methods.

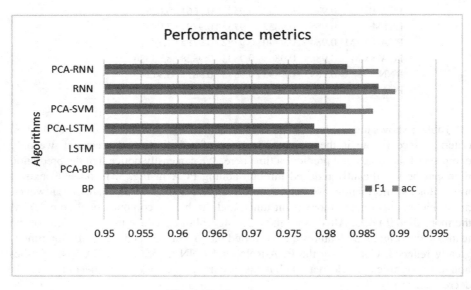

Fig. 4. Performance metrics

We also compare our PCA-RNN with several existing statistical algorithms. As can be seen in Fig. 5, statistical detection algorithms can only perform well on certain types of attacks, while our PCA-RNN algorithm shows good detection accuracy on all testing scenarios.

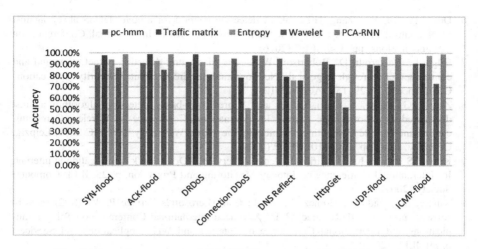

Fig. 5. Detection accuracy of PCA-RNN compared with existing methods.

5 Conclusion

This paper proposed a model to detect DDoS attacks with PCA-based feature reduction and RNN-based prediction method. We compared our PCA-RNN detection method with several existing DDoS attacks detection methods using KDD dataset Experimental results show that our PCA-RNN method has better detection accuracy, higher detection efficiency, and wider applicability. In the future work, we will test the algorithm through more real data set and try to study the inherent characteristics under the selected features.

Acknowledgement. The paper is sponsored by CUC Guangzhou Institute (Project No: 2014-10-05).

References

1. Douligeris, C., Mitrokotsa, A.: DDoS attacks and defense mechanisms: a classification. In: IEEE International Symposium on Signal Processing and Information Technology, pp. 190–193. IEEE (2003)
2. Study: Attack on KrebsOnSecurity Cost IoT Device Owners $323 K. https://krebsonsecurity.com/2018/05/study-attack-on-krebsonsecurity-cost-iot-device-owners-323k/
3. Tao, Y., Yu, S.: DDoS attack detection at local area networks using information theoretical metrics. In: IEEE International Conference on Trust, Security and Privacy in Computing and Communications, pp. 233–240. IEEE (2013)
4. Mousavi, S.M., Sthilaire, M.: Early detection of DDoS attacks against SDN controllers. In: International Conference on Computing, Networking and Communications, pp. 77–81. IEEE (2015)
5. Ren, X.Y., Wang, R.C., Wang, H.Y.: Wavelet analysis method for detection of DDoS attack based on self-similar. J. Commun. 2(1), 73–77 (2006)

6. Dong, P., Du, X., Zhang, H., et al.: A detection method for a novel DDoS attack against SDN controllers by vast new low-traffic flows. In: IEEE International Conference on Communications, pp. 1–6. IEEE (2016)
7. Bilge, L., Balzarotti, D., Robertson, W., et al.: Disclosure: detecting botnet command and control servers through large-scale NetFlow analysis. In: Computer Security Applications Conference, pp. 129–138. ACM (2012)
8. Zhang, G., Jiang, S., Wei, G., et al.: A prediction-based detection algorithm against distributed denial-of-service attacks. In: International Conference on Wireless Communications and Mobile Computing: Connecting the World Wirelessly, IWCMC 2009, Leipzig, Germany, June, pp. 106–110. DBLP (2009)
9. Kumar, S.: Smurf-based distributed denial of service (DDoS) attack amplification in internet. In: International Conference on Internet Monitoring and Protection, p. 25. IEEE Computer Society (2007)
10. Kumar, S., Azad, M., Gomez, O., et al.: Can Microsoft?s Service Pack2 (SP2) security software prevent SMURF attacks?. In: Advanced International Conference on Telecommunications and International Conference on Internet and Web Applications and Services, p. 89. IEEE (2006)
11. Kim, S.J., Lee, S., Bae, B.: HAS-analyzer: detecting HTTP-based C&C based on the analysis of HTTP activity sets. KSII Trans. Internet Inf. Syst. **8**(5), 1801–1816 (2014)
12. Jacob, G., Hund, R., Kruegel, C., et al.: JACKSTRAWS: picking command and control connections from BOT traffic. In: Usenix Conference on Security, p. 29. USENIX Association (2011)
13. Tegeler, F., Fu, X., Vigna, G., et al.: BotFinder: finding bots in network traffic without deep packet inspection. In: Co-Next, pp. 349–360 (2012)
14. KDD Cup Data. http://kdd.ics.uci.edu/databases/kddcup99/kddcup-99.html

Learn a Deep Convolutional Neural Network for Image Smoke Detection

Maoshen Liu[1,2](✉), Ke Gu[1,2], Li Wu[1,2], Xin Xu[1,2], and Junfei Qiao[1,2]

[1] Faculty of Information Technology, Beijing University of Technology,
Beijing 100124, China
LMSbjut@163.com
[2] Beijing Key Laboratory of Computational Intelligence and Intelligent System,
Beijing, China

Abstract. Smoke detection is the key to industrial safety warnings and fire prevention, such as flare smoke detection in chemical plants and forest fire warning. Due to the complex changes in smoke color, texture and shape, it is difficult to identify the smoke in the image. Recently, more and more scholars have paid attention to the research of smoke detection. In order to solve the above problems, we propose a convolutional neural network structure designed for smoke characteristics. The characteristics of smoke are only complicated in simple features, and no deep semantic structure information needs to be extracted. Therefore, there is no performance improvement in deepening the depth of the network. We use a 10-layer convolutional neural network to hop the features of the first layer of convolution extraction to the back layer to increase the network's ability to extract simple features. The experimental results show that our convolutional neural network model has fewer parameters than the existing deep learning method, and the accuracy rate in the smoke database is optimal.

Keywords: Deep learning · Deep neural networks · Smoke detection · Image classification

1 Introduction

The rapid and effective detection of smoke has become an urgent need for industrial automation and fire safety warning, such as torch black smoke detection in petrochemical fields and forest fire warning. Torch black smoke detection and

This work was supported in part by the 18 Connotation Development Quota - Key Discipline - Advanced Manufacturing Discipline Group - Faculty of Information Technology of Beijing University of Technology (Grant 040000514118032), the National Science Foundation of China (Grants 61703009), the Young Elite Scientist Sponsorship Program by China Association for Science and Technology (Grant 2017QNRC001), and Young Top-Notch Talents Team Program of Beijing Excellent Talents Funding (Grant 2017000026833ZK40).

© Springer Nature Singapore Pte Ltd. 2019
G. Zhai et al. (Eds.): IFTC 2018, CCIS 1009, pp. 217–226, 2019.
https://doi.org/10.1007/978-981-13-8138-6_18

pyrotechnic detection in traditional petrochemical plants are mainly through manual observation or sensors. The traditional manual observation method can not keep the rapid and effective identification of smoke for a long time without interruption due to limited human energy. Conventional smoke sensors, based on smoke particle sampling, have a severe delay in the detection of black smoke due to environmental influences, and cannot cover the detection area in all directions. Traditional smoke detection is difficult to meet today's industrial process and safety warning requirements.

In order to solve the above problems, image-based smoke detection methods have been extensively explored. Toreyin et al. [1] proposed a method based on spatial wavelet transform of current and background images to monitor the reduction of high-frequency energy of the scene to detect smoke based on the phenomenon that smoke affects the high-frequency information of the original background image. Gubbi et al. [2] proposed a novel method for smoke characterization using wavelets and support vector machines to identify smoke in video images. Yuan has done a lot of research on the identification of black smoke and made many contributions. Yuan proposed a fast accumulative motion orientation model based on integral image for video smoke detection [3], a video smoke detection by histograms of Local Binary Pattern (LBP) and Local Binary Pattern Variance (LBPV) based on pyramids [4], and a new smoke detection method by integrated learning based on shape invariant features on multi-scale partitions with AdaBoost [5]. Recently, Yuan et al. has proposed a image classification method based on high-order local ternary mode with local preservation projection [6].

Currently, most smoke detection algorithms are based on manually extracting image features to identify black smoke. The complex changes of the characteristics of the smoke makes the artificial smoke extraction image feature used to identify the image smoke to reach a certain bottleneck. Recently, deep convolutional neural network (CNN) have shown unmatched performance in computer vision tasks, breaking the performance bottleneck of traditional algorithms in many fields. Especially in the task of image recognition and image classification, such as convolutional neural networks in the ImageNet contest, the accuracy of the record is frequently refreshed. Several classic convolutional network structures in the ILSVRC (ImageNet Large Scale Visual Recognition Challenge) competition classification project, AlexNet [7], VGGNet [8], Google Inception Net [9] and ResNet [10], these four networks are arranged in order of appearance, while depth and complexity are in turn increment. The ILSVRC's top-5 error rate has made major breakthroughs in recent years, and the main breakthroughs are in deep learning and convolutional neural networks, and the dramatic increase in performance is almost accompanied by deeper layers of convolutional neural networks. Through the visualization of convolutional neural networks [11], researchers have discovered earlier layers in the network tend to capture low level features such as oriented bars and edges, i.e. As the network deepens, deeper layers of high-level semantic patterns, such as wheels and faces, continue to emerge, until the final convolutional layer, and more resolving patterns are captured by convolutional networks. When classifying on the ImageNet dataset, the data content is complex and there are many categories. Therefore, the more layers of the convolutional neural network, the more complicated the structure is, the better the effect can be obtained.

The above classification algorithms based on convolutional neural networks are all aimed at complex content and multi-category application problems. However, research on the identification of smoke is rare. In the identification of smoke, we only need to regard the task as a two-category problem, one is smoke and the other is no smoke. Recently, Yin et al. [12] proposed a deep normalized convolutional neural network (DNCNN) for image smoke detection. The network improves the convolutional layer in the traditional CNN to the batch normalized convolutional layer, effectively solving the problem of gradient dispersion and over-fitting in the network training process, thereby accelerating the training process and improving the detection effect, and performing training samples. The data is enhanced to solve the problem of positive and negative sample imbalance and insufficient training samples.

In this paper, a novel convolutional neural network for smoke detection is proposed. Aiming at the characteristics of smoke recognition as two classification tasks and smoke, mainly focusing on the complexity of simple features and not including the characteristics of deep semantic information, our network enhances the extraction of smoky features by using a skip-connection to preserve information of the preceding layers. Further, replacing the fully connected layer in the network structure with the global average convergence layer, on the one hand, the parameters are greatly reduced, and on the other hand, the risk of over-fitting is reduced. In the experiment, compared with several classic Deep CNNs, such as AlexNet, ZF-Net [11], and VGG16, the proposed algorithm has obvious advantages in performance and number of parameters. Compared with the recent DNCNN algorithm based on convolutional neural networks, the performance of our proposed algorithm is significantly improved and the parameters are reduced by nearly twenty times.

The following structure of the article is arranged as follows. Section 2 details the algorithm principle and parameter settings. In Sect. 3, compared with traditional algorithms and classical convolutional neural networks. Finally, we summarize the whole paper.

2   Proposed Algorithm

Today's classic convolutional neural networks for classification are designed for the task of multi-category and complex scenarios. The problem of directly applying the network to the identification of smoke is likely to cause over-fitting problems. At present, there are few research results on the use of deep learning methods to identify smoke. The recently proposed DNCNN network using batch normalization [13] and dropout [14] technology to reduce the over-fitting method is worth learning. Based on the complex and simple features of smoke and the lack of complex semantic structure, we designed a convolutional neural network structure for smoke recognition. The main idea is to improve the recognition of smoke by transmitting the features obtained by the first layer of convolution to the middle layer of the network to protect the simple features of the image. And by changing the fully connected layer to convolution and global averaging operations, the network parameters are greatly reduced, preventing over-fitting of the network.

2.1   Network Architecture

Our network structure is a convolutional neural network designed for smoke detection, so it is named the smoke detection convolutional neural network, abbreviated as SDCNN. The basic architecture of the network is shown in Fig. 1, and the specific parameters of the network structure are listed in Table 1. The following is a detailed introduction to the design of the network.

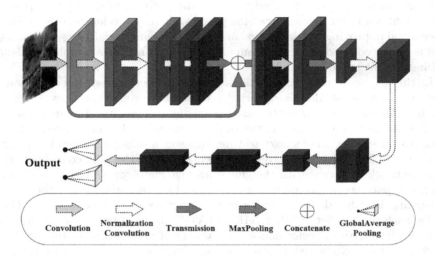

Fig. 1. The basic architecture of SDCNN. The input of the network is an RGB three-channel image, and the image features are extracted by the above operation, and finally two outputs are used to indicate the presence or absence of smoke. The cuboid in the figure represents the features extracted from each layer in the network, and the degree of abstraction of the features is increased by the color from light to dark. (Color figure online)

(1) Batch Normalization and Convolution: Convolution is a local operation that obtains local information of an image by applying a convolution kernel of a certain size to a local image area. Because the training process of the model is based on Mini-batch stochastic gradient descent, the adoption of Batch normalization (BN) can effectively speed up the training of the network and prevent over-fitting. However, batch normalization layers normalize the features of the convolution extraction so that the extracted features are freely constrained [16]. Therefore, the removal of BN in the first two layers of convolutional layers can effectively protect the characteristics of the image of smoke. In the second layer convolution, the convolution kernel size is set to 1, the main purpose is to obtain richer smoke characteristics by combining the features extracted by the front layer without changing the structure of the features.

(2) Skip-connection and Fusion: The network transmits the feature extracted by the first layer of convolution to the input of the first pooling layer through a skip-connection and merges with the features of the previous layer. Fusion is first by joining two features together using a concatenate operation, and

then converging the connected features using a convolutional layer with a convolution kernel size of one. The merged feature map contains the initial simple features and the detailed features of the multi-layer convolution extraction, and the redundant feature pixels are removed by the pooling process of the next layer.

(3) Classification Layers: The feature map obtained earlier requires further feature extraction and feature dimensionality reduction through two layers of convolution (kernel size of 3, number of 128), one MaxPooling process and two layers of convolution (kernel size of 3, number of 256). The general classification layer adopts a fully connected layer, which causes too many network parameters and is likely to cause over-fitting for the two-class task. Replacing the fully connected layer with a layer of convolution (kernel size of 1, number of 2) and a global averaging pooling layer can effectively reduce network parameters and prevent over-fitting and the network is not limited by the size of the input image. The values obtained by the two global averaging pooling get the probability of two class through the softmax function.

2.2 Image Preprocessing

The image preprocessing operations used in this algorithm mainly include: image normalization, and data augmentation. We use the min-max normalization method [17] for image normalization and its operation is calculated in pixels. The formula is defined as follows:

$$x_n = \frac{x_r - x_{min}}{x_{max} - x_{min}} \tag{1}$$

where x_r refers to a pixel value, x_{min} and x_{max} refer to the minimum and maximum values of the pixels in the image, x_n represents the pixel normalization result. We increase the number of smoke images in the smoke identification data set to match the number of smoke-free images by flipping and rotating the image to ensure the balance of the categories.

2.3 Network Training

The method of initializing the network weights is glorot-uniform distribution [18]. In the training process, we use the momentum trick [19] and learning rate decay to improve the training effect and prevent it from falling into local optimum. We train our proposed SDCNN with SGD [20] by setting momentum coefficient to 0.9, the initial learning rate to 0.01 and the learning rate decay coefficient to 0.0001. We set minibatch size as 96. The loss function used by our network during training is cross entropy. The cross-entropy formula is as follows:

$$E(o, \hat{o}) = -\sum_{n=1}^{2} o_n \log(\hat{o}_n) \tag{2}$$

where $[\hat{o}_1, \hat{o}_2]^T$ is category probability vector, $[o_1, o_2]$ is one-hot encoding label.

3   Experimental Results

Tensorflow [21] and Keras [22] are used in the experiment to implement smoke detection algorithms based on convolutional neural network. The experimental environment is the Windows 10 operation system running on a PC with Inter(R)

Table 1. Hyperparameter setting of network structure.

Layer	Layer Type	Hyper-parameters
Input	Input	Image size : 48 × 48 × 3
Conv1	Convolution	Filer size k1 × k1 : 3 × 3, Filer number n2 : 32
		Stride : s1 × s1: 1 × 1, Padding : same
		Activation function : ReLU
Conv2	Convolution	Filer size k2 × k2 : 1 × 1, Filer number n2 : 64
		Stride : s2 × s2: 1 × 1, Padding : same
		Activation function : ReLU
NC1	Normalization and Convolution	Filer size k3 × k3 : 3 × 3, Filer number n3 : 64
		Stride : s3 × s3: 1 × 1, Padding : same
		Activation function : ReLU
NC2	Normalization and Convolution	Filer size k4 × k4 : 3 × 3, Filer number n4 : 64
		Stride : s4 × s4: 1 × 1, Padding : same
		Activation function : ReLU
NC3	Normalization and Convolution	Filer size k5 × k5 : 3 × 3, Filer number n5 : 64
		Stride : s5 × s5: 1 × 1, Padding : same
		Activation function : ReLU
Fusion	Concatenate and Convolution	Filer size k6 × k6 : 1 × 1, Filer number n6 : 64
		Stride : s6 × s6: 1 × 1, Padding : same
		Activation function : ReLU
P1	Pooling	Pooling region size k7 × k7 : 2 × 2
		Stride : s7 × s7: 2 × 2
		Pooling method : MaxPooling
NC4	Normalization and Convolution	Filer size k8 × k8 : 3 × 3, Filer number n8 : 128
		Stride : s8 × s8: 1 × 1, Padding : same
		Activation function : ReLU
NC5	Normalization and Convolution	Filer size k9 × k9 : 3 × 3, Filer number n9 : 128
		Stride : s9 × s9: 1 × 1, Padding : same
		Activation function : ReLU
P1	Pooling	Pooling region size k10 × k10 : 2 × 2
		Stride : s10 × s10: 2 × 2
		Pooling method : MaxPooling
NC6	Normalization and Convolution	Filer size k11 × k11 : 3 × 3, Filer number n11 : 256
		Stride : s11 × s11: 1 × 1, Padding : same
		Activation function : ReLU
NC7	Normalization and Convolution	Filer size k12 × k12 : 3 × 3, Filer number n12 : 256
		Stride : s12 × s12: 1 × 1, Padding : same
		Activation function : ReLU
Conv3	Convolution	Filer size k13 × k13 : 3 × 3, Filer number n13 : 2
		Stride : s13 × s13: 1 × 1, Padding : same
		Activation function : ReLU
Output	Pooling	Activation function : softmax
		Pooling method : GlobalAveragePooling

Core i7-7820X CPU 3.60 GHz and an Nvidia GeForce GTX 1080. The smoke detection database [12] used in the experiment has four types of data sets with certain differences, named Set1, Set2, Set3 and Set4. Set1 and Set2 are used to test the performance of the network, with smokeless maps 831 and 817 and smoke maps 552 and 688, respectively. Set3 originally had 2,201 smoke maps and 8511 smokeless maps. In order to enhance the data for network training, 8804 smoke maps and 8511 smokeless maps were obtained. Set4 is used for network validation and has 2254 smoke maps and 8363 smokeless maps.

3.1 Competing Metrics and Evaluation Methodology

The algorithms participating in the comparison are mainly divided into two categories, including the traditional smoke detection method (HLTPMC and MCLBP), the convolutional neural network, AlexNet (2012 ILSVRC Champion), ZF-Net (2013 ILSVRC Champion) and VGG16, and the convolutional neural network designed for smoke recognition (DNCNN).

We use evaluation indicators [6] Accuracy Rate (AR), Detection Rate (DR), and False Alarm Rate (FAR) to quantitatively compare our proposed SDCNN algorithm with others. The formula is as follows:

$$AR = \frac{P_p + N_n}{M} \times 100\% \qquad (3)$$

$$DR = \frac{P_p}{M_p} \times 100\% \qquad (4)$$

$$FAR = \frac{N_p}{M_n} \times 100\% \qquad (5)$$

where M are the numbers of samples respectively. The subscript indicates the result of the algorithm discrimination. P_p and N_p are the numbers of correctly detected true positive samples and negative samples falsely classified as positive samples. A good algorithm has higher AR and DR and FAR is also very low.

3.2 Performance Comparison

First, by comparing with the traditional smoke recognition algorithm, the data used for comparison are Set1 and Set2. The comparison results are shown in Table 2. The optimal results have been bolded in the table. It can be clearly seen that the proposed algorithm has obvious advantages in all indicators. Second, it is compared with classical algorithms based on convolutional neural networks. The comparison results are shown in Table 3. The optimal results have been bolded in the table. It can be seen that the AR and DR indicators have obvious advantages compared with other algorithms, and the FAR remains at the same level as other algorithms. The parameters that SDCNN needs to learn are one order of magnitude less than other algorithms, and nearly 19 times less than DNCNN.

As shown in Fig. 2, by comparing with the DNCNN training process curve, it can be found that the two networks have the same accuracy for the training set, and the final convergence result of the DNCNN in the verification set accuracy is lower than the SDCNN algorithm. The above results can reflect that our proposed algorithm has better generalization ability and the advantage of preventing over-fitting than DNCNN.

Table 2. Comparisons with traditional algorithms.

Metrics		HLTPMC [6]	MCLBP [15]	SDCNN
Set1	AR(%)	96.46	97.47	**99.13**
	DR(%)	98.00	96.37	**99.04**
	FAR(%)	4.57	1.80	**0.84**
Set2	AR(%)	98.48	97.41	**99.00**
	DR(%)	99.56	96.65	**98.83**
	FAR(%)	2.44	1.95	**0.85**

Table 3. Comparisons with classical deep CNNs including AlexNet, ZF-Net, VGG16 and DNCNN (dedicated for smoke detection).

Metrics		AlexNet [7]	ZF-Net [11]	VGG16 [8]	DNCNN [12]	SDCNN
Input image size		227	224	224	48	48
Set1	AR(%)	97.18	97.18	97.48	97.83	**99.13**
	DR(%)	93.29	93.29	96.19	95.28	**99.04**
	FAR(%)	0.24	**0.24**	0.60	0.48	0.84
Set2	AR(%)	98.04	97.01	97.48	98.08	**99.00**
	DR(%)	96.07	94.33	95.05	96.36	**98.83**
	FAR(%)	**0.12**	0.73	0.48	0.48	0.85
Learnable parameters		60 million	60 million	120 million	20 million	**1.2** million

3.3   Discussions

By comparing existing studies, several spotlights are contained in our work. Firstly, Our convolutional neural network, designed for smoke detection, has a clear advantage over traditional artificial smoke extraction features. The characteristics of smoke are complexly combined with simple features such as texture, color and edges. The Skip-connection and Fusion module designed in our network can effectively extract the smoke features. Secondly, the SDCNN network has significantly improved performance compared to the classical convolutional neural network. It shows that the network designed for complex scenarios and multi-category tasks can not get good performance when it is directly migrated

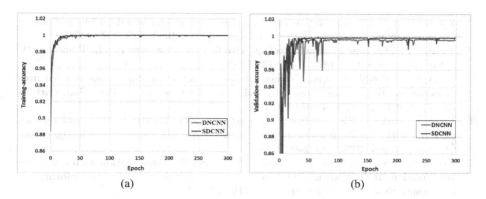

(a)   (b)

Fig. 2. The accuracy curve of the training and validation process of DNCNN and SDCNN. (a) Training process. (b) Validation process.

to the two-category task. Thirdly, compared with other smoke detection convolutional neural networks, the SDCNN uses the global-average-pooling instead of the full connection layer, which effectively reduces the network parameters, improves the generalization ability of the network and prevents over-fitting.

4   Conclusions

The rapid and effective detection of smoke has become an urgent need for industrial automation and fire safety warning. Traditional smoke detection is difficult to meet today's industrial process and safety warning requirements. Convolutional neural networks have made tremendous breakthroughs in computer vision tasks. However, research on the identification of smoke using convolutional neural networks is still relatively rare. We designed a novel convolutional neural network for the identification of smoke based on the characteristics of smoke. The use of the skip-connection and fusion module in the network effectively protects the transmission of simple features of smoke. In order to prevent the network from having too many parameters causing over-fitting, etc., proposed SDCNN uses the global-average-pooling instead of the full connection layer. Compared with the existing smoke recognition algorithm DNCNN, the network parameters have been greatly reduced, and the generalization ability has been significantly improved.

References

1. Töreyin, B.U., Dedeoğlu, Y., Cetin, A.E.: Wavelet based real-time smoke detection in video. In: Proceedings of 13th European Signal Processing Conference, September 2005, pp. 1–4 (2005)
2. Gubbi, J., Marusic, S., Palaniswami, M.: Smoke detection in video using wavelets and support vector machines. Fire Saf. J. **44**(8), 1110–1115 (2009)

3. Yuan, F.: A fast accumulative motion orientation model based on integral image for video smoke detection. Pattern Recognit. Lett. **29**(7), 925–932 (2008)
4. Yuan, F.: Video-based smoke detection with histogram sequence of LBP and LBPV pyramids. Fire Saf. J. **46**(3), 132–139 (2011)
5. Yuan, F.: A double mapping framework for extraction of shape-invariant features based on multi-scale partitions with AdaBoost for video smoke detection. Pattern Recognit. **45**(12), 4326–4336 (2012)
6. Yuan, F., Shi, J., Xia, X., Fang, Y., Fang, Z., Mei, T.: High-order local ternary patterns with locality preserving projection for smoke detection and image classification. Inf. Sci. **372**, 225–240 (2016)
7. Krizhevsky, A., Sutskever, I., Hinton, G.E.: ImageNet classification with deep convolutional neural networks. In: Proceedings of Advances in Neural Information Processing Systems, vol. 25, pp. 1097–1105 (2012)
8. Simonyan, K., Zisserman, A.: Very deep convolutional networks for large-scale image recognition, September 2014. https://arxiv.org/abs/1409.1556
9. Szegedy, C., et al.: Going deeper with convolutions. In: Proceedings of the IEEE Conference on Computer Vision and Pattern Recognition, pp. 1–9 (2015)
10. He, K., Zhang, X., Ren, S., Sun, J.: Deep residual learning for image recognition. In: IEEE Conference on Computer Vision and Pattern Recognition (CVPR) (2016)
11. Zeiler, M.D., Fergus, R.: Visualizing and understanding convolutional networks. In: Fleet, D., Pajdla, T., Schiele, B., Tuytelaars, T. (eds.) ECCV 2014. LNCS, vol. 8689, pp. 818–833. Springer, Cham (2014). https://doi.org/10.1007/978-3-319-10590-1_53
12. Yin, Z., Wan, B., Yuan, F., Xia, X., Shi, J.: A deep normalization and convolutional neural network for image smoke detection. IEEE Access **5**, 18429–18438 (2017)
13. Ioffe, S., Szegedy, C.: Batch normalization: accelerating deep network training by reducing internal covariate shift February 2015. https://arxiv.org/abs/1502.03167
14. Srivastava, N., Hinton, G., Krizhevsky, A., Sutskever, I., Salakhutdinov, R.: Dropout: a simple way to prevent neural networks from overfitting. J. Mach. Learn. Res. **15**(1), 1929–1958 (2014)
15. Dubey, S.R., Singh, S.K., Singh, R.K.: Multichannel decoded local binary patterns for content-based image retrieval. IEEE Trans. Image Process. **25**(9), 4018–4032 (2016)
16. Lim, B., Son, S., Kim, H., Nah, S., Lee, K.: Enhanced deep residual networks for single image super-resolution. In: The IEEE Conference on Computer Vision and Pattern Recognition (CVPR) Workshops, vol. 1, no. 2 (2017)
17. Gonzalez, R.C., Woods, R.E.: Digital Image Processing, 3rd edn. Prentice-Hall, Englewood Cliffs (2006)
18. Glorot, X., Bengio, Y.: Understanding the difficulty of training deep feedforward neural networks. J. Mach. Learn. Res. **9**, 249–256 (2010)
19. Bengio, Y.: Practical recommendations for gradient-based training of deep architectures. In: Montavon, G., Orr, G.B., Müller, K.-R. (eds.) Neural Networks: Tricks of the Trade. LNCS, vol. 7700, pp. 437–478. Springer, Heidelberg (2012). https://doi.org/10.1007/978-3-642-35289-8_26
20. LeCun, Y., Bottou, L., Bengio, Y., Haffner, P.: Gradient-based learning applied to document recognition. Proc. IEEE **86**(11), 2278–2324 (1998)
21. Abadi, M., et al.: TensorFlow: large-scale machine learning on heterogeneous distributed systems, March 2016. https://arxiv.org/abs/1603.04467
22. Chollet, F.: Keras. http://keras.io

Auditing Between Event Logs and Process Trees

Hongxia Li[1,2(✉)], Haixia Hou[1], Yuyue Du[2], and Zhi Liu[3]

[1] College of Science and Information,
Qingdao Agricultural University, Qingdao 266109, China
lovelymelody@163.com
[2] College of Information Science and Engineering,
Shandong University of Science and Technology, Qingdao 266590, China
[3] School of Information Science and Engineering,
Shandong University, Jinan 250100, China

Abstract. Targeting the auditing problem in process mining, this paper proposed a novel approach to carry out auditing between event logs and process trees. Firstly, all the possible problems in auditing of event logs and process trees were analyzed. Then, the set of first activity for a process tree (*FirstSet*) was defined to solve the sub-tree choice problem; and the set of following activity for a process tree (*FollowSet*) was proposed to solve the auto-matching problems. Then, *AnalyForm* and *Process tree auditing* algorithm were provided to audit event logs and a process tree. An example was given to illustrate the given algorithms subsequently. Four sorts of comparison were carried out between *Process tree auditing* and A* alignment algorithm: the computation time for a few traces and batches of traces, the computation time of different noise percent and length of traces. From the comparative experimental results, *Process tree auditing* algorithm was superior to A* alignment algorithm in batches of event logs auditing.

Keywords: Auditing · Process mining · Process tree · Petri nets

1 Introduction

Process mining is a young discipline based on process modeling and data mining. It aims at finding and improving the real process model from the recorded running data of the process (event logs). And there are three cases process mining technologies: process discovery, process conformance checking and process improvement [1].

Process alignment and auditing are the main content of process conformance checking in process mining. Conformance checking aims to find deviations between a process model and an event log of the same process. It can verify the quality of a process discovery algorithm and modify the model to accord with the real world [2, 3]. And so far, many research works have been carried out on process alignment. And there are the optimal alignment based on move step numbers [2, 4] and the optimal alignment based on cost [5] on the basis of whether or not to distinguish the importance of activities. Process decomposition method is used in process alignment for longer traces [6, 7].

© Springer Nature Singapore Pte Ltd. 2019
G. Zhai et al. (Eds.): IFTC 2018, CCIS 1009, pp. 227–237, 2019.
https://doi.org/10.1007/978-981-13-8138-6_19

But in some fields, such as a judicial or an economic field, event logs should fit its process model well. It means each event log should be audited to find abnormal behaviors according to its process model. Particularly, with the emergency of huge amounts of event logs, auditing should be carried out between batches of event logs and process model, not just for a few of traces. Current research about process auditing is still in the stage of concept model. And there has not a specific auditing method to solve it [8]. Thus, process auditing should be paid more attention to.

This paper presents an event log auditing method which can judge if each trace in event logs can fit its process model completely. The algorithm is proposed for dealing with batches of event logs of a process model representing as a process tree. Firstly, process trees, event logs and auditing between them are introduced. Then, *FirstSet* and *FollowSet* are introduced to solve the sub-tree choice and auto-match problem respectively. The auditing algorithm and an example are given subsequently based on above discussion. The experiments and conclusion are showed at the end of the paper.

2   Problem Definition

Due to focusing on the auditing between event logs and process models, we firstly give the related definitions. Then the definition of event log auditing is described.

2.1   Event Logs

Many PAIS systems recorded the whole operational procedure of business processes, and the recorded data are the basis of process mining. The organizational forms of these data can be given as following.

Definition 1 (*instance, trace and event log*). Let Σ be the set of all activities in models, then a run of a business process and its record of activities sequence are called an *instance* and a *trace* respectively. Trace t is a sequence of activities, and t can be empty sequence, i.e. $t \in \Sigma^*$. An event log L is the finite non-empty multi-set of traces, namely $L \in \mathrm{B}(\Sigma^*)$.

2.2   Model Representation

Many kinds of forms are selected to describe process models, and Petri net is an important process model descriptive form. Meanwhile, many other descriptive forms can be converted into Petri nets. A kind of Petri nets, block-structured workflow nets [9], is suitable to denote process models.

A process tree is an abstract representation of block-structured workflow nets. The definition of process trees is in the following.

Definition 2 (*a process tree*). An activities set Σ, a silent activity τ ($\tau \notin \Sigma$) and an operators $\oplus$ are combined to define a process tree M as follows.

- a is a process tree, where $a \in \Sigma \cup \{\tau\}$;
- Let $M_1, ..., M_n, n > 0$, be process trees and $\oplus$ be an operator, then $M = \oplus (M_1, ..., M_n)$ is a process tree. And $M_1, ..., M_n$ are the sub-trees of process tree M.

The operator set has four operators: operator $\times$ means exclusive choice, $\rightarrow$ means sequence, $\wedge$ means parallel (interleave), and $\circlearrowright$ means loop. For the operator $\circlearrowright$, the first sub-tree is loop body, and others are alternative redo parts.

2.3 Auditing Event Logs with Process Models

Given a process model N and its process tree M, let A (M) be the set of activities in M and $A(L)$ be the activities set of event logs in L, then auditing between event logs and process tree can be defined as follows.

Definition 3 (*auditing*). Auditing is to replay each trace in event logs L on the process model M represented by a process tree, and each *step* in auditing is a (x, y) pair:

1. If $x \in A(M)$, $y \in A(L)$ and $x = y$ then (x, y) is called synchronous move;
2. If $x = \tau$ and $y \in A(L)$ then (x, y) is called pending move;
3. If $x \in A(M)$, $y \in A(L)$, and $x \neq y$ then (x, y) is called abnormal move.

Definition 4 (*auditing success*). Auditing between a trace and a process model is successful if and only if each step of auditing is synchronous or pending move until the process tree and the trace completes at the same time.

3 The Problem in Event Logs Auditing

When replaying a trace on a process tree, sub-tree(s) should be selected to match the trace. And the selection of sub-tree(s) depends on its likelihood to conform to the trace. Moreover, auditing will end if sub-tree' first activity don't agree with corresponding activity of the trace. So, the first activity set of process sub-tree is importance in sub-tree selecting.

3.1 The First Activity Set of a Process Tree–*FirstSet*

For a process tree M, the construction of its first activities set *FirstSet(M)* can be expressed in the following.

```
Function FirstSet(M)
1 if M= τ then return {ε}
2 else if M=a then return {a}
3 For M do
4   if M =× (M₁,…, Mₙ) or M =∧(M₁,…, Mₙ), then
5     for 1≤i≤n FirstSet(M)← FirstSet(Mᵢ)
6     else if M = ↻(M₁,…, Mₙ), then
7          FirstSet(M)←FirstSet(M₁)
8       else if  M =→(M₁,…, Mₙ), then
9          FirstSet(M)  ← FirstSet(M₁) \{ε}
10    if 1≤j≤i-1,∀j, ε∈FirstSet(Mⱼ) then
11       FirstSet(M)  ←FirstSet(Mⱼ)\{ε}
12    if  1≤i≤n) ε∈FirstSet(Mᵢ) then  FirstSet(Mᵢ)←{ε}
13  return FirstSet(M)
```

Function *FirstSet(M)* showed that *FirstSet* of a process tree M could be constructed by each sub-tress's *FirstSet* and their operator.

According the construction of *FirstSet*, the following theorem can be obtained.

Theorem 1. Given a process model N and its process tree M, it holds that *FirstSet(M)* can be gotten and is certain.

Proof. Proof by induction on $D(M)$, which is the depth value of process tree M.

- Base cases: $D(M) = 0$ or $D(M) = 1$. Then $M = \tau$ or $M = a$. By the construction function of *FirstSet*, *FirstSet(M)* = $\{\varepsilon\}$ or $\{a\}$. Then, each *FirstSet* is certain.
- Induction hypothesis: for all process trees whose depth value $D(M_i)$, $1 \leq i \leq n$, less than or equal to k, *FirstSet(M_i)* is certain.
- Induction step: assume $D(M) = k + 1$ and the induction hypothesis. Then
  - Case $M = \tau$, see base case;
  - Case $M = a$, see base case;
  - Case $M = \oplus (M_1, ..., M_n)$ where $\oplus \in \{\times, \rightarrow, \wedge, \circlearrowleft\}$. Let $M_1, ..., M_n$ be the process trees whose depth less than or equal to k, that is, $D(M)$ less than or equal to $k + 1$. By the induction hypothesis, $\forall i, 1 \leq i \leq n, D(M_i) \leq k$, *FirstSet(M_i)* is certain. According to the construction method of *FirstSet(M)*, *FirstSet(M)* is decided only by *FirstSet(M_i)*, $1 \leq i \leq n$. Due to the certainty of *FirstSet(M_i)*, we can conclude that *FirstSet(M)* is certain.   □

3.2 The Following Activity Set of a Process Tree–*FollowSet*

Definition of *FirstSet* can solve the problem of which sub-tree should be selected to match the trace. But, the problem should be further analyzed when one trace $t = a...$ matches with its process tree $M = \rightarrow (M_1, ..., M_n)$, but $a \notin FirstSet(M_1)$.

If $a \notin FirstSet(M_1)$, it may not conclude that trace t don't conform to process tree M. According the definition of process tree, a process tree could be ε. Then, if $\varepsilon \in FirstSet(M_1)$, following activity of the process tree M_1 should be considered to match activity a. If the following non-ε activity equals to a, then ε matches with M_1, or else auditing fails. The following activity set of a process tree M_1 is written as *FollowSet(M_1)*. And it is called an auto-matching when a process tree M_1 matches with ε.

Let M be the process tree of a process model N, $M = \oplus (M_1, ..., M_n)$. Then, $M_1, ..., M_n$ are the sub-trees of M. Then, let *FollowSet(M)* equal to $\{\Diamond\}$. $\Diamond$ is a terminal mark. Therefore, the following activity set of a process tree is a set including and the activities in $A(M)$.

For a sub-tree M_i of M, its construction of *FollowSet* can be described in the following.

```
Function FollowSet(M_i)
1  If M =× (M_1,…, M_n)  then
2    FollowSet(M_i)←FollowSet(M) \{ε}
3  Else If M =→ (M_1,…, M_n) then
4    FollowSet(M_i) ← FirstSet(M_{i+1}) \{ε}
5    If for i+1≤j≤k ε∈FirstSet(M_j)  then
6      FollowSet(M_i) ← FirstSet(M_{k+1})\{ε}
7    If for i+1≤j≤n ε∈FirstSet(M_j)  then
8      FollowSet(M_i) ←{ε}
9  Else If M =↺(M_1,…, M_n) then
10   If i=1 then
11     FollowSet(M_i) ←FollowSet(M)
12     For 2≤j≤n FollowSet(M_i) ←FirstSet(M_j)
13   Else
14     FollowSet(M_i) ←FollowSet(M_1)
15   Else
16     FollowSet(M_i) ←FollowSet(M)
17 return FollowSet(M_i)
```

Function *FollowSet* showed that the *FollowSet*(M_i) can be worked out by *FollowSet*(M) and *FollowSet*(M_j) where $M = \oplus (M_1, …, M_n)$. And the following theorem holds.

Theorem 2. Given a process model N and its process tree T, M be the sub-tree of T or T itself, then *FollowSet*(M) can be acquired and is certain.

Proof. Let M be equal to $\oplus (M_1, …, M_j)$. Proof by induction on $n = D(T) + 1 − D(M)$, where $D(T)$ and $D(M)$ is the depth of M and T respectively.

- Base cases: $n = 1$, that is, $M = T$, then *FollowSet*(M) = $\{\Diamond\}$. So, *FollowSet*(M) is certain.
- Induction hypothesis: $n = k$, that is, $D(M) = D(T) − k + 1$, $(1 < k < D(T))$, *FollowSet*(M) is certain.
- Induction step: assume $n = k + 1$, that is, $D(M_i) = D(T) − k$, $(1 < k < D(T) − 1)$, where $M = \oplus (M_1, …, M_j)$ and the induction hypothesis. Then

- Case $M = T$, see base case;
- Case $M = \oplus (M_1, \ldots, M_n)$ where $\oplus \in \{\times, \rightarrow, \wedge, \circlearrowright\}$. Then, $D(M) = D(T) - k + 1$ and $M_1, \ldots, M_j$ be the process trees whose depth less than or equal to $D(T) - k$. By the induction hypothesis, $D(M) = D(T) - k + 1$, $(1 < k < D(T))$, $FollowSet(M)$ is certain. And according to Theorem 1, $FirstSet(M_i)$, $(D(M_i) > 0)$, is certain. By construction of $FollowSet(M_i)$, $(1 \leq i \leq j)$, $FollowSet(M_i)$ can be worked out only by $FirstSet(M_i)$, $(1 \leq i \leq j)$, and $FollowSet(M)$. Due to the certainty of $FirstSet(M_i)$ and $FollowSet(M)$, we can conclude that $FollowSet(M_i)$ is certain. $\qquad\Box$

3.3 Event Log Auditing Algorithm

Based on the above analysis, an auditing algorithm is proposed to replay a trace on a process model. For a process model N, its process tree M and a trace t, the algorithm can judge if a trace t fit the process model N well.

In the following algorithm, the related parameters and functions can be interpreted as follows.

a: the current activity to be matched;
$read(a)$: read next activity a in the trace t;
$LABEL$: an end marker;
$AnalyForm$: the analysis form of process tree M;
$AnalyForm(M, a)$ means the process tree or activity when process tree M confronts an activity a in trace t;

When $M = \oplus (M_1, \ldots, M_n)$ is to match with activity a due to $AnalyForm$, corresponding process tree is called to carry out the matching. In algorithm, terminal symbol $\Diamond$ and M are put into $STACK$ firstly, then next action depends on stack's top element X and a. If $X = a \in \Sigma$, it will be a synchronous move (X, a), and then next activity is read subsequently; if $X = a = \Diamond$, then auditing is successful; if X is not an activity, one process tree may be selected to match activity a according to $AnalyForm$.

```
Algorithm. Process tree auditing
Input: a trace t, the process tree M
Output: auditing result (Boolean: true, false)
1  Initialize STACK
2  push(◊); push(M)
3  read(a)
4  LABEL=True
5  While LABEL do
6    X=pop(STACK)
7    If X=a∈Σ then read(a)
8    Else If X=◊=a then LABEL=False
9    Else If AnalyForm(M,a)={M=⊕(M₁,…, Mₙ)} then
10     If ⊕=→ then push(Mₙ)…, push(M₂), push(M₁)
11     Else If ⊕=× and a∈FirstSet(Mⱼ) then push(Mⱼ)
12     Else If⊕=⊃ then
13       push(Y); push(M₁)
14       FLAG=True
15       While (top(STACK)≠Y and FLAG=True do
16         If pop(STACK) =a then read(a)
17         If (Y=top(STACK)  and a∈FirstSet(Mⱼ)) then
18           push(M₁), push(Mⱼ)
19         Else If (Y=top(STACK) and a∈FollowSet(M)) then
20           pop(STACK)
21         Else If (Y=top(STACK))
22           FLAG=False
23         End If
24     End While
25   Else
26         return False
27   End If
28 End while
29 return True //audit success
```

AnalyForm is mentioned in Algorithm Process tree auditing, and it can be constructed as follows.

Let $M = \oplus\ (M_1, \ldots, M_n)$ be a process tree, then performs the following operations for each sub-tree of process tree M:

1. If $a \in FirstSet(M)$, then put $M = \oplus\ (M_1, \ldots, M_n)$ in *AnalyForm(M, a)*;
2. If $\varepsilon \in FirstSet(M)$, then for all $b \in FollowSet(M)$, put the process sub-tree $M = M_i$ in *AnalyForm(M, b)*, where M_i makes $\varepsilon \in FirstSet(M)$;
3. No defined *AnalyForm(M, a)* is labeled *Error*.

According to algorithm *Process tree auditing*, we can judge if a trace fits its process model well. An example and comparative experiments are given in the following.

3.4   An Example for Process Tree Auditing Algorithm

A trace $t = abcbce$ and a process tree $M = \rightarrow (a, \circlearrowright(b, c), \times (d, \tau), \times (e, f))$ are exampled to explain the algorithm Process tree auditing. Let $M_1 = a$; $M_2 = \circlearrowright(b, c)$, $M_{21} = b, M_{22} = c$; $M_3 = \times (d, \tau), M_{31} = d, M_{32} = \tau$; $M_4 = \times (e, f), M_{41} = e$ and $M_{42} = f$.

Firstly, *FirstSet* and *FollowSet* are calculated. According to function *FirstSet*, *FirstSet*(M_1) and *FirstSet*(M) are equal to $\{a\}$. Similarly, other *FirstSet* of process trees can be calculated, for example, *FirstSet*(M_{32}) is $\{\tau\}$. Meanwhile, we can solve all of the *FollowSet* set, such as *FollowSet*$(M) = \{\Diamond\}$, *FollowSet*$(M_3) = \{e, f\}$, etc.

When replaying trace t on process tree M, because the activity a in trace t is an element of *FirstSet*(M) and it originates from M_1, M_1 is selected to match, then (a, a) is a synchronous move. (We describe the matching procedure briefly; in fact, there are operations of constructing and querying *AnalyForm*). Then, next activity b in trace t is read to be matched. Similarly, each activity of $bcbc$ forms synchronous move with process tree M_2. When e will be matched with M_3, $e \notin$ *FirstSet*(M_3), $\varepsilon \in$ *FirstSet*(M_3) and $e \in$ *FollowSet*(M_3) holds. So, (e, ε) is a pending move. Let M_3 auto-match with ε and e match with *FollowSet*(M_3), then auditing can continue to the next step. Repeat the auditing process, and trace t is audited successfully in the end.

4   Experiments

The source program in this section is developed with Visual C++ and the machine configuration is 2 GHz Quad Core processor, 16 GB memory with the Microsoft Windows 7 platform. The experiments read event logs in the form of text. And we compare Process tree auditing algorithm with A* alignment algorithm in [4]. A* alignment algorithm is a representative alignment algorithm which can find the optimal alignment between a trace and a given process model.

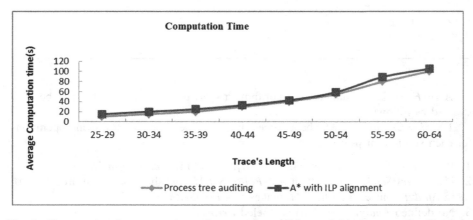

Fig. 1. Computation time comparison of process tree auditing and A* alignment for 50 traces

Dataset in [7] was used here for comparing two algorithms. A process tree could be constructed from the process model firstly. And then, an event log L was produced by running these process models 150 times. In Fig. 1, we compare computation time between Process tree auditing and A* algorithm for randomly selected 50 traces in log L with their lengths ranging from 25 to 64 activities. Then, an event log L_1 was formed by introducing some noises, such as randomly inserting and/or deleting some activities, in the base of log L.

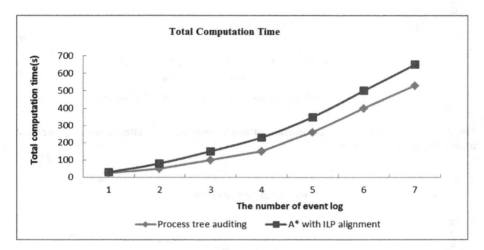

Fig. 2. Total computation time comparison of process tree auditing and A* alignment for batches of traces

From Fig. 1, the computation time of two algorithms increased with the increase of traces' length. None of them has obvious advantage than the other. In Fig. 2, 50 randomly selected traces in the event log L_1 formed a new event log. By comparing the total computation time of two algorithms, Process tree auditing algorithm was obviously superior to A* alignment with the increase of the number of event logs. The result was because each process model's *FirstSet*, *FollowSet* and *AnalyForm* were constant in Process tree auditing algorithm, whereas each product net is needed to construct for each trace in A* alignment algorithm.

In Fig. 3, the event log included 50 traces with noise and the traces' length from 25 to 29. The event log in Fig. 4 is similar to that of Fig. 3, but the length is from 30 to 34. From Figs. 3 and 4, we can see the computation time of Process tree auditing algorithm is much less than that of A* alignment algorithm with the increase of noise percentage and traces' length. It is because Process tree auditing Algorithm would end when an abnormal move occurs, whereas A* alignment algorithm would continue to align till the last activity.

From the experimental results compared with the A* algorithm, the proposed Process tree auditing algorithm is more suitable for event log auditing than the A* alignment algorithm. And when the batches of event logs are audited, the advantage of this algorithm is more obvious.

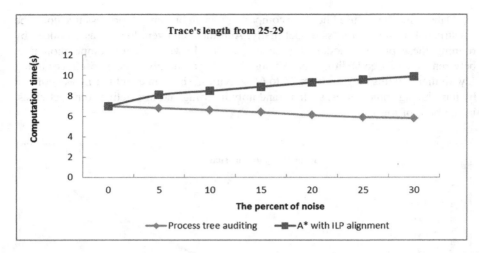

Fig. 3. The computation time comparison of two algorithms with different noise percent and trace's length from 25 to 29

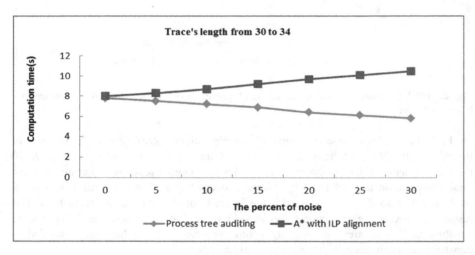

Fig. 4. The computation time comparison of two algorithms with different noise percent and the trace's length from 30 to 34

5   Conclusion

From the comparative experiments, Process tree auditing algorithm has the advantage in auditing batches of event logs which is fitting or nearly fitting the model well, because *FirstSet* and *FollowSet* are computed only once for a definite process tree regardless of diverse traces. Nevertheless, A* alignment algorithm have to construct a special product net and find the shortest path from product net for each trace and the process model. So, when batch of event logs compare with the process model, Process tree auditing in this paper is more efficient.

The computing time of Process tree auditing algorithm is much lesser than that of A* alignment algorithm when dealing with traces with noises. It's the major difference of alignment and auditing. And it can indicate Process tree auditing algorithm is suitable to auditing event logs.

Although Process tree auditing has some advantages than current algorithms, it has its limitations, such as it mainly deals with process models which can be translated into a process tree, only control-flow of the model is considered. Meanwhile, it is suitable for not so long traces. So, furthermore work will focus on auditing for arbitrary process models and any length's traces. And the auditing for the other aspects of process model, such as resource, time, will be carry out in the next step.

Except for monolithic replay, some work has been carried out about decomposing method in process alignment [6, 7]. But, how to decompose a process model is a bottleneck and limits its further application. Meanwhile, it has no obvious advantages when dealing with shorter traces.

References

1. Van der Aalst, W.M.P.: Process Mining: Discovery, Conformance and Enhancement of Business Processes, pp. 95–124. Springer, Heidelberg (2011). https://doi.org/10.1007/978-3-642-19345-3
2. Fahland, D., Van der Aalst, W.M.P.: Model repair-aligning process models to reality. Inf. Syst. **47**, 220–243 (2015). https://doi.org/10.1016/j.is.2013.12.007
3. Kharbili, M.E., De Medeiros, A.K.A., Stein, S., et al.: Business process conformance checking: current state and future challenges. In: MobIS 2008. LNI, vol. 141, GI, 008, pp. 107–113 (2008)
4. Adriansyah, A.A.: Aligning observed and modeled behavior. Technische Universiteitndhoven (2014)
5. Adriansyah, A.A., van Dongen, B.F., van der Aalst, W.M.P.: Conformance checking using cost-based fitness analysis. In: 5th IEEE International EDOC, pp. 55–64 (2011)
6. Verbeek, H.M.W.: Decomposed replay using hiding and reduction as abstraction. In: Koutny, M., Kleijn, J., Penczek, W. (eds.) Transactions on Petri Nets and Other Models of Concurrency XII. LNCS, vol. 10470, pp. 166–186. Springer, Heidelberg (2017). https://doi.org/10.1007/978-3-662-55862-1_8
7. Wang, L., Du, Y.Y., Liu, W.: Aligning observed and modelled behaviour based on workflow decomposition. Enterp. Inf. Syst. **11**(8), 1207–1227 (2017). https://doi.org/10.1080/17517575.2016.1193633
8. Van der Aalst, W.M.P., Van Hee, K., Van der Werf, J.M., et al.: Conceptual model for online auditing. Decis. Support Syst. **50**, 636–647 (2011). https://doi.org/10.1016/j.dss.2010.08.014
9. Leemans, S.J.J., Fahland, D., van der Aalst, W.M.P.: Discovering block-structured process models from event logs - a constructive approach. In: Colom, J.-M., Desel, J. (eds.) PETRI NETS 2013. LNCS, vol. 7927, pp. 311–329. Springer, Heidelberg (2013). https://doi.org/10.1007/978-3-642-38697-8_17

Application of Extreme Learning Machine to Visual Diagnosis of Rapeseed Nutrient Deficiency

Jing Hu[1,2], Xianbin Xu[1], Lingmin Liu[2(✉)], and Yuanhua Yang[1]

[1] School of Computer, Wuhan University, Hubei 430074, China
jhu1983@whu.edu.cn
[2] School of Computer, Wuhan Qingchuan University, Hubei 430204, China
hujing031115@126.com

Abstract. The nondestructive and accurate diagnosis of nutrient deficiency is the key to the adoption of appropriate remedial measures in agriculture. This paper proposes an intelligent visual diagnosis technique for the diagnosis of nutrient deficiency in rapeseed based on the leaf features. To this end, the experimental image library of four types of deficiencies was established, including normal, nitrogen deficiency, phosphorus deficiency and kalium deficiency. First, through employing the GrabCut algorithms, an image with remarkable features was divided into the foreground and background images. Then, the foreground one was employed to extract color, texture and shape features using the average grayscale and color moments in R/G/B and H/I channels, grayscale co-occurrence matrix and wavelet moments, respectively. Second, the initial features were normalized and filtered based on the gain for recognition rate so as to reduce their dimensions for improving the speed and accuracy of the diagnosis. Finally, the core features were imported into the extreme learning machine and the diagnosis of the input rapeseed leaf image could be accomplished. The experimental results showed that the proposed method could accurately identify the common nutrient deficiency, which sets a good example for the diagnosis technique of nutrient deficiency based on image analysis.

Keywords: Nutrient deficiency diagnosis · Rapeseed · Feature extraction · Extreme learning machine

1 Introduction

The lack of necessary nutrient elements during plant growth will seriously affect rapeseed production [1]. In agricultural production, experts or experienced farmers usually diagnose nutrient deficiency using naked eyes to observe the external features, which is far from accurate and is rather subjective. This traditional method has difficulty in identifying the early symptoms of nutrient deficiency, which may hinder the timely adoption of remedial measures [2]. Development of rapid and non-destructive testing technology of nutrient deficiency has become an important issue to guarantee a good harvest [3].

© Springer Nature Singapore Pte Ltd. 2019
G. Zhai et al. (Eds.): IFTC 2018, CCIS 1009, pp. 238–248, 2019.
https://doi.org/10.1007/978-981-13-8138-6_20

Methods for the detection of nutrient deficiency include chemical analysis, chlorophyll meter and image analysis [4]. The chemical method is highly accurate but with a complex process and is unfit to be applied to the diagnosis of nutrient deficiency of rapeseed seedlings in the field. The chlorophyll meter is very suitable to be employed in the field, but it can only detect nitrogen deficiency. One of image analysis methods, spectral analysis, is commonly used to measure the SPAD value and nitrogen content in crop leaves [5], while it requires chemometrics technology and an expensive spectrometer [6]. Another method, multispectral and hyperspectral image analysis, is widely applied in accurate measurement of water nitrogen deficiency and other conditions. However, it has a low energy efficiency and is difficult to achieve the requirements of high resolution, high signal-to-noise ratio and high stability [7]. Visible image analysis method based on external features arising from nutrient deficiency in crop organs is a simple technique with fast detection, but the accuracy may be limited due to the complexity of natural environment [8–10]. In fact, a real-time and accurate diagnosis method can be established with color images of rapeseed taken by a digital camera or cell phone [10]. This kind of method has advantages in diagnosing nutrient deficiency in the field and is suitable to be applied and popularized by ordinary agriculturists [11].

As the most important physiological organ of rapeseed plant, the leaf can reflect the state of the nutrition of the plant. Its color, texture and shape are directly related to the type and degree of nutrient deficiency [12, 13]. Based on the detection and analysis of the abnormal features of rapeseed leaves, we proposed an innovative technique for nutrient deficiency diagnosis, which facilitates an easy detection of the deficiency in fundamental nutrient elements. All algorithms are realized by using C++ programming and can be run on a common mobile computing platform, and any ordinary technician can operate this system in the field for evaluation of nutrient conditions.

2 Method

In this section, details of the proposed method will be introduced. The algorithm flowchart of this paper is presented in Fig. 1. The procedures of the method are shown as follows.

- All experimental images are pre-processed to extract the foreground images using the GrabCut algorithm [14].
- The foreground images are converted to HSV format and then the average grayscale and the color moments of both R/G/B and H/S channels are calculated.
- The grayscales of the foreground images are employed to get the GLCM and the two-level wavelet moment, which demonstrate the features of the image.
- Eigenvector needs to be normalized to eliminate deviation due to the different physical meanings or value ranges of the feature components.
- The dimensions of features are reduced and used to train the extreme learning machine to obtain the classification rules.
- The features of the testing image are input into the classifier to obtain the diagnosis results according to the classification rules.

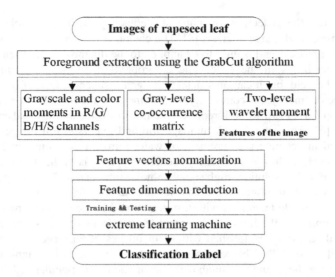

Fig. 1. Algorithm flow chart.

2.1 Feature Extraction

2.1.1 Color Features Extraction

The red and green channels are critical to nutrient deficiency diagnosis especially. The HIS color model is more suitable for image processing because of its three components including hue, saturation and brightness in the HSI color space. The first two components contain the information of image color and are not affected by the outside light. The color moment is extremely robust and efficient to describe color characteristics. The color image in RGB format will be converted to HSI color space. R/G/B/H/S channels are used for color moments, it has been added the grayscale of each channel to form a 20-dimensional vector marked as formula (1):

$$X_{C-20} = \left[R, G, B, H, S, M_R^{1-3}, M_G^{1-3}, M_B^{1-3}, M_H^{1-3}, M_S^{1-3}\right] \tag{1}$$

which describes the color features of the leaf image. M^{1-3} is the vector consists of the first three orders of color moments in R/G/B and H/S channel. For example, the first three orders of color moments of the hue component can be calculated using formula (2).

$$M_I^k = \left[\frac{1}{N}\sum_{j=1}^{N}(p_{i,j} - \mu)^k\right]^{\frac{1}{k}} \quad \begin{cases} k = 1, \mu = 0 \\ k \geq 2, \mu = \mu_1^i \end{cases} \tag{2}$$

where $p_{i,j}$ is the probability of the occurrence of the pixel whose grayscale is j in the I color channel, N is the total number of pixels in the image, and $k(1, 2, 3)$ is the order of the color moments.

2.1.2 Texture Features Extraction

GLCM (gray level co-occurrence matrix) is a matrix function of pixel distance and angle to describe the texture features of the image [15], through which the correlation in grayscale between two pixels at a certain distance and direction is calculated. In an image with k grayscale and $M * N$ image resolution, for a pixel point $P(x, y)$ with g_1 grayscale and another pixel point $P'(x+a, y+b)$ with g_2 grayscale, the grayscale (g_1, g_2) is applied to replace the space coordinates (x, y). The frequency of the occurrence of (g_1, g_2) marked as $k_{(g_1, g_2)}$ is then counted and normalized to a probability of occurrence, forming the square matrix GLCM. (a, b) is termed as the selected different distance according to the characteristics of texture distribution. The grayscale of the image is generally compressed to decrease the amount of calculation. In this paper, the grayscale will be compressed from 256 to 8. The normal calculating direction of GLCM is 0°, 90°, 45°, 135°. The normalized formula is shown as formula (3).

$$P_{(g_1, g_2)} = \frac{k_{(g_1, g_2)}}{R}, R = \begin{cases} N(N-1) & \theta = 0°, 90° \\ (N-1)^2 & \theta = 45°, 135° \end{cases} \tag{3}$$

The three scalars including angular second moment (reflecting the degree of image gray distribution and texture fineness), entropy (representing non-uniformity of the complexity of the image or texture), the autocorrelations (showing the consistency of image texture) in four directions are used to describe the texture features of rapeseed leaves. All of these scalars form a 24-dimensional vector marked as formula (4).

$$X_{T-24} = [Asm_{(a,b)}, Ent_{(a,b)}, Cor_{(a,b)}]$$
$$(a, b) \in \{(0, 1), (0, -1), (1, 0), (-1, 0), (-1, 1), (1, -1), (1, 1), (-1, -1)\} \tag{4}$$

2.1.3 Shape Features Extraction

Geometric shape features of the image area can be represented by the moment features. Both Zernike moments and wavelet moments have the most comprehensive performance, but the latter requires less calculation. Wavelet moment contains the multi-resolution feature of wavelet, enabling the simultaneous output of the partial and whole characteristics of the image. Wavelet decomposition of leaf image labeled as f(x, y) can be processed with two-dimensional Mallat decomposition algorithm. K layer wavelet decomposition can be obtained by formula (5).

$$f(x, y) = A_k + \sum_{(x,y)} d_k^s, s = 1, 2, 3 \tag{5}$$

Ak is the low-frequency component in this scale, and $d_k^1 d_k^2 d_k^3$ are the high-frequency components in horizontal, vertical, and diagonal directions, respectively. In this paper, the coefficients of high-frequency detail components are defined to describe the shape features of leaves. The 6-dimensional feature vector is marked as formula (6).

$$X_{S-6} = [d_1^1, d_1^2, d_1^3, d_2^1, d_2^2, d_2^3] \tag{6}$$

2.1.4   Normalization of the Feature

Eigenvector needs to be normalized to eliminate deviation due to the different physical meanings or value ranges of the feature components. Training samples are noted with {xi}, in which the maximum, minimum and average values of each component are identified as xmax, xmin and $\bar{x}$. x' is the sample which has been normalized. The normalization is conducted as algorithm (7).

$$x' = (x - \bar{x})/(x_{max} - x_{min}) \tag{7}$$

After normalization, the normalized eigenvalues can be compared with each other.

2.2   Pattern Recognition

Classifier is a way for classifying samples in data mining. In the process of classification, a model is constructed to map the data recorded from the database to a given category for data forecasting. Extreme Learning Machine (ELM) has the advantages of high learning efficiency and strong generalization ability, which has been widely used in classification, regression, clustering, feature learning and so on. ELM has been a typical single-hidden layer forward neural network structure, including input layer, hidden layer and output layer. The connection weights and thresholds of the input layer and the hidden layer have been randomly or artificially given when creating the network, the learning process only needs to calculate the output weights, so the extreme learning process has been very time-sensitive, so it has been easy to converge in the global minimum. For a given n-Group of training data (N is greater than 100 in this article), using ELM to study the single-layer feedforward neural Network (SLFN) with L-suppressed layers (L = 1000 in this article) and M-Output layers (M = 4 in this article) has the following steps:

(1) Set the number of hidden layer nodes L is 1000, randomly initialize the input layer and the hidden layer of the link weights and hidden layer neurons threshold.
(2) Select the ReLU function as the activation function of the hidden layer neurons.
(3) Calculate the hidden layer output matrix.
(4) Solve the output weight.

For the image of a rape leaf to be detected, the ELM can be output by calculating its characteristic input.

2.3   Reduction of Feature

The feature vector consisting of the characteristics of color, texture and shape is 50-dimensional. Some features have little relevance to the symptoms of nutrient deficiency. In other words, these features cannot indicate the differences among different types of nutrient deficiency. The application of these features will increase the error and time consumption of the proposed algorithm. Therefore, the strongly correlated characteristics need to be chosen from the 50-dimensional feature vector. In deficiency diagnosis based on different characteristic values, more differences among nutrient deficiency types will contribute to simplicity and accuracy of the diagnosis. To explore the impact of different feature combinations on recognition rates, an indicator has been defined, called the gain for recognition rate, such as the formula (8).

$$K_x = E_{none} - E_x \tag{8}$$

x has been any one of the 50 normalization features; E_{none} has been the average recognition rate without removing any features; K_x has been the gain after remove the x feature; E_x has been the average recognition rate after the x feature is removed.

The effect of each characteristic on K_x has been investigated one by one, if K_x has been less than a certain threshold (0.05), then the character has been judged to have negative effect on the recognition rate, removed it.

3 Results and Discussion

3.1 Experimental Image and Data Acquisition

Rapeseed plants were soilless-cultured with the Kawasaki formula for image acquisition of the experiment. To avoid sediment caused by chemical reaction, the nutrient liquor was prepared with three different methods according to chemical characteristics. The incubation time was from September to December 2017. Perlite with a particle size of 2–4 mm was selected as the substrate and nutrient solution was prepared according to the Japanese Yamasaki formula, with a PH value of 6.0–6.5 and EC value of 1.2 ms/cm. Besides, the YN-4000 intelligent soil analysis meter was employed to measure the N/P/K contents and PH value of the rapeseed leaves, so as to make sure that the experimental conditions were correct. The test software is window 10 64 Ultimate Edition and VS2015 with OpenCV 3.1. The hardware is configured with core i7 7700HQ 2.8GHZ/8G DDR3/1T+128G SSD/GTX1060 6G graphics cards.

To simulate the plant growth under four conditions, including normal conditions, nitrogen deficiency, phosphorus deficiency, and kalium deficiency, 30 pots of rapeseed were grown for each condition. The experimental images of the cultivated rapeseed plants were shot under indoor lighting using Canon EOS 600D (Lens: EF-S 18–135 mm f/3.5–5.6 IS, Resolution: 18 million pixels, Mode: auto-exposure mode). The pictures of the sample plants were taken every other day at a fixed time and the leaf images and canopy images were saved as JPEG format. In addition, more experimental images were obtained through the Internet, books, other literature and rapeseed field shooting. Experimental images were divided into four categories noted as B/N/P/K, which respectively correspond to normal, nitrogen deficiency, phosphorus deficiency and kalium deficiency. Figure 2 shows a set of experimental images.

Especially, the images with the most obvious color characteristics were chosen to be the template images, which were divided into 5 levels according to the severity of nutrient deficiency. Because the experimental image background would affect the accuracy of the algorithm, the leaf regions were segmented from all those images by using the GrabCut algorithm. The minimum bounding rectangle of the leaf regions was figured out, then the rectangular regions (50 × 50 pixels) close to the rectangle center were cut out as training images. There are 4 types of training images with 5 gradients,

Fig. 2. Partial experimental images.

meaning that one group of training images includes 20 template images. Generally, more than 6 groups were employed in the EML training. Some template images are shown in Fig. 3.

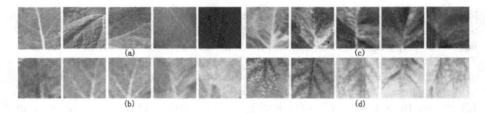

Fig. 3. (a)–(d) Four types of template images respectively for B/N/P/K.

3.2 Feasibility Analysis of Diagnosis Based on Image Feature

The color and texture of the leaves of rapeseeds suffering from nutrient deficiency usually exhibit obvious distinctions [11]. Severe nutrient deficiency will cause the change in leaf shape. As shown in Fig. 4, from left to right are the images of color histogram back projection of kalium deficiency template image to all the four template images in the second level of deficiency. Histogram back projection reflects the similarity of two images in color. From Fig. 4, we can see a generally strong correlation between the type of nutrient deficiency and color feature. Figure 4(c) and (d) have the lowest overall brightness while Fig. 4(e) has the highest brightness. However, Fig. 4(b) is the image of normal leaves but exhibits a high brightness as well. In this case, it cannot be judged whether the image type belongs to the leaves of nitrogen or phosphorus deficiency. Therefore, not one feature but a set of features are needed for nutrient deficiency diagnosis with the maximum probability by using advanced data mining techniques.

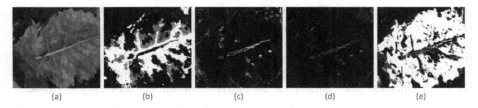

Fig. 4. Histogram back projection between template images (normal, Nitrogen deficiency, Phosphorus deficiency, Kalium deficiency) and the image of Kalium deficiency. Note: (a) rapeseed image in Kalium deficiency, (b)–(e) color histogram back projection images.

3.3   Test of Deficiency Diagnosis

48 testing images of 4 types are classified and labeled as B/N/P/K, which are also the classification labels. Multi-dimensional feature parameters of nutrient deficiency and corresponding classification labels together form the multi-dimensional feature vector matrix. The matrix is put into the EML for training and generating classification rules. Both the number of features and the kind of classification influence the accuracy and time consumption of the nutrient deficiency algorithm. First, removed a feature from the 50 original features, input other features into the EML record recognition rate, and filtered by formula (8) to remove the feature of the large negative gain. Finally, $B, M_B^1, M_B^2, M_B^3, Ent_{(0,1)}, 16$ features have been rejected, with an average gain rate of -2.4%.

The overall accuracy ratio of the test is 91.6%. Table 1 shows the results of diagnosis by using the proposed method. The suffix of the label such as B, N, P, and K is the right attribute.

Table 1. Test results of nutrient deficiency diagnosis

No.	1	2	3	4	5	6	7	8	9	10	11	12
Label_B	B	B	B	B	B	K	B	B	N	B	B	B
Label_N	N	N	P	N	N	N	N	N	P	N	N	N
Label_P	P	P	P	P	P	P	P	P	P	P	P	P
Label_K	K	K	K	K	K	K	K	K	K	K	N	K

The column "OPERATION" is the operation of EML without feature reduction, EML with feature reduction, SVM with feature reduction, random forest classifier (RFC) with feature reduction, naive Bayes classifiers (NBC) with feature reduction respectively. The column "NUM" is the number of the features. The column "ACCURACY" and "TIME" are the test results when the operation is executed. From Table 2, we can infer that the decrease in the feature number improves both the accuracy and speed of the recognition. These results indicate that the feature number may influence the recognition results because fewer features can reduce the time consumption of the algorithm. Those features of nutrient deficiency without stable consistence will cause confusion and reduce the accuracy of the algorithm. SVM's recognition rate has been slightly lower than RFC and ELM, but it's time consuming has been 10 times more than them. NBC has the lowest recognition rate and medium time-consuming. RFC and ELM have the highest recognition rates, but the ELM has taken the shortest time. It has been concluded that the extreme learning machine has been an application most suitable for the diagnosis of nutrient deficiency in rapeseed.

Table 2. Accuracy and time consumption of algorithms with different classification

Operation	Num	Accuracy				Time (S)
		B	N	P	K	
OR with EML	50	58.3%	75.0%	75.0%	50.0%	6.6
R-F with EML	34	83.3%	91.6%	100%	91.6%	2.5
R-F with SVM	34	75.0%	91.6%	91.6%	91.6%	32.5
R-F with RFC	34	83.3%	91.6%	100%	91.6%	3.1
R-F with NBC	34	75.0%	75.0%	91.6%	91.6%	5.9

We also tested the effect of the group numbers of training images (Fig. 5). Generally speaking, the accuracy of the diagnosis will be improved with increasing numbers of training images, but it will be stabilized eventually. If the number of training images is too small (less than 8 groups), the diagnosis results would be valueless; if the number exceeds a certain number (9 in this experiment), the accuracy rate would stay stable. Two factors may be responsible for this phenomenon: first, the various sources of the experimental images; second, different rapeseed breeds with small variations in color feature. These two factors lead to the lack of absolute consistency of the experimental images.

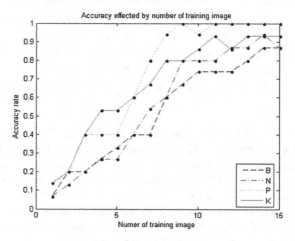

Fig. 5. Influence of the number of training images on diagnosis accuracy. (affected, number)

4 Conclusion

This article introduces an intelligent image diagnosis technique of nutrient deficiency diagnosis in rapeseed on the basis of color characteristics of the leaves. Image library of rapeseed was created for four types of nutrient deficiencies, i.e. normal and N/P/K deficiency. The template image sets with five gradients were set up and the color feature was calculated by using the color histogram back projection. The Bayesian classifier was employed for the classification of nutrient deficiency types in article [11]. By using that method, the accuracy was 87.5% and time consumption was 3.1 s. The proposed method has advantages in precision and speed of the algorithm. Deficiency diagnosis is based on the image features, and thus demands the high quality of image source. Preprocessing of the images with the GrabCut algorithm can effectively reduce the interference of the background. The template images with 5 gradient grades and plenty of training images will help to generate a stable and accurate decision parameter for the extreme learning machine classifier. The dimension reduction improves both the accuracy and speed of the diagnosis. The overall diagnosis accuracy rate is 91.6%, and the accuracy rate of phosphorus deficiency can be up to 100%, which can be attributed to the significant color characteristics. However, the error of the normal samples is remarkable due to the chromatic aberration caused by illumination variations. The experimental results show that this problem can be addressed by raising the number of training images in different environments.

Overall, this paper shows that the nutrient deficiency diagnosis method based on color features of rapeseed leaves is efficient and accurate. Compared with the spectral analysis, the proposed method can be easily applied and popularized. People only need one hand to hold the devices (such as mobile phone) to take images of rapeseed in the field and send the images to the server, and then the diagnosis results can be generated. However, the method only employs rapeseed leaves or canopy without considering other different parts of rapeseed plants. Further study will help to improve the accuracy and practicability of this technique, which can be used to detect the nutrient deficiencies of other crops.

References

1. Yu, Z., Lei, Y., Li, J., Hu, L.: Effects of application amounts of nitrogen, phosphate and potassium and planting density on yield and quality of rapeseed. Plant Nutr. Fertil. Sci. **18**(1), 146–153 (2012)
2. Xu, S., Liu, J., Zhou, J., Zhao, H., Ke, X., Zheng, Y., Yang, F.: Major nutrient elements deficiency diagnosis based on the color and texture features of rapeseed leaves using random forest classifier. Int. Agric. Eng. J. **26**(1), 212–221 (2017)
3. He, Y., Peng, J., Fei, L., Chu, Z., Kong, W.: Critical review of fast detection of crop nutrient and physiological information with spectral and imaging technology. Trans. Chin. Soc. Agric. Eng. **31**(3), 174–189 (2015)
4. Kong, W., Liu, F., He, Y.: Nondestructive estimation of nitrogen status and vegetation index of oilseed rape canopy using multi-spectral imaging technology. Sensor Lett. **9**(3), 1126–1132 (2011)

5. Zhang, X., Liu, F., He, Y., Gong, X.: Detecting macronutrients content and distribution in oilseed rape leaves based on hyperspectral imaging. Biosys. Eng. **115**(1), 56–65 (2013)
6. Sun, H., Li, M., Zhang, Y., Zhao, Y., Wang, H.: Spectral characteristics of corn under different nitrogen treatments. Spectrosc. Spectral Anal. **30**(3), 715–719 (2010)
7. Liu, F., Nie, P.: Nondestructive determination of nutritional information in oilseed rape leaves using visible/near infrared spectroscopy and multivariate calibrations. Sci. China Inform. Sci. **54**(3), 598–608 (2011)
8. Guan, H., Yi, S., Jiao, F., Xu, S., Zuo, Y., Jin, B.: Diagnosis model of crop nutrient deficiency symptoms based on regularized adaptive fuzzy neural network. Trans. Chin. Soc. Agric. Mach. **43**(5), 162–167 (2012)
9. Zhu, H., Zheng, L., Yin, J., Wu, F.: Nitrogen evaluation of winter wheat based on color features of canopy images. Trans. Chin. Soc. Agric. Eng. **26**(s2), 16–20 (2010)
10. Yuan, S.Y., Haiou, G., Lu, C.Z., Ning, H., Ke, W.: Diagnoses of rice nitrogen status based on characteristics of scanning leaf. Spectrosc. Spectral Anal. **29**(8), 2171–2175 (2009)
11. Zhao, H.-T., Xu, S.-Y., Lin, W.-G., Wu, W.-B.: Nutrient deficiency image diagnose of rapeseed based on color feature. Chin. J. Oil Crop Sci. **37**(4), 576–582 (2015)
12. Wang, F., Liao, G., Wang, X., Li, J., Li, J., Shi, W.: Feature description for nutrient deficiency rape leaves based on multifractal theory. Trans. Chin. Soc. Agric. Eng. **29**(24), 181–189 (2013)
13. Zhu, J., Deng, J., Lin, F., Wang, K.: Determination of suitable leaf for nitrogen diagnosis in rice based on computer vision. Trans. Chin. Soc. Agric. Mach. **41**(4), 179–183 (2010)
14. Ren, D., Jia, Z., Yang, J., Kasabov, N.: A practical GrabCut color image segmentation based on Bayes classification and simple linear iterative clustering. IEEE Access **5**(99), 18480–18487 (2017)
15. Yang, P., Yang, G.: Feature extraction using dual-tree complex wavelet transform and gray level co-occurrence matrix. Neurocomputing **197**(c), 212–220 (2016)

Nonlinear Contextual Face Hallucination

Kangli Zeng[1], Tao Lu[1(✉)], Junjun Jiang[2], and Zhongyuan Wang[3]

[1] Hubei Key Laboratory of Intelligent Robot, Wuhan Institute of Technology,
Wuhan 430073, China
lut@wit.edu.cn
[2] School of Computer Science and Technology, Harbin Institute of Technology,
Harbin 150001, China
[3] School of Computer Science, Wuhan University, Wuhan 430072, China

Abstract. Face hallucination, which refers to the restoration of single
or multiple low-resolution face images into clear high-resolution one, is
a challenging research issue. Most existing methods use local or global
patches for image representation and achieve good performance. However, they ignore that the local patch limits the area of the receptive
field and the priori information used in reconstruction is limited. And the
global patch expands the receptive field but introduces irrelevant information to degrade the reconstruction performance. In order to improve
the performance of reconstruction, we propose a nonlinear contextual
face hallucination method. First, contextual information can effectively
improve the receptive field area to make full use of priori information.
Then, the nonlinear model can make the proposed model more suitable
for practical application and make the correlation of data in kernel space
more compact. Finally, combining contextual and residual learning can
improve the stability of the solution of the super-resolution model and the
accuracy of reconstruction performance. The experimental results show
that the proposed face hallucination method has superior performance
than the state-of-the-art method.

Keywords: Context-patch · Face hallucination · Kernel space ·
Weighted collaborative representation

1 Introduction

In recent years, face analysis has received great interest and made impressive
achievements, especially in video surveillance, identity recognition, security and
so on. However, in practical applications, people often observe unclear low resolution (LR) images instead of high resolution (HR). Super-resolution (SR) technology plays an important role in improving the resolution of face images.

The purpose of learning-based SR algorithm is to find the correspondence
between high-resolution image and low-resolution image. The commonly used
method is to represent the image according to the training sample learning
dictionary or to establish some mapping between HR image and LR image in

© Springer Nature Singapore Pte Ltd. 2019
G. Zhai et al. (Eds.): IFTC 2018, CCIS 1009, pp. 249–258, 2019.
https://doi.org/10.1007/978-981-13-8138-6_21

feature space. Patch-based face SR approaches divide a facial image into small patches, then represent and reconstruct images in patch level, they yield satisfactory results rather than other global-face approaches. From the manner of how to represent patch-prior, patch-based face SR can distinguish into local-patch (position-patch) based and nonlocal patch based.

Local-based methods assumes that image patches at the same location have similar prior information, which reconstructs a given LR position patch primarily by linearly combining the position patches in the training set. Roweis et al. [1] first introduced locally neighbor embedding for local patch to reconstruct. Ma et al. [2,3] used the same position image patches of each training image to construct HR image patches and achieved good reconstruction results. Jung et al. [4] and Wang et al. [5] discussed position-patch based sparse representation how to undo the over-fitting problem. Jiang et al. [6,7] argued locality regularization has better reconstruction performance with position priori. Gao et al. [8] used a locally constrained dual low-order representation (LCDLRR) based on position patches for effective facial hallucinations. Moreover, low-rank constraint [9], smooth regularization [10] were used to boost the reconstruction performance. On the other hand, kernel methods [11,12] were adopted to explore the high-order information for better performance. Due to the highly structured attributes of facial image, the above position-based patch method provides semantic constraints to improve the reconstruction performance. However, position prior requires alignment preprocessing of the original image, which limits the representation ability of prior information from training data.

In image super-resolution reconstruction, high-frequency detail recovery using nonlocal information of images is another research idea. This type of algorithm uses the similarity of the image's own structure to define the difference between pixels, and reconstructs the high-resolution image based on the complementary information provided between similar image patches, thereby more effectively protecting the structural information of the image. Chang et al. [13] first proposed a neighborhood embedding scheme, which linearly represented input patches by finding most similar non-local patches, and trained the database by using local manifold prior. Yang et al. [14]improved reconstruction performance by learning nonlocal coupled pixel dictionaries. Clustering and collaborative representation approach [15] was proposed to cluster nonlocal dictionaries to boost super-resolution performance. Although nonlocal-based methods achieves satisfactory results, the location information of facial structure is neglected, and the large receptive field region will introduce unrelated prior information which will lead to performance degradation.

More recently, deep learning offers an end-to-end solution for super-resolution tasks. The deep architecture owes power nonlinear ability to describe the image feature. Dong et al. [16] first proposed convolutional neural network for super-resolution using nonlinear mapping. Kim et al. [17] used very deep residual neural network for accurate image representation by recursive subnetwork units. Efficient sub-Pixel convolutional neural network [18] was used to accelerate the reconstruction speed. Ledig et al. [19] used generative adversarial network to render photo-realistic image. Deep learning based approaches has strong ability of image representation but training the network is hardware (GPU) dependent and time-consuming.

As far as receptive field is concerned, the local region of the position patch contains facial structure prior, and the self-similarity priori of the image representation comes from the global region of the nonlocal patch. The receptive field area is very important for obtaining prior knowledge that is beneficial to image representation. Inspired by context-patch [20,21], we propose a simple yet powerful nonlinear contextual face hallucination for better reconstruction performance. **First**, we use context to obtain more prior information for reconstruction, so it provides a reasonable receptive field area. **Second**, the nonlinear model can well describe the complex relationship between LR and HR to explore high-frequency information, and the proposed nonlinear method is simple and effective. **Third**, contextual residual learning can obtain more accurate high-frequency information and make reconstruction better.

2   Related Work

2.1   Notations and Assumptions

Let $\{A_i\}_{i=1}^N$ and $\{B_i\}_{i=1}^N$ be the LR and HR training face images, $n = 1, ..., N$, where N is the number of training sample, $A_i \in \Re^{p \times q}$ and $B_i \in \Re^{pt \times qt}$, where t is the scale factor. Each face image is divided into M small overlapping patches. Given an input image $Y^L \in \Re^{p \times q}$, the purpose of SR is to render a high resolution HR image $Y^H \in \Re^{pt \times qt}$. For every LR patch $\boldsymbol{y}_i^L \in \Re^{\varepsilon \times 1}$ (patch size is $\sqrt{\varepsilon} \times \sqrt{\varepsilon}$ and it is column vectors) to infer the potential HR patch $\boldsymbol{y}_i^H \in \Re^{(t^2 \times \varepsilon) \times 1}$. Suppose D_i^L and D_i^H are the LR and HR dictionaries of the i–th patch, respectively.

2.2   Collaborative Representation

Recent theoretical results in machine learning have shown that sparsity is a strong constraint on the weight vector α which suffers slow optimization speed and unstable solution. Then, collaborative representation [22–25] came into being, which can produce better results with affordable computational cost. Then, the objective function becomes:

$$\min_{\boldsymbol{\alpha}_i} \sum_{i=1}^M \left\{ \left\| \boldsymbol{y}_i^L - D_i^L \boldsymbol{\alpha}_i \right\|_2^2 + \beta \left\| \boldsymbol{\alpha}_i \right\|_2^2 \right\}, \tag{1}$$

where M is the number of patches, the second term is the constraint term. $\|\cdot\|_2$ denotes the l_2-norm and β is a regularization parameter.

This objective function is a typical regularized least squares with analytical solution:

$$\boldsymbol{\alpha}_i^* = \left((D_i^L)^T D_i^L + \beta I \right)^{-1} (D_i^L)^T \boldsymbol{y}_i^L, \tag{2}$$

where I is the identity matrix and $(D_i^L)^T$ is the transpose matrix of D_i^L. Then the desired HR image Y^H can be optimized by,

$$Y^H = \sum_{i=1}^{M} D_i^H \boldsymbol{\alpha}_i^*. \qquad (3)$$

3 Proposed Method

3.1 Contextual Dictionary Learning

Different from the traditional position-patch based face hallucination methods, we leverage all the contextual patches [20, 21] around position i−th in Fig. 1. Compared with the position-patch based methods, the number of patches taken by context-patch is greatly improved, providing more nonlocal details information for reconstruction. Let define c is the number of context-patches at one LR face image and the patch size $ps \times ps$. Then, the window size centered on position i−th is $ws \times ws$ and in this bigger window we use step size ss (in this paper, we fix the step size to 2) to sample multiple patches. Therefore, c can be calculated by $c = \left(1 + \frac{ws-ps}{ss}\right)^2$.

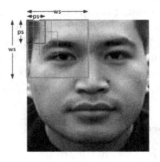

Fig. 1. Contextual information sampled by context-patch.

Therefore, the HR and LR dictionaries of the i−th are $C_i^H = [c_1^H, c_2^H, \cdots, c_{c \times N}^H]$ and $C_i^L = [c_1^L, c_2^L, \cdots, c_{c \times N}^L]$. Here, we interpolate LR images into the same size of HR image. At the same time, we use $K - NN$ to reduce the dimension of the dictionary and get new dictionaries D_i^H and D_i^L. In our experiment, K is set to 800.

As we know, residuals are common for image super-resolution to get accurate high frequent components. In this paper, we use context-patch residual learning to replace traditional pixel-wised learning scheme. The contextual information residual is $R_i = D_i^H - D_i^L$. We use R_i to take place of D_i^H in learning, and this simple modification boosts super-resolution performance.

3.2 Nonlinear Contextual Face Hallucination

In practical applications, in order to overcome the limitation that linear models can not handle nonlinear relationships, we use Gaussian kernel function to induce infinite dimensional RKHS [26,27] to capture the nonlinear similarity of patches. Since the nonlinear structures of patches are taken into account, it is more effective to estimate reasonable HR patches.

Let us define the nonlinear mapping operator $\varphi \colon \Re^\varepsilon \to F$. The kernel function $f\left(x_i, x_j\right) = \varphi(\boldsymbol{x}_i)^T \varphi\left(\boldsymbol{x}_j\right)$ describes the nonlinear similarity between two features $\boldsymbol{x}_i$ and $\boldsymbol{x}_j$ in the RKHS, where $\langle \cdot, \cdot \rangle_F$ is the inner product in the kernel feature space F. Among the best-known nonlinear kernel functions is the Gaussian kernel:

$$f\left(\boldsymbol{x}_i, \boldsymbol{x}_j\right) = \exp\left(-\tau \|\boldsymbol{x}_i - \boldsymbol{x}_j\|^2\right), \tag{4}$$

where τ is a scalar parameter.

Nonlinear contextual face Hallucination is formulated and solved as follows:

$$\alpha_i^* = \min_{\alpha_i} \sum_{i=1}^{M} \left\| \varphi\left(\boldsymbol{y}_i^L\right) - \Phi\left(D_i^L\right)\boldsymbol{\alpha}_i \right\|_2^2 + \beta\left\| \Pi_i \otimes \boldsymbol{\alpha}_i \right\|_2^2$$

$$s.t. \sum_{j=1}^{K} \boldsymbol{\alpha}_{i[j]} = 1 \tag{5}$$

where $\Phi\left(D_i^L\right) = \left[\varphi\left(\boldsymbol{l}_1\right), \varphi\left(\boldsymbol{l}_2\right), \cdots, \varphi\left(\boldsymbol{l}_K\right)\right]$, $\otimes$ denotes the Hadamard product. $\Pi_i = diag\left(\left\|\varphi\left(\boldsymbol{y}_i^L\right) - \varphi\left(\boldsymbol{l}_1\right)\right\|_2, \cdots, \left\|\varphi\left(\boldsymbol{y}_i^L\right) - \varphi\left(\boldsymbol{l}_K\right)\right\|_2\right)$ serves as a penalty which describes the kernel similarities between $\varphi\left(\boldsymbol{y}_i^L\right)$ and corresponding training samples $\varphi\left(l_j\right)$ from LR dictionary $\Phi\left(D_i^L\right)$ in the kernel-mapped space,

$$\left\|\varphi\left(\boldsymbol{y}_i^L\right) - \varphi\left(\boldsymbol{l}_j\right)\right\|_2$$
$$= \sqrt{\varphi(\boldsymbol{y}_i^L)^T \varphi\left(\boldsymbol{y}_i^L\right) - 2\varphi(\boldsymbol{y}_i^L)^T \varphi\left(\boldsymbol{l}_j\right) + \varphi(\boldsymbol{l}_j)^T \varphi\left(\boldsymbol{l}_j\right)}. \tag{6}$$
$$= \sqrt{f\left(\boldsymbol{y}_i^L, \boldsymbol{y}_i^L\right) - 2f\left(\boldsymbol{y}_i^L, l_j\right) + f\left(l_j, l_j\right)}$$

Then, Eq. 5 can be solved as:

$$\boldsymbol{\alpha}_i^* = \left(G + \beta \Pi_i^T \Pi\right)^{-1} f\left(\bullet, \boldsymbol{y}_i^L\right), \tag{7}$$

where $G = f\left(l_i, l_j\right)$ and $f\left(\bullet, y_i^L\right) = \left[f\left(l_1, y_i^L\right), \cdots, f\left(l_K, y_i^L\right)\right]$.

Finally, the reconstructed HR can be obtained by

$$X = \sum_{i=1}^{M} \{R_i \boldsymbol{\alpha}_i^* + \boldsymbol{y}_i^*\}, \tag{8}$$

where $\boldsymbol{y}_i^{L*}$ is the interpolated version of $\boldsymbol{y}_i^L$.

4   Experiments and Result Analysis

4.1   Database Description

We select 1000 images as the training samples on CAS-PEAL-R1 [28] face database, the rest 40 images for testing. The size of HR image is 112×96 pixels. The LR images are formed by average blur (blur kernel is 4 pixels) and down-sampling (scale factor $t = 4$) from corresponding HR images, thus the size of LR face images are 28×24 pixels. Here, we interpolate the LR images into the size of HR one. Some training and testing samples from CAS-PEAL-R1 face database are shown in Fig. 2. We set image patch at size of 12×12 with 4 pixels overlapped. All experiments are conducted at same condition for fair comparison.

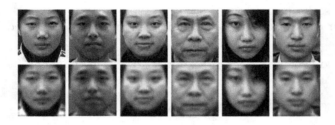

Fig. 2. Samples from CAS-PEAL-R1 face database. The first row is the HR ground-truth, and the second row is the corresponding LR sample (with the same size of HR).

4.2   Experimental Parameters Setting

The Contextual Window Size *ws*. The contextual window size ws is set to get more contextual information, as shown in Fig. 3. The performance achieves the best when ws is equal to 28. With larger ws, it not only takes a long time, but also reduces the performance of the algorithm. Too big ws brings more different patches for image reconstruction which degrades the performance.

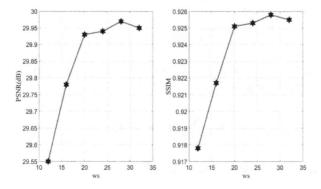

Fig. 3. The average SSIM and PSNR performance of different contextual windows ws.

The Nonlinear Scalar Parameter τ. We test the performance of our method with different τ. As shown in Fig. 4, it is easy to see that the nonlinear scalar parameter τ have a significance for the performance of the proposed method. Gaussian kernel function improves solution stability which boosts the super-resolution performance. Therefore, we select a proper nonlinear scalar parameter $\tau = 10^{-8}$, the proposed method gains best performance.

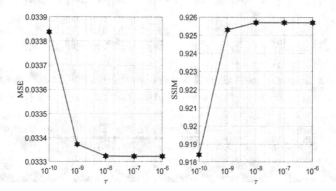

Fig. 4. The average SSIM and MSE values of different τ.

4.3 Results Comparison

In this section, we compare the proposed approach with some state-of-the-art super-resolution algorithms. As usual, commonly used PSNR and SSIM are utilized to evaluate the image reconstruction performance.

Figure 5 shows some visual results generated by different hallucination methods. From the visual results of hallucinated faces, we learn that the proposed ours method generates the best visual results with more facial details and are much more similar to the ground-truth HR faces in the red box parts.

Table 1. The average of PSNR and SSIM values with different methods

Methods	LSR	WSR	LLE	LCR	CLNE	TLCR	NC	Remove border		
								SRCNN	VDSR	NC
PSNR (dB)	27.04	27.20	27.58	27.61	28.12	29.72	30.01	29.28	30.38	**31.03**
SSIM	0.875	0.874	0.886	0.887	0.896	0.921	0.926	0.914	0.927	**0.928**

The average PSNR and SSIM of different super-resolution reconstruction methods are shown in Table 1 on the CAS-PEAL-R1 database. Intuitively speaking, context-patch contains more information than position patch due to a larger

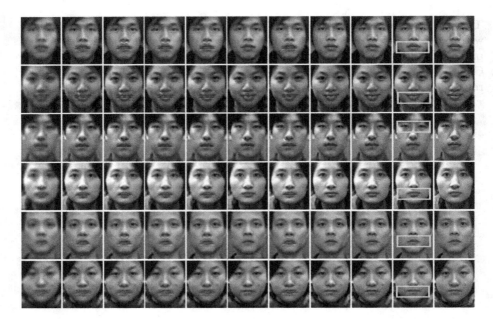

Fig. 5. Some hallucinated results by state-of-the-art hallucinations. From left to right: LR faces, LSR [3], WSR [5], LLE [1], LCR [6], CLNE [7], TLCR [21], SRCNN [16], VDSR [17], ours and ground-truth HR image. (Color figure online)

receptive field. We compare the proposed method with some representative position-based approaches, e.g., LCR [6], CLNE [7] respectively. We can find that in the first and second testing results in Fig. 5, position-based approaches render aliasing in mouth part, because position-based approaches rely on alignment. What's more, we observed that TLCR (used context-patch) achieves the second best performance among patch-based approaches. However, our method has higher PSNR and SSIM than TLCR because the nonlinear extension on contextual information. From this point, we can conclude that nonlinear representation scheme promotes the reconstruction performance than linear manner. Although deep learning is getting more and more attention, as can be seen from Table 1, our method shows encouraging performance and is more effective than the referred deep learning methods through context residual-learning. In small data setting, shallow learning manner combining with nonlinear scheme has considerably performance with some deep-learning based models.

5   Conclusion

In this paper, we propose a novel face hallucination, termed nonlinear contextual face hallucination. Instead of local patches or nonlocal patches, the proposed method uses context information to obtain more valid information patches for image representation. At the same time, the nonlinear relationship is effectively applied to the proposed method and combined with the residual learning scheme, which improves the stability of the cooperative representation solution and the accuracy of reconstruction performance. Experimental results on CAS-PEAL-R1 face database demonstrate the effectiveness of the proposed approach. In future, the fast algorithm on nonlinear representation scheme will be fully investigated.

Acknowledgement. This work is supported by the National Natural Science Foundation of China (61502354, 61501413, 61671332, 41501505), the Natural Science Foundation of Hubei Province of China (2015CFB451, 2014CFA130, 2012FFA099, 2012FFA134, 2013CF125), the Central Government Guided Local Science and Technology Development Projects (2018ZYYD059), Provincial Teaching Research Project of Hubei Province Higher Education (2017324), Wuhan Institute of Technology Key Teaching Project (Z2017009), Scientific Research Foundation of Wuhan Institute of Technology (K201713).

References

1. Roweis, S.T., Saul, L.K.: Nonlinear dimensionality reduction by locally linear embedding. Science **290**(5500), 2323–2326 (2000)
2. Ma, X., Zhang, J., Qi, C.: Position-based face hallucination method. In: IEEE International Conference on Multimedia and Expo, pp. 290–293 (2009)
3. Ma, X., Zhang, J., Chun, Q.: Hallucinating face by position-patch. Pattern Recogn. **43**(6), 2224–2236 (2010)
4. Jung, C., Jiao, L., Liu, B., Gong, M.: Position-patch based face hallucination using convex optimization. IEEE Signal Process. Lett. **18**(6), 367–370 (2011)
5. Wang, Z., Hu, R., Wang, S., Jiang, J.: Face hallucination via weighted adaptive sparse regularization. IEEE Trans. Circuits Syst. Video Technol. **24**(5), 802–813 (2014)
6. Jiang, J., Hu, R., Han, Z., Lu, T., Huang, K.: Position-patch based face hallucination via locality-constrained representation. In: IEEE International Conference on Multimedia and Expo, pp. 212–217 (2012)
7. Jiang, J., Hu, R., Han, Z., Wang, Z., Lu, T., Chen, J.: Locality-constraint iterative neighbor embedding for face hallucination. In: IEEE International Conference on Multimedia and Expo, pp. 1–6 (2013)
8. Gao, G., Jing, X.Y., Huang, P., Zhou, Q., Wu, S., Yue, D.: Locality-constrained double low-rank representation for effective face hallucination. IEEE Access **4**(99), 8775–8786 (2016)
9. Lu, T., Xiong, Z., Zhang, Y., Wang, B., Lu, T.: Robust face super-resolution via locality-constrained low-rank representation. IEEE Access **5**(99), 13103–13117 (2017)
10. Jiang, J., Ma, J., Wang, Z., Wang, Z., Hu, R.: SRLSP: a face image super-resolution algorithm using smooth regression with local structure prior. IEEE Trans. Multimed. **19**(1), 27–40 (2017)
11. Yu, K., Zhang, T., Gong, Y.: Nonlinear learning using local coordinate coding. In: International Conference on Neural Information Processing Systems, pp. 2223–2231 (2009)
12. Yang, W., Yuan, T., Zhou, F., Liao, Q.: Face hallucination via position-based dictionaries coding in kernel feature space. In: 2014 International Conference on Smart Computing, pp. 131–135, November 2014

13. Chang, H., Yeung, D.Y., Xiong, Y.: Super-resolution through neighbor embedding. In: Proceedings of the 2004 IEEE Computer Society Conference on Computer Vision and Pattern Recognition, CVPR 2004, p. I (2004)
14. Yang, J., Wright, J., Huang, T., Ma, Y.: Image super-resolution as sparse representation of raw image patches. In: IEEE Conference on Computer Vision and Pattern Recognition, CVPR 2008, pp. 1–8 (2008)
15. Zhang, Y., Zhang, Y., Zhang, J., Dai, Q.: CCR: clustering and collaborative representation for fast single image super-resolution. IEEE Trans. Multimed. 18(3), 405–417 (2016)
16. Dong, C., Loy, C.C., He, K., Tang, X.: Image super-resolution using deep convolutional networks. IEEE Trans. Pattern Anal. Mach. Intell. 38(2), 295–307 (2016)
17. Kim, J., Lee, J.K., Lee, K.M.: Accurate image super-resolution using very deep convolutional networks. In: Computer Vision and Pattern Recognition, pp. 1646–1654 (2016)
18. Shi, W., et al.: Real-time single image and video super-resolution using an efficient sub-pixel convolutional neural network. In: 2016 IEEE Conference on Computer Vision and Pattern Recognition (CVPR), June 2016, pp. 1874–1883 (2016)
19. Ledig, C., et al.: Photo-realistic single image super-resolution using a generative adversarial network. In: 2017 IEEE Conference on Computer Vision and Pattern Recognition (CVPR), July 2017, pp. 105–114 (2017)
20. Romano, Y., Elad, M.: Con-patch: when a patch meets its context. IEEE Trans. Image Process. 25(9), 3967–3978 (2016)
21. Jiang, J., Yu, Y., Tang, S., Ma, J., Qi, G.J., Aizawa, A.: Context-patch based face hallucination via thresholding locality-constrained representation and reproducing learning. In: IEEE International Conference on Multimedia and Expo, pp. 469–474 (2017)
22. Li, H., Lam, K.M.: Fast super-resolution based on weighted collaborative representation. In: International Conference on Digital Signal Processing, pp. 914–918 (2014)
23. Timofte, R., Gool, L.V.: Adaptive and weighted collaborative representations for image classification. Pattern Recogn. Lett. 43(1), 127–135 (2014)
24. Timofte, R., De Smet, V., Van Gool, L.: A+: adjusted anchored neighborhood regression for fast super-resolution. In: Cremers, D., Reid, I., Saito, H., Yang, M.-H. (eds.) ACCV 2014. LNCS, vol. 9006, pp. 111–126. Springer, Cham (2015). https://doi.org/10.1007/978-3-319-16817-3_8
25. Timofte, R., De, V., Gool, L.V.: Anchored neighborhood regression for fast example-based super-resolution. In: IEEE International Conference on Computer Vision, pp. 1920–1927 (2013)
26. Williams, C.K.I.: Learning with kernels: support vector machines, regularization, optimization, and beyond. Am. Stat. Assoc. 98(462), 489–489 (2002)
27. Saitoh, S.: Theory of reproducing kernels. In: Begehr, H.G.W., Gilbert, R.P., Wong, M.W. (eds.) Analysis and Applications — ISAAC 2001. ISAA, vol. 10, pp. 135–150. Springer, Boston (2003). https://doi.org/10.1007/978-1-4757-3741-7_10
28. Gao, W., et al.: The CAS-PEAL large-scale Chinese face database and baseline evaluations. IEEE Trans. Syst. Man Cybern. Part A Syst. Hum. 38(1), 149–161 (2008)

Quality Assessment

What Is the 3D Comfort Difference Experienced via VR Glasses and 3D-TV

Bo Zang[1,2], Jun Zhou[1,2(✉)], and Jian Xiong[1,2]

[1] Institute of Image Communication and Network Engineering,
Shanghai Jiao Tong University, Shanghai 200240, China
zhoujun@sjtu.edu.cn
[2] Shanghai Key Lab of Digital Media Processing and Transmissions,
Shanghai Jiao Tong University, Shanghai 200240, China

Abstract. Nowadays, many people use virtual reality (VR) glasses such as Oculus instead of 3D-TV to watch stereoscopic 3D (S3D) videos. However, few subjective 3D visual comfort assessment works that related to VR glasses were reported. In this paper, we explore the difference of visual comfort experienced while viewing the same S3D videos via VR glasses and 3D-TV. A S3D video database was built including 10 original S3D videos and their corresponding shifted, geometric distorted, and frame desynchronized version of videos for subjective comfort test. Subjective experimental results show that the subjective comfort experienced on 3D-TV is generally higher than on VR for original and shifted S3D videos, but the visual comfort for geometric distorted and frame unsynchronized S3D videos on VR is higher than on 3D-TV.

Keywords: Comparative study · Subjective quality experienced ·
3D comfort · VR glasses · 3D-TV

1 Introduction

Binocular parallax principle is the theoretical basis for stereoscopic 3D (S3D) TV. S3D videos are usually shot with two cameras mounted side by side, which encoded disparity between left and right images. The human eyes receive slightly different prospective retinal images horizontally when viewing S3D videos by using 3D glasses, then the brain generates relative stereoscopic depth information [1]. There are many potential causes related to visual discomfort such as vergence-accommodation conflict, which is existed in all conventional stereo displays [2]. Vergence-accommodation conflicts also leads to fatigue and visual discomfort while viewing S3D videos [3–5]. Low-quality S3D videos can lead to a very unpleasant experience such as dizziness, eye strain, fatigue and so on [6].

Subjective assessment is an effective method to obtain the comfort for S3D content. The Likert Scale is generally used to measure the full extent of viewers' experience [7]. Many research papers about subjective evaluation on S3D videos have been presented such as [8–10].

© Springer Nature Singapore Pte Ltd. 2019
G. Zhai et al. (Eds.): IFTC 2018, CCIS 1009, pp. 261–272, 2019.
https://doi.org/10.1007/978-981-13-8138-6_22

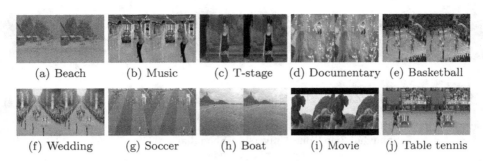

(a) Beach	(b) Music	(c) T-stage	(d) Documentary	(e) Basketball
(f) Wedding	(g) Soccer	(h) Boat	(i) Movie	(j) Table tennis

Fig. 1. Sample scenes of original videos.

With the rise of Virtual Reality (VR), many new ways to view S3D videos have been appeared. However, current researches in video quality assessment (VQA) fields mainly focus on 3D-TV.

VR glasses have been widely used due to the development of virtual reality technology. Numerous video types in VR glasses can be chosen such as panoramic videos and live videos. More and more people enjoy using VR glasses such as Oculus instead of 3D-TV to watch S3D videos due to the high portability and good immersion of VR glasses. For 3D-TV display, human watch S3D videos from the same planer screen. However, when using VR glasses, left and right image of S3D are projected to human eyes separately. Considering that the way to watch S3D videos on VR glasses is different on 3D-TV, it is very meaningful to study the comfort difference experienced while viewing the same S3D videos via VR glasses and 3D-TV.

A S3D video database was built for subjective comfort test, which includes 10 original 15s long S3D video clips. The contents of these original videos include movies, sporting events, natural landscapes and so on. In order to compare the subjective comfort difference experienced while viewing shifted and degraded versions of S3D videos, a shifted, geometric distorted, and frame desynchronized version of original S3D videos were also added into the database. Two formats videos used by VR and 3D-TV were encoded for each sample. Both formats use the same processed criteria for viewing on VR glasses and on 3D-TV respectively. 20 people were invited to participate in this subjective comfort test. Mean Opinion Score (MOS) was used to assess the S3D video quality.

The rest of the paper is organized as follows: In Sect. 2, we introduce the details of the S3D video database and the procedure details of the subjective comfort test. Section 3 shows the subjective experimental results and analyzes the comfort difference while watching the same videos via VR glasses and 3D-TV. Conclusion of this paper is in Sect. 4.

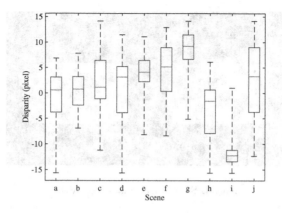

Fig. 2. The disparity range of all original videos.

2   Experiment Set-Up

2.1   Database

In the database, 10 high quality S3D video clips were selected as the original videos with 15 s long for each. In order to avoid the influence of voice, we removed the audio track of all videos. The content of original S3D videos include movies, documentaries, natural scenery, sports competitions and so on. Figure 1 shows the screen-shot of all original S3D videos in side-by-side (SbS) format used by 3D-TV and VR glasses. These videos include dramatic scenes (b, e, g, i, j) and mild scenes (a, c, d, f, h). The resolution of all videos are 1920×1080. All S3D videos have a frame rate of 25 fps. The disparity range of all S3D videos are shown by using boxplot [11] in Fig. 2.

Considering the defects that usually existed in S3D videos and related to visual comfort, 3-type of defection including shifting, geometrical distortion, and frame synchronization, were applied on each original video.

(1) Shifting. In order to comfortably view S3D contents, it is necessary to arrange the main object within a comfortable disparity range which allow binocular fusion. Excessive disparity can cause ghosting which leads to eye strain and unpleasant sensations [12]. According to the 3DC Safety Guidelines [13], ± 60 min ($\pm 1°$) is a guide for the range of comfortable viewing. To compare the subjective comfort difference experienced while viewing shifted S3D videos, each original video was processed to 4 shifted S3D videos ($-50'$, $-25'$, $25'$, $50'$) for the database, which include two types of negative parallax shifted videos and two types of positive parallax shifted videos. Considering that the parallax was related with viewing distance, two formats videos used by VR and 3D-TV were encoded for each original videos and both formats use the same processed criteria.

The view distance of each observer for 3D-TV was set as 3H (H = screen height), which was proposed in ITU-R BT.1438 [14]. The VR glasses we used

Fig. 3. S3D videos played on VR.

was StormMojing IV VR glasses. When people watching S3D videos by using this glasses, the S3D videos will be processed by two separated lens. The virtual screen is designed to be at ten meters apart, which is the zero disparity plane for 3D video. The virtual screen have a size of 470 in., giving a person an immersive feeling in a movie theater. Therefore, according to official data of StormMojing, the viewing distance was calculated to 1.71H.

According to [13], the shifted distance S for each format of 4 shifted types was calculated as follows:

$$S = 2 \times L \times tan(\frac{\theta}{2}) \tag{1}$$

where L is the viewing distance and θ is the parallactic angle. θ is computed as:

$$\theta = \alpha - \beta \tag{2}$$

where α is the angle at which the eyes focus at the center of the display and β is the angle between the eyes relative to the stereo virtual content. When considering the disparity factor, using the corresponding number of pixels as a unit is more convenient for content creation [13]. The shifted pixels p of each S was calculated as follows:

$$p = \frac{S}{W} \times 1920 \tag{3}$$

where W is the screen width. The W and H have the following relationship:

$$\frac{H}{W} = \frac{9}{16} \tag{4}$$

The shifted pixels for each format corresponding to 4 shifted types are shown in Table 1.

Since that S3D videos have barrel distortion when playing through VR glasses, the software of StormMojing will process videos automatically to compensate the barrel distortion as shown in Fig. 3.

Table 1. Shifted pixels on 3D-TV and VR

Shifted minutes	3D-TV (pixel)	VR (pixel)
$-25'$	-24	-13
$-50'$	-47	-27
$25'$	24	13
$50'$	47	27

(2) Geometrical Distortion. Since that S3D videos are usually shot with two cameras, geometric distortion often exited in S3D videos. Three types geometric distortion are described in [1]. We only focus on the type-α distortion since that it is one of the most common distorted type. When watching type-α distorted S3D videos, eyes will be forced to rotate in opposite direction, which will cause visual discomfort [15]. In order to compare the subjective comfort difference experienced while watching geometric distorted S3D videos, 4 types of type-α distorted videos (0.5°, 1°, 1.5°, 2°) were generated on each original video in the database.

(3) Frame Synchronize. There often exist frame desynchronize in S3D videos when shooting with two cameras, which will lead to motion disparity and visual discomfort. The motion disparity is related to the motion direction of the object. In order to study the comfort difference experienced while watching frame desynchronized S3D videos, 4 types of frame desynchronized videos were generated in the database. We set the frame desynchronized degrees as 1f, 2f, 3f, 4f based on the original S3D videos.

Since that the geometric distortion degree and frame desynchronized degree are not affected by the viewing distance. The two type versions of S3D videos which played on 3D-TV and VR have the same formats. Hence the database was built, which includes 10 original S3D videos and their corresponding 40 shifted videos, 40 geometric distorted videos, and 40 frame desynchronized videos. Each shifted video have two formats for viewing on VR and 3D-TV.

2.2   Test Procedure

Twenty observers with normal stereo vision were invited to participate in the test (14 men and 6 women, with ages between 21 to 26). All subjects were instructed to give the score based on their subjective comfort experienced. A 47-in. polarized HD 3D displays (LG 47LA6600) and a StormMojing IV VR glasses were used to display the S3D videos to human subjects. Figure 4 shows the 3D-TV and VR glasses we used in this experiment.

The view distance of each observer for 3D-TV was set as 1.76 m which was 3 times of the screen height. Before each test, a set of reference videos would be played first, including one original S3D video and its shifted, geometric distorted, and frame desynchronized version of video. In each test, all videos were sorted randomly and videos of the same scene were ordered at least two videos apart.

(a) 3D-TV   (b) Storm Mojing IV VR glasses.

Fig. 4. Test on 3D-TV and VR glasses.

There would be a five-second scoring time right after the end of each video. Since that observers may feel dizziness or eye strain when watching S3D videos for too long, they would take a rest with each eight minutes viewing.

The absolute category rating (ACR) which described in [16] includes two different rating methods. In order to get more accurate subjective experimental results, we used the nine-point grading scale to rating the quality of S3D videos. Mean Opinion Score (MOS) was computed under this scale.

After the experiment, each observer was asked to do a questionnaire about the subjective comfort experienced. The mean comfort line of all observers was calculated to 5.6 from the questionnaire results. The results also show that many observers have the feelings that videos played on VR glasses were less comfortable than on 3D-TV. The reasons for voting in the top three are: (1) The VR glasses was too heavy and observers would feel uncomfortable when wearing the VR glasses for a long time. (2) The resolution of S3D videos under VR viewing condition was lower than that on 3D-TV. (3) Dizziness still exist on VR glasses which may be caused by oclar-vestibular conflict.

3   Comparative Evaluation of 3D-TV and VR

3.1   Score Processing

MOS was used as an indicator of subjective video quality. We calculated the MOS of each video by the following formula:

$$MOS_j = \frac{\sum_{i=1}^{N} m_{ij}}{N} \tag{5}$$

where MOS_j is the MOS of video j, N is the number of testers and m_{ij} is the score assessed by tester i to video j.

Before calculating MOS, we removed the outliers for all the scores according to ITU-R BT.500-11 [17]. The scores may include noise due to a variety of

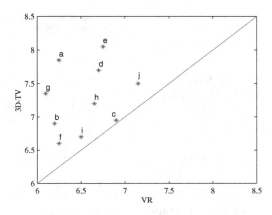

Fig. 5. The MOS scatter plot of all 10 scenes original videos on 3D-TV and VR.

factors such as visual fatigue of subjects, so excluding outliers was conducive to the analysis of data. After removing the outliers, we used the remaining data to calculate MOS.

All VR/3D-TV MOS pairs of 10 original S3D videos were shown as scatter plot in Fig. 5. In the figure, the area above the line indicates that videos on 3D-TV are more comfortable than on VR, and the area under the line shows that videos on VR are more comfortable than on 3D-TV. We can see from Fig. 5 that all the points are above the line, so the subjective comfort experienced on 3D-TV is higher than on VR for original videos. Weight, resolution and dizziness are main reasons according to questionnaires. Another reason is that the angle of convergence when watching videos on VR is different from that on 3D-TV. As shown in Fig. 6, since that the viewing distance was set as 3 times of the screen height, the viewing distance of VR glasses was 10 m while the viewing distance of 3D-TV was 1.76 m. So the angle of convergence β_2 is smaller than β_1, which may lead to different comfort experienced when watching S3D videos on 3D-TV and VR.

In order to compare the comfort difference experienced when watching shifted, geometric distorted and desynchronized versions of S3D videos, all MOSs with 10 scenes on 3D-TV and VR are plotted by using boxplot in Fig. 7. The mean MOS values of all scenes for each type and the mean comfort line of all observers were also plotted in the figure.

(1) Figure (a) shows that the stereo content in front of the screen (with negative shifting) on VR is generally more comfortable than on 3D-TV, but the stereo content behind the screen (with positive shifting) on TV is generally more comfortable than on VR. The main reason is that there will appear a virtual screen when viewing S3D videos with VR glasses, so there is no reference plane and we will not experience border conflicts.

(2) Figure (b) shows that the visual comfort on VR is higher than on 3D-TV if the angle of rotation become more than 1°. MOS on VR have a

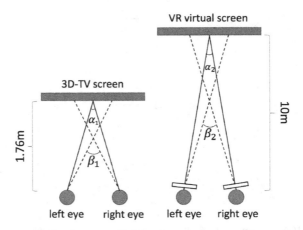

Fig. 6. Binocular parallax model for watching S3D videos on 3D-TV and VR.

smaller variation range in different distorted types of videos than on 3D-TV. Since that S3D videos will be processed by two separated lens when observers using VR glasses, human eyes are comparative insensitive to type-α geometric distortion with separated view from VR glasses.

(3) Figure (c) shows that human visual are sensitive to frame desynchronize and feel discomfort. The visual comfort for frame desynchronized S3D videos on VR is relatively higher than on 3D-TV. The reason is the same as the geometric distortion that human eyes receives the separated view when watching S3D videos on VR glasses.

In order to study the comfort difference experienced when viewing frame desynchronized videos in dramatic scenes and mild scenes, two sets of MOS samples of scenes were chosen for analysis. The MOS of all videos in scene (a) and scene (i) are shown in Fig. 8. Scene (a) describes a relaxing beach scene and scene (i) describes a fierce fighting scene. In the figure, we can see that when watching slow motion scene frame desynchronized S3D videos, observers were more tolerant on VR glasses than on 3D-TV, and observers could feel comfortable if the frame desynchronized degree was weak. However, when watching fast motion scene frame desynchronized S3D videos, observers would feel very uncomfortable both on VR and on 3D-TV. The figure also shows that no matter in which scene, the visual comfort for frame desynchronized S3D videos on VR is generally higher than on 3D-TV.

The Mann-Whitney U test was proposed by Mann and Whitney in 1947 [18]. It can test whether there is a significant difference between the means of the two populations. In this paper, the two-sided Mann-Whitney U test was used to measure whether there is a significant difference in comfort experienced between VR glasses and 3D-TV while viewing shifted and frame desynchronized videos. We calculated the p values for the Mann-Whitney U test of the negative shifted videos and positive shifted videos respectively. In addition, the p values of frame

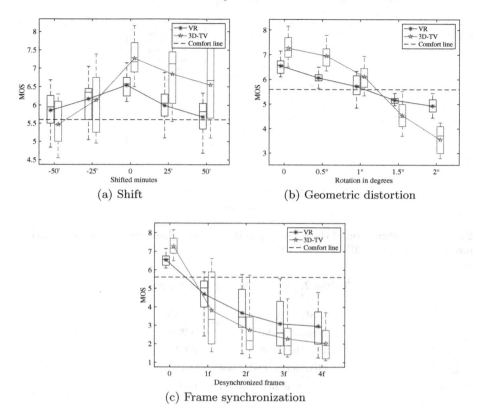

(a) Shift

(b) Geometric distortion

(c) Frame synchronization

Fig. 7. The MOS of three versions of S3D videos on 3D-TV and VR.

desynchronized videos and geometric distorted videos are also calculated. We set the null hypothesis that there was no significant difference in comfort while watching S3D videos on 3D-TV and VR glasses. If the test rejects the null hypothesis ($p < 0.05$), then we could conclude that 3D-TV and VR have significant differences in comfort.

The p values of S3D videos are shown in Table 2. We can conclude from Table 2 that there is a significant difference in visual comfort on 3D-TV and VR when watching positive shifted S3D videos and frame desynchronized S3D videos.

Subjective experimental results show that the subjective comfort experienced on 3D-TV is generally higher than on VR for original videos. While watching shifted S3D videos, the negative parallax (stereo content in front of the screen) on VR is more comfortable than on 3D-TV, but the positive parallax (stereo content behind the screen) on TV is more comfortable than on VR. The visual comfort for geometric distorted and frame unsynchronized S3D videos on VR is higher than on 3D-TV.

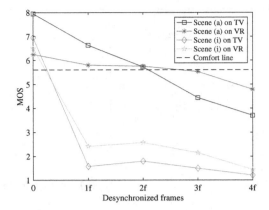

Fig. 8. The comparison of the Scene (a) and Scene (i) when viewing frame desynchronized S3D videos on 3D-TV and VR.

Table 2. Mann-Whitney U test p value

Distorted type	p value
Negative shift	0.208
Positive shift	0.001
Geometric distortion	0.400
Frame synchronization	0.003

The main factors of the comfort difference are due to: (1) S3D videos were processed by the lens of VR glasses, the resolution under VR viewing condition is lower than 3D-TV. (2) There is no reference plane when viewing S3D videos with VR glasses, so we will not experience border conflicts. (3) Human eyes are comparative insensitive to geometric distortion and frame desynchronization with separated view from VR glasses.

4   Conclusion

In this paper, we built a S3D video database and performed a subjective S3D comfort comparative study on 3D-TV and VR glasses. The database contains 130 videos include 10 different scenes. Each scenes includes 1 original video, 4 shifted videos, 4 geometric distorted videos and 4 frame desynchronized videos. The subjective S3D comfort comparative assessment is conducted on VR glasses and 3D-TV. MOS was collected from 20 testers and we analysed the experiment results. Through this experiment we compared the subjective comfort difference experienced while watching S3D videos on 3D-TV and VR. Main reasons about the result were analyzed.

Acknowledgements. The work for this paper is supported in part by MOST under 2015BAK05B03, NSFC under 61471234 and 61527804, Shanghai Pujiang Program under 16PJD029, and the Shanghai Key Laboratory of Digital Media Processing and Transmissions.

References

1. Zhou, J., Gu, X., Zhang, Y.: On evaluation the quality of subjective S3D comfort assessment. In: IEEE International Symposium on Broadband Multimedia Systems and Broadcasting, pp. 1–6 (2017)
2. Shibata, T., Kim, J., Hoffman, D.M., Banks, M.S.: The zone of comfort: predicting visual discomfort with stereo displays. J. Vis. **11**(8), 11 (2011)
3. Okano, F., Emoto, M., Niida, T.: Repeated vergence adaptation causes the decline of visual functions in watching stereoscopic television. J. Disp. Technol. **1**(2), 328–340 (2005)
4. Takatalo, J.: Simulator sickness in virtual display gaming: a comparison of stereoscopic and non-stereoscopic situations. In: Conference on Human-Computer Interaction with Mobile Devices and Services, pp. 227–230 (2006)
5. Hoffman, D.M., Girshick, A.R., Akeley, K., Banks, M.S.: Vergence-accommodation conflicts hinder visual performance and cause visual fatigue. J. Vis. **8**(3), 1–30 (2008)
6. Urvoy, M., Barkowsky, M., Le Callet, P.: How visual fatigue and discomfort impact 3D-TV quality of experience: a comprehensive review of technological, psychophysical, and psychological factors. Ann. Telecommun. Annales des télécommunications **68**(11–12), 641–655 (2013)
7. Lambooij, M., Ijsselsteijn, W.A., Heynderickx, I.: Visual discomfort of 3D TV: assessment methods and modeling. Displays **32**(4), 209–218 (2011)
8. Goldmann, L., De Simone, F., Ebrahimi, T.: A comprehensive database and subjective evaluation methodology for quality of experience in stereoscopic video. In: Proceedings of SPIE, vol. 7526 (2010)
9. Cho, S.H., Kang, H.B.: Subjective evaluation of visual discomfort caused from stereoscopic 3D video using perceptual importance map. In: TENCON 2012 - 2012 IEEE Region 10 Conference, pp. 1–6 (2013)
10. Kawano, T., Yamagishi, K., Hayashi, T.: Performance comparison of subjective assessment methods for 3D video quality. In: 2012 Fourth International Workshop on Quality of Multimedia Experience (QoMEX), pp. 218–223. IEEE (2012)
11. Hoaglin, D.C.: Some implementations of the boxplot. Am. Stat. **43**(1), 50–54 (1989)
12. Wöpking, M.: Viewing comfort with stereoscopic pictures: an experimental study on the subjective effects of disparity magnitude and depth of focus. J. Soc. Inf. Disp. **3**(3), 101–103 (1995)
13. 3D Consortium: 3DC Safety Guidelines for Popularization of Human-friendly 3D (2006)
14. ITU-R, Subjective Assessment of Stereoscopic Television Pictures, Technical report BT. 1438 (2000)
15. Barkowsky, M., Cousseau, R., Le Callet, P.: Is visual fatigue changing the perceived depth accuracy on an autostereoscopic display? In: SPIE 2011 Stereoscopic Displays and Applications XXII, vol. 7863, p. 78631V (2011)
16. Telephone Installations and Local Line, ITU-T P.910. Subjective video quality assessment methods for multimedia applications, Recommendation ITU-T P.910, vol. 12, no. 2, pp. 3665–3673 (2007)

17. ITU-R BT. Recommendation, 500-11, Methodology for the Subjective Assessment of the Quality of Television Pictures, Recommendation ITU-R BT. 500-11, ITU Telecom. Standardization Sector of ITU, vol. 7 (2002)
18. Mann, H.B., Whitney, D.R.: On a test of whether one of two random variables is stochastically larger than the other. Ann. Math. Stat. **18**, 50–60 (1947)

Quality Assessment of Virtual Reality Videos

Pei Wu, Ping An[⊠], and Jian Ma

Shanghai Institute for Advanced Communication and Data Science,
School of Communication and Information Engineering,
Shanghai University, Shanghai 200444, China
anping@shu.edu.cn

Abstract. 360-degree spherical images/videos, also called virtual reality (VR) images/videos, can provide an immersive experience of real scenes in some specific systems. This makes it widely used in VR games, sporting events and VR movies. However, due to its high resolution, it is so difficult to transmit, compress or store VR images/videos. Therefore, it is significant to study how noise affects the quality of VR images. To this end, this paper builds a VR video database, and carries out subjective and objective experiments on them. Specifically, first, six standard panoramic videos are processed by inputting three kinds of distorted types to establish a VR video database which comprises 96 videos. Second, we utilize the Double Stimulus Injury Scale (DSIS) for subjective experiments. All subjective scores are from 20 non-professional viewers. Third, we utilize 6 existing objective metrics to validate our database. Finally, experimental results demonstrate that the established VR database is suitable for subjective and objective quality evaluation of VR video. Our work has alleviated the problem of missing VR databases.

Keywords: Panoramic video database · Subjective quality assessment · Objective quality assessment · Performance comparison

1 Introduction

With the development of multimedia technology and computer graphics, VR technology has attracted much attention due to its good user experience and efficient human-computer interaction. Users can access VR through a variety of Head Mounted Displays (HMD) such as HTC VIVE [1], Oculus Rift [2], etc. In this paper, a panoramic video display system is built based on the HTC vive platform to provide users with a clear and smooth panoramic video viewing experience. While enjoying the immersive and technological sense brought about by virtual reality technology, users are also paying more attention to their display quality. However, unlike the traditional video or image, the VR videos always have very high resolution, which makes them very hard to be transmitted, compressed or stored. So how to improve the display quality and provide users with a better visual experience has become a hot topic in this field.

The VR video/image quality evaluation is still in the beginning of development. As we know, at present, many 2D image quality assessment (IQA) databases have been built, such as LIVE [3], TID2008 [4] and CSIQ [5]. However, few databases are relevant to VR images/videos. To the best of our knowledge, Sun established a

© Springer Nature Singapore Pte Ltd. 2019
G. Zhai et al. (Eds.): IFTC 2018, CCIS 1009, pp. 273–283, 2019.
https://doi.org/10.1007/978-981-13-8138-6_23

Compressed VR Image Quality Database (CVIQD) by Insta360 4K Spherical VR Video Camera [6]. The CVIQD database consists of 165 VR images form five original images, but it is not standard enough because of the effects of various noises in the environment. Therefore, in this paper, we attempt to build a new VR video database from six standard panorama original video. Due to the H264/HEVC protocol is the crystallization of the development of traditional graphic video coding technology, it can not directly support the spherical panorama video, so the standard panorama video is projected in 2D form of video. Projection formats include Equirectangular (ERP), Cubemap (CMP), Equal-area (EAP) types and so on. Most of panoramic video databases are used in ERP projection format, as shown in Fig. 1.

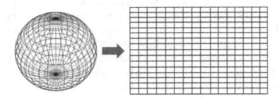

Fig. 1. Schematic diagram of ERP projection process.

In general, similar to 2D IQA methods, VR video quality assessment methods are divided into subjective quality assessment and objective quality assessment. Subjective test methods commonly used are Single Stimulus (SS) method, Double Stimulus Continuous Quality Scale (DSCQS) and DSIS method. Zhang proposed a new subjective evaluation method SAMPVIQ [7] and compared with the other two subjective test methods, they calculated the four coefficients between the data of the three subjective methods and the objective model of VQM. However, it is questionable because they regard VQM as a standard. On the other hand, there is no standard objective model for VR video quality assessment. So all VR video objective quality assessment models refer to the traditional models. Traditional objective quality assessment method is mainly divided into full reference, reduced reference and no reference method for whether to refer to the original image information. The methods currently used for VR video quality assessment are mostly based on full reference methods.

To identify the key influence factors affecting VR video and solve the problem of that there is no standard VR video database, in this paper, we build a VR database and perform subjective and objective assessment on it. The main contributions are summarized below.

- We build a VR video database. Specifically, we treat the original six standard panoramic videos with three kinds of distorted types, each with five levels of distortion to build a new VR videos database. The database contains a total of 96 panoramic videos and can be used to facilitate the studies of VR videos quality assessment.
- Subjective and objective experiment tests are performed on the database. Specifically, the subjective experiments use the DSIS method. Meanwhile, six full reference models are used in the objective experiments. Finally, we analyze experimental results by comparing with four parameter values.

The rest of the paper is arranged as follows. Section 2 introduces the panoramic video database of subjective quality evaluation, the evaluation method, and the processing and analysis of subjective experimental results. Objective assessment and performance evaluation are presented in Sect. 3. Finally, Sect. 4 provides some concluding remarks.

2 Subjective Quality Assessment

2.1 Panoramic Video Database

Six standard panoramic videos recommended by IEEE 1857.9M1053 proposal [8] are used as test sequences. The video format is yuv420p, and the projection format is the ERP format. Based on the experience of VR, all the video sequences have a resolution of 4096 * 2048 and a frame rate of 30 fps.

Each video is ten seconds long. Figure 2 shows their example frames. These standard panoramic videos are processed by inputting three kinds of distorted types to set up a VR video database which comprises 96 videos. The three kinds of distorted

(a)Video01(Talk)   (b)Video02 (The Pagoda)

(c)Video03(Lake)   (d)Video04(The Great Wall)

(e)Video05(Auditorium)   (f)Video06(Boat)

Fig. 2. Thumbnails of the source video sequences

types are: Gaussian white noise, JPEG compression and Motion blur [9]. Each distorted type is processed into five levels. Table 1 shows the results: the higher the level, the worse the quality of video.

Table 1. The types of distortion and parameters of each level

Distortion	Level 1	Level 2	Level 3	Level 4	Level 5
Gaussian white noise	0.001	0.003	0.005	0.008	0.01
JPEG compression	13	11	9	7	5
Motion blur	6	12	18	24	30

- Gaussian white noise: To generate the noise, we employ the Matlab imnoise command with standard normal probability density function of variance σ_N^2 (0.001, 0.003, 0.005, 0.008, 0.01) on each of three color channel, R, G and B.
- JPEG compression: we use the Matlab imwrite command to create JPEG compressed images by setting the Q parameter as 13, 11, 9, 7 and 5.
- Motion blur: we use the Matlab fspecial and imfilter commands to create Motion blurred images by setting the motion angle as 0 and motion length parameter as 6, 12, 18, 24 and 30.

2.2 Subjective Experiment Methodology

The subjective quality evaluation can be made after setting up the VR video database. The ITU-R BT500-13 [10] has defined several subjective testing methodologies to assess image quality, for instance, SS, DSIS and DSCQS. The methodology selected for this test is based on DSIS. The test process contains a total of 18 test sequences, and a short 20-s break was performed to relieve the fatigue of the eyes after completing a set of video comparisons. The test subjects will repeatedly compare the quality of the original video sequence with the damaged sequence, and then give a score of 1 to 5. Due to the VR video shows the entire field of view of a scene, the observers can rotate their heads to see any place from any angle when put on the HMD. There is no requirement for the surrounding environment after wearing an external helmet. Figure 3 shows the test environment.

We chose the HTC VIVE as the HMD because of its excellent graphic display technology and high precision tracking ability. The average age of the 20 participants was 23.4, including 13 boys and 7 girls. They both reported normal or corrected vision. Before starting the experiment, the goal of this subjective test and instruction were introduced to each subject. The test totally lasted 15 days.

Fig. 3. Subjective experimental environment.

2.3 Data Processing and Analysis

From the subjective test, we have collected all the subjective MOS (Mean Opinion Score) values. Outlier detection is performed according to the guidelines defined in ITU recommendation [11]. The MOS is computed for each distortion condition j as follows:

$$MOS_j = \frac{1}{N} \sum_{i=1}^{N} m_{ij}, \tag{1}$$

where N is the number of subjects; m_{ij} is the score for stimulus j by participant i.

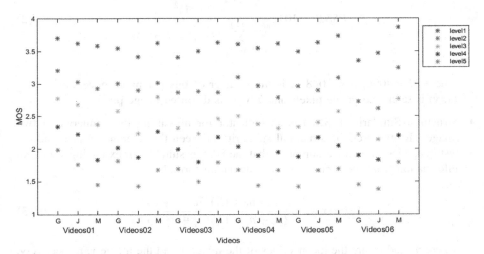

Fig. 4. Scatter plots of MOSs in the database

We plot all MOS values in Fig. 4 after calculating the subjective MOS value of all video sequences. Note that, the ordinate is the subjective MOS value, and the "G", "J" and

"M" on the abscissa refer to Gaussian white noise, JPEG compression and motion blur, respectively. Level 1 to level 5 stand for that the degree of compression increases in turn.

It can be found from the figure that the subjective score of gaussian white noise is slightly higher than the subjective score of the other two noises.

3 Objective Quality Assessment

Since image quality assessment (IQA) plays a crucial role in the guidance and optimization of image/video applications, it has always been a hot topic in digital image processing, such as: compression [12], enhance [13], denoising [14], and so on. For 2D IQA metric, there are many algorithms have been proposed. The most classic one is the PSNR algorithm, which is widely used due to its mathematical convenience. However, it was found to be not always consistent with the quality perceived by the human visual system (HVS). Therefore, some classic IQA methods [15, 16] rely mainly on structural information or statistical information. In addition, some modern IQA models use HVS features to obtain more accurate quality predictions. For example, the Gradient Magnitude Standard Deviation (GMSD) [17] is based on this fact. Since there is no standard for the objective algorithm of VR video, we use the traditional objective algorithm to calculate it. This paper uses the following six algorithms:

- Peak Signal to Noise Ratio (PSNR) is a traditional image quality assessment method [18]. It is the ratio between the maximum power of the signal and the power of the difference signal between the reference and test images. Its calculation formula is as follows:

$$PSNR = 10 \lg \frac{(2^n - 1)^2}{\sum\limits_{x=0}^{M-1} \sum\limits_{y=0}^{N-1} [T(x,y) - R(x,y)]^2} \tag{2}$$

where $M = 4096$, $N = 2048$. n is the number of bits per pixel, generally is 8. $R(x, y)$ is reference image pixels and $T(x, y)$ is distorted image pixels.

- Structural Similarity (SSIM) is an indicator for measuring the similarity of two images. It measures the structural similarity between the reference image and the test image based on the assumption that the HVS is suitable for extracting structural information from the scene [15]. Its calculation formula is:

$$SSIM(x, y) = \frac{(2u_x u_y + C_1)(2\sigma_x \sigma_y + C_2)}{(u_x^2 + u_y^2 + C_1)(\sigma_x^2 + \sigma_y^2 + C_2)} \tag{3}$$

where u_x and u_y are the mean values of the image x and the image y, respectively. σ_x and σ_y are the standard deviations of image x and image y, respectively.

- Mean Structural Similarity (MSSIM) [15]. It is an improvement to the structure similarity SSIM algorithm. Because SSIM has some limitations on some types of distortions such as blurring, noise distortion, and geometric distortion, MSSIM has been derived on this basis. Its calculation formula is as follows:

$$MSSIM(x, y) = \frac{1}{M} \sum_{j=1}^{M} SSIM(x_j, y_j) \tag{4}$$

where x_j and y_j are the image contents at the j th local window; and M is the number of local windows of the image.

- Gradient Magnitude Standard Deviation (GMSD). It is a global variation of gradient based local quality map for overall image quality prediction. The GMSD algorithm is much faster than most state-of-the-art IQA methods and provides highly predictive accuracy. Its calculation formula is as follows:

$$GMSD = \sqrt{\frac{1}{N} \sum_{i=1}^{N} (GMS(i) - GMSM)^2} \tag{5}$$

$$GMSM = \frac{1}{N} \sum_{i=1}^{N} GMS(i) \tag{6}$$

The GMS map is computed in a pixel-wise manner, and other details can refer to the article [17].

- Feature Similarity (FSIM): It is image quality assessment based on image structure and congruency similarity. It is for the evaluation of image denoising effect and closer the value is to 1, better the denoising result is [19].

$$FSIM = \frac{\sum_{x \in \Omega} S_L(x) \cdot PC_m(x)}{\sum_{x \in \Omega} PC_m(x)} \tag{7}$$

Where $PC_m(x) = \max(PC_1(x), PC_2(x))$, Ω is the whole image spatial domain and SL(x) is similarity measure [19].

- Most Apparent Distortion (MAD). Local brightness and contrast masking are used to estimate based on detection of perceptual distortion in high quality image, whereas changes in the local statistics of spatial frequency components are used to estimate appearance-based perceived distortion in low quality images [20].

$$MAD = (d_{det\,ect})^{\alpha}(d_{appear})^{1-\alpha} \tag{8}$$

$$\alpha = \frac{1}{1 + \beta_1 (d_{det\,ect})^{\beta_2}} \tag{9}$$

$$d_{det\,ect} = \left\{ \frac{1}{P} \sum_p \lceil \xi(p) \times D(p) \rceil^2 \right\}^{1/2} \tag{10}$$

$$d_{appear} = \left[\frac{1}{P}\sum_p \eta(p)^2\right]^{1/2} \tag{11}$$

where $MAD \in [0, \infty]$ denotes the overall perceived distortion. The weight $\alpha \in [0, 1]$ is chosen based on the (predicted) overall level of distortion [20]. P is the total number of blocks and the summation is over all blocks. The quantity $D(p)$ is the local MSE computed for each 16 * 16 block p.

The above six kinds of objective algorithms are adopted in this paper. For details, reference can be made to their respective documents. Ultimately, we evaluate the performance and map the objective quality metric predictions to subjective evaluations using a five-parameter logistic function for eliminating non-linear values:

$$mos = \beta_1\left(\frac{1}{2} - \frac{1}{1 + e^{\beta_2(x-\beta_3)}}\right) + \beta_4 x + \beta_5 \tag{12}$$

where x denotes the predicted score, MOS denotes the corresponding subjective score. β_1, β_2, β_3, β_4 and β_5 are the parameters to be fitted. These five statistical indicators are used to compare the performance of the consensus and are compared with the predicted scores obtained from objective indicators and subjective MOS. They are Pearson's linear correlation coefficient (PLCC), Spearman rank correlation coefficient (SROCC), Kendall rank order correlation coefficient (KROCC), average absolute prediction error (AAE) and root mean square error (RMSE) [21–23].

We find that the MSSIM algorithm performs best on PLCC and RMSE and the MAD algorithm performs best on SROCC and KROCC by calculating the four values of SROCC, PLCC, KROCC, and RMSE. Table 2 shows the result.

Table 2. The types of distortion and parameters of each level

Method	PLCC	SROCC	KROCC	RMSE
PSNR	0.8017	0.7662	0.5657	0.4248
SSIM	0.7428	0.7723	0.5842	0.4758
MSSIM	**0.8370**	0.7925	0.6071	**0.3889**
GMSD	0.8237	0.8149	0.6256	0.4029
FSIM	0.8078	0.7899	0.6211	0.4188
MAD	0.8341	**0.8346**	**0.6519**	0.3920

- PLCC is the covariance of the two variables divided by the product of their standard deviations [21].
- SROCC and KROCC mainly evaluate the ranked relevance of the two sets of data. They are used to give monotonicity prediction [22].
- RMSE is the square root of the mean square error, which is used to measure the prediction accuracy [23].

Figure 5 shows the subjective MOS values fitted to four objective algorithms. SSIM, MSSIM and FSIM values are distributed between 0and 1, with the value of

PSNR ranging from 20 to 50. The larger of the three metrics indicates the better video quality. In contrast, the distribution of GMSD values is from 0 to 0.2 and the distribution of MAD values is from 40 to 160, where a smaller value means better video quality. According to the calculation and drawing results, the relative results of MSSIM and MAD are better. However, compared with the normal video where the correlation coefficient value of the MSSIM model can reach 0.9 or more, the objective model for the panoramic video has a lot of room for improvement.

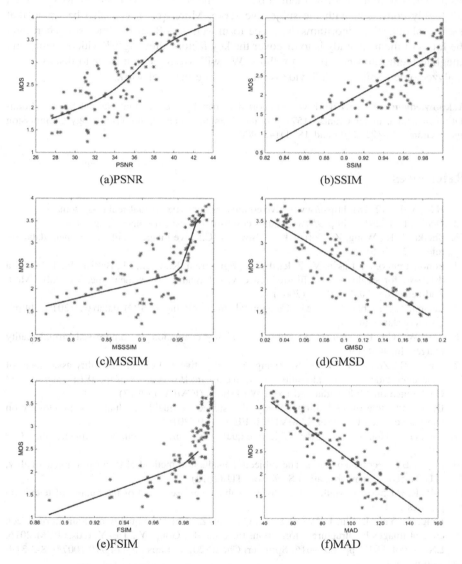

Fig. 5. MOS values fitted with results of objective algorithms

4   Conclusion

In this paper, a VR video database is constructed, which contains 96 panoramic videos. Subjective and objective experiments are performed on our database. The DSIS method is used for subjective experiments. Subjective experimental results demonstrate that the quality of experience has changed due to different losses and video content. In addition, we compare six objective 2D IQA models on our database. Objective experimental results show that the MSSIM method based on multi-scale model and the MAD model are highly consistent with the subjective score. Moreover, it can also be found that traditional objective algorithms do not perform well on VR video databases. Therefore, the focus of the next study is to discover the key factors affecting VR video quality and integrate them into objective algorithms. We will use the eye tracker to discover and analyze some features of VR videos on our future plans of work.

Acknowledgement. This work was supported in part by the National Natural Science Foundation of China, under Grants 61571285, and Shanghai Science and Technology Commission under Grant 17DZ2292400 and 18XD1423900.

References

1. HTC Valve (2018). https://www.vive.com/us/product/vive-virtual-reality-system/
2. Oculus Rift (2018). https://www.oculus.com/rift/#oui-csl-rift-games=mages-tale/
3. Sheikh, H.R., Wang, Z., Cormack, L., Bovik, A.C.: Live image quality assessment database release 2 (2005)
4. Ponomarenko, N., Lukin, V., Zelensky, A., Egiazarian, K., Carli, M., Battisti, F.: Tid 2008-a database for evaluation of full-reference visual quality assessment metrics. Adv. Mod. Radioelectron. **10**(4), 30–45 (2009)
5. Larson, E.C., Chandler, D.M.: Categorical image quality (CSIQ) database (2010). http://vision.okstate.edu/csiq
6. Sun, W., Gu, K., Zhai, G.G.: Subjective quality evaluation of compressed virtual reality images. In: ICIP (2017)
7. Zhang, B., Zhao, J.Z., Yang, S., Zhang, Y.: Subjective and objective quality assessment of panoramic videos in virtual reality environments. In: Proceedings of the IEEE International Conference on Multimedia and Expo Workshops (ICMEW) (2017)
8. Beijing Institute of Technology, Study of a subjective quality evaluation methodology on panoramic video based on SAMVIQ. IEEE 1857.9 (2016)
9. Yue, G.H., Hou, C.P., Gu, K.: Subjective quality assessment of animation images. In: VCIP (2017)
10. ITU-R BT Recommendation, The subjective evaluation method of television image quality, ITU Telecom. Standardization Sector of ITU (2012)
11. I.-R. R. BT.500-11, Methodology for the subjective assessment of the quality of television pictures (2002)
12. Fang, Y., Yan, J., Liu, J., Wang, S., Li, Q., Guo, Z.: Objective quality assessment of screen content images by structure information. In: Chen, E., Gong, Y., Tie, Y. (eds.) PCM 2016. LNCS, vol. 9917, pp. 609–616. Springer, Cham (2016). https://doi.org/10.1007/978-3-319-48896-7_60

13. Gu, K., Zhai, G.G., Lin, W.S., Liu, M.: The analysis of image contrast: from quality assessment to automatic enhancement. IEEE Trans. Cybern. **46**(1), 284–297 (2016)
14. Mittal, A., Moorthy, A.K., Bovik, A.C.: Noreference image quality assessment in the spatial domain. IEEE TIP **21**(12), 4695–4708 (2012)
15. Wang, Z., Bovik, A.C., Sheikh, H.R., Simoncelli, E.P.: Image quality assessment: from error visibility to structural similarity. IEEE TIP **13**(4), 600–612 (2004)
16. Wang, Z., Simoncelli, E.P., Bovik, A.C.: Multiscale structural similarity for image quality assessment. In: Proceedings of IEEE 37th Asilomar Conference Signals Systems & Computers, Pacific Grove, CA, USA, November 2003, pp. 1398–1402 (2003)
17. Xue, W.F., Zhang, L., Mou, X.Q., Bovik, A.C.: Gradient magnitude similarity deviation: a highly efficient perceptual image quality index. IEEE TIP **23**(2), 684–695 (2014)
18. Hore, A., Ziou, D.: Image quality metrics: PSNR vs SSIM. In: ICPR pp. 2366–2369 (2010)
19. Zhang, L., Zhang, L., Mou, X.Q., Zhang, D.: FSIM: a feature similarity index for image quality assessment. IEEE TIP **20**(8), 2378–2386 (2011)
20. Larson, E.C., Chandler, D.M.: Most apparent distortion: full-reference image quality assessment and the role of strategy. J. Electron. Imaging **19**(1), 011006-1–011006-21 (2010)
21. Pearson, K.: Note on regression and inheritance in the case of two parents. Proc. R. Soc. Lond. **58**, 240–242 (1895)
22. Yang, J.C., Lin, Y.C., Gao, Z.Q., Lv, Z.H., Wei, W., Song, H.B.: Quality index for stereoscopic images by separately evaluating adding and subtracting. PLoS ONE **10**(12), e0145800 (2015)
23. Kim, S.J., Chae, C.B., Lee, J.S.: Subjective and objective quality assessment of videos in error-prone network environments. Multimed. Tools Appl. **75**(12), 6849–6870 (2016)

Modulation Spectral Features for Intrusive Measurement of Reverberant Speech Quality

Sai Ma$^{(\boxtimes)}$, Hui Zhang, Lingyun Xie, and Xi Xie

Communication University of China, Beijing, China
{saima,zhanghui0931,xiely,cici.xie}@cuc.edu.cn

Abstract. Temporal fine structure includes temporal envelope and fine structure which also called carrier, and instantaneous frequency is the partial derivative of the carrier. An intrusive reverberant speech quality measurement is investigated with the representation of corresponding instantaneous frequency. A Gammatone filterbank is used to simulate auditory mechanism and a modulation filterbank is used to improve frequency resolution. The mean mutual information between reference and reverberant modulation spectral instantaneous frequency probability distribution is taken as the final measurement score. Experimental results show the proposed method outperforming two benchmark algorithms in some practical application conditions.

Keywords: Reverberation · Direct-to-Reverberant energy ratio · Modulation · Instantaneous Frequency · Mutual Information

1 Introduction

When speech signals propagate in an enclosed environment, they are distorted by the features of room acoustics, including room dimensions, reflection path and sound absorption of the enclosure, which make them reverberate. Reverberation is known to degrade human-perceived speech quality and intelligibility [1] as well as many other applications, e.g. automatic speech recognition (ASR) system [2] and cochlear implant users [3]. A lot of work has been done for speech quality measurement, and many classical methods have been presented, e.g. frequency segmental signal-to-noise ratio, weighted-spectral slope, log-likelihood ratio, Itakura-Saito distance, and ITU-T P. 862 Perceptual Evaluation of Speech Quality (PESQ) [4]. Recently, more researchers focus on evaluation of reverberant speech. Falk proposes a non-intrusive objective evaluation method for reverberant speech quality, which is called Speech-to-Reverberant Modulation energy Ratio (SRMR) [5,6]. In [7], three PESQ empirical factors have been refitting from, reverberant speech coloration, reverberation tail effect and overall quality, three aspects in order to achieve the reliable prediction. [8] utilizes Blind Estimation of Spectral Standard Deviation (BESSD) and [9] uses variation of first

© Springer Nature Singapore Pte Ltd. 2019
G. Zhai et al. (Eds.): IFTC 2018, CCIS 1009, pp. 284–295, 2019.
https://doi.org/10.1007/978-981-13-8138-6_24

three formant locations as an indicator of reverberation level for low and high fundamental frequency sound, respectively. Nowadays, Temporal Fine Structure (TFS) exemplifies the current state-of-the-art in speech signal processing based on human auditory system. TFS contains two parts: temporal envelope and fine structure. Temporal envelope is mainly related to the energy, and fine structure which also called carrier is tightly bound to the details [10]. The carrier can be obtained through the analytical form of speech signal, and then the instantaneous frequency, which effectively improves speech recognition accuracy [11], is available.

In this research, an intrusive objective reverberant speech quality measurement algorithm based on modulation spectral instantaneous frequency is proposed. The remainder of this paper is organized as follows: Section 2 describes models of room reverberation as well as introduces methods to artificially generate reverberant speech. Section 3 presents the algorithm framework and illustrates Gammatone filterbank and modulation filterbank in details. Section 4 shows how to calculate the final measurement score and the comparison with baseline algorithms. Conclusions are in Sect. 5.

2   Room Reverberation

2.1   Models of Room Reverberation

Reverberation can be described as the persistence of sound in space from a source, the relationship between physical environment and the reverberation produced can be described in mathematical terms by its impulse response C the output of a dynamic system (the room) from an external change (impulse sound input) as a function of time. In room acoustics, the impulse response describes the acoustic characteristics of a room, particularly the reverberation [12].

The reverberated speech, $s_{Reverb}(n)$, is usually modeled as the convolution of a given speech signal, $s_{Ref}(n)$, with room impulse response (RIR), $r(n)$, which is mathematically expressed by [13]

$$s_{Reverb}(n) = r(n) * s_{Ref}(n). \tag{1}$$

As is well known, the ensemble average of the squared room impulse response decays exponentially with time under the diffuse sound field assumption [14]

$$\langle r^2(n) \rangle = A exp(-kn), \tag{2}$$

where A is a gain term, and k is damping factor given by

$$k = \frac{(log10^6)}{(F_s \times T_{60})}, \tag{3}$$

where F_s is the sampling frequency and T_{60} is the so-called reverberation time.

2.2   Room Reverberation Property

Numerous reverberation parameters can be predicted from room impulse response (RIR), which is the transfer function between sound source and receiver. Reverberation Time (RT) and Direct-to-Reverberant energy Ratio (DRR) are two significant indicators of room reverberation characteristics. RT is defined as the time for the sound to die away to a level 60 dB below its original level, which is commonly noted as T_{60}. Generally, the Schroeder integral is used to calculate T_{60} from the room impulse response [15]. DRR is the energy ratio between direct and reverberant speech signals, which is an important cue to sound source distance, and is given by [16]

$$DRR = \frac{E_d}{E_r} = \frac{\sum_{(n_d - n_1)}^{(n_d + n_{1.5})} r^2(n)}{\sum_{(n_d + n_{1.5})}^{N} r^2(n)}. \tag{4}$$

Furthermore, other parameters that characterize room acoustics and obtained from RIR include early decay time (the slope of the decay curve should be determined from the slope of the best-fit linear regression line of the initial 10 dB of the decay), speech clarity index (early-to-late arriving sound energy ratio which can be calculated for either a 50 ms or an 80 ms early time limit) [17], and so on.

2.3   Simulated Reverberant Speech

In this research, Image-Source Model (ISM) [18] is used to artificially generate different RIRs. T_{60} is roughly a function of the room size (for reflection constant) but not the Source C Microphone Distances (SMDs), taking three different

Table 1. SMD and corresponding DRR

RT = 300 ms		RT = 600 ms		RT = 1000 ms	
SMD (m)	DRR (dB)	SMD (m)	DRR (dB)	SMD (m)	DRR (dB)
0.174	15.0403	0.101	15.0083	0.072	15.0710
0.262	12.0170	0.151	12.0281	0.105	12.0789
0.387	9.0259	0.217	9.0200	0.155	9.0290
0.578	6.0290	0.315	6.0321	0.219	6.0517
0.857	3.0026	0.456	3.0044	0.314	3.0279
1.275	0.0030	0.647	0.0183	0.466	0.0196
1.877	−3.0042	0.954	−3.0067	0.645	−3.0011
2.848	−6.0006	1.376	−6.0011	0.945	−6.0007
4.580	−9.0420	1.980	−9.0121	1.360	−9.0273
6.962	−12.0011	2.831	−12.0080	1.867	−12.0033
7.999	−15.0290	3.985	−15.0254	2.806	−15.1267

T_{60}, (e.g. 300 ms, 600 ms and 1000 ms). Table 1 shows a number of SMDs which make the DRR spans from 15 to −15 dB, and the room dimensions (length * width * height) = 9 * 4 *6 m^3. Therefore, 33 room impulse responses are generated.

The reverberant speeches are obtained by the convolution of generated room impulse responses and clean speeches. Critical distance is defined as that distance from source to receiver where the direct sound energy is equal to the total reverberant sound energy, which means DRR = 0 dB. The waveforms depicted in Fig. 1 exemplify reverberant speech signals produced at critical distance for T_{60} = 300, 600 and 1000 ms.

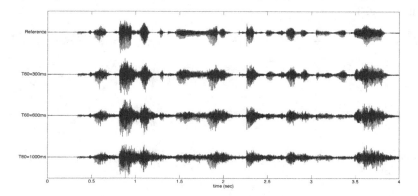

Fig. 1. Waveforms, top to bottom: reference and reverberant, T_{60} = 0.3, 0.6 and 1 s, at critical distance

3   Algorithm

The proposed reverberant speech quality measurement is accomplished using the signal processing steps illustrated in Fig. 2. Both reference and reverberant speech signals, $s_{Ref}(n)$ and $s_{Reverb}(n)$, are filtered by a bank of critical-band filters. A critical-band Gammatone Filterbank, with 23 filters, is used to simulate the processing performed by the cochlea [19,20]. And then, both reference and reverberant signals at each critical-band are filtered by a 32-channel Modulation Filterbank, and instantaneous frequency in every modulation band are extracted. Training the features with Gaussian Mixture Model (GMM) in order to obtain their probability distribution, respectively. Therefore, the reverberation affection can be expressed by mutual information between them.

Fig. 2. Reverberant speech quality measurement framework

3.1   Gammatone Filterbank

Filter center frequencies range from 125 Hz to nearly half the sampling rate (e.g., 6947.85 Hz for 16 kHz sampling rate). Filter bandwidths are characterized by the Equivalent Rectangular Bandwidth (ERB). The ERB for filter l, $l = 1, 2, \cdots, 23$, is given by

$$ERB_l = \frac{f_l}{Q_{ear}} + B_{min}, \tag{5}$$

where f_l represents the center frequency for the filter and Q_{ear} and B_{min} are constants set to 9.265 and 24.7, respectively. Select 23-channel which means 23 critical-band in this research, and Gammatone filterbank frequency response is shown in Fig. 3.

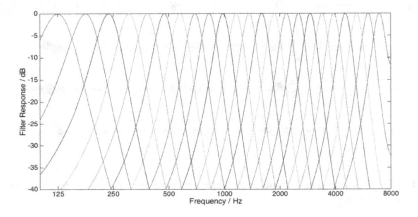

Fig. 3. Frequency response for the 23-channel Gammatone filterbank

3.2   Modulation Filterbank

The filtered signal, $s_l(n)$ ($l \in L$), still has interference from other frequency components, and we still consider it as a full band signal [21]. Let $s_l(n)$ pass through a filterbank which is characterized by a set of LTI bandpass filters $h_k(n)$

$$s_{lk}(n) = s_l(n) * h_k(n), \ for \ k = 1, \cdots, K. \tag{6}$$

The resulting sub-band signals $s_{lk}(n)$ are passed to the envelope detector and carrier estimator, which estimate a modulator signal $a_{lk}(n)$ and a carrier signal $cos(\varphi_{lk}(n))$, respectively. The modulation framework is depicted in Fig. 4.

In practical modulation systems care should be taken to realign the modulators after filtering, since each filter $g_k(n)$ may have a different group delay. Furthermore, the carriers should also be delayed appropriately before recombining them with the filtered modulators. After filtering, the modulators are recombined with the original sub-band carriers into modified sub-band signals

$$\widetilde{s}_{lk}(n) = \widetilde{a}_{lk}(n) \cdot cos(\varphi_{lk}(n)). \tag{7}$$

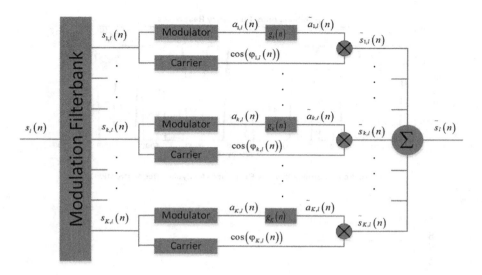

Fig. 4. Modulation filterbank framework

From the modified sub-band signals, a modulation filtered full band signal is obtained. This process, commonly referred to as filterbank reconstruction, is done by the filterbank summation method, which is given by

$$\widetilde{s}_{lk}(n) = \sum_{k=1}^{K} \widetilde{s}_{lk}(n). \tag{8}$$

We evenly divide the full band to 32 parts (for $fs = 16000\,\text{Hz}$), and only consider the frequency components under Nyquist. The sub-band filter frequency response and modulation filterbank impulse response are shown in Fig. 5.

The outputs of critical-band are modulated to sub-band, and the carriers are obtained, and then accordingly instantaneous frequencies are extracted. It can be seen from the upper bottom diagram that the modulation filterbank satisfy the signal reconstruction condition, however, it is not the interest of this paper.

4   Experiment

4.1   Instantaneous Frequency Extraction

The output of lth ($l \in L$) critical-band Gammatone filter and k^{th} ($k \in K$) sub-band modulation filter is denoted by $s_{lk}(n)$, the Hilbert transform $\mathcal{H}\{\cdot\}$ is then used to obtain the analytical form of $s_{lk}(n)$

$$z_{lk}(n) = s_{lk}(n) + j\mathcal{H}\{s_{lk}(n)\} = a_{lk}(n)\,e^{j\varphi_{lk}(n)}, \tag{9}$$

$$a_{lk}(n) = \sqrt{s_{lk}^2(n) + \mathcal{H}^2\{s_{lk}(n)\}}, \tag{10}$$

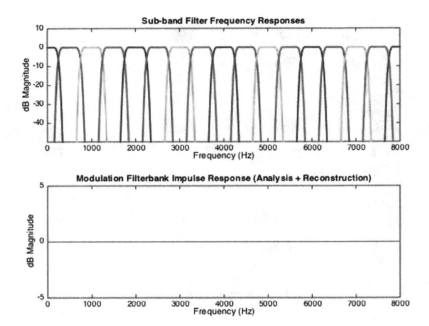

Fig. 5. Sub-band filter frequency response and modulation filterbank impulse response

$$\varphi_{lk}(n) = arctan\left(\frac{\mathcal{H}\{s_{lk}(n)\}}{s_{lk}(n)}\right), \tag{11}$$

where $a_{lk}(n)$ is instantaneous amplitude, $\varphi_{lk}(n)$ is instantaneous phase. Then, the expansion form of $z_{lk}(n)$ is

$$z_{lk}(n) = s_{lk}(n) + j\mathcal{H}\{s_{lk}(n)\} = a_{lk}(n)cos(\varphi_{lk}(n)) + ja_{lk}(n)sin(\varphi_{lk}(n)). \tag{12}$$

Obviously, it can be seen that

$$s_{lk}(n) = a_{lk}(n)cos(\varphi_{lk}(n)). \tag{13}$$

The decomposition of a signal into a modulator and a carrier is most meaningful for narrowband signals. $cos(\varphi_{lk}(n))$ is the carrier of $s_{lk}(n)$, and instantaneous phase $\varphi_{lk}(n)$ commonly has the following form

$$\varphi_{lk}(n) = 2\pi fn + \theta, \tag{14}$$

where f is carrier frequency, n is time index, and θ is the original phase. Clearly, instantaneous phase $\varphi_{lk}(n)$ has time-frequency properties, and $f(n)$ is partial derivatives of $\varphi_{lk}(n)$ to time called Instantaneous Frequency (IF), which can reflect frequency variation of the carrier. The instantaneous frequency tracks at critical-band 15 and sub-band 5 for reference and reverberant, $T_{60} = 300, 600$ and 1000 ms, at DRR = 0 dB are depicted in Fig. 6.

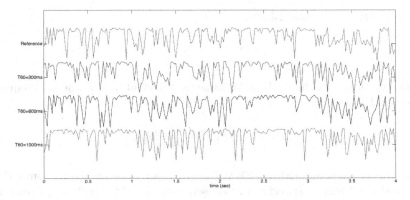

Fig. 6. IF tracks, top to bottom: reference and reverberant, $T_{60} = 0.3$, 0.6 and 1 s, at DRR = 0 dB

4.2 Modulation Spectral Instantaneous Frequency Ratio

Both the reference and reverberant signals IF at l^{th} ($l \in L$) critical-band and k^{th} ($k \in K$) sub-band are noted as Ref_{lk} and $Reverb_{lk}$, respectively. After trained by Gaussian Mixture Model (GMM, M components), their marginal Probability Distribution Function (PDF) and joint probability distribution function are as following

$$p\left(F_{t,lk}|\lambda_{lk}\right) = \sum_{i=1}^{M} \omega_{lk,i} g_t\left(F_{t,lk}|\mu_{lk,i}, \Sigma_{lk,i}\right), \ t = 1,2,3, l \in L, k \in K, i \in M,$$
(15)

where

$$\begin{cases} g_t\left(F_{t,lk}|\mu_{lk,i}, \Sigma_{lk,i}\right) \\ = \frac{1}{(2K)^{D/2}|\Sigma_{lk,i}|^{1/2}} exp\{-\frac{1}{2}\left(F_{t,lk} - \mu_{lk,i}\right)^T \Sigma_{lk,i}^{-1}\left(F_{t,lk} - \mu_{lk,i}\right)\}, \\ \lambda_{lk} = \{\omega_{lk,i}, \mu_{lk,i}, \Sigma_{lk,i}\}, \ l \in L, k \in K, i \in M, \\ F_{t,lk} = Ref_{lk}, \ t = 1, \\ F_{t,lk} = Reverb_{lk}, \ t = 2, \\ F_{t,lk} = (Ref, Reverb)_{lk}, \ t = 3. \end{cases}$$
(16)

Suppose IF Mutual Information (MI) at l^{th} critical-band k^{th} sub-band is

$$MI_{lk} = \sum_{Ref_{lk}} \sum_{Reverb_{lk}} g_3 \cdot log\left(\frac{g_3}{g_1 \cdot g_2}\right),$$
(17)

and define MI at l^{th} critical-band is

$$MI_l = \overline{\sum_k MI_{lk}},\qquad(18)$$

and then we define the final MI as Modulation Spectral Instantaneous Frequency Ratio (MSIFR), which is

$$MSIFR = MI = \overline{\sum_l MI_l}.\qquad(19)$$

Two benchmark algorithms, SRMR and PESQ, are selected as comparison. Clean male and female speeches are chosen from TIMIT database as reference, and the corresponding reverberant speeches are generated by the convolution of reference and RIRs which are illustrated in Section II. All of the average assessment scores are shown in Tables 2 and 3. We divide them into two parts, SMD shorter than critical distance which means DRR $\geqslant 0$ dB, and SMD longer than critical distance which means DRR $\leqslant 0$ dB, the Pearson Correlation coefficients between scores and DRR are depicted in Figs. 7 and 8. Clearly, MSIFR has a high linear correlation with DRR in both parts, and the benchmarks have a better performance in the first part, however, MSIFR can more accurately reflect DRR variation in the second part which is more suitable for practical application according to SMDs in Table 1.

Table 2. MSIFR and baselines comparison for male

DRR (dB)	$T_{60} = 300$ ms			$T_{60} = 600$ ms			$T_{60} = 1000$ ms		
	MSIFR	SRMR	PESQ	MSIFR	SRMR	PESQ	MSIFR	SRMR	PESQ
15	0.1418	4.2635	3.5855	0.1396	3.9702	3.1596	0.1350	3.6880	2.9771
12	0.0765	4.1656	3.3344	0.0905	3.7145	2.9538	0.0910	3.5272	2.7915
9	0.0434	4.0199	3.0446	0.0539	3.4756	2.7651	0.0549	3.1927	2.6116
6	0.0237	3.6137	2.8248	0.0277	3.0852	2.5363	0.0337	2.8511	2.4040
3	0.0136	3.2982	2.6412	0.0167	2.5307	2.3318	0.0163	2.3230	2.1747
0	0.0107	3.2641	2.4234	0.0093	2.2069	2.0849	0.0092	1.7369	1.9728
−3	0.0085	3.2458	2.3066	0.0068	1.7825	1.6283	0.0050	1.5158	1.6447
−6	0.0080	3.4811	2.3348	0.0055	1.9488	1.7873	0.0041	1.3935	1.5395
−9	0.0055	3.5245	2.3491	0.0044	1.7653	1.6338	0.0037	1.3695	1.5278
−12	0.0043	3.8757	2.4877	0.0044	1.8267	1.7058	0.0030	1.2117	1.5996
−15	0.0036	3.9366	2.5675	0.0034	1.6383	1.7137	0.0028	1.2417	1.6803

Table 3. MSIFR and baselines comparison for female

DRR (dB)	$T_{60} = 300\,\text{ms}$			$T_{60} = 600\,\text{ms}$			$T_{60} = 1000\,\text{ms}$		
	MSIFR	SRMR	PESQ	MSIFR	SRMR	PESQ	MSIFR	SRMR	PESQ
15	0.1634	12.0982	3.6405	0.1647	11.0438	3.1836	0.1553	10.5501	2.9782
12	0.0877	11.0876	3.4846	0.1073	9.5192	2.9791	0.1058	9.1170	2.7850
9	0.0503	10.0718	3.1520	0.0618	8.3053	2.7463	0.0646	7.3246	2.5529
6	0.0283	8.1034	2.9680	0.0332	6.3371	2.4675	0.0374	6.0463	2.3288
3	0.0212	6.4036	2.6616	0.0190	5.3529	2.3014	0.0192	4.2010	2.0698
0	0.0183	5.1384	2.5217	0.0125	4.2505	2.0184	0.0106	3.3836	1.9155
−3	0.0121	5.3560	2.4438	0.0092	3.0439	1.7134	0.0074	2.8284	1.5898
−6	0.0105	5.3585	2.4271	0.0072	3.0478	1.6685	0.0051	2.1848	1.5030
−9	0.0077	5.1147	2.4583	0.0055	2.9722	1.6324	0.0038	2.3121	1.4792
−12	0.0061	5.7518	2.5403	0.0049	3.4331	1.8634	0.0032	2.0656	1.4432
−15	0.0053	5.9139	2.6293	0.0032	2.5116	1.7229	0.0029	2.4013	1.5368

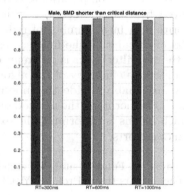
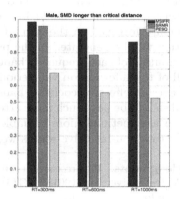

Fig. 7. Pearson Correlation coefficients between assessment scores and DRR for male

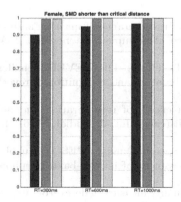
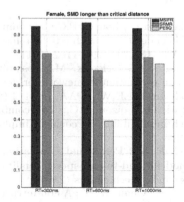

Fig. 8. Pearson Correlation coefficients between assessment scores and DRR for female

5   Conclusion

In this paper, an intrusive objective reverberation evaluation algorithm based on instantaneous frequency is proposed. Two filterbanks are introduced in the algorithm, the Gammatone filterbank used to mimic the mechanism of cochlear, and the modulation filterbank used to further improving the frequency resolution. The analytic form of speech signal can be obtained by instantaneous amplitude and instantaneous phase via Hilbert transform, and then get the carrier feature. Instantaneous phase has time-frequency characteristics, and its partial derivative is instantaneous frequency, which can reveal the frequency variation of the carrier. The probability distribution of both reference and reverberant speech signal instantaneous frequency can be acquired by GMM, and the reverberation effect will be expressed by the final mean mutual information between them which is called MSIFR.

Experiments shows that MSIFR has a higher linear correlation with the change of DRR in practical application, however, lots of work should be done in the future. The training is based on GMM, and its computational consumption is very large, which should be improved by Neural Networks with GPU acceleration. Moreover, in the current algorithm, a huge number of redundant information will be generated in the process of calculating the final scores, and the contribution of each frequency band of the two filterbanks is different, calculating all of the information will seriously affect the efficiency of the algorithm. How to extract effective cochlear band and reasonably divide the modulation sub-band should be pay much more attentions. Furthermore, the method of blind estimation is sometimes more valuable, which means transforming the existing algorithm to a non-intrusive way is worth more efforts.

Acknowledgments. This research is supported by the Fundamental Research Funds for the Central Universities (2018XNG1810). The authors thank Prof. W.-Y. Chan for his guidance for this research.

References

1. Kokkinakis, K., Loizou, P.C.: The impact of reverberant self-masking and overlap-masking effects on speech intelligibility by cochlear implant listeners (L). J. Acoust. Soc. Am. **130**(3), 1099–1102 (2011)
2. Kinoshita, K., Delcroix, M., Yoshioka, T., et al.: The REVERB challenge: a common evaluation framework for dereverberation and recognition of reverberant speech. In: IEEE WASPAA, pp. 1–4 (2013)
3. Hazrati, O., Loizou, P.C.: The combined effects of reverberation and noise on speech intelligibility by cochlear implant listeners. Int. J. Audiol. **51**(6), 437–443 (2012)
4. ITU-T P. 862 Perceptual Evaluation of Speech Quality (PESQ): An objective method for end-to-end speech quality assessment of narrow-band telephone networks and speech codecs (2000)
5. Falk, T.H., Chan, W.-Y.: A non-intrusive quality measure of dereverberated speech. In: Proceedings of International Workshop on Acoustic Echo and Noise Control (2008)

6. Falk, T.H., Chan, W.-Y.: Temporal dynamic for blind measurement of room acoustical parameters. IEEE Trans. Instrum. Meas. **59**(4), 978–989 (2010)
7. Kokkinakis, K., Loizou, P.C.: Evaluation of objective measures for quality assessment of reverberant speech. In: IEEE ICASSP, pp. 2420–2423 (2011)
8. Ma, S., Xie, X.: Blind estimation of spectral standard deviation from room impulse response for reverberation level recognition based on linear prediction. Commun. Comput. Inform. Sci. **685**, 231–241 (2017)
9. Ma, S., Li, H., Zhang, H., et al.: Reverberation level recognition by formants based on 10-fold cross validation of GMM. Commun. Comput. Inform. Sci. **815**, 161–171 (2018)
10. Moon, I.J., Hong, S.H.: What is temporal fine structure and why is it important? Korean J. Audiol. **18**(1), 1–7 (2014)
11. Vijayan, K., Reddy, P.R., Murty, K.S.R.: Significance of analytic phase of speech signals in speaker verification. Speech Commun. **81**, 54–71 (2016)
12. Tu, A.: Reverberation simulation from impulse response using the image source model (2014)
13. Habets, E.A.P., Gannot, S., Cohen, I.: Late reverberation spectral variance estimation based on a statistical model. IEEE Signal Process. Lett. **16**(9), 770–773 (2009)
14. Kuttruff, H.: Room Acoustics, 4th edn. Elsevier, London (2000)
15. Schroeder, M.: New method of measuring reverberation time. J. Acoust. Soc. Am. **37**(3), 409–412 (1965)
16. Del Vallado, J.M.F., De Lima, A.A., Prego, T.D.M., et al.: Feature analysis for the reverberation perception in speech signals. In: IEEE ICASSP, 8169–8173 (2013)
17. ISO 3382–1 Acoustics C Measurement of Room Acoustic Parameters C Part 1: Performances Spaces (2009)
18. Allen, J.B., Berkley, D.A.: Image method for efficiently simulating small-room acoustics. J. Acoust. Soc. Am. **65**(4), 943–950 (1979)
19. Patterson, R.D., Robinson, K., Holdsworth, J., et al.: Complex sounds and auditory images. In: Auditory Physiology & Perception, pp. 429–446 (1992)
20. Slaney, M.: An efficient implementation of the Patterson-Holdsworth auditory filter bank. Apple Computer Technical report #35, Perception Group C Advanced Technology Group (1993)
21. Schimmel, S.M., Atlas, L.E., Nie, K.: Feasibility of single channel speaker separation based on modulation frequency analysis. In: IEEE ICASSP, vol. 4, pp. 605–608 (2007)

Telecommunications

Channel Estimation over Doubly Selective Channels Based on Basis Expansion Model and Compressive Sensing

Xin Fang[1](✉), Xiong Jian[1], Bo Liu[2], Lin Gui[1], Meikang Qiu[3], and Zhiping Shi[4]

[1] Department of Electronic Engineering, Shanghai Jiao Tong University,
Shanghai, China
{fxdd001,xjarrow,guilin}@sjtu.edu.cn
[2] Department of Engineering, La Trobe University, Melbourne, VIC 3086, Australia
b.liu2@latrobe.edu.au
[3] Department of Computer Science, Pace University, New York, USA
mqiu@pace.edu
[4] National Key Laboratory of Science and Technology on Communications,
Electronic Science and Technology of China, Chengdu, People's Republic of China
szp@uestc.edu.cn

Abstract. This paper proposes a novel channel estimation (CE) algorithm over doubly-selective (DS) channels based on basis expansion model (BEM) and compressive sensing (CS). In high speed scenarios, the coefficients of DS channel introduce inter-carrier interference (ICI) to orthogonal frequency division multiplexing (OFDM) broadband system; and it needs a large number of pilot subcarriers to estimate the channel matrix. The CE for the system over DS channels is very challenging. Distributed compressive sensing (DCS) theory combined with the BEM is a very efficient way to accurately estimate the channel state information (CSI) of DS channels, but at the overhead cost of the guard pilots around the effective pilots. A novel ICI cancellation based CE algorithm is proposed to estimate the CSI of pilots by eliminating the ICI from the neighborhood subcarriers. The guard pilots around the effective pilots are no longer needed; as results, the number of pilots needed is only 1/5 of the traditional pilot pattern scheme, but at the cost of a limited performance loss. If the same pilot pattern without guard pilots is employed, the proposed algorithm outperforms the traditional CE algorithms.

Keywords: Basic expansion model · Channel estimation · Compressive sensing · Double selective channel · ICI estimation

This work was supported in part by the National Natural Science Foundation of China (61671295, 61471236, 61420106008), the Shanghai Key Laboratory of Digital Media Processing and the National Key Laboratory of Science and Technology on Communications (KX172600030); it is also partly sponsored by Shanghai Pujiang Program (16PJD029), the 111 Project (B07022).

© Springer Nature Singapore Pte Ltd. 2019
G. Zhai et al. (Eds.): IFTC 2018, CCIS 1009, pp. 299–311, 2019.
https://doi.org/10.1007/978-981-13-8138-6_25

1   Introduction

The orthogonal frequency division multiplexing (OFDM) technique is one of the ways to implement multi-carrier transmission scheme. The robustness of OFDM technique against frequency-selective (FS) fading makes it develop rapidly in the past few decades. OFDM has developed into a popular scheme for broadband digital communication applications such as digital television, audio broadcasting and wireless networks. In most scenarios of these applications, the channel impulse response (CIR) changes slowly with frequency within one OFDM symbol, so the conventional channel estimation (CE) method such as least square (LS) algorithm is sufficient to estimate the CIR accurately [1].

But the channel under high-speed scene scenarios [2] is usually double-selective channel due to the Doppler shift [3]. Different from the FS channel case, it is extremely challenging to estimate the doubly-selective (DS) channel accurately with limited pilot resources due to its time-frequency-double-selectivity. The DS channel impulse response changes rapidly within one OFDM symbol. Therefore, there are a large amount of channel coefficients needed to be estimated within one OFDM symbol.

The channel under the high-speed scene of the suburbs is a sparse channel, which means the channel impulse responses are dominated by a small number of relatively dominant resolvable paths. Thus, compressive sensing theory provides a potential solution to estimate numerous channel coefficients with fewer pilot subcarriers. In [4], the Distributed compressive sensing (DCS) based estimation methods are proposed for a mildly time-selective fading channel, but the effect of a large Doppler shift is not considered in these two researches. It is found in [5] that with a large Doppler shift, the Doppler leakage can notably reduce the sparsity in Doppler domain.

Through a combination of basis expansion model (BEM), the channel coefficients can be transformed into few joint sparse BEM coefficients; then CS theory can be adopted to estimate the channel by BEM coefficients. The authors of [6] used BEM to model the time-varying channel and introduced a novel DCS based CE approach to track the fast fading DS channel. A novel sparse pilot pattern is also introduced in [6], which features an ICI-free structure due to the presence of guard pilots. The authors of [7] proposed differential simultaneous orthogonal matching pursuit (DSOMP) algorithm to estimate the dynamic sparse channel based on DCS theory. The authors of [8] proposed a novel structured DCS (SDCS) based joint multi-symbol CE scheme. However, all of these algorithms are based on the pilot pattern with guard pilots, which lead to low spectrum efficiency and is compatible with most of the existing communication standards.

To overcome the disadvantages of the guard pilots, an ICI estimation algorithm that can avoid using guard pilots is proposed. The contributions of this paper are as follow: the difference of the signal at the guard pilots produced by the iteration ICI estimation algorithm is considered as the approximation of ICI, and it can replace the received signals at the guard pilots position based on the pilot pattern with guard pilots. Thus, the guard pilots are no longer needed and the original position of them can be used to send more data.

2   System Model

2.1   The Sparse CE-BEM Channel Model

Based on the narrow-band characteristics of time-varying channels, the BEM convert the time-varying channel into a weighted linear superposition of a few orthogonal components, and the channel coefficients can be recovered by estimating only a small number of BEM coefficients, which greatly reduces the computation complexity of CE.

The complex exponential basis expansion model (CE-BEM) is used to represent the double-selective channel impulse response $h_{n,l}$ in time delay domain in this paper, where n represents the n-th subcarriers and l represents l-th channel tap. We define that the l-th channel tap of j-th OFDM symbol is $h_l^{(j)} \triangleq [h_{0,l}^{(j)}, h_{1,l}^{(j)}, \dots, h_{N-1,l}^{(j)}]^T$. Using BEM to re-model it, $h_l^{(j)}$ can be expressed as

$$h_l^{(j)} = [b_0, \cdots, b_{Q-1}] \left[c^{(j)}[0, l], \cdots, c^{(j)}[Q-1, l] \right]^T, \tag{1}$$

where $Q\,(Q \ll N)$ denotes the BEM order, $b_q \in \mathbb{C}^{N \times 1}$ is the q-th ($q \in [0, Q-1]$) CE-BEM basic function and $c^{(j)}[q, l]$ is the corresponding CE-BEM coefficients of the j-th OFDM symbol. $\xi_l^{(j)}$ represents the error generated by CE-BEM modeling, which is regarded as noise in the following illustration.

However, the channel under high-speed scene has some sparsity [9], which means only a small number of channel coefficients in the delay domain are non-zero. We define the channel sparsity during the j-th OFDM symbol as $K^{(j)}$ satisfies $K^{(j)} \ll L$. If $\ell^{(j)}$ is a set consisting of the non-zero position of coefficient vectors of the sparse channel with cardinality $\left|\ell^{(j)}\right| = K^{(j)}$. The sparsity of channel under high-speed scene is reflected in $h_l^{(j)} = 0$ for $l \notin \ell^{(j)}$.

As shown in (1), it can be concluded that the CE-BEM coefficient vector $c_q^{(j)}$ has jointly-sparsity with the channel coefficient $h^{(j)}$. This characteristic can be expressed as follow

$$c^{(j)}[0, l] = \cdots = c^{(j)}[Q-1, l] = 0 \left(l \notin \ell^{(j)} \right). \tag{2}$$

After CE-BEM modeling, the problem of a set of channel coefficients estimation has been transformed into the estimation of the corresponding CE-BEM coefficients and the number of coefficients to be estimated is greatly reduced in this way.

2.2   DCS Framework for OFDM Symbols Based on CE-BEM

Unlike the CS theory, which can only reconstruct a single sparse signal alone, DCS theory can be used to reconstruct a set of jointly-sparse signals by the same measurement matrix. In this subsection, a DCS framework for OFDM symbols based on the channel after CE-BEM modeling is introduced.

We assume that the received signals is

$$\mathbf{R}^{(j)} = \mathbf{H}^{(j)}\mathbf{S}^{(j)} + \mathbf{W}^{(j)} = F_N h^{(j)} F_N^H \mathbf{S}^{(j)} + \mathbf{W}^{(j)}, \tag{3}$$

in which F_N stand for the N-point FFT matrix while F_N^H stand for the IFFT matrix. And $W^{(j)}$ is the addictive noise. The channel impulse response in the frequency domain can be rewritten in the form of CE-BEM coefficients as [6]

$$\mathbf{H}^{(j)} = F_N h^{(j)} F_N^H = F_N \sum_{q=0}^{Q-1} b_q c_q^{(j)} F_N^H = \sum_{q=0}^{Q-1} B_q C_q^{(j)}, \tag{4}$$

where $B_q \triangleq F_N \vartheta\{b_q\} F_N^H$ and $C_q^{(j)} \triangleq \vartheta\{V_L c_q^{(j)}\}$, $\vartheta\{m\}$ are diagonal matrixes with m on its diagonal. And V_L represents the matrix formed with the first L columns of the matrix $\sqrt{N} F_N$. Then, we can express the received signal as

$$\mathbf{R}^{(j)} = \sum_{q=0}^{Q-1} F_N \vartheta\{b_q\} F_N^H \vartheta\left\{V_L c_q^{(j)}\right\} \mathbf{S}^{(j)} + \mathbf{W}^{(j)}. \tag{5}$$

In this way, the estimation of channel coefficients has been converted to the estimation for a series of joint-sparse CE-BEM coefficients $c_q^{(j)}$. And each OFDM symbol shares the same CE-BEM basic functions b_q but different CE-BEM coefficients $c_q^{(j)}$.

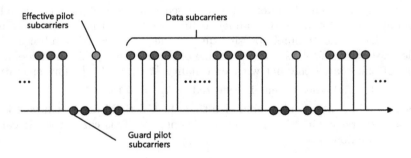

Fig. 1. Pilot pattern for BEM ($Q = 3$)

In order to present the DCS framework, a conventional pilot pattern [6] is introduced firstly. Taking the estimation model with the CE-BEM order $Q = 3$ for example, this pilot pattern is shown in Fig. 1.

As we can see from Fig. 1, each pilot group P consists of one effective pilot P_e and $2Q - 2$ guard pilots P_g with zero-value. The exist of guard pilots is to prevent the effective pilot subcarriers from the ICI produced by data subcarriers.

The pilot position index set ρ can be divided into two parts, the effective pilot position index set ρ_e can be expressed as

$$\begin{aligned} \rho_e &= \{p_0, \cdots, p_{E-1}\}, \\ 0 &\le p_0 \le \cdots \le p_{E-1} \le N - 1. \end{aligned} \tag{6}$$

The guard pilot position index set ρ_g can be expressed as

$$\rho_g = \{\rho_e - Q + 1\} \cup \cdots \cup \{\rho_e - 1\} \\ \cup \{\rho_e + 1\} \cup \cdots \cup \{\rho_e + Q - 1\}, \tag{7}$$

where E is a total number of effective pilots in one OFDM symbol, $N < E \ll L$.

It is clear that the received signals at the subcarriers position $\left\{\rho_0, \cdots \rho_{\frac{Q-3}{2}}\right\} \cup \left\{\rho_{\frac{Q+1}{2}}, \cdots \rho_{Q-1}\right\}$ are the ICI from the effective pilots and data subcarriers. In order to save the pilots overhead, which means the original guard pilots need to be utilized to send data. Then, the iteration ICI estimation algorithm proposed in this paper is utilized to estimate the ICI of the received signals at the subcarrier positions $\left\{\rho_0, \cdots \rho_{\frac{Q-3}{2}}\right\} \cup \left\{\rho_{\frac{Q+1}{2}}, \cdots \rho_{Q-1}\right\}$.

$\mathbf{R}_\rho^{(j,0)}$ is used to represent the original received signal at the subcarrier position, and $\mathbf{R}_\rho^{(j,k)}$ represents the received signal after k-time iteration ICI cancellation. The estimated ICI value at the subcarrier position ρ can be presented as

$$\mathbf{R}_{ICI\rho}^{(j)} = \mathbf{R}_\rho^{(j,k)} - \mathbf{R}_\rho^{(j,0)}. \tag{8}$$

Then, the Eq. (27) in [6] can be rewritten as

$$\begin{cases} R_{ICI\rho_m}^{(j)} = \Phi^{(j)} s_m^{(j)} + W_m^{(j)} \\ R^{(j)}{}_{\rho_n} = \Phi^{(j)} s_n^{(j)} + W_n^{(j)} \end{cases}, \tag{9}$$

where $m = (0, \cdots \frac{Q-3}{2}, \frac{Q+1}{2}, \cdots, Q - 1)$ and $n = \frac{Q-1}{2}.\Phi^{(j)} \stackrel{\Delta}{=} \vartheta\left(P_e^{(j)}\right)$ $[V_L]_{\rho_{\frac{Q-1}{2}}}$ and $s_q^{(j)} \stackrel{\Delta}{=} \Lambda_q c_q^{(j)}$, and Λ_q is the diagonal matrix with each CE-BEM basic function on its diagonal as

$$\Lambda_q = \vartheta\left(1, e^{-i\frac{2\pi}{N}(q-\frac{Q-1}{2})}, \cdots, e^{-i\frac{2\pi}{N}(q-\frac{Q-1}{2})(L-1)}\right). \tag{10}$$

It can be deduced that vector in $\left\{s_q^{(j)}\right\}_{q=0}^{Q-1} = \left\{\Lambda_q c_q^{(j)}\right\}_{q=0}^{Q-1}$ is jointly-sparse due to the co-sparsity of CE-BEM coefficient vectors $\{c_q\}_{q=0}^{Q-1}$ and each equation in (9) shares the same measurement matrix $\Phi^{(j)}$. As results, applying the DCS theory to recover the CE-BEM coefficient vectors becomes possible. And (9) can be written in the form of DCS model into

$$\left(R_{ICI\rho_m}^{(j)}, R_{ICI\rho_n}^{(j)}, R_{ICI\rho_m}^{(j)}\right) \\ = \Phi^{(j)} \left(s_m^{(j)}, s_n^{(j)}, s_m^{(j)},\right) + W^{(j)}. \tag{11}$$

Until now, the problem of estimation for CE-BEM coefficient vectors has been transformed into the frame of DCS theory. Therefore, the DSC-SOMP algorithm presented in [6] can be utilized to recover a series of joint-sparse CE-BEM coefficient vector with low computational complexity and fewer pilot subcarriers.

3   Proposed Channel Estimation Scheme

3.1   Inter-carrier Interference Analysis Under High-Speed Scenarios

The Doppler shift caused by high-speed movement brings the Doppler shift to each subcarrier in OFDM symbols, which destroys the orthogonality between the adjacent subcarriers. The frequency shift caused by the Doppler effect can be expressed as:

$$f_d = \frac{f_c}{c} \times v \times \cos\theta, \tag{12}$$

where f_c denotes the carrier frequency, v denotes the relative velocity between the signal receiver and transmitter. θ is the arrival angle of received signal while c represents the speed of light.

Figure 2 shows the ICI energy from the effective pilot subcarriers at the subcarrier positions around the effective pilot position ρ_e, in the condition of normalized Doppler frequency $v_{\max} = \frac{f_c v}{c \Delta f} = 0.065$ and $[E_{\rho_e}] = P_e = 2$.

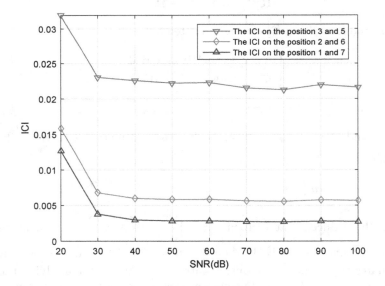

Fig. 2. ICI energy from the effective pilot subcarriers

As shown in Fig. 3, all pilot subcarriers are set to zero except for the effective pilot subcarriers. When the signal to noisy ratio (SNR) is large enough, the value of the received signals at the position $\{1, 2, 3, 5, 6, 7\}$ is approximately equal to the ICI from the effective pilots. Among them, the pilots at position 3 and position 5 are adjacent to the effective pilot; thus the subcarriers at these two positions are most affected by ICI. The ICI at the position 2 and 6 are much smaller than those at the position 3 and 5; however, they still cannot be ignored

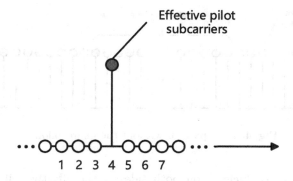

Fig. 3. The transmitted signals for ICI analysis

when we estimate the channel coefficients. Moreover, as the pilots at position 1 and position 7 are a little far from the effective pilot subcarriers, the ICIs have smaller order of magnitude; and they need not to be considered when estimating the channel state information.

To sum up, in the proposed channel estimation scheme, the proposed iteration ICI estimation only considers the ICIs at the effective pilot subcarriers and another $Q-1$ received data subcarriers on both sides of the effective pilot subcarriers. The proposed algorithm estimates the ICI of the received signals at these $Q-1$ subcarrier positions and eliminate the ICI of received signals at the effective pilot positions. To employ the algorithm, the CE-BEM with the order Q is needed to model the double-selective channel under high-speed scenarios firstly; and then the DCS theory can be utilized to reconstruct the CE-BEM coefficients.

3.2   The Proposed ICI Estimation Iteration Algorithm

As mentioned above, for the conventional CE scheme under CE-BEM modeling, the pilot pattern with guard pilots is essential to eliminate the ICI. In order to save more pilot overhead for CE under CE-BEM modeling, we propose a novel pilot pattern without the guard pilots, and 80% of the total pilot subcarriers can be saved. Then, the proposed iterative ICI estimation algorithm will be applied to the $Q-1$ received data subcarriers on both side of each effective pilot subcarriers to get the estimated value of the ICI of these $Q-1$ data subcarriers $R^{(j)}_{ICI \rho \frac{Q-3}{2}}$ and $R^{(j)}_{ICI \rho \frac{Q+1}{2}}$, which will be input into the DCS-SOMP based CE-BEM Coefficient vectors estimation algorithm for the proposed system model with a ICI-free structure. And the pilot pattern without the guard pilots is shown in Fig. 4.

Algorithm 1 presents the pseudocode of the proposed iteration ICI estimation algorithm. Before the iteration begins, we need to initialize some channel parameters. The initial channel coefficient at the effective pilot position can be approximate by LS channel estimation algorithm: $\hat{h}^{(j,0)}_{\rho \frac{Q-1}{2}} = R^{(j,0)}_{\rho \frac{Q-1}{2}} / E^{(j)}_{\rho}$. Then,

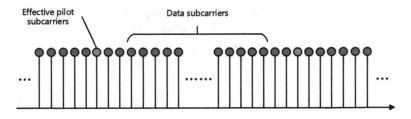

Fig. 4. Pilot pattern without the guard pilots

the initial channel coefficients on both sides of the effective pilot $\hat{h}_{\rho_{\frac{Q-3}{2}}}^{(j,0)}$ and
$\hat{h}_{\rho_{\frac{Q+1}{2}}}^{(j,0)}$ can be estimated by linear interpolation algorithm.

In the first step of each iteration, the transmitted signals at both sides of the effective pilot $S_{\rho_{\frac{Q-3}{2}}}^{(j)}$, $S_{\rho_{\frac{Q+1}{2}}}^{(j)}$ are equalized using ZF equalization algorithm as

$$\begin{cases} \hat{S}_{\rho_{\frac{Q-3}{2}}}^{(j)} = R_{\rho_{\frac{Q-3}{2}}}^{(j)} / \hat{h}_{\rho_{\frac{Q-3}{2}}}^{(j)} \\ \hat{S}_{\rho_{\frac{Q+1}{2}}}^{(j)} = R_{\rho_{\frac{Q+1}{2}}}^{(j)} / \hat{h}_{\rho_{\frac{Q+1}{2}}}^{(j)} \end{cases} . \tag{13}$$

In order to calculate the ICI coefficients, we need to do the constellation demodulation on the equalized received signals $\hat{S}_{\rho_{\frac{Q-3}{2}}}^{(j)}$ and $\hat{S}_{\rho_{\frac{Q+1}{2}}}^{(j)}$ firstly to get the demodulated values $\bar{S}_{\rho_{\frac{Q-3}{2}}}^{(j)}$ and $\bar{S}_{\rho_{\frac{Q-3}{2}}}^{(j)}$. Then, the decision gain from the last step can be used to update the channel coefficients at both sides of the effective pilot

$$\begin{cases} \hat{h}_{\rho_{\frac{Q-3}{2}}}^{(j,k)} = R_{\rho_{\frac{Q-3}{2}}}^{(j,k)} / \bar{S}_{\rho_{\frac{Q-3}{2}}}^{(j)} \\ \hat{h}_{\rho_{\frac{Q+1}{2}}}^{(j,\bar{k})} = R_{\rho_{\frac{Q+1}{2}}}^{(j,\bar{k})} / \bar{S}_{\rho_{\frac{Q+1}{2}}}^{(j)} \end{cases} . \tag{14}$$

At the same time, the ICI coefficients of the left and the right data subcarrier relative to the effective pilot subcarriers can be obtained respectively by

$$\begin{cases} \hat{h}_{2\rightarrow1}^{(j)} = (\hat{S}_{\rho_{\frac{Q-3}{2}}}^{(j)} - \bar{S}_{\rho_{\frac{Q-3}{2}}}^{(j)})/T_{\rho_{\frac{Q-3}{2}}} \\ \hat{h}_{2\rightarrow3}^{(j)} = (\hat{S}_{\rho_{\frac{Q+1}{2}}}^{(j)} - \bar{S}_{\rho_{\frac{Q+1}{2}}}^{(j)})/T_{\rho_{\frac{Q+1}{2}}} \end{cases} , \tag{15}$$

where $\hat{h}_{2\rightarrow1}^{(j)}$ denotes the ICI coefficients of the left data subcarrier relative to the effective pilot subcarriers and $\hat{h}_{2\rightarrow3}^{(j)}$ denoted the ICI coefficients of the right data subcarrier relative to the effective pilot subcarriers.

In addition, the ICI coefficients of the adjacent subcarriers can be assumed to be equal. So, it can be obtained that $\hat{h}_{3\rightarrow2}^{(j)} = \hat{h}_{2\rightarrow1}^{(j)}$ and $\hat{h}_{1\rightarrow2}^{(j)} = \hat{h}_{2\rightarrow3}^{(j)}$.

The ICI coefficients calculated above will be utilized to eliminate the ICI from the received signals. The ICI of the received signals at the effective pilot is presented as

Algorithm 1. The proposed Iteration ICI Estimation Algorithm

Input Received signals: $R^{(j)}$; Effective pilot transmission signals: E_ρ
Output Estimated ICI value: $R_{ICI}^{(j)}$

1: Initialization: iteration coefficient $k = 0$, received signals $R_{\rho\frac{Q-3}{2}}^{(j,0)} = R_{\rho\frac{Q-3}{2}}^{(j)}$,
$R_{\rho\frac{Q-1}{2}}^{(j,0)} = R_{\rho\frac{Q-1}{2}}^{(j)}$, $R_{\rho\frac{Q+1}{2}}^{(j,0)} = R_{\rho\frac{Q+1}{2}}^{(j)}$, CIR $\hat{h}_{\rho\frac{Q-1}{2}}^{(j,k)}, \hat{h}_{\rho\frac{Q-3}{2}}^{(j,k)}, \hat{h}_{\rho\frac{Q+1}{2}}^{(j,k)}$.

2: The start iteration index: $k = k + 1$.

3: Obtain the transmitted signals:$\hat{S}_{\rho\frac{Q-3}{2}}^{(j)} = R_{\rho\frac{Q-3}{2}}^{(j)}/\hat{h}_{\rho\frac{Q-3}{2}}^{(j)}$, $\hat{S}_{\rho\frac{Q+1}{2}}^{(j)} = R_{\rho\frac{Q+1}{2}}^{(j)}/\hat{h}_{\rho\frac{Q+1}{2}}^{(j)}$.

4: Hard decision for the equalized estimated signals:$\bar{S}_{\rho\frac{Q-3}{2}}^{(j)} = sign(\hat{S}_{\rho\frac{Q-3}{2}}^{(j)})$,$\bar{S}_{\rho\frac{Q+1}{2}}^{(j)} = sign(\hat{S}_{\rho\frac{Q+1}{2}}^{(j)})$

5: Update the CIR at each position: $\hat{h}_{\rho\frac{Q-3}{2}}^{(j,k)} = R_{\rho\frac{Q-3}{2}}^{(j,k)}/\bar{S}_{\rho\frac{Q-3}{2}}^{(j)}$,$\hat{h}_{\rho\frac{Q+1}{2}}^{(j,k)} = R_{\rho\frac{Q+1}{2}}^{(j,k)}/\bar{S}_{\rho\frac{Q+1}{2}}^{(j)}$.

6: Calculate the ICI coefficients, which is detailed in (15), then $\hat{h}_{3\to2}^{(j)} = \hat{h}_{2\to1}^{(j)}$,$\hat{h}_{1\to2}^{(j)} = \hat{h}_{2\to3}^{(j)}$.

7: Eliminate the ICI from received signals, which is detailed in (18), (19) and (20).

8: Repeat 3–7 until meeting a certain stop criterion, when the number of iteration $k = K$.

9: The ICI can be obtained by: $R_{ICI\,\rho\frac{Q-3}{2}}^{(j)} = R_{\rho\frac{Q-3}{2}}^{(j,K)} - R_{\rho\frac{Q-3}{2}}^{(j)}{}^{[0]}$, $R_{ICI\,\rho\frac{Q+1}{2}}^{(j)} = R_{\rho\frac{Q+1}{2}}^{(j,K)} - R_{\rho\frac{Q+1}{2}}^{(j)}{}^{[0]}$.

$$\begin{aligned} R_{ICI\,\rho\frac{Q-1}{2}}^{(j,k)} &= \hat{h}_{1\to2}^{(j)}R_{\rho\frac{Q-3}{2}}^{(j,k-1)} + \hat{h}_{3\to2}^{(j)}R_{\rho\frac{Q+3}{2}}^{(j,k-1)} \\ &= \hat{h}_{2\to3}^{(j)}R_{\rho\frac{Q-3}{2}}^{(j,k-1)} + \hat{h}_{2\to1}^{(j)}R_{\rho\frac{Q+3}{2}}^{(j,k-1)}. \end{aligned} \tag{16}$$

In the same way, the ICI value of the data subcarriers on both sides of the effective pilot can be obtained as

$$\begin{cases} R_{ICI\,\rho\frac{Q-3}{2}}^{(j,k)} = h_{2\to1}^{(j)}R_{\rho\frac{Q-1}{2}}^{(j,k-1)} \\ R_{ICI\,\rho\frac{Q+1}{2}}^{(j,k)} = h_{2\to3}^{(j)}R_{\rho\frac{Q-1}{2}}^{(j,k-1)} \end{cases}. \tag{17}$$

At last, the received signals after once iteration of ICI cancellation can be expressed in (18), (19) and (20).

$$R_{\rho\frac{Q-1}{2}}^{(j,k)} = R_{\rho\frac{Q-1}{2}}^{(j,k-1)} - \hat{h}_{2\to3}^{(j)}R_{\rho\frac{Q-3}{2}}^{(j,k-1)} - \hat{h}_{2\to1}^{(j)}R_{\rho\frac{Q+1}{2}}^{(j,k-1)} \tag{18}$$

$$R_{\rho\frac{Q-3}{2}}^{(j,k)} = R_{\rho\frac{Q-3}{2}}^{(j,k-1)} - \hat{h}_{2\to1}^{(j)}R_{\rho\frac{Q-1}{2}}^{(j,k-1)} \tag{19}$$

$$R_{\rho\frac{Q+1}{2}}^{(j,k)} = R_{\rho\frac{Q+1}{2}}^{(j,k-1)} - \hat{h}_{2\to3}^{(j)}R_{\rho\frac{Q-1}{2}}^{(j,k-1)}. \tag{20}$$

When the iteration stops, the difference between the received signals at the data subcarriers after the iteration and the original received signals is considered as the ICI, and it can be expressed as

$$
\begin{cases}
R^{(j)}_{ICI\rho_{\frac{Q-3}{2}}} = R^{(j,K)}_{\rho_{\frac{Q-3}{2}}} - R^{(j,0)}_{\rho_{\frac{Q-3}{2}}} \\
R^{(j)}_{ICI\rho_{\frac{Q+1}{2}}} = R^{(j,K)}_{\rho_{\frac{Q+1}{2}}} - R^{(j,0)}_{\rho_{\frac{Q+1}{2}}}
\end{cases}. \tag{21}
$$

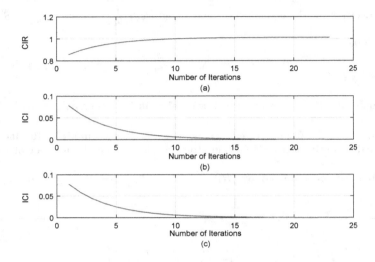

Fig. 5. ICI iterative elimination process, (a) CIR at the effective pilot position, (b) ICI from a left position of the effective pilot, (c) ICI from a right position of the effective pilot

In this way, the ICI of data subcarriers around the effective pilot and the received signals at the pilot position after ICI cancellation are obtained, and they can be brought into the DCS-SMOP algorithm proposed in [6] to do the CE for DS channel. The ICI elimination performance of the proposed algorithm is shown in Fig. 5. It is obviously that in the channel condition of $SNR = 20\,\text{dB}$ and $v_{\max} = 0.065$, the ICI of the received signal can be completely eliminated using the proposed algorithm.

Compared to the conventional CE scheme based on CE-BEM modeling, our proposed CE scheme with the iterative ICI estimation algorithm saves 80% of pilot overhead but can also achieve similar performance, which will be discussed in detail in next section.

4   Simulation Results and Discussion

In this section, Matlab will be used to implement CE scheme proposed in this paper into simulation and compare it with the conventional CE scheme based on CE-BEM modeling presented in [6]. The parameters of the simulation system are shown in Table 1.

In this proposed system, the double-selective channel is modeled into a Rayleigh fading channel with the length $L = 64$; and the channel sparsity K is 6, which means only 6 CIR of the paths are non-zero in the total 64 multi-paths of the channel. The variation of the DS channel is characterized by the Doppler shift and the normalized value $v_{max} = \frac{f_c v}{c \Delta f} = 0.065$.

The parameters of OFDM symbols meet the LTE standard with $\Delta f = 15\,\text{kHz}$ and $f_c = 3\,\text{GHz}$. The bandwidth B is 20 MHz, which means there are 2048 subcarriers in each OFDM symbol and all the subcarriers are assumed to be available for data transmission. Meanwhile, the length of CP is set to 64 to remove the inter symbol interference (ISI). All the pilot subcarriers are equally distributed in all subcarriers of one OFDM symbol, and every three OFDM symbols are arranged with pilot subcarriers.

Table 1. Simulation parameters

Parameters	Value
Number of subcarriers	$N = 2048$
Length of CP	$L_{CP} = 64$
Length of CIR	$L = 64$
Channel sparsity	$K = 6$
Subcarriers spacing	$\Delta f = 15\,\text{kHz}$
Bandwidth	$B = 20\,\text{MHz}$
CE-BEM order	$Q = 3$
Carrier frequency	$f_c = 3\,\text{GHz}$
Modulation	$QPSK$
Number of effective pilots	$G = 88$
Relative velocity	$v = 350\,\text{km/h}$

4.1 NMSE Comparison Against SNR Under the Condition of Same Effective Pilot Density

In Fig. 6, the normalized mean square error (NMSE) comparison under the condition of same effective pilots density between three different CE scheme is shown. It is clear that the proposed channel scheme with iteration ICI cancellation (ICIC) can achieve 2.5 dB performance gain compared with the CE scheme without iteration ICIC. And it is also our expectation that the proposed CE with iteration ICI cancellation has 1.5 dB performance loss compared with the conventional CE scheme, for the ICI is estimated. But because of the pilot pattern without guard pilots, the proposed CE scheme can save 4/5 of the pilot cost compared with the conventional one, but at the cost of a little performance loss.

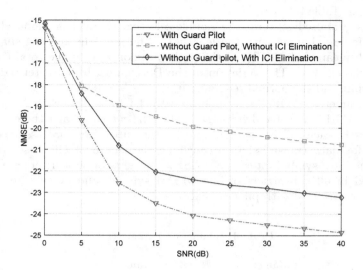

Fig. 6. NMSE comparison against SNR under the condition of same effective pilot density

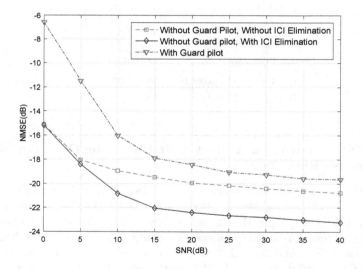

Fig. 7. NMSE comparison against SNR under the condition of same total pilot density

4.2   NMSE Comparison Against SNR Under the Condition of Same Total Pilot Density

It can be obviously concluded from Fig. 7, the performance gain of the proposed CE scheme is obvious when the total effective pilots density is the same, especially in the condition of low SNR. And the total pilot density of this simulation is 1.43%. It is clear that we can get about 5 dB NMSE performance gain when $SNR = 10\,\mathrm{dB}$ or can get a 4 dB NMSE performance gain when $SNR = 20\,\mathrm{dB}$ at the cost of iteration ICIC complexity.

5   Conclusion

In this paper, a novel CE scheme based on BEM modeling and CS is proposed by using ICIC under high-speed scenarios. The BEM model converts the original CE problem into estimating jointly sparse CE-BEM coefficients; and the CS can make the system work even at very low pilot density. The CE algorithm based on iteration ICIC is proposed to eliminate the ICI from data carriers, which are used as guard pilots in the traditional wireless communication systems. Simulation results show that the proposed CE scheme can save about 80% overhead cost of guard pilots but with limited performance lose under the same effective pilot density; and it outweights the conventional schemes under the same total pilot density.

References

1. Coleri, S., Ergen, M., Puri, A., Bahai, A.: Channel estimation techniques based on pilot arrangement in OFDM systems. IEEE Trans. Broadcast. **48**, 223–229 (2002)
2. Liu, C., Zakharov, Y.V., Chen, T.: Doubly selective underwater acoustic channel model for a moving transmitter/receiver. IEEE Trans. Veh. Technol. **61**, 938–950 (2012)
3. Ma, X., Giannakis, G.B.: Maximum-diversity transmissions over doubly selective wireless channels. IEEE Trans. Inf. Theory **49**, 1832–1840 (2003)
4. Duarte, M.F., Eldar, Y.C.: Structured compressed sensing: from theory to applications. IEEE Trans. Signal Process. **59**, 4053–4085 (2011)
5. Taubock, G., Hlawatsch, F., Eiwen, D., Rauhut, H.: Compressive estimation of doubly selective channels in multicarrier systems: leakage effects and sparsity-enhancing processing. IEEE J. Sel. Top. Signal Process. **4**, 255–271 (2010)
6. Cheng, P., et al.: Channel estimation for OFDM systems over doubly selective channels: a distributed compressive sensing based approach. IEEE Trans. Commun. **61**, 4173–4185 (2013)
7. Zhang, X., Gui, L., Qin, Q., Gong, B.: Dynamic sparse channel estimation over doubly selective channels: differential simultaneous orthogonal matching pursuit. In: 2016 IEEE International Symposium on Broadband Multimedia Systems and Broadcasting (BMSB), pp. 1–6 (2016)
8. Qin, Q., Gui, L., Gong, B., Ren, X., Chen, W.: Structured distributed compressive channel estimation over doubly selective channels. IEEE Trans. Broadcast. **62**, 521–531 (2016)
9. Zhao, J., Xiong, L., Zhang, Y., Zhou, T., Tan, Y.: SFN MIMO channel model for high-speed railway. In: 2017 XXXIInd General Assembly and Scientific Symposium of the International Union of Radio Science (URSI GASS), pp. 1–4 (2017)

Mixed Tiling Scheme for Adaptive
VR Streaming

Jingxing Xu, Yiling Xu$^{(\boxtimes)}$, Yunfeng Guan, and Wenjun Zhang

Shanghai Jiao Tong University, 800 Dongchuan Road, Minhang, Shanghai, China
yl.xu@sjtu.edu.cn

Abstract. VR technology is rapidly progressing in recent years with incremental consumption demand of immersive media. Transmission is one major challenge to be overcome for ultra high resolution 360 VR video streaming, requiring large throughput and strict latency. Conventional monolithic streaming scheme transfers the entire panorama and impose heavy burden to network load. Tiling based video streaming tackles such problem that it discriminates the FOV (field of view) and surrounded field out of sight then tiles are transmitted in appropriate quality according to viewing probability and network condition. Existing tiling method divides video frame into fixed-size uniform rectangles and encoding efficiency is inevitably decremented. The optimal mesh of video frame tiling is content dependent but typically tiling dimension is fixedly configured by service provider, without elasticity and content awareness. Several proposed optimization methods for tile dimension needs to enumerate all possibility and these offline manner requires specific transcoded samples to be prepared beforehand.

In this paper, a bandwidth-efficient mixed tiling scheme is proposed to improve the situation where diverse tiles are spliced into integral frame and tile selection is processed within multiple correlative meshes. We apply a graph algorithm to search the optimal case within multiple meshes and the online manner demands neither exhaustive enumeration nor intensive calculation.

We develop an adaptive VR video streaming system and mixed tiling scheme reflects advantage in bandwidth consumption and pixel overheads, compared to existing fixed size tiling scheme and traditional monolithic video streaming approach.

Keywords: Virtual reality · 360-degree video ·
Tile-based adaptive streaming

1 Introduction

Propelled by developments in computing hardware and network technology, virtual reality (VR) has become increasingly popular nowadays. Virtual reality

This paper is supported in part by National Natural Science Foundation of China (61650101), Scientific Research Plan of the Science and Technology Commission of Shanghai Municipality (16511104203), in part by the 111 Program (B07022).

© Springer Nature Singapore Pte Ltd. 2019
G. Zhai et al. (Eds.): IFTC 2018, CCIS 1009, pp. 312–323, 2019.
https://doi.org/10.1007/978-981-13-8138-6_26

market is estimated to USD 33.90 billion by 2022 [1]. One major virtual reality application scenario is 360 VR video streaming, where user wears head-mounted displays (HMDs), e.g. HTC Vive [2] and Oculus Rift [3], and obtains immersive experience surrounded by virtual panorama. 360-degree video, also known as spherical video, comprises of omnidirectional view and can be mapped as sphere graphical textures. 360 VR video typically features ultra high resolution, i.e. 4K or more, and issues a challenge for video delivery. Conventional transmission scheme to stream entire 360 video is bandwidth inefficient because only field of view (FOV) is consumed by end user and another solution to transmit only FOV region requires intensive computation for real-time frame cropping and transcoding.

Tile based adaptive streaming [4] are previously proposed to overcome aforementioned drawbacks by spatially splitting the video frame into tiles which are independently encoded into multi-bitrate segments and transmitted in appropriate quality version according to viewport tracing and network state. Bitrate control is achieved by either configuring quantization level or resolution downsampling and it grades the video segment with various selectable quality levels.

Current typical tiling mesh is fixed and single, e.g. 8×4 mesh or 12×6 mesh, and for a 8K UHD 360 VR video, each tile approximates half resolution of the 1080p full video, lacking in scalability and potentially bringing about significant *pixel overheads* if only marginal portion of a tile is consumed. However, enlarging tile quantity with smaller tile scale neither necessarily means preferable performance since boundary cuts off reference between distant *macro blocks* and deteriorates encoding compression ratio (Fig. 1).

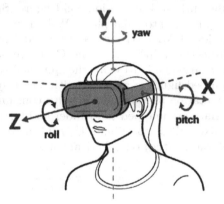

Fig. 1. Viewing omnidirectional video on HMDs [7]

In this paper, we propose a mixed tiling scheme with a graph algorithm to process optimal tile selection. Several tiling meshes are configured according to video source resolution and mesh dimensions are disposed in multiple relation. Tiles are therefore capable of merging/splitting into ones within other mesh and selected tiles of varied scale are mixed to represent the full resolution frame. Then multiple meshes are transformed into graph structure and tile selection for optimal bandwidth consumption is induced from the shortest path searching in the graph. Since small tile reduces aforementioned pixel overheads and large tile characterize superior encoding compression ratio, mixed nonuniform tiles readily approximates or even exceeds the performance of uniform optimal tile, without requirement of preliminary experiments or permutation.

2   Background and Related Work

In this section, we probe into solutions for adaptive VR video streaming and retrospect state-of-the-art optimized tiling method relevant to our approach.

2.1   Adaptive Video Streaming

The primary solution for bandwidth-efficient multimedia transferring is adaptive streaming. MPEG-DASH [5] is a standardized adaptive streaming protocol which utilizes Spatial Relationship Description (SRD) to indicate relations between spatially partitioned frame regions. Splice and combination of tiles within single mesh is operated according to SRD descriptor. [6] explores how spatial access can be performed in an adaptive HTTP streaming context and experiment different adaptation policies for tiled video content.

Spatial Projection. Current encoding/decoding techniques, e.g. AVC/HEVC, are mostly applied for 2-dimension video content but for 360 VR video, it's inherently a 3-dimension solid figure. Spatial projection is required for paving solid faces onto a flat plane. Well known projection comprises of Cube Map Projection (CMP), Truncated Pyramid Projection (TSP) [9] and Equirectangular Projection (ERP). TSP and CMP are both proposed by Facebook and the general rationale is to wrap the spherical surface in the specific solid figures. Each mapped figure is assigned with varied quality level according to user viewport orientation to reduce bandwidth consumption. And in ERP approach, spherical surface are mapped to cylinder and further unfold to rectangular surface. Given a pixel whose coordinate is (x, y) in equirectangular frame, its original position $(\angle yaw, \angle pitch)$ on spherical surface is derived as

$$\angle yaw = 2\pi \cdot \frac{x}{width}, \ \angle pitch = \pi \cdot (\frac{1}{2} - \frac{y}{height}).$$

Tile-Based Streaming. In tile-based adaptive streaming scheme, integral video frame is mapped in one of previously mentioned projections and then partitioned into several smaller scale rectangulars called tile. Each tile is encoded independently with multiple quality levels and user can prefetch preferable quality version referring to head orientation prediction and available bandwidth volume. Tile prefetching policy is explored in [20], using a target buffer control method, and [14] propose a rate adaptation algorithm which leverages future bandwidth and head orientation distribution to determine tile quality.

For the purpose of economical bandwidth consumption and focalizing the frame pixels nearby FOV, viewpoint prediction is widely adopted to make hypothesis of future viewpoint position. Linear regression analysis method is generally utilized to fulfill the prediction from recorded viewpoint samples during past time sequence and this is also the method we deployed in our VR system. Further viewpoint prediction method is experimented in [7,12] and their mentioned methods, including weighted linear regression and machine learning, gain a slight improvement in predicted accuracy but have drawbacks in non-trivial time complexity. The most significant factor influencing prediction accuracy is merely the size of time sliding windows for prediction.

2.2 Optimal Tiling

Tiling scheme has an impact on encoding efficiency since originally optional motion vectors are cut off by tile margins and deteriorated compression ratio makes more storage volume and network capacity wasted. And total storage size of tiles significantly grows when tiling mesh is fine-grained and can hold plenty of tiles, depicted in Fig. 2. To optimize the tiling method, several solutions are presented from different aspects. Codec enhancement approach is proposed in [8] which adopts inter-view prediction in intra random access point pictures and enables stereoscopic video coding. They suggest using motion-constrained tile sets (MCTS) to make tiles within one column predictable but this method doesn't take viewpoint tracing and content dependent characteristics into consideration. A spatio-temporal activity metrics based tiling scheme is explored in [11] and video samples are preprocessed for pixel domain analysis to derive the optimization model. And non-uniform tiling is proposed in [10] and their named Optile optimizes combined use of storage and download bandwidth as Integer Linear Program. These methods call for preprocessing in offline manner and present as amendment of conventional single-mesh tiling scheme.

Since adjacent tiles are possible to be attributed to same quality level and apparently larger tile has advantage of better encoding efficiency, our multi-mesh tiling scheme is inspired which splices mixed non-uniform tiles to construct monolithic frame. Furthermore, we translate multiple meshes to one acyclic graph structure and operate a shortest path searching algorithm to induce optimal tiling selection. The graph establishment is accompanied with topological sorting for vertexes and thus shortest path question is able to be solved in linear time. Benefited from such performance advantage, optimal tiling is executed online without requirement of weighty preprocessing or re-encoding and also gains superior bandwidth saving than single-mesh fixed-size tiling.

3   Methodology

3.1   Multiple Tiling Meshes Configuration

In tile-based approach for adaptive 360 VR video streaming, a full resolution *equirectangular* video frame is divided horizontally and vertically into multiple uniform tiles. Video segment resolution and mesh dimension jointly decide the tile dimension $\langle width, height \rangle$. Proposed solution adopts multiple tiling meshes within mesh set $\mathcal{M}$ and base mesh 1 represents a current common partition case, characterized by ordered pair $Dim_1^{\mathcal{M}} = \langle horizontal_{base}, vertical_{base} \rangle$ and naturally all $Dim_i^{\mathcal{M}} \in \mathbb{Z}_+^2$. Size of tile or full frame is estimated by resolution or pixel quantity and their relationship is formulated as:

$$S_i^{\mathcal{M}} = S_{frame} \cdot \det(\text{diag}(Dim_i^{\mathcal{M}})^{-1})$$

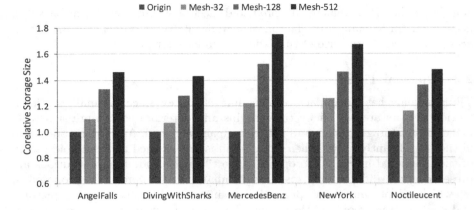

Fig. 2. Total storage size along with increment of tile amount

Multiple relation is applied for identical dimension between variant meshes and the densest mesh is limited by tile size threshold S_{min}, empirically decided by service provider and assuring finiteness of $\mathcal{M}$. Followed equations can interpret element characteristic and size of $\mathcal{M}$:

$$N_c = \left\lceil \log_{\alpha_h \alpha_v} \left(\frac{S_1^{\mathcal{M}}}{S_{min}} \right) \right\rceil$$

$$Dim_i^{\mathcal{M}} = Dim_1^{\mathcal{M}} \operatorname{diag}(\alpha_h^{i-1}, \alpha_v^{i-1}), \ i \in \{1 \ldots N_c\}$$

where $\alpha_h, \alpha_v \in \mathbb{Z}_+$ are the multiple factors for horizontal/vertical dimension of mesh and tile size threshold is subject to $S_{min} \leq S_1^{\mathcal{M}}$ in order that $\mathcal{M}$ has at least one element. Note that tile in mesh i covers the area $\alpha_h \alpha_v$ times of mesh $i+1$ tile and tile quantity of mesh i is derived as:

$$N_i = \det(\operatorname{diag}(Dim_i^{\mathcal{M}})), \ \forall i$$

Let encoded bitrate profile $\mathcal{B}$ represents collection of multi-bitrate levels sorted in ascending order, i.e. $b_1 < b_2 < \ldots < b_{|\mathcal{B}|}$, and denote view probability of all tiles within mesh i as probability vector p_i, $i \in \{1 \ldots N_c\}$. Then bandwidth cost of j-th tile in mesh i is deduced as:

$$b_{i,j}^* = b_{\lceil p_{i,j}|\mathcal{B}|\rceil}, \ j \in \{1 \ldots N_i\}$$

Given that diverse mesh dimension entails corresponding variation of tile quantity and each mesh only contributes partial tiles, a set of binary vector for filtering purpose is utilized to manipulate binary selection for tiles, denoted as $\mathcal{F} = \{f_i \mid f_{i,j} \in \{0,1\}\}$. Thus optimization procedure is modelled as:

$$\min_{\mathcal{F}} \ \sum_{i=1}^{N_c} \sum_{j=1}^{N_i} f_{i,j} \, b_{\lceil p_{i,j}|\mathcal{B}|\rceil}$$

$$s.t. \ \sum_{i=1}^{N_c} \mathcal{R}^{N_c-i}(f_i) = \mathbf{1} \tag{1}$$

where $\mathcal{R}(f_i)$ transform filtering binary vector f_i with N_i elements into f^*_{i+1} with N_{i+1} elements, i.e. $\alpha_h \alpha_v N_i$, and f^*_{i+1} from mesh i indicate the *equivalent* tile selection for mesh $i+1$. Successive conversion for each f_i occurs $N_c - i$ times so as to match the dimension of f_{N_c} for densest mesh N_c. Avoidance of *tile overlap* is attained by constrain summation of equivalent tile selection in mesh N_c, where only single selection is permitted for each underlying region of tile.

In mesh i, let $n_h = Dim^{\mathcal{M}}_{i,1}$ denote its horizontal dimension and j-th tile can be mapped into 2-dimension coordinate:

$$\langle\, x = (j-1) \bmod n_h + 1, \quad y = \left\lceil \frac{j}{n_h} \right\rceil \,\rangle$$

Then after transformation $\mathcal{R}$, j-th tile splits into $\alpha_h \alpha_v$ smaller tiles, covering same spherical regions, its index becomes

$$j^* = \alpha_h \alpha_v (y-1) n_h + \alpha_h (x-1) + 1$$
$$= \alpha_h \alpha_v n_h \left\lceil \frac{j - n_h}{n_h} \right\rceil + \alpha_h [\,(j-1) \bmod n_h\,] + 1$$

and generated tile group is correspondingly indexed by integer union set:

$$\mathcal{I}^{\mathcal{R}}_j = \bigcup_{k=1}^{\alpha_v} \{\, j' \in \mathbb{Z} \mid j' \in [\,\eta(k), \eta(k) + \alpha_h\,)\,\} \tag{2}$$
$$s.t. \quad \eta(k) = j^* + \alpha_h n_h (k-1)$$

3.2   Viewpoint Prediction

In adaptive VR streaming system, mixed tiles of video segments requires to be pre-fetched in appropriate quality level in accordance with view probability distribution. Head orientation tracking typically reflects user pattern and shows strong temporal auto-correlation in short time period [12]. Future motion can be predicated by statistical regression method and probability distribution is referred to estimate aforementioned cost vector. In this paper, *linear regression* model is utilized to fulfill such motion prediction.

User viewpoint at time point t is denoted by angular velocity vector $v_t = [\angle\theta_t \;\; \angle\phi_t]^\top$. Then let τ denote the *sampling interval* for head tracking and $T_{t,\tau}$ represents the discrete time sequence which recently elapsed from time point t and characterize interval τ. Viewpoint prediction for next period Δt is hence modeled as

$$\hat{v}_{t+\Delta t} = v_t + \Delta t \left[\, \beta^\theta_{T_{t,\tau}} \, \beta^\phi_{T_{t,\tau}} \,\right]^\top \tag{3}$$

where $\beta^\theta_{T_{t,\tau}}$ is the regression coefficient for yaw angle, calculated from FOV variance in time sequence $T_{t,\tau}$ and likewise $\beta^\phi_{T_{t,\tau}}$ for pitch angle. In ordinary linear regression model for viewpoint prediction, predicted error term is feasibly assumed to be *normally distributed*, and predicted viewing probability per angle, for j-th tile in mesh i, is estimated by adjusted cumulative distribution as

$$p_{i,j}^{\theta} = \text{erfc} \left| \frac{\theta_{i,j} - \hat{\theta}_{t+\Delta t}}{\sigma_{T_{t,\tau}}^{\theta} \sqrt{2}} \right|, \ p_{i,j}^{\phi} = \text{erfc} \left| \frac{\phi_{i,j} - \hat{\phi}_{t+\Delta t}}{\sigma_{T_{t,\tau}}^{\phi} \sqrt{2}} \right|$$

where mutually independent $<\theta_{i,j}, \phi_{i,j}>$ is spherical position projected from central pixel of the represented tile. Thus aforesaid viewing probability vector p_i in previous subsection is constructed from N_i tiles probability, each derived as

$$p_{i,j} = \gamma \cdot p_{i,j}^{\theta} \cdot p_{i,j}^{\phi} \tag{4}$$

where $\gamma \in (0, 1]$ is empirically determined in order to proportionally distribute varied tile qualities and it's rational to associate γ with average fetched quality in a certain time sliding windows. For simplicity, intact interpretation and formulation proof for this subsection are presented in full paper and then viewpoint prediction topic will be discussed in detail.

3.3   Optimal Tiling Inference

Since tile property can be described by bitrate cost $b_{i,j}$ for bandwidth consumption and viewing probability $p_{i,j}$ for potential visible quality, we could assign each tile a composed weight

$$w_{i,j} = -\lambda b_{i,j}^* / b_{i,j}^{max} + (1 - \lambda) p_{i,j} \tag{5}$$

and λ indicates the preference between bandwidth saving and tile quality. Then multiple meshes can be used to construct a directed acyclic graph based on pixel coordinate of tile margin and edge weight tile is $w_{i,j}$. To be specific, each graph edge represents a tile from one mesh whose source vertex is the tile top-left corner and destination vertex is the tile bottom-right corner. Multiple relationship of the mesh span assures that each tile shares same vertexes of its sub-tiles and any path that traverses the parent tile can cover entire underlying frame region without neglect. Optimal tiling can be inferred from the directed graph by shortest path searching and the searched path represents the optimal tile selection from multiple meshes covering the integral frame without deduplication. Since the edge weight is possibly negative and linear-time searching is preferred in a directed acyclic graph, we adopt the topological-sort based shorted path searching in our proposition. To summarize the path searching algorithm, graph nodes are firstly preprocessed by depth-first-searching to generate a post reverse order as its topological order and then graph node relaxation in ordinary path searching is applied according such order. Once the shortest path is inferred, optimal tile selection from multiple meshes is mapped from the path. Note that topological order deduction is one pass preprocessing and shortest path searching is ongoing runtime routine since the graph edge weight changes dynamically.

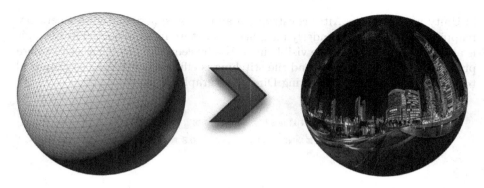

Fig. 3. Video frame texture UV mapping to graphical sphere.

4 System and Evaluation

To evaluate our proposed scheme, a VR system is implemented to evaluate proposed mixed tiling scheme. We develop a VR video streaming server deployed on cloud service provider *Aliyun* and accompany a VR player on client side to let user experience immersive 360 panorama with the HTC Vive headset.

4.1 Media Streaming Server

On server side, video is partitioned into tiles graded by quality and transcoded independently. Each tiling mesh partitions uniform tiles which belong to the same mesh group. Tile selection from multiple meshes is determined by aforementioned graph algorithm that searches the optimal path in the graph to cover the integral video frame by optimal tiles. Server program manipulates multiple video streamings and synchronizes the transferring pace to evenly consume the bandwidth for each streaming. We adopt versatile HTTP protocol and set the chunked-encoding to stream the segmented video part by part. Each HTTP chunk is 1 s tile segment. All streaming connections request the tile video and user client notifies the prefetching indication in another dedicated control connection. Prefetching policy is based on aforementioned FOV prediction. Given the fixed bandwidth capacity, the less consumed tile video gains higher priority for subsequent network transfer of its stream. Chunk-extension of each HTTP chunk is filled with the metadata of the streaming status to let client software adjust receiving buffer and once the tile relevant to the chunk is replaced by the ones in other mesh, chunk-extension also includes referred streaming indexes and corresponding mesh index. To monitor the bandwidth consumption and network status, we use *Nload* software on server side and record the measurement log file.

4.2 VR Playback Client

On client side, our developed VR player is based on Unity engine for graphical transition and SteamVR for driving HTC Vive headset. Additional functionalities of network I/O, video decoding, graphical texture stitching are implemented in Unity *native plugin*. After constructing an inverse sphere material, where UV mapping happens on its underlying spherical texture mesh, depicted in Fig. 3, it is able to make current scene visible in HMDs by centrally placing a user camera provided by SteamVR SDK and tile stitching is efficiently achieved as graphical texture manipulation by invoking DirectX11 graphical interface.

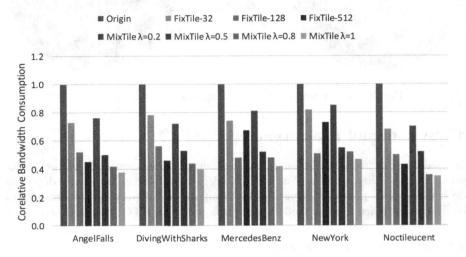

Fig. 4. Bandwidth evaluation of tiling scheme with 1-s time sliding window for FOV prediction.

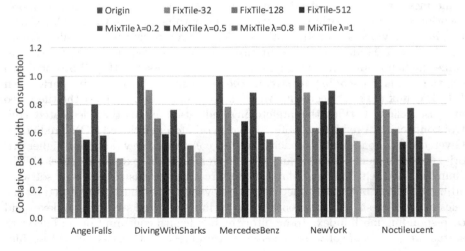

Fig. 5. Bandwidth evaluation of tiling scheme with 3-s time sliding window for FOV prediction.

4.3   Performance Evaluation

To evaluate our proposed mixed tiling scheme, we preliminarily download 5 high resolution VR videos from YouTube and MPEG website, transcode by *FFmpeg* with same codec parameters and remove the audio stream. Then we crop the raw video into tiles with multiple meshes configuration as previous section demonstrates. To be specific, in this implementation, quality level for tile is graded by resolution downsampling varied from $\frac{3}{4}, \frac{1}{2}, \frac{1}{3}, \frac{1}{4}$ and base tiling mesh dimension $Dim_1^{\mathcal{M}}$ is 8×4 with multiple factors $\alpha_h = \alpha_v = 2$. Tile size partitioned by mesh dimension for each video is illustrated in Table 1. We evaluate the performance of proposed scheme from the average result of 42 user sample data. Time sliding window of 1-s and 3-s are both experimented and compared which shows the performance variation when prediction accuracy deteriorates.

Table 1. Video details and tile specification within multiple meshes.

Video	Resolution	Tile size		
		mesh 8×4	mesh 16×8	mesh 32×16
MercedesBenz	3840×1920	480×480	240×240	120×120
NewYork	3840×1920	480×480	240×240	120×120
AngelFalls	7680×3840	960×960	480×480	240×240
DivingWithSharks	7680×3840	960×960	480×480	240×240
Noctileucent	7856×3928	982×982	491×491	245×245

Performance evaluation is shown in Figs. 4 and 5 where FixTile-32 represents conventional single mesh tiling scheme with mesh dimension 8×4 and FixTile-128 for mesh 16×8, FixTile-512 for mesh 32×16. Fact can be observed in FixTile scheme that for 8K resolution video, the most fine-grained tiling mesh 32×16 performs best since large tile size causes significant pixel overheads while for 4K resolution video, tiling mesh 16×8 performs best since too small tile size in mesh 32×16 gains deteriorated encoding efficiency. Then for our proposed mixed tiling scheme (shortname MixTile in figure), the bandwidth performance is in positive correlation with the factor λ. When λ is larger which means few bitrate of tile segment is more preferred than high visible quality, bandwidth consumption is more saved. Mixed tiling scheme outperforms conventional fixed tiling scheme in the aspect of bandwidth consumption and reduces at most 65% bandwidth compared with original non-tiling approach and up to 31% relative to fixed tiling scheme. The superiority benefits from combination of encoding efficiency inherent in large tile and lessened pixel overheads inherent in small tile. In regions close to FOV, viewing probability is high but tile with better quality causes significant pixel overheads if only tile margin is within FOV. Cost comparison with other mesh tiles makes it possible to substitute wasteful large tile by fine-grained small tiles, covering equivalent sphere area. While in regions far from FOV, tiny derivative from viewing probability variance entails portion of tiles in same quality merge into larger tiles featuring higher encoding compression ratio. Therefore, proposed mixed tiling scheme combines merits of tiles varied in size and intrinsic multiple selectivity also qualifies it for relieving bandwidth fluctuation when prediction accuracy decrements, that can be observed by comparing same x-axis column from two figures.

5   Conclusion

Tile based adaptive VR streaming enables user to enjoy FOV in high quality and reduces overall transmission bandwidth. Optimal tiling depends on content characteristics and existing methods require preliminary inference for a circumscribed case and demand high computing complexity. In this paper, we propose a versatile solution where several correlative meshes jointly determine tile division and the mixed tiling scheme can dynamically select the optimal tile set in linear time during each iteration. Mesh dimension grows in multiple along with video resolution and the extensibility is attained from capabilities of tile merging and splitting. We formulate the cost optimization and viewpoint prediction, assisted with a graph algorithm for tile selection from multiple meshes. Performance evaluation in our implemented VR system manifests proposed mixed tiling scheme outperforms native non-tiling approach and fixed tiling scheme. In future work, we plan to apply machine learning model to fulfill viewpoint prediction and probe mesh parameter optimization as well.

References

1. Virtual Reality Market to 2022. https://www.marketsandmarkets.com/Market-Reports/reality-applications-market-458
2. HTC Vive. https://www.vive.com/
3. Oculus Rift. https://www.oculus.com/rift/
4. Inoue, M., Kimata, H., Fukazawa, K., Matsuura, N.: Interactive panoramic video streaming system over restricted bandwidth network. In: Proceedings of the 18th ACM International Conference on Multimedia (MM 2010) (2010)
5. Stockhammer, T.: Dynamic adaptive streaming over HTTP: standards and design principles. In: Proceedings of the Second Annual ACM Conference on Multimedia Systems (MMSys 2011) (2011)
6. Feuvre, J.L., Concolato, C.: Tiled-based adaptive streaming using MPEG-DASH. In: Proceedings of the 7th International Conference on Multimedia Systems (MMSys 2016) (2016)
7. Qian, F., Ji, L., Han, B., Gopalakrishnan, V.: Optimizing 360 video delivery over cellular networks. In: Proceedings of the 5th Workshop on All Things Cellular: Operations, Applications and Challenges (ATC 2016) (2016)
8. Zare, A., Aminlou, A., Hannuksela, M.M., Gabbouj, M.: HEVC-compliant tile-based streaming of panoramic video for virtual reality applications. In: Proceedings of the 2016 ACM on Multimedia Conference (MM 2016) (2016)

9. Next-generation video encoding techniques for 360 video and VR. https://code.facebook.com/posts/1126354007399553/nextgeneration-video-encoding-techniques-for-360-video-and-vr/

10. Xiao, M., Zhou, C., Liu, Y., Chen, S.: OpTile: toward optimal tiling in 360-degree video streaming. In: Proceedings of the 2017 ACM on Multimedia Conference (MM 2017) (2017)

11. Sanchez, Y., Skupin, R., Hellge, C., Schierl, T.: Spatio-temporal activity based tiling for panorama streaming. In: Proceedings of the 27th Workshop on Network and Operating Systems Support for Digital Audio and Video (NOSSDAV 2017) (2017)

12. Bao, Y., Wu, H., Zhang, T., Ramli, A., Liu, X.: Shooting a moving target: motion-prediction-based transmission for 360-degree videos. In: 2016 IEEE International Conference on Big Data (Big Data), pp. 1161–1170 (2016)

13. Hosseini, M., Swaminathan, V.: Adaptive 360 VR video streaming: divide and conquer. In: 2016 IEEE International Symposium on Multimedia (ISM), pp. 107–110 (2016)

14. Ghosh, A., Aggarwal, V., Qian, F.: A rate adaptation algorithm for tile-based 360-degree video streaming. CoRR abs/1704.08215 (2017)

15. El-Ganainy, T., Hefeeda, M.: Streaming virtual reality content. CoRR abs/1612.08350 (2016)

16. FFmpeg. https://www.ffmpeg.org/

17. Boost.Beast. https://www.boost.org/doc/libs/1_66_0/libs/beast/

18. MessagePack. https://msgpack.org/

19. Unity Engine. https://unity3d.com/

20. Xie, L., Xu, Z., Ban, Y., Zhang, X., Guo, Z.: 360ProbDASH: improving QoE of 360 video streaming using tile-based HTTP adaptive streaming. In: Proceedings of the 2017 ACM on Multimedia Conference (MM 2017) (2017)

21. Fan, C.-L., Lee, J., Lo, W.-C., Huang, C.-Y., Chen, K.-T., Hsu, C.-H.: Fixation prediction for 360° video streaming in head-mounted virtual reality. In: Proceedings of the 27th Workshop on Network and Operating Systems Support for Digital Audio and Video (NOSSDAV 2017) (2017)

A Gigapixel Image Browsing Scheme in Edge Computing Environment

Yulin Han, Long Ye$^{(\boxtimes)}$, Wei Zhong, and Li Fang

Key Laboratory of Media Audio and Video,
Communication University of China, Ministry of Education,
Beijing 100024, China
`yolincuc@163.com`, {`yelong,wzhong,fangli`}@`cuc.edu.cn`

Abstract. Gigapixel images have drawn many attentions recently as it can supply ultra-high-definition visual experience, however the strict requirements for user's terminal to display makes the gigapixel image difficult to enter people's daily life. Aiming at this problem, we proposed a novel picture browsing scheme under the edge-computing environment. By receiving the control command from users' terminal, the edge server corresponds the instruction to generate the current field of view (FOV) which needed to be transmitted back to the terminal. Two ways to generate the FOV including block-based image stitching with super resolution reconstruction and quasi video coding are proposed in this paper. Experimental results showed the performances of the two ways on the compression rate and interaction delay, meantime analyzed the relative merits of each way.

Keywords: Gigapixel image · Browsing scheme · Low delay

1 Introduction

As the resolution can reach one billion pixels per image, gigapixel image has a wide range of usage in various fields and it has shown utterly advantages [1]. For example, a gigapixel image of a football field can let you see every face of the audience distinctly and it makes the video-watching process more freely, without the restriction of the director. Because of detailed description property, gigapixel image has played a significant role in military and security industry. However, there are still problems in the browsing of gigapixel images, especially the capacity of real-time processing, and that is the reason why gigapixel images are hard to be introduced into people's daily life [2].

There are two ways, namely local browsing and network-based browsing, to achieve ultra-high-definition image/video browsing. The former method needs to store images in the local equipment, which obviously costs more memory and larger storage space locally [3], causing browsing unfluency when the user do the sliding or zooming process. And the existing compression method, from JPEG [4] to JPEG2000 [5] to HVEC [6] and to the present compression with recurrent neural networks [7], has greatly increased the compression ratio. However, it is still difficult to solve the big storage space problem of gigapixel images.

On the other hand, with the development of cloud storage and cloud computing, we are more inclined to store such a large amount of data in the cloud end and view it in

© Springer Nature Singapore Pte Ltd. 2019
G. Zhai et al. (Eds.): IFTC 2018, CCIS 1009, pp. 324–333, 2019.
https://doi.org/10.1007/978-981-13-8138-6_27

real time through the network on our equipment. Our experiments are performed in the real-time edge computing environment. Compared with cloud computing, edge computing has lower latency, so it is more suitable for real-time data, and greatly reduces the pressure of the network traffic [8]. Meanwhile, the hardware with superior computing and storage capabilities have greatly promoted the applications of edge computing, leading to the rapid development of cloud games. The cloud game is a good attempt of real-time service, in which way a game is running on a server and the game pictures are compressed and transmitted to the users in the form of a video stream [9]. In this case, the gaming device in users' console does not need any high-end processors and graphics cards any more, and an ordinary device with video decoding capability is enough. The key point of this edge-computing based solution is the delay of network transmission. So it is advisable to deploy the cloud game server to the edge nodes. The data size of the gigapixel image is very huge and there is high demand for real time processing, as explained above, we use the edge computing environment to conduct the experiments. Moreover, we draw lessons from the cloud game. By receiving the control command from user's terminal, the edge server corresponds the instruction to generate the current view which needed to be transmitted back to the terminal. The key is to generate image blocks in large images. Tile loading method, as a general method of ultra high definition image browsing, is to segment the pictures in a fixed way [10]. The first method proposed in this paper is optimized on this basis. The second method is to generate the image block in real time and transmit the video to the front end.

The main contribution of this paper is that we proposed novel browsing schemes for gigapixel images including both panoramas and 2D images. To sum up, the main contents of the paper can be concluded into three key points. First of all, the experiments are carried out in the edge computing environment for real time processing. Secondly, it allows not only the computer but also mobile as the terminal. And all the method we proposed can provide us with a more convenient way to see gigapixel images, because we don't need to download any software [11]. Thirdly, we have proposed two different modes for gigapixel image browsing. The first mode is the an upgraded version of the tile loading technique, we mainly use interpolation super-resolution reconstruction to reduce the amount of data method when users zoom in and zoom out the images. The second one is the conversion of images into video to show users the selected FOV currently. The two modes have their own advantages, and that is what we will introduce in Sects. 2 and 3.

2   The Gigapixel Image Browsing Scheme Based on Fixed Block

This image browsing scheme which we named scheme A, divides large images into blocks in different resolution. And we used super-resolution reconstruction to reduce the amount of data transmission, mainly to solve the application of zoom-in and zoom-out. All the transmission of scheme A is image block. Using the block transmission with super-resolution reconstruction technology can further reduce the delay.

For the ultra-high definition pictures, we should split the picture into appropriate blocks and encode each blocks. That means the image data is divided into tiles in terms of the two-dimensional grid plane, and map each tile to an object stored in the object-based storage system. And because the general resolution of the mobile phone and the ordinary display is 1920 * 1080, the size of the block should be smaller than the resolution to avoid redundant information. We ought to transmit the block which seen by the user, then, when the users have received the block, it can directly display for ultra-high definition pictures, and if the pictures are panoramic, we can adjust it to form a panoramic image. We also take good advantage of caching technology to avoid bandwidth waste. When the user views the image displayed by the view, the blocks next to the view are being transmitted, and the splice work is performed at the front end. In this way, we can minimize users' waiting time and improve their experience. At the same time, image segmentation is also beneficial to protect users' privacy and enhance users' trust in image cloud storage. However, The above method has solved the sliding problem in the same scene, but the zooming operation has not been solved yet (Fig. 1).

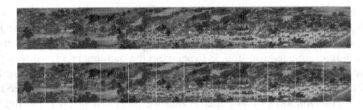

Fig. 1. The picture is segmented into blocks and each block is transmitted separately.

The tile loading technology as a mature technology has already played an important role in ultra high definition image browsing in the cloud, which is generally used for map browsing. Tile loading technology is mainly based on image pyramid [12]. It means the high resolution images of each layer of pyramid are divided into a series of low resolution small image blocks for storage and browsing. The adjacent image blocks are continuous regions in the large image and there is no overlap between each other. Assuming that the resolution size of the base image block is set to $a_0 \times b_0$ and the resolution size of the whole image is $A \times B$, then the resolution of the j level is $(A/2^j) \times (B/2^j)$, and the number of image blocks after the partition is $\frac{A}{2^j \times a_0} \times \frac{B}{2^j \times b_0}$. Our method which needs less data is based on it (Fig. 2).

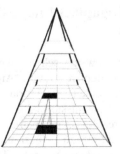

Fig. 2. The image pyramid

Therefore, based on tile loading technology, we propose a more suitable scheme for image browsing. We try to use the existing simple super-resolution reconstruction method to reduce the data of the transmission. For example, if a user amplifies a block, the block of the front end will interpolate itself to generate a block with twice the length and width, and the server side only needs to transmit the calculated residual image to the front end. This method saves more bandwidth than tile loading technology for gigapixel image browsing. As shown in Fig. 3, if we have got the red box image, we need to transmit the residual image of the red box in the right picture in order to get the image of the green box. Compared with tile loading technology, this method greatly reduces the amount of data transmitted (Fig. 4).

Fig. 3. Image Pyramid with interpolated super-resolution reconstruction (Color figure online)

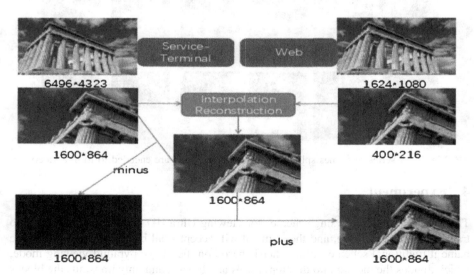

Fig. 4. Specific operation scheme based on super-resolution reconstruction

3 The Gigapixel Image Browsing Scheme of Quasi Video Coding

For the gigapixel image browsing, we can also convert pictures into video. By receiving the control command from user's terminal, we convert the pictures the user would like to see into the video in real time, and transmit the video. When it comes to video encoder, although the compression ratio of H.265 is very high, its coding efficiency is too low [13]. For Ultra HD video, only one frame can be programmed in about one minute. Therefore, we still use H.264 encoder. If the user sends a slide or a zoom-in request, the server will pick out the desired picture and code it into video in real time. Then the video will be transmitted to the display in a 25-frame-per-second. The reason for the conversion of pictures to video is that the live-broadcasting video technology is more mature, which can be set to bandwidth adaptation to meet user's viewing, on the other hand, it can reduce the size of the data by using the interframe prediction of video, also this method can be well applied to the transmission of full view video or VR games (Fig. 5).

Fig. 5. A series of frames splited from the whole image are encoded to form a video

4 Experiment

There are two main browsing schemes for viewing Ultra HD images: the first one is to transmit the entire image, and the terminal will accept it all before viewing it, and we name it traditional scheme 1; the other is based on the image pyramid viewing mode, which divides the picture into different levels and blocks, and only transmits the blocks the user currently sees, and we name it traditional scheme 2. With the proposed the gigapixel image browsing scheme based on fixed block (scheme A) and scheme of quasi video coding (scheme B), we have there are four browsing schemes. We first conducted the subjective experience experiments of these four browsing schemes. Subsequently, since our scheme A is an optimization of the traditional scheme 2, we compare the delay and data quantity of scheme A with that of the traditional scheme 2. At the same time, we compare the delay and data quantity between the scheme B and the traditional scheme 1.

4.1   Subjective Evaluation of Satisfaction of the Four Schemes

In this experiment, we asked 20 people to make subjective evaluations. They were asked to browse the pictures online displayed by the three schemes. They told us if they are satisfied after viewing them. The transmission speed is limited to 1M/s.

Table 1.   Subjective evaluation of satisfaction of the three schemes

Satisfaction rate	Traditional scheme		Our scheme	
Method	One	Two	A	B
Pictures (>10M)	30%	85%	95%	80%
Pictures (<1M)	90%	90%	90%	85%

The first traditional scheme is to load the whole picture and wait for a longer time. The experience is acceptable when the image is small and the wait time is short, but when the picture is large, the experience is poor because of the longer wait time. The second traditional scheme is based on the image pyramid, so no matter the size of the picture, it guarantees the fluency of browsing, but there are still some delays between each layer switching in the big picture, so the subjective feeling is not particularly good. Our scheme A is to make the picture into blocks and using super-resolution while zooming. As is indicated in the table, the effect of this mode is the best among the four schemes, especially in the situation of large image. Our scheme B is the mode of converting the picture into video, and because of the short-time delay, it also has extraordinary performance when the bandwidth is not very high. The conclusion is that the user is more likely to accept the transmission mode which will let them view the picture quickly. They usually do not have enough patience to wait for a long time to load the picture. Compared with all loading pictures, the satisfaction of the Scheme A and scheme B are both better than the traditional one when the picture is large.

4.2   The Time Delay and Total Data of Scheme B and Traditional Method

This experiment compares the scheme B to convert pictures into videos with the traditional method which transmits the whole picture. The amount of data required to view the entire panorama through video and the delay we need to view the panorama picture are tested. The transmission speed is limited to 1M/s. The Table 1 gives an example of three experiment. And we got Fig. 6 by carrying out several experiments for images between 200K and 10M (Table 2).

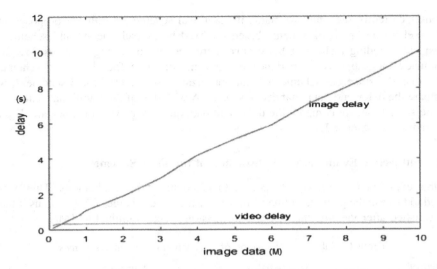

Fig. 6. The delay of video transmission and picture transmission vary with the amount of data

Table 2. The delay and total data volume between scheme B and traditional method

	Image data	Our video data	Image delay	Our video delay
Test1	1.27M	3.84M	1.27 s	354 ms
Test2	12.3M	27.82M	12.3 s	370 ms
Test3	95.6M	220.7M	95.6 s	390 ms

We summarize the conclusion of the experiment below:

Compared with the traditional method, the total amount of data from scheme B is roughly 3–4 times larger, but people are more concerned about whether the current picture can be quickly displayed when viewing the image. And the video can be transmitted in real time, so that the delay has a significant improvement. In the case of the rate of 1M/s, it can realize real-time display. At the same time, experiments have found that when the amount of image data is less than 400 KB, the traditional image transmission mode is more advantageous. As pictures become larger and larger, our scheme B shows a strong ability to reduce delay.

4.3 The Delay of Our Scheme A and Tile Loading Transmission While Zooming

In this experiment, the time delay of the tile loading technique and our scheme A is compared. The magnification of each layer of the image Pyramid is selected as the default 2 * 2. The time delay of the scheme is the sum of the time needed for transmission and the time of the display. Therefore, we also calculate the time of the reconstructed image in the client server of the scheme A (Table 3).

Table 3. Delay of traditional transmission and our scheme A transmission

	Tile loading delay	Our scheme A delay
Test1	410 ms	125 ms
Test2	356 ms	96 ms

The experimental conclusion is obvious, in most cases, our scheme A can achieve lower delay than tile loading. This is mainly because in the image Pyramid, the tile loading technology is still transmitting all the image blocks while zooming. However, our scheme optimizes it, that is, only the image residuals are transmitted and the image blocks will be reconstructed on the client server. Although it will produce more computation on the client server, the fluency of image browsing is greatly improved.

4.4 Data Size of Scheme A and Tile Loading Technology Under Different Gain

The purpose of the experiment is to explore the size of the amount of data used for super-resolution reconstruction and traditional tile loading when the user performs different magnification operations on the picture. At the same time, this experiment is also to explore the relationship between the size and number of blocks of adjacent layers in Pyramid. Because of most people's operating habits, it can not be enlarged to a large extent, we set the magnification between 1.2 * 1.2 and 4 * 4 (Table 4 and Fig. 7).

Table 4. Data size of Scheme A and tile loading technology under different gain

Gain	Data of scheme A (KB)	Data of tile loading (KB)
1.2 * 1.2	95.9	1150
1.5 * 1.5	118	
1.8 * 1.8	121	
2 * 2	132	
2.5 * 2.5	150	
2.8 * 2.8	159	
3 * 3	166	
3.5 * 3.5	169	
3.8 * 3.8	172	
4 * 4	176	

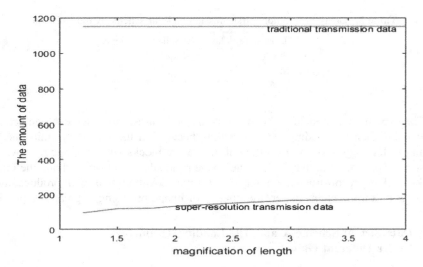

Fig. 7. Relationship between the amount of data and the magnification after super-resolution reconstruction

When using the tile loading, no matter what kinds of the proportional relationship between the two adjacent layers of image Pyramid, it is necessary to transmit the complete image block. So the data amount does not change with the magnification. But when using our scheme A, the larger the size of the block between the two layers, the larger the amount of image residuals block data needed to be transmitted. In fact, it is not difficult to see from the whole that the amount of data we need to transmit in our scheme A is significantly less in the case of the amplification factor. So our method can be well adapted to the usage of audience in reality.

5 Conclusion

From what has been discussed above, we can safely draw the conclusion that converting ultra-high definition pictures into real-time video can provide users lower delay and better experience. However, its total data is much bigger than the pictures itself. The Improved differential transmission for tile loading technology has smaller data and lower delay especially when zooming in. But it will increase the computational complexity of the display side. Both methods have better performance than traditional methods. So they will be more suitable for the transmission of gigapixel images. It will also provide a good foreshadowing for the transmission of panoramic video and ultra-high definition video.

Acknowledgment. This work is supported by the National Natural Science Foundation of China under Grant Nos. 61631016 and 61371191, and the Project of State Administration of Press, Publication, Radio, Film and Television under Grant No. 2015-53.

References

1. Brady, D.J., Gehm, M.E., Stack, R.A., Marks, D.L., Kittle, D.S., Golish, D.R.: Multiscale gigapixel photography. Nature **486**(7403), 386–389 (2012)
2. Hosseini, M., Swaminathan, V.: Adaptive 360 VR video steaming: divide and conquer (2016). arXiv preprint: arXiv:1609.08729
3. Perra, C., Giusto, D.D.: An image browsing application based on JPEG XR. In: CBMI 2008, pp. 396–401 (2008)
4. Belyaev, E., Mantel, C., Forchhammer, S.: Low-complexity compression of high dynamic range infrared images with JPEG compatibility. In: VCIP 2017, pp. 1–4 (2017)
5. Sánchez-Hernández, J.J., Garcia Ortiz, J.P., González Ruiz, V., Muller, D.: Interactive streaming of sequences of high resolution JPEG2000 images. IEEE Trans. Multimed. **17**(10), 1829–1838 (2015)
6. Liao, W., Yang, D., Chen, Z.: A fast mode decision algorithm for HEVC intra prediction. In: VCIP 2016, pp. 1–4 (2016)
7. Toderici, G., et al.: Full resolution image compression with recurrent neural networks. In: CVPR 2017, pp. 5435–5443 (2017)
8. Cao, Y., Chen, Y.: QoE-based node selection strategy for edge computing enabled Internet-of-Vehicles (EC-IoV). In: VCIP 2017, pp. 1–4 (2017)
9. Xu, Y., Shen, Q., Li, X., Ma, Z.: A cost-efficient cloud gaming system at scale. IEEE Netw. **32**(1), 42–47 (2018)
10. Lv, D., Tao, W., Ying, X., Cui, Y.: The design and implementation of massive map tile storage technology oriented to the mobile terminal. In: Geoinformatics 2015, pp. 1–510 (2015)
11. Maged, B., Jeffrey, W., Jianya, G., Peng, Y.: Web GIS in practice VIII: HTML5 and the canvas element for interactive online mapping. Int. J. Health Geograph. **9**, 14 (2010)
12. Kim, Y., Kang, B.-N., Kim, D.: Detector with focus: normalizing gradient in image pyramid. In: ICIP 2017, pp. 420–424 (2017)
13. Yang, K., Wan, S., Gong, Y., Wu, H.R., Feng, Y.: Perceptual based SAO rate-distortion optimization method with a simplified JND model for H.265/HEVC. Signal Process. Image Commun. **31**, 10–24 (2014)

Performance Analysis of Full-Duplex Cooperative Systems over Correlated Fading Channels

Bicheng Wang, Ruoqi Shi, Jian Tang, and Jianling Hu[✉]

School of Electronic and Information Engineering,
Soochow University, Suzhou 215006, Jiangsu, China
jlhu@suda.edu.cn

Abstract. In this paper, the effects of correlated fading channels in full-duplex cooperative systems are discussed. Due to the diversity of actual channel environments, the correlations between different channels need to be considered specifically. We first present the state of art research on the channel correlations in cooperative systems. Then, the transmission performance of a typical full-duplex relaying network is analyzed in detail. The system adopts opportunistic relay selection scheme to find the global optimal relay for two-hop communication. The assumption that the correlations between channels are approximately equal is adopted. The closed-form expression of transmission outage probability is analytically derived, which can be described by the correlation coefficients among source-relay links and the relay-destination links. Finally, numerical simulations are performed to verify the derived analytical expressions and the influences of the channel correlations under different transmission conditions are discussed.

Keywords: Full-duplex · Cooperative systems · Correlated channels · Outage probability

1 Introduction

Full-duplex (FD) cooperative systems are considered as one of the promising candidate applications, and it's hopeful to be standardized to 5G in the near future [1]. As an alternative to MIMO schemes, cooperative systems utilize distributed relays to contribute a spatial diversity for wireless communication [1,2]. Therefore, it has been widely employed in D2D, Mobile Ad Hoc Network, IoT and so on.

As a promising scheme for signal enhancement and coverage extension, half-duplex (HD) cooperative systems were applied in LTE systems. However, in HD mode, the systems only adopt devices with single antenna, so that the process of signal receiving and forwarding commonly requires two time slots. This phenomenon leads to a reduction of spectral efficiency, and makes it extremely

© Springer Nature Singapore Pte Ltd. 2019
G. Zhai et al. (Eds.): IFTC 2018, CCIS 1009, pp. 334–345, 2019.
https://doi.org/10.1007/978-981-13-8138-6_28

difficult for cooperative systems to meet the strict synchronization requirements. In fact of the forwarding delay caused by HD relays, the decoding complexity of receivers is also increased, correspondingly. Therefore, the FD mode is proposed to solve these problems. In FD mode, the main challenge used to be the ill effect of self-interference. However, with the improvement of antenna technology and signal processing algorithm, the self-interference between the input and output of FD devices can be evidently restrained. Yet in some cases, the residual self-interference (RSI) is still out of tolerance. Considering that the RSI may not be enough canceled, the authors in [3,4] proposed a hybrid duplex communication mechanism for cooperative systems. This scheme is a compromise between the pure FD or HD mode. Meanwhile, how to combine FD cooperative systems with non-orthogonal multiple access (NOMA) and physical layer security (PLS) has also attracted widespread attention. It is shown in [5–7] that FD cooperative systems contribute a huge potential to resource utilization and security performance for wireless data transmissions.

On the other hand, spatial correlation is one of the major challenges for the multi-antenna transmission channels. Once the correlation is excessively high, it is hard for receivers to correctly decode the signal transmitted in each antenna channel. It leads to a serious decrease in the performance of systems. In fact, even if the FD cooperative systems do not employ the multi-antenna technology, there are also correlations among the fading channels. For example, the correlations can be strong if the relays distribute unevenly in the system, the relays may be relatively concentrated in location, or some strong scatterers may emerge in the neighborhood of the nodes. As a result, the correlations need to be analyzed specifically. In [8,9], the correlations between the source-relay (S-R) and relay-destination (R-D) links was investigated. It is shown that this form can bring a benefit to the network, which means that a larger correlation coefficient leads to a better system performance. While in [10], the source-to-destination (S-D) link was also added to the study of correlations in relaying networks. The authors in [10] considered two wireless communication scenarios: one for S-D correlated to S-R, and the other for S-D correlated to R-D. Meanwhile, in the actual transmission process, the estimated CSI is ordinarily out of date due to the feedback delay caused by the design of transmission strategy. The relationship between outdated CSI and actual CSI can also be expressed as a function of a power correlation coefficient. The authors in [8,11,12] provided the mathematical expressions of the correlation factor, respectively. In terms to the different distributions of signal envelope (e.g., Rayleigh, Rician or Nakagami-m distribution), the corresponding mathematical characteristics of the channel correlations, which were utilized to evaluate the system performance, were also investigated in [13]. In the NOMA system, partial channel correlation may exist in a pair of users. The correlation between the relay user and the indirect communication user is considered in [14,15]. In addition, channel correlations also play a positive role in PLS. Its influence on the secure transmission performance in cooperative systems was studied in [16,17].

Although the channel correlations in traditional HD relaying networks have been widely investigated, the transmission performance of the FD cooperative system in the correlated fading channels is still far from being meticulously understood. In this article, we consider the correlations among the S-R channels. At the same time, the R-D channels are also correlated. It is generally believed that the direct transmission link is approximately ignored due to the influence of large-scale path fading or numerous obstacles. There are two most popular forwarding modes for relays – amplify-and-forward (AF) and decode-and-forward (DF). The former one is utilized in this study. In order to facilitate the performance analysis, the correlations in each hop are approximately equal. The opportunistic relay selection (ORS) scheme is adopted to find the globally optimal relay. Thus, the source signal is transmitted in two hops. Also we assume that perfect CSI is available [18]. It means that the feedback delay is tolerable or the reciprocity of channels is accessible. Note that the correlations analyzed in this paper exist among fading channels, which is different from the antenna correlations in MIMO relaying networks in [9].

The rest of this paper is organized as follows. Section 2 describes the investigated FD cooperative system model in correlated environments. In Sect. 3, we analytically derive the closed-form of transmission outage probability (TOP) described by the correlation coefficients among the S-R channels and the R-D channels. We conduct extensive simulations and use a series of numerical results to verify the mathematical expression of TOP in Sect. 4. Finally, Sect. 5 concludes the paper.

2   System Model

Figure 1 shows the diagram of a FD cooperative system under correlated fading channels. The transmitter-receiver pair (S and D) is equipped with single antenna due to size limitation. There are N intermediate relays R_i randomly located in this network, i $\in \{1, \ldots, N\}$. Each relay has two antennas, one for receiving while the other for transmitting. The relays assist the transmission from the source S to the destination D. All of them are working in the AF relaying mode. In this article, we utilize the ORS scheme for relays with fixed-gain transmission to illustrate the advantages of relaying networks. Since the assumption that the direct link between the S and D suffers severe shadowing, the source signal can only transmit with the $S - R_i - D$ link. The wireless links of S-R_i and R_i to D are respectively denoted as h_{SR_i} and h_{R_iD}, which are correlated with each other and assumed as zero-mean complex Gaussian random variables (RVs) with variance $|\sigma_{SR}|^2$ and $|\sigma_{RD}|^2$. We hold the believe that the self-interference between each two FD relays is impossible to be completely cancelled. Referring to the S-R channels, the RSI can also be modeled as a fading channel [4]. The channel variable of the i-th relay's RSI is h_{ii}, and it also follows a zero-mean complex Gaussian distribution with variance σ_{RR}^2. All channels above are modeled as Rayleigh fading. In order to make the model stochastic and persuasive, the channel coefficients are set to change constantly from one time slot to another.

In this scenario, the noise between each two nodes is set as an additive white Gaussian noise (AWGN). Its variance can be described as N_{mn}, m, n $\in \{S, R, D\}$.

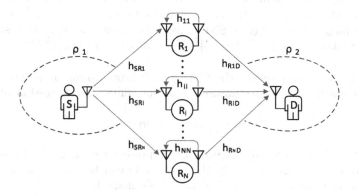

Fig. 1. FD cooperative system under correlated fading channels.

The discussions of variable transmission gain and power optimization are beyond the scope of this article, so the source and relays send signals at fixed power P_S and P_R, respectively. Additionally, the transmission rate is also fixed.

With regard to the relays in this scenario, the transmission and reception of signals are completed in one time slot. Therefore, when the R_i acquires the signal x_S from source broadcast, it is also interfered with the repeated signal y_{R_i} from the output of itself at the same time. Considering the computational simplicity, the source signal x_S is normalized to $|x_S|^2 = 1$. We can express the signals received at R_i and D as

$$y_{R_i} = \sqrt{P_S}h_{SR_i}x_S + \sqrt{P_R}h_{ii}y_{R_i} + N_{SR}, \tag{1}$$

$$y_D = \sqrt{P_R}h_{R_iD}y_{R_i} + N_{RD}. \tag{2}$$

According to the previous assumption of channel parameters, the SNR at D is

$$\gamma_D = \frac{GP_S|h_{SR_i}|^2|h_{R_iD}|^2}{GN_{SR}|h_{R_iD}|^2 + G|h_{ii}|^2|h_{R_iD}|^2\left(P_S|h_{SR_i}|^2 + N_{SR}\right) + N_{RD}}, \tag{3}$$

where G represents the amplification gain of the relay R_i. Each AF relay amplifies the source signals by the fixed transmitting power P_S. Thus, G can be expressed by P_S as

$$G(P_R) = \sqrt{\frac{P_R}{P_S|h_{SR_i}|^2 + N_{SR}}}. \tag{4}$$

In case of good channel conditions (high γ_{SR_i} and γ_{R_iD}), substituting Eqs. (4) into (3), we can approximately derive the following expression

$$\gamma_D = \min\left(\frac{\gamma_{SR_i}}{1 + \gamma_{ii}}, \gamma_{R_iD}\right). \tag{5}$$

The received SNRs of R_i and D are obtained as $\gamma_{SR_i} = P_S|h_{SR_i}|^2/N_{SR}$ and $\gamma_{R_iD} = P_R|h_{R_iD}|^2/N_{RD}$. The SNR of RSI link is represented as $\gamma_{ii} = P_R|h_{ii}|^2/N_{RR}$. They indicate the instantaneous SNRs of each link. It is known that the variance of the channel variable is $|\sigma_{SR}|^2$, $|\sigma_{RD}|^2$ and $|\sigma_{RR}|^2$. Correspondingly, the received SNRs also obeys an exponential distribution with the variances $\lambda_{SR} = P_S|\sigma_{SR}|^2/N_{SR}$, $\lambda_{RD} = P_R|\sigma_{RD}|^2/N_{RD}$, $\lambda_{RR} = P_R|\sigma_{RR}|^2/N_{RR}$.

The ORS scheme requires the CSI of each link, aiming at maximizing the available capacity of the destination. The mathematical expression of ORS is given by

$$b = \arg\max_{i \in \{1,\ldots,N\}} \{min\,(\gamma_D)\}. \tag{6}$$

After b is obtained by (6), we use R_b to represent the optimal relay employed in this strategy. According to (5), the SNR at D can be expressed as γ_{D_b}. The system capacity obtained at D with the ORS scheme is

$$C_b = \log_2\,(1 + \gamma_{D_b}). \tag{7}$$

We utilize the power correlation coefficient ρ to measure the correlations between each two channels. This coefficient is a constant in the range of $[0,1]$. When $\rho = 0$, it means that each channel is independent with each other; when it comes to $\rho = 1$, we deem that the statistical parameters of each channel are exactly the same, i.e., the receiver cannot distinguish any two channels at this point. The magnitude of ρ depends on the distribution of the nodes in the actual communication scenario. For example, if a huge scatterer emerge in neighborhood of the source, the channel correlations of the first hop will increase as a result. For the first hop communication, we denote the covariance matrix of S-R channels

formed by ρ as $\begin{bmatrix} 1 & \rho_{SR_1SR_2} & \cdots & \rho_{SR_1SR_{N-1}} & \rho_{SR_1SR_N} \\ \rho_{SR_2SR_1} & 1 & & \rho_{SR_2SR_{N-1}} & \rho_{SR_2SR_N} \\ \vdots & & \ddots & & \vdots \\ \rho_{SR_{N-1}SR_1} & \rho_{SR_{N-1}SR_2} & \cdots & 1 & \rho_{SR_{N-1}SR_N} \\ \rho_{SR_NSR_1} & \rho_{SR_NSR_2} & & \rho_{SR_NSR_{N-1}} & 1 \end{bmatrix}_{N*N}$.

The channel correlations of the second hop communication can also be indicated as a similar form, so it will not be repeated here. In addition, since the forwarding of the signals in this paper is performed by a single relay, there is no need to consider whether the fading channel between a relay's input and output is correlated or not.

The calculation of ρ is regarded as a forward process, and the way to add ρ into a cooperative communication strategy is regarded as a reverse process. In the forward process, the ρ can be obtained by normalizing the covariance matrix when transmitting the same set of bit streams over each channel, which can be expressed as

$$\rho_{ij} = \frac{|cov\,(h_i, h_j)|}{\sigma_i\sigma_j}, \tag{8}$$

where cov() indicates the covariance of two sets of random data sequences, and σ represents the standard deviation of each sequence. For each hop, a $N * N$ covariance matrix is then constituted via ρ. In the reverse process, we factorize the covariance matrix and then multiply it with a matrix of the independent-channel variables. Thus, the case in the independent channel scenario is transferred into the correlated channels.

3   System Outage Probability

According to the expression in the previous section, the TOP can be easily recorded as

$$P_{outage} = \Pr\left(C_b \leq R_0\right) = \Pr\left(\gamma_{D_b} \leq 2^{R_0} - 1\right) = F_{\gamma_{D_b}}\left(2^{R_0} - 1\right), \quad (9)$$

where R_0 is the normalized system transmission rate, i.e., spectral efficiency. $\Pr\left(\cdot\right)$ is the probability distribution function, and $F_{\gamma_{D_b}}\left(\cdot\right)$ is the cumulative distribution function of γ_{D_b}.

In the actual communication scenario, it is unrealistic for receivers to perform lots of numerical statistics. What we are concerned with is the closed-form expression of TOP, so we try to derive an exact function for the CDF of γ_{D_b}. For simplicity, we specify that $\gamma_0 = 2^{R_0} - 1$ indicates the appointed instantaneous SNR when R_0 is obtained. According to (5), the $F_{\gamma_{D_b}}\left(\cdot\right)$ can be expressed as an intersection or union of the probabilistic events, which is written as

$$
\begin{aligned}
F_{\gamma_{D_b}}\left(\gamma_0\right) &= \Pr\left(\gamma_{D_b} \leq \gamma_0\right) \\
&= \Pr\left\{\bigcap_{i=1}^{N}\left[\min\left(\frac{\gamma_{SR_i}}{1+\gamma_{ii}}, \gamma_{R_iD}\right) \leq \gamma_0\right]\right\} \\
&= 1 - \Pr\left\{\bigcup_{i=1}^{N}\left[min\left(\frac{\gamma_{SR_i}}{1+\gamma_{ii}}, \gamma_{R_iD}\right) > \gamma_0\right]\right\},
\end{aligned}
\quad (10)
$$

It can be understood that no channel that satisfies the SNR condition can be found at the current moment. Because of the union of a set of events, it's hard to parse the probability distribution from the above formula. Therefore, we convert the union form into the following form [19],

$$
\begin{aligned}
&\Pr\left\{\bigcup_{i=1}^{N}\left[min\left(\frac{\gamma_{SR_i}}{1+\gamma_{ii}}, \gamma_{R_iD}\right) > \gamma_0\right]\right\} \\
&= \sum_{n=1}^{N}\sum_{m_1,\ldots,m_n}(-1)^{n+1}Pr\left\{\bigcap_{i=1}^{n}\left[\left(\frac{\gamma_{SR_{m_i}}}{1+\gamma_{m_im_i}} > \gamma_0\right) \cap \left(\gamma_{R_{m_i}D} > \gamma_0\right)\right]\right\},
\end{aligned}
\quad (11)
$$

where the values of $m_1, \ldots, m_n$ depend on n, i.e., for each n, $\Sigma_{m_1,\ldots,m_n}$ selects n probability events for summation. There are a total of C_N^n cases. Since we consider the identically distributed channels, a set of binomial coefficients can be used to simplify the equation above. The improved form is as follows,

$$
\Pr\left\{\bigcup_{i=1}^{N}\left[min\left(\frac{\gamma_{SR_i}}{1+\gamma_{ii}},\gamma_{R_iD}\right)>\gamma_0\right]\right\}
$$

$$
=\sum_{n=1}^{N}(-1)^{n+1}\binom{N}{n}\Pr\left\{\bigcap_{i=1}^{n}\left[\left(\frac{\gamma_{SR_i}}{1+\gamma_{ii}}>\gamma_0\right)\cap(\gamma_{R_iD}>\gamma_0)\right]\right\},
$$

(12)

where $\binom{N}{n}$ is the coefficient of the n-th term in the N-power binomial formula. The model shown in Fig. 1 does not consider the correlations between two hops. Therefore, the γ_{SR_i}, γ_{ii} and γ_{R_iD} are mutually independent, i.e., $\frac{\gamma_{SR_i}}{1+\gamma_{ii}}$ is also independent with γ_{R_iD}. Thus, we can split them apart and get the following expression,

$$
\Pr\left\{\bigcap_{i=1}^{n}\left[\left(\frac{\gamma_{SR_i}}{1+\gamma_{ii}}>\gamma_0\right)\cap(\gamma_{R_iD}>\gamma_0)\right]\right\}
$$

$$
=\Pr\left[\bigcap_{i=1}^{n}\left(\frac{\gamma_{SR_i}}{1+\gamma_{ii}}>\gamma_0\right)\right]*\Pr\left[\bigcap_{i=1}^{n}(\gamma_{R_iD}>\gamma_0)\right]
$$

(13)

$$
=\left\{1-\Pr\left[\bigcup_{i=1}^{n}\left(\frac{\gamma_{SR_i}}{1+\gamma_{ii}}\leq\gamma_0\right)\right]\right\}*\left\{1-\Pr\left[\bigcup_{i=1}^{n}(\gamma_{R_iD}\leq\gamma_0)\right]\right\}.
$$

Then, we can convert $\Pr\left[\bigcup_{i=1}^{n}\left(\frac{\gamma_{SR_i}}{1+\gamma_{ii}}\leq\gamma_0\right)\right]$ into $\Pr\left[\bigcap_{i=1}^{n}\left(\frac{\gamma_{SR_i}}{1+\gamma_{ii}}\leq\gamma_0\right)\right]$ with the same method in (12). In addition, the processing of $\Pr\left[\bigcup_{i=1}^{n}(\gamma_{R_iD}\leq\gamma_0)\right]$ is similar to the foregoing.

$\Pr\left[\bigcap_{i=1}^{n}\left(\frac{\gamma_{SR_i}}{1+\gamma_{ii}}\leq\gamma_0\right)\right]$ describes the transmission performance of the first hop with the consideration of RSI, i.e., the CDF of the first hop when the SNR is less than γ_0. It is equivalent to the TOP of partial relay selection (PRS) scheme. As long as the CSI and ρ of the first hop is acquired, we can calculate the TOP with PRS strategy. Its expression is as follows [13],

$$
\Pr\left[\bigcap_{i=1}^{n}\left(\frac{\gamma_{SR_i}}{1+\gamma_{ii}}\leq\gamma_0\right)\right]
$$

$$
=\int_{0}^{\infty}\left[1-Q\left(\sqrt{\frac{2u}{\rho_{SR_i}^{-1}-1}},\sqrt{\frac{2u(1+\lambda_{RR})}{\lambda_{SR}(1-\rho_{SR_i})}}\right)\right]^{N}e^{-u}du,
$$

(14)

where $Q(.)$ is the first-order Marcum Q function. Thus, the closed-form CDF expression of γ_{D_b} in (9) can be obtained.

We assume that the channel correlations are equal, i.e., $\rho_{SR_i} = \rho_1$, $\rho_{R_iD} = \rho_2$, $i \in \{1, \ldots, N\}$. For example, when the number of relays N is 2, the TOP can be depicted as (15).

$$F_{\gamma_{D_b}}^{N=2}(\gamma_0)$$

$$= 1 - e^{-\gamma_0\left(\frac{1+\lambda_{RR}}{\lambda_{SR}} + \frac{1}{\lambda_{RD}}\right)}$$

$$+ \left\{\int_0^\infty \left[1 - Q\left(\sqrt{\frac{2x\rho_1}{1-\rho_1}}, \sqrt{\frac{2x(1+\lambda_{RR})}{\lambda_{SR}(1-\rho_1)}}\right)\right]^2 e^{-x}dx - 1 + 2e^{-\frac{\gamma_0(1+\lambda_{RR})}{\lambda_{SR}}}\right\}$$

$$* \left\{\int_0^\infty \left[1 - Q\left(\sqrt{\frac{2x\rho_2}{1-\rho_2}}, \sqrt{\frac{2x}{\lambda_{RD}(1-\rho_2)}}\right)\right]^2 e^{-x}dx - 1 + 2e^{-\frac{\gamma_0}{\lambda_{RD}}}\right\}.$$

$$(15)$$

Further unfolding the unary integral, we can get (16).

$$F_{\gamma_{D_b}}^{N=2}(\gamma_0)$$

$$= 1 - e^{-\gamma_0\left(\frac{1+\lambda_{RR}}{\lambda_{SR}} + \frac{1}{\lambda_{RD}}\right)}$$

$$+ \left\{2e^{-\frac{\gamma_0(1+\lambda_{RR})}{\lambda_{SR}}}\left[1 - Q\left(\sqrt{\frac{2\gamma_0(1+\lambda_{RR})}{\lambda_{SR}(1-\rho_1^2)}}, \rho_1\sqrt{\frac{2\gamma_0(1+\lambda_{RR})}{\lambda_{SR}(1-\rho_1^2)}}\right)\right]\right.$$

$$\left. + e^{-\frac{\gamma_0(1+\lambda_{RR})}{\lambda_{SR}(1-\rho_1^2)}} I_0\left[\frac{2\rho_1\gamma_0(1+\lambda_{RR})}{\lambda_{SR}(1-\rho_1^2)}\right]\right\}$$

$$* \left\{2e^{-\frac{\gamma_0}{\lambda_{RD}}}\left[1 - Q\left(\sqrt{\frac{2\gamma_0}{\lambda_{RD}(1-\rho_2^2)}}, \rho_2\sqrt{\frac{2\gamma_0}{\lambda_{RD}(1-\rho_2^2)}}\right)\right] + e^{-\frac{\gamma_0}{\lambda_{RD}(1-\rho_2^2)}} I_0\left[\frac{2\rho_2\gamma_0}{\lambda_{RD}(1-\rho_2^2)}\right]\right\}.$$

$$(16)$$

4   Numerical Results

In this section, we give some numerical results and simulation to verify our presented studies. The target spectral efficiency of the system is set as $R_0 = 0.5$ $bit \cdot (s \cdot Hz)^{-1}$. The channel correlations are $\rho_{SR_i} = \rho_1$, $\rho_{R_iD} = \rho_2$, $i \in \{1, \ldots, N\}$. Regarding the statistical parameters of each channel, the AWGN is normalized to $N_{mn} = 1$ mw $= 0$ dBm, m, n $\in \{S, R, D\}$, and the variance of channels is normalized to $\sigma_{SR_i}^2 = \sigma_{R_iD}^2 = 1$. It can be found that a cancellation of more than 30 dB is possible to be achieved for the RSI of FD relays. In this paper, we assume that the cancellation of RSI reaches 20 dB [20], i.e., $\sigma_{ii}^2 = 0.01$.

In Fig. 2, we assume that P_S is from -5 dBm to 35 dBm. The relay provides fixed transmission power $P_R = 20$ dBm, and the power correlation coefficients are $\rho_1 = 0.8$, $\rho_2 = 0.5$ [13]. The TOP is given as a function of the source transmitting power P_S. We find that when N = 2 or N = 3, there is a great agreement between the numerical analysis and the simulation.

In order to show the universality of the proposed expressions, we also analyze the situation of the independent channels. As we can see from Fig. 2, when
$\rho_1 = \rho_2 = 0$, the expression can also accurately describe the TOP under the independent channels. Regardless of transmitting power, the system performance of
independent channels is always better than that of the correlated fading channels.
Meanwhile, it is obvious that the TOP under the same channel environments is
significantly improved with the increase of N. In addition, it can be found that
as the transmission power increases, the decline speed of TOP goes through two
phases – the first to increase, and the later to slow down. In the first phase, the
channel status of the first hop is suffering from a low P_S. At this point, λ_{SR_i}
is the decisive factor that limiting the system performance. The increase of the
transmitting power will significantly increase the SNR of the $S - R_i$ link. It
contributes to an obvious improvement of system performance. However, with a
gradual increase of λ_{SR_i}, the decisive factor of the TOP gets changed from λ_{SR_i}
to λ_{R_iD}. Even if the transmitting power is enhanced, the SNR of the $R_i - D$
link will not be significantly improved. To increase the SNR in the second phase,
the relays require to raise the transmitting power P_R. Therefore, high P_S is
not able to reduce the TOP, but resulting into a waste of resources. Accordingly, we can observe that there is a balance between the system performance
and resource utilization. Interestingly, the TOP ratio between the correlated
environment and the independent environment also follows the same pattern of
change. We use $Pout_c$ and $Pout_i$ to represent the TOP of the correlated fading
channels and the independent channels, respectively. Figure 3 shows the variation of $Pout_c/Pout_i$ with the source transmitting power P_S. Before the transmit
power reached about 11 dBm, the influence of the correlation on TOP gradually
increased. Subsequently, we find that the effects of correlations decrease with
the enhancement of transmit power. It shows that the correlated environment
greatly affects the system within the range of $P_S \in [5\,\text{dBm}, 20\,\text{dBm}]$. When
N = 3, the system performance decreased over 4 times. In wireless local area
networks, the transmit power of LTE terminals is usually not more than 23 dBm,
and the maximum transmit power of mobile phones is within 30 dBm.

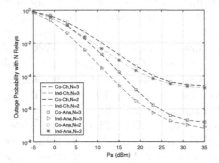

Fig. 2. TOP of a FD cooperative system
versus P_S.

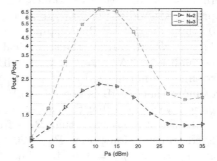

Fig. 3. Outage probability ratio over
two channel environments.

In Fig. 4, we assumed that both S and R employ a fixed power $P_S = P_R = 20$ dBm, and the TOP is written as a function of the power correlation coefficients. In Fig. 4(a), ρ_1 takes the value between $(0, 1)$, while ρ_2 is fixed to 0; in Fig. 4(b), $\rho_1 = \rho_2 \in (0, 1)$. It shows that the curves of the two figures are extremely similar. Especially when ρ is small (less than 0.5), the correlated environment has an especially slight impact on the system performance, even if the correlations among each hop change simultaneously. When $\rho > 0.6$, the influence of channel correlations on the TOP gradually enhances. It is worth noting that in both cases, the TOP tends to be the same value when $\rho \to 1$, regardless of the number of relays. At this point, the TOP corresponds to the result when $N = 1$. This phenomenon results from the fact that the distribution of each channel are approximately the same when $\rho \to 1$, i.e., each relay has almost the same SNR. Therefore, the receiver cannot distinguish the relays, and the ORS scheme loses its function. The system is equivalent to being equipped with a single relay.

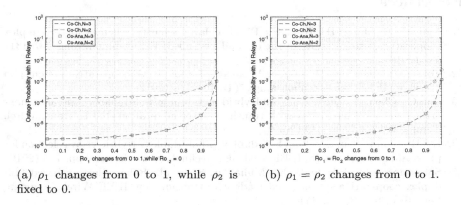

(a) ρ_1 changes from 0 to 1, while ρ_2 is fixed to 0.

(b) $\rho_1 = \rho_2$ changes from 0 to 1.

Fig. 4. TOP of a FD cooperative system versus correlations.

5 Conclusion

In this work, we studied the correlated fading channels in FD cooperative systems with ORS scheme. We focused on analyzing the effect of the correlations over a FD relaying network. The closed-form expression of the TOP was derived under the condition of equal correlations. This expression can be depicted as a function of the power correlation coefficient, source transmitting power, or transmission rate. We showed that the correlation always deteriorates the performance of the FD system, but only a strong correlation ($\rho > 0.6$) can significantly worsen the TOP. In addition, with the increase of transmitting power, it was proved that the TOP goes through two phases – the first to increase, and the later to slow down.

This paper also opens up several interesting research directions. It is worth noting that only single relay is selected in this system. This method makes the channel correlations interfere with the relaying strategy, but cannot be utilized by systems. However, for multi-relay selection or multi-hop transmission scenarios, we can introduce the power correlation coefficient between each hop to evaluate the relay selection strategy and optimize the transmission scheme. In an actual communication scenario, the correlation coefficient of each channel can be calculated with the information of feedback links or the reciprocity of channels. Therefore, it is not complex to calculate and analyze the correlations. Another possible direction for future research is to study the randomness of channel correlations. It is also a promising solution for proposing an adaptive and intelligent criterion to optimize the working mode, e.g., a hybrid forwarding mode for relays, or a hybrid duplex communication mechanism for FD nodes.

References

1. Nguyen, B., Jung, H., Kim, K.: Physical layer security schemes for full-duplex cooperative systems: state of the art and beyond. IEEE Commun. Mag. **56**, 131–137 (2018)
2. Torabi, M., Haccoun, D., Frigon, J.: Relay selection in AF cooperative systems: an overview. IEEE Veh. Technol. Mag. **7**(4), 104–113 (2012)
3. Liu, G., Chen, X., Ding, Z., et al.: Hybrid half-duplex/full-duplex cooperative non-orthogonal multiple access with transmit power adaptation. IEEE Trans. Wirel. Commun. **17**(1), 506–519 (2018)
4. He, H., Ren, P., Du, Q., et al.: Full-duplex or half-duplex? Hybrid relay selection for physical layer secrecy. In: IEEE Vehicular Technology Conference, pp. 1–5 (2016)
5. Sofotasios, P.C., Fikadu, M.K., Muhaidat, S., et al.: Relay selection based full-duplex cooperative systems under adaptive transmission. IEEE Wirel. Commun. Lett. **6**(5), 602–605 (2017)
6. Fan, L., Lei, X., Yang, N., et al.: Secrecy cooperative networks with outdated relay selection over correlated fading channels. IEEE Trans. Veh. Technol. **66**(8), 7599–7603 (2017)
7. Fan, L., Zhao, R., Gong, F., et al.: Secure multiple amplify-and-forward relaying over correlated fading channels. IEEE Trans. Commun. **65**(7), 2811–2820 (2017)
8. Nguyen, B., Kim, K.: Performance analysis of amplify-and-forward systems with single relay selection in correlated environments. Sensors **16**(9), 1–15 (2016)
9. Cheng, X., Wang, C., Wang, H., et al.: Cooperative MIMO channel modeling and multi-link spatial correlation properties. IEEE J. Sel. Areas Commun. **30**(2), 388–396 (2012)
10. Chen, Y., Shi, R., Long, M.: Performance analysis of amplify-and-forward relaying with correlated links. IEEE Trans. Veh. Technol. **62**(5), 2344–2349 (2013)
11. Michalopoulos, D.S., Suraweera, H.A., Karagiannidis, G.K., et al.: Amplify-and-forward relay selection with outdated channel estimates. IEEE Trans. Commun. **60**(5), 1278–1290 (2012)
12. Jiang, W., Kaiser, T., Vinck, A.J.H.: A robust opportunistic relaying strategy for co-operative wireless communications. IEEE Trans. Wirel. Commun. **15**(4), 2642–2655 (2016)

13. Chen, Y., Tellambura, C.: Distribution functions of selection combiner output in equally correlated Rayleigh, Rician, and Nakagami-m fading channels. IEEE Trans. Commun. **52**(11), 1948–1956 (2004)
14. Xu, D., Ren, P., Du, Q., Sun, L., et al.: Design in power-domain NOMA: eavesdropping suppression in the two-user relay network with compensation for the relay user. Mob. Netw. Appl. **23**, 1068–1079 (2017)
15. Xu, D., Ren, P., Du, Q., Sun, L., et al.: Combat eavesdropping by full-duplex technology and signal transformation in non-orthogonal multiple access transmission. In: IEEE International Conference on Communications, pp. 1–6 (2017)
16. Lang, F., Deng, Z., Wang, B.: Secure communication of correlated sources over broadcast channels. In: IEEE Information Theory Workshop, pp. 416–420 (2014)
17. Sun, X., Wang, J., Xu, W., Zhao, C.: Performance of secure communications over correlated fading channels. **19**(8), 479–482 (2012)
18. Wang, D., Li, Y., Bai, B., et al.: Green communications based on physical-layer security for amplify-and-forward relay networks. J. Electron. Inf. Technol. **38**(4), 841–847 (2016)
19. Bogart, K.P., Stein, C., Drysdale, R.: Discrete Mathematics for Computer Science. Thomson Brooks/Cole, Pacific Grove (2006)
20. Chen, G., Gong, Y., Xiao, P., et al.: Physical layer network security in the full-duplex relay system. IEEE Trans. Inf. Forensics Secur. **10**(3), 574–583 (2015)

An Implementation of Capture and Playback for IP-Encapsulated Video in Professional Media Production

Lu Han[1(✉)], Jinyao Yan[2], and Yang Cai[1]

[1] School of Information Engineering,
Communication University of China, Beijing, China
miah_hl@163.com, fengjianyun11456@cuc.edu.cn
[2] Laboratory of Media Audio & Video,
Communication University of China, Beijing, China
jyan@cuc.edu.cn

Abstract. With the rapid development of the Ultra-High-Definition (UHD) television, the SDI technology for video transmission in traditional broadcast and TV production is in awkward circumstances. In the meantime, for the sake of flexibility, scalability and versatility, it is an excellent choice to transmit the IP-encapsulated video with SMPTE ST 2022-6 or SMPTE ST 2110 protocol in professional media facility. For the IP-encapsulated uncompressed video, we implement a system for capture and playback in real time, and measure the system performance with the end-to-end delay and packet loss rate during the process. It implements a system from video signal capture to processing and playback, and implements decoding and playback of IP video signals with software, which has strong reproducibility and high flexibility.

Keywords: IP-encapsulation · SMPTE ST 2022-6 · SMPTE ST 2110

1 Introduction

In recent years, the development of new technologies has intensified competition in the media industry. The concept of media convergence has been repeatedly emphasized. Therefore, it is an inevitable trend to converge professional quality audio, video, data, and production communications to a common networked infrastructure [1]. As bitrates increase and equipment prices drop, IP-based communication technologies are pushing more and more dedicated communication systems into retirement. Traditional SDI (Serial Digital Interface) technology develops slowly relatively and it is difficult to integrate with new media technology. As the name indicates, video data is transported serially line-by-line, frame-by-frame. Each frame has vertical ancillary data (VANC) where no video is transmitted and each line also contains horizontal ancillary data (HANC). These usually contain audio, time code and other packetized data, accompanying the video, which for most cases is transmitted as uncompressed YCbCr 4:2:2 with 10-bit color depth [2]. While the demand of high bit rate media such as UHDTV, 4K and 8K video signals is getting larger and larger, and the transmission capacity of

© Springer Nature Singapore Pte Ltd. 2019
G. Zhai et al. (Eds.): IFTC 2018, CCIS 1009, pp. 346–355, 2019.
https://doi.org/10.1007/978-981-13-8138-6_29

SDI is far from meeting the demand. IP-encapsulation can enhance the agility and flexibility of the broadcast plant, reduce the amount of cabling through aggregating multiple signals onto Ethernet connections. The emergence of protocols such as SMPTE ST 2022-6 and SMPTE ST 2110 standardizes the format for IP-based packaged uncompressed video. However, for the IP-encapsulated video signal, there is no display device to facilitate monitoring directly. Different from traditional hardware devices that usually expensive restoring the signal to SDI, the software can realize the parsing and playing of data packets on common equipments, which can reduce the cost greatly.

For the IP-encapsulated uncompressed HD video, this paper implements a system for capture and playback in real time, and measures the system end-to-end delay and packet loss rate during the process. However, as professional media video signals, in addition to the large amount of data and real-time characteristics, the requirements for delay and packet loss of the transmission network are very strict. This paper also takes these factors into account, analyzes the measurement results and gives suggestions for further improvement.

2 Related Work

A similar work was done in Edwards' "Demonstration of COTS Hardware for Capture, Playback and Processing of SMPTE ST 2022-6 Media Streams" to capture and playback video from the SMPTE ST 2022-6 standard IP package [1]. The authors examine the capture, clean editing, graphics insertion, and playback of uncompressed HD video using the SMPTE ST 2022-6 packetized video standard. However, it uses the Nevion VS902 codec module to decode and recover the IP video signal, and the recovered SDI signal is sent to the Video Clarity system for display, relying more on hardware operation.

Klein and Edwards in the paper "All-IP Video Processing of SMPTE 2022-6 Streams on an All Programmable SoC" describe a fully networked broadcast platform based on the Xilinx Zynq-7000 All Programmable System on a Chip (SoC) that performs live video processing, similar to that of traditional broadcast equipment switchers and routers, but uses 10 GbE networking interfaces for uncompressed video transport [2]. It also depends on expensive professional hardware equipment to achieve video processing.

Levy and Richardson in the paper "4K Video over SMPTE 2022-5/6 Workflows" explore the issues uncompressed 4K video at 60fps 4:2:2 requires 12 Gbps and even more for 4:4:4, which causes a problem for video transport across 10 Gbps Ethernet networks [3]. For the industry's existing and deployed infrastructure, the compression has to be capable of leveraging already deployed SMPTE 2022 5/6 equipment. Visually lossless compression for a single 4K stream over a 10GE link is also ideal.

To ensure stable video transmission, Kawamoto and Kurakake in "XOR-Based FEC to Improve Burst-Loss Tolerance for 8K Ultra-High Definition TV over IP Transmission" propose an exclusive OR-based FEC method for improving burst-loss tolerance and developed transmission equipment for an uncompressed 8K UHDTV signal over IP-transmission using 100-Gb/s Ethernet packets implemented with the proposed method [4].

The work of this paper focuses more on the software implementation, using C++ programming to capture the IP video signal, and calling the underlying image interface to display the video in real time locally.

3 SMPTE ST 2022-6/SMPTE ST 2110 Video

The SMPTE ST 2022 series of standards specifies the IP packet encapsulation format for professional video, providing a means of transmitting high quality video signals over IP. An IP packet starts with several different protocol headers and finally the innermost layer will contain the actual payload. The entire IP packet is then put inside an Ethernet frame. The outermost layers (Ethernet, IP) contain address information, for the network to know where to deliver the packet to, followed by UDP (or TCP) that define which networking socket within the destination machine should receive the packet. There are application-specific protocols that contain metadata, timing information, etc. about the actual payload itself. SMPTE ST 2022-6 defines the encapsulation format of SDI signals based on RTP (Real-Time Transport Protocol) and HBRMT (High Bit Rate Media Transport Protocol). The data encapsulation structure from the outermost layer to the innermost layer are: Ethernet, IP, UDP, RTP, HBRMT and SDI payload [5]. The standard encapsulates 1376-octet SDI video payload into an RTP packet, while the packets for one frame are neatly arranged, and the last package shall have additional null octets added to achieve a total length of 1376 octets [6]. The RTP header and RTP payload header specified by SMPTE ST 2022-6 are shown in Figs. 1 and 2.

```
 0                   1                   2                   3
 0 1 2 3 4 5 6 7 8 9 0 1 2 3 4 5 6 7 8 9 0 1 2 3 4 5 6 7 8 9 0 1
+-+-+-+-+-+-+-+-+-+-+-+-+-+-+-+-+-+-+-+-+-+-+-+-+-+-+-+-+-+-+-+-+
|V=2|P|X|  CC   |M|     PT      |         sequence number       |
+-+-+-+-+-+-+-+-+-+-+-+-+-+-+-+-+-+-+-+-+-+-+-+-+-+-+-+-+-+-+-+-+
|                          timestamp                            |
+-+-+-+-+-+-+-+-+-+-+-+-+-+-+-+-+-+-+-+-+-+-+-+-+-+-+-+-+-+-+-+-+
|           synchronization source (SSRC) identifier            |
+=+=+=+=+=+=+=+=+=+=+=+=+=+=+=+=+=+=+=+=+=+=+=+=+=+=+=+=+=+=+=+=+
```

Fig. 1. ST 2022-6 RTP header

```
 0                   1                   2                   3
 0 1 2 3 4 5 6 7 8 9 0 1 2 3 4 5 6 7 8 9 0 1 2 3 4 5 6 7 8 9 0 1

+-+-+-+-+-+-+-+-+-+-+-+-+-+-+-+-+-+-+-+-+-+-+-+-+-+-+-+-+-+-+-+-+
|Ext    |F|VSID |  FRCount      | R | S | FEC | CF    | RESERVE |
+-+-+-+-+-+-+-+-+-+-+-+-+-+-+-+-+-+-+-+-+-+-+-+-+-+-+-+-+-+-+-+-+
|  MAP  |     FRAME     |     FRATE     |SAMPLE | FMT-RESERVE   |
+-+-+-+-+-+-+-+-+-+-+-+-+-+-+-+-+-+-+-+-+-+-+-+-+-+-+-+-+-+-+-+-+
|                Video timestamp (only if CF>0)                 |
+-+-+-+-+-+-+-+-+-+-+-+-+-+-+-+-+-+-+-+-+-+-+-+-+-+-+-+-+-+-+-+-+
|                Header extension (Only if Ext > 0)             |
+-+-+-+-+-+-+-+-+-+-+-+-+-+-+-+-+-+-+-+-+-+-+-+-+-+-+-+-+-+-+-+-+
```

Fig. 2. ST 2022-6 RTP payload header

The marker bit (M) shall be set to 1 to denote the last packet of the video frame, and shall be set to zero for all other packets.

The FRCount field is the video frame count, FRAME is the frame structure, FRATE is the frame rate, and SAMPLE is the color sampling structure. In this experiment, we focus on 1080i/60 and 1080p/50 video source, and the color sampling is 422/10bit. The SDI signal output by the video source is encapsulated by the gateway of the SMPTE ST 2022-6 standard format by the gateway of Gefei.

The SMPTE ST 2110 protocol is different from SMPTE ST 2022-6, which combines the signal of video signals, audio signals and other auxiliary data into one IP stream. When the receiver only needs one of the elements, it still needs to obtain the complete IP stream to separate the parts they want, which brings inconvenience to people to a certain extent. While the 2110 standard puts each part of the signal into a different stream. Video, audio and auxiliary data can be sent separately, and the receiver can directly obtain the stream they want [7]. The 2110-20 standard is for uncompressed video, which only transmits the active pixels of image, leave blanking data alone. Compared with ST 2022-6, It has a quite obvious advantage to save the bandwidth. The RTP payload header is shown in Fig. 3.

```
 0                   1                   2                   3
 0 1 2 3 4 5 6 7 8 9 0 1 2 3 4 5 6 7 8 9 0 1 2 3 4 5 6 7 8 9 0 1
+-+-+-+-+-+-+-+-+-+-+-+-+-+-+-+-+-+-+-+-+-+-+-+-+-+-+-+-+-+-+-+-+
|      Extended Sequence Number   |        SRD Length           |
+-+-+-+-+-+-+-+-+-+-+-+-+-+-+-+-+-+-+-+-+-+-+-+-+-+-+-+-+-+-+-+-+
|F|         SRD Row Number        |C|        SRD Offset         |
+-+-+-+-+-+-+-+-+-+-+-+-+-+-+-+-+-+-+-+-+-+-+-+-+-+-+-+-+-+-+-+-+
|          SRD Length             |F|       SRD Row Number      |
+-+-+-+-+-+-+-+-+-+-+-+-+-+-+-+-+-+-+-+-+-+-+-+-+-+-+-+-+-+-+-+-+
|C|        SRD Offset             |
+-+-+-+-+-+-+-+-+-+-+-+-+-+-+-+-+-+
```

Fig. 3. ST 2110 RTP payload header

It contains Extended Sequence Number (i.e. the upper 16 bits of the extended sequence timer) and no more than three SRD (Sample Row Data) headers. Each SRD header is composed of SRD Length, F (field flag), SRD lines, C (continuous flag), and SRD offset [8].

4 Capture of Video Packets

The IP-encapsulated data is transmitted to a common computer equipped with Intel 82599ES 10 Gigabit NIC with optical fiber. And sniff the 10 Gigabit NIC to receive the data packets through the WinPcap programming interface.

WinPcap is an open source library based on the Win32 platform for capturing network packets and analyzing. Most web applications access the network through widely used operating system components, such as sockets. This is a simple implementation because the operating system has properly handled the underlying implementation details (such as protocol processing, encapsulating data packets, etc.) and provides a familiar interface similar to reading and writing files. However, in some cases, this "simple way" does not meet the needs of the task, because some applications need to directly access the packets in the network. Those applications need to access the original data packet, that is, the data packet that has not been processed by the operating system using the network protocol.

WinPcap provides two libraries: packet.dll and wpcap.dll. The former provides a underlying API, along with a programming interface that is independent of the Microsoft operating system. These APIs can be used directly to access driver functions. the latter exports a more powerful set of high-level capture primitives that are consistent with LibPcap. These primitives allow the capture of packets to be done in a way that is independent of the network hardware and operating system. The Pcap_loop function provided in WinPcap is used to continuously monitor the 10 Gigabit NIC, and after the packet is acquired, the callback function handle pcap_handler is called to process the packet. Then the packet will be stored in the PCAP file in a write-only manner.

5   Display of PCAP Video

SDL (Simple Direct Media Layer) is a set of open source cross-platform multimedia development library, which provides a variety of functions for controlling image input and output. Its general flow of function call is shown in the following Fig. 4. The most important one is the SDL_UpdateTexture function. After the window is created, the SDI effective pixel data in the data packet is cyclically read. And sent one frame size of data to the function as a parameter, thereby realizing the update of each frame of the video picture.

After reading the data packet, the flag field in the SMPTE ST 2022-6 standard is detected to determine the frame structure, color sampling, and the size of the image to be displayed. In addition, whether it is interlaced is determined as well. The TRS (Time Reference Signal) of HD video differs from SD video, which is the serial data stream merged by two parallel data streams. The EAV/SAV is 3FF 3FF 000 000 000 000 XYZ XYZ, which needs to be processed differently [9, 10]. For the SDI payload in the data packet, the first data packet starting of one image frame is locked according to the TRS [11]. Then the data packet containing the image information of the frame is processed one by one to remove synchronization and ancillary data, retaining only active pixels that actually displayed. This involves the process of splicing and recovering 10-bit data from the adjacent two bytes. Subsequent determination of the ancillary data is based on the 10-bit tuple. Then, the 10-bit tuple is shifted to the right by two bits into 8-bit data for display, and the line number and column number in the image are calculated according to interlaced or not information, and stored in the corresponding position of the frame buffer array. This process is repeated until it is determined that the marker bit is 1 which means the last packet of one frame, then the loop of the current frame will be terminated [12].

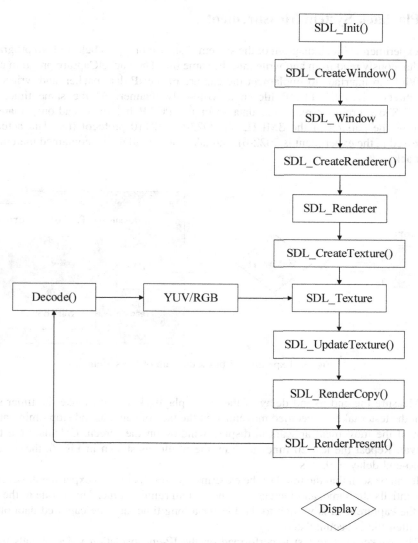

Fig. 4. Function call flow of SDL

In the experiments in this paper, the packet loss caused by the experimental condition limit was processed. In order to avoid the occurrence of the loss of active data in the case of continuous packet loss, the FRCount field of the data packet is detected. When a data packet that does not belong to the current frame is read in a loop of one frame, the whole frame data will be discarded in time. Re-lock the next frame according to the TRS detection, in which way to solve the problem of the static frame to achieve smooth video playback.

6 Playback System Measurement

The experimental block diagram of the system is shown in Fig. 5 below. Two programs simultaneously read from and write into the same file. The PacketCapture program calls the WinPcap interface to implement the capture of the IP data packet, and writes the data directly into the PCAP file in a write-only manner. At the same time, the SMPTEShow program reads the data from the PCAP file in a read-only manner, performs the parsing of the SMPTE ST 2022-6 or 2110 protocol (the data actually processed in the experiment is 2022-6), and takes out the SDI data contained therein for playback.

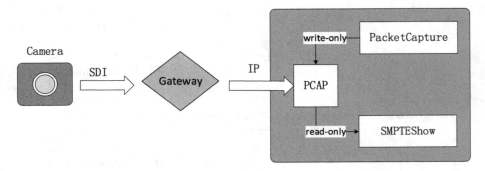

Fig. 5. Experimental block diagram of the system

Measure the end-to-end delay of the entire playback system: make the timer start when the tester takes a specified movement in the face of camera, and stop timing at the point of the movement appears in display window on the screen. Calculate the time interval. Repeat the test 20 times to draw the results as shown in Fig. 6, the average end-to-end delay is 9.05 s.

It can be seen that the trend of the experimental results in each experimental cycle is substantially the same, and increases as the system running time. This is due to the fact that the capture data is written to the file for a long time, and the captured data of the unwritten file is accumulated.

The packet capture test is performed on the IP-encapsulation video signals transmitted in 1080i/60 and 1080p/50, 10-bit format respectively. Each time the packet capture lasts for 10 s, a total of 10 times packet capture has been done. The result is shown in Fig. 7 below. The average packet loss rate is shown separately for 4.17% (1080i/60) and 8.05% (1080p/50).

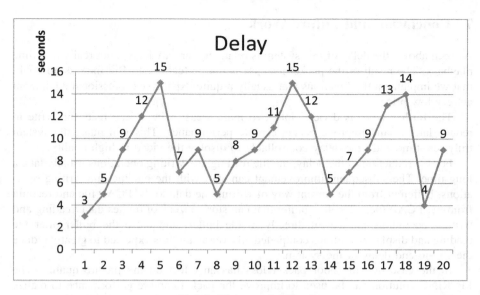

Fig. 6. End-to-end delay

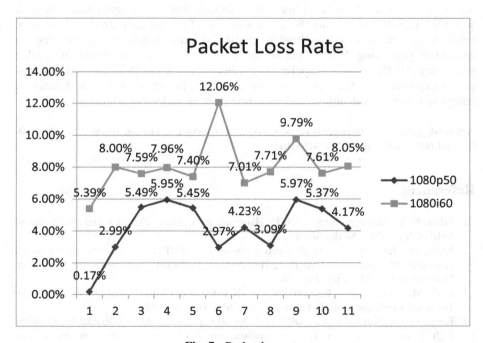

Fig. 7. Packet loss rate

7 Conclusion and Future Work

As seen above, the delay of this system is relatively large, which is not really real-time playback. The result of the packet loss test is not perfect either. But there is no doubt that we implement the functions that usually require expensive professional equipment at very low prices.

The further work is divided into two main areas: using cache read and write to reduce latency and improve packet capture performance. This will make the system truly real-time and time-delay controllable to display the video in high quality.

For the reduction of the delay, the file reading and writing operations usually take a long time. The subsequent improvement can start with the reading and writing operations. Different from the current way of writing the data to the PCAP file and reading from the PCAP file, allocate a buffer that can store dozens of frames data. reading and writing operations implement directly in the buffer, and reuse the buffer after the reading and display operations completed all over again. It is expected to greatly reduce the end-to-end delay of the system.

In the case that the poor packet loss has an effect on the picture quality. The PF_RING solution can be used to improve the packet capture performance to realize the loss-free transmission recovery to the utmost extent. One solution is the use of a TCP/IP "stack bypass" system such PF_RING from ntop.org [13]. This provides a new socket service in the form of a Linux kernel module that more directly communicates with the NIC with fewer of the "bells and whistles" of the standard Linux TCP/IP stack (such as the crafting of packet headers, routing, or error detection). By reducing the amount of processing done by the kernel, PF_RING dramatically speeds up packet processing [1]. This project is applicable to Linux systems, but WinPcap itself also has its corresponding LinPcap programming interface. Therefore, it is not difficult to complete network card sniffing and capturing packets under Linux system.

Acknowledgement. The paper is supported by CUC Guangzhou Institute (Project No: 2014-10-05) and NSFC under grant No. 61631016.

References

1. Edwards, T.: Demonstration of COTS Hardware for Capture, Playback and Processing of SMPTE ST 2022-6 Media Streams
2. Klein, M., Edwards, T.: All-IP video processing of SMPTE 2022-6 streams on an all programmable SoC. In: SMPTE 2013 Annual Technical Conference & Exhibition, Hollywood, CA, USA, pp. 1–20 (2013)
3. Levy, M., Richardson, L.R., Rouvroy, G.: 4K video over SMPTE 2022-5/6 workflows. In: Technical Conference and Exhibition, Smpte SMPTE, pp. 1–12 (2016)
4. Kawamoto, J., Kurakake, T.: XOR-based FEC to improve burst-loss tolerance for 8K ultra-high definition TV over IP Transmission. In: 2017 IEEE Global Communications Conference, GLOBECOM 2017, Singapore, pp. 1–6 (2017)
5. Laabs, M.: SDI Over IP-Seamless Signal Switching in SMPTE 2022-6 and a Novel Multicast Routing Concept. EBU Technical Review, Q4 (2012)

6. Transport of High Bit Rate Media Signals over IP Networks (HBRMT), SMPTE ST 2022-6 (2012)
7. Understanding SMPTE ST 2110. https://www.smpte.org/education/courses/st2110
8. Professional Media Over Managed IP Networks: Uncompressed Active Video. SMPTE Standard 2110-20 (2017)
9. SMPTE STANDARD for Television—3 Gb/s Signal/Data Serial Interface. SMPTE Standard 424M (2006)
10. 1.5 Gb/s Signal/Data Serial Interface. SMPTE Standard 292-1 (2012)
11. 10-Bit 4:2:2 Component and 4fsc Composite Digital Signals—Serial Digital Interface. SMPTE Standard 259M (1997)
12. Small program to generate and view video carried by the SMPTE2022-6 protocol for testing purposes. https://github.com/CiaranWoodward/smpteViewer
13. PF_RING: High-speed packet capture, filtering and analysis. http://www.ntop.org/products/pf_ring/

Video Coding

A Novel R-λ Rate Control Algorithm for HEVC

Jialing Xu, Guowei Teng$^{(\boxtimes)}$, Guozhong Wang, and Zhenglong Yang

School of Communication and Information Engineering,
Shanghai University, Shanghai, China
teng_gw@163.com

Abstract. In this paper, a novel R-λ rate control algorithm is proposed. Firstly, different from the conventional R-λ rate control for the predefined bit ratio of the frame level rate control, an adaptive bit allocation ratio, which is mainly determined by mean bi-directional frame difference, is proposed for more reasonable frame level bit allocation. Then, according to the rate distortion optimization (RDO) process, a special relationship between frame λ and the mean coding tree unit (CTU) λ can be built. Finally, a CTU λ clipping method is proposed to get the optimal RDO of every CTU in a frame. The experimental results show that the coding quality of the proposed algorithm is increased by 0.35 dB at Random Access (RA) configuration and by 0.66 dB at Low Delay (LD) configuration.

Keywords: HEVC · Rate control · Bit allocation · CTU λ clipping

1 Introduction

High efficiency video coding (HEVC) [1] is the latest video coding standing developed by ISO/IEC Moving Picture Experts Group (MPEG) and ITU-T Video Coding Experts Group (VCEG) standardization organizations, working together in a partnership known as the Joint Collaborative Team on Video Coding (JCT-VC). Compared with H.264/AVC [2], it has obtained great performance gains, and many coding tools are adopted.

As rate control plays a key role in HEVC, lots of the excellent rate control algorithms are proposed. Choi et al. [3] propose a unified rate quantization (URQ) rate control, where the quantization parameter (QP) is regarded as the most important factor to determine the bit rate. However, Li et al. [4] suggest that only when the coding parameters are not flexible, the bit rate is effected by the QP, and then the R-λ rate control model is proposed with a better coding performance. Latterly, some typical improved R-λ rate control algorithms are proposed. In [5], a multiple scalable rate control algorithm is proposed, which is including the temporal, spatial and quality scalability. Li et al. [6] propose a bit allocation scheme for CTU level rate control. An adaptive bit allocation scheme [7] is proposed and gets a better rate control performance. In this paper,

© Springer Nature Singapore Pte Ltd. 2019
G. Zhai et al. (Eds.): IFTC 2018, CCIS 1009, pp. 359–368, 2019.
https://doi.org/10.1007/978-981-13-8138-6_30

we most concern about the bit rate ratio of the frame level and the λ decision of every CTU in a frame. Gao et al. [8] propose a frame-level bit allocation algorithm based on the DCT coefficient distribution and the quality dependency analysis.

In this paper, we propose a novel rate control algorithm. The major contributions of this paper are described as follows: (1) We explore the relationship between the bit cost and the mean bi-directional difference of the current frame. (2) For the RDO process of a frame, a special relationship, where the mean CTU λ should be equal to the frame λ, is built. (3) A CTU λ clipping method is proposed to get a optimal RD characteristic of a frame. The rest of this paper is organized as follows. Section 2 reviews the R-λ rate control. In Sect. 3, we introduce the proposed algorithm. Section 4 presents the experimental results. The conclusions are given in Sect. 5.

2   Overview of the R-λ Rate Control

For R-λ rate control, the R-D relationship is modeled by the Hyperbolic function, which is defined as

$$d(r) = \sigma \cdot r^{-\gamma} \tag{1}$$

Where σ and γ are model parameters related to the characteristics of the video source. Here, r is modeled in terms of bpp, and d is modeled in terms of mean square error (MSE) of luma component. As is well known, λ is the slop of R-D curve and (1) can be calculated by

$$\lambda = -\frac{\partial d}{\partial r} = \sigma \cdot \gamma \cdot bpp^{-\gamma-1} \triangleq \alpha \cdot bpp^{\beta} \tag{2}$$

where $\alpha = \sigma \cdot \gamma$ and $\beta = -\gamma - 1$ are parameters related to the video content. Until now, the R-D model is built for rate control. For the GOP level, the target bits of a GOP is calculated by

$$t_{GOP} = \frac{r_{Frame} \cdot (n_{coded} + SW) - r_{coded}}{SW} \cdot n_{GOP} \tag{3}$$

Where $r_{Frame} = T_{bitrate}/fr$, in which $T_{bitrate}$ is the target bit rate and fr is the frame rate. n_{coded} is the number of the encoded frames and r_{coded} is the used bits. SW is the smooth window. Then, the target bit rate t_{frame} of the k-th frame in this GOP is calculated by

$$t_{frame} = \frac{t_{GOP} - \Sigma_{i=0}^{k-1} r_i}{\Sigma_{i=k}^{N_{GOP}} \omega_i} \cdot \omega_k \tag{4}$$

Where r_i is the bit cost of i-th frame, ω_i is the predefined bit ratio. Finally, the target bit per pixel is calculated by

$$bpp = \frac{t_{frame} - \tilde{t}}{n \cdot \Sigma_{i=1}^{N_{CTU}} \overline{\omega}_k(i)} \cdot \overline{\omega}_k(j) \tag{5}$$

$$\bar{\omega}_k(j) = \frac{1}{n^2}\Sigma_{x=1}^n \Sigma_{y=1}^n \left(p_{x,y} - \bar{p}_{x,y}\right)^2 \tag{6}$$

It can be seen from (6) that the weight of every CTU for bit allocation is measured by the predicted error. However, Li et al. [9] propose an adaptive bit allocation strategy. Then, (6) will be modified as

$$\bar{\omega}_k(j) = n \cdot \left(\frac{\lambda_F}{\alpha_{CTU}}\right)^{\frac{1}{\beta_{CTU}}} \tag{7}$$

Where λ_F is the frame λ. α_{CTU} and β_{CTU} are the parameters from the collocated CTU in the encoded frame. During the adaptive process, bit rate will be allocated according to the characteristics of video contents. Then, QP is determined by the given λ as

$$QP = a \cdot ln(\lambda) + b \tag{8}$$

Where a and b are set to 4.2005 and 13.7122, respectively.

3   The Proposed Algorithm

Normally, when the two frames are exactly the same, it will use little bits to code the frame. However, if the two frames are quite different, it is hard to find the reference regions for the current frame, and this will lead to cost a lot of bits for encoding. The mean bi-directional frame difference of k-th frame is defined as

$$mbdd_k = (md_{k-1} + md_{k+1})/2 \tag{9}$$

where md_{k-1} and md_{k+1} are calculated by

$$
\begin{aligned}
md_{k-1} &= \frac{1}{W \cdot H} \sum_{x=1}^{W} \sum_{y=1}^{H} \left| p_{x,y}^k - p_{x,y}^{k-1} \right| \\
md_{k+1} &= \frac{1}{W \cdot H} \sum_{x=1}^{W} \sum_{y=1}^{H} \left| p_{x,y}^k - p_{x,y}^{k+1} \right|
\end{aligned}
\tag{10}
$$

In (10), W and H are the width and height of the frame respectively. $p_{x,y}^k$, $p_{x,y}^{k-1}$ and $p_{x,y}^{k+1}$ are the pixel values of the current frame, the first forward frame and the first backward frame respectively.

3.1   Frame Level Bit Rate Ratio

For the frame level rate control, we explore the relationship of the bit cost and $mbdd$. We ran the HEVC encoder for four sequences (RaceHorses, BasketballDirll, Cactus and ParkScene) numerous times without opening rate control function, observing the relation for each encoded frame. Figure 4(a) and (b) show the relationship of the bit cost and $mbdd$ at Random Access (RA) and Low Delay (LD) configuration.

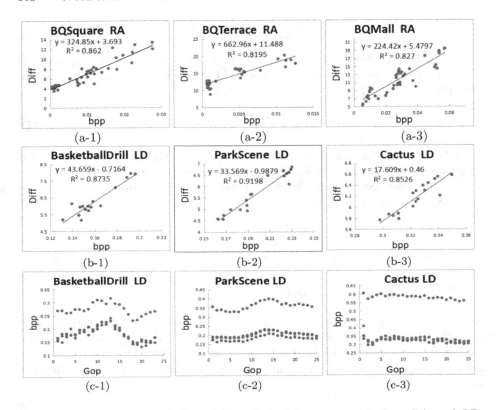

Fig. 1. The relationship of the *mbdd* and the bit cost per pixel at RA and LD configuration

From Fig. 1(a-1)–(a-3), we can see that they obey an approximate linear relation between the mean bi-directional difference and bit cost at RA configuration. However, at LD configuration, we find that the last frame in a GOP always costs more bits than other frames, shown in Fig. 1(c-1)–(c-3). We can see that the bit cost of first three frames in a GOP is close to each other, and the bit cost trend of the four frames is the same. So we design two experiments. For the first one, we make a statistics of only the first three frames in a GOP for mean bi-directional difference and bit cost. The results are shown in Fig. 1(b-1)–(b-3). We can see that they also obey an approximate linear relationship. The other experiment will obtain the bit cost ratio about the bit cost of the last frame and the mean bit cost of first three frames. The results are shown in Table 1.

According to the above analysis, the bit rate ratio for the frame is determined by *mbdd* and the Eq. (4) will be redefined as

$$t_{frame} = \frac{t_{GOP} - \Sigma_{i=0}^{k-1} r_i}{\Sigma_{i=k}^{N_{GOP}} \widehat{\omega}_i} \cdot \widehat{\omega}_k \tag{11}$$

Table 1. The bit cost ratio for the bit cost of the last frame and the mean bit cost of the first three frames in a GOP

LD	Bit ratio
Class A	1.92
Class B	2.86
Class C	2.60
Class D	2.57
Class E	3.89
Class F	2.06
Average	**2.65**

Where

$$\widehat{\omega}_k = mbdd_k \tag{12}$$

When at Low Delay configuration, $\widehat{\omega}_k$, in (12), of the last frame in a GOP will be defined as

$$\widehat{\omega}_k = 2.65 \cdot (\widehat{\omega}_{k-1} + \widehat{\omega}_{k-2} + \widehat{\omega}_{k-3})/3 \tag{13}$$

3.2   Optimal CTU λ Decision

To minimize the distortion of a frame, the RDO problem can be modeled as

$$min_{\{r_{CTU}(i)\}_{i=1}^{N_{CTU}}} \quad D_F = \sum_{i=1}^{N_{CTU}} d_{CTU}(i) \quad s.t. \quad R_F = \sum_{i=1}^{N_{CTU}} r_{CTU}(i) \leq T_F \tag{14}$$

where D_F and R_F are the distortion and the bit rate of the current frame. $d_{CTU}(i)$ and $r_{CTU}(i)$ are the distortion and the bit rate of i-th CTU. N_{CTU} is the number of the CTU in current frame. T_F is the target bit rate of the frame. Then, the Lagrange multiplier method can be converted to an equivalent unconstrained problem as

$$min_{\{r_{CTU}(i)\}_{i=1}^{N_{CTU}}} \sum_{i=1}^{N_{CTU}} d_{CTU}(i) + \lambda_F \cdot \sum_{i=1}^{N_{CTU}} r_{CTU}(i) \tag{15}$$

where λ_F is the Lagrange multiplier of current frame, and (15) can be solved via setting its derivative zero,

$$\frac{\partial \sum_{i=1}^{N_{CTU}} d_{CTU}(i)}{\partial r_{CTU}(z)} + \lambda_F \cdot \frac{\partial \sum_{i=1}^{N_{CTU}} r_{CTU}(i)}{\partial r_{CTU}(z)} = 0 \tag{16}$$

where $z \in [1, N_{CTU}]$. As the CTU in a frame can be considered separately, so

$$\sum_{z=1}^{N_{CTU}} \left(\frac{\partial \sum_{i=1}^{N_{CTU}} d_{CTU}(i)}{\partial r_{CTU}(z)} + \lambda_F \cdot \frac{\partial \sum_{i=1}^{N_{CTU}} r_{CTU}(i)}{\partial r_{CTU}(z)} \right) = 0 \tag{17}$$

Then, (17) can be converted equally as

$$\sum_{i=1}^{N_{CTU}} \frac{\partial d_{CTU}(i)}{\partial r_{CTU}(i)} + \lambda_F \cdot \sum_{i=1}^{N_{CTU}} \frac{\partial r_{CTU}(i)}{\partial r_{CTU}(i)} = 0 \tag{18}$$

taking $\lambda_{CTU}(i) = \partial d_{CTU}(i)/\partial r_{CTU}(i)$ into (18). Finally, we can obtain

$$[\sum_{i=1}^{N_{CTU}} \lambda_{CTU}(i)]/N_{CTU} = \lambda_F \tag{19}$$

(19) indicates that the mean λ of the CTUs in a frame should equal to the λ of the current frame. So the CTU λ clipping scheme for k-th CTU is calculated by

$$Clip(max([\Sigma_{i=1}^{k-1}\lambda_{CTU}(i)]/(k-1) \cdot 2^{-\frac{1}{3}}, \lambda_F \cdot 2^{-\frac{2}{3}}),$$
$$min([\Sigma_{i=1}^{k-1}\lambda_{CTU}(i)]/(k-1) \cdot 2^{\frac{1}{3}}, \lambda_F \cdot 2^{\frac{2}{3}}), \lambda_{CTU}(k)) \tag{20}$$

From (20), current CTU λ is effected not only by the frame λ, but also by the mean CTU λ of the encoded CTUs. So (20) can be approximately met.

Table 2. Experimental results at RA configuration

RA	Proposed				HM16.9			
	T_{target}	T_{actual}	$M\%$	PSNRY	T_{target}	T_{actual}	$M\%$	PSNRY
BlowingBubbles	15000	14917.892	0.547	52.24	15000	15002.634	0.018	51.97
	16500	16376.592	0.748	53.69	16500	16503.744	0.023	53.33
	16000	15898.716	0.633	53.24	16000	16003.842	0.024	52.82
BQSquare	17000	17002.990	0.018	53.79	17000	17001.972	0.012	52.88
	18000	18004.426	0.025	54.42	18000	18002.328	0.013	53.89
	16000	16001.688	0.011	52.85	16000	16002.317	0.014	52.22
BQMall	75000	75001.586	0.002	53.68	75000	75002.779	0.004	53.35
	80000	80002.589	0.003	54.80	80000	80002.440	0.003	54.38
	85000	84998.623	0.002	55.92	85000	85001.892	0.002	55.70
RaceHorses	11000	11000.147	0.001	41.74	11000	11003.196	0.029	41.48
	13000	13000.183	0.001	42.67	13000	13002.660	0.020	42.45
	12000	12000.203	0.002	42.20	12000	12001.896	0.016	41.96
BasketballDrive	20000	20003.126	0.016	39.23	20000	20008.736	0.044	39.17
	40000	40002.018	0.005	40.52	40000	40008.084	0.020	40.32
	160000	159999.954	0.000	46.65	160000	160000.026	0.000	46.55
AVE	\	\	0.134	49.18	\	\	0.016	48.83

4   Experimental Results

The proposed algorithm is implemented on HM16.9 platform. All of the sequences are encoded with 200 frames in the default profile of RA and LD configuration respectively.

The bit rate accuracy is defined as

$$M = |T_{actual} - T_{target}|/T_{target} \tag{21}$$

where T_{actual} and T_{target} are the actual bit rate and target bit rate respectively. The experimental results at RA configuration are shown in Table 2.

Table 3. Experimental results at LD configuration

LD	Proposed				HM16.9			
	T_{target}	T_{actual}	$M\%$	PSNRY	T_{target}	T_{actual}	$M\%$	PSNRY
BlowingBubbles	13000	12783.430	1.666	51.23	13000	12999.626	0.003	50.30
	14000	13651.668	2.488	52.24	14000	13999.356	0.005	51.14
	12000	11895.050	0.875	50.10	12000	11999.608	0.003	49.54
BQSquare	13000	12922.303	0.598	51.15	13000	12999.948	0.000	49.81
	14000	13810.445	1.354	51.95	14000	14000.011	0.000	50.49
	12000	11985.701	0.119	49.66	12000	12000.005	0.000	49.13
BQMall	50000	49996.010	0.008	49.49	50000	50000.254	0.001	49.24
	60000	59029.709	1.617	52.05	60000	60000.312	0.001	50.76
	55000	54638.076	0.658	50.96	55000	55000.289	0.001	50.00
RaceHorses	30000	29438.045	1.873	49.35	30000	29999.928	0.000	49.13
	40000	38246.003	4.385	53.29	40000	39999.991	0.000	53.10
	35000	33984.640	2.901	51.41	35000	34999.993	0.000	50.78
BasketballDrive	60000	60000.024	0.000	41.65	60000	60001.050	0.002	41.52
	70000	70000.088	0.000	42.20	70000	70001.080	0.002	42.04
	80000	80000.154	0.000	42.66	80000	80000.720	0.001	42.56
AVE	\	\	1.236	49.29	\	\	0.001	48.63

From Table 2, we can see that the average bit rate accuracy of the proposed algorithm is 0.134%, while the average value of the HM16.9 is 0.016%. Even though the bit rate accuracy of the proposed algorithm has a little degradation, it is still kept at high accurate level. For the PSNRY indexes, it can be seen that the average PSNRY indexes of the proposed algorithm and HM16.9 are 49.18 dB and 48.83 dB respectively. At the LD configuration in Table 3, the bit rate accurate indexes of the proposed algorithm and HM16.9 are 1.236% and 0.001%. Both of them are kept a well bit accurate level. For the proposed algorithm, we can see that the actual bit rate are always less than the target bit rate. However, the PSNRY index of the proposed algorithm is increased by 0.66 dB on average, in which the PNSRY index of HM16.9 is 48.63 dB. This result indicates that the proposed algorithm uses less bit rate to achieve a better coding quality. The improvement should be own to the more reasonable frame level bit allocation and the optimal CTU decision.

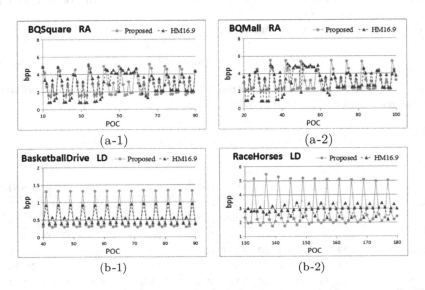

(a-1)   (a-2)

(b-1)   (b-2)

Fig. 2. bpp per frame for (a-1) *BQSquare* @17000 kbps, (a-2) *BQMall* @75000 kbps and (b-1) *BasketballDrive* @60000 kbps, (b-2) *RaceHorses* @35000 kbps at RA and LD configuration respectively

Figure 2 shows the bpp per frame at RA and LD configuration respectively. At the RA configuration, the bits of HM16.9 fluctuate a little largely than that of the proposed algorithm. However at the LD configuration, the bit fluctuation of HM16.9 is steadier than that of the proposed algorithm. As mention in Fig. 1 (c-1)–(c-3), when the rate control function is closed, the bpp of the last frame is much bigger than the first three frames in a GoP. So the bpp distribution of the proposed algorithm is the same as the situation in Fig. 1(c-1)–(c-3). This is the mainly reason for improving the coding quality at LD configuration.

Figure 3 shows the PSNRY for every frame at RA and LD configuration respectively. At RA configuration, some frames of the proposed algorithm is better than the other frames in a GoP, the most important is that the lowest points of the proposed algorithm are almost the same to the lowest points of the HM16.9. So the proposed algorithm has a better coding quality than HM16.9. At LD configuration, the PSNRY distribution of the proposed algorithm is the same to the bpp distribution. This is because the last frame in a GoP is always be referenced by all the frames in the next GoP. When the quality of the last frame is improved, this is useful for the frame which refers it. So the coding quality of the proposed algorithm will be increased. The next, we will illustrate

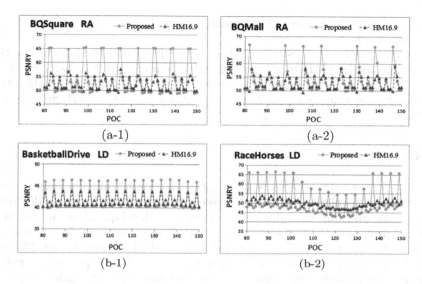

Fig. 3. PSNRY per frame for (a-1) *BQSquare* @17000 kbps, (a-2) *BQMall* @75000 kbps and (b-1) *BasketballDrive* @60000 kbps, (b-2) *RaceHorses* @35000 kbps at RA and LD configuration respectively

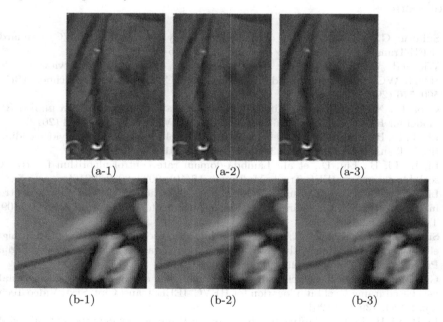

Fig. 4. Subjective performance. (a-1)–(a-3) are the partial pictures getting from *Race-Horses* @1000 kbps 66th frame for the original frame, proposed algorithm, HM16.9 respectively at RA configuration. (d-1)–(d-3) are the partial pictures getting from *BasketballDrill* @1000 kbps 39th frame for the original frame, proposed algorithm and HM16.9 respectively at LD configuration.

the subjective performance of the proposed algorithm and HM16.9. The results are shown in Fig. 4.

From Fig. 4(a-2) and (a-3), we can see that the face of the horse in (a-2) is clearer than that in (a-3), especially the region near the eye. For (b-2) and (b-3), the coding quality of region near the elbow in (b-2) is much better than that in (b-3). So the proposed algorithm has a better subjective performance than HM16.9.

5   Conclusion

In this paper, we propose a novel rate control algorithm. Different from the previous works, we explore relationship between the bit cost and the mean difference of the frame and find the approximate linear relationship. Then, according to the RDO process of the frame level rate control, an equation of the frame λ and the mean CTU λ is built. Finally, based on the calculated results, a CTU decision scheme is proposed with a CTU clipping method. The experimental results show that the proposed algorithm increase the coding quality significantly with a little bit rate accurate degradation.

References

1. Sullivan, G.J., et al.: Overview of the high efficiency video coding (HEVC) standard. IEEE Trans. Circ. Syst. Video Technol. **22**(12), 1649–1668 (2012)
2. Wiegand, T., Sullivan, G.J., Bjontegaard, G., Luthra, A.: Overview of the H.264/AVC video coding standard. IEEE Trans. Circ. Syst. Video Technol. **13**(7), 560–576 (2003)
3. Choi, H., Nam, J., Yoo, J., Sim, D., Bajic, I.: Rate control based on unified RQ model for HEVC, ITU-T SG16 contribution, JCTVC-H0213, pp. 1–13 (2012)
4. Li, B., Li, H., Li, L., Zhang, J.: Domain rate control for high efficiency video coding. IEEE Trans. Image Process. **23**(9), 3841–3854 (2014)
5. Li, L., Li, B., Liu, D., et al.: Lambda-domain rate control algorithm for HEVC scalable extension. IEEE Trans. Multimed. **18**(10), 2023–2039 (2016)
6. Li, S., Xu, M., Wang, Z., Sun, X.: Optimal bit allocation for CTU level rate control in HEVC. IEEE Trans. Circ. Syst. Video Technol. Idea https://doi.org/10.1109/TCSVT.2016.2589878
7. Sun, H., Gao, S., Zhang, C.: Adaptive bit allocation scheme for rate control in high efficiency video coding with initial quantization parameter determination. Signal Process. Image Commun. **29**(10), 1029–1045 (2014)
8. Gao, W., et al.: DCT coefficient distribution modeling and quality dependency analysis based frame-level bit allocation for HEVC. IEEE Trans. Circ. Syst. Video Technol. **26**(1), 139–153 (2016)
9. Li, B., Li, H., Li, L.: Adaptive bit allocation for R-lambda model rate control in HM. In: JCT-VC of ITU-T SG16 WP3 and ISO/IEC JTC1/SC29/WG11 13th Meeting, Incheon, Republic of Korea, Doc JCTVC-M0036 (2013)

Research on a Parallel Rate Control Algorithm of Macro-Block Layer

Min Ding, Lulu Huang, Guoping Li$^{(\boxtimes)}$, and Guozhong Wang

School of Communication and Information Engineering, Shanghai University,
Shanghai 200444, China
liguoping@shu.edu.cn

Abstract. In order to efficiently transmit video data while satisfying the
channel bandwidth and transmission delay constraints, bit rate control of
the video encoding process is required. According to ultra-high-definition
video, traditional coding algorithms have a large amount of caculation
and high computational complexity, thus, parallel coding methods such
as inter-frame parallel coding and wavefront parallel coding (WPP) are
proposed. However, the rate control of parallel coding is a difficult problem, especially the intra-frame rate control under the WPP coding mode,
so this paper proposes a bit rate control algorithm within macro-block
layer. By contrasting the PSNR, the encoding speed and the VBV (Video
Buffer Verifier) buffer condition of the video sequences, the algorithm
proposed in this paper has advantages of less computing cost and faster
coding speed than the traditional algorithms.

Keywords: Parallel coding · Rate control · Intra-frame coding ·
Quantization parameter · Wavefront parallel processing

1 Introduction

In video communication, the communication channel bandwidth is limited, and
the bits for coding each frame of the video sequence changes. Therefore, in
order to make full use of the channel bandwidth and guarantee that the coding
bit stream can be transferred smoothly, the rate control is needed for video
coding. In the actual video encoding process, there are different frame types:
IBP, the bits allocated to each frame is different. As the reference frame, I frame
need more bits and B frame needs the least. Bits allocated for each frame is
determined first when coding, and then the bits are allocated to the macro-
blocks of the current frame. The target bits of each macro-block is directly
related to video content. For example, the coding residual of background area is
smaller, and the bit rate should be small; the coding residual of the regions with
more details and more intense movement are larger, and the bit rate should be
larger. A parallel coding framework is proposed in literature [2], the achieved
speedup is 12 while the PSNR decreased about $0.01-0.02$ dB. The algorithm
proposed in this paper implements the macro-block layer rate control based

© Springer Nature Singapore Pte Ltd. 2019
G. Zhai et al. (Eds.): IFTC 2018, CCIS 1009, pp. 369–378, 2019.
https://doi.org/10.1007/978-981-13-8138-6_31

on this framework. Before coding, the framework uses the original frame as a reference frame to compute the sum of absolute difference (SAD) [1] of the current frame, and then uses the calculated SAD to predict the bits of the current frame. The top ten percent macro-blocks of the current frame are pre-coded, the complexity coefficient (coeff) of the macro-block is updated every ten percent of the row macro-blocks to guarantee that the update frequency of coeff doesn't change in order to ensure the precision of coding. When the pre-coding is finished, the quantization parameter (QP) is predicted by the updated *coeff*. The results of experiment shows that this algorithm can achieve better effect and less computation.

2   Parallel Coding Framework

The parallel coding framework used in this paper [2] is shown in Fig. 1:

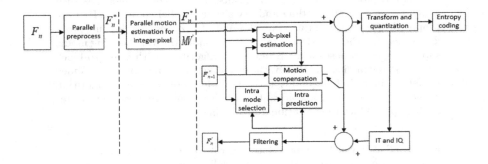

Fig. 1. Video parallel coding framework.

Parallel preprocessing module: In addition to the basic preprocessing such as denoising filtering, smoothing filtering and RGB to YUV color space conversion of the original video sequence, it is most important to perform scene detection and frame type judgment on the sequence by calculation of correlation parameters. Since the frames are independent of each other, they can be processed in parallel.

Parallel motion estimation module: using the frame type of each image frame obtained by the previous module, this module selects the corresponding original frame as a reference frame according to the frame type parameter, so that multiple frames can simultaneously perform an integer pixel motion vector search to obtain an integer pixel motion vector MV'. After the motion estimation is over, the next stage is the coding module. This parallel method parallelizes the most time-consuming motion estimation of the integer pixel in the coding, greatly improving the parallelism and coding efficiency of the entire parallel coding framework.

Parallel coding module: Using interlaced coding, each field acts as a slice, and inter-frame coding with reference dependencies is performed independently between fields. After the macro-block mode selection, this module performs motion estimation of the sub-pixel search using MV' as a starting point, and ultimately gets the motion vector MV. And then through motion compensation, transform quantization and entropy coding finally gets the code stream.

3   Wave Parallel Processing

Wavefront parallel processing coding [3] is proposed according to parallel coding. This method has many advantages, such as high speed and high amenability to parallel computing. However, it is difficult to deal with rate control. In WPP mode, each frame of a video sequence is divided into several rows of Largest Coding Units (LCUs) [3]. Coding each LCU depends on the information of the left, the upper, the left upper, the right upper LCUs [4], therefore, in WPP mode, the first row of each frame is processed normally, and the second will be processed after processing two CTUs of the first row, and the third row will be processed after processing two CTUs of the second row. All the rest are processed in the same way.

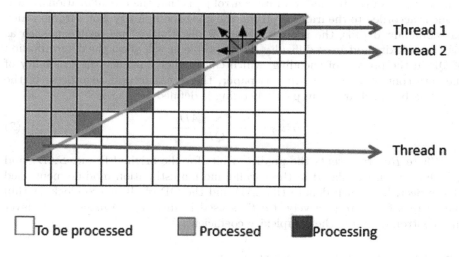

Fig. 2. WPP mode.

As Fig. 2 shows that in WPP mode, the arrangement mode of macro-blocks doesn't change. The difference is that these macro-blocks are encoded according to each oblique line. Open a thread for each macro-block on each oblique row and encode these macro-blocks simultaneously. In this way, the macro-blocks of the oblique line can be encoded in the encoding time of a macro-block. When the macro-blocks of the oblique line are encoded completely, all the threads will be turned to the next oblique line.

4   A Macro-Block Layer Rate Control Algorithm in Parallel Coding Framework

In the parallel coding framework proposed in this paper, there is a parallel motion estimation module. In this module, the original frame is regarded as a reference frame to compute the sum of absolute difference (SAD) of the current frame. The calculated SAD is used to predict the bits of the current frame. Then, the bits of the current frame will be allocated to the macro-blocks of it. When the intra-frame macro-block layer rate control is carried out, the calculated SAD (macro-block layer) is used as the input to determine the QP (macro-block layer), and then use the determined QP to encode. The SAD's formula can be written as:

$$SAD = \sum_{(x,y) \in A} |S_k[x,y] - P_k[x,y]| \tag{1}$$

Where A represents a pixel area; $S_k[x,y]$ is the pixel value of the video image at $[x,y]$; $P_k[x,y]$ is a prediction value of $S_k[x,y]$.

4.1   Frame-Level Rate Control

The core idea of the frame-level rate control [1] is that the bits allocation of each frame is accorded to the frame type and the image complexity. For a frame which has abundant details, the process of the bit distribution has problems such as high complexity and great difficulty. These problems will affect the determination of QP in the process of encoding, which can further influence the feasibility of the rate control algorithm. In this paper, the dynamic update process of the encoding bits each frame in parallel coding is defined as:

$$Bits = \frac{coeff \times SAD_f}{QP_f} \tag{2}$$

Where *Bits* represents the predicted bits for the original frame, SAD_f and QP_f have been calculated in the parallel motion estimation module mentioned before Sect. 4.1, which denote the SAD and the QP of all macro-blocks within the current frame respectively. *Coeff* is used in intra-frame macro-block layer rate control, denoting the complexity coefficient.

4.2   Macro-Block Layer Bit Control

The rate control algorithm proposed in this paper implements the parallel AVS+ video encoder and is based on AVS+ standard. The formula of macro-block layer rate control can be written as formula (3):

$$Bits = \frac{coeff \times SAD_{MB}}{QP_{MB}} \tag{3}$$

Assume that the bits pre-distribution of per frame is known, there are two traditional intra-frame macro-block layer rate control algorithms:

(a) Encoding the original frame only once, the *coeff* is updated when a row of macro-blocks are coded. The QP of each row of macro-blocks is predicted according to the formula (2). The original QP is solved referring to the QP of the encoded frame and frame level bit-rate control (2). Because the original QP is not accurate, therefore, the QP of other rows of macro-blocks which takes the original QP as a reference will be more inaccurate. If the predicted original QP is smaller, and the bits predicted is less, the QP of later macro-blocks of the current frame will be larger. If the predicted original QP is larger, and the bits predicted is more, then the QP of the later macro-blocks of the current frame will be smaller [6]. Obviously, this method will lead to that the allocation of QP of the current frame's macro-blocks is not uniform and fluctuates fiercely. Meanwhile, the subjective effect of the current frame won't be satisfying.

(b) The current frame will be encoded twice. In the first pass, the bit stream will not be outputted, and the original *coeff* equals to the previous frame's. The *coeff* is updated when a row of macro-blocks are coded until all the macro-block slices are encoded completely. QP is predicted by each row's *coeff* according to the formula (2). When the first pass is finished, average all the macro-blocks' QP and then use the average value or the updated *coeff* to solve the new original QP according to the formula (2). In the second pass, the algorithm use the new QP to code. The QP has been steady in the second pass and almost doesn't need to be updated. This algorithm has high coding accuracy and great effect. However, the computational complexity of this algorithm is high.

(c) The algorithm proposed in this paper has made improvements according to the disadvantages of the two traditional algorithms mentioned above. Also, the original frame will be encoded twice. The difference between it and the second traditional algorithm mentioned above is shown in the first pass.

The first pass: Pre-coding.

Only the top 10% macro-blocks of the original frame will be encoded. The *coeff* is updated when per $Wb * 10\%$ macro-blocks are coded, and QP can be predicted according to formula (3). In this process, the *coffe* is updated Hb times. This is to prove that the updating frequency of *coeff* is the same as the traditional algorithm's to guarantee the precision of coding.

The second pass:

Using the *coffe* got in the first pass to solve the original QP according to the formula (2), and then use the new QP for the second encoding. We denote the new QP as QP_0. The *coeff* is updated while per Wb macro-blocks are coded, and QP is predicted according to formula (3). After updating, QP of each row of macro-blocks is ranged in $[QP_0-4, QP_0+4]$. The QP of each macro-block within the current frame is fluctuated in a small range which can guarantee the coding quality of the frame.

The calculation of *coeff* is written as formula (4) [1]:

$$coffe = \frac{bits \times QP'}{SAD' \times count} \tag{4}$$

where the QP' and the SAD' denote the average QP and SAD of the previous row of macro-blocks respectively, *bits* denotes the previous row of macro-blocks' actual coding bits and *count* is the updating times.

As the formula (5) and (6) show that *count* and *coffe* are updated with attenuation coefficient (*decay*) [1]:

$$count'' = count' \times decay + 1 \tag{5}$$

$$coeff'' = coeff' \times decay + coeff \tag{6}$$

4.3 Process of the Intra-frame Macro-Block Layer Rate Control Algorithm

The steps of the algorithm proposed in this paper are as follows:

(1) The initial QP of the current frame can be obtained from formula (3) based on the number of predictive coding bits and the SAD of the current frame.
(2) Pre-coding. Only the top 10% macro-blocks of the current frame will be encoded. The *coeff* is updated when per $Wb * 10\%$ macro-blocks are coded. Then, QP is predicted according to formula (3). In this process, the *coffe* is updated Hb times.
(3) After the pre-coding, we use the updated *coffe* to solve the original QP according to the formula (2), and then use the new QP to encode the current frame for the second pass. The *coeff* is updated when per Wb macro-blocks are coded, and QP is predicted according to formula (3) for the actual encoding process.
(4) We use the updated *coffe*, SAD and QP to predict the rest bits of the current frame. And then we update the buffer of the current frame.
(5) For each frame in parallel coding, perform the above steps (1)–(4).

5   Experiment Results Analysis

To verify the performance of the intra-frame macro-block layer rate control algorithm proposed in this paper, the experimental configuration is shown as Table 1.

In this paper, PSNR, VBV buffer condition and coding speed are tested. The proposed method is compared with other two traditional algorithms to verify the effectiveness. To be easily understood and show results intuitively, we refer the three algorithms as tradition algorithm 1, tradition algorithm 2 and the new algorithm respectively.

Table 1. Experimental configuration

Environment	Value
Machine configuration	Xeon E5-2690 v32 cpu, 48 cores2.6 GHZ
Tested sequences	parterredialbasketballvolleyballleafbirdcage
Resolution	1920 * 1280
Bit Rate	12000 kbps
NumberBFrames	1
Thread number	6
FrameFieldCoding	Field

5.1 Frame Rate

In order to compare the real-time encoding speed of the three algorithms, the frame rate comparison curves of the six tested sequences under the three algorithms are shown in Fig. 3.

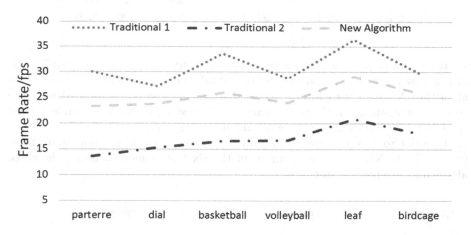

Fig. 3. The frame rate comparison

Table 2 shows that the comparison of frame rate (fps) of six YUV sequences under the three algorithms.

It can be seen from Table 2 that although the coding speed of the new algorithm is slower than the traditional algorithm 1, it is much faster than the traditional algorithm 2. This is because that the traditional algorithm 1 encodes each frame only one pass. Therefore, the coding speed is faster although the encoding quality of the image is not high. The traditional algorithm 2 encodes each frame two passes so that the calculation is large and the encoding precision is high. However, the encoding speed is the slowest. The new algorithm reduces the coding time by 90% compared to the traditional algorithm 2, so the encoding speed is much higher than the traditional algorithm 2.

Table 2. Frame rate of 6 tested sequences under three algorithms

Algorithms	Parterre	Dial	Basketball	Volleyball	Leaf	Birdcage
Traditional 1	30.07	27.18	33.68	28.78	36.38	29.81
New algorithm	23.32	23.82	25.96	24.06	29.09	25.85
Traditional 2	13.60	15.30	16.62	16.72	20.89	18.02

5.2 PSNR Comparison

Table 3 shows the comparison results of Y PSNR of the six YUV sequences under the three algorithms.

Table 3. PSNR of 6 tested sequences under three algorithms

Algorithms	Parterre	Dial	Basketball	Volleyball	Leaf	Birdcage
Traditional 1	31.4	37	33.5	32.3	24.9	32.7
New algorithm	31.7	37.7	33.7	32.9	25.9	33.3
Traditional 2	32.1	37.9	34.2	33.3	26	33.6

It can be seen from Table 3 that, for these six sequences, the PSNR (dB) of the new algorithm is reduced by 0.1−0.5 dB compared with the traditional algorithm 2, which is within an acceptable range. However, compared with the traditional algorithm 1, the performance of the new algorithm has been improved by 0.7−1.1 dB which makes a significant improvement.

In order to compare the coding quality of the three algorithms more intuitively, the PSNR comparison curves of the six test sequences under the three algorithms are plotted in Fig. 4.

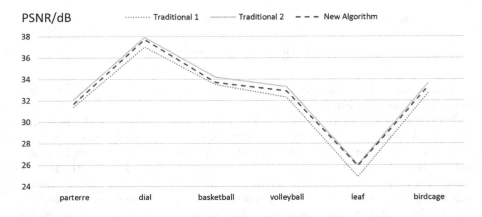

Fig. 4. The PSNR comparison

From the comparison of PSNR and average frame rate of these six sequences, we can see that the performance of the new algorithm proposed in this paper is nearly closed to the traditional 2 algorithm, but the coding speed is improved, which solves the problem that the real-time coding speed cannot keep up.

5.3   VBV Buffer Condition Comparison

The leaf sequence and the volleyball sequence are selected as shown in Figs. 5 and 6.

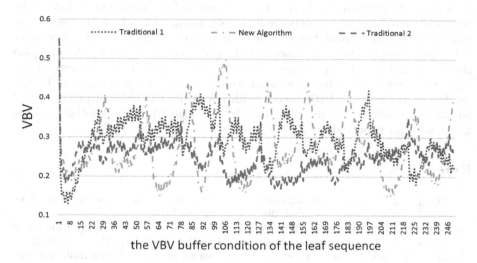

Fig. 5. The VBV buffer condition of the leaf sequence under three algorithms

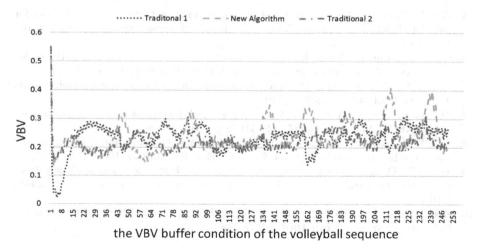

Fig. 6. The VBV buffer condition of the volleyball sequence under three algorithms

From the comparison of the VBV buffer condition of the sequences under the three algorithms, we can see that there is no overflow or underflow in VBV buffer. The volleyball sequence has a larger fluctuation range under the new algorithm relative to the traditional two algorithms. This is because the QP of the new algorithm ranges in $[QP_0-4, QP_0+4]$, but it's within the normal range and the subjective effect of the image is also guaranteed to be better.

6   Conclusion

This paper focuses on the intra-frame rate control of macro-blocks layer. The proposed algorithm makes improvements according to the high computational complexity of traditional intra-frame rate control algorithms. The new algorithm pre-codes the top 10% macro-blocks and updates the *coeff* while keeping the updating frequency unchanged. Thus, the new algorithm can guarantee the coding accuracy and reduce the calculation. At last, by comparing the PSNR, the frame rate and the VBV buffer condition of the HD video sequences based on the two traditional algorithms and the new algorithm, the feasibility of the new algorithm is proved.

References

1. Xiaoguang, W., Li, G., et al.: Research on rate control algorithm based on video parallel coding. Telev. Technol. **39**(16), 78–82 (2015)
2. Jiang, X., Li, G., Wang, G., et al.: Multi-core parallel video coding algorithm based on AVS+ real-time encoding. J. Electron. Inf. Technol. **36**(4), 810–816 (2014)
3. Chen, K., Sun, J., Duan, Y., et al.: A novel wavefront-based high parallel solution for HEVC encoding. IEEE Trans. Circuits Syst. Video Technol. **26**(1), 181–194 (2016)
4. Gu, J., Han, Y., Wen, J.: A novel low delay in-loop filtering WPP process for parallel HEVC encoding. In: Visual Communications and Image Processing, pp. 1–4. IEEE (2017)
5. Chen, M., Liu, P., Yao, Q., et al.: Macroblock level rate control algorithm for H.264/AVC. J. Zhejiang Univ. (Eng. Edn.) **41**(6), 925–929 (2007)
6. Cheng, F., Zou, X., Teng, G., et al.: A macroblock level code rate control scheme. Telev. Technol. **34**(6), 23–25 (2010)
7. Zhang, Y., Xu, X., Yang, Y.: A new macroblock level rate control algorithm for H.264/AVC. Chin. J. Image Graph. **10**, 2019–2022 (2008)
8. Wei, F., Liang, J., Han, J.: An X264 parallel coding algorithm based on inter-frame and intra-frame macroblock level. Comput. Eng. Sci. **33**(07), 106–111.2 (2011)
9. Wang, Z., Dong, S., Wang, R., Wang, W., Gao, W.: Dynamic macroblock wavefront parallelism for parallel video coding. J. Vis. Commun. Image Represent. **28**, 36–43 (2015)
10. Zou, B., Fan, L.: A parallel video coding method based on CPU + GPU. J. Shanghai Univ. (Nat. Sci. Edn.) **19**(03), 235–239 (2013)

Motion Adaptive Intra Refresh for Low Delay HEVC Encoding

Zhaoliang Ma[1(✉)], Li Song[1,2], Rong Xie[1,2], and Wenjun Zhang[1,2]

[1] Institute of Image Communication and Network Engineering,
Shanghai Jiao Tong University, Shanghai, China
{mazhaoliang, song_li, xierong, zhangwenjun}@sjtu.edu.cn
[2] Cooperative Medianet Innovation Center, Shanghai Jiao Tong University,
Shanghai, China

Abstract. Low delay video coding is a critical technology for real-time applications. The method of periodic intra refresh (PIR) can obtain the low delay effect by embedding the intra-coding columns or slices into inter frames (e.g. P or B frames). However, due to the diversity of video motion direction, this method still cannot achieve the optimal coding performance. In this paper, we propose a motion adaptive intra refresh method, which can choose the optimal refresh direction adaptively according to the video motion direction. Experimental results show that the proposed scheme can achieve 2.2% and 2.5% BD-rate gain in average compared with the periodic intra refresh method for PSNR and SSIM, respectively, with a similar low delay effect under the low delay P configuration in HM16.14. At the same time, the encoding time ratio is 99.85%, which means the time complexity of the two algorithms remains at the same level.

Keywords: Low delay · Intra refresh · Video coding · HEVC · Error recovery

1 Introduction

In recent years, there has been a growing demand for such industries as video broadcast, video conference, and remote video education. The requirements for end-to-end delay are increasingly harsh in the real-time interaction. Especially for the VR industry, the issue of delay is still outstanding. A high latency makes a poor virtual reality experience (motion sickness and nausea). In May 2011, Google released an open source project known as WebRTC [1], which enable real time communication of audio, video and data in Web and native apps. This project is still in the process of rapid development although it has some problems. Therefore, low delay is a key technology and design goal for any video transmission system where needs real-time video interaction.

Schreier and Rothermel [2] analyzed the overall delay in the video transmission system. At the encoder side, the encoder latency contains capture latency, frame-reordering latency, encoder processing latency and buffer latency. Among them, the capture latency is determined by the hardware. The use of B-frames (Bi-directional predicted frames) will cause the frame-reordering latency because its display and coding order is different, so the coding structure of IPPP is commonly used in low-delay

© Springer Nature Singapore Pte Ltd. 2019
G. Zhai et al. (Eds.): IFTC 2018, CCIS 1009, pp. 379–390, 2019.
https://doi.org/10.1007/978-981-13-8138-6_32

applications. To reduce the latency of encoder processing, parallel acceleration in multi-core or heterogeneous platform is an important technology and it works well.

Actually, the dominant delay contributor is the buffer delay in most video-streaming applications. Low delay and error resilience are critical features in real-time communications. In order to meet the requirement of low delay, the buffer size must maintain a very small level. In addition, to get the characteristic of error resilience, the common practice is to insert I frames periodically, and it can avoid error propagation and accumulation effectively. However, I frame usually consume up to 10 times more data than P frame, the periodically insertion of I frames will cause a large buffer delay. To achieve short buffering delay, it is generally desirable to have a constant bit rate (CBR) in short time intervals with minimum intervention of the rate control. Although this approach leads to a decrease in rate-distortion performance and drastic fluctuation of the encoded quality between frames, we still have to do this for low latency. It is desirable to do intra refresh (IR) coding instead of inserting an entire I frame periodically. That is to say, a portion of the P frame is encoded by using intra coding mode to recover the error.

There are many intra refresh algorithms, such as random intra refresh (RIR) [3, 4], adaptive intra refresh (AIR) [5–7] and periodic intra refresh (PIR) [8, 9]. RIR selects a certain number of macroblocks randomly to adopt the intra coding mode, but this refresh method is random, the effect of error resilience is not obvious. Based on the characteristics of video content or the feedback of network, the AIR method can select some macroblocks adaptively to do intra coding. This method is more efficient compared with RIR method.

In these above three refresh strategies, only PIR method can guarantee full recovery of errors within a defined refresh cycle. The video frames are completely refreshed within the specified refresh period of the PIR. Also for each frame, a fix subset of macroblocks must be intra coded which leads to more constant bitrate than inserting a key frame. This method is recommended for video streaming applications as it provides low-delay and good error-resilience. Moreover, many excellent open source encoders (such as x264, x265, etc.) use PIR technology due to its simplicity and practicality. However, there are still some weaknesses in the PIR method, the coding performance will significantly decrease when the video motion direction is opposite to the intra refresh direction because of the limitation of the search range of the refreshed area. Therefore, this method still cannot achieve the optimal coding performance owing to the diversity of video motion direction. Schreier [10] first made improvements to this shortcoming of PIR, and a motion adaptive intra refresh method was proposed for H.264/AVC based on PIR method, but the refresh cycle size of the article is a constant, which means that the scheme cannot be implemented if the refresh cycle size changed. In addition, the method proposed in [10] also needs to use the motion vector information obtained by standard IP encoding, which makes the method unable to be used in practical real-time applications.

In this paper, we propose a motion adaptive intra refresh method developed by the PIR method, which can choose the optimal refresh direction adaptively according to the video motion direction. It can effectively reduce the degradation of the rate distortion performance when the direction of video motion and the direction of refresh are inconsistent. Compared with [10], the refresh cycle size could be changed in our design, and there is no need to use standard IP encoding to obtain motion vector information.

The rest of this paper is organized as follows. We first introduce the periodic intra refresh method in Sect. 2. The proposed motion adaptive intra refresh method is described in Sect. 3. The experimental results are presented in Sect. 4, and Sect. 5 draws the conclusion.

2 Intra Refresh Introduction

Intra refresh is a method of video error control that adopts the intra coding mode for macroblock or whole frame forcibly. This method leads to the corresponding inter prediction no longer continuous, that is, the subsequent picture or macroblock cannot be encoded and reconstructed according to the previous frame or macroblock information. Thereby this method can prevent the spread of errors between video frames.

The PIR method is done by inserting intra columns into each P frame in a sequential order as shown in Fig. 1. In this refresh scheme, the whole frame will be divided into N regions according to the given refresh cycle size (for example, N = 4 in Fig. 1). In the encoding process, these regions use the intra coding mode in turn. The area that has been intra-coded is called the clean region. The area to be intra-coded (intra coded region in Fig. 1) and not intra-coded are called the dirty region.

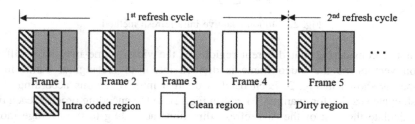

Fig. 1. Periodic intra refresh principle.

In the process of mode decision, the encoder needs to determine whether the macroblock is in the intra-coded region and then decide whether to take the forced intra-coding mode. Notice that the entire frame will be fully refreshed in a refresh cycle. For example, if an error occurs in the second column of frame 1, then in frame 2, the second column will be coded by using intra coding mode, so the error could be eliminated immediately.

In the PIR method, in addition to the above mentioned operations of sequentially refreshing the columns, it is also necessary to limit the search range of the refreshed regions. As seen in Fig. 1, the second column in frame 2 is coding by using intra coding mode. If the recent refreshed macroblocks in the first column use an error occurred region in the second column for motion estimation, then the error will propagate in the subsequent frames. An argument can be made this case occurs when the motion direction of the object in the frame is opposite to the intra refresh direction.

To protect the clean regions, [11] suggests restricting the search range for the clean region. That is to say, the clean region cannot refer to the dirty region for motion estimation, and the dirty region can use anywhere of the previous frames as a reference.

3   Motion Adaptive Intra Refresh Method

3.1   Motion Adaptive Intra Refresh for HEVC

When the video content has motility, especially it is moving at high speed, the traditional PIR method cannot get the optimal coding performance. To prevent the error propagating to the clean region, when the motion vector (MV) of the clean region points to the dirty region, the MV needs to be limited, that is, the search range of the clean region is limited. In order to minimize the occurrence of this situation, we propose the motion adaptive intra refresh method.

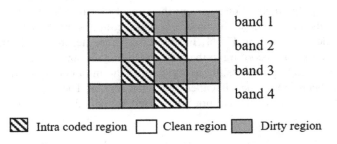

Fig. 2. Motion adaptive intra refresh method.

Firstly, considering that different regions of the video frame may have different motion vectors, so the video frame is divided into four rectangular bands in our scheme, as shown in Fig. 2. Each band is divided into M regions according to the refresh cycle size M (for example, M = 4 in Fig. 2). In the encoding process, each band will calculate the cost of the two refresh directions according to the average motion vector of the band (the cost calculation method is as shown in Eqs. (1), (2) and (3)), and adaptively select a lower cost refresh strategy (from the left to the right or from right to left).

The cost estimation principle is illustrated in Table 1 for the example in Fig. 3. As mentioned earlier, when the MV of clean region points to the dirty region, the MV needs to be limited, which can also be understood as border protection. This is done to protect clean regions. In this case, a penalty will be generated and we need to select the method with the minimum penalty to determine the refresh direction for each band. Here we take one of the bands for example. The Table 1 shows that for frame 1, region 1 is intra-coded and there is no border protection, thus the cost is 0. For frame 2, region 1 belongs to the clean region, and its MV points to the dirty region (region 2). So it is necessary to prevent this region obtaining reference information from the dirty region, and this will result in a penalty of 3. For frame 3, region 1 belongs to the clean region, but its MV points to the clean region (region 2). So the penalty for region 1 is 0. Region 2 belongs to the clean region, and its MV points to the dirty area (region 3). So the penalty for region 2 is 3. As shown in Table 1, the accumulated cost of all frames in a refresh cycle is 9. We can easily verify that the optimal refresh direction for this example is from right to left with 0 cost.

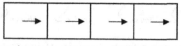

region 1   region 2   region 3   region 4

Fig. 3. An example of cost estimate. Average motion vectors for all regions (x, y) = (3, 0). The refresh direction of this example is from left to right.

Table 1. Cost estimation example.

Frame 1		No border protection
Frame 2		Region 1: 3
Frame 3		Region 1: 0 Region 2: 3
Frame 4		Region 1: 0 Region 2: 0 Region 3: 3
Accumulated cost		9

In the actual coding process, the MV of each frame can be known after encoding each frame, and it has been refined due to the limitation of the search range of the clean region. So it cannot be used to estimate the cost. In [10], the cost estimate is based on the motion vectors of standard IP-coding of the same video frames. However, this method is too troublesome, and it cannot be used in a real environment. In our scheme, the motion information of the previous refresh cycle is replaced by the motion information of the last frame of the previous refresh cycle. The coding experiments discussed in Sect. 4 show that this approach is simple yet effective. The cost function of band m (m = 1, 2, 3 and 4) between adjacent regions i and j in frame n is defined as follow.

If region i is "clean" and j is "dirty", and the motion vector of region i is pointing to region j:

$$C_{m,n,i,j} = \sum |MV_{xi}| \tag{1}$$

Where MV_{xi} is the horizontal motion vector of region i.

For other cases:

$$C_{m,n,i,j} = 0 \tag{2}$$

Based on this, the total cost for the last refresh cycle can be obtained by calculating and accumulating the cost of all adjacent regions and all frames of the refresh cycle.

$$C_m = \sum_{frames\,n} \sum_{regions\,i} \sum_{neighbors\,j} C_{m,n,i,j} \tag{3}$$

Calculate the cost of the two refresh strategies (from left to right and from right to left) respectively through formulas (1) (2) and (3), and then select the refresh direction with smaller cost for the next refresh cycle.

When the refresh direction of each band is the same, it can be used as the final refresh strategy to go to the next refresh cycle. However, if the refresh directions of the two adjacent bands are inconsistent, then the two bands cannot refer to each other. Therefore, it is necessary to investigate the dependence of the two bands in order to select the optimal direction for the final refresh direction.

We use the following method to determine the final refresh direction of the two bands:

Firstly, the band with the larger cost will be selected as a benchmark. This is because when the cost is larger, change of the refresh direction will result in more degradation in coding performance.

Secondly, the average motion vector of the two bands are calculated to determine whether the refresh direction needs to be changed. For example, suppose that band i and band j are two adjacent bands with different refresh directions. Assuming that band i is the benchmark, the refresh direction of the band j will be changed if the conditions in the following formula are satisfied:

$$MV_{yi} + MV_{yj} > |MV_{xj}| \tag{4}$$

Where MV_{yi} is the vertical MV component of band i pointing to band j, MV_{yj} is the vertical MV component of band j pointing to band i, MV_{xj} is the horizontal MV component of band j, and Algorithm 1 summarizes the process of performing the proposed low delay scheme.

3.2   Processing of the First Frame

In our low delay design, only one I frame is used at the beginning of the encoded bitstream. Since all macroblocks in the first frame are intra coded, its bitrate will be high. When the first frame passes through a fixed rate channel, the transmission time will be longer, resulting in a larger video delay. Therefore, in order to reduce the video delay, the bitrate of the first frame (I frame) must be greatly reduced. So we need to do some processing on the I frame.

When encoding the I frames, we can reduce the data number of I frames by reducing the allocated frame number, thus reducing the buffer delay. At the same time, the reduction of frame number will lead to the decrease of image quality in the first frame. But the quality degradation of the first frame is acceptable in low delay applications. What's more, the intra columns could be embedded in the subsequent P frames. This approach can restore the quality of the video in a refresh cycle.

Our experimental platform is HM16.14 [12] and the configuration file is Lowdelay P. In this platform, the target bitrate of I frame will be refined due to the intra coding mode. In order to maintain the stability of the bit rate, we forbid the refinement of bitrate for I frame in the experiment, making the bitrate of I frame and P frame almost the same.

Algorithm 1 Proposed intra refresh method.

Step 1: Obtain the motion vector information.

   1: Divide the video frame into 4 bands and the motion vector information of each band is counted.

Step 2: Calculate the cost of two refresh strategies.

   2: If this refresh cycle is not completed, jump to **Step 1**;

   3: If region i is "clean" and j is "dirty", and the motion vector of region i is pointing to region j:

$$C_{m,n,i,j} = \sum |MV_{xi}| \text{, Otherwise, } C_{m,n,i,j} = 0$$

   4: Calculate the total cost for the last refresh cycle by:

$$C_m = \sum\nolimits_{frames\ n} \sum\nolimits_{regions\ i} \sum\nolimits_{neighbors\ j} C_{m,n,i,j}$$

Step 3: Determine the refresh strategy.

   5: Choose the strategy with a smaller cost as the refresh method for the next refresh cycle;

   6: If the refresh direction of the 4 bands is the same, then go to the next refresh cycle, jump to **Step 1**;

Step 4: Check the vertical direction.

   7: Choose the band with the largest cost as a benchmark;

   8: If the refresh direction of the adjacent band(s) (not compared before) is(are) different from the benchmark. If the formula

$$MV_{yi} + MV_{yj} > |MV_{xj}|$$

is satisfied, change the direction of the adjacent band;

   9: If all bands have been compared, jump to **Step 1**. Otherwise, set the adjacent band(s) as the benchmark, jump to **Step 4.2**.

4 Experimental Results

In order to evaluate the performance of our design, we implement the traditional periodic intra refresh method and the proposed scheme in HM16.14 with low delay P coding structure. We aim to prove that the proposed refresh strategy has a better video quality, and the buffer delay of two methods maintain at the same level. The standard test sequence in class C and class D provided by HEVC are adopted, besides, we also test some sequences in CIF/HD/UHD format which have obvious movement. Different target bitrates are tested for the anchor algorithm and the proposed scheme as Table 2 shows.

According to [13], many encoders, such as x264 and x265, set the number of reference frames at 1 when IR is opened. Therefore, in this experiment, the number of reference frames is set to 1, and Table 3 lists the setting of encoder rate control parameters. This experiment uses the encoding structure under the configuration file of Low Delay P in HM, which is suitable for low latency applications.

Table 2. Target bitrate setting.

Resolution	352 × 288 416 × 240	832 × 480	1280 × 720	1920 × 1080
Target bitrate	256	384	512	2000
	384	512	1000	3000
	850	1200	2000	7000
	1500	2000	4000	10000

Table 3. Rate control parameter setting.

RateControl	Enabled
KeepHierarchicalBit	Disabled
LCULevelRateControl	Enabled
RCLCUSeparateModel	Enabled
InitialQP	Disabled
RCForceIntraQP	Disabled

The ability to keep the buffer away from overflow and underflow is one of the critical criterion for measuring the effect of low delay. If the size of the accumulated data is too large, the encoder has to skip some frames to reduce the buffer delay and prevent the buffer overflow. To the contrary, if the encoder output bit rate is lower than the channel bandwidth, buffer underflow will happen and cause a waste of channel. In order to observe low delay effect of the two methods, the buffer size is set as:

$$Buffer = T_{Delay} \times R_{Target} \qquad (5)$$

Where T_{Delay} is the delay time for the real-time video bitstream, and R_{Target} is the target bitrate. T_{Delay} is set at two frames in the simulation.

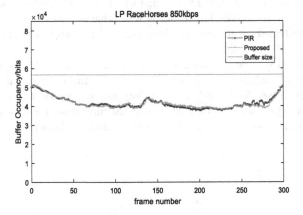

Fig. 4. Comparison of frame by frame CPS fullness: RaceHorses@850kbps

Figure 4 shows the coded picture buffer occupancy of *RaceHorses* by using the PIR method and proposed scheme. In the case of a small buffer setting, there are no buffer overflow and underflow in both of them. Experiments show that the proposed scheme can achieve a similar low delay effect compared with the traditional PIR method.

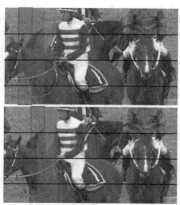 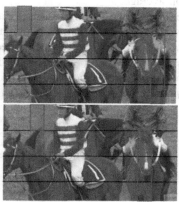

(a)Using the PIR method at the first refresh cycle.   (b)Using the proposed scheme at the first refresh cycle.

Fig. 5. Comparison of refresh effect between two methods: RaceHorses@850kbps

The effect of the two methods is shown in Fig. 5. It should be noted that the loss of performance of PIR method is mainly due to the fact that the search range of the boundary blocks (marked with a red box in the figure) near the dirty region is limited. As can be seen from Fig. 5(a), the refresh direction is from left to right, and the boundary blocks are frequently intra-coded which lead to a big loss of coding performance. In Fig. 5(b), the first band is refreshed from left to right, and the last three bands are refreshed from right to left. The proposed method avoids the frequently intra-coded situation and therefore has a better effect compared with the PIR method.

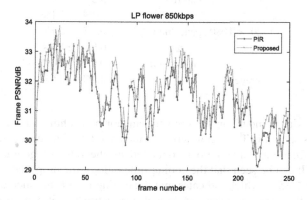

Fig. 6. Comparison of fluctuation of frame PSNR: flower@850kbps.

It is well-known that high quality and low delay are contradictory and cannot be achieved at the same time. When the delay is decreased, the coding performance is bound to have some loss. However, the proposed scheme cannot only keep a similar effect of low delay, but also get better video quality compared with the PIR method. As seen in Fig. 6, the proposed scheme has a higher frame PSNR compared with the PIR method on average.

Table 4 states the performance comparison of the anchor algorithm and the proposed low delay scheme. The two columns of "psnr" and "ssim" list the BD-rate on quality metric with PSNR and SSIM, respectively. It can be observed that rate distortion (RD) has about 2.2% gain on PSNR for the proposed scheme, while on SSIM, about 2.5% gain is achieved. At the same time, for the sequences with obvious movement (like *city* and *flower*), the proposed scheme can get significantly BD-rate gain.

Table 4. Performance comparison of two methods

Resolution	Sequence	BD-Rate (proposed VS PIR)	
		psnr	ssim
352 × 288	city	−4.3%	−4.9%
	coastguard	−2.8%	−2.9%
	flower	−5.1%	−5.6%
	paris	−3.4%	−3.3%
	stefan	−2.6%	−3.3%
416 × 240	BasketballPass	−1.0%	−1.1%
	BlowingBubbles	−1.4%	−1.5%
	RaceHorses	−1.8%	−1.9%
832 × 480	BasketballDrill	−1.6%	−1.3%
	PartyScene	−2.1%	−2.4%
	RaceHorses	−0.9%	−0.7%
1280 × 720	ducks_take_off	−0.5%	−0.6%
	parkrun	−5.3%	−7.7%
	stockholm	−2.3%	−3.1%
1920 × 1080	pedestrian	−0.7%	−0.7%
	Cactus	−0.9%	−1.3%
	crowd_run	−0.9%	−1.0%
Average		−2.2%	−2.5%

The complexity comparison between the anchor algorithm and the proposed low delay scheme is shown is Table 5 in terms of the encoding time under the low delay P configuration. Encoding time ratio is obtained as the ratio of geometric means of encoding time. It can be seen that the coding time ratio of the proposed scheme and the PIR method is 99.85%, which indicates that the coding time is not increased. Although the solution in this paper requires additional cost estimates, it can be seen from the results that this part has little effect on the overall coding time.

Table 5. Complexity comparison of two methods

Resolution	Sequence	Encoding time ratio	Average
352 × 288	city	101.89%	100.86%
	coastguard	100.73%	
	flower	101.54%	
	paris	99.90%	
	stefan	100.05%	
416 × 240	BasketballPass	99.85%	99.61%
	BlowingBubbles	99.33%	
	RaceHorses	99.91%	
832 × 480	BasketballDrill	98.80%	99.55%
	PartyScene	99.45%	
	RaceHorses	100.41%	
1280 × 720	ducks_take_off	98.97%	100.31%
	parkrun	100.64%	
	stockholm	101.33%	
1920 × 1080	pedestrian	100.09%	98.90%
	Cactus	96.72%	
	crowd_run	99.90%	
Average			99.85%

5 Conclusions

In this paper, we propose a motion adaptive intra refresh method, which can choose the optimal refresh direction adaptively according to the video motion direction. The experimental results show that compared with the PIR method, the proposed scheme can obtain better rate-distortion performance while maintaining the same level of low-latency effects. Also higher rate distortion gain can be obtained for motion-sense sequences. At the same time, the time complexity of the proposed algorithm is equivalent to the PIR method, and the additional cost estimation part has less influence on the overall coding time.

Acknowledgment. This work was supported by NSFC (61671296 and 61521062) and the Shanghai Key Laboratory of Digital Media Processing and Transmissions.

References

1. Carlucci, G., De Cicco, L., Holmer, S., et al.: Analysis and design of the Google congestion control for web real-time communication (WebRTC). In: Proceedings of the 7th International Conference on Multimedia Systems, p. 13. ACM (2016)
2. Schreier, R.M., Rothermel, A.: A latency analysis on H.264 video transmission systems. In: International Conference on Consumer Electronics, ICCE 2008, pp. 1–2. Digest of Technical Papers. IEEE (2008)

3. ISO/MPEG & ITU-T, H.264/AVC Reference Software. http://iphome.hhi.de/suehring/tml/download/. Accessed 14 Feb 2017
4. Tourapis, A.M., Leontaris, A., Suhring, K., et al.: H. 264/14496-10 AVC reference software manual. Doc. JVT-AE010 (2009)
5. Zhou, Y.R., Li, G.Q., Ning, S.S.: A new feedback-based intra refresh method for robust video coding. In: 2015 International Conference on Computer Science and Applications (CSA), pp. 218–221. IEEE (2015)
6. dela Cruz, A.R., Cajote, R.D.: Low complexity adaptive intra-refresh rate for real-time wireless video transmission. In: 2014 Asia-Pacific Signal and Information Processing Association Annual Summit and Conference (APSIPA), pp. 1–5. IEEE (2014)
7. Chen, H., Zhao, C., Sun, M.T., et al.: Adaptive intra-refresh for low-delay error-resilient video coding. J. Vis. Commun. Image Represent. **31**, 294–304 (2015)
8. Tran, T.D., Liu, L.K., Westerink, P.H.: Low-delay MPEG-2 video coding. In: Visual Communications and Image Processing'98, vol. 3309, pp. 510–517. International Society for Optics and Photonics (1998)
9. Slice decision Options x265 documentation. http://x265.readthedocs.io/en/default/cli.html#slice-decision-options. Accessed 24 May 2017
10. Schreier, R.M., Rothermel, A.: Motion adaptive intra refresh for the H.264 video coding standard. IEEE Trans. Consum. Electron. **52**(1), 249–253 (2006)
11. Krause, E., Paik, W.H., Liu, V.C., et al.: Method and apparatus for refreshing motion compensated sequential video images. U.S. Patent 5,057,916, 15 October 1991
12. Rosewarne, C., Bross, B., Naccari, M., Sharman, K., Sullivan, G.: High Efficiency Video Coding (HEVC) Test Model 16 (HM 16) Improved Encoder Description Update 7. Document JCTVC-Y1002, Chengdu, CN, 14–21 October 2016
13. Moiron, S., Ali, I., Ghanbari, M., et al.: Limitations of multiple reference frames with cyclic intra-refresh line for H.264/AVC. Electron. Lett. **47**(2), 103–104 (2011)

Deep Integer-Position Samples Refinement for Motion Compensation of Video Coding

Sifeng Xia, Yueyu Hu, and Jiaying Liu[✉]

Institute of Computer Science and Technology, Peking University, Beijing, China
liujiaying@pku.edu.cn

Abstract. Motion compensation is a critical technology in video coding for temporal redundancy removal. In the motion compensation process, previously coded frames are utilized as the reference for generating the prediction of the blocks which are to be coded. However, despite being filtered after reconstruction, there are still some artifacts in the reference, which may affect the motion compensation performance. In this paper, we propose a deep convolutional neural network (CNN) based integer-position samples refinement method to additionally enhance the references before the motion compensation process. A lightweight convolutional neural network is designed to learn to remove the artifacts of the integer-position samples and facilitate motion compensation. 8 convolutional layers with 10 channels are designed to obtain a wider receptive field with fewer parameters for feature extraction. The residual learning technique is also utilized in the feature extraction process for accelerating the convergency of the network. Experimental results have demonstrated the efficiency of our CNN-based integer-position samples refinement method.

Keywords: Integer-position samples refinement ·
Convolutional neural network · Motion compensation · Video coding

1 Introduction

Temporal redundancy removal is a significant component of video coding, which can be accomplished by motion compensation. Specifically, during the inter prediction, one or more coded frames are used as the references for compressing the current frame. For each block which is to be coded, reference blocks are searched for it from the references. With the reference block, only the motion vector and residual between the two blocks need to be coded, which is more efficient than encoding the original block and many bits can be saved.

Considering the spatial sampling of digital video, the adjacent pixels in a video frame are not continuous. Reference blocks at integer positions may have sub-pixel motion shifts to the current block. For the purpose of better prediction,

© Springer Nature Singapore Pte Ltd. 2019
G. Zhai et al. (Eds.): IFTC 2018, CCIS 1009, pp. 391–400, 2019.
https://doi.org/10.1007/978-981-13-8138-6_33

many video coding standards like MPEG-4/H.264 AVC [11] and the state-of-the-art High Efficiency Video Coding (HEVC) [10] additionally utilize fractional interpolation technique to generate sub-pixel position reference samples from the integer-position sample. A better reference sample will be selected among the integer-position sample and the sub-pixel position samples.

Unluckily, despite being filtered after reconstruction, heavy compression artifacts still exist in the integer-position samples. Since the reference samples are all derived from the integer-position samples, the underlying artifacts in the integer-position samples will degrade the derived samples, which will finally affect the motion compensation performance. So it's meaningful to refine the integer-position samples before motion compensation to acquire a better coding performance.

Recently, many deep learning based methods have been proposed for image processing problems, *e.g.* image interpolation [14], inpainting [8], and super-resolution [1]. These works have demonstrated the potential of deep learning technology and generated impressive results. In [14], different from traditional interpolation methods [6,9] which utilize limited information of similarities in the image for interpolation, Yang *et al.* utilized a variational learning network to effectively exploit the structural similarities among images for image interpolation. Pathak *et al.* [8] designed a context encoder to inpaint an arbitrary image region according to its surroundings. Dong *et al.* proposed a super-resolution method called SRCNN [1], which is the first to use CNN for the image super-resolution problem and has obtained significant performance gain over traditional super-resolution methods.

Considering the great performance brought by the deep learning based methods in image processing problems and the high implementation efficiency of deep learning based methods brought by GPU acceleration, it is a new opportunity to utilize the deep learning technology for video coding. Jia *et al.* [3] explored to introduce CNN in loop filter to further enhance the coded frames. Yan *et al.* [13] first proposed a CNN-based interpolation filter to replace the half-pixel interpolation part of HEVC. Xia *et al.* [12] proposed a group variational transformation neural network to generate sub-pixel position samples of different positions with one network.

Inspired by the great success brought by the deep learning technologies for video coding, in this paper, we adopt the deep learning technique for the integer-position samples refinement. An integer-position sample refinement network (ISR-Net) is designed to efficiently extract features from the integer-position sample and learn to remove the artifacts in it. We integrate the trained network into HEVC and test it with different configurations. Experimental results have shown the superiority of our ISR-Net in integer-samples refinement which further benefits video coding.

The rest of the paper is organized as follows. Sect. 2 introduces the proposed integer-position sample refinement network. The architecture of the network is first presented. Training and integration details are introduced later. Experimental results are shown in Sect. 3 and concluding remarks are given in Sect. 4.

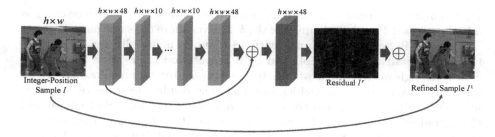

Fig. 1. Framework of the proposed ISR-Net. The network first extracts feature maps from the integer-position sample. Then the residual is inferred from the feature map. The final result of integer-position sample refinement can be obtained by adding the residual to the integer-position sample.

2   Integer-Position Sample Refinement Network for Motion Compensation

In this section, we first introduce the integer-position sample refinement network of our method. Details of the network architecture and the process of deriving refined integer-position samples are illustrated. Then the details of the implementation and training techniques are demonstrated. Moreover, we will introduce the method to integrate the trained model into HEVC and analyze how the refined integer-position sample will benefit the coding performance.

2.1   Architecture of ISR-Net

Given an integer-position sample I, the proposed ISR-Net extracts a feature map from the integer-position sample and then infers a residual map I^r from the feature map. The final refined sample I^t is derived from I and I^r.

Figure 1 shows the architecture of ISR-Net. The integer-position sample I is the input of the network. $h \times w \times c$ represents the size of each convolutional layer, where h and w are the height and the width of the feature map respectively, and c is the channel number of the feature map. The parametric rectified linear units (PReLU) [2] are utilized for nonlinearity between the convolutional layers.

Specifically, we define f_k^{out} to be the output of the k-th convolutional layer. f_k^{out} is obtained by:

$$f_k^{out} = P_k \left(W_k * f_{k-1}^{out} + B_k \right), \tag{1}$$

where f_{k-1}^{out} is the output of the previous layer, W_k is the convolutional filter kernel of the k-th layer and B_k is the bias of the k-th layer. f_0^{out} is the inputted integer-position sample. The function $P_k (\cdot)$ is the PReLU function of the k-th layer:

$$P_k (x) = \begin{cases} x, & x > 0, \\ a_k * x, & x \leq 0. \end{cases} \tag{2}$$

x is the input signal and a_k is the parameter to be learned for the k-th layer. a_k is initially set as 0.25 and all channels of the k-th layer share the same parameter a_k.

In the ISR-Net, a feature map with 48 channels is initially generated from the integer-position sample, followed by 8 convolution layers with 10 channels which are lightweight and cost less to save the learnt parameters. The 10-th layer later derives a 48 channel feature map. The residual learning technique is utilized here for accelerating the convergency of the network. So that we add the output of the 1-st layer to the output of the 10-th layer and then activate the sum with PReLU function to derive a 48 channel feature map. After 10 convolutional layers, the receptive field of each point in the derived feature map is 17×17, which means that a large nearby area in the integer-pixel position sample has been considered for the feature extraction of each pixel.

Table 1. The configurations of each convolutional layer of ISR-Net.

Layer	Kernel size	Output number	Padding
Conv1	3×3	48	1
Conv2_1	1×1	10	0
Conv2_2 conv2_8	3×3	10	1
Conv3	1×1	48	0
Conv4	3×3	1	1

The detailed configuration parameters for each layer of ISR-Net are shown in Table 1. The second column shows the convolutional kernel size of each layer. Number of the feature map of each layer is shown in the third column and the last column is the padding size.

The final refined integer sample I^t can be obtained as:

$$I^t = I + f(I, \Theta), \tag{3}$$

where Θ is the set of learnt parameters and $f(I, \Theta)$ is the mapping function that represents inferring the residual I^r from the inputted integer-position sample I.

2.2   Training ISR-Net

ISR-Net is built for removing the compression artifacts in the integer-position sample I. The compression artifacts are caused by the lossy compression of the video coding tools. So we adopt HEVC coding tools to generate training data with the same compression artifacts.

200 training images and 200 testing images in *BSDS500* [7] at size 481×321 and 321×481 are used for training data generation. The images are previously coded by HM 16.4 under the All-Intra configuration. And then the coded images are used as the input and the original images are used as the label.

In real applications, the integer-sample refinement method is measured by the coding performance. However, the entire coding system is too complex to be integrated into the training process. So we can not train ISR-Net in an end-to-end framework. Alternatively, mean square error is adopted as the loss function in this paper, which is also widely used in many deep based image restoration methods.

Let $F(\cdot)$ represent the learnt network that infers the refined samples from the integer-position samples and Θ denote the set of all the learnt parameters including the convolutional filter kernels, bias and a_k of the PReLU function in each layer. The loss function can be formulated as follows:

$$L(\Theta) = \frac{1}{n} \sum_{i=1}^{n} \| F(x_i, \Theta) - y_i \|^2,\tag{4}$$

where pairs $\{x_i, y_i\}_{i=1}^{n}$ are the generated training pairs of the coded images and the raw images without coding artifacts. n is the total number of the pairs.

2.3   Integration into HEVC

In this subsection, we introduce how we integrate the trained ISR-Net into HEVC. In HEVC inter prediction, a reference picture set will be built for the inter prediction of each P frame or B frame. When the reference frames of the current frame are decided, we previously refine the reference frames before coding the current frame with the trained ISR-Net. The refined frames are cached in the system and will be used in the later inter prediction process.

In HEVC inter prediction, the motion estimation will be first performed for each current block which is to be coded. The block will search the blocks in reference frames for one or two matched candidates. However, there are coding artifacts in the reference frames, which may affect the accuracy of motion estimation. By replacing the reference frame with a refined sample of higher quality, a better searching result can be achieved.

After the motion estimation, fractional interpolation technology is utilized to generate samples at sub-pixel positions from the searched best matched integer-position sample. A final reference block will be selected from the integer-position sample and the generated sub-pixel position samples. With the reference block, only the motion vector and the residual between the reference block and the current block need to be coded. We hold that the reference block generated from the refined integer-position sample will have far fewer artifacts. And it is intuitive that the residual between the current block and the refined reference sample will also be smaller. As a result, more bits can be saved in inter prediction if we adopt the refined integer-position sample for motion compensation.

Table 2. BD-rate reduction of the proposed method compared to HEVC under the LDP configuration.

Class	Sequence	BD-rate		
		Y	U	V
Class B	Kimono	−1.9%	0.8%	1.3%
	BQTerrace	−5.1%	−1.0%	−1.3%
	BasketballDrive	−2.6%	0.2%	0.4%
	ParkScene	−0.2%	−0.5%	−0.7%
	Cactus	−2.9%	0.5%	0.5%
	Average	−2.6%	0.0%	0.0%
Class C	BasketballDrill	−1.9%	−0.2%	0.8%
	BQMall	−3.1%	−0.4%	0.3%
	PartyScene	−1.2%	−0.3%	−0.3%
	RaceHorsesC	−1.7%	0.1%	−0.6%
	Average	−2.0%	−0.2%	0.1%
Class D	BasketballPass	−1.4%	1.1%	0.2%
	BlowingBubbles	−2.6%	−0.2%	−0.6%
	BQSquare	−2.2%	−0.3%	0.7%
	RaceHorses	−2.7%	−0.3%	−0.7%
	Average	−2.2%	0.1%	−0.1%
Class E	FourPeople	1.9%	4.1%	3.9%
	Johnny	−2.1%	2.9%	3.9%
	KristenAndSara	0.9%	4.2%	5.1%
	Average	0.2%	3.7%	4.3%
All sequences	Overall	−1.8%	0.7%	0.8%

3   Experiments

3.1   Experimental Settings

During the training process, the training images are decomposed into 32×32 sub-images with a stride of 16. The ISR-Net is trained on Caffe platform [4] via Adam [5] with standard back-propagation. The learning rate is initially set as a fixed value 0.0001 and dropped after 30,000 iterations by a factor of 10. The batch size is set as 128. Models after 50,000 iterations are used for testing. The network is trained on one Titan X GPU.

The proposed method is tested on HEVC reference software HM 16.4 under the Low-Delay P (LDP) and Random-Access (RA) configurations. BD-rate is used to measure the rate-distortion. The quantization parameter (QP) values are set to be 22, 27, 32 and 37. The integer-position samples of different QPs are all refined by the same model. We only apply this refinement to the luma component.

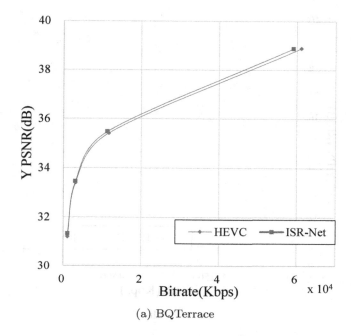

(a) BQTerrace

Fig. 2. Example R-D curve of the sequence *BQTerrace* under LDP configuration.

3.2   Experimental Results and Analysis

Table 2 shows the BD-rate reduction of our method in class B, C, D and E under the LDP configuration. Our method has obtained on average 1.8% BD-rate saving and up to 5.1% BD-rate saving for the test sequence *BQTerrace*. The results demonstrate that the performance of inter prediction is improved with the refined integer-position samples. For better comparison, two example rate-distortion (R-D) curves are shown in Figs. 2 and 3. It can be seen that our method is superior to HEVC under most QPs.

For the purpose of further verification, we additionally test our method under the RA configuration. As shown in Table 3, our method still obtained gain over HEVC. The average BD-rate saving of our method is 1.9% for class C and class D. The results identify that our ISR-Net can benefit both the unidirectional and bi-directional inter prediction.

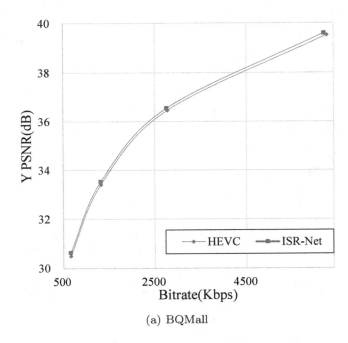

(a) BQMall

Fig. 3. Example R-D curve of the sequence *BQMall* under LDP configuration.

Table 3. BD-rate reduction of the proposed method compared to HEVC under the RA configuration.

Class	Sequence	BD-rate		
		Y	U	V
Class C	BasketballDrill	−2.0%	−0.3%	0.2%
	BQMall	−2.8%	−0.2%	−0.4%
	PartyScene	−0.9%	−0.3%	−0.4%
	RaceHorsesC	−1.5%	−0.7%	0.4%
	Average	−1.8%	−0.3%	−0.1%
Class D	BasketballPass	−1.4%	0.5%	0.2%
	BlowingBubbles	−2.4%	0.0%	0.0%
	BQSquare	−2.4%	−0.6%	0.3%
	RaceHorses	−2.0%	−0.1%	−0.1%
	Average	−2.1%	0.0%	0.1%
All sequences	Overall	−1.9%	−0.2%	0.0%

4   Conclusion and Future Work

In this paper, we proposed an integer-position sample refinement network (ISR-Net) for motion compensation of video coding. The network removes compression artifacts in the coded reference integer-position samples so that the inter coding performance can be improved with the higher quality reference samples. Experimental results show that the coding performance can be further improved with our refinement method. For the future work, a coding unit level RDO is considered to be added to decide whether to use the refined reference block for the inter prediction of a coding unit. Besides, it is meaningful to explore the problem of training data generation. Training data generated by inter coding can be closer to the problem domain, which may further improve the performance of integer-position sample refinement.

References

1. Dong, C., Loy, C.C., He, K., Tang, X.: Learning a deep convolutional network for image super-resolution. In: Fleet, D., Pajdla, T., Schiele, B., Tuytelaars, T. (eds.) ECCV 2014. LNCS, vol. 8692, pp. 184–199. Springer, Cham (2014). https://doi.org/10.1007/978-3-319-10593-2_13
2. He, K., Zhang, X., Ren, S., Sun, J.: Delving deep into rectifiers: surpassing human-level performance on ImageNet classification. In: Proceedings of the IEEE International Conference on Computer Vision, pp. 1026–1034 (2015)
3. Jia, C., Wang, S., Zhang, X., Wang, S., Ma, S.: Spatial-temporal residue network based in-loop filter for video coding. In: Proceedings of the IEEE Visual Communication and Image Processing (2017)
4. Jia, Y., et al.: Caffe: convolutional architecture for fast feature embedding. In: Proceedings of the ACM International Conference on Multimedia, pp. 675–678 (2014)
5. Kingma, D., Ba, J.: Adam: a method for stochastic optimization (2015)
6. Li, M., Liu, J., Ren, J., Guo, Z.: Adaptive general scale interpolation based on weighted autoregressive models. IEEE Trans. Circuits Syst. Video Technol. 25(2), 200–211 (2015)
7. Martin, D., Fowlkes, C., Tal, D., Malik, J.: A database of human segmented natural images and its application to evaluating segmentation algorithms and measuring ecological statistics. In: Proceedings of the IEEE International Conference on Computer Vision, vol. 2, pp. 416–423 (2001)
8. Pathak, D., Krähenbühl, P., Donahue, J., Darrell, T., Efros, A.A.: Context encoders: feature learning by inpainting. In: Proceedings of the IEEE International Conference on Computer Vision and Pattern Recognition, pp. 2536–2544 (2016)
9. Ren, J., Liu, J., Bai, W., Guo, Z.: Similarity modulated block estimation for image interpolation. In: Proceedings of the IEEE International Conference on Image Processing, pp. 1177–1180 (2011)
10. Sullivan, G.J., Ohm, J., Han, W.J., Wiegand, T.: Overview of the high efficiency video coding (HEVC) standard. IEEE Trans. Circuits Syst. Video Technol. 22(12), 1649–1668 (2012)
11. Wiegand, T., Sullivan, G.J., Bjontegaard, G., Luthra, A.: Overview of the H.264/AVC video coding standard. IEEE Trans. Circuits Syst. Video Technol. 13(7), 560–576 (2003)

12. Xia, S., Yang, W., Hu, Y., Ma, S., Liu, J.: A group variational transformation neural network for fractional interpolation of video coding, pp. 127–136 (2018)
13. Yan, N., Liu, D., Li, H., Wu, F.: A convolutional neural network approach for half-pel interpolation in video coding. In: IEEE International Symposium on Circuits and Systems (2017)
14. Yang, W., Liu, J., Xia, S., Guo, Z.: Variation learning guided convolutional network for image interpolation. In: Proceedings of the IEEE International Conference on Image Processing (2017)

An Adaptive Rate-Distortion Optimization Algorithm for HEVC-SCC with High Perceptual Quality

Jiajun Ding[1,2], Jing Chen[1,2(✉)], and Huanqiang Zeng[1,2]

[1] School of Information Science and Engineering,
Huaqiao University, Xiamen 361021, China
1261758319@qq.com, {chenjing8005,zeng0043}@hqu.edu.cn
[2] Xiamen Key Laboratory of Mobile Multimedia Communications,
Xiamen 361021, China

Abstract. Considering the characteristics of screen content video, an adaptive rate-distortion optimization algorithm based on CTU level of HEVC-SCC is proposed in this paper. By extracting the perceptual features from the spatial and temporal domain, a new perceptual feature for screen content video is proposed. In spatial domain, the gradient magnitude information of CU is used; in temporal domain, gradient direction as well as gradient magnitude is considered to utilize the correlation of adjacent frames. Then, an adaptive Lagrange operator is proposed to improve the rate-distortion performance of the screen content video coder. Experimental results show that the proposed algorithm can save 9.76% and 12.21% bitrate in random access mode and low delay mode, respectively, while maintaining the perceptual quality of screen content videos; for the same bitrate consumption, the proposed algorithm can improve 0.0057 and 0.006 perceptual quality in random access mode and low delay mode, respectively.

Keywords: Screen content coding · HEVC · Rate distortion performance · Perceptual quality

1 Introduction

With the widely used of screen content (SC) image/video applications, such as 3-D games, computer desktop sharing, remote video conferencing, remote video education, the study on screen content coding (SCC) becomes a hot topic [1]. An HEVC-SCC extension was proposed by Joint Collaborative Team on Video Coding (JCT-VC) to improve the compression capability for SC videos [2]. For rate control [3], which can effectively improve the bandwidth utilization of coding, the unique characteristics of screen content video must be considered. Those characteristics including large area of uniform plane, less captured noise, duplicate patterns and characters, colors with high saturation but limited types, high image contrast, sharp edges, etc. Therefore, it is worthwhile to study on SCC. Guo et al. [4] proposed a rate control method with a sliding window to allocate the bits and adjust the model parameter of SCC adaptively, which achieves high performance of rate control while maintaining the video quality. In [5], a delay constraint method with a pre-analyzer and more rational bit allocation

© Springer Nature Singapore Pte Ltd. 2019
G. Zhai et al. (Eds.): IFTC 2018, CCIS 1009, pp. 401–409, 2019.
https://doi.org/10.1007/978-981-13-8138-6_34

strategy was proposed to improve the accuracy of rate control and the video quality. In [6], the concept of key frame and non-key frame was defined by inter-frame correlation, and then an effective bit allocation method was established to improve the rate control accuracy and the rate distortion performance.

Although these works have good results, the human vision characteristics of SC video are not considered. Therefore, the video perception information extracted from both spatial and temporal domains is utilized in this paper. In spatial domain, the gradient magnitude is extracted by a simple differential operator to obtain the spatial perception information at the CTU level. In temporal domain, since there are many text areas with sharp edges in SC videos, the subjective distortion measurement method, named gradient similarity (GS) [7], is used. Then, the spatial and temporal perceptual features are merged to achieve new perceptual features. With the new measurement of this perceptual feature, an adaptive Lagrange operator is proposed to do the rate-distortion optimization, which can adjust the bit allocation reasonably, and guarantees the subjective quality of SC video.

The rest of the paper is organized as follows. Section 2 explains how to extract perceptual features both in spatial and temporal domain. Section 3 presents how to adjust the Lagrange operator adaptively with the extracted perceptual information. Section 4 shows the experimental results and Sect. 5 provides the conclusion.

2   Extraction of Perceptual Features for Screen Content Video

2.1   Feature Extraction in Spatial Domain

According to the human visual system, if the same objective distortion is added to a block with flat texture and a block with complex texture, the distortion of flat area can be easily detected, while the human eyes cannot distinguish the complex area well. This characteristic of human eyes enables to assign less bit rate to the complex blocks of the frame and more bit rate to the flat blocks.

To distinguish the complex and flat area, [7] proposed an edge operator at CTU level to extract the edge information of the image. Authors of [8] and [9] also adopt the idea. The extracted gradient magnitude is used to determine whether the CTU is a complex block or a flat one.

In this paper, the classical differential operator method is used to calculate the reciprocal of the horizontal and vertical directions of the luminance components in the screen contents.

$$G_H = I(x+1, y) - I(x, y) \tag{1}$$

$$G_V = I(x, y+1) - I(x, y) \tag{2}$$

Where, I represents the luminance component.

The gradient magnitude (GM) of a pixel (x, y) in a CTU and the GM of the whole CTU is denoted as follows, respectively.

$$G(x, y) = |G_H| + |G_V| \tag{3}$$

$$GM_{CTU} = \sum_{i=1}^{M} G(x, y) \tag{4}$$

Where, M represents the number of pixels in current CTU. The average magnitude of current frame is calculated as follows:

$$GM_{Pic} = \frac{\sum_{j=1}^{N} GM_{CTU}}{N} \tag{5}$$

Where, N represents the number of all CTUs in the current frame.

After calculating the gradient value of each CTU and the whole frame, the complexity of the current CTU can be judged. The method of determining whether current CTU is a complex block or a flat is defined as:

$$GM_{weight} = \frac{GM_{CTU} + C_1}{GM_{Pic} + C_1} \tag{6}$$

Where, C_1 is set 20 and it is the experimental value, which is used to make GM_{Weight} gently. From formula (6), it can be noticed that the larger the GM_{Weight}, the more complex the current CTU. On the contrary, the CTU belongs to the smooth region.

2.2   Feature Extraction in Temporal Domain

Since there are large amount of correlations between adjacent frames, the information of current CTU can be predicted by the corresponding CTU of the previous frame. For SC image, [7] proposed a subjective distortion measurement method, named Gradient Similarity (GS), which fuses the gradient magnitude and the gradient direction to evaluate the perceptual quality of SC. Considering that there are many text areas in SC video and these areas have sharp edges, the gradient direction can reflect the perception quality of the SC as well as the gradient magnitude.

The gradient direction value is obtained by convolving the gradient magnitude with the convolution kernel (13 * 13) in each direction. The formula is as follows:

$$D(x, y) = Ker \otimes G(x, y) \tag{7}$$

After obtaining 12 gradient directions, the direction with the strongest response is selected as the required gradient direction.

$$D(x,y) = i \times \frac{\pi}{12}, where \ i = \arg\max\{\{D(x,y)\}, i \in \{0\ldots11\}\} \qquad (8)$$

Like in spatial domain, all the processes are based on CTU level, the gradient magnitude and gradient direction of each CTU in the current frame are calculated as follows:

$$G_{CTU} = \frac{\sum\limits_{i=1}^{M} G(x,y)}{M} \qquad (9)$$

$$D_{CTU} = \frac{\sum\limits_{i=1}^{M} D(x,y)}{M} \qquad (10)$$

Where, M represents the number of pixels in a single CTU. Refer to [7], the gradient magnitude and gradient direction values of CTUs extracted above are processed accordingly, then, the gradient magnitude similarity and gradient direction similarity can be obtained as follows:

$$\begin{aligned} MS &= \frac{2 \times G_{r_{CTU}} \times G_{d_{CTU}} + C_M}{G_{r_{CTU}}^2 + G_{d_{CTU}}^2 + C_M} \\ DS &= \frac{2 \times D_{r_{CTU}} \times D_{d_{CTU}} + C_D}{D_{r_{CTU}}^2 + D_{d_{CTU}}^2 + C_D} \end{aligned} \qquad (11)$$

Where MS represents the gradient magnitude similarity, DS represents the gradient direction similarity; $G_{r_{CTU}}$ and $G_{d_{CTU}}$ represent gradient magnitude of original CTU and distorted CTU, respectively; and $D_{r_{CTU}}$ and $D_{d_{CTU}}$ represent gradient direction value of original CTU and distorted CTU, respectively; C_M and C_D are two constant values.

To represent the similarity of SC better, MS and DS are briefly fused as follows:

$$GS = MS^\alpha \cdot DS^\beta \qquad (12)$$

Where α and β are two values that represent the importance of gradient magnitude and gradient direction. If $\alpha = 0$, then only the gradient direction is used as the perception information, and if $\beta = 0$, then only the gradient magnitude is used as the perception information. Here, the assumption is that the information of gradient direction and gradient magnitude is equally important.

To better reflect the subjective quality of the current CTU, GS_{Weight} is defined by the ratio of the GS of current CTU to the GS of current frame, denote as:

$$GS_{Weight} = \frac{GS_{CTU} + C_2}{GS_{Pic} + C_2} \qquad (13)$$

Where, GS_{Pic} represents the average GS of current frame, denote as:

$$GS_{Pic} = \frac{\sum_{N} GS_{CTU}}{N} \tag{14}$$

Let C_2 is 0.0001, which is to prevent the denominator from being 0. It is clear that the larger the GS_{Weight}, the better the subjective quality of the CTU. On the contrary, the smaller the GS_{Weight}, the worse the subjective quality of the CTU.

3 Rate-Distortion Optimization with a Perceptual Adaptive Lagrange Operator

According to the perceptual information obtained in Sect. 2, It can be seen that the larger the perceptual feature GM_{Weight} in the spatial domain, the more complex the texture of the current CTU; and the larger the perceptual feature GS_{Weight} in the temporal domain, the better the subjective quality of the current CTU. For current CTUs with complex texture and better subjective quality, less bits allocation is reasonable. For current CTUs with flat texture and worse subjective quality should be allocated more bits. Therefore, in this paper, the perceptual features of spatial and temporal domain are combined. The new perceptual feature is defined as follows:

$$ST = GM_{weight^\delta} \cdot GS_{weight^\mu} \tag{15}$$

Where δ and μ represent the importance of spatial information and temporal information, respectively. When the assumption is that they are equally important, then, δ and μ are set to 1. The above information shows that the larger the ST value, the more complex the texture and the better the subjective quality of the current CTU, and less bits should be allocated to these CTUs when coding.

According to the knowledge of rate-distortion optimization in the coding process, the Lagrange operator is adjusted adaptively by the perceptual features, so that each CTU can allocate bit rate resources reasonably, which can improve the performance of rate-distortion optimization. The rate-distortion optimization model with perceptual features is defined as follows:

$$J_{RD} = D + R \times \lambda_{ST} \tag{16}$$

In addition, λ_{ST} is the new Lagrange operator which has added the perceptual features and defined as follows:

$$\lambda_{ST} = (a \times ST + b) \times \lambda_{old} \tag{17}$$

Where a and b are the experimental values, which are set to 1.5 and 0.1, respectively. And λ_{old} is the original Lagrange operator.

4 Experimental Results

The experiment is under the platform of HM-16.9+SCM-8.0. The video test sequences are recommended by HEVC-SCC common test condition [10]. All the video sequences are in YUV 4:2:0 formats. There are two test configurations, random access and low delay. Four different QP values (22, 27, 32, 37) are used for testing.

The proposed algorithm is compared with the original HEVC-SCC standard algorithm. Tables 1 and 2 show the experimental data of the two algorithms when PSNR and GS are used as quality evaluation methods, which represent the rate distortion performance in random mode and low delay mode. The BDGS in the tables represents the compared perceptual quality value under the same bitrate. It can be seen from Table 1, in random access mode, the bit rate consumption can achieve 9.76% saving under the same GS; the perceptual quality can be improved 0.0057 GS under the same bit rate consumption. As can be seen from Table 2, in low delay mode, the bit rate consumption can be reduced 12.21% under the same GS; and the perceptual quality can be improved 0.006GS under the same bit rate consumption.

Table 1. Comparison of perceptual rate distortion performance under Random access mode

Video sequences	Resolution	Random access			
		BDBR (%)	BDPSNR	BDBR (%)	BDGS
ChinaSpeed	1024x768	1.54	−0.1341	−8.63	0.009
web_browsing	1280x720	−0.41	0.0636	−20.78	−0.0003
SlideShow	1280x720	4.08	−0.1027	−3.75	0.0026
Map	1280x720	−0.4482	0.0758	−7.29	0.0017
robot	1280x720	1.39	−0.0809	−8.03	0.0037
flyingGraphics	1920x1080	−0.0612	−0.0442	−10.61	0.0094
MissionControlClip3	1920x1080	2.5994	−0.3454	−6.63	0.0132
Basketball_Screen	2560x1440	−0.067	0.0243	−12.32	0.006
Average		1.08	−0.068	−9.76	0.0057

Table 2. Comparison of perceptual rate distortion performance under Low delay mode

Video sequences	Resolution	Low delay			
		BDBR (%)	BDPSNR	BDBR (%)	BDGS
ChinaSpeed	1024x768	1.38	−0.1171	−8.34	0.013
web_browsing	1280x720	−2.94	0.4792	−1.94	0.001
SlideShow	1280x720	1.07	−0.0952	−8.25	0.0109
Map	1280x720	−0.97	0.1059	−17.74	0.0024
robot	1280x720	2.51	−0.1147	−7.33	0.0044
flyingGraphics	1920x1080	−0.35	0.0828	−17.31	0.0065
MissionControlClip3	1920x1080	2.97	−0.5299	−4	0.0035
Basketball_Screen	2560x1440	0.32	0.3321	−32.77	0.0063
Average		0.5	0.0179	−12.21	0.006

As Figs. 1 and 2 shown, the perceptual quality of two different test sequences reconstructed by the proposed algorithm has no difference with the one which reconstructed by the original HEVC-SCC standard. There are a lot of bits saving while achieves almost the same SCC perceptual quality.

Figure 3 shows the rate-distortion performance curves of HEVC-SCC and the proposed one in diverse mode, which represents the superiority of the proposed algorithm visually.

(a) Original, GS=0.9452, bits=209168   (b) Proposed, GS=0.9455, bits=191896

Fig. 1. Reconstructed frame results (sequence: SlideShow, 29th frame, QP = 27, Random access)

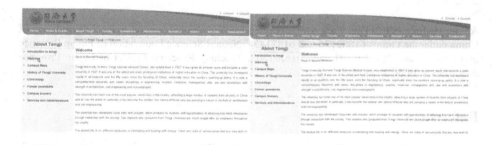

(a) Original, GS=0.9997, bits=547368   (b) Proposed, GS=0.9987, bits=532112

Fig. 2. Reconstructed frame results (sequence: WebBrowsing, 9th frame, QP = 22, Low delay)

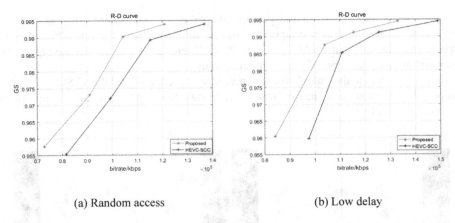

(a) Random access   (b) Low delay

Fig. 3. Rate-distortion curves of compared results (sequence: flyingGraphics)

5 Conclusions

An adaptive rate-distortion optimization algorithm for screen content video is proposed in this paper. With spatial gradient feature and temporal correlation of adjacent frames, an adaptive Lagrange operator is defined to do the rate-distortion optimization for SC video. Experimental results show that the proposed algorithm is superior to the HEVC-SCC standard.

Acknowledgements. This work was supported by the National Natural Science Foundation of China under the Grants 61802136 and 61871434, Natural Science Foundation of Fujian Province under the Grants 2017J05103 and 2016J01308, Teaching Research Project of Fujian Province under Grant FBJG20180038.

References

1. Joshi, R., Xu, J.: High Efficiency Video Coding (HEVC) Screen Content Coding: Draft 2. JCTVC-S1005, Sapporo, JP, July 2014
2. (2018). http://www.hevc.info/scc
3. Li, B.: Rate control by R-lambda model for HEVC. In: Joint Collaborative Team on Video Coding (JCT-VC) of ITU-T 1/SC 29/WG 11, 11th Meeting, Shanghai, CN, October 2012
4. Guo, Y., Li, B., Sun, S., Xu, J.: Rate control for screen content coding in HEVC. In: IEEE International Symposium on Circuits and Systems (ISCAS), pp. 1118–1121 (2015)
5. Xiao, J., Li, B., Sun, S., Xu, J.: Rate control with delay constraint for screen content coding. In: IEEE International Conference on Image Processing (ICIP), pp. 10–13 (2017)
6. Wang, C., Li, J., Wang, S., Ma, S., Gao, W.: A frame level rate control algorithm for screen content coding. In: IEEE International Symposium on Circuits and Systems (ISCAS), pp. 1–4 (2018)
7. Ni, Z., Ma, L., Zeng, H., Cai, C., Ma, K.: Gradient direction for screen content image quality assessment. IEEE Signal Process. Lett. (SPL) **23**(10), 1394–1398 (2016)

8. Xue, W., Zhang, L., Mou, X.: Gradient magnitude similarity deviation: a highly efficient perceptual image quality index. IEEE Trans. Image Process. (TIP) **23**(2), 684–695 (2014)
9. Tang, C., Chen, C., Yu, Y.: Visual sensitivity guided bit allocation for video coding. IEEE Trans. Multimed. **8**(1), 11–18 (2006)
10. Yu, H., Cohen, R., Rapaka, K., Xu, J.: Common conditions for screen content coding tests. In: JCTVC-Q1015, Valencia, ES, April 2014

Video Surveillance

Teaching Assistant and Class Attendance Analysis Using Surveillance Camera

Xiaofei Peng, Zhijun Fang$^{(\boxtimes)}$, and Yongbin Gao

Department of Electrical and Electronic Engineering,
Shanghai University of Engineering Science, Shanghai 201620, China
zjfang@foxmail.com

Abstract. In order to reduce the time spent on class attendance in colleges and universities, an auxiliary sign-in technology based on surveillance cameras was investigated and designed. This paper proposes to use deep learning algorithm to detect and count current number of students and calculate the class attendance rate. Due to the insufficient classroom illumination, densely occluded faces and the blurred image, the system first performs light compensation on the input image, and uses the InceptionV1 convolutional network to generate multiple region proposal for the specific location of the faces, the Long Short-Term Memory is further used to resolve the region proposal to obtain a face frame with maximum confidence. Finally the class attendance statistic is calculated by counting the number of real face frames. Experimental results show that the proposed method significantly improves the detection speed, reducing the computational time from 119 ms to 50 ms per frame on the gtx1060, meanwhile, the detection accuracy is high and robust, which meets the requirements of real-time class attendance detection.

Keywords: Auxiliary sign-in · Illumination compensation · Human face · Real-time

1 Introduction

Along with the popularity of computer aided instruction and the consideration of campus security, almost every classroom in college or university has surveillance camera equiped. However, most surveillance cameras are only used to record and replay, the usages of the surveillance system are not fully excavated. In this paper, we will show how to exploit the classroom video and promote the efficiency of class. We propose an automatic class sing-in system which can calculate the class attendance rate by detecting human heads in classroom video. Before class, the algorithm will analyze the camera records and then the real-time student number will shown on teacher's platform. By means of the system, especially for large classes, teachers can save much time from sign-in and improve the class attendance.

In most cases, classroom surveillance cameras are installed in the front corner of the classroom. The top-down angle and distance of the camera may cause

© Springer Nature Singapore Pte Ltd. 2019
G. Zhai et al. (Eds.): IFTC 2018, CCIS 1009, pp. 413–422, 2019.
https://doi.org/10.1007/978-981-13-8138-6_35

perspective projection, so the objects in camera view may be tiny, crowded and overlapping. Moreover, the indoor brightness is not uniform while the seats far away from the window will have low illumination than those close to. The human heads and faces in dark area are vague and blended with background, increasing the detection difficulty and detection errors. At present, there are many kinds of algorithms to detect head and face, such as background elimination method, inter-frame difference method, clustering, statistical method. However, adaptions are needed considering the low illumination area in indoor images. In this paper, we designs a face detection algorithm based on deep neural network, which fuses appearance information of upper body, etc., hair, as auxiliary detection clues. The proposed detection algorithm achieves processing speed at 50 ms per frame with high accuracy.

In [1], face detection was first conducted to locate human bodies and then Kalman filter was used to estimate the human trajectory. Finally each trajectory was separated according to the trajectory classification. In [2], the person's height in the image was utilized as a scale reference to calculate the pivot relationship and then image features was optimized by smile operation. Finally, the number of human was counted by a Support Vector Regression (SVR) regression model. Original image was divided into several regions with the same perspective range and blocks were sampled in each region by different scales. Then the number in each block was estimated by an order-based spatial pyramid pooling network [3]. The SURF points of moving object were classified and the density map of people was generated [4]. [5] matched image regions based on the optical flow and HOG and color histogram were extracted. [6] embedded the prior knowledge into CNN networks and made the network robust to get a fine estimate. [7] proposed a new FCN network to make a maximum confidence decision on the predicted heat map. [8] adopted the greedy way in booting learning to generate density map. A new classifier (strong classifier) was trained to minimize the training error of a previous classifier (weak classifier), Then a normalized 2D Gaussian kernel generated the density data of the crowd of people in the current image based on the classifier prediction.

Although several methods have good detection results, the images are in good quality or the object is in proper size. As mentioned above, the detection of heads and faces in classroom environment is a relatively challenge task for current methods since the objects are tiny and with low quality. Other methods resort to CNN network to extract good features, but they estimate the density map of crowded people and can not obtain the accurate number of people. In this paper, we combines CNN+LSTM [9] network to effectively solve the problem of dense face and occlusion, taking into account both real-time performance and accuracy.

2 Attendance Rate Calculation

2.1 Illumination Compensation

Due to the seats distribution in classroom, the seats close to the window will have sufficient illumination while those away from the window have low illumination. The low illumination area will affect the robustness of human head detection. In order to alleviate the impact of non-uniform light distribution, the equalizeHist algorithm is utilized to compensate the light of the image. The compensation result is shown in Fig. 1.

Fig. 1. Light compensation result: left (before); right (after)

The equalizeHist algorithm is mainly to enhance the local image by using histogram equalization, and enhance the contrast by stretching the range of pixel intensity distribution. The specific process is to count the number of pixels in each intensity pixel, and then map the original pixel intensity distribution to another distribution. The mapping method is as shown in the following formula:

$$S_k = \sum_{k}^{j=0} n_j/n_k, \quad k = 0, 1, 2...L - 1 \tag{1}$$

Where n is the sum of the pixels in the image, n_j is the number of current gray scale pixels, and L is the total number of possible gray scale levels in the image.

2.2 Head Detection Process and Parameter Settings

The first step of face detection is to extract features, and the feature selection has a great influence on the prediction of face candidates. Traditional face detection is based on Haar [10] feature training using Adaboost [11] learning algorithm to get a cascade of boosted classifiers, and then the classifier is used to detect targets. In addition, Qian [12] achieved good results by applying human face color feature detection to face detection. Because the application scenario of this article is more complicated, the illumination distribution of the image is not uniform, and the faces are dense. This will affect the neural network to extract feature information. It can be proved in [13] that the deeper network structure is more effective for feature extraction. The network structure in this paper is shown in Fig. 2.

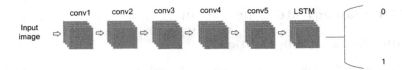

Fig. 2. Network structure

However, during the detection process, the CNN network will output multiple face candidate frames with different confidence levels. Common face detection algorithms will use NMS non-maximal suppression [13] to traverse all candidate boxes and score all candidate boxes. And delete the candidate box larger than the set IOU threshold. Repeat the above steps to finally save the face frame with the highest score. However, due to the phenomenon of occlusion in the classroom, when the two faces overlap, the CNN network will predict the two face frames separately, but the NMS non-maximal suppression will remove the occlusion face candidate frame, resulting in occluded faces Was detected. This paper uses the LSTM long and short-term memory network to jointly predict the candidate CNN output candidate frame, which can effectively solve the face occlusion phenomenon. This article's approach is to use the improved googleNet network feature extraction, and reduce the calculation on the premise of ensuring accuracy, so as to achieve better real-time effect. Specific network parameters are set as shown in Fig. 3.

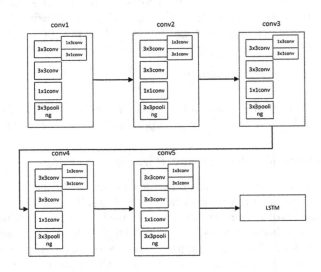

Fig. 3. Network flowchart and parameter settings

In order to achieve better real-time performance, network in this paper is modified based on the GoogleNet network framework, the network modification shown in Fig. 3. Each convolution block of the original network consists of a 5×5 convolutional layer, a 3×3 convolutional layer, a 1×1 convolutional layer, and a 1×1 pooling layer, and the simplified 5×5 convolutional layer is composed of a 3×3 convolutional layer superimposed on 1×3 layers and 3×1 layers. The benefit of this approach is that it reduces the amount of calculation. In principle, a 5×5 convolution equals two 3×3 convolutional sizes, but on the premise of channels, the 5×5 convolution kernel has a parameter size of $5 \times 5 = 25$, and the two 3×3 convolution kernels have a parameter size of $2 \times 3 \times 3 = 18$. As shown in Fig. 2, a 3×3 convolution kernel is modified to a 1×3 and a 3×1 convolution kernel with a parameter size of $3 \times 3 + 1 \times 3 + 1 \times 3 = 15$. Compare the size of the parameter in the convolution block of the original network with the parameter size $25 > 15$ after modification. The network structure of this paper is composed of five basically identical convolution blocks, from which it can be calculated that the modified parameter quantity is $(15/25)^5$ times as the original network.

The CNN encodes the image into a high dimensional descriptor, which is then represented as a set of bounding boxes. As a core mechanism network that can control the prediction variable length output, LSTM is controlled by decoding the 1024-dimensional feature descriptor outputted by CNN. This 1024-dimensional feature descriptor has rich regional information and position information of the object. During each step of the prediction process, the LSTM will output a new bounding box and corresponding confidence, which will be sorted in descending order of confidence. When the LSTM cannot predict another frame in a region with high confidence, the search is stopped. Each prediction of LSTM will output a bounding box bbox {x_min, y_min, w, h} and a confidence score for each bounding box.

3   Experiments and Experimental Results

3.1   Experimental Platform

The experiment is based on Ubuntu 14.04, a 64-bit operating system. The training platform is python2 and caffe. The hardware configuration is gtx1060 6G.

3.2   Data Used for Training

In order to make the network more robust, the training data is acquired using a separate frame and facial images of different angles are acquired, and annotated tools are used for labeling. And get pictures in different scenes to enhance its practicality, the picture resolution is 640 pixel * 480 pixel. Some end-to-end scene training pictures are shown in Fig. 4.

In order to obtain more training data, this task is combined with end-to-end training. Therefore, the amount of data is increased by changing the degree of blur of the image through scaling. In addition, this paper also increases the amount of data by increasing the noise through random noise perturbation.

Fig. 4. Training examples

The performance of loss and accuracy in the training process is very important for the judgment of the quality of the network. The curve of loss and accuracy changes as shown in Fig. 5.

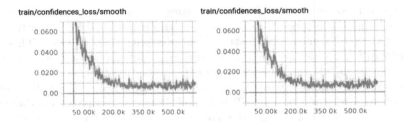

Fig. 5. Training parameter diagram

In order to obtain a better loss performance, this paper trains pre-train the data set of this paper with the pre-training model. In the pre-training phase, the parameters are fine-tuned and the resolution of the network is improved, so that the network can better adapt to different scales of detection tasks under different scenarios. As can be seen from the figure, the numerical value of the loss numerical nuclear accuracy has stabilized at approximately 200K cycles.

During the training process, each candidate box of the network will calculate its own confidence. The formula is:

$$P(O_{obj}) * R_{pred}^{truth} \tag{2}$$

$P(O_{obj})$ in the formula shows whether there is a target in the network, R_{pred}^{truth} is the overlap rate between the prediction candidate box and the real target box. If the overlap rate between the manually labeled box and the network predicted candidate box is greater than the set threshold, $P(O_{obj}) = 1$, otherwise $P(O_{obj}) = 0$.

The confidence level of each candidate box is multiplied with the category information of the network, and a comprehensive score corresponding to each candidate box will be obtained. The formula is:

$$P(C_i|O_{obj}) * P(O_{obj})P * R_{pred}^{truth} = P(C_i) * R_{pred}^{truth} \tag{3}$$

In the formula, $P(C_i\text{—}O_{obj})$ is the category probability score predicted by each network, when i $=0$, which is a non-target, and i $=1$ is a target.

After each candidate box's comprehensive score is obtained, a threshold is set to filter out candidate boxes with low scores, and non-maximal suppression of NMS is performed, that is, a maximum value is taken among several groups of the comprehensive scores that are greater than the threshold, and finally each candidate box is determined by combining with LSTM. The candidate box position is calculated as follows:

$$(i, P_{pred}) = \max_{j, p_{pred}} [P(C_i) * R_{pred}^{truth}], P(C_i) * R_{pred}^{truth} \geq T_{threshold} \qquad (4)$$

In the formula, P_{pred} is the position of target candidate frame, i is 0 or 1, $T_{threshold}$ is a candidate threshold.

In the process of maximizing operation, joint prediction of the candidate frames needs to be performed through LSTM, so that it is possible to prevent accidental deletion of real candidates that are relatively close to each other in the NMS process.

3.3   Experimental Results and Analysis

Loss and accuracy performance during model testing is very important for the pros and cons of the model. The curve changes of the loss and accuracy methods in this paper are shown in Fig. 6.

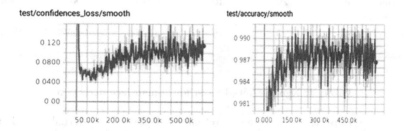

Fig. 6. Testing parameter diagram

During the test, it can be seen that when the number of trainings is in the interval of 0–50k times, the loss value of the test drops sharply and the accuracy rate rises sharply. Obviously, this is a good model performance process. When the number of model training reaches 200k, the loss and accuracy of the model test tend to be stable and achieve a better performance.

It can be seen from Table 1 that the googleNet+LSTM network is used for detection, and the error of the complex environment scene of the classroom reaches -15.2%, and the error of the scene two reaches -40%. It can be seen from Tables 2 and 3 that SSD [14] and YOLOv2 [15] have poor head detection for crowded scenes in the classroom. The main reason is that SSD and YOLOv2

Table 1. GoogleNet+LSTM for human face detection

	Expected number	Detected number	Actual number	Detected attendance	Actual attendance	Error
Scene one examination	46	39	46	84.78%	100%	15.2%
Scene two class	80	46	78	57.5%	97.5%	−40%

Table 2. SSD for human face detection

	Expected number	Detected number	Actual number	Detected attendance	Actual attendance	Error
Scene one examination	46	32	46	69.6%	100%	−30.4%
Scene two class	80	29	78	36.25%	97.5%	−61.3%

Table 3. YOLOv2 for human face detection

	Expected number	Detected number	Actual number	Detected attendance	Actual attendance	Error
Scene one examination	46	29	46	63%	100%	−37%
Scene two class	80	25	78	31.25%	97.5%	−66.3%

Table 4. XgoogleNet+LSTM for human face detection

	Expected number	Detected number	Actual number	Detected attendance	Actual attendance	Error
Scene one examination	46	46	46	100%	100%	0%
Scene two class	80	75	78	78%	97.5%	−3.75%

Table 5. Performance comparison under different network structures

Method	Size of the picture	Time-consuming	Graphics model
GoogleNet+LSTM	640 × 480	119	GTX1060
XgoogleNet+LSTM	640 × 480	50	GTX1060

have small effects on small targets and poor target detection. As can be seen from Table 4, using the XgoogleNet+LSTM network for detection, the scene 1 error reaches 0%, and the scene 2 error reaches −3.75%. It can be seen that the XgoogleNet+lstm network is better represented by the detection accuracy.

It can be seen from Table 5 that the detection speed of the original network googleNet+lstm is about 119 ms per frame, which is difficult to achieve in real time. SSD and YOLOv2 are particularly good in real-time, but the detection accuracy is not suitable for small scenes and dense scenes in classrooms. However, the modified XgoogleNet+LSTM network performs well, the detection speed reaches 50 ms per frame and the detection effect is very good, which can meet the requirements of real-time and high accuracy of the technology.

This paper calculates the number of predicted real candidate boxes, outputs the number of people currently attending the class, and obtains the current class rate by inputting assumptions. The final specific detection results are shown in Fig. 7.

Fig. 7. Result diagram

4 Summary

This paper proposes a method to assist in teaching sign-in by searching the face of the entire picture for counting and obtaining the number of people currently attending class. Using the modified GoogleNet neural network to make a preliminary prediction of the current head count, and then use the LSTM network to predict the candidate faces frame candidates for joint prediction regression, and ultimately obtain accurate numbers. And by presetting the number of people who should arrive at the time, the current number of attendees and the attendance rate will be returned to the screen. The experiment proves that the system has a very high counting accuracy, and the detection speed is increased from 119 ms per frame to 50 ms per frame, which can meet the real-time and high accuracy requirements of the secondary sign-in.

References

1. Qi, Y., Liu, F., Jiao, L.: Adaptive reduction immune algorithm for solving large-scale tsp problems. J. Softw. **19**(6), 1265–1273 (2008)
2. Wu, H.: University classroom occupancy statistics system based on surveillance video. Ph.D. dissertation, Shenyang University of Technology (2015)
3. Shi, Z., Ye, Y., Wu, Y.: Crowd counting method based on ordered spatial pyramid pooling network. Acta Automatica Sinica **42**(6), 866–874 (2016)
4. Liang, R., Liu, X., Ma, X.: High-density population counting method based on surf. J. Comput.-Aided Des. Comput. Graph. **24**(12), 1568–1575 (2012)
5. Jingwei, G.: Research and implementation of Tongji bridge high density population counting method. Ph.D. dissertation, Sun Yat-sen University (2013)
6. Zhao, M., Zhang, J., Porikli, F., Zhang, C., Zhang, W.: Learning a perspective-embedded deconvolution network for crowd counting. In: IEEE International Conference on Multimedia and Expo, pp. 403–408 (2017)
7. Marsden, M., Mcguinness, K., Little, S., O'Connor, N.E.: Fully convolutional crowd counting on highly congested scenes, pp. 27–33 (2017)
8. Walach, E., Wolf, L.: Learning to count with CNN boosting. In: Leibe, B., Matas, J., Sebe, N., Welling, M. (eds.) ECCV 2016. LNCS, vol. 9906, pp. 660–676. Springer, Cham (2016). https://doi.org/10.1007/978-3-319-46475-6_41
9. Stewart, R., Andriluka, M., Ng, A.Y.: End-to-end people detection in crowded scenes, pp. 2325–2333 (2015)
10. Lienhart, R., Maydt, J.: An extended set of haar-like features for rapid object detection. In: International Conference on Image Processing, Proceedings, vol. 1, pp. I-900–I-903 (2002)
11. Freund, Y., Schapire, R.E.: Experiments with a new boosting algorithm. In: Thirteenth International Conference on International Conference on Machine Learning, pp. 148–156 (1996)
12. Qian, H., Chen, G., Shen, R.: People counting system based on face detection. Comput. Eng. **38**(13), 188–191 (2012)
13. Neubeck, A., Gool, L.V.: Efficient non-maximum suppression. In: International Conference on Pattern Recognition, pp. 850–855 (2006)
14. Liu, W., et al.: SSD: single shot multibox detector. In: Leibe, B., Matas, J., Sebe, N., Welling, M. (eds.) ECCV 2016. LNCS, vol. 9905, pp. 21–37. Springer, Cham (2016). https://doi.org/10.1007/978-3-319-46448-0_2
15. Redmon, J., Farhadi, A.: Yolo9000: better, faster, stronger. In: IEEE Conference on Computer Vision and Pattern Recognition, pp. 6517–6525 (2017)

Dynamic Attribute Package: Crowd Behavior Recognition in Complex Scene

Tianqi Shi[1,2], Hua Yang[1,2(✉)], Lin Chen[1,2], and Ji Zhu[1,2]

[1] Institution of Image Communication and Network Engineering,
Shanghai Jiao Tong University, Shanghai 200240, China
{shitianqi1994,hyang,SJChenLin}@sjtu.edu.cn
jizhu1023@gmail.com
[2] National Engineering Laboratory for Public Security Risk Perception
and Control by Big Data (PSRPC), Beijing, China

Abstract. Crowd behavior recognition under complex surveillance scenarios is a fundamental and important problem in crowd management application. In this paper, a comprehensive and specific overall-level dynamic attribute package is proposed by considering local pattern-related motion and group-level motion together to represent crowd movement. Curl and divergence map of normalized average motion vector field act as local pattern-related motion, which represents physical movement tendency of each particle. Group-level motion explores crowd interaction of inter-/intra-group, which focus on depicting crowd's social dynamic property. The complementary characteristic of two motion representation in different level is analyzed and verified. Single frames in video clips and the corresponding dynamic attribute packages are sent into two-branch structured ConvNet, which can extract more discriminative spatial-temporal feature for behavior recognition. Experiment results conducted on CUHK dataset show that the proposed crowd behavior recognition framework outperforms than existing approaches and obtains the state-of-art performance.

Keywords: Crowd behavior recognition · Complex scene ·
Dynamic attribute package · Movement description ·
Convolutional neural network

1 Introduction

With the automatic video surveillance gaining increasing attention, recognizing crowd behavior under extremely complex scenes becomes important and fundamental. It can be applied in citizen safety, security, administration and be the preparatory step for other more meaningful and socially-significant crowd applications, such as crowd planning and anomaly detection.

Crowd behavior is the movement state caused by groups and individuals' various purposes and emotions. In reality, crowd movement always happens in

© Springer Nature Singapore Pte Ltd. 2019
G. Zhai et al. (Eds.): IFTC 2018, CCIS 1009, pp. 423–432, 2019.
https://doi.org/10.1007/978-981-13-8138-6_36

complex scenes with large varieties of densities, locations, points of cameras views, shooting angles, etc, thus information provided by visual characteristics is limited. Accordingly, crowd behavior is the task influenced by social psychology, biological attribute, behavior interaction, etc, rather than a simple video mission. Analyzing crowd's dynamic attributes and giving a comprehensive representation is a key issue. Crowd dynamic can be characterized by physical and social property. Local pattern-related motion derived from the adjacent frames' movement tendency of each particle, represent dynamic physical property. Crowd behavior originates from social interaction between groups and between individuals in one group, thus inter-group and intra-group dynamic should be depicted to represent crowd's dynamic social property.

There now exists many research [1–9] regarding on crowd dynamic from various level. Most of them, such as [10–13], propose video-level feature, which is not suitable for complex scene. [14,15] propose group descriptors, which achieves preferable performance in crowd task, but too little low-level motion information is considered. Many joint-level crowd motion are also utilized. [16,17] propose bilinear CD feature which takes low-level and group-level motion information into consideration, however, PCA and fisher coding used in this algorithm results in loss of information.

To address fore-mentioned problems, in this paper, we unify local pattern-related (curl and divergence deriving from optical flow) and group-level crowd motion together to generate crowd dynamic attribute package which can depict both crowd dynamic physical and social property. From our observation, local pattern-related and group-level motion can complement mutually and represent crowd dynamic more comprehensively. This two crowd motions suitable scenarios are found to be supplementary set according to experiment, thus proves that the power of discriminating crowd behaviors is enhanced. In our paper, A two-branch ConvNet which contains spatial branch and temporal branch is employed for recognition. Deep ConvNet make full use of input information as the input has no compression or coding. For temporal branch, the proposed dynamic attribute package corresponding to each frame are used as input to obtain crowd dynamic feature. Many extensive experiments are performed on the widely utilized CUHK crowd dataset. The experimental results show superior performance of our framework.

The major contributions of this paper can be summarized as three-folders: (1) proposal of the crowd behavior recognition framework, which contains comprehensive crowd dynamic attribute package and the two-branch temporal-spatial ConvNet architecture. (2) proposal of crowd dynamic attribute package, in which pattern-related sub-package (curl and divergence map) depicting crowd motions physical property, while inter- and intra-group level sub-package depicting social property. (3) getting state-of-art result in crowd behavior recognition task.

2   Method

2.1   Overall Framework

As Fig. 1 is shown, the proposed crowd recognition framework mainly includes two portions, i.e, (a) dynamic attribute packaging and (b) network architecture. We first obtain dynamic attribute package from consequent frame sequences. Next, single frame and the corresponding package are sent into two-branch deep ConvNet to extract temporal and spatial feature separately, then fuse into the combined feature for final predicting.

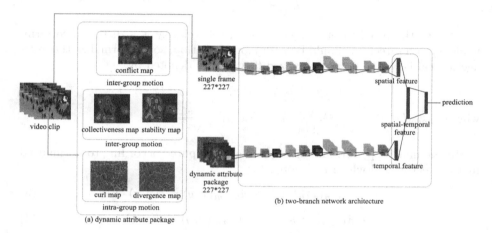

Fig. 1. General structure of our proposed crowd behavior framework. There are two main modules: (a) dynamic attribute packaging, (b) two-branch network architecture, both branch contains multiple layers, including convolution (yellow), maxpooling (blue), normalization (red), fully connected (green). Two fully-connected (green) are employed to fuse the two branches. (Color figure online)

2.2   Crowd Dynamic Attribute Packaging

The dynamic attribute package contains: pattern-related part (curl, divergence map) and group-level part (collectiveness, stability and conflict map) as shown in Fig. 1(a). They describe crowd behavior in different and complement perspectives. For video clip with size m $\times n \times l$ ($m \times n$ size of single frame and totally l frames), the corresponding dynamic package is in size of $m \times n \times 5$ ($m \times n$ size of curl, divergence, collectiveness, stability and conflict map respectively) and $(l - s)$ total number, where s represents the length of frame sequences which can generate one dynamic package. Group-level dynamic sub-package is in size of $m \times n \times 3$, while local pattern-related dynamic sub-package is in size of $m \times n \times 2$. Dynamic attribute package is computed by concatenating two sub-packages' channel dimension directly.

Local Pattern-Related Motion. Optical flow has the intrinsic advantage for describing motion vector field for sequential movements. We first use Epicflow algorithm [18] to capture crowd motion for all particles. $M(x,y) = u(x,y) \cdot i + v(x,y) \cdot j$ between two consecutive frames τ and $\tau+1$, where u and v represent velocity component in x and y directions, i and j are the unit vectors parallel to x and y axes respectively. Due to small difference between adjacent frames, which cause severe noises in optical flow, we compute average optical flow in L frames with step of 1, which is denoted by

$$M_{ave}(x,y) = \frac{1}{L} \sum_{k=f}^{f+L} (u_k(x,y) \cdot i + v_k(x,y) \cdot j) \tag{1}$$

Due to the problem of complex scenes, the velocity is a disturbance term, while motion direction should be paid more attention, so we normalize the average optical flow. the final normalized flow can be denoted by:

$$M_{norm}(x,y) = u_{norm}(x,y) \cdot i + v_{norm}(x,y) \cdot j \tag{2}$$

where $u_{norm}(x,y) = \frac{u_{ave}(x,y)}{\sqrt{u_{ave}^2+v_{ave}^2}}$, $v_{norm}(x,y) = \frac{v_{ave}(x,y)}{\sqrt{u_{ave}^2+v_{ave}^2}}$

In the final step, curl and divergence are computed according to normalized motion vector field which is denoted by:

$$curl M_{norm}(x,y) = \nabla \times u_{norm}(x,y) = c(x,y) \cdot k \tag{3}$$

$$div M_{norm}(x,y) = \nabla \cdot u_{norm}(x,y) = d(x,y) \tag{4}$$

$$c(x,y) = \frac{\partial v_{norm}(x,y)}{\partial x} - \frac{\partial u_{norm}(x,y)}{\partial y} \tag{5}$$

$$d(x,y) = \frac{\partial u_{norm}(x,y)}{\partial x} + \frac{\partial v_{norm}(x,y)}{\partial y} \tag{6}$$

where $c(x,y)$ represent rotation degree of motion vector field $M_{norm}(x,y)$ at point (x,y), while $d(x,y)$ represent gathering/dispersal degree at point (x,y). Different sings of c and d indicate different motion types [17], such as:

- $c(x,y) > 0$: the point's rotation is clockwise.
- $c(x,y) < 0$: the points rotation is counter-clockwise.
- $c(x,y) = 0$: there is no rotation at this point.
- $d(x,y) > 0$: the points motion tends to dispersal.
- $d(x,y) < 0$: the points motion tends to gather.
- $d(x,y) = 0$: there is no motion tendency at this point.

As Fig. 2 is shown, many crowd movement patterns can be depicted by curl and divergence. Given different curl and divergence value, many real-life scenarios can be represented. For example, Splitting and merging can be discriminable with divergence value, walking in same direction and walking with rotation angle are distinguishable with curl value. Thus, curl and divergence can provide local motion pattern information in crowd dynamics.

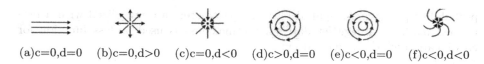

(a)c=0,d=0   (b)c=0,d>0   (c)c=0,d<0   (d)c>0,d=0   (e)c<0,d=0   (f)c<0,d<0

Fig. 2. (a)–(e) represent 5 simple motion vector fields with various value of c and d, where c and d denote curl and divergence respectively. (f) represents a complex motion vector field which has both convergence and counter clock-wise rotation.

Group-Level Motion. Although local pattern-related motion (curl and divergence) can provide pixel level dynamic information, it has no capability to depict crowd movement from an overall perspective. Thus, high-level motion should be add to improve crowd dynamic package.

Shao proposed group-level descriptors [19] in scene-independent group detection task. The descriptor can depict and quantify inter- and intra- groups correlation and variation. Curl and divergence are unified and complemented with these group descriptors mutually, which combine the local pattern-related and group-level movement information together and generate an dynamic attribute package of crowd video.

- Collectiveness: the property indicated the degree of individuals acting as a union in collective motion and is used as a universal measure to study crowds [14].
- Stability: this property characterizes whether a group can keep internal topological structure overtime [14].
- Conflict: the conflict property characterizes interaction/friction between groups when they approach each other [14].

2.3 Two-Branch Network and Feature Fusion

The crowd video can be naturally decomposed into temporal and spatial components. Spatial information comes from single RGB frames, which depicting crowd and scenes appearance in the video. Temporal information comes from crowd dynamic attribute package.

We propose our network with two independent branches, as shown in Fig. 1(b). Both branch is implemented using same deep convolutional network architecture(modified from AlexNet [20]). The parameters in single branch are: $conv(7 \times 7 \times 96)$, $relu$, $pool(3 \times 3)$, $norm(5)$, $conv(5 \times 5 \times 384)$, $relu$, $pool(3 \times 3)$, $norm(5)$, $conv(3 \times 3 \times 512)$, $relu$, $conv(3 \times 3 \times 512)$, $relu$, $conv(3 \times 3 \times 384)$, $relu$, $pool(3 \times 3)$, $fc(4096)$. In last fully-connected layer of single branch, spatial feature vector $S_{4096 \times 1}$ and temporal feature vector $T_{4096 \times 1}$ are obtained. The two features are concatenated to vector of size (8192×1) and sent into $fc(256)$, where spatial and temporal feature interact and fuse into combined temporal-spatial feature vector $TS_{256 \times 1}$. Finally, we have $fc(8)$ producing 8 categories probability predictions. Spatial branch's parameters are initialized with a pre-trained model of ImageNet dataset. Softmax loss is used as loss function for classification which is denoted by:

$$J\left(\theta\right) = -\frac{1}{m}\left[\sum_{i=1}^{m}\sum_{j=1}^{k}\mathbf{1}\left\{y^{(i)}=j\right\}\log\frac{e^{\theta_{j}^{T}x^{(i)}}}{\sum_{l=1}^{k}e^{\theta_{l}^{T}x^{(i)}}}\right] + \frac{\lambda}{2}\sum_{i=1}^{k}\sum_{j=0}^{n}\theta_{ij}^{2} \qquad (7)$$

where m denotes the number of data samples, k denotes the number of labels, $\mathbf{1}\left\{y^{(i)}=j\right\}$ denotes the function, which value is 1 where $y^{(i)}=j$ (the prediction is correct), 0 where $y^{(i)}\neq j$ (the prediction is uncorrect). $\frac{\lambda}{2}\sum_{i=1}^{k}\sum_{j=0}^{n}\theta_{ij}^{2}$ is the regular expression.

3   Experimental Result

3.1   Dataset and Data Preprocessing

CUHK crowd datase [14] is utilized in our experiments, which is summarized in Table 1. 474 video clips are included captured from 215 different scenes, and each of them is assigned to one of the 8 class label. The data is randomly separated into 5 parts, and guarantee crowd scenes in each part are non-intersect, which achieves the purpose of cross-scene validation. Leave-one-out evaluation is used as evaluation protocol which is similar to [14,21]. To solve data imbalance problem, data in each class are upsampled by cropping/mirroring/direct-copying to increase data volume. Due to the fact that videos have various resolution, all frames of video clips after augmentation are resized into 227 × 227 resolution.

Table 1. Summary of the CUHK crowd dataset [14]

Class label	Class name
1	Highly mixed pedestrian walking
2	Crowd walking in mainstream in well organized manner
3	Crowd walking in mainstream in poorly organized manner
4	Crowd merge
5	Crowd split
6	Crowd crossing in opposite direction
7	Intervened escalator traffic
8	Smooth escalator traffic

3.2   Parameter Setting

To obtain dynamic attribute package, frames in consecutive sequence represented by $\{\tau, \tau + 1, \tau + 2, ..., \tau + L\}$ contains L pairs of adjacent frames $\{\tau, \tau+1\}, ...\{\tau + L-1, \tau+L\}$. L optical flow can be computed separately and then get one average normalization motion vector field, and then generate one local pattern-related sub-package and one group-level sub-package. Step s is taken to get next dynamic attribute package resulting in frame sequence $\{\tau + s, \tau + s + 1, ..., \tau + s + L\}$. In our experiment, we set $L = 60$, $s = 1$.

For training process, the learning rate is set to 10^{-2} initially, and then decreases according to a fixed schedule, which is kept same for all training sets. Iteration is set to 50k. In the fine-tuning scenario, the rate is changed to 10^{-3} and training stops after $20\,\mathrm{K}$ iterations.

3.3   Results Analysis

In this paper, Accuracy and confusion matrix are used as performance matrices in this experiment. Confusion matrix is a standard evaluation format in multi-classification task. Holistic feature [21], group descriptors [14] and CD feature [16] which performs as state-of-art are used as baselines.

Performance comparisons between our method and three fore-mentioned methods are shown in Table 2. we can observe that our method performs better than other approaches. The obtained average accuracy of our approach is around 77%, which is higher than the result of holister feature (44%), group descriptors (70%) and CD feature (76%). The noticeable margin demonstrates the proposed dynamic package and two-branch network give more comprehensive crowd behavior's representation.

Table 2. Classification accuracy of different methods

Method	Accuracy
Holistic [21]	44%
Shao Jing's [14]	70%
CD Feature [16]	76%
Our's	**77%**

Confusion matrices results are shown in Fig. 3. Compared with result of group descriptors, the accuracy of categories which have apparent appearance characteristics such as intervened escalator traffic and smooth escalator, increase by 26% and 14%. It indicates that spatial branch is vital for crowd behavior depicting. Crowd merge and crowd split categories' accuracy also raise substantially, as crowd behaviors in these scenarios have obvious motion pattern, which can be depicted by pattern-related motion attributes. It manifests it's more comprehensive to package holistic-level (curl and divergence map) together with group-level

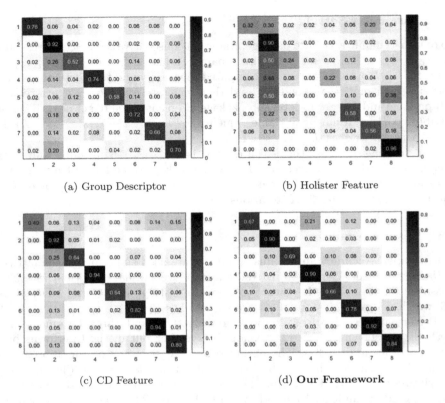

(a) Group Descriptor

(b) Holister Feature

(c) CD Feature

(d) **Our Framework**

Fig. 3. Confusion matrices of crowd behavior recognition. (a) The result by using group descriptors [14]. (b) The result using holistic features [21]. (c) The result using CD feature [16]. (d) The result of our method.

motion attribute. CD feature can't discriminate all crowd videos as highly mixed pedestrian walking class's accuracy is low, while our framework performs well in all classes.

For more detailed analysis, results of training on single-branch are shown in Table 3. The CNN architecture is same as the first row in Fig. 1 without last fully-connected layer. In spatial single branch, entire dynamic package, local pattern-related sub-package and group-level sub-package are sent to neural network for training alone. The accuracy of entire dynamic package increases by 20% and 3% respectively compared with pattern-related sub-package and group-level sub-package, which again indicate the dynamic attribute's superior power in representing crowd behaviors in complex scene.

Table 3. Classification accuracy using single-branch deep ConvNet with various settings.

Branch	Method	Accuracy
Spatial	With Fine-tune	64%
Temporal	Local Pattern-related	52%
	Group-level	69%
	Dynamic Package	72%

4 Conclusion

In this paper, we propose a dynamic attribute package to represent crowd behavior in complex scene, which prove to be effective for crowd behavior recognition. Raw frames in video clips and corresponding dynamic attribute packages are sent into two-branch structured ConvNet to extract spatial and temporal feature for classifying. Experiment results conducted on widely utilized CUHK dataset show that the proposed crowd dynamic attribute package can outperform other crowd motion representations and obtain state-of-art result in crowd behavior recognition in complex scene task. Accuracy of scenes with apparent appearance characteristics and obvious motion pattern improve by noticeable margin. It indicates that local pattern-related and group-level crowd dynamics complement mutually and have powerful discernibility in recognizing crowd behaviors in complex scene when unified together.

Acknowledgement. This work was supported in part by National Natural Science Foundation of China (NSFC, Grant No. 61771303 and 61671289), Science and Technology Commission of Shanghai Municipality (STCSM, Grant Nos. 17DZ1205602, 18DZ1200-102, 18DZ2270700), and SJTUYitu/Thinkforce Joint laboratory for visual computing and application. Director Fund of PSRPC.

References

1. Wu, S., Moore, B.E., Shah, M.: Chaotic invariants of lagrangian particle trajectories for anomaly detection in crowded scenes. In: Computer Vision and Pattern Recognition, pp. 2054–2060 (2010)
2. Ali, S., Shah, M.: A lagrangian particle dynamics approach for crowd flow segmentation and stability analysis. In: IEEE Conference on Computer Vision and Pattern Recognition, CVPR 2007, pp. 1–6 (2007)
3. Mehran, R., Moore, B.E., Shah, M.: A streakline representation of flow in crowded scenes. In: Daniilidis, K., Maragos, P., Paragios, N. (eds.) ECCV 2010. LNCS, vol. 6313, pp. 439–452. Springer, Heidelberg (2010). https://doi.org/10.1007/978-3-642-15558-1_32
4. Tang, X., Wang, X., Zhou, B.: Understanding collective crowd behaviors: learning a mixture model of dynamic pedestrian-agents. In: Computer Vision and Pattern Recognition, pp. 2871–2878 (2012)

5. Mehran, R., Oyama, A., Shah, M.: Abnormal crowd behavior detection using social force model. In: IEEE Conference on Computer Vision and Pattern Recognition, CVPR 2009, pp. 935–942 (2009)

6. Zhao, J., Xu, Y., Yang, X., Yan, Q.: Crowd instability analysis using velocity-field based social force model. In: Visual Communications and Image Processing, pp. 1–4 (2011)

7. Rodriguez, M., Ali, S., Kanade, T.: Tracking in unstructured crowded scenes. In: IEEE International Conference on Computer Vision, pp. 1389–1396 (2009)

8. Yang, C., Yuan, J., Liu, J.: Abnormal event detection in crowded scenes using sparse representation. Pattern Recogn. 46(7), 1851–1864 (2013)

9. Li, T., Chang, H., Wang, M., Ni, B., Hong, R., Yan, S.: Crowded scene analysis: a survey. IEEE Trans. Circ. Syst. Video Technol. 25(3), 367–386 (2015)

10. Su, H., Yang, H., Zheng, S., Fan, Y., Wei, S.: The large-scale crowd behavior perception based on spatio-temporal viscous fluid field. IEEE Trans. Inform. Forensic. Secur. 8(10), 1575–1589 (2013)

11. Kratz, L., Nishino, K.: Tracking pedestrians using local spatio-temporal motion patterns in extremely crowded scenes. IEEE Trans. Pattern Anal. Mach. Intell. 34(5), 987–1002 (2012)

12. Wu, S., Yang, H., Zheng, S., Su, H., Fan, Y., Yang, M.H.: Crowd behavior analysis via curl and divergence of motion trajectories. Int. J. Comput. Vis. 123(3), 1–21 (2017)

13. Ali, S.: Measuring flow complexity in videos. In: IEEE International Conference on Computer Vision, pp. 1097–1104 (2013)

14. Shao, J., Chen, C.L., Wang, X.: Scene-independent group profiling in crowd. In: Computer Vision and Pattern Recognition, pp. 2227–2234 (2014)

15. Shao, J., Chen, C.L., Wang, X.: Learning scene-independent group descriptors for crowd understanding. IEEE Trans. Circ. Syst. Video Technol. 27(6), 1290–1303 (2017)

16. Wu, S., Su, H., Yang, H., Zheng, S., Fan, Y., Zhou, Q.: Bilinear dynamics for crowd video analysis. Journal of Visual Communication Image Representation (2017)

17. Wu, S., Su, H., Zheng, S., Yang, H., Zhou, Q.: Motion sketch based crowd video retrieval via motion structure coding. In: IEEE International Conference on Image Processing, pp. 1–29 (2016)

18. Revaud, J., Weinzaepfel, P., Harchaoui, Z., Schmid, C.: Epicflow: edge-preserving interpolation of correspondences for optical flow. In: Computer Vision and Pattern Recognition, pp. 1164–1172 (2015)

19. Shao, J., Kang, K., Chen, C.L., Wang, X.: Deeply learned attributes for crowded scene understanding. In: Computer Vision and Pattern Recognition, pp. 4657–4666 (2015)

20. Krizhevsky, A., Sutskever, I., Hinton, G.E.: Imagenet classification with deep convolutional neural networks. In: International Conference on Neural Information Processing Systems, pp. 1097–1105 (2012)

21. Kratz, L., Nishino, K.: Anomaly detection in extremely crowded scenes using spatio-temporal motion pattern models. In: IEEE Conference on Computer Vision and Pattern Recognition, CVPR 2009, pp. 1446–1453 (2010)

Sequentially Cutting Based the Cluster Number Determination for Spatial Feature Classification

Hong Lu[1(✉)], Ke Gu[2(✉)], Chen Yang[1], and Yunceng Hu[1]

[1] School of Automation, Nanjing Institute of Technology,
Nanjing 211167, China
zdhxlh@njit.edu.cn
[2] Faculty of Information Technology, Beijing University of Technology,
Beijing, China
guke.doctor@gmail.com

Abstract. Clustering the spatial feature of the object region plays an important role in object modeling, detecting and tracking etc. However, many clustering methods adopt the pre-set cluster number, which cannot adapt to full automatic system. In this paper, a novel frame work for adaptively determining the number of clusters is proposed based on hierarchically kernel cutting. We firstly extract the value contour of object region and rank the peaks of the contour in descending order. And then we utilize a group of gauss kernels located at peaks to sequentially segment the contour into several subintervals. When the residual area being not cut is lower than a threshold value, the cutting process is compulsively terminated. Furthermore, we merge adjacent kernels according to the intersection area ratio and take the retained kernel number as the cluster number k. We finally classify the object region with k and K-means algorithm. Both theoretical reasoning and experimental comparing illustrate the proposed method is rational, adaptive and efficient.

Keywords: Gauss kernel · Sequentially cutting · Adaptive cluster number · Object region classification

1 Introduction

Clustering the object spatial feature to improve the representation power is very important in computer vision applications [1–3]. Since clustering can partition an object image into meaningful classes or different groups, so it can simplify the image representation, make the object image more easily be analyzed, and ultimately enhances the efficiency of applications such as traffic surveillance [4] and medical image understanding [5].

The early best-known and most widely used member of the clustering algorithm family is K-means or ISODATA algorithm [6]. Yip et al. [7] further summarized clustering algorithms into five classes (density and grid based methods, etc.).

K-means clustering [8] is an important classification algorithm in highlighting the main color or texture features. Wang et al. [9] presented a regularized K-means

© Springer Nature Singapore Pte Ltd. 2019
G. Zhai et al. (Eds.): IFTC 2018, CCIS 1009, pp. 433–443, 2019.
https://doi.org/10.1007/978-981-13-8138-6_37

formulation to improve the pattern discovery results. Mignotte [1] fused several K-means clustering under different color spaces to get a more accurate segmentation result. However, all methods mentioned above need to pre-set the cluster number k. Thereby they cannot achieve full-automatically clustering. Mai et al. [10] proposed a semi-supervised clustering based fuzzy C-means (FCM) algorithm where they utilized the multiple kernel technique to separate the highly complex shaped data. Yin et al. [11] compared K-means with FCM algorithm in arterial input function (AIF) detection, and demonstrated that K-means analysis could yield more accurate and robust AIF results. Nevertheless, in their experiments, both clustering methods adopt the pre-set cluster number k.

ISODATA (Iterative Self-Organizing Data Analysis) is the well-known extension of K-means [12, 13], and can adaptively achieve k. Sabin [14] further studied the convergence and consistency of the fuzzy ISODATA. However, ISODATA generally run very slowly, particularly on large data sets. To fulfill the fast implementation, Memarsadeghi et al. [15] stored the points in a kd-tree, modified the way estimating the dispersion of each cluster and attained better running times.

In density-based methods, DBSCAN (density-based spatial clustering of applications with noise) algorithm [16] is very effective in filtering noises and automatically generating k. However, when clusters touch each other, DBSCAN may not get desired results since both the cluster centers and cluster boundaries become difficult to determine [7]. To handle this problem, Guan et al. [17] divided the laser scanner data into several regions and determined the clustering parameters in each local region. Lu et al. [18] computed the optimal split points for dividing the region of interest, and fused multiple local DBSCAN classification to improve the segmentation performance. Zhang et al. [19] presented a superpixels and DBSCAN-based method for entirely segmenting cavitary nodules.

In experiments, we find that the Value component histogram of the object region, in HSV color space, possesses some relation with k. Thus, this paper concentrates on making certain this relevance so as to adaptively determine k. To the best of our knowledge, our research is the first work to deduce k by sequentially cutting the value contour of the object region, which is more objective than the pre-set parameter based clustering algorithm. Furthermore, our method performs better both in clustering quality and efficiency on relevant object images than noted DBSCAN and ISODATA algorithms.

The structure of this paper is as follows: Sect. 2 describes the overview of the proposed method, Sect. 3 shows the peak contour analysis and the principle of cluster number determination, Sect. 4 illustrates the process of cutting the value contour with sequential kernels and merging kernels for getting k. Section 5 provides the experimental results and comparisons. Finally some conclusion and discussion are given in Sect. 6.

2   The Overview of Proposed Algorithm

Here, the motion region of the vehicle in input image I_{in} is firstly extracted [20]. Then, the peak contour of the Value component histogram in the motion region is extracted to obtain the contour peak and valley values. A group of hierarchical Gauss kernels corresponding to peaks are used to cut the value component contour into different intervals. When intersection area A between adjacent gauss kernels is larger than a threshold value γ, they are merged into one kernel, or else they keep independent and are regarded as two possible clusters. Once the residual energy is smaller than a threshold value, the cutting process is terminated. The final number of gauss kernels is k. Finally, we apply k and K-means algorithm to classify the intensity matrix constructed with the Saturation and Value components of the moving pixels in vehicle region. The flow chart of the proposed clustering algorithm is shown in Fig. 1.

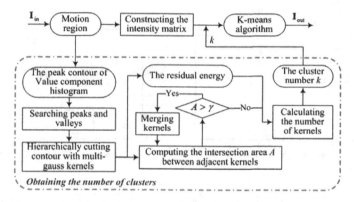

Fig. 1. The flow chart of the proposed algorithm.

3   Analyzing and Reasoning the Number of Clusters

Figure 2 gives a detected vehicle region (Fig. 2(a)). Due to the Saturation and Value components are independent of the color information, more easily processed and suitable for clustering, we classify them and acquire the spatial color feature in object region.

Figures 2(b)–(f) show clustered results of K-means algorithm under different k. Here, we analyze the representative results of $k = \{2, 3, 4, 5, 6\}$ to find the optimal k. Compared with Fig. 2(b), it is obvious that the clustered subregions in Fig. 2(c) are more in line with the true feature distribution of object appearance. Under $k = 3$, three classes correspond to the car outside, windshield and shadow respectively. In Figs. 2(d)–(f), overmuch subregions are obtained, which divide the car outside into several parts. However, too many meaningless details may not keep pace with a strong description power. We also find that the subregion distributions under $k = \{4, 5, 6\}$ are similar. To ensure the integrity of subregion, $k = 3$ here is optimal.

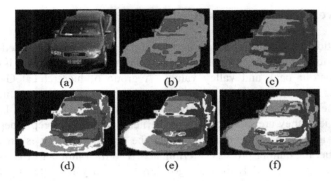

Fig. 2. The vehicle region and the clustered results under different cluster numbers. (a) vehicle region; (b) $k = 2$; (c) $k = 3$; (d) $k = 4$; (e) $k = 5$; (f) $k = 6$.

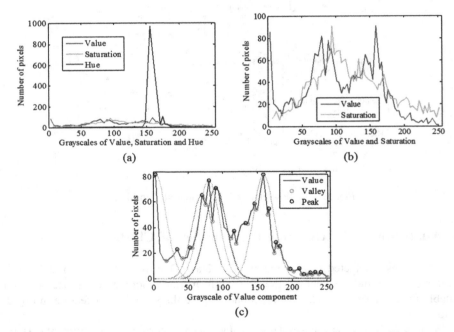

Fig. 3. The peak contours of HSV in object region and the process cutting the Value contour. (a) peak contours of HSV; (b) peak contours of Value and Saturation; (c) cutting Value contour for obtaining k.

To study the association between k and the color distribution of the object appearance, the color histogram contours of the object region are extracted as in Fig. 3(a). The Hue contour (blue solid line) shows an outstanding main peak and a very low sidelobe. To illustrate the legible details of Saturation and Value contours, we specifically illustrate them in Fig. 3(b). It is obvious that the Saturation contour (blue-green solid line) reflects only a prominent contour peak. In comparison, the Value contour (red solid line) embodies several outstanding contour peaks, which may represent car outside, wind-shied and shadow etc. The number of peaks in value contour shows some certain relation with k in the object appearance. To make certain this relation, we apply sequentially gauss kernels (dot lines), whose peaks coincide exactly with the peaks detected in the Value contour, to cut the contour into several sections as demonstrated in Fig. 3(c). Then the intersection area between adjacent gauss kernels is computed and employed to decide if adjacent kernels need to be merged. Furthermore, the residual energy is compared with a threshold value to judge if the cutting process should be terminated. After above merging, the final kernel number is taken as k (here $k = 3$). As in Fig. 3(c), the car outside and its shadow are classified into 2 clusters, while the windshied and the front chassis are divided into a same cluster due to their similar appearance color.

4 Determining the Number of Clusters Using Kernel Cutting

4.1 Cutting the Value Contour with Multiple Gauss Kernels

To reserve the dominating peaks which may correspond to the real clusters, we rank the peak in descending order and sequentially cut the value contour with multiple gauss kernels. Some contour peaks, being far away from all kernels, will be summed to obtain the residual peak energy which is further used to control the termination of cutting process. The steps are as follows.

(i) Extract and smooth the peaks from the Value component histogram H_t to get the Value contour f_l as shown in Fig. 3(c). $l = 1, 2 \cdots, L$ is the number of peaks. $t = 0, 1 \cdots, 255$ denotes the grayscale of Value component.

(ii) Find the contour peak value p_s (black circle) and the contour valley value v_r (green circle) from f_l via (1)–(3), where $sign$ is the plus and minus signs, and $\Delta sign$ describes the sign change. $\Delta sign = 0$ illustrates that the peak and valley of f_l are in increment or decrement state. $s = 1, 2 \cdots, S$ and $r = 1, 2 \cdots, R$ denote the peak number and the valley number respectively.

$$\Delta sign = sign(f_{l+1} - f_l) - sign(f_l - f_{l-1}) \tag{1}$$

$$p_s = f_l \left| \left\{ f_l := \arg_l (\Delta sign < 0) \right\} \right. \tag{2}$$

$$v_r = f_l \left| \left\{ f_l := \arg_l (\Delta sign > 0) \right\} \right. \tag{3}$$

With above judgement, the first and final contour peaks f_1 and f_L may lose because they are only used to reason the adjacent middle peak. To deal with this problem, the follow process is adopted as in (4)–(7). If $f_1 > v_1$ or $f_L > v_R$, increase a peak. Meanwhile, if $f_1 < p_1$ or $f_L < p_S$, increase a valley. v_1 and p_1 correspond to the first peak and valley, and p_S and v_R are the last peak and valley.

$$\text{if } f_1 > v_1, \; p_{s+1} \Leftarrow p_s \text{ and } p_1 \Leftarrow f_1 \tag{4}$$

$$\text{if } f_L > v_R, \; S \Leftarrow S+1 \text{ and } p_S \Leftarrow f_L \tag{5}$$

$$\text{if } f_1 < p_1, \; v_{r+1} \Leftarrow v_r \text{ and } v_1 \Leftarrow f_1 \tag{6}$$

$$\text{if } f_L < p_S, R \Leftarrow R+1 \text{ and } v_R \Leftarrow f_L \tag{7}$$

(iii) Sort p_s in descending order to get a new peak sequence ϕ_i, and orderly build Gauss kernel $g_i(c)$ at each ϕ_i via (8) to segment the value contour via (9). ϕ_i, c_i and h_i are the i-th peak value, peak location (the grayscale of Value component) and kernel radius. $\phi_i > \phi_{i+1} > \phi_{i+2}$ and $i = 1, 2 \cdots, S$. $g_i(c)$ gets to the maximum peak value ϕ_i at $c = c_i$, while $g_i(c)$ is close to zero at $c = c_i \pm 2h_i$. $A_1^{cont} = \sum\limits_{t=\min(v_1, p_1)}^{\max(v_R, p_S)} H_t$ is the overarea of the initial peak contour and A_1^{ker} describes the first kernel overarea being used to segment A_1^{cont}. The remainder area A_{i+1}^{cont} is calculated after each segmentation and compared with αA_1^{cont}. Once $A_{i+1}^{cont} > \alpha A_1^{cont}$, the next kernel at ϕ_{i+1} will be triggered to cut the value contour via (9). When $A_{i+1}^{cont} \leq \alpha A_1^{cont}$, the cutting process is compulsively terminated. $A_i^{ker} = \sum\limits_{t=c_i-h_i}^{c_i+h_i} H_t$ and $\alpha \leq 0.1$ is a scale parameter which is employed to evaluate if the remainder peak contour (which may be consisted by noise, trifle border or little region etc.) needs to be further cut.

$$g_i(c) = \phi_i \cdot \exp\left(-\frac{1}{2}\left(\frac{c-c_i}{h_i}\right)^2\right) \tag{8}$$

$$A_{i+1}^{cont} = A_i^{cont} - A_i^{ker} \tag{9}$$

4.2 Merging Kernels for Acquiring the Number of Clusters

The adjacent gauss kernels used for cutting the peak contour often possess high overlap ratio. Therefore, they may repeatedly illustrate a common cluster. Thus, we need to judge associated kernels and merge them into an effective one. Here, we compute the overlap area between adjacent gauss kernels via (10) and (11), and incorporate the kernel being with higher overlap ratio into the other adjacent kernel according to (12) and (13). Where $\beta \geq 0.6$ is a threshold value which is utilized to judge if a kernel needs to be merged. A_i^{ratio} and A_j^{ratio} are the overlap ratios of the i-th kernel regions G_i^{ker} and the j-th kernel regions G_j^{ker} respectively. $A_{\left(G_i^{ker} \cap G_j^{ker}\right)}^{cross}$ denotes their overlap area. The number of retained kernels after above merging is taken as the clusters number k.

$$A_i^{ratio} = \frac{A_{\left(G_i^{ker} \cap G_j^{ker}\right)}^{cross}}{A_{G_i^{ker}}} \tag{10}$$

$$A_j^{ratio} = \frac{A_{\left(G_i^{ker} \cap G_j^{ker}\right)}^{cross}}{A_{G_j^{ker}}} \tag{11}$$

$$\text{If } A_i^{ratio} \geq \beta > A_j^{ratio} \text{ or } A_i^{ratio} > A_j^{ratio} \geq \beta \text{ or}$$
$$A_i^{ratio} = A_j^{ratio} = \beta, \text{ merge } g_i(c) \text{ into } g_j(c) \tag{12}$$

$$\text{If } A_i^{ratio} < \beta \text{ and } A_j^{ratio} < \beta, \text{ retain } g_j(c) \text{ and } g_i(c) \tag{13}$$

With k and K-means algorithm, we cluster the Saturation and Value components of the object region. The cluster centroid intensities are initialized randomly.

5 Experimental Results

The proposed algorithm is implemented on a PC with a 2.1 GHz AMD A8-5550 M CPU, MatLab implementation and Windows 7 operation system. To evaluate our method, we selected the other object image with different posture and resolution as described in Fig. 4. Furthermore, we compare the proposed method with ISODATA and DBSCAN algorithms (both of them being able to adaptively get the number of clusters). The experimental results are shown in Figs. 4 and 5. The quantitative comparisons are listed in Table 1 to illustrate the adaptivity of k and the efficiency of classified result.

5.1 Classified Results Comparison Under Different Cluster Numbers

The object in Fig. 4(a) is with blurry appearance. In Fig. 4(b), the Value contour of the object region is cut by sequential kernels and ultimately merged into 4 clusters according to Sect. 4. The corresponding clustered result is shown in Fig. 4(c).

In contrast, we also give the clustered results of K-means under $k = \{2, 3, 5\}$. Figures 4(d) and (e) give the classified subregions under fewer cluster numbers, but both cases obviously lose some details such as vehicle wheel. However, Fig. 4(f) presents the similar cluster distribution with larger k as Fig. 4(c). It is clear that increasing k may not apparently enhance the appearance description of the object. Here, $k = 4$ is optimal.

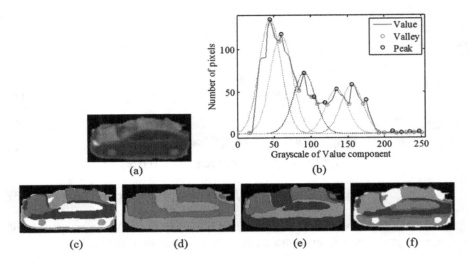

Fig. 4. The low-resolution vehicle region and the clustered results under different cluster numbers. (a) vehicle region; (b) the Value contour cut by sequential kernels; (c) $k = 4$; (d) $k = 2$; (e) $k = 3$; (f) $k = 5$.

5.2   Clustered Results Comparison Under Different Classifying Methods

The first column in Fig. 5 shows original object regions, where the objects show are different resolution (object sizes from top to bottom are 84×123, 65×95, 71×154 and 85×164 respectively), noise and appearance subregions distribution. Columns 2–4 present the clustered results under the proposed, ISODATA and DBSCAN algorithms respectively. ISODATA and DBSCAN here are gave consideration to all color components (i.e. H, S and V). Since the initial cluster centroids are set randomly, the pseudo-colors marking every subregion are randomly, e.g. shadows in row 1 are labelled with red, purplish red and blue respectively. The clustering time comparisons are illustrated in Table 1. We set the initial cluster number of ISODATA method as 10. Adjusting parameters *Eps* and *Minpts* of DBSCAN method, k will change, but the optimal clustered results concentrate on or are similar with the representative cases as in column 4.

In row 1 (Fig. 5), the proposed method ($k = 3$) and DBSCAN method ($k = 6$, and DBSCAN parameters are set as *Eps* = 2 and *Minpts* = 15) acquire more integrated subregions than ISODATA method. Under $k = 5$, ISODATA divides the car outside into several pieces and runs slowly (20.30 s) than the other two methods (Table 1). Both the proposed and ISODATA algorithms in row 2 show many effective details such as the vehicle wheel and the plate area. Nevertheless, DBSCAN (*Eps* = 4 and *Minpts* = 15) finds the fewest cluster number ($k = 2$) with a fuller description of car outside along with losing the above mentioned local appearance features. In addition, DBSCAN spends more time (0.86 s) than our method (0.22 s). Similar results occur in row 3, where ISODATA ($k = 5$) and our method ($k = 4$) obtain almost identical subregions distribution, but the former is with more cluster number and a long time consumption (26.16 s).

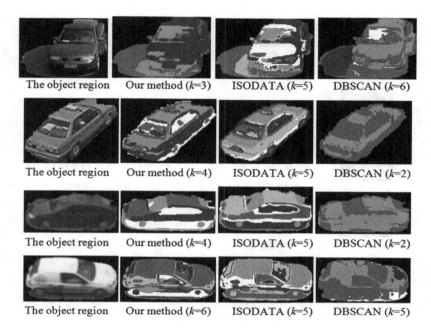

The object region   Our method (*k*=3)   ISODATA (*k*=5)   DBSCAN (*k*=6)

The object region   Our method (*k*=4)   ISODATA (*k*=5)   DBSCAN (*k*=2)

The object region   Our method (*k*=4)   ISODATA (*k*=5)   DBSCAN (*k*=2)

The object region   Our method (*k*=6)   ISODATA (*k*=5)   DBSCAN (*k*=5)

Fig. 5. Clustered results comparison. (Column 1 is the object image; Columns 2–4 are the proposed, ISODATA and DBSCAN algorithms respectively.)

Meanwhile, DBSCAN (*Eps* = 3 and *Minpts* = 35) also classifies the object region into two clusters, where the car outside is described as a connected area. Under $k = 5$ in row 4, ISODATA receives clearly appearance subregions, while DBSCAN (*Eps* = 3 and *Minpts* = 45) gets many trivial blocks which may correspond to noise. Although our method use more cluster number ($k = 6$) to achieve the same clustered result similar to ISODATA, the time spend in our method is only 0.89 s.

In all tests, the number of clusters under ISODATA keeps 5 and the classifying process is much time-consuming. DBSCAN and our method spend far less time than ISODATA. However, DBSCAN seems to suffer from overfitting and results in some fractional and spurious subregions. In comparison, our algorithm achieves the optimal output where the connection regions possess less noise, are more in line with the true spatial feature distribution and can model the object easily. Furthermore, the proposed method is efficient and effective in computing k and takes good use of the fast characteristic of K-means clustering.

Table 1. Clustering performance analysis and comparison.

Object image	Algorithm	Cluster number	Time-consuming (second)
	Proposed	3	0.27
	ISODATA	5	20.30
	DBSCAN	4	3.13
	Proposed	4	0.22
	ISODATA	5	11.08
	DBSCAN	2	0.86
	Proposed	4	0.32
	ISODATA	5	26.16
	DBSCAN	2	4.79
	Proposed	6	0.89
	ISODATA	5	36.03
	DBSCAN	5	8.05

6   Conclusion

In this paper, we have presented a new approach for adaptively getting the number of clusters. We extract and cut the value contour of object region with a group of sequential kernels to obtain several sections containing possible clusters. Adjacent kernels merging according to the intersection area ratio among kernels is utilized to derive k. Both theoretical reasoning and experimental comparing are employed to illustrate the rationality of our method. Experimental results demonstrate that the proposed algorithm provides superior adaptivity and efficiency to ISODATA and DBSCAN algorithms.

Acknowledgments. This work was supported by the National Natural Science Foundation of China (61305011, 61703009), the Young Elite Scientist Sponsorship Program by China Association for Science and Technology (2017QNRC001), and Young Top-Notch Talents Team Program of Beijing Excellent Talents Funding (2017000026833ZK40). We thank the anonymous reviewers for their constructive comments.

References

1. Mignotte, M.: Segmentation by fusion of histogram-based K-means clusters in different color spaces. IEEE Trans. Image Process **17**(5), 780–787 (2008)
2. Wang, L., Wang, Y.Z., Jiang, T.T., et al.: Learning discriminative features for fast frame-based action recognition. Pattern Recogn. **46**, 1832–1840 (2013)
3. Lu, H., Gu, K., Lin, W.: Tracking based on stable feature mining using intraframe clustering and interframe association. IEEE Access **5**, 4690–4703 (2017)
4. Zhang, T.Z., Liu, S., Xu, C.S., et al.: Mining semantic context information for intelligent video surveillance of traffic scenes. IEEE Trans. Ind. Inf. **9**, 149–160 (2013)
5. Thangavel, K., Manavalan, R.: Soft computing models based feature selection for TRUS prostate cancer image classification. Soft. Comput. **18**, 1165–1176 (2014)
6. Su, M.C., Chou, C.H.: A modified version of the K-means algorithm with a distance based on cluster symmetry. IEEE Trans. Pattern Anal. Mach. Intell. **23**(6), 674–680 (2001)
7. Yip, A.M., Ding, C., Chan, T.F.: Dynamic cluster formation using level set methods. IEEE Trans. Pattern Anal. Mach. Intell. **28**(6), 877–889 (2006)
8. Duda, R.O., Hart, P.E., Stork, D.G.: in: Pattern Classication. Wiley, New York (2001)
9. Wang, H.X., Yuan, J.S., Wu, Y.: Context-aware discovery of visual co-occurrence patterns. IEEE Trans. Image Process. **23**(4), 1805–1819 (2014)
10. Mai, S.D., Ngo, L.T.: Multiple kernel approach to semi-supervised fuzzy clustering algorithm for land-cover classification. Eng. Appl. Artif. Intel. **68**, 205–213 (2018)
11. Yin, J., Sun, H., Yang, J., et al.: Comparison of K-means and fuzzy c-Means algorithm performance for automated determination of the arterial input function. PLoS ONE **9**(2), 1–8 (2014)
12. Haghverdi, A., Leib, B.G., Washington-Allen, R.A., et al.: Perspectives on delineating management zones for variable rate irrigation. Comput. Electron. Agr. **117**, 154–167 (2015)
13. Girma, A., de Bie, C.A.J.M., Skidmore, A.K., et al.: Hyper-temporal SPOT-NDVI dataset parameterization captures species distributions. Int. J. Geogr. Inf. Sci. **30**(1), 89–107 (2016)
14. Sabin, M.J.: Convergence and consistency of fuzzy c-means/ISODATA algorithms. IEEE Trans. Pattern Anal. Mach. Intell. **9**(5), 661–668 (1987)
15. Memarsadeghi, N., Mount, D.M., Netanyahu, N.S., et al.: A fast implementation of the ISODATA clustering algorithm. Int. J. Comput. Geom. Ap. **17**(1), 71–103 (2007)
16. Ester, M., Kriegel, H.P., Sander, J., et al.: A density-based algorithm for discovering clusters in large spatial databases with noise. In: Proceedings of the International Conference on Knowledge Discovery and Data Mining, SIGKDD, Portland, pp. 226–231. ACM, USA (1996)
17. Guan, C.H., Chen, Y.D., Chen, H.Y., et al.: Improved DBSCAN clustering algorithm based vehicle detection using a vehicle-mounted laser scanner. Trans. Beijing Inst. Technol. **30**(6), 732–736 (2010)
18. Lu, H., Li, H.S., Qiang, Y., et al.: Image segmentation using region division and local parameters based density clustering. J. Comput. Inform. Sys. **11**(14), 4985–4994 (2015)
19. Zhang, W., Zhang, X.L., Zhao, J.J., et al.: A segmentation method for lung nodule image sequences based on superpixels and density-based spatial clustering of applications with noise. PLOS ONE **12**(9), 1–25 (2017). 0184290
20. Xin, B., Tian, Y., Wang, Y. Z., et al.: Background Subtraction via generalized fused lasso foreground modeling. In: Proceedings of the IEEE Conference on Computer Vision and Pattern Recognition (CVPR), Boston, Massachusetts USA, pp. 4676–4684 (2015)

Virtual Reality

The Design of Immersion Acrophobia Adjuvant Therapy System (IAATS)

Qisong Fu[1], Haixia Hou[2], Dongmei Jiang[3], and Zhi Liu[1(✉)]

[1] School of Information Science and Engineering,
Shandong University, Qingdao 266237, China
liuzhi@sdu.edu.cn
[2] Qingdao Agricultural University, Qingdao, China
[3] Qingdao University, Qingdao, China

Abstract. A new immersion acrophobia adjuvant therapy system (IAATS) was designed by us to help people with acrophobia escape the fear of heights. We built a realistic virtual scene, in which patients receive Virtual reality exposure therapy (VRET). Scenes of different heights are available to offer patients with different levels of stimulation. Patients can get continuous progress and corresponding feedback in the system. During the patient's treatment, we collected the patient's eye movement data and Electroencephalogram (EEG) data through certain algorithms and different external hardware devices. These two data are involved in Altitude layering agreement we designed to form a more reasonable treatment strategy. They can also be saved and further analyzed after the treatment. The effectiveness of the whole system still needs further experimental exploration.

Keywords: VR · Acrophobia · VRET · EEG · Eye-tracking

1 Introduction

Approximately 2–5% of the general population has acrophobia [1], which has caused varying degrees of damage to their normal life. Furthermore, a related milder form of visually triggered fear or anxiety called visual height intolerance is reflected in 1/3 of the public [2]. When Acrophobia patients stand on a high elevation, their visual information becomes contradictory and missing, and they will show specific psychological factors, anxiety, dizziness, tension and other symptoms. Serious people are even afraid to take a transparent elevator, and dare not stand on the balcony, which has caused great trouble to their lives.

In general, traditional methods of treating acrophobia include behavioral therapy and drug therapy. Among the relatively effective ones are exposure desensitization therapy in behavioral therapy [3]. Specific, Exposure therapy does not perform any relaxation training for the patient, allowing the patient to imagine or directly enter the situation that causes the patient's horror and anxiety, to correct the patient's misunderstanding of the source of the horror and anxiety, allow patients to gradually adapt to the source of stimulation and continue to break the willingness of patients to escape. In a series of escalating stimuli, fear is minimized until it disappears [4, 5].

© Springer Nature Singapore Pte Ltd. 2019
G. Zhai et al. (Eds.): IFTC 2018, CCIS 1009, pp. 447–455, 2019.
https://doi.org/10.1007/978-981-13-8138-6_38

In view of characteristics of exposure therapy, Virtual Reality (VR) technology is considered to be one of the most effective methods to realize exposure therapy. Virtual reality exposure therapy (VRET) has been used in the field of phobia treatment for a long time and has been proved to be a powerful tool [6–8]. VRET demonstrates strong security, controllability, and convenience. Patients do not have to be physically at a higher height to experience the same scene. And with the development of computer technology, the cost of VR equipment and system production has been greatly reduced. The new helmet-mounted VR has gradually replaced the past mode based on display, cave and so on. And this treatment with a more powerful sense of immersive still shows great results in the treatment of acrophobia [9]. We chose helmet-mounted VR with new approaches to realize a more precise treatment of acrophobia.

In addition, traditional acrophobia assessments are mainly based on long-term manual counseling or self-questionnaires. However, these methods are time-consuming and have predictable biases. They cannot quickly and accurately evaluate the acrophobia patients. What's more, the psychological state of the patient during the treatment process is difficult to explore. Therefore, the detection of physiological signals is necessary. Electroencephalogram (EEG) and eye movement can be used as two of our essential tools.

2   Methods

2.1   Scene Design

The scene design should include a stimulus source (i.e., a certain height) that can cause anxiety. It is decided to set the virtual environment background as a modern city, and the tops of different skyscrapers in the city are places where patients would be trained. Some transfer points are reserved on the top of different building. All the training will start at the appropriate height. Wooden bridges and Glass trestles were built connecting two skyscrapers to provide extra stimulation. They are used to give patients a stronger sense of anxiety. The glass trestle has the strongest sense of instability.

As for mobile modes in VR, due to the limitations of the current VR technology, unreasonable movement will bring patients extra sense of vertigo, which will affect the patient's feelings at high places and have an unnecessary impact on the results. Therefore, we have designed different ways of moving for different scenarios. For a small area at the edge of a tall building, patients walk in a small range as moving in reality. While walking in the plank path, patients can switch coordinates by means of the "instant moving". This can greatly reduce the stun of the movement in virtual scenes.

2.2   Electroencephalogram

Electroencephalogram (EEG) is a method of recording brain activity using physiological electrical indicators, which are formed by the synaptic potentials that occur simultaneously in a large number of neurons [10]. When observing brain waves, by recording changes in the brain's movements during activity, we can infer the user's mental state in different situations, such as attention, relaxation, frustration, or other emotions. Frequency of EEG varies from 1 to 30 times per second and can be mainly divided into four bands, namely δ (1–3 Hz) and θ (4–7 Hz), α (8–13 Hz), and β (14–30 Hz) [11]. Among them, the alpha wave is the basic frequency band of ordinary human brain waves, and its frequency is quite constant without external stimulation. This frequency band is most pronounced when people are awake, quiet, and close their eyes. When individuals receive some kinds of stimuli, the alpha waves diminish immediately [12]. While the beta wave will appear when individuals get excited or nervous [13]. By comparing these two waves, we can roughly obtain the emotional fluctuations of the patient throughout the treatment.

2.3 Eye Tracking Technology

Another essential technology to enable us to obtain more information of patients when they are training is eye tracking technology also known as vision tracking technology, which is a technique that uses optical, electronic, mechanical, software algorithms and other detection methods to obtain the current gaze direction of the subject. It is widely used in assisted driving, virtual reality, and human-machine. At present, the main interaction mode of virtual reality is head tracking and accessory tracking, that is, by detecting the position of accessories such as VR helmet and handle. When the user wears a virtual reality helmet, his state in the helmet is completely unrecordable. In order to detect the user's precise visual focus or other eye physiological data, it is necessary to configure some hardware to help track the movement of the eye. Eye tracking can help us find the patient's gaze point and determine the height that the patient actually experience. Further, it records the real-time activity status of the virtual scene and screens out the real effective state to reduce the impact of closing eyes or some other conditions away from treatment.

3 System Design

Patients first need to wear hardware equipment. After a period of environmental and operational adaptation, the training is officially started. The hardware part of the system includes the VR helmet and the EEG detector. The VR helmet provides the patient with a way to enter the virtual scene, while the EEG detector detects the patient's brain waves and transmits them to the computer for processing. The eye movement device is mounted on the VR helmet to provide precise gaze point positioning in virtual scene. The patient completes the training according to the established procedure, and his eye movement data and brainwave data will be treated as part of our altitude layering agreement. The specific architecture of the system is shown in Fig. 1. After the training, the recorded focus distribution of the patient's gaze and brain wave map will be compared and analyzed.

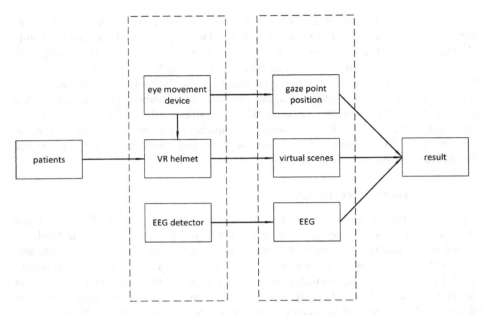

Fig. 1. The overall architecture of the system

3.1 Virtual Environment

In the implementation of the virtual environment, the immersion of the tester is vital. Immersion means individuals concentrate on the current virtual environment, creating the feeling of being in a virtual environment, and get individuals forgetting the real-world situation. The more realistic the virtual environment, the stronger the immersion that the tester feel, and the better the results of the assessment and treatment. We use a combination of a game engine that enable us to create a virtual reality scene and a virtual reality helmet to create a frightening, realistic high-altitude environment as our source of stimuli.

The virtual object model is designed by 3DMAX software. The overall scene is based on Unity 5.6.3f1 software. By deploying various models such as buildings, streets, trees, street lamps, etc., a virtual city as shown in Fig. 2 is built. The design of the object and the arrangement of the scene try to simulate the scene of real life.

We chose the VR helmet HTC VIVE and the Steam VR plugin to enter the virtual scene. VIVR offers 1200 * 1080 pixels per eye and a 90fps refresh rate. Accordingly, we utilized the computer equipped with a NVIDIA GeForce® GTX 1080 GPU and an i7-7700 CPU. The combination of hardware is enough to run our virtual environment smoothly.

Fig. 2. A view of the top of different buildings

3.2 Altitude Layering Agreement

We design an altitude layering agreement as the basic principles of training: success increases height, failure reduces height, and patients can manually reach a certain height at any stage or return directly to the comfort zone, the lowest height. Among them, success or not are decided by the physiological signals we detect as well as the patient's performance in the virtual scene. For the patient's brainwave data, a certain period of time when the beta wave is significantly stronger than the alpha wave and this difference remains a certain threshold means that the patient has a certain degree of anxiety or panic. This situation will be judged to be a failure. However, a certain degree of anxiety does not mean that the patient really feels an unbearable panic.

Therefore, after each specific height failure, the threshold of the corresponding height will rise. In addition, if the height difference between the gaze point and the position of the patient has not remained the height of the patient position within a certain period of time, the failure is also determined. If these two failed judgment conditions do not appear, the patient is judged to be successful. Until the patient returns to the comfort zone or success in the highest floor, one training session ends.

3.3   EEG Detection

To efficiently detect brain waves, Emotiv Epoc+ are taken as our EEG detection. Epoc+ is a wireless EEG detector, designed for contextual research and advanced brain computer interface (BCI) applications. It applies a saline solution to the electrode pads, providing a comfortable wearing experience for users and reducing unnecessary anxiety of users.

Epoc+ has fourteen channels. We sample up to 2048 Hz for a single frequency wave in each channel. This helps us get more accurate waveform data. The waveform data is independently passed through a high-pass filter, a low-pass filter and a band-stop filter to filter out the interference and then processed by a band-pass filter to obtain approximate α, β waves. Then, we can visualize the different waves according to their strength and corresponding time information, so that they can be recorded more vividly and provide real-time emotional recognition. The visualization effect is shown in Fig. 3.

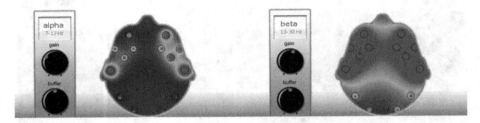

Fig. 3. The state of the brain waves intercepted during the volunteers' experiment.

3.4   Eye Tracking Implementation

We use the VR eye tracker of Shanghai Qingyan Technology, which is divided into external modules and built-in modules. The external module is a stand-alone accessory that can be easily combined with a VR helmet. Built-in modules are embedded in SDK for Unity, providing enterprise users with tightly controlled hardware modules and analysis algorithms.

Through the corresponding interface in the SDK, the relative coordinates of the eye gaze point in the virtual environment and the eye movement gaze rays (i.e., the rays emitted from the position of the eye) can be obtained. According to the location and angle of the ends of the two rays, the exact gaze point can be calculated. One simplest simulation calculation is to take the vertical angle of two eyes as the same and then calculate the focus of two eyes in the horizontal direction as shown in Fig. 4.

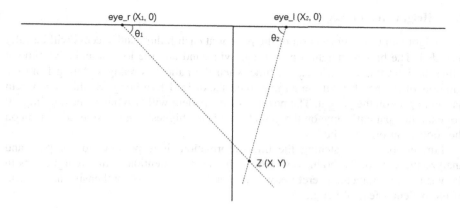

Fig. 4. The sketch map of eye tracking under simplified circumstances, which cannot represent the real algorithm. The coordinate system takes the patient's head as the reference system, and the final coordinates need to be transformed into the world coordinate system in the virtual scene.

The position of gaze point can be roughly simulated by the following equations.

$$-\tan\theta_1(X - X_1) = Y \tag{1}$$

$$\tan\theta_2(X - X_2) = Y \tag{2}$$

Then we get the specific gaze position of the patient through a certain algorithm of compensation and correction. Finally, we combined the current time information with gaze position to achieve better visualization. In order to obtain a reliable eye track, the eye tracker will perform an eye control calibration before use, and the exact eye movement gaze point will be obtained after the calibration.

4 Discussion

In the whole process of training patients in the VR scene, some data is worthy of in-depth analysis.

4.1 System Acceptability

At the end of each experiment, patients should be released with a questionnaire for their treatment. These include: training experience scores, sense of dizziness in the comfort zone, how this performance, and the willingness to recommend to others. Each item has a scale of 10 to 1. The results of these questionnaires are of great significance to our judgment of System acceptability.

4.2 Height Acceptance

The height and time information of the patient at each failure and success will be fully recorded. The highest height a patient can withstand and the longest effective time at which he is at this height (i.e., the time when the patient is really suffering from the stimulus of the height) will be an important factor in determining whether the system has an impact on the patient. The position of the patient will also have a certain impact. For example, patient's time on the glass trestle is the highest is more significant than on the roof of an ordinary building.

Furthermore, by matching the time information, it is possible to compare and analyze the state of the brain wave when patients pay attention to different pictures in the virtual environment. Therefore, we can conduct a more comprehensive assessment of the patient's fear of heights.

5 Insufficient and Outlook

There are still some obvious shortcomings in the system. The first is the realistic level of the scene. The more realistic the scene, the more the patient feels the stimulus, and the better the patient switches from the virtual scene to the real world. But limited by the cost of money and time, it is difficult to make the scene more realistic. In addition, the accuracy of EEG testing is not that satisfactory. Due to the General precision of EPOC, it is difficult to accurately grasp the emotional state of the patient, but it is of great value as a reference. These problems will be solved step by step in subsequent studies. Eye movement brain wave detection technology have the potential to gain more development. In the future work, we first need to address the deficiencies we mentioned. More sophisticated algorithm design is conducive to improving the accuracy of different data results, and well-designed experiments with a sufficient number of volunteers can help us test and improve the system.

6 Conclusion

We have built a new type of acrophobia exposure therapy using the latest immersive VR technology, in which patients gradually recover from acrophobia by regularly exposing themselves to the stimulus source set in the virtual scene under the rules of altitude layering agreement we developed. The altitude layering agreement can promote patients to receive stimulation in a more rational way and simply quantify the patient's acrophobia. This quantification allows patients to experience a more intuitive experience of their own progress, providing patients with a steady stream of positive feedback incentives. The application of EEG and eye tracking technology will help us achieve breakthroughs. The emotional changes in the virtual scene for different situations will be carefully recorded. We can therefore have a clearer understanding and assessment of the patient's acrophobia details. Careful attention to the subtle manifestations of patients in virtual environments has rarely occurred on previous systems. Regarding the actual application of the system, we still need to conduct large sample experiments in the future to verify this.

References

1. Juan, M.C., et al.: An augmented reality system for the treatment of acrophobia. Presence **15** (4), 315–318 (2005)
2. Huppert, D., Grill, E., Brandt, T.: Down on heights? One in three has visual height intolerance. J. Neurol. **260**(2), 597–604 (2013)
3. Foa, E.B., Kozak, M.J.: Emotional processing of fear: exposure to corrective information. Psychol. Bull. **99**(1), 20–35 (1986)
4. De Silva, P., Rachman, S.: Is exposure a necessary condition for fear-reduction? Behav. Res. Ther. **19**(3), 227–232 (1981)
5. Miltenberger, R.G.: Behavioral Modification: Principles and Procedures, p. 552. Thomson/Wadsworth, Belmont (2008)
6. Costa, J.P., Robb, J., Nacke, L.E.: Physiological acrophobia evaluation through in vivo exposure in a VR CAVE. In: 2014 IEEE Games Media Entertainment (GEM), Toronto, ON, pp. 1–4 (2014)
7. Emmelkamp, P.M.G., Krijn, M., Hulsbosch, A.M., de Vries, S., Schuemie, M.J., van der Mast, C.A.P.G.: Virtual reality treatment versus exposure in vivo: a comparative evaluation in acrophobia. Behav. Res. Ther. **40**(5), 509–516 (2002)
8. Krijn, M., Emmelkamp, P.M.G., Biemond, R., Wilde de Ligny, C., Schuemie, M.J., van der Mast, C.A.P.G.: Treatment of acrophobia in virtual reality: the role of immersion and presence. Behav. Res. Ther. **42**(2), 229–239 (2004)
9. Schäfer, P., Koller, M., Diemer, J., Meixner, G.: Development and evaluation of a virtual reality-system with integrated tracking of extremities under the aspect of Acrophobia. In: SAI Intelligent Systems Conference (IntelliSys), London, pp. 408–417 (2015)
10. Niedermeyer, E., Lopes da Silva, F.H.: Electroencephalography: Basic Principles, Clinical Applications, and Related Fields. Lippincott Williams & Wilkins, London (2004). ISBN 0-7817-5126-8
11. Tatum, W.O.: Ellen R. Grass lecture: extraordinary EEG. Neurodiagnostic J. **54**(1), 3–21 (2014)
12. Niedermeyer, E.: Alpha rhythms as physiological and abnormal phenomena. Int. J. Psychophysiol. **26**(1–3), 31–49 (1997)
13. Pfurtscheller, G., Lopes da Silva, F.H.: Event-related EEG/MEG synchronization and desynchronization: basic principles. Clin. Neurophysiol. **110**(11), 1842–1857 (1999)

Virtual Reality Based Road Crossing Training for Autistic Children with Behavioral Analysis

Yicong Peng[✉], Wei Zhu, Fangyu Shi, Yi Fang, and Guangtao Zhai

Institute of Image Communication and Network Engineering,
Shanghai Key Laboratory of Digital Media Processing and Transmission,
Shanghai Jiao Tong University, Shanghai, China
{jack-sparrow,sujszw,fangyu.shi,yifang,zhaiguangtao}@sjtu.edu.cn

Abstract. Autism Spectrum Disorder (ASD) is a collection of multiple neural developmental disorders, which can cause deficits in social activities, stereotype or repetitive behaviors, as well as cognitive difficulties. Road crossing is a typical daily activity which requires the ability that autistic individuals are usually deemed to be in lack of and thus became a training method for autistic people. While both real-world and virtual training experiments have been conducted over the years, little attention has been paid to the intrinsic characteristics and behavioral patterns exhibited by the subjects during the process. By utilizing virtual reality technology, both the characteristics and patterns of autistic people can be monitored in a more precise and detailed way. We conducted a virtual reality road crossing training experiment measuring spacial distribution pattern and attention pattern of the autistic subjects. To further exploit these major behavior properties, we extract several parameters from the data to quantitatively analyze the characteristics and evaluate the performance of autistic people in road crossing. Several distinctive behavioral pattern changes were found in the subjects both before and after the training experiment. These patterns changes may be further utilized in the future to improve the training process.

Keywords: Virtual reality · Autism Spectrum Disorder · Behavioral analysis · Road crossing training

1 Introduction

Autism Spectrum Disorder is a developmental disorder diagnosed on the basis of early-emerging social impairments and repetitive behavioral patterns [6]. A survey focused on the travel patterns of autism people in New Jersey showed that the inability to cross roads has become the dominant mobility barrier for autism people [5]. As road crossing is a typical daily activity which involves the abilities that autistic people are deemed to be in the lack of, it has become a major point of interest in autism training practice.

© Springer Nature Singapore Pte Ltd. 2019
G. Zhai et al. (Eds.): IFTC 2018, CCIS 1009, pp. 456–469, 2019.
https://doi.org/10.1007/978-981-13-8138-6_39

Traditional road crossing training was often conducted with the help of the local community and government. It usually requires a prearranged enclosed area, controlled traffics, and limited pedestrians [4]. All of which not only consume a substantial amount of social resources, but also are highly susceptible to real world conditions such as weather, security, and public transportation. The inconsistency in the experiment conditions along with the unpredictable environmental factors may cause the result of the experiment to be inaccurate or even prevents the research to be conducted.

Considering the limits of real world experiments and the flexibility as well as controllability the virtual environment provides, the forms of research have been shifting towards virtual environment simulations. The research by Young and a study led by Mccomas has proved the effectiveness of virtual reality in teaching normal children pedestrian safety [11,19]. A research led by Parsons has proved that the virtual reality can be effective as a tool in the social skills training of the autistic people [12]. Studies led by Joshman and Goldsmith using virtual reality in teaching both children and adolescents with autism have proved the effectiveness of virtual environment training [7,8]. Several researches as well as training programs regarding autistic people road crossing ability have been conducted using virtual environment technology and have achieved promising outcomes [15]. A study led by Mario Saiano, focused on teaching adults with Autism Spectrum Disorder of street crossing and path following skills using virtual environment [14]. Autistic participants who completed the training session showed significant improvement in their navigation performance. Another study further verified the generalization possibility of virtual reality training by conducting real world road tests on school students both before and after the virtual reality intervention [2]. The results indicated that participants showed a noticeable greater improvement in road safety after the virtual reality intervention compared to those participants who had no virtual reality intervention. Both studies led by Saiano and Bart proved that the skills acquired from virtual reality can later be generalized into real life skills for both normal and autistic people.

While previous work explored the effectiveness and performance of virtual environment training, little attention has been paid to the intrinsic behavioral patterns exposed during the process. The implementation limits introduced additional uncertainties into the experiment since the subjects can be affected by real world influences while interacting with the virtual environment [9,16]. And since the virtual environment used in previous work [10,14] requires specific interaction commands to navigate through the scenes, the performance of the subjects in the virtual environment is no longer solely decided by the mastery of the skills but also the mastery of the commands adopted by the experiment.

In order to address the problems mentioned above, we introduce a new way of road crossing training method as well as a new scheme to monitor and analyze the behaviors of the subjects in virtual reality. Virtual reality can provide a more realistic immersive first person experience compared to previous virtual environment implementations. Therefore it can reduce the generalization barrier and make the transfer of skills acquired in the virtual scene into real world practise more easily. We also proposed a new method to evaluate the performance and analyze the properties of autistic subjects by their spacial distribution and head pose patterns, which can provide more detailed behavioral information of the subjects.

2   Experiment

In this experiment, new criteria and standard were adopted to evaluate the performance and analyze the behavioral patterns of the subjects in a quantitative way. Several parameters were extracted from the data to act as the characterization of the behavioral properties as well as the evaluation benchmark. A new training method based on the statistical results were proposed which emphasizes both the behavioral intervention as well as the road crossing skills of the autistic subjects.

In order to examine how the complexity of the training objective affect our training method performance, the experiment contains two virtual scenes with different environment complexity and skill level requirements. Both scenes have typical daytime modern city environment with road crossings and traffic lights. We use L and H to refer to the scene with lower and higher scene complexity respectively. The detailed information of the scenes are listed in Table 1. The traffic flow (F), defined by formula (1), is used to describe the traffic condition. F is the average number of cars (N) passed trough the zebra crossing divided by unit time (t), N_I is the number of the road crossing intersections in the scene, and l is the number of lanes of each road in question. The higher value of F means more traffic on the road and higher average vehicle speed. T_G and T_R represent the duration of green and red traffic lights measured in seconds respectively. The deviation angle (θ_0) is the maximum deviation of direction allowed in the training stage before the subject receives instructions. Larger values of the deviation angle means less instructions were given during the training stage. We sampled both the position and the head pose of the subject at 60 Hz along with the time information during the road crossing experiment for our analysis. A three-stage process was adopted for each scene, which includes the profiling stage, training stage and evaluation stage. Every subjects were required to go through all three stages of each scene sequentially for their data to be valid in the analysis.

By exploiting the statistical properties of both the position and the head orientation data sampled during the experiment, several parameters were extracted from the data to describe the performance and behavioral characteristics of the subject quantitatively. The definition of the parameters used in our evaluation are listed in Table 2 and will be explained in detail later in Sect. 2.2. Comparisons were made regarding the parameters between different stages of the experiment to determine whether the subjects have improved after the training.

$$F = N/lN_It \tag{1}$$

2.1 Participants

This experiment involves 11 male and 6 female subjects recruited from multiple autistic children caring centers in Shanghai, China. All subjects have been diagnosed with autism spectrum disorder according to DSM-5 criteria [1] and aged from 6 to 12 years old. All subjects have taken a simple test to ensure that they have approximately the same degree of understanding regarding colors, traffic rules and traffic relevant objects such as cars and traffic lights. However, all of the subjects are incapable of crossing roads in the real world on their own. We excluded several candidates during the screening process due to their sensory disorder [13] such as hypersensitive tactile sensory which may cause the subjects to refuse wearing the virtual reality helmet [17]. 7 out of 11 male subjects and 5 out of 6 female subjects completed the experiment and qualified for the final analysis. The subjects were randomly assigned to two groups of the same size. The group labeled L used the low complexity scene as their training environment while the group labeled H used the high complexity scene for their training.

Table 1. The comparison of the environment parameters between the two scenes in detail

Scene	F	T_G	T_R	m	N_I	M	θ_0
L	0.2	20	10	8	1	4	40°
H	0.4	15	10	12	4	8	40°

Table 2. The denotation and definition of the parameters used in this experiment

Parameter	Definition
R	The success ratio in **Profiling Stage** and **Evaluation Stage**
$\hat{\sigma}_l$	The standard deviation of the route
β_θ	Velocity bias coefficient
$R_{\Sigma L}$	The routing efficiency ratio
F_θ	The Frobenius norm of the normalized orientation matrix

2.2 Procedure

The experiment was carried out in a 6 m × 8 m room, with sound proof materials and no windows in order to isolate possible real world influence. The room is also facilitated with a stereo sound playback system which is capable of simulating real world sound field. A 3 m × 3 m area was marked out for the subjects to walk around safely and interact with the virtual scene. The area is calibrated according to the virtual scene so that the size and orientation of the accessible area in the virtual scene matches the real world area. The experiment area covers the zebra crossing and a part of the pavement on both sides of the road. When subject walks from one side to the other in real world area, he can go across the road from one side of the pavement to the other in the virtual scene. We use three dimensional Cartesian coordinate system in this experiment. The origin as well as the axis direction are showed in Fig. 1. To ensure the safety of the subjects when they walk around in the scene, we placed the experiment area in the center of the room, with at least one meter of safety margin of empty space surrounding the area to avoid any possible collisions.

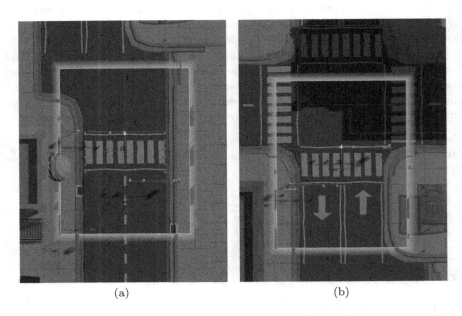

(a)   (b)

Fig. 1. The top view of the two scenes. (a) is the scene L and (b) is the scene H, and the blue boxes indicate the area of the virtual scenes in which the subjects are allowed to move. The red axis is the x axis and the blue axis is the y axis, the green intersection marks the origin of the scene. (Color figure online)

All zebra crossings in the scenes have traffic lights for pedestrians on both sides of the road. The green light indicates that the road is safe to go across while the red lights indicates the opposite. The traffic lights will blink multiple times to notify the subject before changing the color. The lanes are separated by white traffic dash lines. Figure 2 shows the first person view of the two scenes. Cars of different types are generated randomly on each direction, and drives on the right hand side of the road. The cars are programmed to keep a certain distance between each other and follow the traffic rules. The pavement on both sides of the road is 1.5 m wide and has yellow safety bars to mark the boundaries between the pavement and the traffic road. Before the commencement of every stage, subjects were asked to put on the virtual reality helmet and were escorted to one side of the experiment area. They were given up to 30 s to adjust the position and get ready for the experiment. Once the subject is ready for the experiment, the subject will be placed on the safe area in the virtual scene, which is the area on the pavement behind the safety bar. The sampling and recording of the data will also start simultaneously with the scene. We define a successful trial when the behavior of the subject met the following requirements:

1. The road crossing attempt happened during the green light.

2. The subject walked on the zebra crossing in the whole process.

3. The subject got to the safe area on the other side before the traffic light turns into red.

4. The subject stayed in the safe area after crossing the road.

(a)   (b)

Fig. 2. The first person view of the two scenes. (a) is captured in the scene L and (b) is captured in the scene H. (Color figure online)

All three stages were conducted sequentially according to the following descriptions:

Profiling Stage: Subjects from both groups are required to attempt to go across the road 10 times independently without any instructions. The sampled data as well as the success ratio will be recorded as the baseline of the subjects' performance.

Training Stage: During this stage, subjects will be given both visual and auditory instructions to help them navigate towards the other side of the road. During the green light. Arrows indicating the correction will appear on the road in the virtual scene along with the voice instructions. Another direction arrow will appear in front of the subject when they deviation angle (θ) to the correction direction is greater than θ_0. Subjects will also receive instructions when they step out of the zebra crossing zone. During the red light, the subject will be warned when they try to step into the road. Additional prompts which reminds the subjects to notice the traffic lights will be given to the subjects every time the traffic light changes. We also provided boy and a girl characters which can go across the road following the traffic rules to give subjects demonstrations when the system detects that the subjects failed more than three times consecutively.

Evaluation Stage: Subjects from both groups are required to attempt to go across the road 10 times independently without any instructions. The sampled data as well as the success ratio will be recorded as the subjects' performance after the training stage.

While profiling of every subject from both groups is conducted only once at the beginning of the experiment, both the training and the evaluation stage were conducted every other day on the subjects over a two month period.

2.3 Data Analysis

We wanted to evaluate the performance of the autistic subject in road crossing by considering the attention distribution, routing quality and how well the subjects followed the traffic rules during the process. We proposed the following evaluation criteria for our analysis.

Evaluation Criteria:

1. Subjects should pay due attention to both sides of the zebra crossing when they go across the road.

2. We encourage the subjects to choose the shortest route possible to reduce the time they spend on the road.

3. Subjects should show consistency in their speed during the road crossing process. Halt, slow down or speed up unnecessarily will be regarded as unwanted behaviors.

4. Subjects should be able to maintain the direction when try to go across the road. We encourage the subject to remain as directly as possible towards the other side of the road without altering their directions.

5. The subject should follow the traffic rules and respond correctly to the traffic signals.

And by applying the definition of a successful trial, we can calculate the success ratio of the subject in both profiling (R_p) and evaluation (R_e) stage by applying the formula (2), where the N_S is the number of successful trial and N_T is total number of trial.

$$R_{p,e} = \frac{N_S}{N_T} \tag{2}$$

To measure the routing quality, we first analysed the spacial distribution of the subject in every stage. Initially we obtain the position data which is a 2 by N matrix (D), where N is the total number of the samples. Each row of D stores a position vector $\boldsymbol{p}(x, y)$. S is the size of the matrix H. Suppose the size of the area is $A \times A$, then S can be calculated from $S = A/\Delta$, Δ is the spacial resolution of the heat matrix. The detailed spacial distribution information of the baseline and the evaluation stage can be visualized by calculating the normalized spacial heat matrix, which are denoted as $\overline{H}_B$ and $\overline{H}_E$ respectively. Both $\overline{H}_B$ and $\overline{H}_E$ can be calculated using the same formula (3) and (4), where Δ is the spacial resolution of the position heat matrix and N is the total number of the sampled position data. We define the square neighborhood $\Omega_{i,j}(\frac{\Delta}{2})$ in formula (5) and (6).

$$\forall \boldsymbol{p}(x, y) \text{ in } \boldsymbol{D}, \ \boldsymbol{H}(i, j) = \begin{cases} \boldsymbol{H}(i, j) + 1 & \text{if } x \in \Omega_{i,j}(\frac{\Delta}{2}) \\ \boldsymbol{H}(i, j) & \text{otherwise} \end{cases} \forall i, j \in [1, S] \tag{3}$$

$$\overline{H}_{B,G} = (\frac{1}{N}H_{B,G}) * G \tag{4}$$

$$\forall q(x,y) \in \Omega_{i,j}(\frac{\Delta}{2}) : x \in (x_i - \frac{\Delta}{2}, x_i + \frac{\Delta}{2}), y \in (y_j - \frac{\Delta}{2}, y_j + \frac{\Delta}{2}) \tag{5}$$

$$x_i = -\frac{A}{2} + i\Delta, y_j = -\frac{A}{2} + j\Delta \tag{6}$$

We used the sampled position (p_h) of the helmet to estimate the actual position of the subject (p_s), however the position of the helmet is not necessarily the actual position of the subject. According to studies led by Winter [18] and Bauby [3], the balance and posture control of the human body during walking and standing can be described by the inverted pendulum model. Assume the maximum swing angle of the pendulum is θ_{max}, by applying the formula 7, where h denotes the height of the subject, we can obtain the maximum deviation (Δx_d) of the helmet from the subject's position. The values $h = 1.52$ m and $\theta_{max} = 8°$ were chosen based on the demographics of our subjects. To compensate the deviation as well as reduce the high frequency noise introduced by the sampling process, the two dimensional Gaussian filter G was applied to H_B, H_E. Formula (8) and (9) are the shape of G expressed in continuous and discrete forms ($\sigma = 1.5$). The value of sigma is chosen according to the formula (10), so that the Gaussian filter applied will not filter out the details of the spacial distribution. Figure 3 shows the visualized spacial heat matrix, where the spacial resolution $\Delta = 0.03$ m, brighter color indicates that the longer time subject stayed in that region.

$$\Delta x_d = \overline{p_s p_h} = h \sin \theta_{max} \tag{7}$$

$$G(x, y) = \frac{1}{2\pi\sigma^2}e^{-\frac{x^2+y^2}{2\sigma^2}} \tag{8}$$

$$\mathbf{G}_{\sigma=1.5} = \begin{pmatrix} 0.095332 & 0.118095 & 0.095332 \\ 0.118095 & 0.146293 & 0.118095 \\ 0.095332 & 0.118095 & 0.095332 \end{pmatrix} \tag{9}$$

$$P\{|\Delta x_d| \le 2\sigma\Delta\} \ge 0.9545 \tag{10}$$

Another aspect of the routing quality we can explore by analysis the position data is the standard deviation of the route ($\hat{\sigma}_l$), which reflects the subject's ability to travel consistently towards the target location. The higher value of $\hat{\sigma}_l$ indicates more unwanted drift from the original route. ($\hat{\sigma}_l$) can be obtained by applying the formula (11), where $\bar{x}$ is the mean value of the horizontal coordinates.

$$\hat{\sigma}_l = \sqrt{\frac{\sum_{i=1}^{N}(x_i - \bar{x})^2}{N}} \tag{11}$$

And as mentioned above in the evaluation criteria, we wanted the subjects to go across the road as efficiently as possible. Therefore we encourage the subjects to choose the shortest route possible. By comparing the actual travel distance to the shortest perpendicular distance, we can obtain the routing efficiency $(R_{\Sigma L})$ of the subject. The routing efficiency can be calculated using formula (12), where d_m is the shortest route.

$$R_{\Sigma L} = \frac{d_m}{\sum_{i=1}^{N} |\boldsymbol{v}_i| \Delta T} \tag{12}$$

While the spacial heat matrix and the standard deviation of the route emphasizes the overall spacial distribution of the subject, we wanted to further explore the detailed motion performance of the subject. The statistical characteristics of both the magnitude and the direction of the sampled instantaneous velocity (v_i) can be used to analyze the behavioral patterns and real time performance of the subject. The instantaneous velocity (v_i) is defined by the formula (13), where $\boldsymbol{p}_i$ is the ith position vector sampled from the original position sequence by the time interval of ΔT. We used the velocity bias factor (β_θ) to evaluate the performance quantitatively. Figure 4 shows the magnitude as well as the direction of the sampled instantaneous velocity of the subjects during the green light. The velocity bias factor can be calculated by formula (14) and (15). The velocity near the y direction will make positive contribution to the bias factor while the velocity near the opposite direction will make negative contribution to the bias factor. Better motion performance will result in higher value of velocity bias factor.

$$\boldsymbol{v}_i = \frac{\boldsymbol{p}_{i+1} - \boldsymbol{p}_i}{\Delta T} \tag{13}$$

$$\beta_\theta = \frac{\sum_{i=1}^{N} |\boldsymbol{v}_i| f(\theta_i)}{N|\overline{v}|} \tag{14}$$

$$f(\theta_i) = \begin{cases} 1 & \theta_i \in (\pi/4, 3\pi/4) \\ 0 & \theta_i \in (3\pi/4, 5\pi/4) \bigcup (-\pi/4, \pi/4) \\ -1 & \theta_i \in (5\pi/4, 7\pi/4) \end{cases} \tag{15}$$

In order to examine the attention distribution of the subjects, we analyzed the head orientation of the subject during the green light. We assume that the pointing direction of the face can roughly represent the direction which the person pay attention to. Since we expect the subject to pay due attention to both sides of the zebra crossing when he walk across the road, the horizontal span of the head pose should be as wide as possible. Additionally we wanted the subjects to be able to notice the surrounding environment, and thus more evenly distribute their attention. We plotted the head attention heat matrix at an angular resolution of 1°, as is shown in Fig. 5. The normalized attention matrix (A_θ), which is the size of 180×360, can be calculated using the similar method adopted in calculating the spacial heat matrix. We use the Frobenius norm F_θ of the normalized orientation matrix to indicate how evenly the subjects has distributed their attention. The F_θ can be calculated by applying the formula (16).

$$F_\theta = ||A_\theta||_F = \sqrt{\sum_{i=1}^{180} \sum_{j=1}^{360} |a_{ij}|^2} \tag{16}$$

3   Results and Discussion

As we can see from the spacial heat map in Fig. 3, the spatial distributions of subjects from group L is more concentrated than those of subjects from group H. Which indicates that subjects tend to have more sense of direction and clear objective in environment with lower complexity. Another conclusion can be drawn from the results by comparing the heat matrix from the baseline and evaluation stage. The first subject used to spend more time in the middle region while crossing the road during the baseline stage. However this behavior is suppressed in the evaluation stage and gained more time efficiency when crossing the road. The second subject showed more consistency in the routing and a decrease in the total travel distance after the training. The overall routing is converging towards a line perpendicular to the traffic directions which is the optimal solution in the scenario.

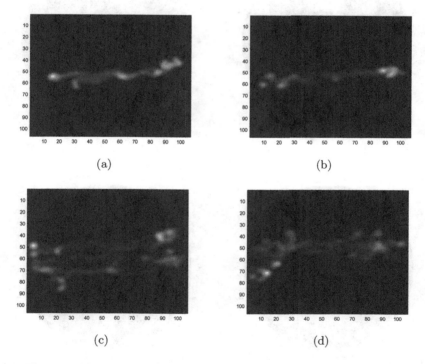

Fig. 3. The spacial heat matrix ($\Delta = 0.03$ m). (a) and (b) are generated from a subject in group L while (c) and (d) are generated from a subject in group H. The left column shows the profiling results and the right column shows the evaluation results. The x axis is placed along the horizontal direction, brighter color indicates that the longer time subject stayed in that region.

The velocity distribution shown in Fig. 4 indicates that subjects from both group L and group H, have improved in choosing the correct direction. Subjects are less likely to go in the wrong direction while crossing the road. The direction angle is more concentrate in the evaluation stage, which means the subjects have better performance in identifying and maintaining the correct direction. However both groups have a lower average speed and halt more likely during the green light. This can be explained by the subjects tends to pay more attention and observe the surrounding environment more carefully after the training. And the subjects may have trouble coordinating observation and body movement. Generally by comparing the velocity bias factor from the profiling and evaluation stage, results showed that both groups have gained improvement after the training stage.

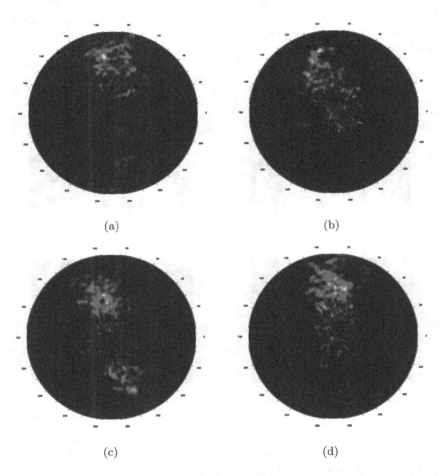

(a)   (b)

(c)   (d)

Fig. 4. The velocity distribution graph. (a) and (b) are generated from a subject in group L while (c) and (d) are generated from a subject in group H, with the sample interval $\Delta T = 0.1$ s. The left column displays the profiling results and the right column displays the evaluation results. The numbers on the rim is the angle measured from x axis to the velocity, the radius is the normalized magnitude of the velocity. Brighter regions indicates the velocity preference of the subject. (Color figure online)

The subject's attention distribution is shown in Fig. 5. We observed a general improvement in the attention distribution performance from both groups. Subjects from both group L and H showed a larger attention angle in the evaluation stage, indicating that the subjects paid more attention to the incoming traffic and surrounding environment. Particularly, we find that the Frobenius norm has a greater decrease ratio in group H than that in group L. Which indicates that environment with higher complexity may have applied a stronger information stimuli to the subjects during the training stage, which propelled the subjects to actively search for the information needed for the task and thus subjects tends to have a better attention distribution.

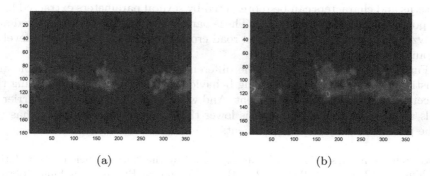

(a)   (b)

Fig. 5. The attention heat matrix. (a) is the attention distribution of a subject from group H in profiling stage ($F_\theta = 0.0120$), (b) is the attention distribution of the same subject in evaluation stage ($F_\theta = 0.0108$). Brighter color indicates that the longer time subject looks in that direction. (Color figure online)

The detailed results of group L and group H are listed in Tables 3 and 4.

Table 3. The average profiling and evaluation results of group L.

	R	$\hat{\sigma}_l$	β_θ	$R_{\Sigma L}$	F_θ
Profiling	0.56	1.5961	0.2193	0.4157	0.0152
Evaluation	0.72	1.0670	0.6254	0.7392	0.0124

Table 4. The average profiling and evaluation results of group H.

	R	$\hat{\sigma}_l$	β_θ	$R_{\Sigma L}$	F_θ
Profiling	0.43	1.8326	0.1136	0.3913	0.0146
Evaluation	0.66	1.2719	0.5220	0.6920	0.0108

4 Conclusion

By utilizing the virtual reality technology, we proposed a virtual reality road crossing training system for autistic people, which is more realistic and thus may have a better performance in the generalization of the skills acquired in the virtual environment. The additional control commands required in previous implementation to navigate through the virtual scene, such as the body language and the keyboard input, is deprecated in this system, which makes it more applicable to a wider range of autistic people and easier to use. We monitored and analyzed the road crossing process in detail and find several patterns which are strongly related to the behavioral characteristics of the autistic people. These patterns and characters can be represented by several parameters extracted from the position and head status data. These parameters can then be quantified and analyzed to reflect and evaluate the road crossing performance and skill level of the autistic people.

Further research can explore the difference between the normal people and autistic people in their road crossing behaviors by comparing and analyzing the aspects mentioned in this experiment. And whether the generalization barrier of skills acquired in this experiment is lower than those in previous work has yet to be proven by real world experiments.

Acknowledgements. This work was supported by the National Science Foundation of China (61831015, 61521062, 61527804) and Equipment Pre-research Joint Research Program of Ministry of Education of China (6141A020223).

References

1. Association, A.P.: Diagnostic and statistical manual of mental disorders, fifth edition (DSM-5). Int. J. Offender Ther. Comp. Criminol. **57**(12), 1546–1548 (2013)
2. Bart, O., Katz, N., Weiss, P.L., Josman, N.: Street crossing by typically developed children in real and virtual environments. OTJR Occup. Particip. Health **28**(2), 42–46 (2008)
3. Bauby, C.E., Kuo, A.D.: Active control of lateral balance in human walking. J. Biomech. **33**(11), 1433–1440 (2000)
4. Cowan, G., Earl, R., Falkmer, T., Girdler, S., Morris, S.L., Falkmer, M.: Fixation patterns of individuals with and without autism spectrum disorder: do they differ in shared zones and in zebra crossings? J. Transp. Health **8**, 112–122 (2018)
5. Deka, D., Feeley, C., Lubin, A.: Travel patterns, needs, and barriers of adults with autism spectrum disorder. J. Transp. Res. Board 4(2542), 9–16 (2016)
6. Frith, U., Happé, F.: Autism spectrum disorder. Curr. Biol. **15**(19), R786–R790 (2005)
7. Goldsmith, T.R., Leblanc, L.A.: Using virtual reality enhanced behavioral skills training to teach street crossing skills to children and adolescents with autism spectrum disorders. In: International Meeting for Autism Research (2008)
8. Josman, N., Benchaim, H.M., Friedrich, S., Weiss, P.L.: Effectiveness of virtual reality for teaching street-crossing skills to children and adolescents with autism. Int. J. Disabil. Hum. Dev. **7**(1), 49–56 (2008)

9. Matsentidou, S., Poullis, C.: Immersive visualizations in a VR cave environment for the training and enhancement of social skills for children with autism. In: 2014 International Conference on Computer Vision Theory and Applications (VISAPP), vol. 3, pp. 230–236, January 2014
10. Matsentidou, S., Poullis, C.: Immersive visualizations in a VR cave environment for the training and enhancement of social skills for children with autism. In: International Conference on Computer Vision Theory and Applications, pp. 230–236 (2015)
11. Mccomas, J., Mackay, M., Pivik, J.: Effectiveness of virtual reality for teaching pedestrian safety. Cyberpsychol. Behav. 5(3), 185–190 (2002)
12. Parsons, S., Mitchell, P., Leonard, A.: The use and understanding of virtual environments by adolescents with autistic spectrum disorders. J. Autism Dev. Disord. 34(4), 449–466 (2004)
13. Robertson, A.E., Simmons, D.R.: The relationship between sensory sensitivity and autistic traits in the general population. J. Autism Dev. Disord. 43(4), 775–784 (2013)
14. Saiano, M., et al.: Natural interfaces and virtual environments for the acquisition of street crossing and path following skills in adults with autism spectrum disorders: a feasibility study. J. NeuroEng. Rehabil. 12(1), 17 (2015)
15. Schwebel, D.C., Mcclure, L.A.: Using virtual reality to train children in safe street-crossing skills. Inj. Prev. 16(1), 1–5 (2010)
16. Tzanavari, A., Charalambous-Darden, N., Herakleous, K., Poullis, C.: Effectiveness of an immersive virtual environment (cave) for teaching pedestrian crossing to children with PDD-NOS. In: 2015 IEEE 15th International Conference on Advanced Learning Technologies, pp. 423–427, July 2015
17. Wiggins, L.D., Robins, D.L., Bakeman, R., Adamson, L.B.: Breif report: sensory abnormalities as distinguishing symptoms of autism spectrum disorders in young children. J. Autism Dev. Disord. 39(7), 1087–1091 (2009)
18. Winter, D.: Human balance and posture control during standing and walking. Gait Posture 3(4), 193–214 (1995)
19. Young, D.S., Lee, D.N.: Training children in road crossing skills using a roadside simulation. Accid. Anal. Prev. 19(5), 327–341 (1987)

Author Index

Printed in the United States
by Baker & Taylor Publisher Services

Printed in the United States
By Bookmasters